W9-CSX-175

from reviews of

THE INTERNET NAVIGATOR

" . . . a gem ."

> *Andrew Kantor*
> *PC Magazine*

". . . If there's only one book on the Internet that you can afford on your shelf, this is your best choice. . . ."

> *Library Journal*

"This is an Internet reference work whose time has come . . . a 'must have' for all online users . . ."

> *Richard Huleatt*
> *Online Newsletter*

"The best tutorial I've seen yet on the Internet. . . . Gilster has done millions of newcomers a great service . . ."

> *Alex Johnson*
> *Knight Ridder News*

". . . probably the most descriptive and useful strategy we've seen in print for getting on the Internet . . ."

> *Jack Rickard*
> *Boardwatch Magazine*

". . . Everything non-techies need to know. . . ."

> *U.S. News & World Report*

". . . one of the best places for new Internet users to start. . . ."

> *Brian Livingston*
> *PC/Computing*

THE INTERNET NAVIGATOR

Paul Gilster

1689301

John Wiley & Sons, Inc.

NEW YORK • CHICHESTER • BRISBANE • TORONTO • SINGAPORE

Associate Publisher: Katherine Schowalter
Editor: Paul Farrell
Managing Editor: Frank Grazioli
Editorial Production and Design: Editorial Services of New England, Inc.

Copyright © 1993 John Wiley & Sons, Inc.

All rights reserved. Published simultaneously in Canada.

Reproduction or translation of any part of this work beyond that permitted by Section 107 or 108 of the 1976 United States Copyright Act without the permission of the copyright owner is unlawful. Requests for permission or further information should be addressed to the Permissions Department, John Wiley & Sons, Inc.

This publication is designed to provide accurate and authoritative information in regard to the subject matter covered. It is sold with the understanding that the publisher is not engaged in rendering professional services. If legal, accounting, medical, psychological, or any other expert assistance is required, the services of a competent professional person should be sought. ADAPTED FROM A DECLARATIONS OF PRINCIPLES OF A JOINT COMMITTEE OF THE AMERICAN BAR ASSOCIATION AND PUBLISHERS.

Trademarks
Many words in this publication in which the Author and Publisher believe trademark or other proprietary rights may exist have been designated as such by use of Initial Capital Letters. However, in so designating or failing to designate such words, neither the Author nor the Publisher intends to express any judgment on the validity or legal status of any proprietary right that may be claimed in the words.

Library of Congress Cataloging-in-Publication Data
Gilster, Paul A., 1949-
      The Internet navigator
      Paul A. Gilster.
          p.   cm.
      Includes index.
      ISBN 0-471-59782-1 (pbk.)
      1. Internet (Computer network) I. Title
TK5105.875.I57G55 1993
384.3—dc20

                                                    93-23133
                                                    CIP

Printed in the United States of America

10 9 8 7 6 5

94-2196

For Eloise

Contents

12. Resource Discovery: Knowing Where and How to Look **279**

Foreword

Unlike frontiers with well-defined and precisely fixed boundaries, the Internet frontier is in a constant state of flux and renewal. As quickly as the frontier is settled, new islands, oceans, and even whole continents become part of it. As a virtual space of software, networking, and computers, the Internet is infinitely renewable and infinitely adaptable, and it grows and changes every day.

The increasingly eclectic character of the Internet and its penetration into almost every corner of the globe have created a rich and sometimes unpredictable environment in which common interests and experience are sometimes more important than the geopolitical and social boundaries that separate its users. This mix of diversity and cohesion has created a collection of global villages with the unusual property that many people on the Internet live in more than one virtual village at a time. The scope, complexity, and richness of the system we have today was far from predictable. Looking at the Internet of 1993 with 1973 eyes, one can only wonder at this evolution. And evolution is exactly the right term. Just as complex life forms arise from simpler ones, genetic experiment by genetic experiment, the Internet is an evolving and organic virtual environment.

The extraordinary freedom of expression and accessibility of information on the Internet suggests that it may well represent a whole new revolution in human communications. In a way, the Internet has made every author a publisher, and given new meaning to the phrase "desktop publishing." And it has required that consumers of information or their proxies (e.g., "knowbots") become truly selective and thoughtful voyagers, ceaselessly sorting through and evaluating the information available to them as they sail the electronic oceans and cast their nets wide (no pun intended).

There are of course downsides to the flood of information on the Internet. The most obvious is the difficulty of simply *finding* items in the vast seas of available material. Another is that not all of the information on the Internet is of equal quality or value. We already know about some unwelcome side effects—such as "flaming," which seems to be exacerbated by a medium of communication that invites instant responses rather than thoughtful consideration. But much of what users *will* find, offered as a labor of love and sharing, is of extraordinary quality and value. We can doubtless look forward to extensions of the Internet that will lead to richer, more expressive modes of communication—including enhanced sound, graphics, and video—just as we can hope that users will avail themselves of these tools in humane and intelligent ways. The late Ithiel de sola Pool called these electronic and computer-based tools the "technologies of freedom." Of course, that, too, has its downside. Hidden in that phrase is all the good and not-so-good of the human condition. Charity and fellowship will cross paths with the coarse and the venal, but that is the price to pay for freedom of information.

The virtual communities found in the Internet make me think of Stephen Hawking's description of the universe at the sub-nuclear level. The seemingly placid vacuum of space is in fact a roiling mass of energy in which particle pairs form and merge in fleeting femto-seconds. These vacuum fluctuations have no energy limits, and an entire universe, such as the one we know, could possibly arise as a consequence. The Internet seems to me a bit like that, vibrant with the energy and ideas of millions of producers and consumers. Communities will form and coalesce, with some subsiding and many persisting and evolving.

To take just one example, consider one interesting effect of the Internet—the growing worldwide use of English. Other languages *are* used on the Internet, and there has even been some recent work to improve the standards for email and other communications protocols to accommodate more than the limited ASCII (English-language-based) character set. But in the larger international discourse that makes up much of the traffic in the net, English has become the common coin. Nonetheless, I learned recently of an effort by M. Bruno Oudet, who is the scientific attaché at the French Embassy here in Washington, to increase the opportunity for the use of the French language. He has created FROGNET (French Research Organization Net) to link by email French researchers around the Internet to their colleagues and institutions in France. In this effort, he has also encouraged schools with Internet access around the world to join in, so that children taking French can correspond in that language with others. I take this as an encouraging sign that while the *lingua anglica* prevails in the net, other tongues will thrive there as well.

In this book, Paul Gilster has done a remarkable job in describing the dynamic, daily growth and change that characterize the Internet. He has also ably summarized the important points in the history of the Internet, and suggested the breadth and diversity of the communities that use it today. And, perhaps most important, he has amassed a truly astonishing list of resources and service providers. I had not known about many of these before, so his book has already found a welcome place in my reference collection.

As Gilster points out, any medium such as print has the simultaneous blessing and curse of a fixed nature. The Internet is changing so rapidly that anything written about it in immutable form is bound to be out of date. This book, however, unlocks many doors and leads you to sources of information on the Internet itself that you can use to stay up-to-date. By decoding the argot of the Internet and empowering its readers to become modern day Lewises and Clarks, this book will show you how the Internet offers an endless journey of discovery along its infinitely changing frontier. You'll be welcome there.

Vinton G. Cerf
Annandale, VA

Preface

···

Although the Internet is the world's largest information network, access to it has been restricted for many years to researchers, academics, and scientists. But all that is changing. Today there are abundant opportunities for individual users to become involved with this exciting medium. If you have a modem and want to dial in to the Internet, this book is for you. It will explain how to gain access and what to do when you're there.

The *Internet Navigator* begins with a description of various network destinations, a kind of whirlwind tour of the Internet. The next chapter explains what the Internet is, how and why it was created, and where it is going. Chapter 3 is all about access; it is supplemented by the appendix which lists dial-up service providers all over the world.

The bulk of the book is a primer on how to use the Internet, from retrieving files through File Transfer Protocol, or FTP, to manipulating remote computers using Telnet. We'll look at USENET, the sprawling worldwide network of newsgroups, relating them to the familiar forums and special interest groups of the commercial on-line world. We'll also explore BITNET, a key tool for academic research and shared knowledge, whose mailing lists have grown to encompass an encyclopedic variety of subjects. We'll consider electronic mail in depth, and discuss how you can use a mail-only gateway to the Internet to perform many of the same functions available through a full Internet connection.

Perhaps the most exciting area of Internet growth is information discovery. The Internet is so huge that tracking down its resources can be a fulltime occupation. Tools like Wide Area Information Servers, **gopher, archie,** and World Wide Web, all fully described here, make the job much easier. The book concludes with a resource directory and a glimpse of future developments as the Internet develops new tools and evolves toward what may, in the United States, become a National Research and Educational Network, the so-called "data highway."

The Internet has always been about networks—as many as 10,000 are now connected worldwide. But with many new dial-up options on the market, the Internet is also about individuals. All it takes is a personal computer and a modem to get started. This book will show you how.

CONVENTIONS

In this book, we use the following conventions:

- Command names are printed in **bold;** for example **telnet** or **archie.**
- Names of services or protocols are printed in uppercase or with the initial letter capitalized; for example TELNET or Archie.
- Input typed literally by the user is printed in **bold;** for example, **get hosttable.txt**
- Internet names and addresses are printed in **bold;** for example, **ora.com.**
- Filenames are printed in *italic;* for example, */etc/hosts.*
- Names of USENET news groups are printed in *italics;* for example, *rec.music.folk.*
- "Variables—"placeholders that the reader will replace with an actual value—are printed in *italic.* For example, in the command **ftp** *hostname,* you must substitute *hostname* for the name of some computer on the Internet.
- Within examples, output from the computer is printed in a constant width type.
- Within examples, text typed literally by the user is printed in constant bold type.

ACKNOWLEDGMENTS

Writing a book about the Internet bore out my belief that the network has become a pervasive influence in the lives of those who use it well. I received countless tips, suggestions, reminders, and corrections from the on-line community, interviewed sources by electronic mail, retrieved files through anonymous FTP, and queried databases through Telnet. It was great fun, and I owe many people my thanks.

Bill Washburn, executive director of the Commercial Internet Exchange Association, provided useful insights into the evolution of the network, particularly with regard to its increasing commercialization. Vinton G. Cerf, president of the Internet Society and creator of the TCP/IP protocols which make the Internet possible, was more than generous with his time; his insights were not only authoritative, but delivered with a clarity unusual in so complex a subject. The Internet has no more stalwart champions than Dr. Cerf and the Internet Society.

At the National Science Foundation Network Service Center, Corinne Carroll's assistance was invaluable in helping me to locate the best sources for network maps. I also owe a debt to Larry Landweber, a key figure in the Internet's growth through his work at CSNET and his provocative seminars, for supplying me with the latest figures on network expansion. At CREN, Jim Conklin helped me locate BITNET information, and the assistance of Michael Gettes at Princeton was invaluable in tracking down the complete set of BITNET maps.

A special note of thanks to Ira Fuchs, the creator of BITNET. Despite a hectic schedule, he was kind enough to offer a line-by-line critique of my BITNET materials which helped me to sharpen their focus and clarified several points I had misunderstood. Fuchs' work has provided scholars with a communications tool no previous generation could have imagined.

Working on the exploding field of resource discovery was difficult; things are changing so fast that it's hard to keep up with events. Brewster Kahle was a major help in my understanding of WAIS, offering his time on the telephone and reading through selections of the manuscript. Likewise, Mark McCahill helped me to understand **gopher,** and Michael Schwartz provided useful information about **netfind.** No better testament to the power of the Internet exists than its ability to let a writer like me go straight to the source to ask questions, quickly and efficiently. At the Clearinghouse for Networked Information Discovery and Retrieval, George Brett, and Jane Smith contributed useful insights into a field that refuses to sit still. Peter Deutsch supplied helpful background material on **archie** and made me realize how rapidly this tool is evolving. Both Peter Scott, creator of HYTELNET, and Fred Barrie, one of the developers of **veronica**, reviewed the manuscript on their respective subjects.

I received similar help from a number of other Internet figures. No one explains Project Gutenberg with the enthusiasm of the man behind it, Michael Hart; his energy and drive should keep this remarkable text-creation project on course. Tom Grundner at the National Public Telecomputing Network not only clarified my views on the burgeoning network of Free-Nets, but also explained why the emerging National Research and Education Network may not be all it's cracked up to be. Gordon Cook, editor of the seminal **COOK Report on Internet→NREN** provided numerous thoughts on the relationship between the National Science Foundation, Advanced Network & Services and the NREN.

Susan Eldred and Sarah Glinka at Advanced Network and Services helped clarity the relationship between ANS, NSFNET, and the Internet; their assistance was patient and thorough. John Quarterman, author of *The Matrix, Computer Networks and Conferencing Systems Worldwide,* as well as editor of the indispensable *Matrix News,* shared information about the Internet's growth.

Linda Millington at the PARADISE Project helped keep me updated with traffic figures for this intriguing directory implementation. And fellow freelancer Jayne Levin proved a friend indeed by forwarding the Department of Defense's Internet Host Table on short notice in a pinch. At NASA, April Marine was kind enough to direct me to the information I needed and ensure my network description was accurate.

Among the service providers, a special thanks to Mary Riendeau at The World; her insights helped this dial-up user understand the changes in network access that have occurred over the past two years. Rusty Williams, DELPHI's general manager, provided me with information about his network's access to the Internet. And Kimberly Brown at PSInet was a great help in providing me with useful data about PSILink.

Michael A. Banks, technology writer extraordinaire, knows how much this book owes to his encouragement and assistance. There is no way to repay the many kindnesses he's shown me over the years. Thanks, Mike. Thanks, too, to Paul Farrell and Allison Roarty at John Wiley & Sons for their encouragement, frequent updates of Internet material, and belief in this project. Nan Fritz and the team at Editorial Services of New England, Inc. had their hands full with me and my manuscript, laboring under an extremely tight schedule. I appreciate their patience and good work.

Here in North Carolina, I owe special thanks to Lisa Stroud, a fellow writer who listened day after day by electronic mail as I discussed the vicissitudes of creating a book about the Internet. Alan Clegg, at CONCERT-CONNECT, patiently answered more questions than a system administrator should be required to field, and Joe Ragland, also at CONCERT-CONNECT, helped to clarify the hardware that moves networked data. John Killebrew, at Southern Bell in Raleigh, was likewise helpful in guiding me through the thickets of telecommunications hardware. Cliff and Carolyn Allen, of Allen Marketing Group in Raleigh, helped often when I needed quick print-outs of network maps. Their son Chris, an up-and-coming network guru if ever there was one, provided many a tip on UNIX and other Internet subjects.

Finally, a special work of thanks to my family, all of whom saw much less of me than they normally would have during the time it took to write this book.

1

A Wild Surmise

John Keats didn't know anything about computers, and he wasn't much on history, either. He evidently thought Cortez discovered the Pacific Ocean, when in fact it was Balboa. But in a poem written 180 years ago, Keats captured the essence of what the newcomer experiences when confronted with the Internet. Listen to him as he compares a translation of Homer by George Chapman to that first glimpse of the Pacific:

> Much have I travelled in the realms of gold,
>   And many goodly states and kingdoms seen;
>   Round many western islands have I been
> Which bards in fealty to Apollo hold.
> Oft of one wide expanse had I been told
>   That deep-browed Homer ruled as his demesne;
>   Yet did I never breathe its pure serene
> Till I heard Chapman speak out loud and bold:
> Then felt I like some watcher of the skies
>   When a new planet swims into his ken;
> Or like stout Cortez, when with eagle eyes
>   He stared at the Pacific—and all his men
> Looked at each other with a wild surmise—
>   Silent, upon a peak in Darien.[1]

A wild surmise indeed. Realizing at the revelation of the Pacific that there was yet another huge ocean to cross—must have struck early explorers with the force of thunder. In the late twentieth century, the sensation Keats so exquisitely depicts is alive and well, thanks to computer networking. The Internet, a worldwide, interconnecting, communicating amalgam of more than eleven thousand networks, ten million users, and a growth rate that makes attempts to quantify it in print necessarily obsolete, inspires just that sense of awe. The moment you run your first Telnet session, logging on to a remote computer, or use FTP to retrieve a file from another continent, you know the boundaries that separate us are being redefined.

But how do you know what to do? Unlike commercial on-line services, the Internet provides few pointers. Most users, logging on through a UNIX-based service provider, work with a cryptic prompt as simple, and in some ways as profound, as a Japanese watercolor's brushstroke. You can make your modem take you around the world in seconds, retrieving files, reading mail, subscribing to electronic journals, using remote databases, but you have to know where you're going and the commands you'll need once you're there. That's what this book is about—a guide to navigating the Internet, assembled with the dial-up user in mind.

DESTINATIONS YOU HAVEN'T THOUGHT OF

There can be no complete printed directory of the Internet. Those who write about this globe-spanning network are destined to labor forever behind the technological wave. Simply put, the Internet is changing so rapidly, with so many new databases, services, addresses, and projects, that it can't be neatly encapsulated in any one set of commands or maxims. The more you use the Internet, the more you will realize that each day is itself a learning process.

Each discovery leads to another, for the Internet is self-referential. A casual reference on a BITNET mailing list may point to a hitherto unknown resource on a computer halfway across the country. A file on that computer may remind you of the existence of a USENET newsgroup which, once subscribed to, updates you on new Internet services. You will seldom find yourself exactly where you planned when you embark on an Internet voyage.

This book will construct a set of strategies that will allow you to get started. The book provides mapping to put you in the neighborhood of your destination, just as early maps of the New World sketched out the coast of Cuba, or Hispaniola, or Virginia, but left it to later cartographers to bring further precision to the task. Even today, maps are continually being refined as more precise methods of measurement are developed. So too on the Internet, new directories are coming into being that attempt to solve the problem of locating resources—the INTERNIC, or Internet Network Information Center, is but one such attempt; the INTERNIC will be explored in subsequent chapters. By necessity, some of the destinations will have subtly changed before this book is printed, but you should be close enough to them to catch on to the changes and proceed. You'll need to be attentive and creative in your dealings with a network as powerful and elastic as this.

INTERNET ECHOES FROM ALL OVER

There are thousands of Internet destinations. Network links remain largely a phenomenon of the developed world, but even Eastern Europe, South America, and Africa are beginning to sprout network nodes. Traffic on Internet mailing lists regularly reveals addresses from countries only now establishing their connectivity, and the clear benefits of network access in terms of tying together the academic communities of developing areas ensures this trend will only accelerate. After a short time on-line, you begin to take international connectivity almost for granted.

A newsgroup on the USENET network, called **misc.test,** exists so that people who send test messages don't tie up the daily reading of newsgroups with greater content. A number of sites around the world monitor this newsgroup, and if you send a test message on it, you'll receive a set of replies, letting you know your message was indeed received and where.

When I posted a test message on **misc.test,** the replies began immediately. The first was from the University of Zurich in Switzerland. Next was Ingres Corporation in Alameda, CA, acknowledging reception of my two-line message "General Test." After that was a Free-Net in Youngstown, OH; Free-Nets provide community services and offer Internet gateways to their local audience. I heard from a site in Lyon, France, as well as Harper Community College in Palatine, IL. Lund, Sweden responded, and so too did Network Architecture Consulting, a firm in Fremont, CA. And I heard from a commercial site in Hollywood, CA (just below the Hollywood sign, said the message), and the University of Natal in Durban, South Africa.

The Internet crosses borders and oceans with daredevil ease. There is no greater challenge to a parochial outlook than a day or two monitoring message traffic.

VIA THE INTERNET TO THE ASTEROIDS

What seems outlandish when you begin your Internet journeys becomes commonplace with experience. Yet in all the time I've been making these voyages, I've never lost a sense of wonder at the bounty available out on the network. Take images, for example. You'll find plentiful files in a variety of formats and subject matter, ranging from museum exhibits on the Vatican library to photographs of landscapes and people. One of my favorite sites is a NASA archive containing imagery from agency missions, including photos of Jupiter, Venus, and the Space Shuttle.

An asteroid named Toutatis, for example, made a close pass to the Earth on December 8, 1992, closing to within 2.2 million miles. NASA's Deep Space Network site in Goldstone, CA, bounced radar off the asteroid, creating a set of images which can be retrieved on-line. By using the Internet procedure known as anonymous FTP, you can log on to the computer at this site (its Internet address is **ames.arc.nasa.gov**) to download this material. There is also a text file, **toutatis.txt,** which presents the captions for these photographs. Figure 1.1 shows the images.

Whether you're interested in photos from Viking, Voyager, Magellan, or a host of other astronomical vistas, NASA's site is bound to contain what you're looking for.

FTP, as you'll quickly learn, is a primary tool for Internet exploration. Using FTP, dial-up users can move into remote computers, change directories and examine their contents, and transfer copies of their holdings to their service provider's computer. From there, they can download the files they've chosen onto their own hard disks. We'll go through the procedures for FTP and use it frequently to retrieve documents as we build an Internet file library.

Figure 1.1
Images from NASA of
the asteroid Toutatis.

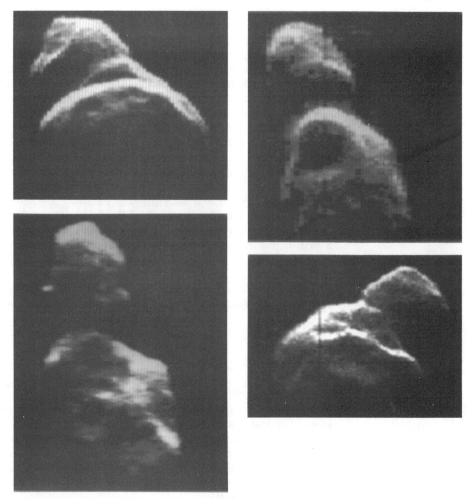

FINDING A MAP OF FINLAND

When my son needed a topographical map of Finland for a school report, it
seemed a simple enough project, but the problem was time. It was too late to
head for the library. Fortunately, I recalled a computer site in Finland—
garbo.uwasa.fi at the University of Vaasa—that maintained GIF files. GIF is a
format used to encode many of the images found on the Internet (the Toutatis
pictures discussed earlier were downloaded as GIF files, and then run through
a file viewer for presentation). Could the computer at Vaasa help?

FTP is fast. Enter the appropriate commands and you're there before you
know it. Searching through the directories in Finland, I found a directory called
pc/gif. Moving to it, I requested a listing of its contents, selected a file called
suomi.gif, and moved it to the computer I dial in to in Research Triangle Park.
I then downloaded it to my PC and printed a copy on my laser printer. Problem
solved. The map is shown in Figure 1.2.

SOFTWARE IN PROFUSION

I was lucky, because I happened to remember a collection of GIF files in Finland at this site. Multiply the number of FTP sites around the world by the number of available files and you quickly realize there is software out there by the gigabyte, waiting to be accessed. There are collections of shareware and public domain software, not to mention text files on a wide variety of subjects, so extensive as to boggle the mind. Looking for telecommunications programs, I turned to the huge archive at Washington University in St. Louis, at the address **wuarchive.wustl.edu.** Like the Finnish computer, this site is accessible by anonymous FTP.

Figure 1.3 shows a screen from a recent visit to Washington University. It may give you some idea of the scope of the contents there.

Note that each of these entries has a name, listed on the far right. There's a section on PostScript, one on the communications program Qmodem, one on security, and one on spreadsheets. At the far left, you'll see that each entry is marked with the letter **d.** Every entry so marked is itself a directory, containing an abundance of software. We are looking at a single, tiny corner of a vast software archive. It is but one of many such archives on the Internet. The tools that help you track down just the file you need are covered later in this book.

TRACKING WHITE HOUSE PRESS RELEASES

Are you hoping to chase down the White House line on a particular issue? The Internet offers several ways to do just that. A number of USENET newsgroups

Figure 1.2
A map of Finland,
direct from the source.

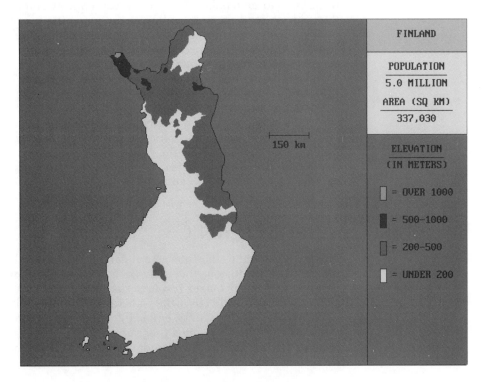

Figure 1.3
A world of software
awaits in Internet-linked
machines.

```
drwxr-xr-x   2 root     archive       1536 Jun 18 02:38 postscript
drwxr-xr-x   2 root     archive        512 Jun 18 02:39 preprocess
drwxr-xr-x   2 root     archive       3584 Jun 29 00:32 printer
drwxr-xr-x   2 root     archive       1024 Jun 18 02:39 procomm
drwxr-xr-x   2 root     archive        512 Jun 18 02:39 prodigy
drwxr-xr-x   2 root     archive       1024 Jun 18 02:39 progjourn
drwxr-xr-x   2 root     archive        512 Jun 18 02:39 prolog
drwxr-xr-x   2 root     archive       2048 Jul  1 00:28 qbasic
drwxr-xr-x   2 root     archive       1024 Jun 18 02:39 qedit
drwxr-xr-x   2 root     archive        512 Jun 18 02:39 qemm
drwxr-xr-x   2 root     archive       1024 Jun 18 02:39 qmodem
drwxr-xr-x   2 root     archive        512 Jun 18 02:39 qpascal
drwxr-xr-x   2 root     archive       1024 Jun 18 02:39 qtrdeck
drwxr-xr-x   2 root     archive        512 Jun 18 02:39 ramdisk
drwxr-xr-x   2 root     archive       2048 Jun 18 02:39 rbbs-pc
drwxr-xr-x   2 root     archive        512 Jun 18 02:39 satellite
drwxr-xr-x   2 root     archive       4608 Jul  1 00:28 screen
drwxr-xr-x   2 root     archive        512 Jun 18 02:39 security
drwxr-xr-x   2 root     archive        512 Jun 18 02:39 simulation
drwxr-xr-x   2 root     archive        512 Jun 18 02:39 small-c
drwxr-xr-x   2 root     archive        512 Jun 18 02:39 smalltalk
drwxr-xr-x   2 root     archive        512 Jun 18 02:39 snobol4
drwxr-xr-x   2 root     archive       1536 Jun 18 02:39 sound
drwxr-xr-x   2 root     archive       1024 Jun 18 02:39 spreadsheet
```

distribute press releases. Or you might want to receive them by electronic mail. By sending e-mail to **clinton-info@campaign92.org,** I was able to request press releases on foreign policy. The process was entirely automated; the computer at this address read the subject line of my incoming message—**receive foreign policy**—and knew this was a request to send press releases to my Internet address. You can also specify releases on the economy, on social policy, even speeches by administration officials.

Maybe you want to track down older information. The press releases are being archived at various sites. At some sites, you can use a search engine called WAIS to fine-tune your search strategy. We'll cover WAIS in Chapter 13. Other sites allow you to sign on by anonymous FTP, just as we did previously when we looked for files, maps, and photographs. You can join in the action too, by sending electronic mail to the White House. The current address is **president@whitehouse.gov.** As you see, one of the strengths of the Internet is the variety of ways resources can be retrieved.

Burrowing into the INTERNIC

Is there any logic to the Internet? It can be hard to find, for just as resources may exist in profusion, they may be hidden from us by the proliferation of network sites. That makes resource discovery a major theme of the network, and later chapters will cover the wide range of tools available.

Works is underway to assemble information in a central repository known as the INTERNIC. By using a program called Telnet to access the site **rs.internic.net,** we can look at the abundance the INTERNIC has to offer. Figure 1.4 shows some resources using the Internet tool called **gopher.**

Figure 1.4
The INTERNIC offers Internet information through a variety of tools, including the easy-to-use **gopher.**

```
           Internet Gopher Information Client v1.11

                  InterNIC Directory of Directories

  -->  1.  Keyword Search of the InterNIC Directory Listings <?>
       2.  Archive Sites/
       3.  Bulletin Board Systems/
       4.  Communication Documents Archive Sites/
       5.  Computing Centers/
       6.  Databases/
       7.  Dictionaries/
       8.  Directories/
       9.  Documents/
      10.  Education/
      11.  FTP Sites/
      12.  Internet Introductory Materials/
      13.  Libraries/
      14.  Mailing Lists/
      15.  Multi-media/
      16.  Network Administration/
      17.  Network Associations/
      18.  Network Information Centers/

  Press █ for Help, █ to Quit, █ to go up a menu              Page: 1/2
```

The INTERNIC has just come on-line as this book is being written; it's sure to expand as users think of new information sources they'd like to see there. A look even now, though, can answer many basic Internet questions. As we proceed, I'll show you how to use Telnet procedures to make this connection. Chances are the INTERNIC will become a regular supply station as you continue your explorations.

ROCKY MOUNTAIN HIGH

The advantage of Telnet is its range; you can use it to take the controls of computers worldwide. Each machine you access will make different options available. Some are full featured indeed, as in the case of the CARL System, the Colorado Alliance of Research Libraries' contribution to data proliferation. Take a glance at the menu in Figure 1.5 and you'll realize how abundant the information is on this system. I got here simply by entering a Telnet command: **telnet pac.carl.org.**

It's not a bad list—there are library catalogs, including government publications, as well as a range of databases and an on-line encyclopedia, among other entries. The ERIC database of education resources is a frequently tapped source. Some of CARL's services require an account, but many are available for public access.

CHECKING OUT THE NEWS ON CAMPUS

Throughout North America and, increasingly, around the world, universities are beginning to implement on-line services called Campus Wide Information Systems, or CWIS. Because I have a friend at Cornell University in Ithaca, NY, I occasionally want to find out what's happening at the school. It's easy to use a

Figure 1.5
The Colorado
Association of
Research Libraries
offers plentiful
information sources.

```
        CARL offers access to the following groups of databases:


              1. Library Catalogs
                    (including Government Publications)

              2. Current Article Indexes and Access
                    (including UnCover and ERIC)

              3. Information Databases
                    (including Encyclopedia)

              4. Other Library Systems

              5. Library and System News



        Enter the NUMBER of your choice, and press the <RETURN> key >>
```

variant of Telnet, called **tn3270,** to zip up to Cornell and see what's on the bill. In addition to campus events, CWIS systems often include other information such as directories of students and faculty, services like Cornell's Uncle Ezra (wherein students can discuss problems with an on-line advisor), dictionaries or encyclopedias, weather, sports, and news. Figure 1.6 shows you the sign-on screen at Cornell's Electronic Information Source.

ALL THE WAY TO THE SUPREME COURT

Project Hermes is the result of efforts to make United States Supreme Court decisions available on-line. A consortium involving Case Western Reserve University, EDUCOM, and the National Public Telecomputing Network is behind this new means of distribution. Now, when a decision comes out, you can retrieve the full text of the Court's opinions minutes after release, at no charge. The files are distributed over the Internet and BITNET, as well as the growing network of community computer systems called Free-Nets. You can also have Court opinions mailed to you.

Figure 1.7 shows a small sample of the opinions available in the *hermes* directory of the FTP site at **ftp.cwru.edu.**

TO NEW ZEALAND BY WAY OF USENET

From Case Western Reserve in Cleveland, it's time to hop across the Pacific. Intrigued since childhood with New Zealand, I used to try to keep up with Kiwi news by means of a shortwave receiver and Radio New Zealand, which was almost impossible to catch except at late hours. Now I keep up by USENET,

Figure 1.6
A look at happenings
at Cornell University.

```
        C U I N F O - Cornell University's Electronic Information Source

                                 MAIN MENU
    Select...  For items such as...

     NEWS      Weather, World/Local News, Grad. Bulletin, Safety Reports, Updates
     EVENTS    Calendars, Athletics, Colloquia, Theatre, Music, Movies...
     DIALOGS   DrugIQ Net, Mr. Chips, Uncle Ezra, Auntie Em, Nutriquest, Suggest
     SERVICES  Careers, Computing, Directories, Food, Health, Housing, Jobs,
                  Library, Just The Facts, OEO, Support, Transport, Volunteer...


    Or select a more general category like...

     ACADEM    Information about Cornell instruction and research
     ADMIN     Items from and about Cornell administrative offices
     ITHACA    General information for and about the Ithaca area


    Or type the name of any specific CUINFO entry such as WEATHER, DIRECT, or EZRA.
    (Type INDEX for a list of available items, or DETAILS for descriptions.)

          Please select a topic or type HELP for hints.  (Blank to exit.)


    --
                                                          C U I N F O
```

where a newsgroup called **soc.culture.new-zealand** carries on a lively discussion of topics related to the North and South Islands. A major bonus of this newsgroup is the presence of one Alan Murray of the University of Canterbury in Christchurch. The indefatigable Murray updates the list frequently with a digest of local news events drawn from his morning paper.

ON-LINE TO ANCIENT GREECE

Electronic books offer certain advantages over their hard-copy brethren. While you can't hold them in your lap for idle browsing, they're nonetheless excellent

Figure 1.7
Supreme Court
opinions are readily
available online.

```
File            Title
----            -----
7-2048S:        TEXACO INC. v. HASBROUCK, Syllabus
7-2048O:        87-2048--OPINION, TEXACO INC. v. HASBROUCK
7-2048C1:       87-2048--CONCUR, TEXACO INC. v. HASBROUCK
7-2048C2:       87-2048--CONCUR, TEXACO INC. v. HASBROUCK


74-ORIG.S:      GEORGIA v. SOUTH CAROLINA, Syllabus

74-ORIG.O:      No. 74, Orig.--OPINION, GEORGIA v. SOUTH CAROLINA
74-ORIG.D1:     No. 74, Orig.--DISSENT, GEORGIA v. SOUTH CAROLINA
74-ORIG.D2:     No. 74, Orig.--DISSENT, GEORGIA v. SOUTH CAROLINA
74-ORIG.D3:     No. 74, Orig.--DISSENT, GEORGIA v. SOUTH CAROLINA
74-ORIG.D4:     No. 74, Orig.--DISSENT, GEORGIA v. SOUTH CAROLINA


88-1125.S:      HODGSON v. MINNESOTA, Syllabus
88-1125.O:      88-1125 & 88-1309--OPINION, HODGSON v. MINNESOTA
88-1125.C:      88-1125 & 88-1309--CONCUR, HODGSON v. MINNESOTA
88-1125.CD1:    88-1125 & 88-1309--CONCUR/DISSENT, HODGSON v. MINNESOTA
```

for text searching. Do you want to find every reference to fate in Sophocles' Oedipus Trilogy? With an ASCII text file of the material, it's a simple matter to load Sophocles' work into a text editor and use its *find* function to track down the word. No wonder CD-ROMs full of text material are becoming common. An electronic version of *Roget's Thesaurus* allows you to locate the word you need almost instantly. An electronic encyclopedia makes it possible to search for cross-linkages between referenced citations. Commonplace reference books suddenly spring into three-dimensional life.

Project Gutenberg, run by Michael Hart at Illinois Benedictine College in Lisle, IL, is an attempt to make ASCII texts of classic works available to as wide an audience as possible. Using FTP, I frequently visit the archive site at **mrcnext.cso.uiuc.edu,** heeding the system's request not to tap the service between 10 A.M. and 5 P.M. local time. There, I can find and download everything from *Paradise Lost* to *Aesop's Fables,* from *Alice in Wonderland* to *The Federalist Papers,* along with recent references like the *CIA World Factbook* and *The Hackers' Dictionary.* We'll examine Project Gutenberg, along with another text project—the Online Book Initiative—in Chapter 10.

A NICE DAY FOR NETWORKING

The University of Michigan can help if you're looking for a weather forecast. The Weather Underground is menu-driven, providing current weather information and forecasts in a strictly noncommercial setting. Figure 1.8 illustrates the outlook for Raleigh, NC.

BITNET AND THE OVERSTUFFED MAILBOX

USENET isn't the only place to keep up with news. BITNET can send information through gateways into the Internet and straight into your electronic mailbox. Every day, when I sign on, I have messages about subjects I've culled from a list of thousands. There are astronomy postings, physics musings and discussions, a genial argument about Anglo-Saxon poetry, and a wild and woolly debate about the future of the Internet and the National Research and Education Network. And, every now and then, I receive messages about the formation of new lists, to which I can subscribe or not, as the inclination moves me.

NORWAVES is a new mailing list developed by four students in Norway who are working with the Norwegian Information Council through its NORINFORM press office. Subscribers (subscriptions are free) will receive weekly news in English from Scandinavia. The address is **nwnews@nki.no.** Norway is but one of many countries you can follow on the network.

Through mailing lists, USENET newsgroups, and electronic mail itself, it's possible to keep abreast of news in just about any part of the world. This will continue to develop as the Internet expands into the nations of Africa and South America.

By now, you should be getting the idea. The problem with the Internet is its vastness; a description could start almost anywhere. Every time you sign on, there are new services available and new databases to explore. Mailing lists seem to pop up overnight, and with the current trend toward commercial use of the network, services like ClariNet and Msen Reuters News Service are turning your electronic mailbox into a digital newspaper, with stories chosen according to

Figure 1.8
Weather forecasts can
be generated for just
about anywhere.

```
Weather Conditions at 11 AM EDT on 29 JUN 93 for Raleigh-Durham, NC.
Temp(F)     Humidity(%)     Wind(mph)     Pressure(in)     Weather
=======================================================================
  86           54%           SW at 7        29.96          Clear

TRIANGLE AREA FORECAST
NATIONAL WEATHER SERVICE RALEIGH/DURHAM NC
1143 AM EDT THU JUL 1 1993

 THIS AFTERNOON...VARIABLY CLOUDY WITH SCATTERED SHOWERS AND
THUNDERSTORMS. HIGH NEAR 90. LIGHT WIND. CHANCE OF RAIN 30
PERCENT.
 TONIGHT...PARTLY CLOUDY WITH A SLIGHT CHANCE OF THUNDERSTORMS
DURING THE EVENING. LOW AROUND 70. LIGHT WIND. CHANCE OF RAIN 20
PERCENT.
 FRIDAY...PARTLY CLOUDY WITH A SLIGHT CHANCE OF AN AFTERNOON OR
EVENING THUNDERSTORM. HIGH NEAR 90. CHANCE OF RAIN 20 PERCENT.
 FOURTH OF JULY FORECAST...PARTLY CLOUDY. CHANCE OF THUNDERSTORMS.
LOWS IN THE 70S. HIGHS IN THE 90S.

HIGH AND LOW SINCE MIDNIGHT  82  70
    Press Return to continue, M to return to menu, X to exit:
```

profiles you select. On-line journals are changing the boundaries of the publishing industry, making retrieval of past issues as simple as querying the proper server computer. Newsletters on a wide variety of subjects have begun to appear; their numbers can only increase. Believe it or not, there's even an Internet radio program, available through the network itself.

THE INTERNET CATCH

There's also a catch. Many of the best resources for accessing and using the Internet are found on-line. The development of the new INTERNIC as a central repository for Internet materials ensures there will always be a place to turn when problems arise. Across the Internet, there are lists of access providers, suggestions on how to use everything from e-mail to remote databases, tutorials, lists of frequently asked questions, newsgroups for beginners. If you spend some time reading through just a fraction of this material, you will quickly become proficient at using the network.

The Internet catch: How do you learn what you need to know about the Internet? You read the Internet materials that can help you. How do you obtain the Internet materials that can help you? You have to be on the Internet.

That's why I wrote this book. I fumbled around making every mistake possible as I first tried to gain access to, then learn how to use, the Internet. This is the book I wish I had had available to me when I began my first voyages. If it can help you as you set sail, I will be gratified indeed.

CHAPTER ONE NOTES

1. "On First Looking into Chapman's Homer." From *The New Oxford Book of English Verse*, chosen and edited by Helen Gardner. New York: Oxford University Press, 1972.

2

The Internet Defined

The Internet is a vast and sprawling network reaching into computer sites worldwide. By its very nature, this interlinked web of networks defies attempts at quantification. Some sources cite Internet penetration into over one hundred countries, with eleven thousand separate networks feeding into it containing up to 1.7 million host computers and ten million users.[1] Other sources give higher user figures, citing fifteen million people in the United States and twenty-five million worldwide who have used the Internet.[2] Indeed, estimates about the Internet's growth are proliferating almost as fast as new host computers on the network.

Consider that by 1985, approximately one hundred networks formed the Internet. By 1989, that number had risen to five hundred. The Network Information Center of the Defense Data Network Information Center found 2,218 networks connected as of January 1990. By June 1991, the National Science Foundation Network Information Center pegged it at close to four thousand, and, as we've seen, connections have more than doubled within the last two years. If we extrapolate based on current numbers, the Internet could reach forty million people by 1995, one hundred million by 1998. Its current growth rate is 15 percent monthly.

Couple that information with an estimated 120–150 million personal computers in use worldwide and you've created a situation with dramatic possibilities. Few of the desktop computers in the average home, for example, are networked together. But many home and business computer users would like to access the Internet's rich resources.

Until recently, it was difficult to access the Internet on a dial-up basis using a modem, but the increase in Internet service providers offering such services has improved that situation. In the past year and a half, estimates John Eldredge of Performance Systems International, a major service provider in Reston, VA, the number of individuals connecting to the Internet by dial-up has increased from 50 to 80 percent.[3] And commercial providers such as CompuServe, GEnie, and Prodigy have either made Internet mail access available or announced plans to do so. DELPHI and BIX have full Internet connections with access to all major services. Demand is intense. "We've seen an incredible response to our offering of full Internet services," says DELPHI general manager Rusty Williams. "It's been well received by current members and by other people looking for Internet service options—people in business, students, researchers, families."[4] UNIX-based service providers tell much the same story of growth in the individual user market.

A BRIEF HISTORY OF THE INTERNET

The Internet's beginnings gave no hint it would evolve into a network accessible by the public. Like many other great ideas, the "network of networks" grew out of a project that began with far different intent: a network called ARPANET, designed and developed in 1969 by Bolt, Beranek, and Newman under contract to the Advanced Research Projects Agency of the U.S. Department of Defense (ARPA).

The ARPANET was a network connecting university, military, and defense contractors; it was established to aid researchers in the process of sharing information, and not coincidentally to study how communications could be maintained in the event of nuclear attack. From humble beginnings—the ARPANET's founders originally contemplated letting only researchers log on and run programs on remote computers—the network grew. They soon added file transfer capabilities, electronic mail, and mailing lists to keep people interested in common subjects in communication.

But even as the ARPANET proceeded, other networks were under development, and it became clear that new methods of communicating were necessary. As early as 1973, in an era of mainframe computing a decade before the desktop revolution took hold, ARPA, under its new acronym DARPA (Defense Advanced Research Projects Agency),[5] began a program called the Internetting Project to study how to link packet networks together. Central to the concept of internetting—networking different networks together—is the need to overcome network-specific protocols. Now, special *gateways* can connect networks and pass traffic from one to the next.

Finding the Right Protocol

The solution for creating such internetwork links was to find the right protocol. A *protocol* is simply a set of conventions that determines how data will be exchanged between different programs. Protocols specify how the network is to move messages and handle errors; using them allows the creation of standards separate from a particular hardware system. TCP/IP, or Transmission Control Protocol/Internet Protocol, is a system of protocols commonly used for wide area networking; its success has made the Internet possible. These powerful protocols were developed in 1974 by Robert Kahn, a major figure in ARPANET development, and now president of the Corporation for National Research Initiatives (CNRI), and computer scientist Vinton G. Cerf, now president of the Internet Society and vice-president of CNRI.

If you think of the Internet as a metanetwork, a network made up of interconnected networks, you'll see the distinction between this highly decentralized structure and the commercial on-line services, which are managed from the top by a single business, and which route traffic to one or more mainframe computers. Around the world, Digital Equipment Corporation's minicomputers work with Sun Microsystems' workstations and a wide variety of other equipment, connected through special computers called routers and hubs. Computers ranging from standalone PCs and Macintoshes, to Intel machines connected as an office network, to large-scale regional networks connected to high-speed network backbones, all participate in the network's development.

Incidentally, TCP/IP is not the only protocol for connecting a variety of differing networks. The Internet is becoming a multi-protocol network, integrating other standards such as Open Systems Interconnection (OSI), a protocol suite developed by The International Organization for Standardization (ISO). OSI implementations became available in the early 1990s. Systems using other protocols, like BITNET, connect through gateways into the Internet, allowing Internet users to tap their riches. The UNIX-to-UNIX Copy Program (UUCP) network connects thousands of computers by dial-up telephone lines; its e-mail destinations are likewise available to the Internet user.

What Is Packet Switching?

The ARPANET and the networks that grew from it highlight the differences between two ways of moving information. *Circuit switching* is one-to-one contact like a telephone call; if you set up a data session between two computers by using ordinary phone lines, placing a call when you needed to move data, you would be using circuit switching. It's useful when you need to connect two computers for the transfer of large amounts of data.

But circuit switching isn't as workable for complex applications requiring contact with two or more computers. That's where *packet switching* comes in. Data carried by packet switching is reduced to chunks and given header information containing the necessary routing. Computers on the network (they're called *packet switches*) examine these headers and move the data packet to another site. Each time, the packet gets closer to its destination. A major bonus of packet switching is that the computers routing the data can select alternate routes when a given link fails. Another bonus: the computers at either end of a packet network connection can operate at different speeds. The network itself acts as a buffer that adjusts for the difference.

The Internet Emerges

When the U.S. Defense Communications Agency mandated TCP/IP for all ARPANET hosts, it established a standard by which the Internet could grow. From this point forward, it would be possible to add more gateways, connecting more networks, while the original core networks remained intact. Most people date the true arrival of the Internet at 1983, the year when the original ARPANET was split into MILNET—to be used for military communications—and the ARPANET—for continuing research into networking. But CSNET, a network linking computer science departments in several states, was the first autonomous network DARPA allowed to connect to the ARPANET as early as 1980.[6]

CSNET eventually merged with BITNET in 1989 (BITNET's story will be told in Chapter 9). The ARPANET itself was decommissioned in June of 1990, its functions absorbed into the broader structure of the Internet. But the two had established a principle: let networks communicate by a set of workable protocols, with new networks being added into an ever-growing metanetwork communicating through gateways. By the time of the ARPANET's demise, the National Science Foundation had taken over much of its functionality through a network of its own.

Connecting Supercomputers

That network, the National Science Foundation Network, or NSFNET, grew out of a particular networking need. NSF wanted to connect its six supercomputer centers around the country and began a network program to link the sites to the scientific community. TCP/IP would be the protocol of choice. By 1986, NSF had expanded these efforts into a backbone network called NSFNET; it also helped fund regional networks whose purpose was to connect universities to NSFNET to give researchers access to supercomputers.

The original NSFNET backbone connected six sites by 56-kilobits-per-second (Kbps) data circuits, a topology that quickly became overloaded as traffic increased. This backbone carried some 115 million packets per month in the first half of 1988.[7] In 1987, NSF awarded a contract to Merit, Inc. (the Michigan Education and Research Infrastructure Triad), working in partnership with MCI Corporation and IBM, to manage and operate the NSFNET backbone, as well as to continue its development. The growing backbone now connected some thirteen sites, six of them supercomputer centers, the others regional networks.

By July 1988, the network comprised thirteen nodes using T-1 connections at 1.5 megabits per second (Mbps). Traffic flow quickly expanded to fill the communications channels, averaging a 20-percent-per-month growth between July 1988 and July 1989. A fourteenth node was added and connections were put in place for FIX East and FIX West (FIX stands for Federal Interagency eXchange), which are governmental interagency connection points. FIX West is located at the NASA Ames Research Center near San Francisco; FIX East is near the University of Maryland.

In September 1990, the National Science Foundation announced the formation of Advanced Network & Services, Inc. ANS was the creation of Merit, IBM, and MCI. The three proposed its formation to provide structure to the NSFNET operation. Operating under contract to Merit, ANS would operate the T-1 backbone for NSFNET and build a new T-3 (45 Mbps) backbone to supersede it.

The T-3 backbone became an operational reality on December 2, 1992, creating a 700-fold increase in power since the 56-Kbps days. T-3 speeds carry data at the equivalent of fourteen hundred pages of single-spaced, typed text per second.[8] These remarkable numbers were no less noteworthy than the traffic figures behind them. NSFNET traffic had grown from 195 million packets in August 1988, to almost 24 billion by November 1992. In that month the network reached the billion-packet-a-day mark, and network traffic growth continued at a rate of 11 percent per month.

With the T-3 backbone functioning, a new arrangement was developed that would allow ANS to operate two separate networks over the same equipment. NSFNET itself would continue to support institutions reliant on government subsidies for their connections. But ANS would also create a subsidiary called ANS CO+RE which would support commercial users of the network. In doing this, ANS thus joined UUNET Technologies and Performance Systems International in the ranks of commercial providers.

NSFNET is therefore no longer *the* backbone for Internet traffic in the United States; it's merely another ANS customer (albeit a major one). NSFNET has become a national research network, deeply involved with the ongoing debate over the creation of a National Research and Education Network. With its high-speed connections now in place, it links agency networks such as ESnet (Department of Energy) and NSInet (National Aeronautics and Space Administration), as well as providing access to local and regional networks.

Add to this complicated picture the varying conditions of the so-called mid-level networks. Some are operated by their states, as is PREPnet in Pennsylvania. Others are run by university consortia operating large regional networks, such as SURAnet or MIDnet. Some of the regionals are run commercially, as is CERFnet, while others are managed by university computer scientists. Some of these networks have become independent from NSF subsidies; others retain close NSF connections. NSF has encouraged regional networks to connect to new sites even as it maintained the general expectation that the regionals would become financially independent within three to five years. At the same time, the regionals have also been encouraged to offer network services as a way of achieving that independence.

THE STRUCTURE OF THE INTERNET

A strict definition is useful for describing what the Internet has become. In his book *The Matrix: Computer Networks and Conferencing Systems Worldwide* (Digital Press, 1990), John S. Quarterman describes the Internet as "an internetwork of many networks all running the TCP/IP protocol suite..., connected through gateways, and sharing common name and address spaces."[9]

There you have an operating definition: The Internet is held together by TCP/IP. What then of networks operating under different protocols which, however, can be contacted through the Internet? BITNET, an academic network many of whose resources are reachable through an Internet connection, isn't a part of the Internet because it uses its own protocols. So does UUCP, the UNIX-to-UNIX Copy Program where USENET began. USENET is commonly read by people on the Internet, but because it propagates by different protocols, it's not strictly speaking *on the Internet*.

What should we make of such distinctions? They have value in helping us understand what we're dealing with, to be sure, but for the purpose of hands-on network use, let's broaden our scope to what Quarterman, following the lead of science-fiction novelist William Gibson, calls the "Matrix." Quarterman again: "The Matrix is a worldwide metanetwork of connected computer networks and conferencing systems that provides unique services that are like, yet unlike, those of telephones, post offices, and libraries."[10]

Most of us will continue to refer to this metanetwork as the Internet, though in the back of our minds we have Quarterman's distinctions in mind. What we mean is access to the Internet and the various networks it comprises, including its gateways into networks that run under widely different protocols. For me, for example, BITNET is invaluable; I probably spend more time reading BITNET mailing lists than any other on-line activity. I don't need a separate network connection to mine its riches, but I concede that the technology behind it is considerably different from that which drives the Internet proper.

When we get down to examining individual network resources, we'll see that a wide range of skills must be employed to use them. I can search for information in a variety of ways on the Internet, including through the use of a developing generation of resource discovery tools. But searching an Internet database through hot new techniques such as Wide Area Information Servers is vastly different from using the BITNET protocols to rummage through files on one of its server computers. Don't be surprised by this; it's the necessary result of the Internet's (and related networks') diversity. We are not yet at a sufficiently advanced state of technology where rival approaches to presenting information have all been subsumed under a single user interface. Nor are we likely to be there soon.

An Internet Cartography

Early explorers of the New World constructed their first maps by following alien coastlines, tracing out river mouths, bays, and harbors as their ships proceeded. The only way to assemble a complete picture, even of a small section of coast, was to sail its entire length. Later, charts could be compared with the work of other navigators, until out of shared experience more accurate maps emerged. Even now, maps are under constant refinement, as satellite observations allow cartographers to measure distance and size to an extent hitherto considered impossible. Other kinds of maps also preoccupy us, for humans are mapping creatures. Thus we map the structure of galaxies, of chemical compounds, and, audaciously, the hidden coding of the human genome, perhaps the greatest challenge of all.

Each mapping project proceeds with its own set of assumptions and difficulties. Surprisingly, mapping the Internet takes us into the realm of metaphysics. We can trace out network connections throughout the world, even as we realize that the network's constantly changing parameters ensure no printed map, not even an electronic one posted online, can be completely up to date. But given a chart of major network connections, applying it to on-line navigation is another challenge. Maps show distance and proximity to other landmasses. Yet how do we measure distance in a network where it's as simple for me to send and receive mail from Taiwan as it is to read a campus directory at the University of North Carolina at Chapel Hill? How much does distance actually count in the electronic world?

As opposed to conventional geographic maps, which reveal the shapes and contours of land masses and oceans, an Internet map is like a diagram of a brain. What we see as we draw the various local and regional networks together with the high-speed backbone networks that link them is a set of clusters, places where connectivity is widespread. The map becomes hard to read; even computer scientists call this phenonmenon a *cloud* of connections, because it becomes impossible to trace out each pathway in the interweaving cyberspace. Move away from the densest intersections and network pathways begin to emerge from the cloud; as we move to less-networked areas—South America, say, or West Africa—each linkage becomes distinct.

A network map without connection overlays is easiest to decipher. Figure 2.1 shows a map prepared by Lawrence H. Landweber, founder of CSNET and a major figure in the development of the Internet, and the Internet Society; the map is used with their permission. This world view can't be considered an Internet map alone; it also displays the status of other networks, including BITNET, UUCP, and FidoNet, each of which runs under a different set of networking protocols than the Internet's TCP/IP. But because network linkages between the Internet and these other networks are so well established that Internet users routinely move between them, it seems reasonable to include them. As the map makes clear, many countries currently boast BITNET connections but do not as yet have Internet capability. This means they can move electronic mail between BITNET and the Internet, but they do not possess the Internet's Telnet and file transfer capabilities.

At the end of this chapter, you'll find a list of domain names, also compiled by Landweber, along with information about the status of the named country in terms of network linkages. The information presented in each column shows connections, sites and protocols available.

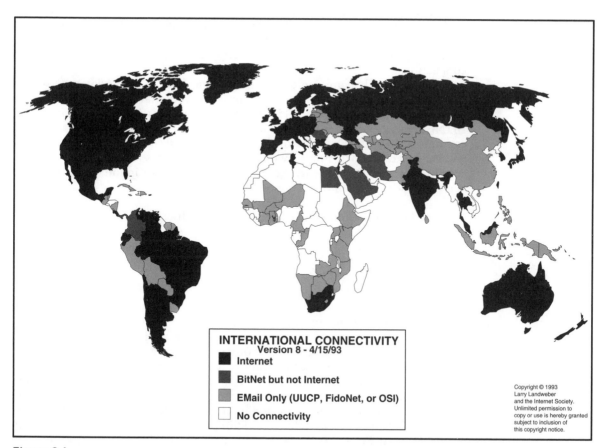

INTERNATIONAL CONNECTIVITY
Version 8 - 4/15/93
■ Internet
■ BitNet but not Internet
■ EMail Only (UUCP, FidoNet, or OSI)
□ No Connectivity

Copyright © 1993
Larry Landweber
and the Internet Society.
Unlimited permission to
copy or use is hereby granted
subject to inclusion of
this copyright notice.

Figure 2.1
International network connections are shown in this map prepared by Lawrence H. Landweber and the Internet Society.

When *Matrix News,* a monthly newsletter covering Internet and other network developments, set out to survey the state of the Internet, its conclusions were somewhat different from Landweber's.[11] *Matrix News,* for example, considers Russia to be on the Internet, whereas the Landweber list does not because networks there do not yet have permission for their trafic to move across the NSFNET backbone, making them inaccessible to many academic sites. The newsletter, because it used its own techniques for data discovery, also tracked networked sites in a number of countries which are not listed in the Landweber list. Clearly, the process of network mapping is collaborative and will draw on the resources of numerous network cartographers as we compile an authoritative picture.

Some intriguing notes from *Matrix News:* U.S. bases at the South Pole exchange electronic mail with the various networks through a satellite link to a NASA computer in Florida; otherwise, the most southerly network connection is Hobart, Tasmania. The northernmost network appearance seems to be a node on the NASA Science Network in Thule, Greenland; the second, a UUCP connection in Atqasuk, Alaska. Iceland's most northerly site is at Kopasker, with Internet and UUCP connections. The network connection farthest west in longitude is Hawaii; easternmost is Fiji, at the Department of Mathematics at the University of the South Pacific in Suva, which maintains UUCP links to New Zealand. Russia's easternmost network connection is at Magadan, running both FidoNet and UUCP; even Sakhalin Island appears on a network map with UUCP connections.

The constantly changing dimensions of the Internet and related networks make this kind of mapping an on-going process. As of March, 1993, *Matrix News* estimated there were some 2,152,000 host computers between the Internet, BITNET, FidoNet, UUCP, and various corporate IP connections. This led to its estimate of 18,150,000 users worldwide in some 130 countries. These numbers will have grown considerably by the time this book sees print.

If you are interested in tracking such issues, a subscription to *Matrix News* is a good idea. You can reach the publication at:

Matrix Information and Directory Services, Inc.
P. O. Box 14621
Austin, TX 78761
Voice: 512-329-1087
Fax: 512-327-1274
E-mail: **mids@tic.com**

It's a vast and evolving structure, this Internet, an interlinked entity made of fiber-optic and copper cable and microwave links, reaching all the way from the depths of the world's fastest supercomputers to 1200 bps dial-up modems moving electronic mail traffic into some of the world's poorest countries. Clearly, a directory of all its constituent networks would be a massive volume which would quickly pass out of date. Users interested in tracking down network structure will, however, be interested in Tracy L. LaQuey's *The User's Directory of Computer Networks* (Digital Press, 1990) as well as John S. Quarterman's *The Matrix* (Digital Press, 1990); both are excellent starting points. And anyone seriously attempting to monitor network growth will learn that an active on-line presence is critical.

The Big Three Internet Applications

As Douglas Comer points out in his *Internetworking with TCP/IP. Vol 1: Principles, Protocols, and Architecture,* what you as an end user see of the TCP/IP protocols is a set of application programs that enable you to use the network to good advantage.[12] You and I don't need to know the intricacies of how TCP/IP functions, though if you're curious, there's no better or more respected guide than Comer's work. But running the programs themselves is simple, as we'll see.

Users of dial-up computer services, like users of bulletin board systems (BBS) and commercial on-line services, have come to expect certain capabilities from their providers, which the Internet provides in its own way through TCP/IP.

ELECTRONIC MAIL

Electronic mail is the most elementary service, and for many users, the most useful. Many people on the Internet have used nothing but electronic mail and still find the network indispensable. You can send messages to one or more people, deliver text files, retrieve information by automated computer programs like LISTSERV (by a gateway to BITNET), and more. While access to all three of the major Internet services is vastly preferable, it's possible to do quite a lot with electronic mail alone. A good thing, too, for aside from DELPHI and BIX, the only major on-line services with a full-fledged Internet connection, there is no access to the Internet from the other commercial services except by e-mail. That means, as we'll see in Chapter 3, you have three choices:

1. Learn to use the Internet through mail alone (Chapter 8 shows you how much you can do with such a connection).

2. Use DELPHI or BIX's full-service connection.

3. Get an account with one of the full-service dial-up providers discussed in Chapter 3 (more on these options there).

Ironically, in the early days of the ARPANET, electronic mail was considered an insignificant add-in to network capabilities. No one anticipated the high volume of traffic that began to flow as scientists exchanged ideas with geographically distant colleagues. Today electronic mail is taken for granted, from small companies with office networks to giant corporations linking remote offices worldwide. Its growth has been just as strong on the commercial networks, many of whose members maintain accounts solely for the e-mail connectivity they provide.

FILE TRANSFER

Moving files between computers is one of the handiest features of the networking revolution. If you can find something you can use—and if it's made publicly available, as are thousands of computer files on the Internet—you can transfer it to your computer. The process is called *file transfer protocol*, or FTP. You access documents made available to the public through a procedure called *anonymous FTP.* This procedure allows you to log on to remote computers and use the resources in directories the administrators have made available. Anonymous FTP will be a major tool as we retrieve files and build an Internet library later in this book.

With FTP procedures, the Internet gets challenging indeed. Instead of consulting a single library source, as on CompuServe or GEnie, for a catalog of files, you are faced with hundreds of computer sites offering programs and text files. To easily track down the program you need, you should learn about the access tools we'll discuss later. With them, you can locate programs, then use FTP to move them from the source computer to your service provider's computer at high speed, and subsequently download them to your own machine.

REMOTE LOGIN

Remote login, otherwise known as Telnet, provides the ability to connect to a remote computer and work with it on an interactive basis. Again, the Internet opens the doors to a worldwide computing environment, on many of whose connected machines are services, databases, and other resources that can be examined and manipulated. By using Telnet, you can log onto the library catalogs of distant universities, look for information about everything from the formation of distant galaxies to recipes for potato soup, and examine Supreme Court decisions or the lyrics of popular songs. All the while, your computer will act as a terminal of the remote computer, which will wait for your command. In many cases, menu-driven systems at the other end make interactive sessions fairly intuitive, but some systems are considerably easier to work with than others.

Note that when the network called "the Internet" is referred to in print, it always has a capital I. But you may also see abundant references, if you prowl your bookseller's shelves for computer books or read the computer press, to general terms such as "internets," "internetting," and "internetworking." Remember that TCP/IP can pass information among computers that aren't on *the* Internet. Your company, for example, might have local area networks in a number of sites. At some point, it would make sense for management to link those LANs together. One way of linking them is through TCP/IP. Your company would have established an *internet*, but you're not on *the Internet* unless you decide to be.

Public Packet Switching Networks

The ARPANET was the first major packet-switched network, running on an experimental basis for the use of DARPA contractors and not open to the general public. But out of the ARPANET's development came the birth of public packet-switched networks. Two companies were formed in the early 1970s—Packet Communications Inc. (PCI), created by former BBN employees, and Telenet Communications Inc., which BBN itself formed. PCI didn't last long, but Telenet grew into a public network which was eventually purchased by a subsidiary of GTE. By 1987, Telenet offered some eighteen thousand local telephone numbers nationwide and access from 70 foreign countries. Now known as SprintNet, Telenet continued to flourish, its growth paralleled by the development of other public packet networks like BT Tymnet, now owned by British Telecom, and CompuServe Packet Network.

Let's consider what packet switching does for dial-up telecommunications users. If you're calling a local bulletin board system, or BBS, your call moves through standard, voice-grade telephone lines. This is not a problem when calling locally, but calling a BBS half a continent away costs you long-distance charges. One reason public packet networks make sense is they allow you to call a local number that connects you to a computer known as a *node*, which routes your call through the packet network's system to its destination. Your on-line charges decrease and you have access to a wide range of services.

Another reason for using packet networks is the stability of the X.25 protocol, which retains its integrity even when line conditions are less than optimum; your chances of getting accurate data thereby increase. Most callers to commercial services such as CompuServe, GEnie, BIX, and DELPHI use packet networks to place their calls, and a number of Internet service providers are also available through the packet network, as we'll see in Chapter 3. Packet-switching networks bill the on-line services themselves for your connect time, so the bill you receive from the service includes network charges.

Although X.25 and TCP/IP are different protocols, the idea behind packet switching remains the same—route data to its destination by sorting it into clearly addressed packets which can move from machine to machine until delivered. If you do access the Internet via a public packet network, your traffic to and from your service provider will be handled by the public network's packet-switching protocols. But the traffic going between the Internet and your service provider's equipment will be managed by the Internet's TCP/IP protocols.

Put another way, the service provider's computer carries an IP (Internet Protocol) address—it is part of the functioning Internet. You can use that computer in a dial-up session to perform Internet functions, but your own computer, lacking an IP address of its own, is not itself on the Internet. As we'll see in Chapter 3, there are ways to provide a dial-up connection which includes an IP address—they're called SLIP and PPP. But most dial-up users will likely forego the extra costs associated with these options. For them, hitchhiking on a service provider's IP address provides more than sufficient connectivity.

How Data Moves—Transmission Media

It's easy to imagine a computer network in terms you may have encountered in a business office: computers connected by cables, moving information back and forth behind the scenes while users work at keyboards. In fact, however, the Internet's connectivity can't be visualized as a network of wires or even fiber-optic cabling alone. Digital data moves through special hardware devices called *routers* which connect networks and use sophisticated algorithms to choose the best route for network traffic.

How does the packetized data flow? Perhaps it flows through telephone lines, standard dial-up or leased lines, perhaps by satellite networks. And that's not all. Traffic can also flow through microwave radio transmission, fiber-optic cable connections, and even so-called *packet radio*. Let's look at each possibility.

DIAL-UP LINES

The telephone line running into your house is a dial-up line; the connection you make when calling a number lasts until you hang up. A dial-up link between two networks could be established for data transfer and then closed back down. The lowering cost of long-distance service has made this a workable alternative for people running small office networks. And as we'll see in Chapter 3, it's possible to call into an Internet site and access Internet services—even to become an on-line IP site yourself—using dial-up connections alone.

LEASED LINES

A leased line works differently. It's established as a full-time connection, always available for traffic flow between sites; leased lines are frequently called *dedicated lines*. Leased lines for digital data transmission come in various grades ranging from a speed of 2.5 kilobits per second to 45 megabits per second. **T1** service boasts a transmission rate of 1.544 megabits per second. A **T3** link is faster still, moving data at 45 megabits per second.

MICROWAVE

Microwave equipment can link networks without wires, using a transmitter to send data to a receiving antenna at the destination. Between the two are repeaters, whose job is to receive the signal, amplify it, and pass it along to the next station. Spacing between repeaters can vary depending on terrain since microwave is a line-of-sight medium.

SATELLITE COMMUNICATIONS

From geosynchronous orbits 22,500 miles above the equator, communications satellites offer advantages in the realm of very long distance communication. Transponders aboard the satellites receive signals from ground stations and re-broadcast them back to Earth. A *very small aperture terminal*, or VSAT, is the receiving antenna.

DATA BY RADIO

Radio modems allow users on the road to have access to network connections. Anterior Technology in Menlo Park, CA has developed an electronic mail gateway to the Internet and UUCP. The company's RadioMail, using a packet radio network called Mobitex, connects other major e-mail systems as well. Performance Systems International of Herndon, VA, is also active in this market.

NEARnet: A Representative Network

Let's take a look at a representative network, a mid-level regional funded initially by NSFNET, to see how it operates. Founded in 1988 by Boston University, Harvard, and the Massachusetts Institute of Technology, the New England Academic and Research Network includes member organizations from New England's universities, technology industries, and both government and private agencies. Management and operation of the network are contracted out to Bolt Beranek and Newman Inc. in Cambridge, MA, the private sector contractor that built the original ARPANET, and that until recently housed the NFSNET's Network Service Center, or NNSC. NEARnet offers its members leased-line and microwave connectivity, as well as supporting dial-up access using the SLIP (Serial Line Internet Protocols) we will discuss in the next chapter.

We can represent such a network on a map in one of two ways. Figure 2.2 depicts the more familiar structure, superimposing network lines upon recognizable geographical features. As you can see, NEARnet connects sites throughout the New England states. Figure 2.3 is a map showing the network topology of NEARnet. In many respects, this form of map is both more accurate and more revealing, for it depicts the routes information takes and highlights the major member organizations. Naturally, since the Internet is a network of networks, we should look for connectivity points with the outside world, depicted on this

Figure 2.2
Superimposing
network lines upon
recognizable
geographical features.
Map courtesy of
NEARnet.

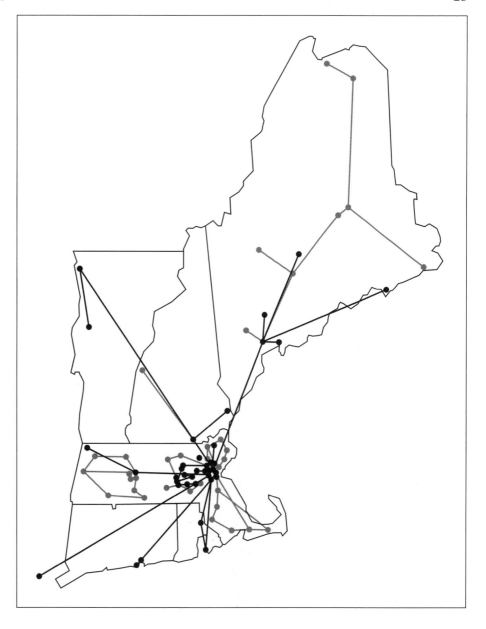

map as ellipses, the oval shapes containing a network name. We can see that NEARnet connects through MIT to ESnet, AlterNet, and NSNFNET, for example, and through Bolt Beranek and Newman in Massachusetts to DSInet.

As the major provider of Internet services to New England, NEARnet has also explored commercial routing for its member organizations. Through an agreement with ANS CO+RE Systems and the Commercial Internet Exchange, NEARnet offers the ability to pursue commercial activities like sales and technical support. Traffic is carried over the ANS CO+RE backbone network

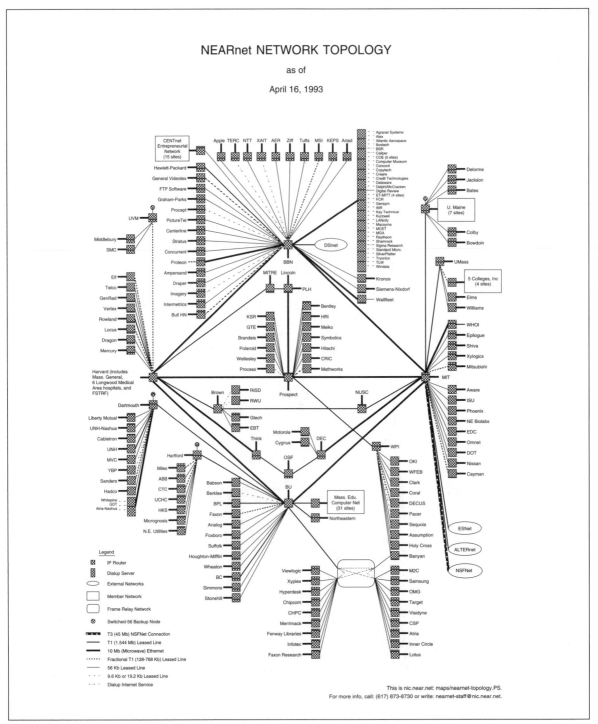

Figure 2.3
A map showing the network topology of NEARnet.

service either directly to the destination or to the Commercial Internet Exchange for interchange with other commercial network service providers.

Note what's happening on the NEARnet map. The NEARnet member organizations, only a few of which are shown here (the total in January of 1993 was 188), link to the major network nodes at BBN, MIT, Boston University, and Harvard through a variety of physical media. As the map shows, there is a 10 Megabits-per-second microwave link between MIT and Boston University; indeed, the major nodes all connect to each other by microwave. Also available are T1 (1.544 Megabits per second) leased lines, like those connecting Boston University with the Naval Undersea Warfare Center in Rhode Island, or the one that connects Boston University with the University of Hartford. T3 (45 Mbps) connections feed NEARnet traffic onto the NSFNET backbone out of MIT, while T1 lines shunt traffic to Alternet and ESnet. 56 Kb leased lines connect a host of businesses, like Aware, Inc. and Phoenix Technologies, Ltd., to MIT. Dial-up connections provide network links for smaller businesses, linking their local area networks via dial-up routers to NEARnet. At the same time, NEARnet provides SLIP connections, using 9600-bps modems to move traffic. These connections are shown on the map as a series of dots.

Perhaps now you can understand why network connections are sometimes referred to as a cloud. The important thing for the user at, say, Wellesley College, is that he or she have access to the same Internet resources as users anywhere else in the world, and indeed, Wellesley is as accessible as anywhere else on the Internet. Its faculty and students don't have to know a complicated network topology to make this work, and even if we tried to work out the precise path a given packet took on its route to a distant computer—out of MIT to NSFNET, perhaps, thence across the ocean to NORDUnet, and so on—we probably couldn't pin it down with any degree of reliability. The point is, it works, thanks to the magic of TCP/IP.

Managing the Internet

Does anyone actually manage the Internet, or does it just happen? Sketched out in its most elementary form, there is an underlying system of networks, called the *backbone*. In the United States, the largest of these is the Advanced Networking & Services Network (ANSnet) over which the National Science Foundation Network (NSFNET) and ANS CO+RE commercial services operate. The Commercial Internet Exchange presides over a healthy and growing backbone of commercial providers. Mid-level networks are regional in nature, connecting one or more states to the high-speed backbone. On the local level, institutional networks are linked to the regional networks which, in turn, give them access to the traffic flow of the backbone. Overseas, we can include EBONE, the pan-European IP backbone network, as well as NORDUnet, EUROPANet, and EUnet, which are providing broad European connectivity.

Each of these networks is responsible for the traffic that flows within it and can route that traffic as necessary. If two computers located within the same university need to exchange information, for example, there is no need for that traffic to flow out of the local network. The same principle applies to the regional networks. If an Internet user wants to send electronic mail to someone at an address connected to the same regional network, that traffic would stay within the regional network and would not need to cross the network backbone. This has significant ramifications, as we'll see when we discuss the issue of commercialization of the Internet.

A related operating principle is that each network bears the responsibility for connecting to the network at the next higher level. Let us go back to the example of the university and assume its computer science department chooses to gain Internet access. There is no central body the department must contact to achieve its new status. Instead, someone will make arrangements with the appropriate service provider. Meanwhile, the department remains autonomous. Its responsibilities include providing information about the computers it maintains to the next higher level of the network. The routing and addressing information within the local network remains in the hands of local administrators.[13]

Who pays for all this? Each network system is responsible for its own funding, just as each system must develop its own administrative procedures. This, more than anything, accounts for the rapid increase in Internet communications. If figures like the widely cited 15 percent increase in network connections per month are to be believed, they can be accounted for only by realizing that networks joining the Internet retain control of their own administration. The political dilemmas that might arise are thus muted, while the benefits of connectivity loom large.

Because there is no single service provider, agencies fund their own networks, each of which is considered a part of the overall Internet. We also find private backbone systems, frequently offering commercial access to the Internet to the growing number of corporations and private individuals interested in going on-line. Many regional networks have been created through initial funding from the National Science Foundation, with the understanding that the emerging networks become self-supporting entities. The result is a series of self-administering networks whose funding, management, and policies differ widely from each other. Some networks, for example, allow commercial traffic while others specifically forbid it.

Internet Addressing

Considering the vast number of networks connecting to form the Internet, how can all those information packets in search of a destination be sure they're going to the right address? How, for that matter, can we specify an Internet address so that it makes sense not only to the machines routing it, but also to the end users of the system? Let's examine how Internet addressing works.

At each step of the Internet hierarchy, a participating network is responsible for maintaining its own organization. In addressing terms, this means each network-linked organization maintains a database of the computers it connects to the network. The numbers used to identify Internet computers are called *IP addresses*. Each machine on the Internet has a unique IP address.

An IP address contains four numbers connected by periods. **192.33.33.22** is an IP address; so is **138.40.11.1.** The numbers farthest to the left are the broadest, representing a larger network and then, working to the right, increasingly specific network information until we arrive at a particular computer.

Let's say you wanted to reach a computer at Washington & Lee University in Lexington, VA. Perhaps you could track down its IP address, **137.113.10.35.**

But the immediate problem with IP addresses is that they're lengthy and difficult to remember. To provide a bit of mnemonic help, computers came to be identified with particular names. The computer above is also known as **liberty.uc.wlu.edu.** Now we've got some information that's easier to work with, because the consistent nature of these names provides us with a ready way to identify what they refer to.

The Domain Name System which describes computers and the organizations they support works in opposite fashion to numerical IP addressing. Whereas an IP address presents its most *general* information at the far left, names are chosen with the most *specific* information at the left. Consider the machine I commonly work on: **rock.concert.net.** At the left is the name of the computer: **rock.** Computers tend to be given names with a certain whimsical similarity. Thus, several companion computers to **rock** at my North Carolina service provider's site are **banjo** and **jazz.** The musical theme is just one possibility. You'll encounter computers named after colors, or movie stars, or flowers.

We continue reading from left to right. **concert** is the name of the network I connect to. Based in Research Triangle Park, it's a statewide network called CONCERT-CONNECT. Its status as a network is shown by the final word in the address: **net,** which is the top-level domain for this address. Again, in the world of Internet *names,* moving from left to right takes us from greater to lesser specificity.

Domain names tell you a great deal about a given address, as should be obvious from the following breakdown:

com   These are U.S. commercial domains, indicating they're a corporate or company site. **allen.com,** for example, is the name of the high-tech marketing firm Allen Marketing Group in Raleigh, NC.

edu   Found in U.S. addresses, **edu** denotes an educational site. **wisc.edu** stands for the University of Wisconsin.

gov   The domain name for a U.S. government site. **nih.gov** is the National Institutes of Health.

mil   A U.S. military site. **ddn.mil** is the Defense Data Network, run by Government Systems, Inc. in Chantilly, VA.

net   Refers to an administrative organization for a network, as in the name **concert.net** above.

org   Organizations, usually private, which don't fit the above categories. Thus the Internet Society is **isoc.org.**

While **.com, .edu, .gov,** and **.mil** apply solely to U.S. organizations, individual countries have their own top-level domain names. Thus **.de** is the domain name for Germany, **.ch** for Switzerland, **.it** for Italy, and there is also a **.us** domain for the United States. The address of an Internet resource tool in Germany is **archie.th-darmstadt.de,** while another such tool in New Zealand is **archie.nz.** At the end of this chapter, you'll find a complete listing of country domain names, along with information about the status of networking in each country.

Reaching a specific user at a given computer address is a matter of adding that person's user name to the address. My Internet mailbox address, then, is

gilster@rock.concert.net. gilster is my user name at CONCERT-CONNECT, which is connected to the address of the machine where my account is located by the @, or "at," symbol.

Now that we have domain names, are IP addresses obsolete? Hardly. The numbers allow computers on the network to return information about the addresses in question. When you specify a particular computer by using domain names, such as **quake.think.com,** an appropriate translation into an IP address will be made for you by a computer in the relevant area, or domain. This computer, called a *nameserver,* will return the proper IP address for the computer you're trying to reach. Depending on the location of the machine you're searching for and its geographical relation to you, such requests may go through one or more nameservers before targeting the final address. The beauty of the system is twofold:

1. You don't have to handle any of these transactions, because they take place automatically.

2. As opposed to a central list of Internet addresses (which, incidentally, used to be the way addressing was managed), the Domain Name System allows the Internet to grow with far less organizational overhead.

Acceptable Use

The question of what can and can't be done on the Internet has always been tricky. The ARPANET, after all, was designed with an explicit mission—to provide an experimental platform for designing computer networks that could undergo various calamities and still function. The redundancy of routing options that gets your electronic mail message through derives from the recognition that networks would have to possess "self-healing" characteristics if they were to work unimpeded when partially shut down. Hence the Internet's ability to send information packets by whatever route necessary to ensure their delivery.

The later involvement of the National Science Foundation, and its key role in propagating regional networks, defined the network's charter in support of research and education. It would be reasonable to expect the NSFNET backbone to carry traffic from a university's computer science department, for example, but unreasonable to expect it to furnish the data highway for a large corporation doing commercial work via the Internet. Accordingly, a set of core principles regarding network usage grew up and was codified in the form of NSFNET's Acceptable Use Policy. Figure 2.4 shows what it has to say.

A careful reading of this document will show that commercial use is not forbidden *ipso facto*; in fact, paragraph 1 explicitly exempts "research arms of for-profit firms when engaged in open scholarly communication and research." But the document rules out "...extensive use for private or personal business."

Exactly how these lines are drawn can be problematic. Perhaps your company produces a software product used in mapping molecular structures. And perhaps that product is about to be released in a version which will present significant new features. Presumably, your decision to use the Internet to acquaint interested parties—particularly those in the academic and research communities—with such a product would not be in violation of the NSFNET policy. But using NSFNET as a medium for general advertising certainly does

Figure 2.4
NSFNET's Acceptable
Use Policy.

THE NSFNET BACKBONE SERVICES ACCEPTABLE USE POLICY

GENERAL PRINCIPLE:

(1) NSFNET Backbone services are provided to support open research and
    education in and among US research and instructional institutions,
    plus research arms of for-profit firms when engaged in open
    scholarly communication and research. Use for other purposes is
    not acceptable.

SPECIFICALLY ACCEPTABLE USES:

(2) Communication with foreign researchers and educators in connection
    with research or instruction, as long as any network that the
    foreign user employs for such communication provides reciprocal
    access to US researchers and educators.

(3) Communication and exchange for professional development, to
    maintain currency, or to debate issues in a field or subfield of
    knowledge.

(4) Use for disciplinary-society, university-association,
    government-advisory, or standards activities related to the user's
    research and instructional activities.

(5) Use in applying for or administering grants or contracts for
    research or instruction, but not for other fundraising or public
    relations activities.

(6) Any other administrative communications or activities in direct
    support of research and instruction.

(7) Announcements of new products or services for use in research or
    instruction, but not advertising of any kind.

(8) Any traffic originating from a network of another member agency of
    the Federal Networking Council if the traffic meets the acceptable
    use policy of that agency.

(9) Communication incidental to otherwise acceptable use, except for
    illegal or specifically unacceptable use.

UNACCEPTABLE USES:

(10) Use for for-profit activities (consulting for pay, sales or
     administration of campus stores, sale of tickets to sports events,
     and so on) or use by for-profit institutions unless covered by the
     General Principle or as a specifically acceptable use.

(11) Extensive use for private or personal business.

This statement applies to use of the NSFNET Backbone only. NSF
expects that connecting networks will formulate their own use
policies. The NSF Division of Networking and Communications Research
and Infrastructure will resolve any questions about this Policy or its
interpretation.

2/92

violate the spirit of that policy, as would clearly commercial activities such as invoicing. In between is a wide and murky area about which controversy continues to swirl.

But note this twist: NSFNET's policy restricts use of the NSFNET backbone only. In fact, connecting networks, according to NSF, "...will formulate their own use policies." So a key question becomes, What kind of traffic are we talking about, and does it cross the NSF backbone on its way to its destination?

Because of the rapid growth in commercial traffic, some method had to be found to promote network traffic without the restrictions of the NSFNET backbone. This is why the Commercial Internet Exchange, or CIX, was created. CIX was founded by Performance Systems International, Inc. (Reston, VA), operators of PSINet, UUNET Technologies Inc. (Falls Church, VA), which operates AlterNet, and General Atomics (San Diego, CA), which operates CERFnet. According to a CIX Association, Inc. press release, "The CIX founders and all new members are Public Data Internetwork (PDI) Service Providers cooperating to provide a nonrestrictive packet interchange for TCP/IP and OSI traffic."

In Elmsford, NY, Advanced Network and Services, Inc., operators of AN-Snet, provides the only network connected to all the major mid-level and regional networks that NSF financed. But ANS, which, as we saw above, is itself a partnership of IBM Corporation, MCI Communications Corporation, and Merit Inc., also runs a commercial backbone service called ANS CO+RE. In this way, regional networks sponsored by the NSF can send and receive commercial traffic across the gateways provided by ANS (not without some controversy regarding ANS' competitive position *vis a vis* the CIX providers). Considering this connection, and the commercial linkages developed through CIX, it's clear that commercial usage of the network is not only acceptable, it's likely to mushroom as companies become aware of the Internet's possibilities.

In a way, commercialization of the Internet is a *fait accompli*. Not only are IBM and MCI deeply involved in ANS, but MCI is also a major player in Infonet, a company that offers global Internet connectivity. And both MCI and Infonet are involved in Government Systems Inc., the company in Chantilly, VA, that operates the Defense Data Network Network Information Center. Not to be outdone, US Sprint, a member of the Commercial Internet Exchange, has announced the commercial availability of SprintLink, described as the first TCP/IP-based data transmission service offered by a national long-distance carrier. Current planning involves linking SprintLink with the company's SprintNet service. European commercial service, meanwhile, is mushrooming, and the Internet Initiative Japan (IIJ) plans to begin commercial networking in that country by summer of 1993.

The best advice I've heard regarding commercialization comes from John Curran, network analyst at the Network Information Center at NEARnet, in a posting on USENET. The group **alt.internet.services** had been discussing these issues, and Curran, after summarizing the current situation, added this:

> What does this all mean? It means that you will find folks who think that the Internet is only for research and education, folks who think that the Internet is a wide-open highway for commercial use, and folks who think something in between. What's most amazing is that they're all correct, due to the eclectic nature of the Internet infrastructure."

For the commercially-minded, Curran adds this comment:

"If you want to provide commercial services over the Internet, talk to your network provider. They should be able to tell you about costs and any specific policies that apply.[14]

KEY INTERNET ORGANIZATIONS

Despite its decentralized nature, the Internet and its activities are coordinated to a greater or lesser extent by a number of organizations. These are names you'll encounter frequently as you prowl the Internet.

The Internet Society

One of the most helpful things you can do for yourself if you plan to become a regular Internet user is to join the Internet Society. This organization was founded to promote the growth of the Internet into a global research and information infrastructure. Quoting from a descriptive document sent out by the Society:

The Internet Society will not operate the Internet. Internet operation will continue to be a collaborative activity which the Society will seek to facilitate. The Society will provide assistance and support to groups and organizations involved in the use, operation and evolution of the Internet. It will provide support for forums in which technical and operational questions can be discussed and provide mechanisms through which the interested parties can be informed and educated about the Internet, its function, use, operation and the interests of its constituents.[15]

Internet Architecture Board

As part of its mission, the Internet Society, or ISOC, has incorporated the Internet Activities Board, now known as the Internet Architecture Board (IAB), into its operations. The IAB has coordinated research and development of the TCP/IP protocols and helped to provide research advice to the Internet community. IAB was formed in 1983 following the reorganization of DARPA's Internet Configuration Control Board. Its early goals were to encourage research into TCP/IP and the Internet, and it gradually evolved into an independent organization.[16] Today, IAB oversees the standards-making activities of the Internet Society, producing standards for the interconnection of information systems. IAB works, naturally, with TCP/IP, but also with a wide variety of protocols involved in computer messaging, data interchange, and resource discovery, including gateways to link TCP/IP networks to other kinds of systems.

IAB relies on several task forces central to the evolution of Internet technology. A brief description of each follows.

The Internet Engineering Task Force (IETF)

Composed solely of volunteers, the IETF is responsible for developing standards for Internet protocols and architecture, with working groups specializing in problem areas as they arise. The mission of IETF is to develop and approve

Internet standard protocols. At its November 1992 meeting, IETF set up a terminal room with dozens of workstations feeding video and audio from concurrent IETF sessions through the network to over one hundred sites around the world.[17] Major issues at that meeting included addressing strategies to accommodate network growth, new transport technologies for moving data, developments in resource discovery tools, and multimedia messaging standards. For further information, contact:

IETF Secretariat
CNRI
1895 Preston White Dr., Suite 100
Reston, VA 22091
Voice: 703-620-8990
Fax: 703-620-0913
E-mail: **ietf-info@isoc.org**

The Internet Research Task Force (IRTF)

Consider the Internet Research Task Force the research wing of the IAB. This group focuses on developing technologies that may be required in the future. This long-term orientation currently includes research groups working on such issues as resource discovery, privacy and security, and library use of the Internet.

The Internet Society publishes *Internet Society News,* a major source for Internet information. Dues are $70 per year for individual membership ($25 per year for student members). For information about the Internet Society, write to:

Internet Society
1895 Preston White Drive, Suite 100
Reston, VA 22091
Voice: 703-648-9888
Fax: 703-620-0913
E-mail: **isoc@isoc.org**

Internet Assigned Numbers Authority (IANA)

The IANA, operated by the University of Southern California's Information Sciences Institute, records protocol identifiers in network-accessible databases and Requests for Comments documents (see below). IANA maintains a registry for all identifiers associated with Internet protocols. This provides a standard way for systems to refer to network resources.

FARNET

The Federation of American Research Networks was established in 1987, creating a nonprofit corporation with a mission to promote the use and improvement of computer networks in research and education. Members include local, state, regional, national, and international network service providers, as well as nonprofit and commercial corporations, universities, supercomputer centers, and other organizations. FARNET offers educational programs for members, works with network organizations to improve information services, and provides a forum for the discussion of technical and policy issues. Its monthly on-line newsletter keeps members abreast of its activities. For further information, contact:

FARNET
100 Fifth Avenue, 4th Floor
Waltham, MA 02154
Voice: 800-72-FARNET
Fax: 617-890-5117

Clearinghouse for Networked Information Discovery and Retrieval

In April of 1992, the National Science Foundation awarded a three-year cooperative agreement to help establish a center supporting the development of wide-area information retrieval tools. These user-friendly systems, like World Wide Web, Wide Area Information Servers (WAIS) and Gopher, are making it possible for Internet users to locate information and retrieve it. They and other software programs now under development are actively supported by CNIDR (pronounced "snyder"), which provides a repository for such systems, and which is also active in the development of standards, as well as the continuing education of new users.

CNIDR's initial funding from NSF and the MCNC Center for Communications in Research Triangle Park, NC is supported by funding from other government agencies as well as a consortium of public and private participants. And although it has not been in operation long, this support center should draw increasing attention as the critical role of information discovery becomes apparent. With over 11,000 networks now feeding data into the worldwide Internet, knowing where to look becomes a critical issue. Tools like WAIS, Gopher, and the rest, all discussed in later chapters, are essential agents in acquiring a mastery of the Internet.

For more information, contact:

CNIDR
MCNC Center for Communications
P.O. Box 12889
Research Triangle Park, NC 27709-2889
Voice: 919-248-1499
E-mail: **info@cnidr.org**
FTP: **ftp.cnidr.org**

Federal Networking Council

This consortium of U.S. government agencies involved in networking, which includes such major movers as ARPA, the National Science Foundation, the Department of Energy (ESnet), and NASA (NASA Science Internet) has been established to foster collaboration in providing network services to the various research communities. The Council has also provided funding for the administration and operational needs of the Internet Architecture Board and the Internet Engineering Task Force.

RARE

The Reseaux Associes pour la Recherche Europeenne is an association of network organizations and users in Europe whose goal is to boost networking cooperation and support the spread of the medium. A supporter of the Open Systems Interconnection (OSI) protocols, RARE has also moved to incorporate TCP/IP, and today stands as the European body most similar to the Internet Engineering Task Force.

RARE makes electronic copies of its publications available over the Internet. To obtain them, you can use several methods. There is a Gopher server at **gopher.rare.nl.** Or use FTP to **ftp.rare.nl,** and look in the directories *doc/reports* or *doc/rtr.*

For further information, contact RARE at:

RARE Secretariat
Singel 466-468
NL-1017 AW AMSTERDAM
Voice: +31 20 639 1131
      +31 20 639 3289
Fax: 020-639 32 89

RIPE

Reseaux IP Europeens is a collaborative organization of European Internet service providers whose aim is to provide technical and administrative coordination towards the creation of a European-wide network. Created in 1989, RIPE now boasts more than 60 member organizations; more than 300,000 computers throughout Europe are accessible through networks RIPE coordinates. RIPE is the major body behind TCP/IP development in Europe; it has been incorporated into RARE.

A particularly valuable collection of documentation is maintained at the RIPE Network Coordination Center, which is accessible via a variety of network tools. A menu-driven service allows users to read documents and retrieve them by electronic mail. You can reach the NCC by Telnet to **info.ripe.net.** All RIPE documents and the full set of Internet RFCs are available via anonymous FTP from **ftp.ripe.net,** and the same documents can be retrieved through a Gopher interface at **gopher.ripe.net;** a WAIS server can be accessed via **wais.ripe.net,** and World Wide Web access is provided via **www.ripe.net.**
For further information about RIPE, contact:

RIPE NCC
Kruislaan 409
NL-1098 SJ Amsterdam

The Netherlands
Voice: +31 20 592 5065
Fax: +31 20 592 5155
E-mail: **ncc@ripe.net**

CCIRN

The Coordinating Committee for Intercontinental Research Networks has a lofty aim—to establish a global research network by coordinating existing network activities internationally. The ocean-spanning nature of CCIRN was clear from its first meeting in 1987, when William Bostwick, chairman of the Federal Research Internet Coordinating Committee, was chosen as co-chairman along with RARE's secretary-general, James Hutton. With initial membership from European network organizations, U.S. governmental agencies, and the Internet Architecture Board, among others, the CCIRN quickly expanded, and now includes members in Eastern Europe, South America, and the Pacific Rim.

INTERNET DOCUMENTATION

Although you'll never have to wade into Internet technical details unless you want to, it's helpful to know something about them. A number of useful documents are available, some called Requests for Comments, others called FYI, or For Your Information documents, that provide background information helpful to any new user.

Requests for Comments (RFCs)

TCP/IP is controlled by the Internet Society through both the IAB and the IETF. A series of Requests for Comments (RFCs) has been established, containing documentation about TCP/IP and the Internet at large. RFCs are managed by the IAB and can be obtained by electronic mail or by file transfer protocol (FTP).

Who writes RFCs? Anyone can put an RFC together, commenting on a particular issue or developing a standard he or she would like to see discussed. The proposed RFC is then reviewed by the RFC Editor. If accepted, it is assigned an RFC number. These documents, begun in 1969 and maintaining a healthy on-line growth, are managed at the Information Sciences Institute of the University of Southern California.

RFCs and the FYI documents mentioned below are available at numerous sites. Although we have not discussed electronic mail yet, the following provides a way to keep up with RFCs now. You may want to return to this section after you've used e-mail so you can send for the relevant material.

What You Need: A Way to Find RFCs

The Document: **Where and How to Get New RFCs**

How to Get It: Send electronic mail to **rfc-info@isi.edu.** In the subject field, enter **Accessing RFCs.** The message should consist of only one line, starting at the far left margin. It should read exactly as follows:

Help: ways_to_get_rfcs

••

RFCs are under active development and are available by file transfer protocol (FTP) from at least 20 on-line repositories around the world. Many of these also provide for automated retrieval by e-mail, so if your only Internet access is a mail gateway, you can still use it to find RFCs. The document previously cited contains full information on these sites.

FYIs

FYI is a familiar acronym; it stands for For Your Information. A subset of the RFCs, the FYIs are documents which provide useful background information about the Internet. However, the FYI documents are generally written with a broader audience in mind, and many documents available at the various FYI sites target beginners. You'll find both an RFC and an FYI number on these documents because, properly speaking, FYIs are a "subset" of the RFC materials and hence are included in a complete listing of RFCs. You retrieve FYIs just as you do RFCs—by locating an appropriate site and using file transfer protocol or electronic mail.

STDs

STDs—the abbreviation means "standards"—are another subset of the RFC materials. STDs identify those RFCs that document Internet standards. Like FYIs, STDs possess both an RFC number and an STD number. You find them the same way you find RFCs.

Internet Monthly Reports

Keeping up with a rapidly moving target like the Internet isn't easy, but Internet Monthly Reports can help. They're distributed by a mailing list and can also be retrieved by FTP from various sites, as well as through electronic mail, much in the fashion of RFCs. Events of significance in the various networks making up the Internet appear here, as well as reports on ongoing research and engineering projects, and a calendar of Internet events.

••

What You Need: A List of Ways to Retrieve Internet Monthly Reports

The Document: **Ways to Get IMRs**

How to Get It: Send electronic mail to **rfc-info@isi.edu.** In the subject field, enter **Getting Imrs.** The message should read:

help: ways_to_get_imrs

This document will also explain how to sign on to the mailing list to receive the Internet Monthly Reports automatically.

•••

NETWORK INFORMATION CENTERS

Network Information Centers (NICs) exist to provide documentation and useful information about the Internet to users. Their role is all the more important given the lack of Internet centralization. By locating abundant information sources in a single site, the Network Information Centers make it possible to find out quickly what is available on the Internet about basic topics. This role becomes even more critical given that the Internet is now moving away from its strictly academic and research focus to comprise users from all walks of life.

Defense Data Network Network Information Center

The DDN NIC is the Internet Registrar for domains and network numbers for MILNET; it also maintains a **whois** database for MILNET users, a kind of on-line directory we'll look closely at later. Like the other NICs, the DDN provides a wealth of publicly accessible files through its anonymous FTP address at **nic.ddn.mil**. Soon, I'll show you how to use such addresses to retrieve a great deal of valuable information. Information is also available through electronic mail. Send to **service@nic.ddn.mil.** If you type nothing in the subject field of the letter and just the word **help** as the message, the NIC will send you information on how to get other documents by e-mail.

Government Systems, Inc.
14200 Park Meadow Dr., Suite 200
Chantilly, VA 22021
Voice: 703-802-4535
Fax: 703-802-8376
E-mail: **hostmaster@nic.ddn.mil**
FTP: **nic.ddn.mil**

INTERNIC

The Internet Network Information Center consists of three organizations known collectively as the INTERNIC. Among the many information services provided here are the complete RFC documents and materials relating to the work of the Internet Society as well as the IETF. The Internet Monthly Report is also available, as are many other documents. The INTERNIC also provides a new directory and database service operated by AT&T. This so-called Directory of Directories is being established to serve as a pointer to resources on the Internet, and will include FTP sites, lists of servers, lists of directories, as well as library catalogs and data archives. AT&T also plans to provide its own directory services to users and organizations. Finally, the INTERNIC serves as the registrar for domains and network numbers for the Internet at large (a function formerly managed at the DDN Network Information Center).

To reach the INTERNIC from the top, you can try several methods:

Voice: 800-444-4345
E-mail: **info@internic.net**

There is also a Gopher system (we'll talk about Gophers later) which provides a user-friendly way to get at INTERNIC resources. Its address is **gopher.internic.net.**
Keeping up with Internet resources is difficult; so many things are happening so fast that it's easy to lose track. I firmly recommend you take advantage of an electronic mailing list being offered by the INTERNIC.

What You Need: Network Information Services (a mailing list containing news about network tools and resources).

How to Get It: Send e-mail to **listserv@is.internic.net.** Leave the subject field blank. In the body of the message, type **subscribe nis** *yourname.*

To reach the INTERNIC's Directory of Directories, you may use several different methods:

1. Telnet to **ds.internic.net.** Login with userid **guest.** No password is required. The default database, *resources*, contains the information for the directory. There is an on-line tutorial and help interface.

2. Anonymous FTP to **ds.internic.net.** The Directory of Directories is stored in the *resource/* directory in the form of ASCII text files in various subdirectories broken out by category.

3. Via electronic mail. Send a message to **mailserv@ds.internic.net.** You can retrieve individual files using the **file** command in the body of the message. For more on this procedure, see Chapter 8.

The INTERNIC replaces the NSF Network Service Center, whose services have been transferred to the INTERNIC team. Three organizations will manage the INTERNIC, with responsibilities broken down as follows:

REGISTRATION SERVICES

This is where IP addresses and domain names for the Internet are assigned. The RIPE NCC performs the same function in Europe. Provided by Network Solutions, Inc. of Herndon, VA.

Voice: 703-742-4757
E-mail: **hostmaster@internic.net**
FTP: **rs.internic.net**

DIRECTORY AND DATABASE SERVICES
Provided by AT&T.

> Directory and Database Services
> 5000 Hadley Road, Room 1B13
> South Plainfield, NJ 07080
> Voice: 908-668-6587
> E-mail: **admin@ds.internic.net**
> Telnet: **ds.internic.net**

INFORMATION SERVICES
Provided by General Atomics of San Diego, CA.

> E-mail: **info@internic.net**
> Voice: 619-455-4600
> E-mail: **info@internic.net**
> FTP: **is.internic.net**

SRI Network Information Systems Center

A research and consulting firm in Menlo Park, CA, SRI maintains a useful archive of Internet information available through anonymous FTP. In addition to such core documents as the Internet Resource Guide, SRI provides a valuable tutorial called *Zen and the Art of the Internet* in a directory called *introducing.the.internet*. There is also a complete set of Requests for Comments documents.

> Network Information Systems Center
> 333 Ravenswood Ave.
> Menlo Park, CA 94025
> Voice: 415-859-6387
> Fax: 415-859-6028
> E-mail: **nisc@nisc.sri.com**

BITNET Network Information Center

Although it's not part of the Internet because it runs its own protocols on top of TCP/IP, BITNET is a valuable resource that Internet users can reach through electronic mail gateways. Its Network Information Center, called BITNIC, was established by EDUCOM, a consortium of universities, colleges, and other institutions promoting computer networking technologies. The holdings at BITNIC are essential for anyone planning to take advantage of BITNET. They include general introductions to using the BITNET system, lists of BITNET servers for particular kinds of information, documents about network etiquette and history, and planning for BITNET's future as it integrates its operations with the TCP/IP protocols.

Corporation for Research and Education Networking (CREN)
Suite 600
1112 16th St. NW
Washington, DC 20036
Voice: 202-872-4200

INTERNATIONAL CONNECTIVITY LIST

Larry Landweber tracks Internet connectivity worldwide from his position at the Computer Science Department at the University of Wisconsin in Madison. The following list summarizes Internet and other network connections. Note that you can retrieve updated versions of this list (and of the world network map shown earlier) by using the FTP address given in Figure 2.5.

Figure 2.5
Larry Landweber's International Connectivity List.*

```
INTERNATIONAL CONNECTIVITY LIST
Version 8—April 15, 1993


Please send corrections, information and/or comments to:


Larry Landweber
Computer Sciences Dept.
University of Wisconsin—Madison
1210 W. Dayton St.
Madison, WI 53706
lhl@cs.wisc.edu
FAX 1-608-265-2635


Include details, e.g., on connections, sites, contacts, protocols, etc.


Thanks to the many people from around the world who have provided informa-
tion. This version (postscript, ditroff, text forms), maps in postscript,
and earlier versions may also be obtained by anonymous ftp from
ftp.cs.wisc.edu in the connectivity_table directory.


In the following, "BITNET" is used generically to refer to BITNET plus sim-
ilar networks around the world (e.g., EARN, NETNORTH, GULF-NET, etc.)


SUMMARY


NUMBER OF ENTITIES WITH INTERNATIONAL NETWORK CONNECTIVITY = 127


BITNET
   Col. 2 (Entities with international BITNET links.)
   b: minimal, one to five domestic BITNET sites, 18 entities
   B: widespread, more than five domestic BITNET sites, 33 entities


IP INTERNET
   Col. 3 (Entities with international IP Internet links.)
   I: = operational, accessible from entire IP Internet, 54 entities
   i: = operational, not accessible via the NSFNET backbone, 2 entities
```

*Copyright 1993 Lawrence H. Landweber and the Internet Society. Unlimited permission to copy or use is hereby granted subject to inclusion of this copyright notice.

```
UUCP
  Col. 4 (Entities with domestic UUCP sites which are connected to the
    Global Multiprotocol Open Internet.)
  u: minimal, one to five domestic UUCP site, 43 entities
  U: widespread, more than five domestic UUCP sites, 64 entities


FIDONET
  Col. 5 (Entities with domestic FIDONET sites which are connected to the
    Global Multiprotocol Open Internet)
  f: minimal, one to five domestic FIDONET sites, 20 entities
  F: widespread, more than five domestic FIDONET sites, 59 entities

OSI
  Col. 6 (Entities with international X.400 links to domestic sites which
    are connected to the Global Multiprotocol Open Internet).
  o: minimal, one to five domestic X.400 sites, 8 entities
  O: widespread, more than five domestic X.400 sites, 23 entities


Email connections to Albania, Algeria, Angola, Gambia, Malawi, Mongolia, Mo-
rocco, Qatar, St. Lucia, and Vietnam have been reported but have not been
verified or are not yet stable and hence are not included in the table or
in the above totals.


-----, AF, Afghanistan (Democratic Republic of)
-----, AL, Albania (Republic of)
-----, DZ, Algeria (People's Democratic Republic of)
-----, AS, American Samoa
-----, AD, Andorra (Principality of)
-----, AO, Angola (People's Republic of)
-----, AI, Anguilla
-I---, AQ, Antarctica
-----, AG, Antigua and Barbuda
BIUF-, AR, Argentina (Argentine Republic of)
--u--, AM, Armenia
-----, AW, Aruba
-IUFo, AU, Australia
BIUFO, AT, Austria (Republic of)
--U--, AZ, Azerbaijan
-----, BS, Bahamas (Commonwealth of the)
b----, BH, Bahrain (State of)
-----, BD, Bangladesh (People's Republic of)
-----, BB, Barbados
--UF-, BY, Belarus
BIUFO, BE, Belgium (Kingdom of)
-----, BZ, Belize
-----, BJ, Benin (People's Republic of)
--uf-, BM, Bermuda
-----, BT, Bhutan (Kingdom of)
--U--, BO, Bolivia (Republic of)
-----, BA, Bosnia-Hercegovina
---f-, BW, Botswana (Republic of)
-----, BV, Bouvet Island
BIUFO, BR, Brazil (Federative Republic of)
-----, IO, British Indian Ocean Territory
-----, BN, Brunei Darussalam
biUF-, BG, Bulgaria (Republic of)
--u--, BF, Burkina Faso (formerly Upper Volta)
-----, BI, Burundi (Republic of)
-----, KH, Cambodia
--u--, CM, Cameroon (Republic of)
BIUFO, CA, Canada
```

(continued)

Figure 2.5
Larry Landweber's
International
Connectivity List
(continued).

```
-----, CV, Cape Verde (Republic of)
-----, KY, Cayman Islands
-----, CF, Central African Republic
-----, TD, Chad (Republic of)
BIUF-, CL, Chile (Republic of)
--ufO, CN, China (People's Republic of)
-----, CX, Christmas Island (Indian Ocean)
-----, CC, Cocos (Keeling) Islands
B-u--, CO, Colombia (Republic of)
-----, KM, Comoros (Islamic Federal Republic of the)
--u--, CG, Congo (Republic of the)
-----, CK, Cook Islands
bIu--, CR, Costa Rica (Republic of)
--u--, CI, Cote d'Ivoire (Republic of)
-Iufo, HR, Croatia
--U--, CU, Cuba (Republic of)
bI---, CY, Cyprus (Republic of)
BIUF-, CZ, Czech Republic
BIUFO, DK, Denmark (Kingdom of)
-----, DJ, Djibouti (Republic of)
-----, DM, Dominica (Commonwealth of)
--Uf-, DO, Dominican Republic
-----, TP, East Timor
bIu--, EC, Ecuador (Republic of)
b-U--, EG, Egypt (Arab Republic of)
-----, SV, El Salvador (Republic of)
-----, GQ, Equatorial Guinea (Republic of)
-IUF-, EE, Estonia (Republic of)
---F-, ET, Ethiopia (People's Democratic Republic of)
-----, FK, Falkland Islands (Malvinas)
-----, FO, Faroe Islands
--u--, FJ, Fiji (Republic of)
BIUFO, FI, Finland (Republic of)
BIUFO, FR, France (French Republic)
--u--, GF, French Guiana
--u--, PF, French Polynesia
-----, TF, French Southern Territories
-----, GA, Gabon (Gabonese Republic)
-----, GM, Gambia (Republic of the)
--UF-, GE, Georgia (Republic of)
BIUFO, DE, Germany (Federal Republic of)
---F-, GH, Ghana (Republic of)
-----, GI, Gibraltar
BIUFO, GR, Greece (Hellenic Republic)
-I-f-, GL, Greenland
--u--, GD, Grenada
b-u--, GP, Guadeloupe (French Department of)
---F-, GU, Guam
--u--, GT, Guatemala (Republic of)
-----, GN, Guinea (Republic of)
-----, GW, Guinea-Bissau (Republic of)
-----, GY, Guyana (Republic of)
-----, HT, Haiti (Republic of)
-----, HM, Heard and McDonald Islands
-----, HN, Honduras (Republic of)
BI-F-, HK, Hong Kong (Hisiangkang, Xianggang)
BIUFo, HU, Hungary (Republic of)
-IUFo, IS, Iceland (Republic of)
bIUfo, IN, India (Republic of)
--u--, ID, Indonesia (Republic of)
b----, IR, Iran (Islamic Republic of)
-----, IQ, Iraq (Republic of)
```

```
BIUFO, IE, Ireland
BIUF-, IL, Israel (State of)
BIUFO, IT, Italy (Italian Republic)
--u--, JM, Jamaica
BIUF-, JP, Japan
-----, JO, Jordan (Hashemite Kingdom of)
--Uf-, KZ, Kazakhstan
---f-, KE, Kenya (Republic of)
--u--, KI, Kiribati (Republic of)
-----, KP, Korea (Democratic People's Republic of)
BIUFO, KR, Korea (Republic of)
-I---, KW, Kuwait (State of)
--U--, KG, Kyrgyzstan
-----, LA, Lao People's Democratic Republic
-IUF-, LV, Latvia (Republic of)
-----, LB, Lebanon (Lebanese Republic)
--u--, LS, Lesotho (Kingdom of)
-----, LR, Liberia (Republic of)
-----, LY, Libyan Arab Jamahiriya
-----, LI, Liechtenstein (Principality of)
--UFo, LT, Lithuania
bIUFo, LU, Luxembourg (Grand Duchy of)
---F-, MO, Macau (Ao-me'n)
-----, ??, Macedonia (Former Yugoslav Republic of)
-----, MG, Madagascar (Democratic Republic of)
-----, MW, Malawi (Republic of)
bIUF-, MY, Malaysia
-----, MV, Maldives (Republic of)
--u--, ML, Mali (Republic of)
--u--, MT, Malta (Republic of)
-----, MH, Marshall Islands (Republic of the)
-----, MQ, Martinique (French Department of)
-----, MR, Mauritania (Islamic Republic of)
---f-, MU, Mauritius
BIuF-, MX, Mexico (United Mexican States)
-----, FM, Micronesia (Federated States of)
--UF-, MD, Moldova (Republic of)
-----, MC, Monaco (Principality of)
-----, MN, Mongolia (Mongolian People's Republic)
-----, MS, Montserrat
-----, MA, Morocco (Kingdom of)
--u--, NA, Namibia (Republic of)
-----, NR, Nauru (Republic of)
-----, NP, Nepal (Kingdom of)
BIUFO, NL, Netherlands (Kingdom of the)
-----, AN, Netherlands Antilles
-----, NT, Neutral Zone (between Saudi Arabia and Iraq)
--U--, NC, New Caledonia
-IUF-, NZ, New Zealand
--u--, NI, Nicaragua (Republic of)
--u--, NE, Niger (Republic of the)
-----, NG, Nigeria (Federal Republic of)
-----, NU, Niue
-----, NF, Norfolk Island
-----, MP, Northern Mariana Islands (Commonwealth of the)
BIUFO, NO, Norway (Kingdom of)
-----, OM, Oman (Sultanate of)
--U--, PK, Pakistan (Islamic Republic of)
-----, PW, Palau (Republic of)
b-uF-, PA, Panama (Republic of)
--u--, PG, Papua New Guinea
--u--, PY, Paraguay (Republic of)
```

(continued)

Figure 2.5
Larry Landweber's
International
Connectivity List
(continued).

```
--Uf-, PE, Peru (Republic of)
--uF-, PH, Philippines (Republic of the)
-----, PN, Pitcairn
BIUF-, PL, Poland (Republic of)
bIUFO, PT, Portugal (Portuguese Republic)
bIUF-, PR, Puerto Rico
-----, QA, Qatar (State of)
--u--, RE, Re'union (French Department of)
B--f-, RO, Romania
BiUF-, RU, Russian Federation
-----, RW, Rwanda (Rwandese Republic)
-----, SH, Saint Helena
-----, KN, Saint Kitts and Nevis
-----, LC, Saint Lucia
-----, PM, Saint Pierre and Miquelon (French Department of)
-----, VC, Saint Vincent and the Grenadines
-----, WS, Samoa (Independent State of)
-----, SM, San Marino (Republic of)
-----, ST, Sao Tome and Principe (Democratic Republic of)
B----, SA, Saudi Arabia (Kingdom of)
--Uf-, SN, Senegal (Republic of)
--u--, SC, Seychelles (Republic of)
-----, SL, Sierra Leone (Republic of)
bIuF-, SG, Singapore (Republic of)
bIUF-, SK, Slovakia
-IUFO, SI, Slovenia
-----, SB, Solomon Islands
-----, SO, Somalia (Somali Democratic Republic)
-IUFO, ZA, South Africa (Republic of)
BIUFO, ES, Spain (Kingdom of)
--U--, LK, Sri Lanka (Democratic Socialist Republic of)
-----, SD, Sudan (Democratic Republic of the)
--u--, SR, Suriname (Republic of)
-----, SJ, Svalbard and Jan Mayen Islands
-----, SZ, Swaziland (Kingdom of)
BIUFo, SE, Sweden (Kingdom of)
BIUFO, CH, Switzerland (Swiss Confederation)
-----, SY, Syria (Syrian Arab Republic)
BIuF-, TW, Taiwan, Province of China
--uf-, TJ, Tajikistan
---f-, TZ, Tanzania (United Republic of)
-IUF-, TH, Thailand (Kingdom of)
--u--, TG, Togo (Togolese Republic)
-----, TK, Tokelau
-----, TO, Tonga (Kingdom of)
--u--, TT, Trinidad and Tobago (Republic of)
bIUfo, TN, Tunisia
BI-F-, TR, Turkey (Republic of)
--U--, TM, Turkmenistan
-----, TC, Turks and Caicos Islands
-----, TV, Tuvalu
---f-, UG, Uganda (Republic of)
--UF-, UA, Ukraine
-----, AE, United Arab Emirates
bIUFO, GB, United Kingdom (United Kingdom of Great Britain and Northern Ire-
land)
BIUFO, US, United States (United States of America)
-----, UM, United States Minor Outlying Islands
--UF-, UY, Uruguay (Eastern Republic of)
--UF-, UZ, Uzbekistan
--u--, VU, Vanuatu (Republic of, formerly New Hebrides)
-----, VA, Vatican City State (Holy See)
```

```
-IU--, VE, Venezuela (Republic of)
-----, VN, Vietnam (Socialist Republic of)
-----, VG, Virgin Islands (British)
---f-, VI, Virgin Islands (U.S.)
-----, WF, Wallis and Futuna Islands
-----, EH, Western Sahara
-----, YE, Yemen (Republic of)
-----, YU, Yugoslavia (Socialist Federal Republic of)
-----, ZR, Zaire (Republic of)
--uf-, ZM, Zambia (Republic of)
--uf-, ZW, Zimbabwe (Republic of)
```

CHAPTER TWO NOTES

1. Telephone conversation with John Quarterman, 12 April 1993.
2. R.E. Calem, "The Network of All Networks." *New York Times*, 6 December 1992, 12-F.
3. *Ibid.*
4. Telephone conversation with the author, 12 April 1993.
5. DARPA is again ARPA, as of early 1993.
6. Malamud, Carl, *Exploring the Internet.* Englewood Cliffs, NJ: Prentice Hall PTR, 1992, p. 355.
7. These figures are from Eric M. Aupperle's "Changing Eras: Evolution of the NSFNET." *Internet Society News* Vol. 1., No. 4, Winter 1993, 3.
8. From Merit press release, 2 December 1992.
9. J.S. Quarterman, *The Matrix: Computer Networks and Conferencing Systems Worldwide*, Burlington, MA: Digital Press, 1990, 278. Quarterman's book, though dated, remains a major source for obtaining an overall view of networks throughout the world.
10. *Ibid.*, xxiii.
11. *Matrix News*, Vol. 3, No. 3, March 1993.
12. Comer, Douglas E, *Internetworking with TCP/IP.* Vol. 1: *Principles, Protocols, and Architecture.* 2d ed. Englewood Cliffs, NJ: Prentice Hall, 547 pages. 1991, 1. Comer's work is regarded as the seminal study of TCP/IP, its growth and development, and its current status.
13. This discussion of network administration owes much to Jay Habegger, who discusses the subject in "Understanding the Technical and Administrative Organization of the Internet." *Telecommunications*, April 1992, 12–14.
14. You'll likely be surprised, as I was, at how much information you begin to acquire simply by following Internet postings. The ultimate goal of a guide like this one is to make you self-sufficient in terms of information, so that your Internet presence keeps you abreast of what you need to know.
15. From "The Internet Society," a document provided by the Society as part of a descriptive packet sent to interested parties. The document is dated 20 February 1992.
16. Comer, *op. cit.*, 9.
17. Developments in the IETF are fully covered in the *Internet Society News*, newsletter of the Internet Society. This particular meeting is covered in Vol. 1, No. 4, Winter 1993, 37.

3

....

Signing On
to the Internet

To work with the Internet, you must remove the notion of one-stop shopping from your thinking. True, you'll be dialing into a single telephone number to gain access to one computer as your first step. At that point, however, all resemblances between the Internet and the commercial on-line services evaporate. You will use your initial computer contact only as the first step in a worldwide journey, although it will always provide a useful home base, and it will be the site where your mail is delivered and stored, and where any files you choose to retrieve are stored. You might consider your home directory on a service provider's computer the analog to Balboa's base camp. From it, you have a glimpse of the broad Pacific.

Just a few years ago, Internet access for dial-up users was hard to acquire because there were few commercial providers. Unless you already worked for a company with network access, or had a compliant friend who was willing to let you use his or her account, you were simply out of luck. The Internet was for network users only, and the individual user with a stand-alone computer and modem was shut out. A different kind of service had grown up for such people—the commercial networks such as CompuServe, GEnie, Prodigy, and DELPHI. Dial-up users, it was assumed, would stay within those confines while the Internet served the networks.

Today, all that has changed, and a growing number of companies offering dial-up access have emerged. Each of these companies lets you use computer space on their machines. That space is your foothold on the network. From there, you are in position to explore the worldwide Internet using whatever tools your provider offers. These tools may vary slightly from place to place, but the basics will remain the same. The point is, you the individual user finally have a choice, and as you'll see when you examine the list of providers, there's no shortage of options.

DIAL-UP CONNECTIVITY AND THE CLIENT/SERVER MODEL

Dial-up connections differ from a continuous on-line network presence. Depending on your choice of service provider, the major Internet services—electronic mail, File Transfer Protocol, and Telnet—are all available to the dial-up user. What's not available are a number of programs called *clients* which run on computers with full network connections. You can still use clients, but they have to be located on your service provider's computer, which does have a full network presence. This restricts your use of clients to those available on that computer.

What are these clients? The client/server model operates this way: client programs request information from *servers*, which are programs running on other computers. There are numerous clients in varying degrees of complexity. A Macintosh user with full connectivity might use a client called WAIStation to gain access to a wide range of Internet databases. The client makes the process of data retrieval far more intuitive than it would otherwise be by providing a helpful interface that prompts the user about what to do. Clients like this are available for computers ranging from **MS-DOS** machines to Sun workstations, from VAX computers to NeXT machines and Macintoshes.

Not all of these client programs are available to the dial-up user. Because you and I are limited to placing a call via modem to our service provider's computer, we must use the clients available *on that system*. In addition, we're limited to those clients that can communicate with our computer over the telephone line. There are such clients—they're referred to as terminal-based, or character-based clients—and, in most cases, they perform very well indeed. We'll use a terminal-based client to explore the hypertext searching tool called World Wide Web, for example, and to sift through gigantic amounts of network data using a client called **archie.** We can explore all network capabilities with a terminal-based client, but the limitations of our connection to the network mean we won't have the snazzy graphic interface WAIStation and some other clients provide.

Public versus Private Clients

A possible source of confusion arises over the difference between two types of clients—public and private. A public client is simply one that has been made available for general use. We'll take advantage of several of these as we discuss Internet resource discovery tools. There is a public client, for example, at Thinking Machines Corporation which allows us to examine the same set of databases that the Macintosh-based WAIStation client does, though without the latter program's elegance and power. This client is public in that it is not running on our local service provider's computer, but rather at a public site that we must access by Telnet procedures.

You might, on the other hand, have a wide range of clients—I call them "private clients"—available on your service provider's machine. Some clients, such as **archie** and **whois,** are widely distributed and are likely to be found at your dial-in site. That means you can launch a search using **archie,** for example, without first having to use Telnet to gain access to a remote computer offering **archie** services. We'll discuss these options as we go, but be aware that if your service provider doesn't offer a client for a given service, I will list public sites that make a client available. This information will be especially necessary for those readers who choose DELPHI or BIX as their providers, since they rely on public sites for such clients.

TERMINAL EMULATION

Why can't a dial-up customer run all available client software? The answer has to do with the nature of the connection. When you place a call to a service provider, you won't necessarily know (unless you ask) what kind of computer you're dialing in to. Whatever it is, your computer has to find some way of talking to it. A mainframe computer, for example, is used to dealing with terminals, which are simply screens that reflect what the mainframe is doing; terminals offer only limited functionality. You may hear such terminals referred to as *dumb terminals* because of this lack of processing muscle. Such a terminal usually contains a video display unit, a keyboard, and the circuitry to communicate with the computer to which it is connected. It can send what you type and display what the main computer returns. Personal computers, on the other hand, offer greater processing power; they can be "smart" terminals.

The problem is we can't use the smarts inside our desktop machines when we make this kind of connection. Because we're not actually networked into the service provider's computer, it regards us as a terminal. To get anything to happen, our computer must emulate a terminal so the remote *host* will know what's going on. This process, called *terminal emulation,* is established through software settings.

Terminal emulation is a critical feature of good communications software. It allows us, even as we pretend to be dumb terminals, to use some nonterminal features such as the ability to capture data and download files. The network client programs examined in this book can all be accessed if you'll set your software to emulate VT100 (VT102 will work just as well), a terminal emulation mode tuned for Digital Equipment Corporation's computers, and widely used no matter where you go on the Internet.

Figure 3.1 shows the settings screen for Crosstalk for Windows 2.0, a popular communications program. Note that the figure shows a menu for terminal emulators.

A wide range of emulators is available. A familiar one might be ANSI PC, which is commonly used to connect to bulletin board systems running on IBM-compatible platforms. There are emulators for Digital Equipment Corporation's computers, from VT52 to VT320, as well as emulators for Hewlett-Packard, IBM, WYSE, and others. You can't see the full list in Figure 3.1 because the menu has to be scrolled to display all the choices.

SIGNING ON—A PERSONAL ODYSSEY

How hard could it be to sign on to the Internet? Many older treatments of the subject make it sound like a snap. "Need access? Just ask your system administrator," they'll blithely say, assuming you wouldn't ask if you weren't already

Figure 3.1
Crosstalk for Windows,
terminal emulation
choices from the
settings menu.

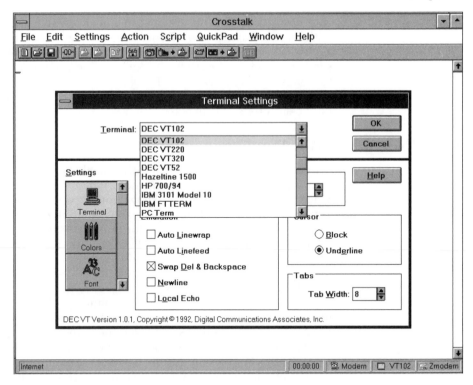

working on a network. If you are, asking your system administrator is good advice. Many people don't realize they can connect through their work site, and in such cases, a simple request is usually enough to get them up and running.

But tell that to someone who's trying to log on by modem from an isolated computer, either from work or home. Someone like me, who spent month after month getting the runaround from people who knew jargon and little else. For me, logging on to the Internet became something of a crusade, deepening into obsession when I realized what a stone wall I was running into. Several years ago, I made the mistake of asking this simple question: "I work out of a home office. I don't have Internet access and I don't have a system administrator. What do I do?" I asked people in my area and looked for answers on various on-line services. I peppered local bulletin boards for advice and called computer gurus in Research Triangle Park, pestering some people for months.

The result? "Try the universities," some people said. I called Duke, UNC, North Carolina State; access there was restricted and no one I spoke with knew how to get it. Maybe if I was a student. Unfortunately, my years at UNC had ended in the mid-1970s. "Call some of the big corporations," I was told. "Someone out there might be able to get you an account." I didn't know what I was doing, but I began to make these calls. Most people didn't know what I was talking about. Those that did seemed incredulous that I would ask. "Network connections are private," they said.

Network connections private? If that doesn't give you something to think about, what does?

The Internet is not CompuServe or Prodigy. Lacking any central organization, the network has no billing address. You can't make a phone call to a network office and say "Sign me up." Then, too, you'll get confused by the plethora of possibilities some of the people who are already on the network will tell you about. "Do you want a full connection?" they'll ask, and you reply, "Sure," not understanding why you would want anything else. "The best we can do is SLIP," you may hear. SLIP? What does it mean? And why do these people I'm talking to have nothing better to offer? Is SLIP some kind of restricted access?

It wouldn't be until CONCERT-CONNECT came along that I made my real plunge into the Internet. CONCERT-CONNECT is a service provider which, among many other options, makes possible local dial-up access to the Internet. It brings order into the North Carolina Internet scene by offering a flat rate per month, allowing you to log on to the computers at MCNC (formerly the Microelectronics Center of North Carolina, now known solely by its acronym, as are many computer organizations). The flat rate was attractive, as were the services; not just USENET newsgroups, but FTP and Telnet as well; not just electronic mail, but the whole panoply of features that make the Internet so fascinating.

As you're about to see, access today has become greatly simplified. Providers are springing up all over the country to offer dial-up service into the Internet. Commercial on-line services have opened mail gateways, and two, DELPHI and BIX, offer Telnet and FTP as well. In what follows, we'll work our way up the access ladder to illustrate the options available. If you are already on the Internet, you won't need to read the following unless you just want to understand why your nonnetworked friends seem so impatient when you talk about what you do on the network.

USING A LOCAL BULLETIN BOARD

The first misconception faced by Internet newcomers isn't about the Internet at all; it's about UNIX. UNIX is an operating system which runs on computers at a wide variety of academic and research sites around the world. Because of its built-in communications capabilities, it has been used for years to carry mail and move messages by way of a cooperative, wide-area network called UUCP. USENET news, the bulletin-board-style messaging service covered in Chapter 11, grew up in this UNIX environment, and thus many novices assume UNIX is *ipso facto* the language of the Internet community. USENET is often the first Internet-reachable tool many novices encounter, usually through a local bulletin-board system (BBS) offering the capability of logging on to some or all of the newsgroups.

We now have two such bulletin boards in my area. With either, you can log on and read USENET postings, responding to them as you please; you can also send electronic mail. Figure 3.2 shows the sign-on screen for one such bulletin board, a Raleigh BBS called Computer Business System. After calling its number, this is what is displayed after a brief log-in message

Ah, the Internet Catch again. Here we have a tool that will guide you into your first glimpse of the Internet, but in true UNIX fashion, it's cryptic. You have to prowl around, in this case entering a **?,** to find out what's available. By working through the help system, the new user discovers how to access USENET newsgroups. Figure 3.3 shows the section of the Help Menu that's applicable.

Figure 3.2
The sign-on screen
from a BBS.

```
*   Please enter your account name and password.

*   Accounts names on this system single words, rather than
    the first and last name. For example,

        Login or NEW: jsmith
        Password:

*   If you do not have an account, type NEW to sign up.

Login or NEW: paulg
Password:

    Logging in: paulg

Previous login: 13-Jan-93


No mail.

[#1: General Forum]
9:53a (?=help!) -
```

Entering **new** at the prompt displays messages that have come in since your last login. The **read** command will also suffice if you want to examine other messages. The help message says we can change the message base by entering the number of the board at the main prompt, although how we know which number to enter isn't yet clear. The **join** command lets us add USENET newsgroups, and so on. Note, too, that we're presented with mail options. The other major form of connectivity that such bulletin boards provide is an electronic mail address for Internet access.

We could continue working through the menus, but it would be pointless to do so, because local bulletin board connections are frequently modified by their system operators, and they often have their own software quirks. You have to explore in your area to find which BBS systems have some kind of connectivity, and then call to see what's available.

The downside to connectivity such as this, in addition to not offering FTP and Telnet, is that such systems are usually available only through a limited number of telephone lines. Prepare yourself for busy signals when you're trying to sign on to read your favorite newsgroups. Many local BBS systems, too, carry only a fraction of the total available number of newsgroups, so you may have to lobby the system operator to add a group you're particularly interested in.

But don't overlook the tremendous upside of these systems. Although they're still relatively rare, a growing number of BBSs with USENET hooks are becoming activated as interest in Internet-related activities grows. For a great many people, a local BBS will be the first glimpse of the world-wide community of users that is the Internet. These callers will have the chance to learn gradually, working through the USENET newsgroups, and asking questions of local people and their own system operator as they go. The system operators of these bulletin boards have a great deal to do with the recent explosion of interest in the Internet.

Figure 3.3
A help screen on a
typical BBS.

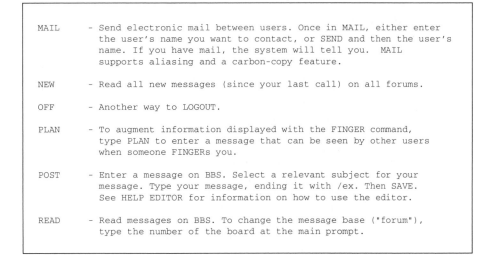

```
    MAIL      - Send electronic mail between users. Once in MAIL, either enter
                the user's name you want to contact, or SEND and then the user's
                name. If you have mail, the system will tell you.  MAIL
                supports aliasing and a carbon-copy feature.

    NEW       - Read all new messages (since your last call) on all forums.

    OFF       - Another way to LOGOUT.

    PLAN      - To augment information displayed with the FINGER command,
                type PLAN to enter a message that can be seen by other users
                when someone FINGERs you.

    POST      - Enter a message on BBS. Select a relevant subject for your
                message. Type your message, ending it with /ex. Then SAVE.
                See HELP EDITOR for information on how to use the editor.

    READ      - Read messages on BBS. To change the message base ("forum"),
                type the number of the board at the main prompt.
```

How can you find local bulletin boards with e-mail access and USENET newsgroups? It can be a tough proposition unless you keep your ear to the ground. If a computer user group in your area is tracking bulletin board activity, they may provide a list of local boards. In my area, an umbrella organization called the Triangle Computer Society maintains a monthly listing of all active boards; your area may also boast such a group. Ask questions in the computer community, at retail stores, and on any bulletin boards you already frequent. And don't forget your newsstand. *Boardwatch Magazine, CONNECT* and *Online Access* all track on-line developments and are expanding their coverage of the Internet.

You could also tap into NixPub, a useful list of open-access UNIX sites worldwide. Unfortunately, NixPub is a prime example of the Internet Catch at work. How do you get it? Through the Internet. What's one way to get access to the Internet? Through the NixPub list. So, while the following tells you where to find the list on-line (later, we'll examine the tools that can help you get it on-line), you will also find information from the most recent NixPub list in the appendix. Once you're on-line, you'll be able to update your lists as follows.

••

What You Need: A list of Public Access UNIX Sites

The Document: **The NixPub List**

How to Get It: By FTP. The address is **vfl.paramax.com.** The directory is *pub/pubnet* and the file is **nixpub.long.** Although this looks like gibberish now, we'll discuss in Chapter 5 how to retrieve documents by FTP. In the meantime, see the list of public access UNIX providers in the appendix, which draws on the NixPub list.

••

COMMERCIAL ON-LINE SERVICES

Thanks to growing interest in Internet connectivity, almost all of the major commercial on-line services have now set up gateways to the Internet. Today you can send and receive electronic mail at CompuServe, BIX, America Online, and at DELPHI, and Prodigy is developing an e-mail gateway as well. With the exception of DELPHI and BIX (more about both later), these are all just gateways into the Internet; they can be used only for electronic mail, and do not provide access to the other two of the big three Internet protocols—Telnet and FTP.

Still, you can do a lot with a mail connection to the Internet, including requesting and receiving programs and other files (they're sent to you in the form of messages, which you must run through decoding routines to restore them to their natural state), following mailing lists and their wide range of discussions, and retrieving a wealth of valuable background information about the Internet. An e-mail link and a little ingenuity can produce startling results— you can even search directories and hunt down programs at remote sites by using the mail versions of Internet tools like **archie.**

Chapter 8 focuses on using the Internet through e-mail alone. Some of the workarounds are cumbersome, but the results may allow you to do everything you need to do.

THE FREE-NET ADVANTAGE

A Free-Net is a superb idea; if there were more of them, Internet access wouldn't pose the level of conceptual difficulty that it does today. A Free-Net, created by volunteers, maintained by people who believe in networking, is a computer system with two principles: broaden a community's access base to local computing resources, and provide hooks into the broader world of networking. To do this, Free-Nets usually tap Internet connections, and that means they're a way for users to log on without the usual hassles. Access is usually restricted to electronic mail and some Telnet capabilities. Free-Nets generally provide easy-to-use menus.

The idea behind Free-Nets is to make telecommunications resources available to all; audience building is what this initiative is all about. Think of National Public Radio (absent any federal funding); then apply the concept to computing. Free-Nets are the brainchild of the National Public Telecommunication Network, or NPTN, which is based in Cleveland, OH. By helping organizers in various parts of the United States, NPTN hopes to construct a network similar to what its media-based counterparts have created, only with the added resources of computing power to spread information. A key word is "cybercasting," the dissemination of network services to NPTN "affiliates" around the country, supplementing local data with high-quality information feeds for all.

Free-Nets, though, aren't yet common. Perhaps the best known is the Cleveland Free-Net, which was the testbed for the concept and remains a driving force behind Free-Net development nationally. The Cleveland Free-Net is accessible by the Internet, as are its relatives such as Tri-State Online and the Heartland Free-Net. Keep a lookout in your area for Free-Net development. These systems can get you up and running on the Internet faster than any other.

Figure 3.4 shows what the Cleveland Free-Net looks like when you sign on from the Internet. The screen will be slightly different when you call directly to the site.

From this point on, you'll be dealing with an unusual menu structure. The Free-Net concept involves community access and involvement, so it's no surprise to find a heavy emphasis on making the system workable for computer novices. Look at the basic menus of the Cleveland Free-Net shown in Figure 3.5 and you'll see what I mean. They're based on the concept of the town hall, with the various services broken out as menu options. The metaphor is that of a town itself; you move through an on-line city, making choices as you go.

Choice 14, for example, *The Communications Center,* breaks into a submenu which offers access to electronic mail, other computer systems, and file transfer options. You also have access to university library systems, databases on agriculture, space science, weather, oceanography, and geography, not to mention USENET news and a host of other features. The menu system is simple to use, but as you begin to find your way around the Internet, mastering the commands on whatever system you use to access its resources, you may find yourself wishing for a leaner interface. Nonetheless, it's hard to imagine an easier introduction for the novice to the Internet than a Free-Net. The only problem: unless you have a local Free-Net, tapping Free-Net resources isn't going to be workable unless you're already on the Internet. So find out what's happening in your area about Free-Nets.

Figure 3.4
The introductory screen to the Cleveland Free-Net.

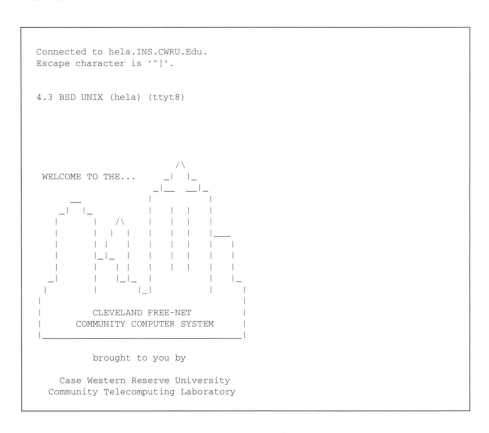

Figure 3.5
An Upper Level menu
on the Cleveland
Free-Net.

```
< CLEVELAND FREE-NET DIRECTORY >

  1 The Administration Building
  2 The Post Office
  3 Public Square
  4 The Courthouse & Government Center
  5 The Arts Building
  6 Science and Technology Center
  7 The Medical Arts Building
  8 The Schoolhouse (Academy One)
  9 The Community Center & Recreation Area
 10 The Business and Industrial Park
 11 The Library
 12 University Circle
 13 The Teleport
 14 The Communications Center
 15 NPTN/USA TODAY HEADLINE NEWS
 16 < SPECIAL FEATURES >
-----------------------------------------------
h=Help, x=Exit Free-Net, "go help"=extended help

Your Choice ==
```

Free-Nets to Watch

The following lists some currently active Free-Nets, along with their phone numbers and Telnet addresses. When you've had a little more experience, you'll be able to use Telnet by way of the Internet to check into any of these sites.

NAME: BIG SKY TELEGRAPH
This highly regarded system is located in Dillon, Montana. Log on as **bbs.**

> Telnet: **192.231.192.1**
> Telephone: 406-683-7680

NAME: BUFFALO FREE-NET
Located in Buffalo, NY. Log on as **freeport.**

> Telnet: **freenet.buffalo.edu**
> Telephone: 716-645-6128

NAME: CLEVELAND FREE-NET
Logging on is handled by choosing options on a menu.

> Telnet: **freenet-in-a.cwru.edu**
> Telephone: 216-368-3888.

NAME: COLOMBIA ONLINE INFORMATION NETWORK
Colombia, MO. Log on as **guest.**

> Telnet: **bigcat.missouri.edu**
> Telephone: 314-884-7000

NAME: DENVER FREE-NET

Denver, CO. Log on as **guest.**

> Telnet: **freenet.hsc.colorado.edu**
> Telephone: 303-270-4865

NAME: HEARTLAND FREE-NET

Sponsored by Bradley University in Peoria, IL. A sister system of the Cleveland Free-Net. Log on as **bbsguest.**

> Telnet: **heartland.bradley.edu**
> Telephone: 309-674-1100

NAME: LORAIN COUNTY FREE-NET

Based in Elyria, OH. Log on as **guest.**

> Telnet: **freenet.lorain.oberlin.edu**
> Telephone: 216-366-9721

NAME: MEDINA COUNTY FREE-NET

Set up in a rural Ohio county, this Free-Net runs at a community hospital southwest of Cleveland.

> Telnet: not presently supported
> Telephone: 216-723-6732

NAME: NATIONAL CAPITAL FREE-NET

Located in Ottawa, Canada. Log on as **guest.**

> Telnet: **freenet.carleton.ca**
> Telephone: 613-780-3733

TALLAHASSEE FREE-NET

Based in Tallahassee, FL. Log on as **visitor.**

> Telnet: **freenet.fsu.edu**
> Telephone: 904-488-5056

NAME: TRI-STATE ONLINE

Cincinnati, OH. Sponsored by Cincinnati Bell Telephone. Log on in the following sequence: **cbos, visitor, 9999.**

> Telnet: **cbos.uc.edu**
> Telephone: 513-579-1990

VICTORIA FREE-NET

Based in Victoria, British Colombia, Canada. Log on as **guest.**

> Telnet: **freenet.victoria.bc.ca**
> Telephone: 604-595-2300

WELLINGTON CITYNET

Wellington, New Zealand. Visitor logins not currently available.

> Telnet: **kosmos.wcc.govt.nz**
> Telephone: +64-4-801-3060

YOUNGSTOWN FREE-NET

Sponsored by St. Elizabeth Hospital Medical Center and Youngstown State University in Youngstown, Ohio. Log on as **visitor.**

> Telnet: **yfn.ysu.edu**
> Telephone: 216-742-3072

A caveat: like other bulletin board systems, Free-Nets do not possess infinite resources. If you're trying to contact them by way of the Internet, you may receive a message like this:

```
telnet freenet-in-b.cwru.edu
Trying 129.22.8.38 ...
Connected to hela.INS.CWRU.Edu.
Escape character is '^]'.
Sorry, this machine already has the maximum allowable number of users.
Please try again later.
Connection closed by foreign host.
```

Nevertheless, people in the areas served by a Free-Net should take advantage of exploring it. Watch for future Free-Net growth in many parts of the country. Figure 3.6 shows cities where NPTN organizing committees have formed, so you can expect these sites to come on-line in the near future.

A NEW ALTERNATIVE—DELPHI AND BIX

At the end of December 1992, General Videotex, a developer of on-line services based in Cambridge, MA, and parent company of the on-line services called DELPHI and BIX, announced that DELPHI had begun to provide full access to the Internet. The term "full access" is now being used in a way we've come to understand—access to the big three Internet protocols of electronic mail, file transfers by FTP, and remote logins to other computers on the Internet using Telnet procedures. The announcement marks the first time the Internet has been made accessible by a broad, consumer-based on-line service in such depth. Shortly before this book went to publication, DELPHI's sister service BIX also announced full Internet access.

Figure 3.6
Free-Nets now
organizing.

```
Freenets of the Near Future

The following are cities now listed by the National Public Telecommunication
Network as having set up organizing committees preparatory to bringing a
Free-Net system on-line.

Akron, OH
Ann Arbor, MI
Austin, TX
Battle Creek/Kalamazoo MI
Champaign-Urbana, IL
Chapel Hill, NC
Chicago, IL
Dallas, TX
Dayton, OH
Eau Claire, WI
Gainesville, FL
Honolulu, HI
Los Angeles-USC, CA
Los Angeles-Valley, CA
Minneapolis/St. Paul, MN
Oklahoma City, OK
Orange County, CA
Palm Beach, FL
Portland, OR
Philadephia, PA
Providence, RI
San Luis Obispo, CA
Santa Barbara, CA
Summit, NJ
Tampa, FL
Tuscaloosa, AL
Washington, DC


International Free-Nets are springing up as well in the following cities:

Bayreuth, Germany
Erlangen, Germany
Helsinki, Finland
Ottawa, Canada
Singapore, R.S.


Further information on NPTN can be obtained by writing:

Dr. Tom Grundner
President, NPTN
Box 1987
Cleveland, OH 44106
216-368-2733
216-368-5436 (fax)
Internet: aa001@cleveland.freenet.edu
```

DELPHI and BIX thus open up a new range of possibilities for Internet users. These are not simply electronic mail gateways, but direct links into full Internet capabilities. With local access numbers in some six hundred cities and towns throughout the United States and many foreign countries, these services have the potential for demystifying the Internet for the broad class of home and office users with modems. DELPHI provides additional on-line support through an Internet forum, or Special Interest Group (SIG), specifically devoted to learning Internet use. DELPHI's Internet SIG makes the transition between commercial on-line service and the Internet about as painless as it can get.

Another helpful factor is DELPHI's menu system. Most commercial on-line services offer menu functions that guide the user through the maze of possible commands. DELPHI is, in effect, providing training for new users by letting them work with familiar commands as they go about their journeys into the Internet. In addition, users can access a range of DELPHI-specific features such as stock quotes, newswires, an on-line encyclopedia, a wide range of special interest groups, files for downloading, and multi-player games. It remains to be seen how many new users are lured into the Internet after first learning on-line methods with DELPHI's basic services, but the huge turnout so far—DELPHI estimates over ten thousand people have signed on for Internet services—suggests the experiment is working. It will be interesting to see whether the new BIX offering matches these levels of growth.

Looking into DELPHI

What can you expect when you try out DELPHI? The following examines the Internet Special Interest Group and what you can find there. Figure 3.7 shows the menu you'll see if you go directly to the Internet SIG (which you can access by typing **internet** at the main system prompt).

There's plenty of material here to keep the novice busy for some time. The first stop for the new user should be the *Using Internet Services* section, accessible by entering **using** at the prompt. This generates the menu shown in Figure 3.8.

You can also examine the *Databases (Files)* area, where you'll find a number of background resources, including many we'll later pick up as part of our Internet library-building project. To move to this area, simply enter **data** at the prompt. DELPHI's menu system is such that entering only part of a word will take you where you want to go, as long as the system can distinguish your command from other commands beginning with the same letters. Figure 3.9 shows some of the on-line resources on DELPHI.

Obviously, DELPHI can be a valuable source of background materials, but how do we actually get into the Internet? Again, the easy-to-use menu structure

Figure 3.7
The DELPHI Internet
SIG main menu.

```
Internet SIG Menu:


About the Internet      Using Internet Services
Announcements           Who's Here
Conference              Workspace
Databases (Files)       Help
EMail                   Exit
Entry Log
Forum (Messages)        Auto-Connect Services
Guides (Books)          FTP
Member Directory        Telnet
Register/Cancel         Utilities


Internet SIGEnter your selection:
```

Figure 3.8
The DELPHI menu for
Using Internet Services.

```
Contents
--------
    1  "I'M NEW! WHAT DO I DO?"
    2  "HOW DO I USE FTP?"
    3  "HOW DO I USE TELNET?"
    4  SENDING INTERNET MAIL
    5  RECEIVING INTERNET MAIL
    6  INTERNET ADDRESSES AND OTHER NETWORKS
    7  FIDONET SPECIAL INSTRUCTIONS
    8  HOW TO MANAGE MAIL TO AVOID STORAGE COSTS
    9  "WHAT IS A LISTSERV? HOW DO I SUBSCRIBE?"
   10  ACCESSING USENET NEWSGROUPS


USING(Enter Number, Scan, "?" or Exit):
```

comes to the rescue. You'll have noticed in Figure 3.7 in the Internet SIG main menu, that there are *FTP* and *Telnet* options. If you were to use either option by way of a conventional dial-up information provider, you'd most likely have to find your way step by step. (There are exceptions—Performance Systems International distributes a software package called PSILink which shields you from some Internet complexities, as does Portal—but these aren't common.)

Figure 3.9
Some of the resources
available on DELPHI.

```
INET.ZIP                         DATA    8-JAN   LAWRENCE2000
HIGH WEIRDNESS BY E-MAIL V2.0    DOCU    6-JAN   MRJOSEPH
IRC LISTING JAN 93               TEXT    2-JAN   TF3
YANOFF LIST (12/28/92)           TEXT    1-JAN   TF3
DECEMBER ANON. FTP LIST          ARTI   21-DEC   CTAVARES
SMITH'S BIG FUN LIST             DATA   12-DEC   WALTHOWE
EJOURNALS, NEWSLETTERS DIRECTORY DATA   11-DEC   WALTHOWE
PDIAL LIST, OCTOBER 92           DATA    9-DEC   WALTHOWE
LIST OF TOP LEVEL DOMAINS        DOCU    7-DEC   WJWHITE
VERONICA                         DOCU   19-NOV   WALTHOWE
DECEMBER LIST OF INFO SOURCES    DATA   16-NOV   WALTHOWE
ANNOTATED INTERNET BIBLIOGRAPHY  DOCU   14-NOV   HTILLMAN
ARCHIE BASICS                    ARTI   11-NOV   JBUCATA
MULTI-USER DUNGEON (MUD) LIST    DATA   10-NOV   WALTHOWE
MORE FTP SITES                   DATA    9-NOV   JBUCATA
LIST OF ARCHIE/FTP SITES         DATA    8-NOV   JBUCATA
ATARINET.TXT                     DOCU    7-NOV   KEN219
RFC1062.TXT                      DOCU    7-NOV   ROBWAT
NETWORKING TERMINOLOGY           DOCU    7-NOV   ROBWAT
ZAMFIELD'S LIST                  DOCU    7-NOV   ROBWAT
USENET SOFTWARE INFORMATION      NEWS    6-NOV   THOMASD
CANCERNET INFO                   DOCU    1-NOV   ALIEN43ET
WHOLE INTERNET GUIDE REVIEW      PROG   SEP-92   WALTHOWE
NEWSGROUP INFO FROM DMC          DOCU   AUG-92   KEN219
COLLEGE.ZIP                      TEXT   SEP-92   COOKY
UPDATED NIXPUB LONG LIST         DATA   AUG-92   ERWINJ
ZEN AND THE ART OF THE INTERNET  DOCU   SEP-92   LAWLESS
DMCONNECTION                     DOCU   AUG-92   RUSTY
INTERNET RESOURCES SHORT GUIDE   DOCU   AUG-92   ROBINTON
SURANET GUIDE TO THE INTERNET    DOCU   JUL-92   WALTHOWE
PUBLIC UNIX SITES--THE LONG VERS DOCU   AUG-92   ERWINJ
PUBLIC UNIX SITES-SHORT VERSION  DOCU   AUG-92   ERWINJ
```

Figure 3.10
DELPHI's Telnet menu.

```
Internet SIGEnter your selection: telnet
"Telnet" is a way of connection from one host to another on the Internet. For
more details, type EXIT and then select About Internet Services.

Several Telnet sites are also accessible through the Auto-Connect menu. Other
options like Gopher, Archie, WWW, and WAIS are now available on the Utilities
menu.


Enter INTERNET address:
```

Figure 3.10 shows DELPHI's *Telnet* option, accessed by entering **telnet** at the SIG prompt.

This is the basic Telnet service. If you simply enter an Internet address at the *Telnet* prompt, you will be taken into a Telnet session at that address. Much the same would happen if you chose *FTP* at the main SIG prompt; again, you would be asked for an address. From this point on, you're on the Internet, and what you see on-screen will depend upon the system you accessed. There is a wide variety of possibilities; they're what this book is about.

Notice that the Internet SIG also has a menu option named *Auto-Connect Services*. This option takes you to menu choices for several major sites by Telnet, including CARL (Colorado Association of Research Libraries), a source of on-line information through library catalogs and databases, as well as NASA Spacelink, the powerful INTERNIC **gopher,** and a Campus Wide Information System at Rutgers University. Figure 3.11 shows the *Telnet* option branching off from the *Auto-Connect Services* menu.

Telnet procedures, though not difficult, will be thoroughly examined later in this book. But it's noteworthy that DELPHI's implementation is crafted to help the new user, who might easily get lost without the help these menus provide. This hasn't been done often in the Internet community, which has long relied on the supposition that anyone who needed to be connected already was. The new DELPHI offering is a healthy symptom that all that is changing, and its success may trigger other on-line services to follow suit.

Figure 3.11
DELPHI's
Auto-Connect Services
menu.

```
Telnet Auto-Connect Services Menu:

DRA/Library of Congress              InterNIC Gopher
Backgammon Server                    Law Library
CARL-Book reviews and databases      NASA Spacelink
Chess Server                         NOAA - Nat'l Oceanic and Atmos. Admin
Cleveland Freenet                    Recordings for the Blind
Geographic Name Server               Rutgers INFO
GO Server                            Spacemet - science/space bbs
Ham Radio Callbook                   Youngstown Freenet
Heartland Freenet                    Exit


AUTO-TELNETEnter your selection:
```

Getting an Account with DELPHI or BIX

Getting on-line with DELPHI or BIX is a competitive way to approach the Internet. DELPHI offers two membership plans. Its 10/4 plan gives you four hours of use each month for $10; additional use is charged at a rate of $4 per hour. The 20/20 Advantage Plan costs $20 per month, and includes twenty hours of use, giving you an effective rate of $1 per hour. Additional hours are billed at $1.80 per hour. These rates are for access speeds up to 2400 bps; you won't be able to roar on-line with that new 9600-bps modem quite yet, although DELPHI is testing 9600-bps access and will surely be offering it in the near future at more locations.

Add to the basic membership plan a $3 per month charge for the Internet connection. This fee sets you up with Internet access and includes a transfer allocation of 10 MB. Note that the 10 MB number does not refer to a *storage* allocation—instead, it's the total volume of incoming and outgoing mail messages and downloaded files by FTP. The 10-MB allocation works out to around three thousand typewritten pages, which should prove adequate for personal messaging tasks. But those who frequently download files or subscribe to multiple Internet mailing lists will have to keep a close watch on the volume of their data transfers.

Using DELPHI, then, and this is true of many dial-up access providers, you must keep a careful eye on your disk space. Standard storage charges on DELPHI are these: the first 25,600 characters are free, while each additional 1K is sixteen cents per month. Assume you've decided to download a file from a remote computer, as you will learn to do in Chapter 5. No problem there using DELPHI's FTP menu. But note what happens to the incoming file; it's placed in an area allocated for you on DELPHI called your *workspace*. Similarly, incoming mail is stored on disk for you, meaning you have to watch how much disk space you're using or you'll be charged for the extra kilobytes. The *Rates* section of the *Using DELPHI* menu contains further information on price changes.

If you decide to use DELPHI, prowl the Internet SIG—there you can learn the disk management process. In general, system operator Walt Howe, who manages the Internet SIG, recommends logging on to check mail at least once per week, and deleting newly read messages immediately. File maintenance is a critical issue for Internet users, since it's so easy to accumulate a huge mass of incoming mail simply by subscribing to mailing lists. Some of these lists can generate hundreds of messages per day, quickly putting you over your limit.

Through a special trial membership plan, new users can learn more about DELPHI and its Internet connection, and can receive five hours of access time for free. To join, dial by modem 1-800-365-4636. After connecting, press the **RETURN** key once or twice to wake up the host computer. At the **Username:** prompt, enter **JOINDELPHI.** At the **Password:** prompt, enter **INTERNET.** Alternatively, you can call DELPHI Member Service Representatives (voice only) at 800-695-4005.

BIX offers two pricing alternatives. Like DELPHI, it features a 20/20 plan—20 hours of evening or weekend use for $20 a month, with additional evening use at $1.80 per hour thereafter (or $1.00 per hour if you use Telnet connections to BIX). The basic pricing plan is $13 per month plus connect charges, which vary depending on time of day and access provider. Accessing BIX by Telnet always involves a flat $1.00 per hour fee, no matter what time of day you call; it's added to the $13 per month charge.

To sign up for BIX, set your communications program for full duplex, 8-N-1, 2400 bps. Dial 800-695-4882 or 617-491-5410. When you connect, press the **RETURN** key until you see the login prompt. Enter **bix.** At the **Name?** prompt, enter **bix.news.** Complete the registration on-line.

BIX, incidentally, offers an interesting wrinkle on the disk storage problem. When you download a file using FTP, the file comes directly to your computer rather than being stored first at the BIX site. This removes one major concern for frequent downloaders; after all, some of those programs and text files can take up a lot of space!

COMMERCIAL DIAL-UP PROVIDERS

We're victims of our own terminology. Isn't "dialing up" what you do with a local bulletin board in the first place? Aren't you using your modem to place a call, and isn't that what dialing up means? You'd think so. But we have to distinguish between calling a bulletin board system and calling into a full-fledged service provider. Most bulletin boards have their own agenda, which may or may not include some kind of hooks into USENET and Internet mail. Bulletin boards may or may not charge a usage fee.

Think of a service provider as someone who makes Internet access a business. This access may come in several guises, as we'll see, and the range of capabilities is up to you, your provider, and your wallet, but moving to this level is almost guaranteed to give you greater functionality and, if you choose, access to things like FTP and Telnet.

What you do with a dial-up connection is simple. You use your modem to place a call to a computer which already has network access. You log on to this remote system and perform your Internet work with its help. The number of service providers offering such connections is growing rapidly, and the cost is reasonable. Usually, you can get by for $20 to $30 per month, sometimes with a per-hour fee tacked on, sometimes not.

Consider The World, run by Software Tool & Die in Brookline, MA. The World offers a full panoply of Internet services, including electronic mail, FTP for file transfers, Telnet for remote login to distant computers, USENET news-groups, and in general, the whole range of Internet features covered later in this book. The World is a local call from Boston, but Software Tool & Die has also made arrangements for connections through CompuServe Packet Network, which means you can call a local number and pay an hourly access fee that's a lot lower than you'd pay through long-distance charges.

The World offers several rate packages. You can pay $5 per month and $2 per hour, or $20 per month and an additional $1 per hour for any time over the 20-hour limit. The charge for access through the CompuServe network is an additional $5.60 per hour. Disk storage in varying amounts is also provided depending on which plan you choose.

A Digression on Downloading and Storage

We've discussed the perils of running up a big bill by violating disk storage requirements. Now we will explore what actually happens when you download a file from the Internet through the mediation of a service provider. It's best understood by contrast to commercial on-line services. When you call a commercial service such as CompuServe or GEnie, your work will involve a direct connection between you and the host computers. Ask to download a file and the file will be sent directly to you, ending on your hard disk. You can watch the modem lights flicker to signal the incoming data.

This is not the case with a dial-up connection to the Internet. Here, when you download a file through FTP procedures, the file is downloaded not to your computer but to *the computer to which you are connected, that is, the service provider's computer.* When I go into a remote computer using Telnet through my connection at MCNC in Research Triangle Park, I am tapping MCNC's resources to help me do my work. The file I retrieve doesn't come directly to me (the modem's lights don't flash); rather, it's sent directly to the MCNC computer over high-speed links and is stored on disk there. I must then download it to my own computer, flashing modem lights and all. So the file transfer process is a two-step procedure. Understand this paradigm or FTP won't make sense to you.

Long-Distance Options

It wasn't that long ago that services such as The World were relatively unknown to the modem-using public, but today, these providers are spreading widely. Like The World, many are available through Public Data Networks (PDNs) like CompuServe Packet Network or BT Tymnet for those who are not within range of a local call. A PDN provides a local number through which, by paying a usage-related fee, you can call the service provider's number and pay significantly less than you would through standard long-distance. PDNs are in the business of moving data packets, and by taking advantage of their offerings, you can cut your on-line costs by a wide margin. The following are the major public data networks.

BT TYMNET

BT Tymnet calls its TYMNET Global Network "the world's largest international network," boasting local access in more than eleven hundred cities and one hundred foreign countries. Call 800-937-2862 or 215-666-1770 for information and local access numbers. This is a voice call, not a modem transaction.

Alternatively, if you already know a local access number, you can call by modem. Set your modem to 7 data bits, even parity, 1 stop to make this call (7-E-1). After the modem at the other end answers, enter **a** (no **RETURN** after the **a**). At the **please log in:** prompt, enter **information.** You'll then be given everything you need to know about the service and you can search for access codes useful to you. Choose #1, *Direct Dial & Outdial Worldwide Access* at the main menu. Figure 3.12 shows the secondary menu you'll be presented with.

As you can see, this database is searchable, and can quickly help you determine the TYMNET number nearest you.

COMPUSERVE PACKET NETWORK

Another widely used network is run by CompuServe, the CompuServe Packet Network, or CPN. Despite some misconceptions, you don't have to be a CompuServe member to use this network. You can obtain further information and local access numbers by dialing 800-848-8199 for a voice call.

Figure 3.12
A TYMNET menu for
access information.

```
                    TYMNET DIRECT DIAL & OUTDIAL ACCESS INFORMATION

    TYMNET has local dial-up access in over 900 cities in the domestic United
    States and over 130 non U.S. cities.  All locations use a variety of indus-
    try standard modem technology.

         1.  Access Location Index and Country Abbreviations
         2.  Worldwide TYMNET Access numbers
         3.  TYMNET Access Numbers for a Specific State or Country
         4.  TYMNET Access Numbers for a Specific Speed or Service
         5.  Regional Bell Operating Company (RBOC) Access Numbers
         6.  New Changes and Scheduled Changes
         7.  Scheduled Outages and Service Interruptions
         8.  X.121 Dialup Origination Addresses
         9.  Search by City, State or Area Code


    If you need assistance, type <H>elp.  To return to the previous menu, type
    <U>p.  To return to the main menu, type <T>op.  When you are finished, type
    Quit.


    Type the number or letter of the desired option at the Select prompt.

    Command:
```

And, just as with TYMNET, you can access CPN numbers by modem. Set
your modem to 7-E-1. Dial a local access number and press the **RETURN** key.
Enter **phones** at the **Host Name:** prompt. You'll see the information shown in
Figure 3.13.

Figure 3.13
The CompuServe
Phone Number Access
Area.

```
    Host Name:  PHONES


    FINDCIS                     PHN-1


    Welcome to the CompuServe Phone Number Access area; a free service of the
    CompuServe Information Service. This area gives you access numbers for the
    CompuServe Information Service and allows you to report any problems you may
    be encountering with an access number.


    *** For 9600bps access, CompuServe supports CCITT standard V.32/V.42 only.
    ***


    Press <CR> for more !


    FINDCIS                     PHN-4


     1 Find Access Numbers
     2 Report Access Number Problems
     3 International Access Information


    Last page, enter choice !
```

PC PURSUIT

There's also the PC Pursuit option by way of SprintNet, offering thirty hours of off-peak 2400 bps access for $30 per month. With PC Pursuit, you can call over forty metropolitan areas in the United States using local access numbers. The net effect is you can reach most of the providers listed in the service provider list in the appendix, even those not listed as having PDN access.

For further information, contact PC Pursuit at 800-736-1130 by voice. You can register for PC Pursuit with a modem call to 800-877-2006. Set parameters to 7-E-1. Press **RETURN** when the modem answers to wake the system up. Figure 3.14 shows what you'll see.

If you're interested in looking up access numbers from Sprint by modem, the number is 800-546-1000. Callers using 1200 bps should press **RETURN** three times after the modem answers; 2400 bps callers should enter **@ RETURN RETURN.** You'll then be prompted for your area code and local exchange, after which a prompt will appear. Enter **mail** at the @ prompt, **phones** at the **User Name?** prompt, and **phones** at the **Password?** prompt. Figure 3.15 shows the menu you'll see.

PSINET

You can obtain information for this network by calling 800-827-7482 or 703-620-6651 by voice. Alternatively, you can send electronic mail (Chapter 7 will show you how) to **all-info@psi.com.** You can also retrieve a list of local access numbers by sending mail to **numbers-info@psi.com.**

Making Internet Music

CONCERT-CONNECT is a program of the MCNC Center for Communications in Research Triangle Park, a high-tech research center located between Raleigh

Figure 3.14
Registering for PC Pursuit.

```
Welcome as a new user to our system!

This is a public system, in support of the PC-PURSUIT service offered by US
Sprint.  There are no files available for download, and this is not a gen-
eral purpose BBS system.

You may exchange messages with the administrators of the PC-PURSUIT system,
as well as read or capture text files explaining the service and the loca-
tions we serve.

You may also register on-line for access to the PC-PURSUIT service, by
using your major credit card.  For more information on how to register for
the service, please display Bulletin 3.

Welcome aboard, see you soon around the country...

PAUL GILSTER from RALEIGH, NC

C)hange FIRST name/LAST name/CITY/STATE, D)isconnect, [R]egister?
```

Figure 3.15
Looking up access
numbers via Sprint.

```
US SPRINT'S ONLINE


        LOCAL ACCESS TELEPHONE NUMBERS DIRECTORY

        1. Domestic Asynchronous Dial Service
        2. International Asynchronous Dial Service
        3. Domestic X.25 Dial Service
        4. New Access Centers and Recent Changes
        5. Product and Service Information
        6. Exit the Phones Directory


   Please enter your selection (1-6):
```

and Durham, NC. MCNC itself is a private, non-profit organization involved in research and education in microelectronics, communications, and super-computing.

CONCERT stands for **CO**mmunications for **N**orth **C**arolina **E**ducation, **R**esearch and **T**echnology. The idea behind the network is to provide North Carolina business and industry with an opportunity to access the rich resources on the Internet. CONCERT-CONNECT thus provides a statewide network operating a high-speed backbone which connects to the Internet through a contract with Advanced Network and Services Inc., the firm currently managing the T-3 backbone network called ANSnet.

A look at CONCERT-CONNECT may give you an idea of what a service provider is all about. Using a connection through CONCERT-CONNECT gives you access to four possible types of Internet access, ranging from those best suited to research and educational institutions to smaller accounts for business and individual use. The network can offer services to business because of an agreement with ANS CO+RE Systems, Inc., the ANS subsidiary providing business access for commercial traffic and communications.

Four types of service are available at CONCERT-CONNECT:

1. On the lowest rung of the ladder, UUCP accounts offering access to mail and USENET newsgroups.

2. Public dial-up UNIX accounts for individual users.

3. Serial Line Internet Protocol, or SLIP, dial-up modem access for local UNIX networks (we'll talk about SLIP in a moment).

4. Direct connections at 56 kbps or T1 circuit speeds.

Callers in North Carolina can tap CONCERT-CONNECT through dial-in access from Asheville, Chapel Hill, Charlotte, Durham, Greensboro, Greenville, Raleigh, and Winston-Salem. A variety of pricing plans are offered.

Each service provider will have its own character, and fee schedules will vary widely, but CONCERT-CONNECT is in many ways representative of the growing access to the Internet now attracting users nationwide. People I've spoken to in North Carolina say that before CONCERT-CONNECT, they simply ruled out Internet usage as prohibitively expensive. Now they're becoming Internet regulars, and the story is being repeated as service options multiply.

PSILink: A User-Friendly Internet

As commercial providers target larger audiences, some are moving aggressively to make Internet connections less difficult to use. We saw earlier that DELPHI's menu system presented users with choices among various Internet tasks. BIX, meanwhile, is updating its BIXnav software to include point-and-click functionality for major Internet chores. PSILink, a software interface provided by Performance Systems International, Inc., makes it easy to send and receive electronic mail, as well as to access the USENET newsgroups and use FTP for retrieval of remote files. With local dial-up numbers in major North American cities, the PSILink Service supports 1200- and 2400-bps access, as well as high-speed 9600 (V.32) to 19200 rates. If PSILink isn't the only user-friendly interface to the Internet—expect many more in the near future—it's certainly one of the best.

Retrieving electronic mail is not only painless but cost-effective, because the PSILink software makes the Internet connection, downloads the relevant material, uploads whatever mail you are sending, and then signs off. You can create your replies at leisure, without worrying about a ticking clock and per-minute charges. Figure 3.16 shows an electronic mail message as read through PSILink software.

Working with USENET newsgroups is likewise simple. In Figure 3.17, you can see how the software works. I'm presented with a complete list of USENET newsgroups, updated every time I sign on. I can choose among them when off-line to determine which I want to receive. As discussed in Chapter 11, signing on to USENET the first time can be a complicated experience, as you weed through the available groups in search of what you want. PSILink automates this process and lets you choose your newsgroups off-line. You can learn more about the service by calling PSInet at the number previously listed.

Public Access Internet Providers

The number of service providers continues to increase as the Internet evolves. You'll need a way to keep up with them, and fortunately, a useful directory exists. The directory is called the Public Dialup Internet Access List (PDIAL), and it's compiled by Peter Kaminski, a software developer in the San Francisco Bay area. The material listed in the appendix draws heavily on both Kaminski's work as well as the NixPub list. Look there for information about service providers you can use. The latest list can be found on-line. Here's how to obtain it.

••

 What You Need: An Updated List of Internet service providers.

The Document: **The Public Dialup Internet Access List**

How to Get It: Send electronic mail to **info-deli-server@netcom.com.** In the subject field of the message, enter **send pdial.** If you wish to receive future editions as they appear, send e-mail with the subject **subscribe pdial** to the same address.

••

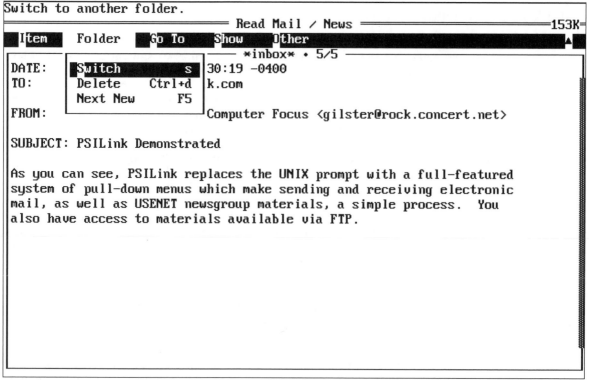

Figure 3.16
Reading electronic mail with PSILink.

SLIPPING ONTO THE INTERNET

Dial-up service is the soundest route to the Internet highway for individual users and for many small businesses. By using these services, we inch closer to the "full access" capabilities many users talk about; in fact, for many, FTP, Telnet, and electronic mail define full access. But there's still a catch. By using dial-up services, you're tapping another computer's power, but you're not actually "on the network." The computer you call maintains a network address, and you're using its resources to do your work.

What happens if you want more? Serial Line Internet Protocol (SLIP) and Point-to-Point-Protocol (PPP) provide the answer, offering a bridge between dial-up and the complete range of Internet connections provided by a dedicated access. SLIP and PPP let us continue to use our regular telephone line while making our own computers true network participants, network address and all. This means that a SLIP or PPP connection will let you handle file transfers directly into your own system, rather than bringing in the file to the dial-up computer and then downloading it to your own system. The same is true of Telnet procedures, which you now control from your machine.

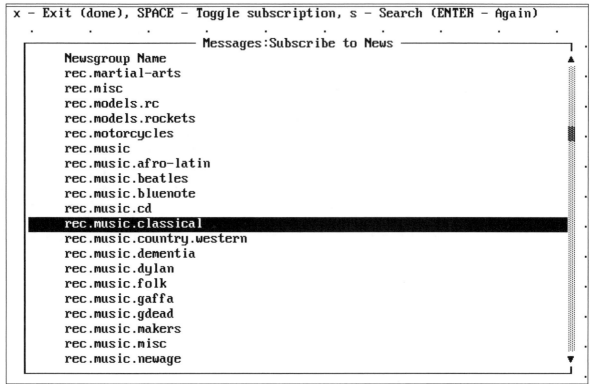

```
 x - Exit (done), SPACE - Toggle subscription, s - Search (ENTER - Again)
    .         .         .         .         .         .         .         .         .
 ┌─────────────────────── Messages:Subscribe to News ───────────────────────┐  .
 │        Newsgroup Name                                                    ▲ │
 │        rec.martial-arts                                                    │  .
 │        rec.misc                                                            │
 │        rec.models.rc                                                       │  .
 │        rec.models.rockets                                                  │
 │        rec.motorcycles                                                     │  .
 │        rec.music                                                         ▓ │
 │        rec.music.afro-latin                                              ▓ │  .
 │        rec.music.beatles                                                   │
 │        rec.music.bluenote                                                  │  .
 │        rec.music.cd                                                        │
 │██████rec.music.classical██████████████████████████████████████████████████│
 │        rec.music.country.western                                           │  .
 │        rec.music.dementia                                                  │
 │        rec.music.dylan                                                     │  .
 │        rec.music.folk                                                      │
 │        rec.music.gaffa                                                     │
 │        rec.music.gdead                                                     │  .
 │        rec.music.makers                                                    │
 │        rec.music.misc                                                      │  .
 │        rec.music.newage                                                  ▼ │
 └────────────────────────────────────────────────────────────────────────┘  .
```

Figure 3.17
Looking at USENET newsgroups with PSILink.

What SLIP Does

By way of providing a half-way station between full Internet access and dial-up capabilities, SLIP and PPP both offer the opportunity to run Internet software over standard telephone lines. That means no high-speed line is necessary, and the user doesn't have to maintain the line only for SLIP purposes, for SLIP connections can be used on a dial-in basis. That leaves your telephone free for other purposes.

Is this similar to dial-up service? Only in the sense that you can call in as you please. Remember, by offering Internet access through a SLIP connection, your provider is making it possible to run various kinds of client programs on your own machine. If you read, for example, about a new client that helps you search databases, you'll be able to locate a copy on-line, download it directly to your computer, and run it there. Dial-up callers wouldn't be able to manage this. They remain dependent on the clients already mounted on their service provider's computer.

Using your own clients can be of large or little benefit depending on your needs. You may find that Internet access, even using terminal emulation in a dial-up connection, can provide so many possibilities that it will suffice. If getting client software running is a major feature for you (and it may well be, especially if you become involved in the growth of such software) then a SLIP connection could make sense. Many of the providers listed in the Appendix offer SLIP as well as standard dial-up options.

FULL ACCESS: THE INTERNET'S HOLY GRAIL

And so you arrive by circuitous path to the ultimate Internet step, full connectivity, or what is otherwise known as "being on the net." This is the domain of large institutions, corporations, educational organizations, and the like, which lease a telephone line and use additional hardware to maintain a network connection. Such organizations generally bring a large number of their computers onto the network. Each machine hooks up to the company network and then to the Internet. Obviously, all the client software options you hear about are accessible to you when running in full access mode. But at this level, you're a long way from the home user dialing in with a modem and a PC on the desktop.

4

One Language
Among Many

The early explorers of the New World could not anticipate what kind of peoples they would encounter. A linguist trained in European languages could do the explorers no good when they confronted native tribes speaking in dialects unlike anything they had ever heard before. But people make contact one word at a time, and language is something that's best acquired through experience. Like the early navigators, those who learn the ways of the Internet will pick up words and phrases as they go. Computer jargon runs rampant on the network—a sea of acronyms and strange abbreviations to be mastered gradually. A welter of operating systems, each with its own set of commands, is in use at various network sites.

Do you really need to master an operating system to work on the Internet? The answer is an emphatic no. But as with travel to any foreign country, the more of the local language you do pick up, the more rewarding the trip will be. It makes sense, then, to acquire a certain proficiency in basic UNIX operations, because they'll make your journey easier and provide a set of tools for manipulating the information you'll discover. Using this operating system—at first alien, then, with experience, logical and powerful—will allow you to draw from the Internet the information you need, download it to your own computer, and send it by electronic mail to other users. It will also make you proficient in file management, a necessary skill when conserving disk space is a high priority.

Why UNIX?

First, a necessary qualification. Although people frequently associate the operating system called UNIX with the Internet, UNIX is no more an official language of the network than is VMS, the operating system driving Digital Equipment Corporation's VAX computers or, for that matter, VM, the IBM mainframe language. It is true, however, that many people first come to the Internet through UNIX implementations. This is because DARPA was concerned with making its TCP/IP protocols available for widespread use in the research community. Since university computer science departments commonly used UNIX, and in particular the UNIX variant known as Berkeley UNIX (developed at the University of California at Berkeley), DARPA funded the integration of TCP/IP into the Berkeley UNIX system.

Today, UNIX is the lingua franca of the dial-up Internet world, and as such, it tends to be intimidating. Like MS-DOS, UNIX presents you with a prompt, usually % or something similar, and then waits for you to act. My service provider, the North Carolina network known as CONCERT-CONNECT, offers me an inscrutable : (colon) prompt. It takes only a few minutes of trying out commands and getting nowhere before you look back on the menu structure of the average BBS or commercial service with great fondness. Doesn't the Internet have any menus? If not, why not?

Some day, of course, there may be an easy-to-use menu structure for Internet operations; some service providers, like Performance Systems International with its PSILink software, and InterCon Systems Corp. with WorldLink, have begun offering one, and both DELPHI and the Free-Nets provide simple menu systems. But many other providers don't. We have to face the fact that this network grew out of a research and academic environment where user friendliness settled in late as a goal. Then, too, there are so many destinations on the Internet that in some ways, a menu structure can seem constricting. The following will help you get your bearings, then, by exploring the UNIX terrain.

Of Interfaces and Complexity

UNIX is unique in that the program that determines its interface runs like an application, like any other program. Therefore, you may choose from a variety of user interfaces. The UNIX interface is known as a *shell*. A shell is a program that accepts keyboard commands, interprets them, and takes action based upon them.

The shell discussed in the following is the C Shell, also known as **csh.** When you log on to a service provider, you may be asked which shell you prefer. Besides **csh,** there may be choices like the Bourne Shell, or **sh,** which uses a $ as its user prompt. This was the original UNIX shell; it comes with all UNIX systems. Other shells include **tcsh, bash,** and **ksh.** In this book, I am using the **csh** shell to illustrate basic Internet procedures. The C Shell uses the percent sign (%) as its user prompt instead of the dollar sign ($); it's the standard shell of Berkeley UNIX.

What you see as your command prompt isn't critical. In fact, it's possible the command prompt will be customized by your service provider. For example, my account at CONCERT-CONNECT gives me the following prompt:

```
rock:
```

where "rock" is the name of the computer I log in to; this is the prompt even though the shell here is **csh,** and we would expect the percent sign (%). On the other hand, my account at The World in Brookline, MA, uses this prompt:

```
world%
```

Again, I am set up to use **csh** at The World; the prompt has simply been customized by the service provider.

DIAL-UP ASSUMPTIONS

For the purposes of this book, I am assuming you are dialing in to a service provider that makes a standard UNIX account available. The examples shown in the text go under this assumption. If you are not—say, for example, you use WorldLink or PSILink software to transact your Internet business, you will find much of the command complexity has been removed from your networking. You'll still proceed with the Internet functions discussed here, but perhaps they'll be easier to access than through a UNIX shell.

If you're accessing the Internet through a mail account at a commercial on-line service such as CompuServe, you'll need to master your system's electronic mail command structure. Chapter 8, which focuses on using the Internet through mail alone, should help you with that. If your entry is through DELPHI, you already have a comparatively easy-to-use command structure to work with, delivered through a series of menus.

But you'll still want to pay attention to this chapter, because when you use Telnet to manipulate a computer at a remote site, you will need some of these commands. You'll learn the core principles of UNIX which should allow you to adapt to these machines, and will make your own interface seem that much friendlier. Using menus is always easier, though often not as powerful, as working from a naked prompt.

THE SMATTERING OF UNIX YOU'LL NEED

Surely you've operated a word processor well enough to write and print out a letter, say, or a report for your school or business. You didn't have to learn a programming language to do it, either, because the program's own interface shielded you from all the problems. UNIX doesn't shield you as completely from a computer's inner workings, but the good news is you don't have to learn much of it. You will return to certain core commands again and again as you familiarize yourself with your service provider's system. But the great bulk of UNIX can safely be left behind. Learn what you need; learn more only if you choose.

The following set of UNIX commands is provided only as a reference. In the chapters that follow, with each step you take into unexplored Internet terrain, you will see what to type and what to expect. You may want to return to this chapter on occasion as you work your way through basic operations like directory listings and file deletion. Above all, don't be afraid to use an operating system that is admittedly powerful, but on the level of its basic commands, not at all difficult to master.

Understanding UNIX Files

UNIX file names must follow certain conventions.

- You should not start a file name with a dash (-) or a plus sign (+).
- You may, however, use a dash (–) or plus sign (+) inside the file name. Any combination of alphabetic characters, digits, periods (.), underscores (_) or dashes, and pluses can make up a UNIX file name;
- UNIX is case sensitive. This is an important consideration; often users of other systems forget about it, and don't understand why they can't access a UNIX file called **WORK.DOC,** for example, by asking for **work.doc.** So remember, case counts. The file **Network.Txt** is a different file from **network.txt.**

UNIX Directory Structure

Like any operating system, UNIX attempts to create order out of the data on your hard disk. An MS-DOS user will have no problem with the UNIX directory structure because it was the model for the MS-DOS system of directories and subdirectories, as well as for Digital's VMS system, so its impact has been wide. But note one crucial difference: UNIX directory path separators are forward slashes, not the backslashes DOS users have become accustomed to. In other words, a DOS directory named *windows\xtalk* would appear in UNIX as *windows/xtalk*. The backslash is the only difference, but it's an important one.

When you establish an account with an Internet system provider (and most providers of dial-up access use UNIX as their operating system), the system administrator at the service provider's site will set up a directory for you to use. This directory is called your *home directory*. Consider it a starting point for your UNIX explorations, and hence your first beachhead into the Internet. There will also be a set of subdirectories available for your use which contain other data related to your account. At CONCERT-CONNECT, for example, when I save a mail message, it's sent to a subdirectory called *Mail*. When I save USENET postings, they go to a subdirectory called *News*.

Basic UNIX Commands

Take a look now at some basic UNIX commands. What's not clear quickly should become so through practice. Some of these commands you won't need to use right away. Others you'll want to experiment with to get the feel of the operating system. You'll put your service provider's UNIX to major use in downloading files (covered in Chapter 5), managing your disk space by deleting (or compressing) the files you save there, and moving and renaming files. These commands will help you manage such tasks.

cat *filename* Displays a file on-screen. This is handy if the file is less than one screen long, or if you prefer to display a long file continuously and capture it with your software's capture buffer. But because the text scrolls through without interruption, you'll also find the **more** command described later useful; it provides page breaks.

cd This command changes your current working directory. Entering it without any specifications causes the system to return you to your home directory.

UNIX distinguishes between absolute and relative path names. An absolute path name begins with a slash and includes the complete path starting with the root directory. */home/gilster/Mail*, for example, is an absolute path name. To reach it, I would type **cd /home/gilster/Mail** (note the upper case on Mail!)

If I were already in the *gilster* subdirectory, however, I could switch to the *Mail* subdirectory by typing a relative path name. **cd Mail** would take me there. Note that the relative path name does not require the complete path statement, as it works in relation to the current working directory. Also note that it requires no slash.

cp Copies a file. Thus **cp internet.intro internet.start** copies the file **internet.intro** to a new file called **internet.start.**

help Don't miss this command. It calls up a screen of help information when you get lost. (Note: not every system will have this function installed. Try yours and see if it's there).

logout Logs off the system.

ls Lists files and directories. **ls** can be tightened up to include more specific commands. Thus **ls -l** lists directories and files in a longer format which includes the type of the file and other information.

Figure 4.1 shows what the **ls -l** command looked like on a particular day at my CONCERT-CONNECT account.

Another useful **ls** variant is the recursive **ls -lR,** which provides a listing of all files in all directories.

Figure 4.1
An **ls -l** directory listing.

```
% ls -l
total 240
drwx------   2 gilster       512 Mar 29 13:05 Mail/
drwx--S---   4 gilster       512 Mar 27 09:33 News/
-rw-r--r--   1 gilster   8442288 Mar 10 08:11 core
-rw-------   1 gilster       625 Mar 15 08:54 date
-rw-------   1 gilster       526 Mar 11 09:47 dial
drwxr-sr-x   2 gilster       512 Jan  9  1992 ftp/
-rw-------   1 gilster      6724 Mar 24 16:24 mbox
-rw-------   1 gilster      5326 Mar 29 13:04 michnet
-rw-------   1 gilster      4094 Mar 27 08:32 nobody1
-rw-------   1 gilster       197 Mar 19 09:16 sig
-rw-------   1 gilster    122423 Mar 27 08:49 world.ps.Z
-rw-------   1 gilster       691 Mar 27 09:04 xmodem.log
```

man   This is another command that may or may not be installed on your
system. The *UNIX User's Manual Reference Guide* is a large document
which can be stored on disk and kept available on-line. If you need
detailed help with a particular command, you can get it by entering
man followed by the name of the command in question. Thus **man ls**
gives you useful information about the **ls** command. Figure 4.2 shows
an example of the **man** command at work.

Be advised: the UNIX *User's Manual Reference Guide* is written by programmers,
and it's pretty heavy stuff. Fortunately, the commands about which you need
detailed information, such as **mail** and **ftp,** will be covered in detail in later
chapters, so you won't need the **man** command often.

mkdir *name*   Creates a new subdirectory. You choose the name; thus **mkdir**
letters creates a subdirectory named *letters*.

more   Allows you to display a file one screen at a time. If, for example, you
wanted to read the file **letter.txt,** you would enter **more letter.txt** to
activate the program. You would then see a prompt at the end of every
page. To move to the next page, use the **space bar.** A carriage return
only moves the text forward one line at a time. Figure 4.3 shows an
example of a file being read with **more.**

mv   Renames a file. You might, for example, not want to keep a file called
net.gloss.txt in quite so verbose a form. So entering **mv net.gloss.txt**
gloss.doc would change the longer title to the simple name **gloss.doc.**

pwd   Shows the name of the current directory.

Figure 4.2
A manual page for **ls**.

```
rock: man ls

LS(1V)                         USER COMMANDS                         LS(1V)

NAME
     ls - list the contents of a directory

SYNOPSIS
     ls [ -aAcCdfFgilLqrRstu1 ] filename ...

SYSTEM V SYNOPSIS
     /usr/5bin/ls [ -abcCdfFgilLmnopqrRstux ] filename ...

AVAILABILITY
     The System V version of this command is available  with  the
     System  V software installation option.  Refer to Installing
     SunOS  4.1  for  information  on  how  to  install  optional
     software.

DESCRIPTION
     For each filename which is a directory, ls  lists  the  con-
     tents  of  the directory; for each filename which is a file,
     ls repeats its name and any other information requested.  By
--More--(8%)
```

Figure 4.3
A file being read using
the **more** command.

```
This article originally appeared in Volume 2 Number 12, (December
1992) of Matrix News, the monthly newsletter of Matrix Information
and Directory Services, Inc. (MIDS).

1.  Which Books

    Here is a list of books related to using the Internet, which is the
    global and exponentially growing network of more than a million
    computers that communicate by interactive use of the TCP/IP
    protocols, for the use of millions of users.  This article was
    prompted by the recent publication of nine or ten books on the
    Internet in the space of a year (some are so new they aren't even
    published yet).  I have also included some books that have been
    around for quite a long time (as long ago as the dim past of 1984).
    I think all of them contain useful information for people new to the
    Internet.

    Some of the books included here are about more than the Internet.
    Some of them are about the Matrix, which is the set of all computer
    networks worldwide that exchange electronic mail.  The Matrix
    includes FidoNet, UUCP, BITNET, USENET, the Internet, and many
    others, but is not limited to any one of those networks.  This
    particular bibliographic collection is oriented around the largest
--More--(6%)
```

rm You'll use this one a lot. **rm** removes, or erases, files. **rm letter.doc** gets
rid of the file **letter.doc.** When you set up an account with a service
provider, your account will include storage limitations which you can't
exceed. Use the **rm** command to keep the files in your directories
pared down to size.

rmdir This command deletes a directory. **rmdir letters** deletes the directory
letters. The directory must be empty for this command to work.

5

Files by the Gigabyte

The best way to learn the Internet is through hands-on experience, which is why we'll begin our discussion of FTP, or File Transfer Protocol, right away. FTP is a way of sending files between computers. One great benefit of the TCP/IP protocols is their ability to give computers using different operating systems a common set of tools, the implements out of which the world-wide internetworking process called the Internet has evolved. That means it doesn't matter if you are using an Apple Macintosh logged on to a Sun Microsystems workstation using UNIX at your service provider's site, and want to tap into a remote IBM mainframe computer using VM. Using the FTP protocol, you can get the file you need with a few simple commands.

For the purposes of this book, FTP is a major tool. As you go through topics from USENET to **gopher,** from database access to BITNET mailing lists, you will learn how to use the Internet itself to generate further information on each of these topics. In many cases, you will be directed to information available as text files on remote computers, which you'll access through the FTP protocol. Intimidating at first, this process quickly becomes second-nature, and you'll soon be zipping around the world with ease. The variety of software and text available is staggering.

But don't be put off by FTP. If you only have electronic mail access to the Internet because you're logging on through one of the commercial dial-up services, you can still retrieve files. Although you won't have the interactive capability offered by FTP to log on to a remote computer and prowl around in its directories, you *will* be able to locate the file you need and have it sent to you by electronic mail. You will learn how in Chapter 8.

We're talking gigabytes of information here. A gigabyte is approximately equal to one billion bytes, meaning one gigabyte equals some 1,000 megabytes. The **archie** program which we'll look at shortly tracks over one thousand sites which you as a public access user can tap. Some estimates of files available over the Internet run as high as 6 terabytes, or 6,000 gigabytes. Granted, there is a great deal of overlap when a successful program appears on the directory listings of multiple sites. But it's clear that ongoing software development and the posting of unique text resources will keep the FTP sites of the world a fascinating and ever-changing place to explore.

SHAREWARE AND PUBLIC DOMAIN SOFTWARE

You won't find commercial software at FTP archive sites because licensing agreements prohibit it from being posted publicly. But you will find shareware and software that's in the public domain. The two differ: public domain software is free, while shareware requires you to pay the author if, after a trial period, you decide to keep and use the program. You'll also find so-called "freeware," software on which the author retains copyright, but which he or she allows you to use for free. The shareware movement has produced some remarkably successful programs; among them are Procomm, a telecommunications program, PC-File, a database which was one of the earliest shareware programs to be marketed, and PC-Write, a full-featured word processor.

The traditional method of dissemination for these programs has been the computer bulletin board. Consumer-driven on-line services such as GEnie and CompuServe have long recognized the importance of software to their user bases. Each provides extensive program libraries, often broken out by specific area of interest, so users can download programs they need. And the mushrooming growth of private bulletin board systems (BBSs) throughout the world has provided thousands of new repositories for shareware and public domain programs. Exec-PC is a case in point. The Wisconsin-based BBS maintains over 450,000 files in its libraries, available to the dial-up caller.

The Internet adds an interesting twist to the shareware story. In the UNIX world, there exists a long tradition of free software development, as exemplified by the continuing work on a project called the Free Software Foundation. FSF's head, Richard Stallman, is of the opinion that software should be shared by the user community. Huge amounts of free software have been produced by programmers associated with Stallman, and the Foundation has been instrumental in developing GNU (**G**nu's **N**ot **U**NIX), an operating system designed as a free work-alike for UNIX. GNU EMACS and GNU C are well-distributed software tools written as part of the overall GNU project.

You probably will not use GNU or its associated utilities, not unless you get involved with networked workstations, but you should understand that the vigorous free software movement on the Internet is in many respects more vocal than the comparable scene on the PC/Macintosh side of the world. Whereas shareware, the idea of paying for software after a trial use, has become fixed and common among commercial service users, there is still a powerful user community insisting on software's free distribution on the Internet.

And unlike the commercial services, the Internet is a vast and unruly landscape. There are few menus to guide the traveler, and even at the largest archival sites, software can be challenging to locate by type or description. Also unlike America Online or DELPHI, the Internet's libraries contain a much higher proportion of professional materials. You'll certainly find Procomm, PC-Write, and the rest of the PC shareware panoply here, but you'll also encounter the client software that drives networked computers of various descriptions and allows them to tap into Internet resources. You'll find archival sites for magazines and newsletters, scientific documents and maps. You'll find the textual treasures of Project Gutenberg and the Online Book Initiative, electronic editions of classic works of literature.

The Internet is a vast realm, most of it yet uncharted, but the tools for exploring it are growing in sophistication, as you'll see when we consider the **archie** program later in this chapter, and the retrieval capabilities of **WAIS, gopher,** and the rest later on. With software available at numerous sites, you'll learn to move around the globe to collect what you need. The process will be fundamentally different from what dial-up users are accustomed to. You will not tap BBS systems but networked computers, using the FTP capabilities provided by TCP/IP. Instead of keeping a list of telephone numbers and dialing up BBS systems in sequence, you'll call one number—your access provider's—and move out from there by FTP, using your provider's network presence and related software to reach your destinations.

DESCRIPTION OF ARCHIVE SITES

As compared to a BBS, run by one or more operators, or a commercial on-line service, run by a company whose business is providing connectivity for the public, Internet FTP sites usually have other things to do. They're working computer systems at a variety of locations worldwide. While their resources, or at least some of them, have been made available for FTP purposes, meaning anyone can go into their archives and download files, they are not designed for the general public, nor are they necessarily "user friendly." You won't find, for example, an FTP site with an easy-to-use interface like CompuServe Information Manager, or a logical menu structure like DELPHI's.

That means a bit more work, but the sheer immensity of the resources available is compelling enough to encourage us up the learning curve. But first, a matter of terminology. Throughout this book you will use *anonymous FTP* as you log on to remote sites and pull down information. Anonymous FTP is the ability to log on and retrieve publicly-accessible files without any special permission to do so. You'll enter **anonymous** when asked for a name, clueing in the remote computer that you are logging on to a part of the disk reserved for public use.

You can see why this would be necessary. Because so many of these systems are providing services to organizations ranging from research laboratories to medical clinics, from military bases to universities, it would present enormous security challenges to simply leave the computer open to FTP without any kind of restriction. A hard disk or an entire computer can be devoted to public information, but the anonymous FTP protocol ensures that you have available the part of their resources the people at the host computer site are willing to share.

Some of these sites are treasure troves. Washington University in St. Louis, for example, offers a huge repository of software and information. Here you find not just public domain and shareware programs, but a wealth of other data including USENET newsgroups (similar to CompuServe Forums and GEnie RoundTables, as you'll see in Chapter 11). There is a wealth of Macintosh programs, and the complete source code to TeX, a powerful text formatter, as well as the X-windowing system, which is widely used on UNIX computers. There's a clone of UNIX for IBM-compatible PCs, and a collection of Graphics Interchange Format (GIF) pictures. No matter what your own computer, there's something for you here.

Washington University isn't much like a dial-up commercial service, and even less so is the US Army Information Systems Command at White Sands Missile Range in New Mexico. You might think getting into this computer could land you in the penitentiary, but remember, controlled access is what anonymous FTP is all about. The directories here, in fact, are stuffed with publicly available software for MS-DOS, Macintosh, UNIX, and a host of other machines. SIMTEL20, as this site is known, is part of the MILNET and is instructive in another way as well. Because SIMTEL20 has things to do other than cater to anonymous FTP visits, the powers that be have limited the number of simultaneous FTP sessions. Each FTP site will have its own rules.

Perhaps the most obvious difference between such Internet archival sites and the libraries of the commercial vendors will be in the nature of their software. Whereas a commercial service will focus on the most popularly available personal computers—those using MS-DOS and Macintosh software— because these represent the dominant equipment base of its user population, an Internet archival site is likely to include a much broader range of materials. You know about UNIX software at Washington University and White Sands, but you'll also find tools for VAX users (VMS is their operating system), IBM minicomputers and mainframe computers, and more. You can expect to see a lot of things that won't interest a dial-up user along with a wealth of programs and text materials that certainly will.

There's still another difference between the commercial on-line services' libraries and the FTP sites of the Internet. CompuServe's forums, for example, are run by system operators (sysops) who are paid by CompuServe. The job of the sysop is to keep a close check on the files uploaded to the libraries, to make sure they contain no viruses, to ensure that they work, and to determine that they're worthwhile. A good sysop also makes sure the programs are current versions. Software at FTP sites, on the other hand, may or may not receive this kind of careful scrutiny. There are so many FTP sites out there, with holdings so diverse, that there is no way to be sure how carefully a particular site has checked a given program.

Assume you've heard about a great new communications program. On CompuServe, you'd log on to a particular forum; perhaps the IBM Communications Forum. There you'd leave a message asking about the program. Because CompuServe offers a central repository for files and messages, others could respond and tell you in which library to look for your program. You could be assured you had the latest version in most cases merely by downloading the most recently dated copy of the program. Updates and new version announcements would generally be made in the same forum, so you could keep up with program developments without difficulty.

The Internet is more challenging. Finding the program requires you to scan a wide range of FTP sites for what you want, using tools like **archie,** which is discussed later in this chapter. Once you've found the program, usually at any number of sites, you must look carefully to determine which version you're getting, and in some cases, it may be impossible to tell without actually downloading the program. Keeping up with updates is likewise decentralized.

The best avenue would be to subscribe to an appropriate newsgroup on USE-NET, watching out for news of your program. Ultimately, you will have the same software up and running, but it takes more ingenuity to achieve the same end on the Internet than on the commercial service.

Internet users, then, must learn to take advantage of the self-referential nature of this metanetwork. A good networker will constantly update information and learn new tricks by following USENET newsgroups, reading mail, and using FTP to pull in publicly available materials. A premise of this book is that the Internet is a moving target, whose constantly shifting parameters impel us to compile our own up-to-date libraries of information. Books are not yet obsolete, nor will they ever be. But supplementing books, constantly revising data, building electronic Alexandrias immune from damage caused by the loss of a single site, is what the Internet does best.

COURTESY WHEN USING FTP

It's time to try out FTP. But first, a word about network courtesy. If we barge into the computers at White Sands or Washington University, or any other working site for that matter, without regard to the effect we're having on local operations, we're committing a newcomer's blunder. The Internet's wide reaches are filled with people trying to get things done. While it's exciting to have software archives accessible at so many different sites, it should also give us pause. With network usage comes network responsibility, and overuse of a privilege can cause the entire user community to suffer.

Basic courtesy, then, involves minimizing the amount of resource drain we put on the Internet. FTP sessions should be run only *after working hours*. And if you fail to take into account the Internet's wide reach, you'll be making a mistake. Sure, it's simple to tie into a computer in Finland. but if it's early morning where you are on the California coast, it's late afternoon in Finland and people are trying to get work done. Base your calling on *the local time at the site you're planning to reach.* Plan on calling between 1900 and 0600 hours *at the site.*

A SAMPLE FTP SESSION

With that in mind, let's now retrieve some information. The format outlined here is the one used in the rest of the book for FTP procedures. Refer back to this section if you have trouble later on, as the basic file transfer and downloading instructions are contained here.

I've chosen a file containing an index of materials available on one prominent network site, the SURAnet Network Information Center in College Park, MD. It's a useful list because it illustrates the resources available at a single network location. A network information center, or NIC, is itself a valuable resource, offering a variety of information about the services available on-line. As we explore the Internet, we'll find many NICs that offer useful material which they make available by anonymous FTP.

We'll get an ASCII file; ASCII stands for the American Standard Code for Information Interchange. To say that a file is in ASCII format has important implications. It means nothing in the file deviates from this standard; the file is therefore readable by virtually any computer. Contrast this with, say, a Word-Perfect file that contains all the formatting codes and other information specific to that word processor. You could download it, but you wouldn't be able to do anything with it unless you had a copy of WordPerfect and could load it into the word processor. ASCII can be viewed by just about anybody. If English is the standard language of commerce worldwide, ASCII is the standard language of computing.

....

What You Need: An Index of Files at a Network NIC

The Document: **A Directory Listing**

How to Get It: Via anonymous FTP to **ftp.sura.net**. The directory is *pub/nic*. The file name is **00-README.FIRST.**

....

Remember, you want to handle this file transaction after business hours at the site, so check the clock. The following is the FTP procedure in a nutshell. At your service provider's command prompt, enter the FTP command, followed by the destination. Figure 5.1 shows what you'll see on-screen. Commands I've entered are shown in bold type.

As you can see, we've logged on by sending the word **anonymous** when prompted for a name, and sending the complete user name as the password. The password doesn't show up in this transaction because it's blanked as you type, but note that we're prompted to enter it by the phrase **Guest login ok, send e-mail address as password;** I then entered **gilster@rock.concert.net** as

Figure 5.1
Logging on at the
SURAnet NIC.

```
% ftp ftp.sura.net
Connected to nic.sura.net.
220 nic.sura.net FTP server
Name (ftp.sura.net:gilster): anonymous
331 Guest login ok, send e-mail address as password.
Password:
230-    SURAnet ftp server running wuarchive experimental ftpd
230-
230-Welcome to the SURAnet ftp server.  If you have any problems with
230-the server please mail the to systems@sura.net. If you do have problems,
230-please try using a dash (-) as the first character of your password
230- -- this will turn off the continuation messages that may be confusing
230-your ftp client.
230-
230-Nifty feature:
230-
230-    Compressed files may be uncompressed by attempting to get the
230-name without the .Z.  Example: to get zen-1.0.tar.Z uncompressed one
230-would get zen-1.0.tar.
230-
230-    Entire hierarchies may also be tarred and optionally compressed.
230-To get, for example, the sendmail hierarchy tarred & compressed, one would
230-get sendmail.tar.Z.
230-
230-
230 Guest login ok, access restrictions apply.
ftp>dir
```

Figure 5.2
A directory listing at
the SURAnet NIC.

```
200 PORT command successful.
150 Opening ASCII mode data connection for /bin/ls.
total 52
drwxrwx--x   3 root      0            512 Jul 29  1992 bin
drwxr-xr-x   2 root      1            512 Aug 13  1992 etc
drwxrwx--x  10 root     10            512 Oct 20 18:54 incoming
drwxr-xr-x   2 root      0           8192 Feb 15  1992 lost+found
-rw-r--r--   1 root      1          13628 Dec  4  1991 ls-lR.Z
drwxrwxr-x  18 root    100            512 Dec  6 16:29 pub
226 Transfer complete.
386 bytes received in 0.21 seconds (1.8 Kbytes/s)
ftp>cd pub/nic
```

my password. We then see a sign-on message followed by the FTP prompt. At the prompt, I asked for a directory listing by entering the command **dir**. Figure 5.2 shows the listing.

Many of the things we tend to look for at FTP sites will be found in directories called *pub;* in this case, we need to move to a subdirectory attached to *pub* called *nic;* in other words, our target is *pub/nic.* Let's check there for the file in question. We'll switch to that directory by entering **cd pub/nic** and again run a **dir** command, as in Figure 5.3.

The file we want is **00-README.FIRST.** Note the capital letters—remember, UNIX is case sensitive! To retrieve this file, we'll use the **get** command. The transfer will take place with the following screen information presented:

```
ftp>get 00-README.FIRST
200 PORT command successful.
150 Opening ASCII mode data connection for 00-README.FIRST (9977 bytes).
226 Transfer complete.
local: 00-README.FIRST remote: 00-README.FIRST
10164 bytes received in 0.22 seconds (45 Kbytes/s)
ftp>bye
221 Goodbye.
```

As you can see, after the file was retrieved I entered the **bye** command to log off.

Note how quick the transfer was. The first thing that strikes dial-up users about FTP is that they've never seen bytes fly through a connection as quickly as they move through the Internet's high-speed hookups. There's a big difference between a standard twisted-pair telephone connection like the one running into your home and a high-speed T-3 line linking supercomputer sites on the NSFNET backbone network, which moves data at 45 Mbps (45 megabits per second). According to Merit Network Inc., a statewide network in Michigan which helped implement the upgrade from T-1 to T-3, 45 Mbps is like moving all the information in a 20-volume encyclopedia in less than 23 seconds.[1]

Your modem connected to an on-line service can't move quite that fast; it's probably a 2400-bps (bits per second) modem, or perhaps a 9600-bps model. At 2400 bps, you're moving data at roughly 240 characters every second; a 9600-bps modem should produce up to 960 characters per second, although actual rates will depend upon such external factors as line noise. A so-called "dial-up" modem is designed to be effective over voice-grade telephone lines, and must cope with their limitations.

Figure 5.3
The *pub/nic* directory
at SURAnet.

```
ftp>dir
200 PORT command successful.
150 Opening ASCII mode data connection for /bin/ls.
total 4702
-rw-rw-r--   1 mtaranto 120        1384 Jan  7 16:30 .message
-rw-r--r--   1 mtaranto 120        9977 Feb 10 15:01 00-README.FIRST
-rw-rw-r--   1 mtaranto 120       47592 Mar  5  1992 BIG-LAN-FAQ
-rw-r--r--   1 mtaranto 120        4266 Dec  8 21:38 ERIC.sites
-rw-r--r--   1 mtaranto 120        3938 Feb 10 14:55 NIC.WORKSHOP.INFO
drwxr-sr-x   2 mtaranto 120         512 Jul 22  1992 NREN
-rw-r--r--   1 mtaranto 120        2351 Oct 19 18:05 NSFNET.acceptable.use
-rw-rw-r--   2 root     120        2565 Oct 14 13:03 SURAnet.acceptable.use
-rw-rw-r--   1 mtaranto 120       85677 May 11  1992 agricultural.list
-rw-rw-r--   1 mtaranto 120       27840 Apr 17  1992 archie.manual
-rw-r--r--   1 mtaranto 120       30500 Oct 14 17:17 bbs.list.10-14
-rw-r--r--   1 mtaranto 120        3030 Nov 11 19:42 bible.resources
-rw-r--r--   1 mtaranto 120        1347 Nov 12 14:05 bionet.list
-rw-r--r--   1 mtaranto 120       41580 Dec  8 21:09 cwis.list
drwxrwsr-x   3 mtaranto 120         512 Apr 28  1992 directory.services
-rw-rw-r--   1 plieb    120        1904 Jan  6  1992 farnet-recommendations
-rw-r--r--   1 mtaranto 120       15968 Oct 28 16:21 holocaust.archive
-rw-r--r--   1 mtaranto 120        2985 Jan 29 19:58 how.to.get.SURAnet.guide
-rw-r--r--   1 mtaranto 120      137525 Feb 10 14:31 infoguide.2-93.txt
-rw-rw-r--   1 mtaranto 120      360853 Aug 20  1992 interest.groups.Z
-rw-r--r--   1 mtaranto 120      879381 Dec  9 13:09 interest.groups.txt
drwxr-sr-x   3 mtaranto 120         512 Jan  5 16:06 internet.literature
-rw-r--r--   1 mtaranto 120       15682 Dec  8 21:18 library.conferences
-rw-r--r--   1 mtaranto 120       69341 Oct  9 16:32 medical.resources.10-9
-rw-r--r--   1 mtaranto 120       15474 Nov 11 19:14 network.law.info
drwxrwsr-x   2 mtaranto 120         512 Apr 14  1992 network.service.guides
-rw-r--r--   1 mtaranto 120       20553 Oct  9 15:54 nnews.9-92
-rw-rw-r--   1 mtaranto 120        6194 Feb 21  1992 obi.directory.index
-rw-r--r--   1 mtaranto 120       39945 Aug 24  1992 search.techniques
drwxr-sr-x   2 1077     120        1024 Nov 12 15:17 training
-rw-rw-r--   1 root     120        6170 Jan  3  1992 wholeguide-help.txt
-rw-rw-r--   1 root     120      499902 Feb  4  1992 wholeguide.txt
226 Transfer complete.
2343 bytes received in 0.58 seconds (4 Kbytes/s)
```

Internet file transfers take advantage of a ride on broadband fiber-optic cables using sophisticated routers to move local network traffic onto the broader backbone; no wonder they're fast. To get used to the Internet, you should remember the varying nature of the communications links it encompasses. Dial-up modems connect some computers to the network, but so do dedicated leased lines, moving traffic at much higher speeds. Some Internet traffic moves by satellite links, some by microwave, and much of it by way of fiber optics. The genius of TCP/IP, of course, is that it can work with such diverse communications capabilities and interconnect them all.

Digression: A Bit More UNIX

Remember that the blink of an eye it took to bring your file from SURAnet to your service provider's computer does not mean that it is now on *your* computer. However, because the file is available through your provider, you can examine it with a series of standard UNIX commands. To make sure it's there, enter **ls** at your command prompt, and you should see the file name, along with whatever else is currently in your home directory. I see the following when I type the **ls** command at my account at CONCERT-CONNECT:

```
% ls
00-README.FIRST News/        ftp/
Mail/           core         xmodem.log
```

Examine this listing for a moment. There's our file, **00-README.FIRST.** Along with it is the name of another file, called **xmodem.log,** which is a record of the uploads and downloads I've done by way of the Xmodem file transfer protocol to this computer.

Note, though, that some of the entries are followed by a slash (/). This indicates they are not files but subdirectories. We can change, for example, to the *News* subdirectory by entering **cd News**. Here, too, we must remember that UNIX is case sensitive; entering **cd news** (small "n") will simply cause the system to tell you no such directory exists. We can enter **cd** to return to the home directory. This wouldn't work in DOS, where entering **cd** with no further commands produces only another display of the command prompt. In UNIX, the **cd** command changes the working directory to your home directory.

Note that UNIX uses a slash (/) in path names for directories; thus */home/gilster* is a statement of the subdirectory *gilster*'s location branching off from the directory *home* which, in turn, branches off from the root directory, known solely by its slash as /. You can change between directories with the **cd** command. If you get lost doing so, a **pwd** command displays the absolute path name for the current working directory. Remember, too, that entering **ls -l** will give you an expanded listing of the directory.

```
-rw-------  1 gilster     11332 Feb 17 11:15 00-README.FIRST
drwx------  2 gilster       512 Feb 17 13:31 Mail/
drwx--S---  4 gilster       512 Feb 16 13:33 News/
-rw-r--r--  1 gilster   8610224 Jan 13 14:47 core
drwxr-sr-x  2 gilster       512 Jan  9  1992 ftp/
-rw-------  1 gilster    172942 Feb 17 11:18 xmodem.log
```

With that bit of UNIX directory lore as reminder, let's take a look at the name of our retrieved file. **00-README.FIRST** is glaringly different from the name of a standard DOS file. With DOS, you're limited to an eight-character (or less) file name along with a three-character extension, in the form **MYFILE.DOS** (this is why DOS users have become so adept at expressive three-letter extension names—they have no choice). **FILE.TXT, FILE.DOC, FILE.NTS,** and so on, are all legitimate DOS file names. So, for that matter, is the DOS equivalent of the file we just downloaded, which could have been something like **00readme.1st.**

UNIX clearly has different conventions. It does not limit you to eight-character names, for one thing. And, unlike DOS, a file name can contain more than a single period (.). Thus you could have a file called **test.ltr.fax** in UNIX, but a DOS file named **tst.ltr.fx** is impermissible. DOS uses the period for one purpose only, to separate the base name from the extension.

Is **00-README.FIRST** a useful document? Let's read it by using the UNIX **more** command, which you can invoke at your service provider's prompt, as shown in Figure 5.4.

Figure 5.4
The **00-READ-
ME.FIRST** file, read
on-line with the **more**
command.

```
% more 00README.FIRST
Welcome to the SURAnet Network Information Center,

        In this directory you will find many materials useful to the
new user of the Internet. Sub-directories have been created which
contain information on Directory Services, "Zen and the Art of the
Internet", copies of all the sessions from Richard Smith's "Navigating
the Internet: An Interactive Workshop", and several "How to Guides" for
better network navigation.  These sub-directories are entitled
directory.services, ZEN, NREN, training, and network.service.guides.
The structure of "nic" directory and sub-directories follows:

nic
-rw-rw-r--   1 mtaranto 120           6122 Jun 29 13:46 00-README.FIRST
-rw-rw-r--   1 mtaranto 120          47592 Mar  5 17:04 BIG-LAN-FAQ
-rw-rw-r--   1 root     120         216594 Jan  3 15:43 Internet-Tour.txt
drwxr-sr-x   2 mtaranto 120            512 Jul 22 13:37 NREN
drwxr-sr-x   2 mtaranto 120            512 Jun 29 13:17 ZEN
-rw-rw-r--   2 root     120           2555 Jan  3 15:43 acceptable.use.policy
-rw-rw-r--   1 mtaranto 120          85677 May 11 17:29 agricultural.list
-rw-rw-r--   1 mtaranto 120          27840 Apr 17 14:10 archie.manual
-rw-r--r--   1 mtaranto 120          23501 Jun 26 15:16 bbs.list.XX-XX
-rw-r--r--   1 mtaranto 120           3030 Nov 11 19:42 bible.resources
--More--(11%)
```

Here we have the first page of the document, broken at the bottom of the screen. As you saw in Chapter 4, the **more** command allows you to page through the file one screen at a time, pressing the **SPACE BAR** at the end of each screen to advance to the next page. Accustomed to pressing the **RETURN** key to move between pages on commercial on-line systems, dial-up users are frustrated when they try this with UNIX, since the **more** program will simply advance the text one line at a time with a **RETURN** key command. It will take you a long time to read any file that way! (A **q** command, incidentally, takes you out of **more** and back to the system command prompt at any point during your reading; you don't have to page through the entire file.)

THE NIC GOLDMINE

Note in Figure 5.4 that the **more** program indicates we have a good bit of the file to go. You might want to page through this file to get an idea of the resources available to you here. The index includes a read-out by means of **ls -lR** (a command that generates not only a fuller directory listing of the current directory, but a list of the contents of all subdirectories as well) of what's in the NIC computers at SURAnet. Figure 5.5 gives you an idea.

There are numerous files in the working directory, which is what you'll find yourself in when you log on by FTP. But notice too that there are subdirectories, marked with their distinctive stamp **drwxr-sr-x**. The files, in contrast, are marked **-rw-r-r-**. A regular file when listed this way always shows up with a dash (–) in front of its listing; a **d** always signifies a directory. The first character in each line of the listing, then, identifies whether it's a file or a directory. The remaining characters contain security information, or *permissions*, explaining who can access the file. We will not discuss UNIX file permissions in this book. For more on UNIX permissions, and on UNIX in general, see *A Student's Guide* *to UNIX,* by Harley Hahn (McGraw Hill, 1993). You may also want to consult *UNIX Power Tools,* by Jerry Peek, Tim O'Reilly, and Mike Loukides (O'Reilly/Bantam, 1993) for a superb collection of UNIX tips and techniques.

NICs, as you can see from the file descriptions in Figure 5.5, go out of their way to provide useful information to their users. A number of how-to guides are presented here, along with useful overall documents like the one called **Internet-Tour.txt.** The following is its file listing:

```
-rw-rw-r--   1 root      120        216594 Jan  3 15:43 Internet-Tour.txt
```

The file size is shown to the left of the date of this file's last modification; it's 216,594 bytes, so we're dealing with a big file. Next to this is the title itself.

A number of interesting files are to be found at SURAnet, some of which we'll call upon later as we build up a network library. One called **networking.terms** looks helpful; it contains basic terminology for people new to the Internet. Another is **netiquette.txt;** it's the Miss Manners document of the network, especially useful for people who have logged on but who don't yet know what is and is not acceptable. And note the subdirectories here; one is filled with information on the NREN, the proposed National Research and Education Network that will eventually become the U.S. part of the Internet for the American research and education community. There's a subdirectory called *Network Service Guides,* and another called *ZEN,* which contains a popular network document known as **Zen and the Art of the Internet.** It provides much useful background material.

GETTING FILES TO YOUR COMPUTER

Before we move on to look at another Network Information Center, let's do something about that index file, **00-README.FIRST.** We want to get it onto

Figure 5.5
A glimpse of the Internet background information available at a Network Information Center.

```
drwxrwsr-x   2 mtaranto 120           512 Apr 14  1992 network.service.guides
-rw-r--r--   1 mtaranto 120         20553 Oct  9 15:54 nnews.9-92
-rw-rw-r--   1 mtaranto 120          6194 Feb 21  1992 obi.directory.index
-rw-r--r--   1 mtaranto 120         39945 Aug 24 15:00 search.techniques
drwxr-sr-x   2 1077     120          1024 Nov 12 15:17 training
-rw-rw-r--   1 root     120          6170 Jan  3  1992 wholeguide-help.txt
-rw-rw-r--   1 root     120        499902 Feb  4  1992 wholeguide.txt


NREN directory

-rw-r--r--   1 mtaranto 120          8225 Jun 29  1992 GPO.bill.6-92
-rw-r--r--   1 mtaranto 120          9848 Jul 22 13:06 GPO.questions
-rw-r--r--   1 mtaranto 120         36482 Jul  7  1992 iita.1992


directory.services directory

-rw-rw-r--   1 mtaranto 120           310 Apr  9  1992 00README
-rw-rw-r--   1 mtaranto 120         25161 Apr  9  1992 FINGER.protocol.info
-rw-rw-r--   1 mtaranto 120          1036 Apr  9  1992 KNOWBOT.email.directory
-rw-rw-r--   1 mtaranto 120           816 Apr  9  1992 NETMAILHOSTS.database
--More--(60%)
```

our own computer because a print-out would be a helpful document to keep. First we will change its UNIX-style file name into something shorter, so we don't have to wrestle with so many characters. The command is simple: **mv.**

```
% mv 00-README.FIRST read.me
```

You can run another directory display by using **ls** to be sure the command took. The **mv** command is called *move* because it does just that; it moves the data in one file to another, and then deletes the original file.

Now we can download the file to our computer. Here the terms begin to seem a bit more familiar. We can use the file transfer protocol Xmodem to download the file. Xmodem, created by telecommunications guru Ward Christensen, is one of a number of error-checking protocols familiar to users of commercial on-line systems; others include Ymodem, Kermit, and Zmodem. I'll rely on Xmodem for our task here because it's so widely distributed throughout the on-line world, and most users of commercial services are familiar with it. You'll also find it installed on virtually any service provider's computers. And it's hard to name a communications software package that doesn't include Xmodem.

Xmodem operates by transferring files in 128-byte blocks, adding an extra bit called the checksum to each block. The extra bit is useful; it allows the receiving computer to determine whether the transmission was accurate (if not, the protocol causes the receiving machine to request a retransmittal of the data packet). In this way, despite the perils of line noise or other communications difficulties, even large, complex files can be transmitted safely to their destination.

Using Xmodem by way of a dial-up UNIX account requires calling up the Xmodem program from the command prompt and specifying the parameters and file name. Typically, the program will support Xmodem and Xmodem/CRC (CRC stands for cyclic redundancy check, which increases error-checking efficiency), as well as Ymodem and Ymodem-G. More on each of these as we go through the Xmodem command options.

We can perform a simple file transfer like the one in question by entering the command shown in the following:

```
% xmodem sb read.me
XMODEM Version 3.9 (November 1990)—UNIX-Microcomputer File Transfer Facility
File read.me Ready to SEND in binary mode
Estimated File Size 12K, 89 Sectors, 11332 Bytes
Estimated transmission time 14 seconds
Send several Control-X characters to cancel
```

As you see, the result is a message from the computer telling us the estimated file size, number of sectors and bytes in the file, and an estimated transmission time. At this point, the service provider's computer is waiting for you to begin receiving the file. You specify the appropriate protocol (Xmodem) in your communications software, enter a file name for the incoming file, and start the download procedure as prompted.

TRANSLATING ASCII FOR YOUR COMPUTER

You've just downloaded a text, or ASCII, file using a binary download protocol. There are other ways you could have retrieved the file, including the simplest:

using the UNIX **cat** command to cause the file to scroll without page breaks, and capturing the results by turning on your communications program's capture buffer. But using Xmodem makes a great deal of sense, even when you're dealing with ASCII. The reason: the download is more accurate, because Xmodem checks for errors and corrects them when it finds them. Make it a habit to use error-checking protocols no matter what kind of file you want to retrieve.

But there's more to this story. I said earlier that ASCII was a file standard. This may have been overly optimistic. In fact, not all ASCII characters are standardized. In particular, computer systems don't always have the same ideas about how to end a line of text. An MS-DOS computer ends lines with a carriage return (CR) and line feed (LF). These characters, CR and LF, are ASCII codes 13 and 10. Macintoshes use only the carriage return to end a line. UNIX systems use only the line feed.

Can you see the problem? A Macintosh doesn't know what to do with the line feed character at the end of every line of a PC file. Open a PC text file on a Macintosh and it displays these characters; it cannot interpret them . On a UNIX system, the text file you upload from your MS-DOS computer has an extra carriage return for every line. Retrieve a file from a UNIX system, on the other hand, and the MS-DOS user has to create the standard carriage return/line feed pairs MS-DOS expects, while the Macintosh user needs the carriage return characters the Mac likes.

Problems like these can be handled by invoking the command line parameters available through the UNIX Xmodem implementation. You've already used parameters; the command **xmodem sb** involves them. **xmodem sb** stands for send by way of Xmodem in binary format. By varying the parameters after the **xmodem** command, you can handle a wide range of possibilities, including uploading as well as downloading to the service provider's computer. Several of these parameters can be useful, depending on the type of computer you're using.

XMODEM PARAMETERS

The basic **xmodem** command structure is:

```
xmodem [parameter] filename.
```

rb   Receive Binary. Here you're sending, rather than receiving files. **rb** means that files are to be placed on the service provider's computer without any conversion. Xmodem destroys existing files of the same name, so be careful. You might upload if you're planning to send a previously prepared file to someone as a message.

rt   Receive Text. This process converts an incoming file in MS-DOS format to a form more familiar to UNIX. The CR-LF pairs are converted to the UNIX line-feed-only format. The result is a file which UNIX editors can use.

ra   Receive Apple. This does the same thing as **rt** only for files sent from Apple Macintosh computers. It translates the CR characters in the incoming file into UNIX line feeds.

sb   Send Binary. Here, files are sent from your service provider's computer to you without conversion, just as they exist on the UNIX disk.

st   Send Text. This translates the UNIX line feed characters into the CR/LF
        pairs MS-DOS wants in a text file.

sa   Send Apple. Does the same thing as the st parameter, but converts UNIX
        line feed characters into CR characters.

OTHER XMODEM OPTIONS

The following options should give you every tool you need to get a file from your
service provider's computer to your own. I generally work with Ymodem because
I transfer more than one file at a time on most occasions; when I download a
series of files, I'll specify **xmodem sbyk** *filename1 filename2*, etc. I then sit
back and let my communications software, Crosstalk for Windows, handle the
transfer.

y   Although still invoked through the **xmodem** command, the **y** option
        (**xmodem y**) selects the Ymodem batch protocol for sending files.
        Ymodem uses CRC error checking and can transfer multiple files.
        Because it transmits data in 1K blocks (Xmodem uses 128-byte
        blocks), Ymodem can be significantly faster than Xmodem, although it
        doesn't function nearly as well when you're working with a poor
        telephone connection.

g   Selects Ymodem-G, a variant of Ymodem which sends files in a con-
        tinuous stream. Ymodem-G works only with error-free connections
        because it contains no built-in error correction. But if you have an
        error-correcting modem, it can transfer files quickly.

m   Uses the Modem7 batch protocol for sending files. This means a list of
        files specified on the command line will be sent in sequence. This
        batch protocol is used automatically if the sending program requests
        it. Use Modem7 only if Ymodem batch protocols aren't available in
        your communications program.

k   Uses the Xmodem-1K mode for sending files. By using 1K packets, speed
        can be increased, but as with Ymodem, excessive transmission retries
        due to line noise or other errors can significantly slow operations.

c   Uses CRC error checking when receiving files. CRC is automatically
        selected for transmission if the receiving modem program requests it.

l   Do not write to the log file. A file called **xmodem.log** in your directory
        area is normally appended to whenever you use Xmodem to handle a
        file upload or download (you saw an example when I listed the files in
        my home directory). You may never need to use this file, but it can be
        useful if you're having problems with file transfers because it records
        when things went wrong.

w   Wait 15 seconds before beginning the startup handshake. The handshake
        is a set of control signals between computer and modem which verifies
        all is ready for the transfer to begin. You may want to use **w** to force
        this delay if the handshaking process is causing characters to appear
        which hinder your own typing as you prepare for the transfer.

RETRIEVING TWO USEFUL FILES

You've now had an opportunity to see how the file transfer process works, from using FTP to gain access to the resources of a remote computer, transferring the file to your service provider's computer, and then downloading it to your own using Xmodem. Let's now get in some practice. We'll look at the holdings of another Network Information Center, the huge repository at the Internet Network Information Center. We want two files, one an introduction to interesting material on the Internet, the other a directory of prime Internet source materials.

••

 What You Need: A Guide to Prime Internet Destinations and a Directory of Internet Resources

The Documents: **There's Gold in them thar Networks!** (RFC 1290), by Jerry Martin and **Information Sources: The Internet and Computer-Mediated Communication,** by John December

How to Get Them: By using anonymous FTP to **is.internic.net.** This time you have some directory switching to do. The directory you need is: *infosource/getting-started/things-to-do-internet/resource-lists.* Look for the files **network-treasures** and **internet-cmc.**
••

Note how deep into the INTERNIC's directory structure we must go for this material. We'll use the **cd** command to change directories. It is best to go one directory at a time. In other words, sign on by means of FTP, as shown in Figure 5.6, and then issue a **cd infosource** command. When you're in the *infosource* directory, issue a **cd getting-started** command (make sure you include the hyphen!) Go one subdirectory at a time until you're in the directory called *resource-lists.* That's where your files are.

And as before, we'll retrieve the files with the **get** command. Thus **get network-treasures** and **get internet-cmc.** You can now download them to your computer using Xmodem.

BASIC FTP PRINCIPLES APPLIED

So far we've had it easy. The file transfers we've managed all involved ASCII data. But FTP procedures can be a bit more complex than that. What if we want to transfer a binary file, for example, or retrieve more than a single file with one set of commands? These things are workable, but we have to know how to find our way around inside the computer at the end of the connection.

Binary vs. ASCII Files

Many files are not ASCII at all; they're binary files—programs, or compressed text files—and to use them, we need to make some changes in the default settings. It's a simple process, but we must remember to do it. Simply enter the command **binary.**

Figure 5.6
An introductory
screen at the Internet
Network Information
Center.

```
& ftp is.internic.net
Connected to is.internic.net.
220-
220-*****************************************************
220-**                                                **
220-**  Welcome to the Internic InfoSource Archive    **
220-**                                                **
220-*****************************************************
220-
220-
220-General Atomics makes no warranty or guarantee, express or
220-implied, concerning the content or accuracy of the information
220-stored and maintained by General Atomics for the InterNIC Information
220-Services and made available to INTERNET users, and General Atomics
220-expressly disclaims any implied warranties of merchantability and
220-fitness for a particular purpose.
220-
220-For REGISTRATION Services,           please ftp to rs.internic.net
220-For DIRECTORY AND DATABASE Services, please ftp to ds.internic.net
220-For INFORMATION Services,            please login as user "anonymous"
220-                                              and cd /infosource
220-
220-
220-
220-Questions? Send e-mail to info@internic.net
220-
220-
220 is FTP server (Version 2.0WU(10) Thu Apr 8 17:52:08 PDT 1993) ready.
Name (is.internic.net:gilster): anonymous
331 Guest login ok, send your complete e-mail address as password.
Password:
230-
230-Logged Access from: rock.concert.net
```

```
ftp> type binary
200 Type set to I
```

Now you're ready to transfer a binary file; the procedure is exactly the same as moving an ASCII file, once you've told the system what you're doing.

Notice the statement "Type set to I" in the example shown. We're using the binary format also known as **I**mage format. When you change back to ASCII setting, you'll see the statement "Type set to A" for ASCII.

The FTP Command Structure

While using FTP, you'll have the opportunity to tap resources in computers around the world. These may range from UNIX-driven workstations to Digital's VAX/VMS computers, from IBM-compatible PCs running MS-DOS, to Apple Macintoshes, and IBM mainframes. The directory structures of some remote systems may require you to experiment with commands to see which work. Entering **cd ..** will generally move you up through the directory tree to the previous directory. But on a VMS system, you may have to use **cdup.** Changing directories with **cd** works with an IBM system running the VM operating system, but instead of changing directories, it actually changes disks.

This may sound extremely intimidating. After all, it took a while to learn to drive that desktop personal computer. But you do not have to master mainframe-style operating systems to get the most out of the Internet. FTP's command structure does almost everything for you; the only help it doesn't provide is converting the output of a remote system into a uniform notation. But you'll almost always be doing one of two things with FTP—looking for a specific file whose name you already know, or asking for a directory listing in a remote computer to confirm a file name before retrieving it.

Let's make sure, then, that you understand the operating parameters of FTP itself. The following describes the major commands you'll be working with.

ascii The default setting. This allows you to transfer ASCII text files. Bear in mind that if you change this setting and subsequently want to transfer an ASCII file, you must reset the option by typing **ascii** at the prompt.

binary The proper mode for transfer of a binary file, such as a program or a compressed file. Once **binary** is set, all subsequent transfers occur in binary mode unless the user specifies otherwise.

bye Ends the FTP session with the remote server, taking you out of the FTP program and back to your system's command prompt.

cd *directory* Changes the directory on the remote computer.

cdup Changes to the parent of the current working directory on a remote VMS machine.

dir Lists contents of the current directory in the remote machine.

get *filename* Retrieves the file you specify and stores it on your service provider's machine.

help Lists the major FTP commands on-screen.

ls Lists contents of the current directory in the remote machine.

mget *filenames* Retrieves the listed file names from the remote computer. Used to retrieve multiple files.

pwd Prints the name of the current working directory on the remote machine.

status Allows you to check your file type, to verify whether you're currently set for ASCII or binary data transfers.

A Closer Look at File Retrieval

File transfer commands under FTP are simple. You use the **get** command to retrieve the file you want. The following command, for example, pulls in a file called **working.groups:**

```
ftp> get working.groups
```

You can rename the file if you choose. The command

```
ftp> get working.groups work.doc
```

will transfer the file to your service provider's computer and also rename it **work.doc.**

Retrieving Multiple Files

The command **mget** handles the transfer of multiple files. You can use wild-card commands to pull such files in. Thus the command **mget book*** will retrieve every file beginning with the four letters **book** and having any further characters. **Book1.doc** would be retrieved, as would **bookbinding.txt.** The wild-card character *****, operates exactly as it does in the DOS environment. It can stand for one or more characters. The **?**, available on UNIX systems, is another wild card. As in DOS, it can stand for any one character. Thus the command **mget paper?.doc** will pull in **paper1.doc, paper2.doc,** etc., but will not retrieve **paperback.doc.** However, the command **mget paper*.doc** would bring in all these files.

Of course, wild-card strategies only apply in particular situations. Perhaps you prefer to get several unrelated files with dissimilar names. To do so, the command is **mget *filename1 filename2*,** etc. The system will prompt you for each file you want to transfer, as in Figure 5.7.

File Compression and Unpacking

Anyone who has worked with a hard disk knows what happens when you think you've got your storage problem licked. That big new disk with seemingly inexhaustible storage space quickly becomes filled; before long, you're casting longing glances at computer catalogs, wondering how soon you'll be able to upgrade to yet another, bigger disk.

And if you've logged much time on local **BBS** systems or commercial on-line services, you know that computer systems big and small all suffer from the same problem. To get around the problem, most **BBS** sysops use file compression. By squeezing extraneous information out of their text, data, and program files, they can store more files on disk. This is frequently the way administrators at FTP sites handle the situation, too, using compression programs not only to shrink files but to combine multiple files into a single archive. A good file compression routine can reduce a file to 40 percent or less of its original size.[2]

Personal computer users are familiar with a number of compression programs. The ARC program from System Enhancement Associates was one of the

Figure 5.7
Prompting for multiple files using **mget**.

```
ftp> mget infosource_contents INDEX
mget infosource_contents? y
200 PORT command successful.
150 Opening ASCII mode data connection for infosource_contents (52068 bytes).
226 Transfer complete.
local: infosource_contents remote: infosource_contents
52836 bytes received in 1.8 seconds (29 Kbytes/s)
mget INDEX? y
200 PORT command successful.
150 Opening ASCII mode data connection for INDEX (25718 bytes).
226 Transfer complete.
local: INDEX remote: INDEX
26308 bytes received in 0.85 seconds (30 Kbytes/s)
```

first programs to achieve wide popularity. PKZIP, from PKware, Inc., is today one of the most commonly-known compression programs. Others include LHARC and ZOO for IBM PCs, while Macintosh users will have encountered StuffIt and Compactor. Amiga users will know about PKAZIP, LZH, ZOO, and more. Most file compression programs are public domain or shareware, available for downloading through the commercial on-line services and local BBS systems.

UNIX users will more frequently encounter a compression utility called **compress.** When **compress** is used to shrink a file into more manageable size, the result appears with a **.Z** extension. For example, **weather.doc** becomes **weather.doc.Z.** Again, if you're an MS-DOS user, you have to get used to the UNIX-style file names; PC people have a hard time getting comfortable with files with more than one extension.

UNCOMPRESSING A FILE

Let's now look at an actual compressed file. This file is the mother lode of mailing list directories, the so-called List of Lists, a file you'll want to keep for future reference when we move to BITNET as well as Internet-based mailing lists.

∙∙∙

What You Need: A Directory of Mailing Lists

The Document: **The List of Lists**

How to Get It: By using anonymous FTP from **ftp.sura.net.** The directory it's located in is *pub/nic.* The file name is **interest.groups.Z.** As we've seen, the **.Z** suffix tells us this is a compressed file.

∙∙∙

Although the file you are interested in is a text file, the fact that it has been compressed means you must treat it as a binary file, and set the binary flag to download it. You do that simply by entering **binary** at the **ftp>** prompt. A **dir** command shows all the files in that directory. You then can change to the *nic* directory using the **cd** command, and retrieve the file with the **get interest.groups.Z** command. You sign off from the session by entering **bye.**

Now you need to uncompress this file. The command is simple: **uncompress interest.groups.Z.** You now have the file you were after. A measure of the significance of the compression process is the total size of the compressed file, which was 360,853 bytes, versus the size of the complete, uncompressed text, some 879,381 bytes. Clearly, file compression can save a lot of space on disk.

But disk saving is significant as well; you don't want to use up your allotment and tax the patience of the system administrator. So let's download this file to our own computer and then remove it from the service provider's computer. The **xmodem** command again does the trick:

```
% xmodem sb interest.groups
```

It's a long download, but it's worth the effort, considering how useful this directory can be. When the downloading is completed be sure to erase the file from your service provider's computer. The command **rm interest.groups** handles this chore. Note, by the way, that when the **uncompress** routine did its work, it removed the old **.Z** file, replacing it with the newly uncompressed file.

tar Files and How to Use Them

The **compress** utility, as we've seen, squeezes the fat out of files to make more room for other files on disk. But another type of compression is needed. PKZIP, for example, can squeeze single files and archive multiple ones. The **tar** utility creates file archives out of multiple files in UNIX. A file created with **tar** is easy to identify because it has the **.tar** extension. Thus we have **recipes.tar,** a file whose name tells us it's an archive of multiple recipe files.

An archive can also be compressed. If we want to shrink our **recipes.tar** archive, we can enter the command **compress recipes.tar.** The result is another file with an unwieldy name: **recipes.tar.Z.** But despite its multiple extensions, **recipes.tar.Z** is easy to decode. The **.Z** at the far right tells us the first thing we must do to get at this file is to uncompress it. The second thing is to unpack the archive of the resulting **recipes.tar** file (a file with a **.tar** extension is commonly called a *tarfile).*

This is handled by invoking **tar** with options. There are two **tar** commands you'll need to know.

tar -xf   Extract all the files in the archive. Thus, to extract everything in **recipes.tar,** you enter **tar -xf recipes.tar.**

tar -tf   List the contents of the **tar** file. To see the contents of **recipes.tar,** then, you enter **tar -tf recipes.tar.**

USING ARCHIE TO TRACK DOWN FILES

One problem arises immediately as we look into FTP. If this is a way of downloading files, how do we know where to look for those files in the first place? With commercial systems, it's easy; call up the local access number and get on-line, move to the file libraries, and browse. The Internet lacks that kind of organization. There's no central repository, no library area clearly set aside for users. Internet rookies have to be aggressive to find what they're looking for, and that often means asking questions, making mistakes, digging for information.

This is where **archie** comes in. The retrieval tool called **archie** helps you find the file you need, no matter which FTP site happens to make it available on the network. And as we'll see in later chapters, it's one of a string of search and discovery tools now being fine-tuned to help the Internet navigator.

Originally developed by researchers at McGill University in Montreal, the **archie** system is now a product of Bunyip Information Systems in the same city.[3] **archie** stores information on what is available at FTP sites in a regularly updated central server. You or I can query this database to find out quickly where a given file is. Finding files on the Internet would be a dicey proposition without **archie.**

Using **archie** is simple. You use Telnet to log on to an **archie** server and search the database. McGill University is where it all began, and the McGill server is available through Telnet to **quiche.cs.mcgill.ca;** the command, then,

is **telnet quiche.cs.mcgill.ca.** You log in as **archie.** We'll cover Telnet procedures shortly. The listings of various FTP sites are stored in the directory
ftp/archie/listings. The file is **archie.mcgill.ca.** By way of anonymous FTP, the
system at McGill taps Internet sites and downloads their directories, storing the
information in its database. Because a portion of the work is done every night,
the **archie** database is eventually updated in its entirety about once every thirty
days.

Having this database is useful indeed, but you'll probably choose to forgo
downloading the information in favor of searching the data. **archie** allows you
to do this by searching for entries containing the search string, and it can provide
other information which can be useful in the hunt for specific files. Figure 5.8
shows you the introductory screen you'll see when you log on through Telnet to
the **archie** server at Advanced Networks & Services (ANS) in Michigan. The
command is **telnet archie.ans.net.** (log on as **archie**).

A variety of commands are available at the prompt. I used the **list** command
to see how many sites were currently tracked here, and received a scrolling
melange of 914 entries. Clearly, there's no shortage of material for software
hunters.

Which archie to Use?

Given that **archie** servers are located around the world, and that your Internet
access is international in scope, you may be tempted to access an **archie** server
in some exotic land. Resist the temptation. A cardinal principle in your Internet
travels should be: *don't be wasteful of network resources.* Why route your work
through Australia when there's a server in the adjacent state? The resources of
archie servers aren't infinite, and if people work with servers nearest to them,
the result is a more distributed workload for the system. Responsiveness drops
when a single server becomes overloaded, and it's even possible to be informed
that a given server is working up to capacity and cannot handle your request at
the moment.

If you look in Figure 5.8, you'll notice the list of **archie** servers. An examination of the addresses of some of these servers shows their origins. Figure 5.9
is a list of **archie** servers with the geographical area they most logically serve.
Staying within these areas makes sense and conserves bandwidth for everyone.

A Sample archie Search

We use the **prog** command to search **archie**; the syntax is simply **prog *searchterm,*** where *searchterm* is whatever you're looking for. I'm interested in shortwave radio, for example, so let's see if we can find any sites that contain files on
the subject. I'll send the **prog radio** command to the server at SURAnet (it's the
nearest server to me, based in Maryland), assuming that the term *shortwave* may
be too precise for the database index. Figure 5.10 shows a fragment of what I
receive.

This is only a segment of the list, but it imparts the flavor of the **archie**
search. As you can see, it has given me a list of FTP sites that contain material
indexed under the term *radio.* Exactly how relevant those sites will be to my

Figure 5.8
Logging on to **archie**
at Advanced Newtorks
& Services.

```
IBM AIX Version 3 for RISC System/6000
(C) Copyrights by IBM and b
login: archie
*------------------------------------------------------------------*
| -- The default search method is set to "exact".                  |
| -- Type "help set search" for more details.                      |
|                                                                  |
| Other Servers:                                                   |
|   archie.unl.edu          129.93.1.14                            |
|   archie.sura.net         128.167.254.179                        |
|   archie.rutgers.edu      128.6.18.15                            |
|                                                                  |
|   archie.au              139.130.4.6                             |
|   archie.funet.fi        128.214.6.100                           |
|   archie.ncu.edu.tw      140.115.19.24                           |
|   archie.doc.ic.ac.uk    146.169.11.3                            |
|   archie.sogang.ac.kr    163.239.1.11                            |
|                                                                  |
| o Questions/comments to archie-admin@ans.net, site add/delete    |
| requests to archie-updates@bunyip.com                            |
|                                                                  |
| Client software is available on ftp.ans.net:/pub/archie/clients; |
| documentation in /pub/archie/doc.                                |
*------------------------------------------------------------------*
# term set to vt100 24 80
archie>
```

search for shortwave information remains to be seen; I would next need to use FTP to go to the sites and check out what files they had available.

Tightening Up Our Search Terms

Is **archie** always this unspecific? Not really. Suppose I needed a specific file. I know there's a shareware program, called **GEOCLOCK,** that calculates the sun's position over the earth and produces a constantly updated map. Such a map is useful for shortwave listeners, because the best times for picking up low-power, difficult-to-hear stations are when the sunrise or sunset line is passing right over them. I'd like to find this program and download it for evaluation, so I will give **archie** the job of finding it. The command will be **prog geoclock.**

Figure 5.9
A list of **archie** servers.

```
Archie Servers
archie.rutgers.edu: northeastern US
archie.sura.net: southern US
archie.unl.edu: western US
archie.ans.net: ANS network sites
archie.mcgill.ca: Canada
archie.au: Australia and Pacific region
archie.funet.fi: Europe
archie.th-darmstadt.de: Germany
archie.doc.ic.ac.uk: United Kingdom
archie.cs.huji.ac.il: Israel
archie.wide.ad.jp: Japanese
archie.kuis.kyoto-u.ac.jp: Japanese
archie.ncu.edu.tw: Taiwan
archie.nz: New Zealand
```

Figure 5.10
Results of an archie
search under the term
"*radio*".

```
Host ccadfa.cc.adfa.oz.au     (131.236.1.2)
Last updated 05:10 18 Jan 1993

    Location: /pub/net/gopher1.03/misc/Radio
       DIRECTORY rwxr-xr-x         512  Jun 12  1992    radio

Host toklab.ics.osaka-u.ac.jp    (133.1.12.100)
Last updated 10:44 12 Jan 1993

    Location: /X/X.V11R5/contrib/lib/elk/examples/xm
       FILE       rw-r--r--        1692  Sep 27  1991    radio

Host think.com   (131.239.2.1)
Last updated 08:14 11 Jan 1993

    Location: /pub
       DIRECTORY rwxrwxr-x         512  Jul  6  1992    radio

Host reseq.regent.e-technik.tu-muenchen.de    (129.187.230.225)
Last updated 07:47  8 Jan 1993

    Location: /informatik.public/comp/networking/communication/in-
fosystems/gopher/gopher-1.1.0/misc/Radio
       DIRECTORY rwxrwxr-x         512  Dec 13 13:43    radio

Host pollux.lu.se    (130.235.132.89)
Last updated 10:50  7 Jan 1993

    Location: /pub/network/gopher/Unix/exe/gopher0.3/Radio
       DIRECTORY rwxr-xr-x         512  Nov  6  1991    radio

Host phloem.uoregon.edu    (128.223.32.35)
Last updated 05:19  7 Jan 1993

    Location: /pub/src/cwis/gopher/gopher1.1b4/misc/Radio
       DIRECTORY rwxr-xr-x         512  Jun 12  1992    radio
```

But when I run the search, this is what I get:

```
# matches / % database searched:    0 /100%
```

Not a single match? **GEOCLOCK** is a well-known program. Either **archie**'s FTP sites aren't that hot, or the program is simply not finding software that's bound to be listed in its database. The latter, it turns out, is the case. Look back at the entry screen we saw when logging on to the **archie** server at ANS. Note the sentence "The default search method is set to 'exact'" in the box containing the addresses of other **archie** servers. This means **archie** is looking for precisely the search string we give it; the search term must be a perfect match for the file name.

Obviously, this might not be the case. What if the file were stored as **GEOCLK.EXE**? If so, **archie** wouldn't find it. Nor would it find **GEO-CLOCK.ZIP** either. We have to tell **archie** to change the terms of its search. Fortunately, this is easy enough to do. The command is **set search** *searchtype* (where *searchtype* is a variable that determines how **archie** looks for information). We can, you see, change the kind of search we want to run. Here are the possibilities.

exact: An exact match to the filename.

regex: Treats the search string as a UNIX regular expression to match filenames.

sub: The search string will find a hit if the filename in question contains it *as a part of* its name. This is a much broader form of search than the two previously listed.

subcase: While **sub** is not sensitive to case, **subcase** is. Thus using this setting will cause your search string to find a hit only if the filename contains it as part of its name, and only if the case matches the case of the substring.

Knowing this, we can return with greater interest to our **archie** search. At the **archie>** prompt, we'll enter **set search sub**, telling **archie** to probe considerably deeper into its listings to look for material possibly buried inside. Having done that, we can run the same search: **prog geoclock.** Figure 5.11 shows what we get.

Aha! The file in question. Examine these file listings and you'll see why we didn't find them the first time. We asked for **geoclock** as our search term. With the **exact** setting on, we wouldn't get a hit because all these files have a three-letter file extension. **archie** looked at a file like **geoclock.lzh** and determined it couldn't be the file we wanted, because it contained additional letters. By setting the search to the **sub** option, we were able to dig out what we needed. All we need do now is use FTP to access the site; **archie** has given us all the directory information we need to find the program.

Directories vs. Files

archie is doubly useful because it doesn't just find files, it also finds directories. Assume, for example, that you're searching for a Spanish language tutorial. It would be of considerable interest to learn that a directory meeting our search

Figure 5.11
Results of a search using the **set search sub** command.

```
Host pinus.slu.se    (130.238.98.11)
Last updated 18:47  7 Jan 1993

    Location: /msdos.nfs.sunet.se/graphics/util/geoclk
        FILE       rw----r--        808  Jan 27  1992     geoclock.dat
        FILE       rw----r--      68081  Jun 21  1990     geoclock.doc
        FILE       rw----r--     101374  Nov 15  1991     geoclock.hlp

Host ux1.cso.uiuc.edu   (128.174.5.59)
Last updated 08:39 13 Jan 1993

    Location: /pc/exec-pc
        FILE       rw-rw-r--     106067  Feb 19  1988     geoclock.zip

Host nic.funet.fi  (128.214.6.100)
Last updated 01:08  5 Jan 1993

    Location: /pub/dx/software/msdos/solar
        FILE       rw-rw-r--     307089  Apr 10  1991     geoclock.lzh
```

Figure 5.12
Results of a search for
a Spanish language
tutorial.

```
Host cs.orst.edu    (128.193.32.1)
Last updated 05:56 19 Jan 1993

     Location: /pub/budd/cs261
        FILE        rw-r--r--       4505   Nov 30 01:01    spanish

Host clover.csv.warwick.ac.uk   (137.205.192.6)
Last updated 20:42 18 Jan 1993

     Location: /pub/tex/babel
        DIRECTORY rwxr-xr-x          512   Sep 28  1991    spanish

Host bric-a-brac.apple.com    (130.43.2.3)
Last updated 05:20 17 Jan 1993

     Location: /dts/mac/sys.soft.intl
        DIRECTORY rwxr-xr-x          512   Sep 15 18:33    spanish

Host skippy.umiacs.umd.edu    (128.8.120.23)
Last updated 05:54  9 Jan 1993

     Location: /pub/bonnie/lisp/lcs
        DIRECTORY rwxr-xr-x          512   Sep 16  1991    spanish

Host quepasa.cs.tu-berlin.de   (130.149.17.7)
Last updated 05:28  8 Jan 1993

     Location: /pub/mac/mirrors/apple/dts/mac/sys.soft.intl
        DIRECTORY rwxrwxr-x          512   Oct 14 05:57    spanish

Host orchid.csv.warwick.ac.uk   (137.205.192.5)
Last updated 07:45 29 Dec 1992

     Location: /pub/tex/babel
        DIRECTORY rwxr-xr-x          512   Sep 28  1991    spanish

Host ftp.denet.dk   (129.142.6.74)
Last updated 05:40 28 Dec 1992

     Location: /pub/wordlists
        DIRECTORY rwxr-xr-x          512   Nov  1 14:01    spanish
```

terms existed, because it would imply considerable resources for us to explore. We can consider this possibility by looking through the **archie** archives under the term *spanish*. After running this search, we come up with seven possibilities (I started with the **exact** setting on), about which we notice something interesting. Look at what I retrieved in Figure 5.12.

What stands out in this list is the fact that all but one of these entries are directories. In the last entry, for example, we're directed to a directory called */pub/wordlists/spanish*. We don't know exactly what's in that directory, but if we use FTP to access the site, we can then run a **dir** command to view what's there. The only actual file we pulled up with this search is the first entry, which is listed as being in the *pub/budd/cs261* directory, and is called **spanish.**

We don't know what this file is, and we don't know from the directory name what it's likely to be. If we reset the search terms, entering **set search sub,** we can generate a much broader list of actual files. I ran that search, again searching under the **prog spanish** command. Figure 5.13 shows a particularly relevant snippet of that list.

As we see, these files look like programs designed to teach the language. We know from the **.hqx** file suffix that these are compressed files in a format generally used by Macintosh computers. The fact that they aren't listed as **.doc** or **.txt** files also tells us they may well be programs, although we won't know for sure until we seek them out. Nonetheless, we're clearly homing in on the tutorial we need.

Using Whatis

archie maintains a software description database which holds the names and descriptions of software packages. This database can also be searched by using the **whatis** command. You'll get back a file name and a short description of that file. The database is useful when you're looking for something but don't know which programs might be able to help. You'll probably use the **whatis** command first in many cases, turning then to the standard **prog** command once you know the name of the file you're interested in.

We might, for example, need to find a conversion program that would switch ASCII text into a format usable by PostScript. To find it, we could use the **prog postscript** command, but asking **archie** for anything with PostScript in the file description could lead to a very long list. Better to be specific, using the **whatis** command to ask for conversion programs. I'll try the command **whatis converter.** Figure 5.14 shows a shortened version of what we'll see on-screen.

Clearly, the file **a2ps** is just what we're after. Having located it through this shortcut, we can now use the standard **prog** command to track it down. **prog a2ps** yields eight locations for this file, such as:

```
Host binkley.cs.mcgill.ca    (132.206.51.9)
Last updated 05:04 17 Jan 1993
    Location: /pub
        DIRECTORY rwxr-xr-x         512  Dec  8 18:02    a2ps
```

Figure 5.13
Results of a tightened
search for the Spanish
language tutorial.

```
Host plaza.aarnet.edu.au    (139.130.4.6)
Last updated 08:11  7 Jan 1993

    Location: /micros/mac/umich/misc/foreignlang
        FILE      r--r--r--      37081  May 28  1992    spanishteacher.cpt.hqx

Host garbo.uwasa.fi   (128.214.87.1)
Last updated 08:30 29 Dec 1992

    Location: /mirror/umich.macarchive/misc/foreignlang
        FILE      r--r--r--      37081  Nov 23 10:13    spanishteacher.cpt.hqx

Host src.doc.ic.ac.uk   (146.169.2.1)
Last updated 15:25 16 Dec 1992

    Location: /computing/systems/mac/umich/misc/foreignlang
        FILE      r--r--r--      37081  May 28  1992    spanishteacher.cpt.hqx
```

Figure 5.14
A whatis search for a
Postscript conversion
program.

```
archie> whatis converter

8to1                     SUN raster file color to mono converter
a2ps                     ASCII to PostScript converter
conv                     Simple numeric base converter
cvtbase                  Generalized base converter
ditroff-to-dvi           Device-independent troff (ditroff) to TeX DVI
                         converter
dvi2ps                   DVI to PostScript converter
dvips                    DVI to PostScript converter
epsonps                  Epson to PostScript converte
f2ps                     A FIG to PostScript converter
fig2ps                   A FIG to PostScript converter
gif2ps                   A GIF to PostScript converter
```

archie's descriptive index is helpful but it can be deceptive. Because the index for the **whatis** function and the (separate) index for **prog** are not simultaneously updated, you may find yourself with a hit using **whatis,** but when you try to locate it, **archie** seems to have no record of it. What has doubtless happened is in the time between updates, the file in question has been deleted from the system. The only thing to do in such a case is to keep searching for other files that meet your criteria.

The following describes a number of other **archie** commands available to provide yet more information to aid in your search.

about Typing this command at the prompt will produce a short overview about **archie** and how to use it.

bugs This command will generate a list of known bugs, useful to know if you run into inexplicable difficulties.

bye Logs you off the system. You can also use **quit** or **exit.**

email Information on how to use **archie** through e-mail.

help This will produce a short help screen; subtopics are available.

list Tells us which FTP sites are listed in the **archie** database.

mail Lets you send the output of your search to a user. Include an e-mail address.

site This handy command lists the files at an archive site. Thus **site uts.mcc.ac.uk** produces everything available at that location.

Putting an archie Client to Work

Do you have an **archie** client on your system? If you're dialing in and you're not sure, enter **archie** at the command prompt and see what happens. You should get a list of **archie** commands usable at the prompt. These commands let you precisely modify the output you'll get from the program, helping you gain control over your search. The most significant of these commands are described in the following. The syntax is simple: **archie [*options*] *searchterm*,** where the search term, as with a Telnet **archie** search, is whatever you are looking for. Note that you're using **archie** as a command here instead of **prog,** the command used in Telnet sessions.

-case Allows you to search with a case-sensitive filter on. You could, for example, search for the term PROCOMM, and **archie** wouldn't flag a file called procomm.

-nocase The opposite of the above. This setting causes **archie** to search for the desired string, no matter whether it's uppercase or lowercase, or any combination of the two.

-exact As we saw above, the exact setting in a Telnet session can be set using the term **set search exact.** If you're using an **archie** client, you flip the same software switch by using the **-exact** modifier. Thus the search command **archie exact geoclk** will only flag files that match the search term letter by letter.

-reg This alerts **archie** that the search string you're using is a UNIX regular expression.

-m # This is a useful modifier indeed; it lets you set a maximum number of hits for a given **archie** search. If my command is **archie -m 15 geoclk,** I'll get a list no larger than 15 for my results. Bear in mind that it may be necessary to expand the list to find the files you need; they could be buried farther down in the sequence of hits.

-server hostname Lets you specify an alternative **archie** server for your search.

-format string Allows you to specify a format string. Assume you want the output from **archie** to appear in a precise order: host first, then directory name, size of file, etc. You could specify this through a format string. Use the **man archie** command at your system prompt to generate more information on how to set up such a format string.

-ffile filename In the event you're specifying a format for your output, this command lets your system read a format file to get the string it will use in the search.

-version Prints the version number of the program.

-sort [date|host] Causes **archie** to sort its output by date or host. When sorting by hosts, the sort key is the domain of the hosts involved.

-domain string Used when you're sorting by hosts. You use the order in the string to sort the hosts. Thus you could tell **archie** to sort by **edu ca.** **archie** would treat these as domain names, and would present its output with all **.edu** domains first, then all **.ca** domains.

Note that you can't do **whatis, site,** or **list** searches in this mode.

Chapter Five Notes

1. Merit press release, 2 December 1992.
2. The best reference on file compression, and many other telecommunication issues, is Michael A. Banks' *The Modem Reference*. 3rd ed. New York: Brady Publishing, 1992.
3. Bunyip Information Systems may be contacted at:
   310 St.-Catherine St. West
   Suite 202
   Montreal, Quebec
   Canada H2X 2A1
   Voice: 514-875-8611
   Fax: 514-875-8134
   Thanks to Peter Deutsch for background information about **archie** and thoughts about where it is heading.

Telnet Shrinks

the World

Telnet is an Internet tool which allows you to log on to remote computers and manipulate them to retrieve data. By using a set of simple commands, you instruct your service provider's computer to make a connection with another computer. You log on to that machine, usually by providing a user identification name and a password. Services that are publicly available often prompt you with the correct log-in sequence, or in many cases the sequence is available through listings of Internet resources like the one you will find in this book in Chapter 15. Once logged on, you can take advantage of the services offered at the remote site.

What's available through Telnet? The variety is impressive. Many universities, for example, make campus information available over publicly accessible Campus Wide Information Systems. You can use these to find out what's happening at schools around the world, to search directories to find student and faculty addresses and, often, to take advantage of services like library catalog searches. When you use Telnet it's as easy to track down a book at the University of Hong Kong as it is at the school around the block.

Database resources are out there as well, many of them openly accessible. The Advanced Technology Information Network, for example, is designed to provide information about agricultural markets in California as well as useful data for exporters. HPCwire tracks high performance computing developments and includes newsletters on computing topics. NYSERNet/PSI's Online X.500 Directory provides address information for personnel at major organizations throughout the United States. The Dartmouth Dante Project makes the corpus of The Divine Comedy available to scholars, along with centuries of scholarly commentary. The Louis Harris Data Center maintains Harris polling information back to 1960 on a wide variety of topics, constituting a treasure trove of data for sociologists.

You can see by this diversity that the range of Telnet-accessible resources is broad and growing. The emphasis, as you would expect, has thus far been on scientific and research topics, but the success of scholarly endeavors such as the Dartmouth Dante Project ensures there will be growing participation from the humanities as well. Telnet thus ranks as one of the most powerful tools available on the Internet, and its ability to allow users of diverse computer systems to tap distant databases is a vindication of the internetworking concept that TCP/IP has made possible.

TELNET VERSUS DIAL-UP SYSTEMS

In order to place Telnet in context, it's useful to contrast using it to using dial-up bulletin board systems. If you call up local bulletin boards, you understand that each offers its own set of features and is slanted toward a particular user community. To tap into a wide variety of bulletin board systems, you must call each in turn, perhaps using a service like PC-Pursuit to cut costs. Each call, however, involves choosing a particular BBS system and making a call to it. Once logged on to a system, you are, in effect, in an electronic building, one filled with a variety of rooms, but one whose only exit is back out the door through which you entered.

When you use Telnet to access a distant computer, you've also entered an electronic building filled with many rooms. But when you've concluded your stay at one address, you need not go off-line, choose another telephone number, and make another call. Instead, your connection to your service provider remains intact. You are returned to its system prompt, from which you can use Telnet again to log on to a different computer. Your modem remains on-line the entire time, but your electronic presence moves from computer to computer, using your service provider's machine as its electronic home base. It's possible in this way to move around the world by means of Telnet at a rapid clip, exploring resources, checking catalogs, and gathering information.

THROUGH TELNET TO THE GATEWAY CITY

Let's take a look at Telnet in action by logging on to Washington University Services, a gateway offering a unique battery of Internet functions under a simple menu structure. To reach this data storehouse, we enter the **telnet** command followed by the address of the site. Figure 6.1 shows what you'll see when you enter this command.

The Login Screen

Let's examine this screen carefully. After giving the **telnet** command and the address of our requested site, we see the message **Trying 128.252.120.1....** This is the IP, or Internet Protocol, address of the computer in question. Remember that Internet computers use addresses with four numbers joined by periods.

Figure 6.1
Initial screen using
Telnet to Washington
University Services.

```
% telnet wugate.wustl.edu
Trying 128.252.120.1 ...
Connected to library.wustl.edu.
Escape character is ' ^ ] '.


ULTRIX V4.2A  (Rev. 47)  (library.wustl.edu)

login: services
```

These numbers are filed with the INTERNIC; each identifies a unique computer on the Internet.

We also know that computers can be identified by names. In this case, the name **library.wustl.edu** has been mapped to the corresponding IP number. Both are addresses, and both refer to the same computer.

Note the statement **Escape character is '^]'.** This is a useful bit of information. During a Telnet session, it's possible something will go wrong. Because Telnet makes it possible to log on to many different kinds of computer systems (this one, for example, uses the ULTRIX software mentioned in the sign-on message), we may lose track of where we are and be unable to get out. Telnet incorporates an escape routine which can be activated by pressing the keys shown. The **^** symbol should be interpreted as the control key. Thus, **^]** means "press the control key at the same time you press the **]** key"; it can also be written as **Ctrl -].** This will return you to a Telnet prompt, at which you can enter the command **quit** to exit. You will see an example later in this chapter.

We're next asked for a log-in name, and I've entered **services.** If you check in Chapter 15 under Washington University Services, you'll find the log-in name listed there, as it is for a variety of other systems. The appropriate log-in allows you to access that part of Washington University's data sources open to the public. Entering **services** opens up the screen shown in Figure 6.2.

We're now asked for information the remote computer needs to know to send data to us. By asking you for your **terminal type,** the computer is determining what kind of special features it can present, from color or graphics to full-screen editing and command keys. The statement **TERM = (vt100):** suggests an answer. By enclosing **vt100** in parentheses, the machine is telling us this is the default choice. If you enter a carriage return here, you announce your intention to use **vt100** as your default terminal emulation. Choosing **vt100** lets your computer function as if it were a Digital Equipment Corporation terminal; it's a standard for terminal-based communications, so press the **RETURN** key to choose it.

A Remote Menu Structure

Once we've told the remote computer how to display its data, the computer presents the menu shown in Figure 6.3.

A quick glance through this menu may reveal why Washington University Services is a popular Telnet destination. University libraries in this country and abroad are available for searching, as are a number of publicly accessible

Figure 6.2
Logging in at
Washington University
Services.

```
  SSSSSSS
SSSSSSSSS
SS           EEEEE   RRRRRR    VV   VV  IIIIII   CCCCC    EEEEE   SSSSS
SSSSSSSS     EEEEEE  RR   RR   VV   VV    II    CCCCCCC   EEEEE  SSSSSS
  SSSSSSSS   EE      RR   RR   VV   VV    II    CCC       EE     SS
        SS   EEEEEE  RRRRRR    VV   VV    II    CCC       EEEEE   SSSS
        SS   EE      RR   RR   VV   VV    II    CCC       EE         SS
SSSSSSSS     EEEEEE  RR   RR   VV VV      II    CCCCCCC   EEEEE  SSSSSS
  SSSSS      EEEEE   RR    RR    VVV     IIIIII  CCCCC    EEEEE   SSSS


       O f f i c e   o f   t h e   N e t w o r k   C o o r d i n a t o r
              W a s h i n g t o n   U n i v e r s i t y
                     i n   S a i n t   L o u i s


       As seen in "Zen and the Art of the Internet" by Brendan P. Kehoe




Washington University Services
Version 2.3.0
==============================
Please enter your terminal type, or hit
return to accept the default.

TERM = (vt100):
```

Figure 6.3
The initial menu at
Washington University
Services.

```
==============================
Please enter your terminal type, or hit
return to accept the default.

TERM = (vt100):


Washington University in Saint Louis            Tue Apr 27 09:47 1993
=[Menu 0: Main
Menu]=============================================================
     1. About Washington University Services
     2. Washington University Services
     3. United States Libraries
     4. Foreign Libraries
     5. Government Libraries and Public Accessible Databases
     6. Campus Wide Information Systems
     7. All Services
     8. Weather Forecast for US/Canada
     9. QUIT the Washington University Services program






==================================================================
/ h: LEFT / j: DOWN / k: UP / l: RIGHT / u: PREVIOUS MENU / ?: HELP / q: QUIT /
```

databases, Campus Wide Information Systems, weather forecasts, and more. The menu system makes it possible to reach these destinations without difficulty.

LEARNING THE COMMANDS

Examine now the bottom of the main menu screen, where you'll find a range of possible commands. Of these, perhaps the most important is the **?** command, which pulls up a help menu. We're now on foreign turf. It would be pointless to go through every command available at Washington University, because you will encounter a wide range of systems using Telnet, and many use their own command structure. So the first rule is: always determine how to call up a help menu. Doing this at Washington University, for example, gives you the screen shown in Figure 6.4.

Notice first of all that this is not the complete help message. Toward the bottom of the screen, the statement **[Text: 33%]** tells us we're looking at one out of three screens. The bottom of the screen gives us commands we can use as we read the help information. Pressing the **n** key, for example, takes us to the next page, while **u** returns us to the main menu.

A Telnet Jump to Another Site

Back at the main menu, look at the material offered under choice 5, "Government Libraries and Public Accessible Databases." We know from the commands at the bottom of the screen that we can move about the menu using several commands, although they're anything but intuitive. A **k** will move up, a **j** down. By repeatedly pressing the **j** key, we can move the highlighted area until it covers our menu choice. At that point, pressing the **RETURN** key will select that item and present us with the submenu shown in Figure 6.5.

Figure 6.4
The help menu at
Washington University
Services.

```
Washington University in Saint Louis              Mon Mar  8 09:10 1993
===============================================================================

                          SERVICES Help Screen
                          ====================

   SERVICES 2.0 represents a step forward in the evolution of the
   library/services account on wugate.  Its main features are:
        -- Hierarchical Menu Interface.
        -- Curses Mode and Dumb Mode.
        -- Terminal Type guesser (that will usually be correct.)
        -- Ability to search for an item.
        -- Ability to jump ahead by typing menu/item number.

   Movement Commands:
     (CURSES MODE)
     Services uses the standard VI command mode movement commands, as
     well as the ARROW keys (if supported by the termcap).

     k, DOWN_ARROW : down              j, UP_ARROW    : up
     h, LEFT_ARROW : left              l, RIGHT_ARROW : right

=============================================================Text: 33%]==
/ b: BACK PAGE / n: NEXT PAGE / u: RETURN TO MENU /
```

Figure 6.5
The menu for libraries
and other databases.

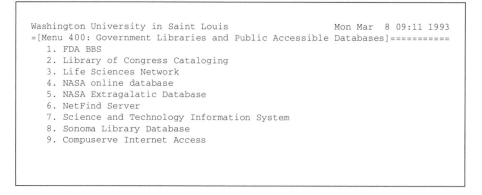

```
Washington University in Saint Louis                    Mon Mar  8 09:11 1993
=[Menu 400: Government Libraries and Public Accessible Databases]===========
    1. FDA BBS
    2. Library of Congress Cataloging
    3. Life Sciences Network
    4. NASA online database
    5. NASA Extragalatic Database
    6. NetFind Server
    7. Science and Technology Information System
    8. Sonoma Library Database
    9. Compuserve Internet Access
```

CompuServe users may find it intriguing that Internet access to their service is provided here (you must, of course, already have an account with CompuServe for this feature to be of any use to you). Also available is a variety of databases, including one we'll take a closer look at, the NASA Online Database. We can get to it by moving around the menu as we did before, using the **j** key to put the highlight on the menu item we need, in this case number 4. Pressing **RETURN** again selects it. At this point, we see an interesting screen indeed, shown in Figure 6.6.

Note what's happening. We're being given the opportunity to connect to this system, which is an archive of space and earth science data. By pressing **c,** we move into NODIS, NSSDC's Online Data and Information Service. Figure 6.7 shows what the process looks like on-screen.

Telnet is taking us on quite a journey. We've accessed computers at Washington University in St. Louis, using their menu structure to find our way around the available services. And then, when we chose a menu item, we were propelled,

Figure 6.6
A Telnet menu at
Washington University
Services.

```
Washington University in Saint Louis                    Mon Mar  8 09:13 1993
=============================================================================
    NASA
    nssdca.gsfc.nasa.gov

        Login with the username of "NSSDC"


                  --- Press "c" to connect to system ---
              --- Press "u" to return to the menu system ---






=========================================================[Text: 100%]=
/ b: BACK PAGE / n: NEXT PAGE / u: RETURN TO MENU / c: CONNECT TO SYSTEM /
```

Figure 6.7
Accessing another
remote site.

```
Accessing service NASA online database:
Internet Address: nssdca.gsfc.nasa.gov
Trying to connect to service 128.183.36.23 ...
Connected to nssdca.gsfc.nasa.gov.
Escape character is '^]'.


     <   NSSDCA    VAX 9410    >     Monday, March 8, 1993

   ANY UNAUTHORIZED ATTEMPT TO ACCESS THIS SYSTEM IS A FEDERAL OFFENSE
   ONLY ACCESS TO THE USERNAME=NODIS(=NSSDC) ACCOUNT IS AUTHORIZED TO ALL


Username:
```

again through Telnet (only this time Telnet as mediated by Washington University's computers) into yet another database. In this way, a menu at one Internet site can actively call up a network connection to another site.

Realize, then, that *such menus are not static entities—they often point to network connections.* You could also reach the NASA database by using Telnet to access it directly once you learned its name or IP address.

Exiting a Telnet Session

Intrigued? I would imagine so. This is Telnet showing off, demonstrating how nimble a person with the basic Telnet know-how can be at moving around the world at light-speed, through fiber-optic cables and microwave transmissions to find information. In this exercise I've traveled from Research Triangle Park to Washington University to a major NASA database, all in one telephone connection, using publicly available sources to find what I need.

But as mentioned before, you must know how to exit. The process is relatively routine, as long as you remember how Telnet operates. If, for example, you took menu choice 10 from the main menu at Washington University, exiting would be simple. The menu says *QUIT the Washington University Services program* and that's exactly what it will do, returning you to your service provider's system prompt.

Things get a little stickier, however, if you get stuck and have to invoke the **Ctrl-]** sequence to quit your Telnet session. Rather than returning you to the friendly local prompt, this command takes you back to the command prompt for the Telnet program itself. You must enter **quit** at this point to return to your system prompt.

```
telnet> quit
Connection closed.
```

THE TELNET COMMAND STRUCTURE

What's the command prompt for? Let's take a look. To get into it, you can enter **telnet** without any further specification at the system prompt. You'll be placed in Telnet's command mode, shown by the prompt **telnet>.** Chances are you will not have much need to use Telnet in command mode, other than to quit from it if you've had to escape from a remote log-in that was going awry. But there are actually a number of commands available at the **telnet>** prompt. The following lists some of the things you can do.

return   Pressing the **RETURN** key without any command takes you out of command mode and returns you to your Telnet connection to the remote computer.

close   Ends the current connection, disconnecting from the remote system.

display   Shows operating parameters for the current session.

open   Connects to a site. Note that you have two ways to reach a remote computer. The first is to give the **telnet** command and specify the remote site at the system prompt. Thus **telnet wugate.wustl.edu** takes you to Washington University Services from your service provider's command prompt. Alternatively, you can issue the **telnet** command by itself at the system prompt; this places you in **telnet** command mode. You follow this up with the **open** command followed by the site specification, as in **open wugate.wustl.edu.** The results are the same.

quit   Exits the Telnet program.

set   Allows you to set a variety of operating parameters. You can enter **set ?** in command mode to see the entire list. Of particular interest to us is the **set escape** command.

The **set escape** command changes the escape character. The default escape character is **Ctrl-],** which moves you into command mode during your Telnet session. Most of the time you can leave the default setting in place, as you won't have any need to change it. However, it is possible that a Telnet session more complicated than usual could require a different escape character.

Why? Because Telnet can involve more than one remote computer. In the example of Washington University Services, we saw that a variety of databases and other services are accessible through the system's menu structure. If you choose one of these, your Telnet connection would have several branches—from your computer to your service provider's computer, then to Washington University, and then to the service you chose at the menu. Your Telnet session would be hopping from site to site. The speed of Telnet makes this kind of connection workable, but it does present a practical challenge.

Suppose, for example, you have made a Telnet connection to a remote computer, followed by another Telnet jump from there to a third. Let's say something went wrong that made you want to exit from the database you're using at the third site and return to the second. If you were to use the standard escape sequence while connected in this way, you would wind up not at the second site's computer, but back in your own service provider's machine; the whole piggy-backed structure would vanish, and you'd have to set up the entire set of connections again.

The **set escape** command allows you to declare a different escape character for each leg of the electronic journey. By choosing which escape character to enter, you give yourself the flexibility to enter into command mode at the connected sites you choose. You do this by entering the command **set escape** followed by the appropriate character. Thus **set escape ^q** establishes **Ctrl-q** as the escape key for that leg. Note that you do this *after you have already established a connection.*

Let's assume your first Telnet site is Washington University Services. Your escape character on the first leg to Washington University is the default, **Ctrl -].** You change that by going into command mode *after* you log on at Washington University, entering a new escape sequence; say, **set escape ^q** (you type the caret, or **^,** character, then the **q.**) Having done so, you now opt for a menu item taking you to the Science and Technology Information System (STIS) at the National Science Foundation in Washington, DC. Once connected to STIS, your escape sequence again defaults to **Ctrl-].** To go into command mode at Washington University, you enter **Ctrl -].** To go into command mode at your home site, you'd enter **Ctrl-q.**

?   Prints help information.

USING COMPUTER PORTS

When more than one service is provided on a given computer, port assignments must be made for each. This is done by assigning a specific port number to each service. Think of it this way. A server is actually a software application that runs on a computer—it's not the computer itself. That means a computer can offer more than one server, and most do, not just for Telnet but for many other applications as well. The server has a particular port assignment to differentiate it from other servers. In this case, the word *port* refers to a software designation which keeps traffic properly routed. It has nothing to do with hardware ports.

For a client program to access the proper server in such an environment, it must specify which port it wants to use. You can spot such servers quickly; their address consists of the computer information followed by a port number. Examples are easy to find. If we were looking around the Internet to find schedules for professional sports teams, we'd encounter a server providing baseball scores at the following address: **culine.colorado.edu 862.** The number 862 is this server's port address. Figure 6.8 shows what it offers, and what's on the other ports.

As you can see, you're offered a list of Major League baseball teams and the chance to generate schedule information for each. On-line help is provided, and by using it, you know that you can create a list of any team's full schedule for the year with the **all** command. I entered **St. Louis all** to get the Cardinals' 1993 schedule. Figure 6.9 shows the results.

The baseball server at this site is only one of several; in fact, this computer also offers hockey, basketball, and football schedules. To separate these services, the system administrators have given each a separate port assignment. National Hockey League schedules are found at the same address with a different port number: **culine.colorado.edu 860.** Basketball is at **culine.colorado.edu 859** and football at **culine.colorado.edu 863.** This is how port assignments can separate specialized traffic from other Telnet operations. Just remember to add the number to the address.

Figure 6.8
A look at
professional sports
schedules.

```
% telnet culine.colorado.edu 862
Trying 128.138.129.83 ...
Connected to ucsu.colorado.edu.
Escape character is '^]'.


Welcome to the MLB Schedule Service.

Type the name of a team or a date or both.
Type help for detailed instructions.

Valid teams are:
   Atlanta,       Cincinnati,    Cubs,           Houston,
   Los Angeles,   Mets,          Montreal,       Philadelphia,
   Pittsburgh,    San Diego,     San Francisco,  St. Louis,
   Baltimore,     Boston,        California,     Cleveland,
   Detroit,       Kansas City,   Milwaukee,      Minnesota,
   Oakland,       Seattle,       White Sox,      Yankees
   Colorado,      Florida
```

Telnet and "Big Blue Iron"

The term "Big Iron" usually refers to big computers—mainframes come to mind, and particularly IBM mainframes. These machines can pose problems for us, because the terminals they're used to dealing with don't work like any others. The 3270 terminals generally function by having users fill in blanks on the screen, entering information in a variety of fields. They also use special keys called programmed function or PF keys. To work with such terminals, we need a terminal emulator that can interpret what the 3270 system needs and allow our keyboards to work within its parameters.

This is where the **tn3270** application comes in. It's a version of Telnet that includes the appropriate 3270 emulation. In most cases, you'll never need to use **tn3270**. Often, the IBM computer you connect to will handle the appropriate terminal emulation automatically. But in some cases, **tn3270** will be a necessity. Some systems will not work with standard Telnet because of their reliance on 3270 features. For these systems, the only way you can establish a connection is with **tn3270.**

Figure 6.9
A segment of the
Cardinals' 1993
schedule.

```
<mlb> st. louis all
            Tuesday,  4/6     SAN FRANCISCO   at ST. LOUIS
          Wednesday,  4/7     SAN FRANCISCO   at ST. LOUIS
           Thursday,  4/8     SAN FRANCISCO   at ST. LOUIS
             Friday,  4/9     CINCINNATI      at ST. LOUIS
           Saturday,  4/10    CINCINNATI      at ST. LOUIS
             Sunday,  4/11    CINCINNATI      at ST. LOUIS
            Tuesday,  4/13    St. Louis       at Los Angeles
          Wednesday,  4/14    St. Louis       at Los Angeles
           Thursday,  4/15    St. Louis       at Los Angeles
             Friday,  4/16    St. Louis       at San Diego
           Saturday,  4/17    St. Louis       at San Diego
             Sunday,  4/18    St. Louis       at San Diego
            Tuesday,  4/20    COLORADO        at ST. LOUIS
          Wednesday,  4/21    COLORADO        at ST. LOUIS
```

Fortunately, doing so is as easy as using Telnet itself. The University of North Carolina at Chapel Hill maintains a database of material from the Harris organization relating to poll results. Over 750 Harris polls are located here; all of them are searchable. This useful archive is stored on an IBM computer which we reach by using **tn3270.** If we try to connect with regular **telnet,** the result is a hung system:

```
% telnet uncvm1.oit.unc.edu
Trying 152.2.21.5 ...
Connected to uncvm1.oit.unc.edu.
Escape character is '^]'.
```

This looks fine, but nothing more happens, and we'll eventually have to use a **Ctrl-]** sequence to get back to the **telnet** prompt, and then to our system prompt. Using **tn3270** works better, as shown in Figure 6.10. We're informed immediately as to the nature of the computer we're using; the message banner tells us it's an IBM 3090.

This sounds imposing. In fact, the publicly available systems you're going to be dealing with are generally much easier to run than specialized setups that are off-limits to outsiders. A good thing, too, for 3270 emulation can be tricky business, and can depend on how special keys have been mapped onto your keyboard. For our purposes, a few tips should provide all you need to use these

Figure 6.10
Signing on at
UNC-Chapel Hill.

```
% tn3270 uncvm1.oit.unc.edu
Trying...
Connected to uncvm1.oit.unc.edu.

VM/XA SP 2.1 ONLINE-PRESS ENTER KEY TO BEGIN SESSION


 VM/XA SP 2.1 ONLINE


     UU     UU NN     NN  CCCCC        OOOOO   IIIIII TTTTTTTT
     UU     UU NNN    NN CCCCCCC      OO   OO    II      TT
     UU     UU NNN    NN CC    CC     OO    OO    II      TT
     UU     UU NN N   NN CC           OO    OO    II      TT
     UU     UU NN  N  NN CC           OO    OO    II      TT
     UU     UU NN   N NN CC           OO    OO    II      TT
     UU     UU NN    NNN CC    CC     OO    OO    II      TT
      UUUUUUU NN     NN CCCCCCC       OO   OO    II      TT
       UUUUU  NN     NN  CCCCC         OOOOO   IIIIII    TT

         UNIVERSITY OF NORTH CAROLINA   IBM 3090 COMPUTING SYSTEM
                     VM/XA  SP 2.1  (9104)


   Fill in your USERID and PASSWORD and press ENTER
   (Your password will not appear when you type it)
   USERID   ===
   PASSWORD ===  ━━━━━━━━━━━━━━━
   Type VMEXIT on AND line to leave VM/XA
   COMMAND  ===
                                          RUNNING   UNCVM1
```

systems, and you can rely on on-line help to provide more clues in the specific situations you find yourself in.

Let's examine the log-on screen in Figure 6.10 for further information. You're asked for a user identification and password. The appropriate ID is **irss1;** the password is **irss.** (This is information you would have to learn before calling the system; it's available in a variety of sources including Chapter 15 of this book.) But note: data entry is a bit different here. Rather than entering your user ID, pressing the **ENTER** key, and then entering your password, you can enter the user ID and use the **TAB** key to move to the next field before entering the password. The 3270 is a full-screen application, meaning it expects you to move around on the screen for data entry, often using the **TAB** key.

When we have entered the password, pressing the **TAB** key takes us to the COMMAND line. Fortunately, the system has prompted us for what to do next. Pressing **ENTER** here takes us to a screen of introductory information, shown in Figure 6.11.

Again, we're prompted for what to do next. Passing through the menu chain, we arrive at a menu that prompts us to search in the extensive data holdings here, as shown in Figure 6.12.

What's matters here is not the methodology of this particular database, but the way the 3270 system works with input and output. You'll notice as you go through such a system that the screen does not scroll upward a line at a time.

Figure 6.11
Introductory information at the Institute for Research in Social Science.

```
LOGON IRSS1
LOGMSG - 06:24:12 EST MONDAY 03/08/93
FILES: 0002 RDR,   NO PRT,   NO PUN
LOGON AT 11:06:47 EST TUESDAY 03/09/93
VM/XA  CMS 5.6  (9104)


            Welcome to the Institute for Research in Social Science
                            Data Services

    The  Institute  for Research in Social Science maintains an extensive
    archive of social science data. Three easy-to-use, menu driven systems
    are available to assist users in locating and accessing these data:

                    * IRSS Data Holdings Catalog *
    An on-line CATALOG of IRSS data holdings arranged by title,principal
    investigator,and subject.

                    * IRSS Public Opinion Item Index *
    Lets you search for public opinion poll questions that contain
    specific words or combinations of words. You can also search using
    study dates or study numbers, separately or with question wordings.




========================================================================

                    Press  ENTER for Data Services Menu
```

Figure 6.12
An Institute for
Research in Social
Science catalog
screen.

```
WELCOME TO THE IRSS CATALOG OF DATA HOLDINGS

This file offers the user the ability to search through the holdings
of the Institute for Research in Social Science.  IRSS is the campus
depository for social science machine-readable data and the national
depository for Louis Harris, Atlanta Journal Constitution, Carolina
Poll, and USA Today polls.

Once a search has been defined and the user is satisfied with
the results, a printout of the questions can be obtained.

If you have any questions or suggestions, please contact:
David Sheaves, IRSS
966-3348
uirdss@uncvm1
-File selected; type HELP DATA HOLDINGS FILE for more information
Type FIND to search this file.
Type SELECT to choose a different file.
YOUR RESPONSE:
f1=Help f2=Find f3=Select
Also:  Setup, Command, Suggest, Lock, Pause, End
```

Instead, the screen goes blank and then reappears. You'll also notice that some keys don't work as advertised.

Take your function keys. The bottom of the screen in Figure 6.12 gives you a set of commands. **f1=Help** seems like a straightforward statement. But it may be that when you press the **F1** function key to generate help, you simply get an error message. If that happens, try using the **ESC** key in combination with a number. Thus, instead of using **F1** for the help screen, it might work to hold down the **ESC** key and press **1** at the same time. One or the other of these methods should produce results. And as we saw earlier, these keys can then be used for help or, in this case, to choose a database and to search it, which is how **F2** and **F3** are used here.

This discussion is necessarily vague because it's impossible to specify which keys will have exactly what function on your system. **tn3270** relies on a file called **map3270** to list how the various keys are mapped to your keyboard. In the absence of a universal method, key assignments vary from one system to another. This often calls for a fair amount of trial and error, and you can wind up, as with Telnet, stuck inside a remote computer without knowing how to get out.

This is where you need the escape sequence, which will take you to command mode. Try **Ctrl-C** if **Ctrl-]** doesn't work. As with Telnet, the escape sequence deposits you at a prompt, after which you can exit.

```
tn3270> quit
Connection closed.
```

On the other hand, as you can see from the screens at UNC, systems designed to be useful to users usually try to give you enough information on-screen to help you get around. If the screen gets filled up with information (and this can easily happen with 3270 emulation), try **Ctrl-Z** or **Ctrl-Home** to clear it.

CHAPTER
7

A World of Electronic Mail

Electronic mail is a core Internet application. Using e-mail, you can communicate with people all over the world, often receiving replies the same day. Your messages are stored in the recipient's mailbox until they are read, so there's little risk of their being overlooked. You can include previous messages in what you write; you can send your mail to one person or a group of users. And because mail management involves no more than mastering a few basic commands, you can gain control over the influx quickly as your daily mail count grows, saving what you need, discarding the rest. Electronic mail is fast, powerful, and addictive; once you've worked with it, you'll wonder how you got along without it.

What appears in my own mailbox changes frequently, as I move into and out of various mailing lists and develop on-line relationships with more and more people. Whether near or far, my correspondents and I have one thing in common—we've learned that an electronic mailbox is a tool that can be customized to meet a wide variety of interests and needs. To make it all work, you have to know the options available to you. Proper navigation techniques are just as important with electronic mail as with any other part of the Internet.

In this chapter, we'll discuss what electronic mail can do for you and how you can use a mail program to continue your on-line explorations. Because Internet addresses are the first thing users see, we'll take the mystery out of these cryptic runes, and move on to a sample log-in session working through the basic commands in the UNIX program called **mail**. Then we'll discuss software options once you out-grow **mail** (and chances are you will). But whatever

127

program you use, I guarantee that your Internet mailbox will soon become one of your most valuable assets.

SHATTERING THE BORDERS

Many people use mail as their *only* Internet application, not realizing how much else is available, or finding that the power of e-mail meets their current needs. Get involved with a number of on-line correspondents and your electronic mailbox can quickly grow to gigantic proportions, particularly when you subscribe to the mailing lists from BITNET and other sources that are described later.

Fortunately, the Internet could not grow to its present complexity without providing tools that make mail management feasible. Many such tools—the lug wrenches and precision screwdrivers of electronic-file maintenance—are there, in varying degrees of power and user-friendliness. But using electronic mail doesn't have to be complicated. A practical knowledge of a few simple programs is all it takes to participate. And the scope of e-mail is wide.

For mail can reach out beyond the Internet itself. You might think of the Internet as the core medium you can use to contact a wide variety of other networks (which use different protocols than the Internet's TCP/IP to provide their own kinds of information and connectivity). If you use local bulletin board systems to exchange messages and download files, you're probably familiar with FidoNet, which allows your local system to be connected with thousands of other computers by telephone link. FidoNet is often a user's first stop on the road to the Internet. By making a local telephone call, users can read and respond to messages that may have been written a city or a continent away.

Then there's BITNET, an academic and research network with powerful mail distribution features explored more fully in another chapter. There's UUCP, which stands for UNIX-to-UNIX Copy Program; its store and forward capabilities keep USENET humming, running newsgroups on countless subjects. There are the big commercial providers, such as CompuServe, GEnie, and DELPHI, not to mention dedicated e-mail specialists like MCI Mail. Users of all these services are available for electronic mail correspondence through your Internet connection, and the Internet's ever-widening series of gateways ensures that connectivity with other providers will only grow.

So the first caveat is this: if you use any other information provider—even if you're an old hand—you must change your thinking as you approach the Internet. You're used to sending a message to a limited audience—people who have accounts with a particular provider. But Internet communications ignore borders. Get used to a communications medium where the transfer of information occurs not just between fellow members of one networked group, but between networks worldwide, no matter what their protocols. And remember, users of those other networks can just as readily get back to you.

A WORD TO USERS OF COMMERCIAL ON-LINE SERVICES

If you are sending electronic mail to the Internet from a commercial service like CompuServe or America Online, you will not be able to use the UNIX **mail** program, or any of the other mail programs available through a UNIX-based service provider. The commands in this chapter will therefore be irrelevant. You need to work through the mail system provided by your service—instead of worrying about UNIX **mail,** you need to know how to handle CompuServe Mail, or DELPHI Mail, or whatever service you use. Time spent brushing up on your system's commands will be time well spent, as we'll see in the next chapter.

ELECTRONIC MAIL DEFINED

Electronic mail provides the ability to send messages by computer. A letter routed electronically has enormous advantages over conventional mail, not the least of which is the speed of its delivery. Internet regulars say it all when they refer to the U.S. Postal Service as "snail mail." Indeed, after only a few days of mastering electronic mail, it seems hard to imagine the days when the mailbox at the end of the driveway was the only way we could communicate with people who were far away. Dazzled by the possibilities of the new medium, we want the rest of the world to operate as smoothly, as usefully, as our electronic mailbox.

Unlike a letter printed on paper, an electronic mail message can be stored on your computer disk. You can handle it like any other file, pulling it into your word processor for editing or printing, or perhaps forwarding it to another person you think would be interested. People who are novices at electronic mail are often surprised at the high rate of return they receive on their Internet mail. The reason is obvious; people find it easier to use a brief computer command to package and send a message than to look up a person's address, print out the letter, address an envelope, and send the whole thing off with a stamp.

The concept of electronic mail is taking time to penetrate the general population. Surprisingly, although office-based computer networks are becoming the norm, only some twenty percent take advantage of e-mail to send messages between workers. And while users of commercial on-line services may have some experience with the medium, most have not glimpsed the full power of e-mail, nor have they guessed that e-mail is headed toward an even brighter future, connecting not just the users of one computer system, but crossing electronic frontiers to reach users across the way. All that is coming, and much of it is here right now.

Every morning when I dial in to the Internet, a mailbox stuffed with messages is waiting for me. Discussing the ins and outs of the writing trade with a fellow practitioner is something I now do at the keyboard. Because my phone is often busy, there's no reason to leave messages on my voice mail system; my correspondents know I'll see any message they leave by e-mail quickly. Is there a hot new restaurant in town? Someone is sure to tell me. Has a nearby company produced an unbeatable software product? My e-mail will soon have news of it. Is a new site available for file downloads? One way or another, e-mail will tell the tale.

But the great thing about this electronic version of the post office is that it's immune to distance. The message left for me this morning at a terminal in Edinburgh, Scotland is already in my mailbox in Research Triangle Park by the time I log on. My response is automatic; by replying to the missive with a simple command, all necessary routing information is added to my message, and it takes but a keystroke to send it flying by high-speed network to its destination. The message I received last week from New Zealand keeping me up on news in

Wellington could as easily have come from Duke University, a mere twenty miles down the road, so transparent is the Internet's mail function.

And there's more, considerably more. Maybe I need to get word to a group of friends that a new market for telecommunications writers is about to open up. Rather than writing a series of letters to various correspondents, I can write one e-mail message and direct it to multiple sites. The recipients can read my message at their leisure and then respond to it. We've set up a circle of interested parties, moving from one to many and back to one, all without the hassle of printing out multiple copies and mailing them.

More than any other medium, e-mail lets you master your own schedule. Writers work on deadline, and the process of composition is susceptible to all kinds of jars—the muse is sensitive and often obstinate. A ringing telephone is intrusive; answering it, I must break my chain of thought and shift attention to an entirely new subject. E-mail, however, lets me handle business when I have time. I can save my correspondence for later in the morning if I choose, preserving those productive early hours for writing. Then, ready for a break, I can respond to ten e-mail messages as a second pot of coffee is brewing.

As with all computer subjects, a high-tech name describes such processes— *asynchronous communications*. The terms means that electronic mail uncouples you from the normal messaging train. Call a phone number and encounter a busy signal—you've run into a brick wall, until you dial back, sometimes repeatedly, and make connections. Dial that same number and reach a voice mailbox and you're into the realm of the asynchronous. Processes don't have to occur simultaneously with this kind of communication; you can leave a message and the person in question will call back when time allows. Electronic mail provides that same service, only the rate of return on e-mail, at least in my experience, is vastly superior to voice mail. Maybe e-mail is just more enjoyable.

ELECTRONIC MAIL PROGRAMS

The Internet is so huge that no one scheme works on all systems. We're not talking about MS-DOS here, nor a single Macintosh on a desktop, but a network comprising a wide variety of operating systems. You may be running an IBM-compatible computer, trained in DOS software applications. Maybe you're dialing in with an Amiga or a Mac. One way or another, you need to be able to deal with the various devices that make up the Internet. Fortunately, most of the dial-up service providers are using UNIX as their operating system, and that gives us a common language with which to work. It also gives us a core program.

I'll work with the UNIX **mail** program in our sample log-on sessions. Bear this in mind: when you dial in to the Internet, you're going through several layers of complexity you don't face when dialing a commercial on-line service. It's easy for me to call up CompuServe and start interacting with its host computers in Columbus. I type a command, which gets sent to the host, which then does something about it and gets back to my computer. In this way, I can do various CompuServ-ish things such as sending e-mail, participating in forum discussions, conferencing, checking the weather patterns, and using on-line databases.

The same paradigm holds with a dial-in Internet account, except there is a wide variety of host computers. The physical location where the message is stored is the host computer you're accessing, only now there's no centralized set of tools for use throughout the network. The software on the machine at your service provider's site determines which tools you can use to read the message. This is why I choose **mail** as the learning vehicle. Because it's plain and ordinary and implemented throughout the UNIX world, **mail** is the program most likely to be found on the greatest number of dial-up systems.

WHAT IS MAIL?

The software program called **mail** reads incoming mail messages. It's one of several such programs. Most of them sport odd, Zen-like names of the kind favored by the UNIX community: **elm, pine, mush.** The tendency toward bizarre cryptography persists in the UNIX world, as we'll see when we cover news readers for USENET, which sport such descriptive monikers as **trn** and **nn.** If you want like to learn more about UNIX alternatives to **mail,** a document available on USENET called "UNIX EMail Software—A Survey" works through the options from the standpoint of a systems administrator, the person who is responsible for setting up a UNIX system to communicate with the outside world.

....

What You Need: A Document on Mail Programs

The Document: **UNIX EMail Software—A Survey, by Chris Lewis**

How to Get It: In one of several USENET news groups: **news.answers, news.admin.misc, comp.mail.misc, comp.answers,** where it appears as a regular posting. We'll discuss how to sign up for such groups in Chapter 11.

....

What should a mail program be able to do? The primary functions are obvious: it should make reading your mail intuitive and logical. It should make it easy to reply to messages in your mailbox, and it should provide general housekeeping chores like save and delete functions, forwarding capabilities, insertion of text files into your messages, and more. The user interface you select for your mail will gradually become second nature, but don't fail to explore the options available. It may be that a particular program suits your temperament better than **mail.** We'll look at another interesting mail program, **elm,** later in this chapter.

PUTTING MAIL TO WORK

To activate **mail,** you need to be at your service provider's command prompt. If you have any messages waiting for you when you log on, you'll see the following:

```
You have mail.
```

The message tells you one or more messages are waiting in your mailbox.

But assuming you're coming to electronic mail for the first time, at the command prompt you will see:

```
No mail for username
```

where *username* is your user identification on the system.

The prompt is telling you the system is waiting for your command. Type **mail** and you'll see the **&** symbol, otherwise known as an ampersand. This is the command prompt for the **mail** program; it tells you the program is now active and waiting to be told what to do. Here's an example of **mail**'s entry screen when you have messages waiting. (I've modified the e-mail addresses other than my own to protect the innocent):

```
Mail version SMI 4.0 Thu Oct 11 12:59:09 PDT 1990 Type ? for help.
"/usr/spool/mail/pag": 8 messages 8 new
>N  1 gilster@rock.concert.net Mon Apr  5 11:12    18/794    Reading the Basic Mai
 N  1 cyborg@extraterr.ucd.edu Mon Apr  5 11:12    14/516    Astronomy Update
 N  3 gcox@handyman.outside.net Mon Apr  5 11:12   14/521    Flooding Fixed
 N  4 jason@entree.std.com Mon Apr  5 12:04    17/498   Re: elm Question
 N  5 shelley@como.zurich.ch Mon Apr  5 14:02   14/514    19th C. Poetry
 N  6 vaughan@sassy.jazz.com Mon Apr  5 14:03   14/529    Remembering Billie
 N  7 beowulf@hrothgar.heorot.gov Mon Apr  5 14:34    16/636    Grendel Sighting
```

The information in the top two lines tells us that eight messages have been received, and that all eight are new (i.e., I'm seeing them for the first time). We also receive the useful information that help is available by pressing the **?** key. We'll look at help options in a moment. Next is a statement of the current mailbox in use; in this case, it's the file **/usr/spool/mail/pag.**

Examining Your Mailbox

We're then given a listing of the messages in the mailbox. Note that the messages are numbered. In the example, the letters to the left of the message entries tell us something about the status of the message they mark. Messages marked **N** are new; you haven't yet looked at either their summary line or their text. A message marked with **U** is one you didn't look at even though it was in your mailbox the last time you checked. **U** thus stands for "unread." You saw the summary line last time but didn't read the message. A **P** signifies a message that has been preserved; i.e., you've elected to leave it in your mailbox even though you've already read it at least once.

Notice that a "greater than," or **>,** symbol points to message 1, flagging this as the current message. Any commands you give will take effect on the current message unless you specify a different message. You'll always find the **>** marker pointing to your first new message or, in the absence of new mail, to the first message in your mailbox that's unread.

After the message status and number, we're given the address from which each message was sent. Depending on circumstances, this may not be the originating address, but may be the address of a mailer that routed the message between you and the original sender. Date and time information appear next. If you look closely, you'll find the messages are listed in the order in which they were received. Following the date and time is a set of numbers separated by a slash. This shows the number of lines and characters in the message, a figure which includes the header information. The subject appears last.

Figure 7.1
A basic electronic mail
message.

```
Message  8:
From gilster@rock.concert.net Mon Apr  5 14:34:17 1993
Return-Path: gilster@rock.concert.net
Received: from rock.concert.net by world.std.com (5.65c/Spike-2.0)
        id AA06628; Mon, 5 Apr 1993 14:34:14 -0400
Received: by rock.concert.net (5.59/tas-rock/8-12-92)
        id AA16175; Mon, 5 Apr 93 14:34:12 -0400
Date: Mon, 5 Apr 93 14:34:12 -0400
From: Paul A Gilster -- Computer Focus gilster@rock.concert.net
Message-Id: p51834.AA16175@rock.concert.net
To: pag@world.std.com
Subject: Reading the Basic mail Message
Status: R


Working through the messages in your mailbox is simple.  You simply
type a RETURN at the end of each line and the next message will come
up on the screen.  If you want to delete the last message you've read,
press the d key; you can also save it to a file name, as we'll see.

&
```

Reading the Mail

To begin reading the current message, you can simply press the **ENTER** key.
The message will appear, as in Figure 7.1.

If the message runs to more than one screen, you can press the **SPACE BAR**
to advance to the next screen. Pressing the **RETURN** key will only advance one
line at a time—definitely NOT the way you want to read your mail.

What if you choose not to read the current message? In the case above, to
read the fifth message, simply enter the number **5**. The message will then be
displayed. Thus:

```
&  5 [RETURN]
```

From which I retrieve the message in Figure 7.2.

Figure 7.2
A message retrieved by
choosing a message
number.

```
& 5
Message  5:
From jason@entree.std.com Mon Apr  5 12:04:23 1993
Return-Path: ason@entree.std.com
Received: from localhost by entree.std.com (5.65c/Jason-2.0)
        id AA11543; Mon, 5 Apr 1993 12:04:20 -0400
Message-Id: Ž4051604.AA11543@entree.std.com
To: pag
Cc: staff
Subject: Re: Irish Ale
Date: Mon, 05 Apr 1993 12:04:20 -0400
From: Joe Murphy ason@entree.std.com
Status: R


        Yes, I agree.  As much as I love Guinness Stout, it's the
regular Guinness ale that I remember from our trip to Dublin.

&
```

The following is a list of some basic **mail** commands you'll use daily as you read through your mailbox.

[RETURN]   Displays next message.

p   Displays current message.

-   Displays previous message.

h   Displays list of headers.

d   Deletes current message.

u   Undeletes current message.

Saving Messages

The **mail** program doesn't throw away messages unless you give it a specific command to do so. Messages are saved automatically into a file called **mbox** after being read. When you've read your mail and taken no further action, you'll receive notice of this fact. If I read through nine messages and then exited mail, for example, I'd see the following:

```
Saved nine messages in /home/gilster/mbox
```

Again, the **/home/gilster/mbox** statement simply tells me where the **mbox** file is located. I could go back and reread these messages, or perform any of the other **mail** commands on them, by the expedient of re-invoking the **mail** program and specifying that I wanted to read the messages currently saved in **mbox.** How? Read on.

Reading Saved Messages

Getting at **mbox** requires you to add a parameter to the **mail** command that invokes the program. Entering **mail -f mbox** brings **mbox** up on-screen, where it will appear exactly as your first list of headers in the **mail** program did. If I enter this command at my prompt, here's what I get:

```
: mail -f mbox
Mail version SMI 4.0 Thu Oct 11 12:59:09 PDT 1990  Type ? for help.
"mbox": 5 messages
>   1 tracer@template.com   Fri Dec  4 16:22   56/2563  Re: DELPHI Conference
    2 rscovill@rsa.com       Tue Dec  8 07:06   17/499   Cyberspace
    3 hostmast@nic.ddn.mil Wed Dec  9 16:57   26/889   Re: Press Information
    4 rscovill@rsa.com        Wed Dec  9 18:28   14/500   Did you get my last messa
    5 stroud@med.unc.edu Wed Dec  9 21:47   21/673   Re:  Lunch Sites
```

With any saved text, the standard **mail** commands function just as they do when handling your new messages.

A brief word about your mailbox. Many new users don't realize **mbox** is there and, as you would imagine, it can grow to remarkable size in a fairly short time. UNIX users have a limited amount of disk space allocated to them; pushing the envelope past the point that will keep your administrator happy is bad policy. But rather than deleting the entire **mbox** file (which you could do if you so desired), why not simply edit it periodically and throw out what you don't need?

File management is the idea, and the following **mail** commands walk you through the primary tools available. Learn them so you can keep your mailbox tidy.

Saving Messages to a File

If a particular message strikes your fancy, it's easy enough to save it to a separate file. Use the **s** command to do the job, paired with a file name of your choice. Because I write a newspaper column, for example, it's frequently necessary for me to save a provocative message for later consideration. I typically type **s column,** which tells the system to save the current message in a file called **column.**

Each time I do this, the message is appended onto the existing **column** file, which I usually let grow to ten or twelve messages before I print it out for scrutiny. Multiple messages can be handled the same way by specifying their message numbers. Thus **s 2 7 8 column** saves the designated messages to my **column** file in sequence.

Deleting Mail

The **d** command can be used to delete the current message. As I work through my new messages, for example, I'll use a **d** to delete the message I've just read, assuming I've decided not to save it. Alternatively, you can delete one or more messages from the **mail** prompt by specifying them: **d 1 2 6** deletes the messages in question. Fortunately for those of us who are sometimes too quick on the keyboard, there's also a **u** command to take care of undeleting a file. The problem with it is you can only undelete a file during the current mail session. Once you've given the command to exit **mail,** it's too late.

Assume I've just read a message and have thoughtlessly pressed the **d** key to send the message into limbo. The command **u 6** will bring it back.

Setting Up Folders

If you're like me, you may receive a wide variety of incoming e-mail, much of it in the form of Internet or BITNET mailing list material from people you don't correspond with personally, the rest in the form of letters directed specifically to you. To organize the e-mail load, consider setting up folders for your regular correspondents and areas of particular interest in mailing lists. That way, when you want to save something and examine it later, you'll have a specific place to look for it. You can respond to, add and delete files from your folder as easily as you can from the mailbox itself.

Folders are easy to establish. Use the **s** *filename* command to save the desired messages in a file. To manage the file, **mail** offers a **folder** command. Think of a folder as a message file that **mail** can manipulate with its standard commands. To move into it, you simply enter **folder** *filename,* which will load the messages in that folder into **mail;** this works the same way as calling up your **mbox** file.

What is the difference between saving to a regular file and saving to a folder? My **column** file is something I want to save for my own use, and I'm not worried about answering the messages in it or forwarding them to anyone else. Once I've saved messages to it, I'm content to manage **column** simply by downloading it regularly to my computer.

Folders, on the other hand, are meant to be handled by the **mail** program. The message that came in this morning might have a question you need to investigate before answering. Filing it in a folder would allow you to store it until you had discovered the right answer. Then, by using the **folder** command, you could use **mail**'s command structure to respond to the message. Think of folders as containing mail material that's still active, messages you may yet want to respond to or manipulate.

Changing folders is simply a matter of invoking the **folder** command with the new filename. A folder called **nets** is where I store messages about current happenings around the Internet, as sent to me by a mailing list called Arachnet. The folder **camelot** is set aside for matters Arthurian, as routed to me from a site in Edinburgh by a list called Camelot. Discussions of food and wine from the Foodwine mailing list reside in a folder called, not surprisingly, **foodwine.**

Responding to Messages

Responding to a message is simple. After reading it, use the **r** command (remember, your command operates on the current message). A lowercase **r** replies to the sender of the message only. An uppercase **R** replies to the sender and anyone else who received the letter. (As we'll see shortly, electronic mail can be sent to a wide group of people simultaneously.)

You'll immediately be asked for a subject. Try to be descriptive, but remember that you have limited space to work with. You want the subject field to make some sense. Having typed it in, you're ready to start your message. The bad news is that **mail**'s editing functions will likely disappoint you. Perhaps you've been writing letters with WordPerfect in the office, or composing that new novel with Microsoft Word for Windows. If so, prepare yourself for culture shock when you start writing with **mail.**

Just remember this. All you need to do at this point is type in your message. You must press **RETURN** at the end of each line. Work about two-thirds of the way across the screen before doing so and check the line for errors before you press **RETURN.** You'll notice that if you made a mistake in line 3 and you've already moved on to line 5, pressing the UP-arrow key will not get you back to line 3. You can, however, work backwards using the **BACKSPACE** key to correct an error on the current line.

Figure 7.3 shows a sample message, along with my reply to it. Note that at the end of the message, we're back at the **mail** command prompt. That's where the action starts.

Notice in the example in Figure 7.3 that it wasn't necessary to supply an address, nor to give a subject. **mail** does this automatically, letting us concentrate on what we have to say. Note, too, that a single period (**.**) ends our message and sends it on its way. Now we can move on to the next message.

Aborting a Message

Sometimes you regret saying something even as you write it, and decide not to send your message. If this happens, you can abort the message in mid-composition with **Ctrl-C** (hold down the **Control** key and press the letter **c**). You'll be prompted for whether you truly want to abort the message. A second **Ctrl-C** aborts it.

The following shows what the process looks like. I began to write a letter, and then changed my mind:

```
% mail pag@world.std.com
Subject: Project On the Rocks
Sorry the project didn't work out. I wonder, though, if you should
have                                        <Here I hit Ctrl-C
(Interrupt—one more to kill letter)
                                     <I hit Ctrl-C again
%                                    <And I'm back to the prompt
```

Figure 7.3
A message and a response.

```
From stroud@med.unc.edu Wed Dec  9 21:47:17 1992
Received: from med.unc.edu (durham.med.unc.edu) by rock.concert.net (5.59/
tas-rock/8-12-92)
id AA02317; Wed, 9 Dec 92 21:47:15 -0500
Received: from cahaba.med.unc.edu by med.unc.edu (4.1/SMI-4.0-ACB-1.0)
id AA13155; Wed, 9 Dec 92 21:48:30 EST
Received: by cahaba.med.unc.edu (4.1/SMI-4.1)
id AA04307; Wed, 9 Dec 92 21:48:21 EST
Date: Wed, 9 Dec 92 21:48:21 EST
From: stroud@med.unc.edu (Phillip Stroud)
Message-Id: ß00248.AA04307@med.unc.edu
To: gilster@rock.concert.net
Subject: Re:  Lunch Sites
Status: R

Pablo:

Yes, the inserted letter also came through. What the hell is Cyberspace?

Lisita


And here's my response:


& r

To: stroud@med.unc.edu
Subject: Re:  Inserted Letter

Lisita:

Cyberspace is just the oddball term for computer-generated
'places' like this network.  In other words, somebody with
a florid imagination would tell you that we are now talking
to each other via 'cyberspace connections.'  It's harmless
doubletalk, like so many computer terms.

Pablo
.
```

You can, incidentally, also abort a message with the **~q** command. More about this and related commands later.

Getting the Headers Back

As you work through your messages, it will occasionally be useful to get an overall view of what's in your mailbox. Maybe you've decided to go back in and delete unnecessary messages, or you want to move immediately to a particular message. The **h** command at the **mail** prompt will restore your list of message headings.

The Extremely Useful :n Command

You're reading through a long message and suddenly realize you don't have the remotest interest in it. Nonetheless, every time you get to the bottom of the screen, there's more message to go. What can you do?

Fortunately, the **mail** program provides for this eventuality. If you're stuck in a long message, enter **:n** and you will be returned to the **mail** prompt (**&**). NOTE: you don't have to press the **RETURN** key after the **:n** command; it will take effect as soon as you enter it. At the **mail** prompt, you can use the **d** command to delete the message and move on to the next, or exit **mail** altogether.

Sending New Messages

The best way to learn **mail** is to send practice messages to yourself. You can send a new message using the sequence **mail** *login@address* at the system prompt. Thus, to send myself a message, I'd enter **mail gilster@rock.con-cert.net,** after which I'd be prompted for a subject. After entering the subject, I type in my text. When finished, a single period (**.**) followed by another **RETURN** ends the message and sends it on its way.

```
% mail gilster@rock.concert.net
Subject: Learning the Ropes
Mail is easy to send; it's more difficult to manage.
```

All of which is to remind you that message management is the core of effective electronic mail.

The message you just sent should blast its way right through your system and pop up in your mailbox. Mail can be sent either from the **&** prompt (from inside **mail**) or the system command prompt; it's your choice.

Looking for Help

Remember that **mail** provides a help function, invoked by pressing the **?** key. Figure 7.4 shows what I see on-screen at CONCERT-CONNECT when I press this key at the **mail** command prompt.

The commands in Figure 7.4 are not the complete set. If you want to see the complete list, you can tap into the on-line manual which UNIX systems make available. Enter **man mail** to call up this storehouse of information as it pertains to the **mail** program. The output will be presented a screen at a time, allowing

Figure 7.4
A help screen in the
mail program.

```
cd [directory]              chdir to directory or home if none given
d [message list]            delete messages
e [message list]            edit messages
f [message list]            show from lines of messages
h                           print out active message headers
m [user list]               mail to specific users
n                           goto and type next message
p [message list]            print messages
pre [message list]          make messages go back to system mailbox
q                           quit, saving unresolved messages in mbox
r [message list]            reply to sender (only) of messages
R [message list]            reply to sender and all recipients of messages
s [message list] file       append messages to file
t [message list]            type messages (same as print)
top [message list]          show top lines of messages
u [message list]            undelete messages
v [message list]            edit messages with display editor
w [message list] file       append messages to file, without from line
x                           quit, do not change system mailbox
z [-]                       display next [previous] page of headers
!                           shell escape

A [message list] consists of integers, ranges of same, or user names separated
by spaces.  If omitted, Mail uses the current message.
```

you to page through it. This is convenient if you have time to read the manual on-line, but a print-out of the commands is preferable if your problem is complicated.

Using the Tilde Escape Commands

Let's talk about forwarding messages for a moment. You're reading your messages and come across one you'd like to pass along to a co-worker. This happens all the time on-line, for the networks are so big that we're constantly running across items of use to others. Recently a friend wanted to know how to get the manual pages for **mail** to scroll. Normally, the manual is set up so that you'll get its pages a screenful at a time, pressing the **SPACE BAR** to move to the next screen. My friend wanted to scroll the output and capture the result to disk, after which he would print it out.

I sent e-mail to the system administrator, who quickly sent the solution. You can save the **mail** section to a file with the command **man mail > filename.** I was then able to send to my friend the administrator's message embedded in a message of my own by using a series of special commands. These commands are preceded by the tilde character (~), common in the Spanish language where its presence above a letter indicates special pronounciation.

For our purposes, the tilde commands (sometimes called *tilde escapes*) help us with the process of sending messages. Here's how they worked in this case: starting a new message, I explained to my friend that I would include in the text the information he'd requested, in the form of a message sent to me from the system administrator. I then typed **~m,** a command that told **mail** to insert the system administrator's message into my letter. I added a few more comments at the end and sent the message on its way.

Keep in mind that your command acts on the current message, and in the case of inserting a previous message, it will insert whichever message is current. It's easy to perform the insertion, only to find to your dismay that you've enclosed the wrong letter. Needless to say, this could lead to some embarrassment. So be certain of what's current, or else insert the appropriate message number!

Figure 7.5 shows what **mail** looks like as you proceed to insert your text.

Note that I've used the **~m** command to insert message #2 in my **mbox** queue into my message. What I see is the statement **Interpolating: 2,** as the host computer puts the message where I want it. At the **(continue)** prompt, I finish my message and sign it. Then I use the **.** command followed by a **RETURN** to send it.

Figure 7.6 shows what the finished message will look like on the receiving end.

The tilde escape commands you'll need most are the following (remember you can generate the complete list with a **man mail** command).

~c   allows you to send a "carbon copy" of the message to another recipient

~b   allows "blind" carbon copies

~v   starts the **vi** editor

~p   displays the entire letter for review

~h   lists message headings, which can then be changed

~r   inserts a file into your letter

~q   cancels the letter you're writing

~m   includes the current message in your letter

~f   includes the current message in your letter

You'll note two sequences for inserting a message. The **~m** I used inserts a tab character in front of each line of the insert, which is what I wanted since I was quoting someone else's message, and the offset made that more clear. Using the **~f** command instead will insert the same text, but without the leading tabs.

Figure 7.5
A message with another being inserted inside it.

```
& mail stroud@med.unc.edu
Subject: Inserted Letter
Lisita:

This is an example of an inserted message.  I've read
the message from my correspondent, a fellow named
Scoville, and have forwarded it to you.

~m 2
Interpolating: 2
(continue)

Let me know if this reaches you.

Pablo
.
```

Figure 7.6
The final message with
insertion.

```
To: stroud@med.unc.edu
Subject: Inserted Letter

Lisa:

This is an example of an inserted message.  I've read
the message from my correspondent, a fellow named
Scoville, and have forwarded it to you.

     From rscovill Tue Dec  8 07:06:34 1992
     Received: by rock.concert.net (5.59/tas-rock/8-12-92)
     id AA25229; Tue, 8 Dec 92 07:06:33 -0500
     Date: Tue, 8 Dec 92 07:06:33 -0500
     From: Richard P Scoville -- Scoville Associates

     Message-Id: Ÿ81206.AA25229@rock.concert.net
     To: gilster@rock.concert.net
     Subject: Cyberspace
     Status: RO

     Got your most recent message. Now I know where DOS got the "" symbol
     for piping stuff to files! (Or is that vice versa?)

     Anyhow, on to cyberspace!

     Richard


Let me know if this reaches you.
Paul
```

Another important point: you must always insert the tilde escape commands at the far left margin of the page. Otherwise, they won't work.

The following sections provide a closer look at the tilde escape commands.

CARBON COPIES

What if I want to send mail to more than one user? **mail** lets you create a **Cc:** field in the outgoing message area. Anyone you list on this line will receive a copy of the same message. Use the **~c** command anywhere in the message (but as with all the tilde escape commands, be sure you enter it at the left margin). Entering **~c gilster@rock.concert.net** sends me a copy of the message you're currently writing. On the other hand, if you don't want the message to be circulated elsewhere, just press the **RETURN** key at this line.

You may find **Cc:** set up as a default on your system, so that the **mail** program prompts for carbon copies whenever you compose a letter. If you'd prefer to have this option activated, a line can be added to **.mailrc**, a UNIX file containing defaults for your mail system; you can do this with the **vi** text editor we'll discuss later.

Another form of carbon copy is accessible through the **~b** command. It creates so-called *blind carbon copies* which go out to a list of recipients just like the conventional copies; the difference is, people who receive blind carbons don't know who else received the message. The sequence **~b** creates the blind carbon capability.

The following is an example of setting up a blind carbon (the same procedure applies for a regular carbon copy):

```
% mail pag@world.std.com
Subject: Meeting Announcement
~b stroud@med.unc.edu
Don't forget the July 16th meeting at The Columns!
.
%
```

Note how this works. After entering the subject, I include a **~b** command followed (after a single space) by the address of the person to whom I want to send a blind carbon copy. The address must be on the same line for this to work—don't enter the tilde escape command and then press **RETURN.**

CALLING UP AN EDITOR

As you work with **mail**'s command structure, you may sometimes find yourself wishing for more features, particularly the ability to go back and rewrite that awkward sentence in the second paragraph, or to fix that misspelled word in line 3. This is where the **~v** command comes into play. Inserting the command at the far left of the screen while you're composing e-mail will call up the **vi** editor program. The lines you've already typed will appear in **vi,** ready to be edited, and you can add additional material as you choose. When you finish writing, exit **vi** by entering **ESC** followed by **:wq** and a RETURN and you will return to the **mail** program. You'll then need to type a period (**.**) to send your message on its way.

The following example shows what a mail message looks like as I begin to compose, and then switch into **vi:**

```
% mail pag@world.std.com
Subject: Showing Off vi
This is designed to illustrate what happens when you use the ~v command
to switch into the vi text editor. I will insert ~v on the far left
margin on the line immediately below.
~v
```

By adding a **RETURN** after the **~v,** I move directly into the **vi** editor. What I have composed so far is already on-screen and is shown in Figure 7.7. I can now edit what I've already written or add to it.

The command structure of **vi** and other text editors is beyond the scope of this book. But remember that you can use the **man** command for further information. Thus **man vi** will call up the basic commands; they're not intuitive, but you'll learn them fairly quickly as you put them to use. I think you'll agree that basic text editors are not a strong point of UNIX systems.

PREVIEWING THE RESULTS

I can't stress enough that you must review the results of your tilde escape commands. Inserting the wrong letter into a sensitive missive can lead to problems. Fortunately, **mail** contains another command, **~p,** which allows you to preview the message. Assume I've just inserted a file into a letter I'm composing. By typing **~p** at the left margin, I get a preview, as the **mail** program

Figure 7.7
Working on a message
with the **vi** editor.

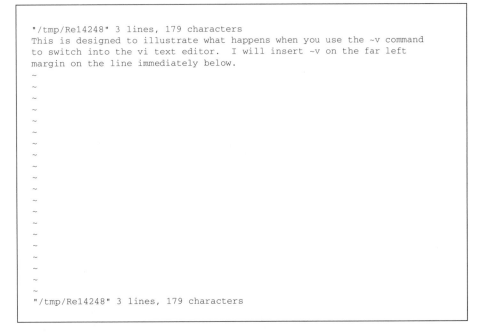

```
"/tmp/Re14248" 3 lines, 179 characters
This is designed to illustrate what happens when you use the ~v command
to switch into the vi text editor.  I will insert ~v on the far left
margin on the line immediately below.
~
~
~
~
~
~
~
~
~
~
~
~
~
~
~
~
~
"/tmp/Re14248" 3 lines, 179 characters
```

scrolls through the letter. When it finishes scrolling, I can either add to the letter or send the letter as is. But now I'm assured it is correct.

CHANGING HEADERS

Another tilde escape command, **~h,** is useful for those times when you're involved in a sequence of back and forth mail conversations. Maybe you began an on-line messaging session with a letter whose subject was "Concert Last Night," in which you solicited opinions on how the local symphony performed. After that subject played itself out, you and your correspondent moved on in a series of e-mail exchanges to discuss his job prospects, the firing of the new supervisor, and the Yankees-Red Sox game last Saturday. As you read and replied to your correspondent's letters, all the mail was still going out and coming back under the heading "Concert Last Night."

You could, of course, simply send a new message with a new subject. But why go to the trouble? Reading the current message, you can go to the left margin and do a **~h** command. Now you'll be prompted as shown in Figure 7.8.

Note what happened here. When I typed the **~h** command, I was prompted with the headers of the message as they were presently constituted. I could use the **RETURN** key to cycle through them until I came to the subject header, which was the one I had decided to change. I backspaced to remove the original header and supplanted it with a new one. I was then given the **(continue)** prompt, at which point I used a single period followed by a **RETURN** to send the letter.

MAILING FILES

As you become more proficient with on-line commands, you'll use **mail's** forwarding capabilities more and more. A friend of mine shares my interest in portable computing, but because of a busy work schedule, had not been

Figure 7.8
Changing message
headers.

```
& mail stroud@med.unc.edu
Subject: Changing Headers

Lisa:

You're going through all this mail wondering when I'm going
to get to the good stuff!  I'm going to keep you wondering.
For now, this is nothing more than an example of how
to change headers.  If I do it right, you won't see
anything in the Subject field except 'New Title.'  Let
me know if it works.

Paul
~h
To: stroud@med.unc.edu
Subject: New Title
Cc:
Bcc:
(continue)
.
```

following events in the industry as closely as she would have liked. Having just completed a column on the subject, I wanted to pass it along, so I saved the column as a file and moved it into the **mail** program. There, I began a message to her and used the **~r** command to insert the file into the message. Since my file was called **column.210,** I sent it with the command **~r column.210.**

Figure 7.9 shows what this looked like.

Again, I see a statement that my file has been added into the message ("**column.210**"); the number of lines and characters in the message is also included. I add after this a final comment and send the message with a period (**.**). On the receiving end, my correspondent sees what is shown in Figure 7.10 (I leave out the superfluous header information).

CREATING A SIGNATURE FILE

As you begin to accumulate e-mail in your mailbox, you'll notice that many correspondents use electronic signatures. Some of these are relatively spare,

Figure 7.9
Mailing a file to
another user.

```
% mail stroud@med.unc.edu
Subject: Recent Computer Column

Lisa:

Here's a computer column I wrote recently.  I'm sending it
to demonstrate how to enclose a file within a letter..

Paul

~r column.210
"column.210" 127/7213
Let me know if this gets through OK.
.
```

Figure 7.10
The letter with a
portion of the inserted
file.

```
Lisa:

Here's a computer column I wrote recently.  I'm sending it
to demonstrate how to enclose a file within a letter.

Paul


    The word out of Las Vegas, where an estimated 145,000
attended the annual Comdex computer show, is that mobile
computing ruled the roost.  Its prevalence was inevitable,
given the fact that computing is about to enter a second,
and far more problematic, wave of growth.  Getting
corporations up to speed on distributed computing was the
theme of the '80s.  Now computers must move into the field...
[and so on].
```

including no more than a name and phone number. Some can be quite elaborate, with inset ASCII figures, and quotations from various sources. Sometimes, in fact, the signature section of a message can be longer than the message itself. But it's not considered good Internet form to work with overly long signatures, which take up unnecessary storage space. So if you're thinking of creating a signature of your own, keep it to the point. Four lines is a reasonable size.

Here's a sample of a signature which could be attached to any electronic message I send:

```
Paul A. Gilster     gilster@rock.concert.net       CompuServe 73537,656
          919-782-5947 (voice)       919-782-7024 (fax)
"Few things are harder to put up with than the annoyance of a good example."
                                                    —Mark Twain
```

To create an electronic signature, you can use **mail**'s **~r** command to insert the appropriate text. The idea is to compose your signature box as you want it to appear and then save it as an ASCII file on your system. Then, as you compose a letter, you can use an **~r** command at the end to insert the signature into the message. Other mail programs, as we'll see, make this process somewhat easier.

EXITING LETTERS

As mentioned before, a **Ctrl-C** aborts the message in progress; a second one returns you to the **mail** program's prompt. But there's another way of exiting which may save you trouble, particularly in those cases where you have composed a partial letter and would like to continue it later. The **~q** command makes this possible. Entering it at the far left margin while you're composing a letter will save the letter you're composing in a file named **dead.letter.** This is helpful, because now you can go back and finish the letter at a later time. Unlike the **mbox** file, **dead.letter** doesn't accumulate abandoned mail. The next time you cancel a letter, the old letter is replaced by the new cancellation.

Handling Longer Messages

Simple messages are one thing, but what if you need to send something more meaty? The easiest solution may be to write your message out in your favorite word processor, save it as a straight ASCII file, and send it along to your recipient. If you're dialing in, this involves uploading the file to your host system first.

We covered file downloading and uploading in Chapter 5 on FTP procedures. You could, for example, compose a file called **story.doc.** Saving it as an ASCII file, you could upload it to your service provider's computer through the command **xmodem rt.**

Once the file is present at your service provider, using mail to send it along to your recipient is a simple matter. The format is **mail address <filename.** Thus **mail stroud@med.unc.edu <burgundy.txt** sends my file on Burgundian vineyards to the address listed.

Setting Up an Alias

There's no need to work with complicated addresses even though you're using a fairly austere program like **mail.** It's easy enough to set up a shortened address which you can use over and over again. This can be a real time-saver, since entering an address as long as **gilster@rock.concert.net** every time you want to write this person, and making the inevitable typing mistakes, can be a pain in the neck. How to proceed? The UNIX file **.mailrc** is where you need to make the changes. You can edit this file with the editor you use on your system, which, at least for starters, will probably be **vi.**

If you enter a quick **ls** command at your service provider's command prompt (asking to see a directory listing), you won't see **.mailrc.** That's because it's a hidden file. But enter an **ls -a** command and you'll see it and other hidden files. Look at the difference between the two commands on my system. First, here's an **ls:**

```
% ls
Mail/     core     mbox      xmodem.log
News/     ftp/     world.ps.Z
%
```

The names with the backslash trailing them are directories; those that stand alone are files. Now we'll do an **ls -a:**

```
% ls -a
./        .gopherrc*    .newsrc      Mail/     world.ps.Z
../       .gopherrc~*   .oldnewsrc   News/     xmodem.log
.article  .letter       .pnewsexpert  core
.cshrc*   .login        .rnlast      ftp/
.elm/     .mailrc       .rnsoft      mbox
%
```

As you can see, the **ls -a** list is a good bit longer, showing more files and directories. Among the files is the one we're looking for, **.mailrc.** Figure 7.11 shows what **.mailrc** looks like when called up into the **vi** editor. I've just added an alias comment.

Figure 7.11
Editing **.mailrc** with
the **vi** editor.

```
% vi .mailrc
".mailrc" 2 lines, 25 characters
set crt=24
set autoprint
alias chris "Chris Allen<callen@tc.cornell.edu>"
~
~
~
~
~
~
~
~
~
~
~
~
~
~
~
~
~
~
".mailrc" 3 lines, 59 characters
```

The idea behind the alias is this. From now on, the line **alias chris "Chris Allen<callen@tc.cornell.edu>"** will allow me to reach this person by simply entering **mail chris** instead of entering the whole address. The alias is handy for frequent correspondents and makes the job of using **mail** that much easier. But make sure you've printed out the **vi** commands before you try any editing. **vi** can be very frustrating to use!

Keeping Your Mailbox Tidy

You'll use the **mail** program to keep your mailbox tidy. That's an easy lesson to learn. Leaving town for what was to have been a short holiday, I was unavoidably detained for over a week. When I returned and logged on to my Internet account, I found 632 messages waiting for me in my mailbox! This is what people mean by "information glut," and it can make dealing with mail an odious proposition unless you know how to handle the overload.

The solution to a mailbox groaning with the weight of hundreds of messages is obvious: read the headers and decide which messages look interesting to you. Scuttle the rest. You already know how to delete files, so a quick **d 4** can dispatch message #4 with a minimum of fuss. Entering **d 6 8 23-29** gets rid of those messages, etc. Note that you can specify a range of messages for deletion.

Be ruthless. You can, of course, work through your messages one by one, but 632 messages in one mailbox makes that a losing proposition. A better way is to jump around. Entering the number of the message that interests you lets you read it. To check the headers again, it's a simple matter to return to **mail**'s command prompt (**&**) at the end of a message and enter an **h,** which puts the headers back up for your perusal. In this way, culling messages of questionable interest, you can pare your mailbox down to size.

Exiting mail

Enter **q** when you've finished reading a particular message and you'll be returned to the **&** prompt. A second **q** will then exit the **mail** program altogether, returning you to the main system prompt. When you do this, all unread mail will be saved in your system mailbox. Any mail that you left undeleted will be saved in the **mbox** file in your home directory.

There's also another way to leave **mail.** Using the **x** command, you can leave **mail** without making any changes to your files. This method also preserves any deleted messages.

INTERNET ADDRESSING—THE LONG WAY HOME

Internet addresses are intimidating to the newcomer, and for good reason. They're long, and they're embedded in a welter of supplementary information that can make the header of a new message longer than the message itself. Look at the example in Figure 7.12, straight out of my mailbox.

Let's take this message header apart. If you look at the top line, marked **From:**, you'll see the Internet address **stroud@med.unc.edu.** We examined domain names in Chapter 2, and this one isn't too difficult to figure out. The **.edu** statement at the far right tells us it's from an educational institution. **unc** is the University of North Carolina at Chapel Hill. **med** in this case refers to the medical school there, and **stroud** is the user name of the person who sent the message. Remember the principle: Internet names go from the most specific,

Figure 7.12
Headers can sometimes overwhelm the message they identify.

```
Message  1:
From stroud@med.unc.edu Thu Apr  1 15:00:48 1993
Return-Path:
@med.unc.edu
Received: from med.unc.edu (durham.med.unc.edu) by world.std.com (5.65c/Spike-
2.0)
    id AA10422; Thu, 1 Apr 1993 15:00:44 -0500
Received: from cahaba.med.unc.edu by med.unc.edu (4.1/SMI-4.0-ACB-1.0)
    id AA02785; Thu, 1 Apr 93 15:02:24 EST
Received: by cahaba.med.unc.edu (4.1/SMI-4.1)
    id AA14297; Thu, 1 Apr 93 15:02:22 EST
Date: Thu, 1 Apr 93 15:02:22 EST
From: stroud@med.unc.edu (Phillip Stroud)
Message-Id: p12002.AA14297@cahaba.med.unc.edu
To: pag@world.std.com
Subject: Re:  Mail Site Problems
Status: R

Paul:

HELP! I'm in the midst of planning a silver wedding anniversary party for
Phil's Dad and stepmother this Saturday for about 100 guests.

So Wednesday won't work.  How about lunch one day the week after
next?
```

the user name, to the most general. As you can see, the name and address are followed by the date and time the message was sent.

What does **Received:** stand for? If you're a technological purist and insist on knowing through what portals a message has passed, these references provide your clues. In this case, the message was routed from the University of North Carolina through a machine called **cahaba** and passed along to my account at The World (**world.std.com**). This information falls into the "nice to know" category; you'll have no need to work with it. In fact, many mail programs simply filter it out; it is of little use to learn that a message was passed through particular computers en route, as long as you are able to read the message and respond to it.

The date appears next—this is the date and time the message was actually sent, as opposed to when it first entered the system (the date and time shown in the first line). The **From:** address is the address you should reply to. In this case, it's the same as the address in the first line, but in many cases, a message may contain an address that shows you where the mail is coming from, as opposed to who sent it.

Message-ID:? Every message identification number is unique, but like routing information, it's of use to UNIX wizards and no one else. **To:** is obvious—it's the address of the recipient and is followed by the subject of the communication in question. If you see a header marked **Cc:,** it's a listing of additional addresses where the message has gone. The good news is, even the simplest mail programs, such as the next one we'll look at, take care of the necessary routing information. Usually, all you'll want to do is check the "From:" and "Subject:" headers as you glance through your mailbox to find out which messages are really worth reading.

You'll occasionally encounter a different kind of tag, an exclamation point (!), which UNIX purists refer to as a "bang." It might look like this: **uunet!check-mate!crk.** When you see the exclamation point, you know you are dealing with a UUCP account. None of this matters to you, the end user, unless you have two address possibilities. Because many UUCP sites are now listing Internet domain names, it's best to try the Internet addressing scheme when you're trying to reach someone. UUCP routing is more restrictive and can fail when a machine somewhere along the line goes down.

Internet routing strategies sound complicated and they are if you examine them from the level of a network administrator. But mastering their intricacies demands nothing more than a few basic principles, knowledge of which can connect you to Internet sites worldwide and to a host of other computer networks. The most exciting thing about Internet e-mail for dial-up users is that this network is now linking up so seamlessly with other networks, including the big commercial providers, that someday you may be able to do everything on-line with a single network address, instead of the variety some of us now use.

Every day, for example, I read and respond to my Internet mail before moving on to check the various news groups I use to keep up on events in the computer industry and elsewhere. Later in the day, I'll use the Internet's Telnet capabilities (discussed in Chapter 6), to log on to BIX, a popular on-line service known for the high level of computer expertise available on it. Checking my mail and messages there, I'll move on to DELPHI, where an active user group now follows Internet developments and participates in network exploration through FTP and Telnet linkages.

Telnet features and file downloading are not electronic mail, of course, and the commercial networks vary in their ability to exchange messages one to one. But the trend is clear. Right now we sail through islands of computer connectivity, pausing where we find something interesting, then moving on to the next island for a fresh look. We're moving toward the gradual firming up of trade routes between those islands, to the point where it won't matter whether you consider your primary account to be on the Internet or on CompuServe or DELPHI or MCI Mail. Through information gateways, your explorations will be world-wide.

The next chapter specifically addresses how to use Internet mail gateways from commercial providers. If your sole entry into the Internet is through a CompuServe or an America Online by means of e-mail, be sure to read that chapter.

HITTING A BRICK WALL

It's not surprising that sometimes, despite your best efforts, things go awry with electronic mail. Because they're complicated, e-mail addresses can fall victim to typographical errors. For that matter, you may simply have your information wrong, and get the address confused, giving someone the wrong domain name or mistaking his or her user name at the site. The Internet mail system will bounce the message right back to you. Along with the failed mail will be a message advising you on the nature of the problem. Figure 7.13 shows what happened to me when I got the user name wrong and sent to a nonexistent address.

Figure 7.13
Results of a mistaken address entry.

```
From gilster Fri Apr  2 16:43:37 1993
Received: by rock.concert.net (5.59/tas-rock/8-12-92)
        id AA18818; Fri, 2 Apr 93 16:43:32 -0500
Date: Fri, 2 Apr 93 16:43:32 -0500
From: Mail Delivery Subsystem AILER-DAEMON
Subject: Returned mail: User unknown
Message-Id: p22143.AA18818@rock.concert.net
To: gilster
Status: R

   ----- Transcript of session follows -----
> RCPT To: arlot@world.std.com
< 550  arlot@world.std.com... User unknown
550 narlot@world.std.com... User unknown

   ----- Unsent message follows -----
Received: by rock.concert.net (5.59/tas-rock/8-12-92)
        id AA18816; Fri, 2 Apr 93 16:43:32 -0500
Date: Fri, 2 Apr 93 16:43:32 -0500
From: Paul A Gilster -- Computer Focus gilster
Message-Id: p22143.AA18816@rock.concert.net
To: narlot@world.std.com
Subject: Test Message

Test.  Please ignore.

&
```

What to do when you have a message returned? The example in Figure 7.13 involved an addressing error. The host computers were unable to locate the person I was mailing to. My mistake, but at least the mail came back. I realized the message had not been delivered, and was then able to contact the person in question to correct the addressing problem. This kind of mistake can occur with people we already correspond with. Used to entering the **r** command to reply and letting **mail** supply the correct address, we forget what that address is when we decide to send new mail to the same user.

Mail sometimes disappears for other reasons. Remember, an active Internet user receives a large number of messages every day. Perhaps the subject on your message wasn't as clear as it should have been; a busy person might simply delete such mail without realizing what it was. Don't assume bad motives on the part of those who don't always respond to all their mail. We all do our best, but I can tell you for a fact how easy it is to overlook a particular message when you're not looking out for it in the first place. If the message is important, resend it. And be sure to make your subject heading germane.

A Brief Look at elm

elm is an electronic mail system developed by Dave Taylor, of Hewlett-Packard Laboratories in Palo Alto, CA, and tweaked by the Elm Development Group. As opposed to the line-oriented **mail** program, **elm** can be configured to let you work full-time with a full-screen text editor like **vi. elm** is also readily customizable; you can manipulate many of its operating characteristics by making additions or changes to a file called **elmrc.** This file is located in the *.elm* directory branching off from your home directory (the *.elm* directory is created when you invoke **elm** for the first time). Chances are your system makes **elm** available; most of the UNIX service providers I consulted for this book offer it along with **mail** and, frequently, other mail programs.

The best way to get a feel for **elm** is to call it up by entering **elm** at your service provider's prompt. When you do this, you should see a screen filled with your incoming mail, much like the one shown in Figure 7.14.

Among the most helpful commands for new users is the help option, invoked with the question mark (**?**) key. But as you can see, the basic **elm** commands are far from difficult—they're laid out for you at the bottom of the screen.

I prefer this list of waiting messages to the interface **mail** offers; it's easier to read, although it provides much of the same information. At the top of the screen is the location of the mailbox, along with the number of messages in it and the **elm** version number. Read from left to right to determine information about the individual messages. Let's look at one in particular:

```
N   4   Apr 5  Chris Allen      (28)    Re:  UNIX Question
```

The status field is at the far left; in this case, the **N** indicates a message that hasn't yet been read. Like **mail, elm** may supply a variety of letters here, including **O** for a message which is not new but has not yet been read, and **D** for a deleted message, among other options.

Following the status field is the message number in the queue; this message is #4, and it was sent on 5 April. The number 28 in parentheses indicates the

Figure 7.14
An opening **elm**
screen with waiting
mail.

```
Mailbox is '/usr/spool/mail/gilster' with 7 messages [ELM 2.3 PL11]


    N  1    Apr 5   Jefferey H. Taylor  (38)    Vatican Exhibit...limited progress r
    N  2    Apr 5   Mike Banks          (19)    Re: Book Clarified
    N  3    Apr 5   JAMES OLSON / UNIV  (143)   Westmont College
    N  4    Apr 5   Chris Allen         (28)    Re:  UNIX Question
    N  5    Apr 5   jayne levin         (31)    Re: Commercial Internet Uses
    N  6    Apr 5   Wesley J. Kaufmann  (35)    Where can you get IEEE specs?
    N  7    Apr 5   Rebecca Wetzel      (38)    NEARnet Description








    You can use any of the following commands by pressing the first character;
    d)elete or u)ndelete mail, m)ail a message, r)eply or f)orward mail, q)uit
     To read a message, press <return>. j = move down, k = move up, ? = help

    Command:
```

total number of lines in the message, while the final field shows the message subject.

On the level of the individual message, **elm** shows off more of its advantages. Figure 7.15, for example, is a message I retrieved by putting the inverse video marker on message 4 above.

One of the great virtues of **elm** is that it can simplify what you see, uncluttering your screen. Figure 7.16, for example, is the same message as displayed by the **mail** program.

As you can see, **elm** has removed extraneous header information, making it easier to concentrate on the message at hand, and tying up less of your time scrolling material you don't need.

Responding to messages is equally simple. Entering an **r** at the **Command:** prompt causes **elm** to prompt us as follows:

```
Command: Reply to message                        Copy message? (y/n) n
```

Answering with a **y** lets you easily copy the message into the message you're about to send, if you so desire. You're then asked for a subject:

```
Subject of message: Re:  UNIX Question
```

You can accept the current subject with a **RETURN,** or enter a new one. Finally, **elm** asks if we want to send copies:

```
Copies to:
```

Pressing **RETURN** sends the message only to the person who sent the original.

Figure 7.15
A message being read
with **elm**.

```
Message 5/8  From Chris Allen                    Apr 5 '93 at 11:53 am -240


Date: Mon, 5 Apr 1993 11:53:08 -0400
To: gilster@rock.concert.net
Subject: Re:  UNIX Question

        Ah!  Glad to help.  That was the best explanation you've seen?  Where
else have you seen explanations?

        Talk to ya later...

chris
---
            Chris Allen            callen@tc.cornell.edu

 Command ('i' to return to index):
```

Now **elm** puts you into the editor you've chosen for your on-line work
(configurable through **elmrc**) and lets you write your message. Having sent this
reply, you can proceed to the next message with a **RETURN,** or move back to
the main screen by pressing the **i** key. This will give you the screen with waiting
mail, showing any deletions you've made, and indicating which messages you've
read and which you still have to read. When you're ready to exit, the **x** command
returns you to your service provider's command prompt.

I'm particularly fond of the way **elm** can be customized. By calling up the
.elmrc file in **vi,** I can make numerous changes to the way **elm** does business.

Figure 7.16
The same message as
displayed by **mail**.

```
Message  4:
From callen@TC.Cornell.EDU Mon Apr  5 11:53:10 1993
Received: from theory.TC.Cornell.EDU by rock.concert.net (5.59/tas-rock/8-12-920
Received: by theory.TC.Cornell.EDU id AA21919
  (5.65c/IDA-1.4.4 for gilster@rock.concert.net); Mon, 5 Apr 1993 11:53:08 -0400
From: Chris Allen allen@TC.Cornell.EDU
Message-Id: Ž4051553.AA21919@theory.TC.Cornell.EDU
To: gilster@rock.concert.net
Subject: Re:  UNIX Question
Status: RO

        Ah!  Glad to help.  That was the best explanation you've seen?  Where
else have you seen explanations?

        Talk to ya later...

chris
---
            Chris Allen            callen@tc.cornell.edu
```

It's a simple matter, for example, to get the program to display a signature after each message I write, just as it is to customize the header information supplied in each message I send. I can also choose which pager program I want to use to display messages, pick the text editor I prefer (the default is a line-oriented editor very similar to the one in the **mail** system), set up aliases for frequent correspondents, and change the prompts that appear when I send messages out. Many more options are available.

The full range of **elm** options is too extensive to summarize here; my intent is simply to give you a quick look at **elm,** and to encourage you to explore the wide range of mail programs out there once you master the basic **mail** program. Intimidating at first, the UNIX shell begins to win your respect when you realize how you can tailor it to meet your own needs. **elm** is distributed with *The Elm Users Guide* and the *Elm Reference Guide,* among other documents. You'll want to explore your service provider's system and ask questions about the availability of these materials.

If **elm** is available on your system, you can also examine these options by using the **man elm** command. You may also be interested in getting further information about the **elm** mailer through an on-line document.

••

 What You Need: A Basic Document on Using **elm**

The Document: **Frequently Asked Questions: elm**

How to Get It: This list of Frequently Asked Question, or FAQ, is regularly posted in two USENET newsgroups: **comp.mail.elm** and **news.answers.** We'll learn how to access USENET newsgroups in Chapter 11. Alternatively, you can use anonymous FTP to retrieve this file. The FTP site is **rtfm.mit.edu.** The directory is *pub/usenet/news.answers/elm,* and the file name is **FAQ.**

••

ELECTRONIC MAIL MANNERS

Electronic mail forces us to use the alphabet and our wits to communicate, but writing skills, as demonstrated by SAT scores and other measures, have reached an all-time low. This decrease in writing ability has a direct impact on the quality of electronic mail. If we write worse than ever before but more and more of us are attempting to communicate using the written word, the result can be misunderstanding, gaffes, poor judgment, bad taste, and a variety of other *faux pas.* You have to expect this with electronic mail and be prepared to overlook some of the more glaring examples.

Little can be done about overt attempts to offend; thankfully, they're not all that common. But precisely because so many of the misunderstandings commonly found in electronic mail are inadvertent, it's useful to bear a set of rules in mind as you master this medium. Before long, the niceties of network behavior will be obvious from experience, but until then, adhering to these simple guidelines will ensure you get off to the right start.

Use Humor with Caution. Don't be misled—humor is more than welcome on the Internet, as a glance through the USENET newsgroup **alt.best.of.internet** will quickly confirm. Judicious use of humor can brighten anyone's day, particularly those of us who spend the majority of our time in front of computer screens.

But be careful. The recipient of your message may not appreciate the sly dig which you, innocently enough, intended as a cheery *double entendre*. Sure, you just finished reading a Henry James novel, and your prose is honed to an incisive clarity that's the envy of your peers. But maybe your recipient prefers *TV Guide*, is in a bad mood this morning, and wouldn't recognize irony if it hit him broadside. How well do you know this person, anyway?

Because innocent epistles can so readily create discord, many people on the Internet, along with the various commercial networks, fall back on a set of pointers to make it clear when they're trying to be funny. The list of these so-called "emoticons" is huge, but the one that's well-nigh universal is some type of smiling face. An imaginative use of the ASCII character set creates it:

:-)

Read it sideways and you've got the picture. Or maybe you'd want to suggest a fine-tuned *bon mot* followed by a wink. A simple character change handles it:

;-)

Try this sentence, with and without an emoticon:

```
Your reference wasn't exactly up-to-date.
```

versus

```
Your reference wasn't exactly up-to-date :-)
```

Or how about this:

```
I doubt Fred was aware of our conversation
```

which suggests a simple fact, versus

```
I doubt Fred was aware of our conversation ;-)
```

which suggests a nod and a conspiratorial wink. And then there's:

```
I doubt Fred was aware of our conversation :-(
```

a way of indicating our disappointment. We can even draw a crude portrait of ourselves as an emoticon:

```
Here's how I might look if wearing glasses and a goatee 8->
```

The set of emoticons has grown to gigantic proportions, a collection of electronic happy and sad-faces too long to recount here. Read a little mail, browse through some USENET news groups, and you'll soon get up to speed with emoticons in all their variety. Then ponder whether or not you want to use them.

What's wrong with emoticons? Those of us who love language find them disturbing. They suggest that their users don't know how to express themselves without the most obvious gesticulating, like the guy who accents every point he makes by waving his arms and making faces. The flip side is that emoticons sometimes take the sting off what might seem a pointed remark. And because, as we use the Internet, we are typing out more messages at greater speed than ever before, it makes sense to take what measures we can to avoid conflict. It's your call.

Be concise. When you write an electronic message to someone, you're asking for a piece of that person's time. Remember what your English teacher told you—say what you have to say with a minimum of verbiage. This doesn't mean you can't enjoy conversations with friends on the topic of your choice, but if you're writing someone you don't already know, remember that your message may be one of hundreds that go through that person's mailbox every day. Most people move from initial wonderment at the capabilities of electronic mail to a sense of being bombarded on days when there are just too many messages to handle in too little time. A short, tight message is more likely to get results.

Make Your References Clear. There's nothing quite so frustrating as receiving a message that says something like "Thanks for the information, but can you clarify what you mean in the third paragraph?" You can't remember who this person is, what information you sent, or what you may or may not have said in the third paragraph. Loose references like these may work if you're only talking to one or two on-line acquaintances, but they quickly become impractical when your list of contacts grows.

Most e-mail software makes provisions for quoting a message so you can avoid this confusion. As we've seen, **mail** lets you incorporate a previous message in the current one, and other programs offer a variety of similar options. Often, the inserted text will be enclosed in brackets, telling you it's your original comment; the text is then followed by whatever thoughts your correspondent has on the subject.

Consider the following message.

```
It's the 23rd. Same place as usual—Fred.
```

This may mean nothing whatsoever to you. However, the following message has meaning.

```
<<I wonder if you know the date of the meteorology seminar?  I've lost my invita-
tion.>>
It's the 23rd. Same place as usual—Fred.
```

The latter is clear, quoting the original question and providing the answer. The key is to avoid ambiguity, to handle the communication in one pass, rather than forcing one party to send yet another message asking to be reminded of the original question.

Don't Waste Bandwidth. Inserting text from a previous message, as in the previous example, can make things clearer. But anyone who has been on the networks for a time has received messages where lengthy e-mail was quoted in its entirety, and for absolutely no reason. The point about quoting is that it pinpoints the area in question. Why enclose an entire message if that message only contains one question needing an answer in the first place?

So be sparing with your quotes even though **mail** doesn't make this as easy as it should. You have to use the **~m** or **~f** command to move text from a previous message into your message. If the message was a long one and you want to pare it down, you have no choice but to call up an editor and edit it. Other mail packages offer different solutions, which is why the search for the perfect mail program is an ongoing one.

Be Discrete. There are any number of ways other people might see what you have entered in your message, so be cautious. If you're pondering saying something you consider absolutely private, talk yourself out of it. Handle that kind of communication in person. Chances are that 99 percent of your electronic mail will reach its destination in utter privacy, but who knows?

Electronic mail and fax machines have this in common: they're both more public than many people realize. The explosion of technology has given us tremendous new tools, but the price of their newfound power is our inability to properly secure them from prying eyes. How often has a critical business proposition been discussed through a fax machine? And how often is the fax left sitting in a place where any number of inquisitive office workers might read incoming material before it gets to the actual recipient? How many electronic mail messages have been read by the wrong person because somewhere along the line a computer routing the message wasn't sufficiently secure?

Don't Get Too Elaborate. Some people have an irresistible urge to pull out all the stops when writing electronic mail or posting messages to USENET. They'll shift back and forth from all caps to all lowercase and any mixture in between. They'll draw odd ASCII pictures that may or may not be decipherable. They'll have so much fun composing the message that they forget the person at the receiving end may want to get on with the day's work and is in no mood for buffoonery.

Know your audience. Special effects can have results different than those desired. Using all capital letters can suggest aggression, as in a shouting match. MAYBE YOU DON'T THINK SO, BUT I DO! In any case, getting the message across with clarity is the fundamental precept of electronic mail.

Choose Your Subjects Wisely. Being as clear and concise as possible in the subject field of your message means the person who receives it can readily decide what to do with the message. Put yourself in that person's shoes. With little time to spare and numerous messages waiting in the mailbox, the recipient wants to know which messages really need attention and which can be deleted quickly in a pinch. A carefully chosen subject will help the recipient keep a tidy mailbox, and you'll also appreciate the effort when you look through your own mail and know exactly what you have waiting.

··

Electronic Mail
as a Gateway
to the Internet

File Transfer Protocol and electronic mail are both key components of Internet connectivity, but what do you do if you only have an Internet mail connection? After all, with the exception of DELPHI and BIX the major commercial on-line services offer only mail connectivity. Fortunately, your on-line mailbox with a commercial provider like CompuServe or GEnie can become a true gateway into the Internet. You won't be able to accomplish everything—in particular, Telnet simply can't be managed by mail alone—but if you are looking for files, you'll be pleased to know you can use electronic mail to retrieve them, without needing to employ FTP procedures yourself.

This chapter is devoted to people with accounts on the CompuServes and GEnies of this world. Let's be clear on this: the optimum connection for a dial-up user is a full-access account with an Internet service provider, because it gives you the ability to use all three key Internet protocols—e-mail, FTP, and Telnet. But maybe you're hoping to shop around on the Internet first, to see what's available. Or perhaps you use CompuServe daily and would like to streamline your operations, running everything through your CompuServe account. Whatever the case, if you have the need to transfer files by mail, you can do it. The solution is workable, and while it's not exactly elegant, it does what you want it to do.

RETRIEVING FILES BY MAIL

You can take several different approaches to using the Internet by mail. It's possible to run a complete FTP routine, sending commands to a remote computer and having it process the request. It's also possible to tap the resources of a specialized mail server, whose job it is to maintain repositories of information, most of it textual in nature, and send requested documents to electronic mail addresses.

Specialized Mail Servers

For a look at mail servers, let's go to the INTERNIC Directory and Database Services site, maintained by AT&T as a "Directory of Directories" about Internet information. The address is **mailserv@ds.internic.net.** Retrieving files from this site is simple; you use the **file** command in the body of your message. You follow this with the pathname for each desired file. You can also request a directory list by using the **ls** command, as in the following example.

```
% mail mailserv@ds.internic.net
Subject:
ls /isoc
.
```

In return, you'll receive by e-mail a document listing the files available in this directory, which is devoted to materials from the Internet Society. See Figure 8.1.

Figure 8.1
A partial listing, retrieved by e-mail, of files in one directory at the INTERNIC.

```
Date: Fri, 16 Apr 93 13:30:04 EDT
To: gilster@rock.concert.net
Subject: Your request

AT&T InterNIC Directory and Database Mail Server 1.0 [ds]

Request arrived - Fri Apr 16 13:17:12 EST
Request processed - Fri Apr 16 13:30 EDT 1993

Processing mail headers ...

Processing message contents...

Command: ls /isoc
=> LS:  /isoc
 => total 1523
 => -rw-r--r--  1 ietfadm      830 Mar  3 11:35 0README
 => -rw-r--r--  1 ietfadm      747 Mar  3 11:34 0README%
 => -rw-r--r--  1 ietfadm    11725 Apr 13 23:51 Internet.host.growth
 => -rw-r--r--  1 ietfadm    16317 Mar  3 11:34 abstract.txt
 There are 65 lines left (29%). Press ace for more, or 'i' to return.
```

Any of these files may then be obtained by sending the appropriate command to the site. Thus, to obtain the file **Internet.host.growth,** I would send the following message:

```
% mail mailserv@ds.internic.net
Subject:
file /isoc/Internet.host.growth
.
```

The file will appear shortly in my mailbox.

To show you the necessary commands, I'm demonstrating a mail session using a UNIX-based service provider. But if you are using an account with a commercial on-line service, you would send the same message through that system's mail gateway to the Internet. You should read on-line documentation for whatever provider you are using if you have any questions about sending such a message. Usually, the process involves specifying the Internet mail address, after which you proceed with the message as above.

You can see how mail servers work to bring you files in response to commands you send through e-mail. It would be useful to have access to the entire range of mail servers. This we can also do by retrieving a document, either by anonymous FTP or by electronic mail. As you'll see, a wide range of mail servers out there can provide information through your electronic mail gateway to the Internet.

•••

What You Need: A List of Mail Servers

The Document: **How to Find Sources,** by Jonathan I. Kamens

How to Get It: By anonymous FTP to **pit-manager.mit.edu.** The directory is *pub/usenet/news.answers.* The file name is **finding-sources.** Although this file largely targets people who are looking for source code, it contains a valuable section on mail servers.

•••

INTERNIC Mail Services

The range of options available through the INTERNIC mail server is remarkable, and serves as a reminder of how much can be done through electronic mail alone. Again, the address is **mailserv@ds.internic.net**. Leave the subject field in your message blank when you use one of these. The following are some highlights.

WHITE PAGES QUERIES

White pages are directories, some of which are built using a standard for directory services called X.500 that is used to find people on the Internet. You can use these services to search for a person or an institution.

To find a person, use the **person** command, followed by the person you're looking for. Thus:

```
person john smith, ATT, us
```

Note that the person command requires the person's name as well as an organization he or she is associated with. Usage of the country name is optional; the default is U.S.

To find an institution, use the **institution** command:

```
institution ATT, us
```

Note that this requires the institution name and country. Figure 8.2 shows the result of the above search.

DOCUMENT QUERIES

You can request a specific document from the INTERNIC if you know its name. This is particularly useful if you're looking for one of the Request for Comments documents, which the INTERNIC maintains in their entirety. To do this for RFC-822, for example, you enter the command **document-by-name** followed by the document name. Thus:

```
document-by-name rfc822
```

You may also search for documents by keyword, through the **document-by-keyword** command. At least one keyword is required; more can be entered if necessary. Thus, I can look for documents on the subject of mail standards by sending a statement as follows:

```
document-by-keyword mail
```

This generates a list of the relevant files available at the site.

FILE LENGTH LIMITS

Some commercial on-line services place limits on the length of incoming messages from the Internet. Because this is the case, you should know that you can limit the size of files you've specified for delivery from the INTERNIC. The

Figure 8.2
A search for AT&T at the INTERNIC.

```
= INSTITUTION:  name = ATT  country = US
= White Pages Query Results:
= ATT                                            +1 212-387-5400
=      aka: AT&T
=      aka: American Telephone
=
= ATT
=   32 Avenue of the Americas
=   New York
=   New York 10013
=   US
=
= Comments about the ATT Directory should be sent to sri@qsun.att.com
=
= Locality:    New York, New York
=
= Name:      ATT, US
= Modified: Wed Jun 16 19:09:32 1993
=       by: manager, att, US
```

command is **limit.** Assume, for example, that your on-line service doesn't let messages longer than 50K come into its system. You could issue the following command to limit the size of INTERNIC materials; files longer than the limit would then be broken into parts. The default length is 64k before this happens. You can change it as follows:

```
limit 50k
```

or whatever limit your system places upon you.

Given the range of options becoming available from the INTERNIC, it would be useful to have a synopsis of mail server commands.

What You Need: Basic Mail-Server Commands From the INTERNIC

The Document: **Mail Server Commands**

How to Get It: Send electronic mail to **mailserv@ds.internic.net.** Leave the subject field blank. In the body of the message, enter the command **help.**

INTERNIC Precautions

Be careful when sending messages to the INTERNIC if you are accessing the Internet from a commercial provider like CompuServe. The reason: you want to be sure your commercial service handles the return mail properly so it's routed to you. To be absolutely sure you'll get what you request, you can add a path statement to your information request. Here's what it might look like when sent from CompuServe:

```
Mail! compose
Enter message. (/EXIT when done)
path 73537.656@compuserve.com
limit 49k
document-by-name rfc822
exit
/exit
```

What you see in the above message is, first, a path statement, giving my CompuServe address for the return reply. It's followed by a command to limit file length to 49K, to get in under the CompuServe length limits. After that is the request for a specific document. The request is followed by the **exit** command, which tells the INTERNIC server to stop processing the message at this point and to ignore any following lines that might be interjected by the system I'm using. The final **/exit** command is the normal CompuServe end-of-message statement.

Using ftpmail

What happens if you need a file that's not located at one of the network information centers or other similar sites? The answer is, you can still retrieve the file using **ftpmail,** a program developed by Paul Vixie at the Digital Western

Figure 8.3
Response to an
ftpmail request.

```
We processed the following input from your mail message:

        connect ftp.sura.net
        chdir pub/nic/internet.literature
        get internet.basics
        quit

We have entered the following request into our job queue
as job number 733006077.12187:

        connect ftp.sura.net anonymous -ftpmail/gilster@rock.concert.net
        reply gilster@rock.concert.net
        chdir pub/nic/internet.literature
        get internet.basics ascii

There are 2309 jobs ahead of this one in our queue.

You should expect the results to be mailed to you within a day or so.
We try to drain the request queue every 30 minutes, but sometimes it
fills up with enough junk that it takes until midnight (Pacific time)
to clear.  Note, however, that since ftpmail sends its files out with
"Precedence: bulk", they receive low priority at mail relay nodes.
```

Research Laboratory and the Digital Network Systems Laboratory, from 1989–1993. To do this, you send a request to **ftpmail@decwrl.dec.com.** (European users only can send to **ftpmail@grasp.insa-lyon.rf**). You can leave the subject field blank or not as you choose. The body of your message will contain the file information needed by the remote computer to process your request. The format is simple, and is best illustrated through an example. I want to retrieve the file **internet.basics,** which I know from my reading of the **00-README.FIRST** file above is located at SURAnet. I also know from the directory that it's in the subdirectory called *pub/nic/internet.literature*. Here's how I can get it.

```
% mail ftpmail@decwrl.dec.com
Subject: internet.basics
connect ftp.sura.net
chdir pub/nic/internet.literature
get internet.basics
quit
.
```

Again, the message address format may look slightly different depending on the provider whose electronic mail gateway you're using. But the text of the message should be as above. You'll receive a return message soon. An excerpt is shown in Figure 8.3.

And in a day or so, just as promised, the file will arrive in your mailbox. Along with it is a separate message showing the actual transaction as it occurred between **ftpmail** and the remote computer. See Figure 8.4.

As you see, **ftpmail** handles the complete transaction, with no help required from your end. This method works well for regular text files, opening up any site that handles anonymous FTP for you to use through your mail gateway to the Internet.

Figure 8.4
Transaction of the
ftpmail request.

```
--- connecting to ftp.sura.net...
Connecting to ftp.sura.net
220 nic.sura.net FTP server (Ve
--- logging in as user=anonymous password=-ftpmail/gilster@rock.concert.net
--- USER anonymous
331 Guest login ok, send e-mail address as password.
--- PASS
230 Guest login ok, access restrictions apply.
--- TYPE A
200 Type set to A.
--- changing working directory to pub/nic/internet.literature...
--- CWD pub/nic/internet.literature
250 CWD command successful.
=== getting 'internet.basics'...
--- PORT 16,1,0,23,8,120
200 PORT command successful.
--- RETR internet.basics
150 Opening ASCII mode data connection for internet.basics (12261 bytes).
... file appears to be 12261 bytes in size
226 Transfer complete.
--- mailing...
internet.basics (pub/nic/internet.literature@ftp.sura.net) (1 part(s),
12261 bytes) sent to gilster@rock.concert.net
---> (end of ftpmail session)
```

Retrieving Binary Files by Mail

Text files are one thing, but when we turn to binary files like executable programs and graphics images, we have to be more careful when using **ftpmail.** Why? Remember that your file will be sent to you as an electronic mail message. That means it must adhere to the standards laid out in RFC-822, which governs how electronic mail is handled on the Internet. This is not a problem when you're receiving text. But for binary files, RFC-822 specifies that they must be converted to 7-bit ASCII characters, because the message header and body can only consist of such ASCII characters.

That means the file must first be converted into ASCII, received by you, and then converted back into a binary file before it can be used. Moreover, if the file is longer than the sixty-four thousand characters that can be sent in a single message, it will be broken into several messages and sent to you in pieces. Some on-line services place limits on the length of messages you can receive as well, so you must have some way to limit the size of a message you'll get in your mailbox.

Fortunately, **ftpmail** provides for such eventualities. First, we'll request a file from a UNIX system. Then we'll get the same file through CompuServe. I'll ask **ftpmail** for a binary file—the **GEOCLOCK** program I discussed in Chapter 5. If you look back at our search there, you'll find that **GEOCLOCK** is available, among other sites, at **ftp.cso.uiuc.edu,** in the directory */pc/exec-pc*. The filename is **geoclock.zip.** We can thus formulate the mail message to retrieve this file. Note that I'm asking it to be sent in binary form:

```
% mail ftpmail@decwrl.dec.com
Subject: geoclock.zip
connect ftp.cso.uiuc.edu
binary
uuencode
chdir pc/exec-pc
get geoclock.zip
quit
.
```

We need to go through these commands one by one to make sure they're clear. First, we've told **ftpmail** which computer we want to connect to: **ftp.cso.uiuc.edu.** With the next line, we've told it we are going to transfer a binary file.

The next line tells **ftpmail** to encode this file according to the **uuencode** utility. We'll use this encoding method to turn the file into ASCII because certain software tools can decode files that have been encoded this way on a standalone PC. That means we can bring the file onto our own hard disk and then **uudecode** it there (more about this later). Incidentally, if you don't specify that **uuencode** be used, the default encoding is **btoa,** which stands for **B**inary **to A**SCII. We'll request **uuencode** because we have the software to decode it.

Don't be surprised if the encoded file is larger than the binary file size listed. The encoding process actually adds about thirty-five percent to the size of the files it translates; the file you receive is, of course, returned to its normal size when restored to binary form.

Finishing out the mail commands, we've then told **ftpmail** to change to the *pc/exec-pc* subdirectory at the FTP site, and to get the file **geoclock.zip.**

When the file arrives, things get interesting. Remember, this is a binary file in ASCII format, so it's going to look funny. Figure 8.5 shows the first of the three messages I received containing **geoclock.zip.** The program was broken into parts because each message defaults to a length of 64,000 bits.

If you were doing this through a UNIX account, you could save the files on-line and decode them there before downloading them to your system. But for now I'm assuming you're using one of the non-UNIX commercial providers by way of a mail gateway. That being the case, you need to save each of these files to your hard disk rather than reading them as mail. Give each of them a separate name. I could, for example, call the three parts of the file in question something like **geo1.uue, geo2.uue,** and **geo3.uue,** showing that they're related but separate parts of the same file.

You're doubtless wondering why I added a **.uue** extension to those files. The answer: the **uudecode** program we're going to use to decode them requires that extension to work. Note that all three files get the same extension.

Finding PC Unix Utilities to Convert Binary Files

Once these files are on your hard disk, you'll have to process them to turn them into the program or graphics file you were expecting. Yes, this is kludgy, but it works—remember that a full Internet account with a commercial provider will save you these additional steps, because you can simply use FTP to go to the site and retrieve the file without the added conversion routines here. Nonetheless, once you've run through this procedure a few times, it won't seem quite so off-putting.

Figure 8.5
A binary file rendered into ASCII.

```
Date: Thu, 25 Mar 93 02:13:08 -0800
To: gilster@rock.concert.net
Subject: part 001 of geoclock.zip (pc/exec-pc@ux1.cso.uiuc.edu) [geoclock.zip]
(binary uncompressed uuencode, last)
X-Complaints-To: ftpmail-admin@inet-gw-2.pa.dec.com
X-Service-Address: ftpmail@inet-gw-2.pa.dec.com
X-Job-Number: 733007825.14099
Precedence: bulk
Reply-To:  y@inet-gw-2.pa.dec.com

MH+060E_',!_;\R2'H@+0/S;'H.++&U:U6F;=SS[_7?X)E@8(.5DS=X0A
MJ&=?V?TM)&#-&%@HJ'-B0I;O"TFB+(1T'^KV'VQ)"PGZ9#L!X^9[%"%N5!@=
M6E0!T**R.FPI0V!+:75(5'0J#;NUO'2PE&A!AL55X83B;A1=3(\::0W*D^&
M.Y$:C'$J08($F8S@.@V@W/ZAE0Q&!U?"'EWM5\NH^V]R0_M1D#U*-(!U
M;9M4T:&90++T"A!C66HT0!^1N*^J&Y',+?80"F8C#!E3B@3965&O:[]:AMT/
MLB1Q7U=(.5#*$@'1)$ZNGT=%L*F8''E%,QJ&3\ZZ?M$4$:J?(^$=T;LQ[B
M_T&R+_@G@'P'0YE;%L@8:N#EBZ'SX7P&_^K=T5R[@W1?T"_''\HSOD1ZT[
MFFL54*KYB^B^98'0?\E^$=T7')E0\^-"0U2Z7P3=#'#"$!0,)&($E,AB
M"&R9(!(HD@!(.EM-F0@-D6J-@UK?#N3E6X'DC+[#U=?[H?-7AK37C_(43-V
M(C1UUB]R4WH0?.A7=%-UU!,94%)_-B5MT$5('1);PL*(J5F=3B"HK$A$PZ%
 There are 286 lines left (8%). Press ace for more, or 'i' to return.
```

To make our new file work, we need a utility program that converts encoded ASCII files back into their functional equivalents. As you saw, the program that encoded the files in the first place was called **uuencode.** Its opposite number is **uudecode.** There are programs for personal computers that convert a uuencoded file on your hard disk. If you were on-line with a UNIX account, you could also do this using the system utilities there.

Where do you get the decoding program? This is the tricky part, since you wouldn't be using FTP through mail like this unless you had no other access to FTP files, and without that access, you can't use FTP to find the unencoded utility program. Fortunately, this program, along with other UNIX utilities for personal computers, can be retrieved on-line. You'll need to dig around in the file libraries at whichever commercial service you're using to find it. Look for any Special Interest Groups or Forums (or your commercial service's equivalent) dealing with telecommunications issues or with UNIX.

On CompuServe, for example, you can use the IBM File Finder (IBMFF) or Macintosh File Finder functions. I searched IBMFF for the **uudecode** program and came up with the following five possibilities:

```
1 Joan Riff's Unix 'uuencode/uudecode' for the PC
   IBMCOM/Comm Utilities [C]  ENCODE.ARC
2 v4.21 (latest) of uuencode/uudecode utilities
   IBMCOM/Comm Utilities [C]  UU421.ZIP
3 Joan Riff's SHAR for the PC and related programs
   IBMSYS/General Utils [S]  JSHAR.ARC
4 Describes JSHAR.ARC.
   IBMSYS/General Utils [S]  JSHAR.DOC
5 How to anonymous ftp from the Internet via C-Mail
   TAPCIS/TAPNEWS/Fact File  FTPNET.ZIP
```

We can take a closer look at one of these files to make sure it's what we're after, as in Figure 8.6.

Figure 8.6
A CompuServe file
description of the
uudecode and
uuencode utilities.

```
   [70473,1567]    Lib: 4
   UENCOD.ZIP/Bin  Bytes:  30118, Count:  379, 06-Jun-92

     Title   : UUencode and UUdecode Utility for DOS.
     Keywords: UUENCODE UUDECODE DOS UNIX TRANSFER BINARY MAIL PROGRAM ASCII
               CODING

     UUencode/UUdecode file coding program. Usually used to convert binary data
     into a coded ascii form to be transmitted between two different computer
     systems, such as Unix and DOS, via electronic mail, but there are other
     similiar uses one can make from this utility.  Both then encoding and
     decoding parts of this program, and documentation is included.  It is also
     very important for the individual or computer system you may be
     transmitting data in this format, to have a UUdecode utility at their end,
     so they can put it back together.
```

And indeed, it is. You can download any of these files and un-zip them with
PKUNZIP (file decompression utilities are also widely distributed on the on-line
services). If you're not on CompuServe but a different service, browse through
the file libraries to find these utilities. They'll form a critical part of your arsenal
if you plan to use the Internet's resources by mail alone. Here, for example, are
the relevant utilities for the Macintosh, found through the Macintosh File Finder
on CompuServe:

```
MAC File Finder

Forum Name: MACCOMM              Library: BBS Systems  (9)
  Accesses: 108                     Size: 402688
      File: UNIX_U.SEA        Submitted: [70641,13]   23-Nov-92

A collection of UNIX utilities collected from the Internet and other CompuServe Fo-
rums, for handling files going to or coming from UNIX hosts. Is a self extracting
archive. Be sure to compensate the shareware authors if you like the utilities.
```

Using the UNIX Utilities to Convert Your Files

When you unpack the **uudecode** package, you'll find two programs, one for
performing the decoding routine, the other for encoding files. We'll just work with
uudecode, since all we want to do is get our files into working order. After all,
we want a program we can run, rather than a document of cryptic-looking ASCII!
    The syntax for using the program is simple:

```
uudecode geo1.uue
```

Note that you don't have to specify the other files; **uudecode** will hop from one
file to another to perform its routine, and when through, you'll have a file
actually called **FTPMAIL.UU.** This is the standard name assigned by **ftpmail** to
the recreated binary file. Once we rename it **geoclock.zip,** we can take the final
step. The **.zip** extension tells us the file has been compressed using **PKZIP**, a file
compression routine available on all on-line services. We can use its counterpart
PKUNZIP to restore it to full size. This will produce a package of files. Figure
8.7 shows what the **uudecode** process looks like from the DOS prompt.
Now we can rename the file and unzip it as shown in Figure 8.8.

Figure 8.7
Using **uudecode** to
re-package
geoclock.zip.

```
C:\uudecode geoclk1

UU-DECODE 4.21 FOR PC.  by Richard Marks

Destination is FTPMAIL.UU
Decoding GEOCLK1.UUE
...
End File encountered in file: GEOCLK1.UUE

Decoding GEOCLK2.UUE
....
End File encountered in file: GEOCLK2.UUE

Decoding GEOCLK3.UUE
...
Completed decode of file FTPMAIL.UU
```

Figure 8.8
Re-naming and
unzipping the program
file.

```
C:\ren ftpmail.uu geoclock.zip

C:\pkunzip geoclock.zip

PKUNZIP (R)    FAST!    Extract Utility    Version 1.1    03-15-90
Copr. 1989-1990 PKWARE Inc. All Rights Reserved. PKUNZIP/h for help
PKUNZIP Reg. U.S. Pat. and Tm. Off.

Searching ZIP: GEOCLOCK.ZIP -

UnShrinking: READ.ME
  Expanding: MAP2.EGA
  Expanding: MAP1.EGA
  Expanding: GEOEGA.EXE
  Expanding: GEOCLOCK.DOC
UnShrinking: GEOCLOCK.DAT
  Expanding: GEO7EGA.EXE
```

A Sample File Download Using CompuServe

Let's look at a sample session, using a commercial on-line service to retrieve another file by electronic mail. For purposes of demonstration, I've chosen CompuServe, but the principles illustrated here apply to any major on-line service. The exceptions will occur in details particular to each service. Each, for example, may have its own addressing methodology for reaching the Internet, and each may vary in terms of the specific layout on-screen of its electronic mail system; the basic message content, however, remains the same. The procedures for retrieving the file to your own hard disk will, again, vary with each system, but the basic download mechanisms should be similar.

To send a message to an Internet address from a CompuServe account, you have to use a special addressing format which includes a standard Internet address and the word INTERNET. The format is as follows:

```
>INTERNET:user@organization.domain
```

Thus, to send a command through **ftpmail,** you must address it this way:

```
>INTERNET:ftpmail@decwrl.dec.com
```

If you're using a different on-line service to retrieve files through **ftpmail,** you should check its conventions about sending mail to the Internet to make sure you know what its particularities are.

We're going to go after the same file we went after before, **geoclock.zip.** Watch the format of the message we'll send carefully, because it contains a

Figure 8.9
An **ftpmail** command
sent via CompuServe.

```
Mail! compose

Enter message. (/EXIT when done)

reply 73537.656@compuserve.com
connect ftp.cso.uiuc.edu-ftp.cso.uirec.edu.
binary
chdir pc/exec-pc
uuencode
chunksize 49000
get geoclock.zip
quit
/exit


Send to (Name or User ID): INTERNET:ftpmail@decwrl.dec.com
Subject: geoclock.zip

To:   INTERNET:ftpmail@decwrl.dec.com
From: Paul A. Gilster
Subj: geoclock.zip


Are your message and address correct? (Y or N)! y

Message sent to INTERNET:ftpmail@decwrl.dec.com
```

change specific to CompuServe. We'll address the request as before: **INTER-NET:ftpmail@decwrl.dec.com.** In the body of the message, we'll insert our request. The message, along with the relevant CompuServe prompts, should look like the example in Figure 8.9.

As before, we've told the system we're requesting a binary file—if we fail to do this, the transfer won't work. We've also asked that the file be transferred into ASCII using the **uuencode** program, which we'll then decode on our own machines. As subject, we've used the name of the file we're requesting—**geoclock.zip.** The subject field could actually contain anything we choose, but by using the file name here, we're making it easier to spot the incoming traffic, because each message from **dec.wrl.com** will have the same subject listed.

But note this difference: we've added two new statements. The first, reply **73537.656@compuserve.com**, tells **ftpmail** where to send the reply. I've added it for safety's sake, because it's not unheard of for errors to creep into the return addresses of messages. I've also added a new command, **chunksize 49000**. We do this because CompuServe mail won't handle messages to and from the Internet that are more than fifty-thousand characters in length. You should check the on-line service you're using to determine whether there are similar restrictions. America Online, for example, demands incoming message lengths for PCs no longer than eight-thousand characters. If a transfer fails mysteriously, this may well be the reason, so be sure to check whether your service has any such limitations.

Downloading the Mailed Files

Having sent the message, we can expect to wait a day or so for the files to arrive. When they do, we'll want to retrieve them by downloading them to our own computer, rather than reading them on-line. The command to do this with CompuServe is **download,** invoked from the **Mail!** prompt.

First, we'll run the **scan** command from the **Mail!** prompt, to make sure we've got the right files. Figure 8.10 shows what it looks like on-screen.

Figure 8.10
Running a scan of a
CompuServe mailbox.

```
  1 Executive News Svc./WP   03/26      Two Big ATM Networks Holding Merger Tas
     29-Mar-93 08:21 EST 73537,656 Length 2309

  2 "ftpmail service on ftp-gw-1.pa.dec.com"/your ftpmail request has been rece]
     29-Mar-93 17:23 EST INTERNET:nobody@pa.dec.com Length 4215

  3 "ftpmail service on ftp-gw-1.pa.dec.com"/results of ftpmail request 7334378]
     29-Mar-93 19:50 EST INTERNET:nobody@pa.dec.com Length 2556

  4 "ftpmail service on ftp-gw-1.pa.dec.com"/part 001 of geoclock.zip (pc/exec-)
     29-Mar-93 19:55 EST INTERNET:nobody@pa.dec.com Length 50517

  5 "ftpmail service on ftp-gw-1.pa.dec.com"/part 003 of geoclock.zip (pc/exec-)
     29-Mar-93 20:44 EST INTERNET:nobody@pa.dec.com Length 49634

  6 "ftpmail service on ftp-gw-1.pa.dec.com"/part 002 of geoclock.zip (pc/exec-)
     29-Mar-93 21:02 EST INTERNET:nobody@pa.dec.com Length 50558

Mail! download 4 5 6
```

As you can see, items 2 and 3 are messages from **ftpmail** about the file transfer. Items 4, 5, and 6 are the actual files which make up **geoclock.zip** in its uuencoded form.

To download them, we give the **download** command followed by the item numbers, as shown before. We'll then be prompted for the file protocol we want to use. I've chosen Xmodem. See Figure 8.11.

CompuServe gives you the option of using several different file-download protocols for this process and prompts you for the one you want to use. I chose Xmodem because it's widely available in communications software programs.

For each file, I chose a different name, with the suffix **.uue.** Thus we have **clock1.uue, clock2.uue,** and **clock3.uue.** Again, this is to meet the demands of the **uudecode** program.

Stripping Off Mail Headers

When the downloads are complete, I'll sign off CompuServe and turn to the task at hand. First, I'll try to decode the files by simply telling **uudecode** to do its stuff. My command will be **uudecode clock1.uue.** As we saw before, this should cause the program to go through each of the retrieved messages in turn and decode them, assembling the whole into the **geoclock.zip** file. The **uudecode** program will link them together, transforming them into the binary file the remote site offered to begin with.

It's possible **uudecode** will stumble over something in the header information, not knowing how to bypass it and thus stalling. For example, take a look at the ASCII read-out of the first lines of the second of our files, **clock2.uue,** shown in Figure 8.12.

You can see that the actual uuencoded file begins after the message header information is over. If **uudecode** stalls, you can edit the files yourself to remove the headers. Remove the header information from the second and third messages, so the uuencoded text is not broken by any header information between the three files. Then try **uudecode** again, and it should work. After all three files are trimmed this way, they're ready to be processed by **uudecode.** The syntax is **uudecode** *filename1.* In this case, then, I'll enter **uudecode clock1.uue.**

Figure 8.11
Beginning the download with Xmodem.

```
Protocol: xmodem

 4 "ftpmail service on ftp-gw-1.pa.dec.com"/part 001 of geoclock.zip (pc/exec-)
   29-Mar-93 19:55 EST INTERNET:nobody@pa.dec.com Length 50517

 5 "ftpmail service on ftp-gw-1.pa.dec.com"/part 003 of geoclock.zip (pc/exec-)
   29-Mar-93 20:44 EST INTERNET:nobody@pa.dec.com Length 49634

 6 "ftpmail service on ftp-gw-1.pa.dec.com"/part 002 of geoclock.zip (pc/exec-)
   29-Mar-93 21:02 EST INTERNET:nobody@pa.dec.com Length 50558

3 messages and 151397 characters ready for download
Starting XMODEM transfer
```

Figure 8.12
The encoded file with
message header.

```
Date:   29-Mar-93 21:02 EST
From:   "ftpmail service on ftp-gw-1.pa.dec.com"   INTERNET:nobody@pa.dec.com
Subj:   part 002 of geoclock.zip (pc/exec-pc@ux1.cso.uiuc.edu) [geocl-
ock.zip] (binary
uncompressed uuencode)
Sender: nobody@ftp-gw-1.pa.dec.com
Received: from ftp-gw-1.pa.dec.com by ihb.compuserve.com (5.65/5.930129sam)
        id AA13535; Mon, 29 Mar 93 19:48:33 -0500
Received: by ftp-gw-1.pa.dec.com; id AA19082; Mon, 29 Mar 93 16:47:15 -0800
Date: Mon, 29 Mar 93 16:47:15 -0800
Message-Id: i00047.AA19082@ftp-gw-1.pa.dec.com
From: "ftpmail service on ftp-gw-1.pa.dec.com" y@pa.dec.com
To: 73537.656@compuserve.com
Subject: part 002 of geoclock.zip (pc/exec-pc@ux1.cso.uiuc.edu) [geocl-
ock.zip] (binary uncompressed uuencode)
X-Complaints-To: ftpmail-admin@ftp-gw-1.pa.dec.com
X-Service-Address: ftpmail@ftp-gw-1.pa.dec.com
X-Job-Number: 733437830.10063
Precedence: bulk
Reply-To: y@ftp-gw-1.pa.dec.com

M!"@#&!P"]$W !B20+__#("K(54_ T^B9@Z\(\,GRWC_"=P @$B!!8HH(QO
M6$$/P+H+H$QL47$\?A?X@' 'P-#F&:EPAY_N!"^0!(PRD+Z!@ %!&/^:?^P)[
M$C10@ /5^0#@#B'31A?2&P )9OV0O ?@!3/2%Ut@0 89D.B0@#R"?G8?PPPD
MR :F@,AO7C@P R"E,'%"DA0(%8=%#"C ,DN3"420%#MR  4$ YTPB0!!@,
```

Downloading the Compression Utilities

Now that we have the principle down, we need another file, one called **comp-430d.zip,** which is found at the site **gatekeeper.dec.com.** This "zipped" file contains another useful utility for MS-DOS called **compress,** and its alter-ego, **decompress.** You'll remember from Chapter 5 that some files are compressed to save space when they're saved; these files contain the **.Z** suffix to their file names; e.g., **worldmap.ps.Z, intro.doc.Z,** etc. People who use UNIX-based service providers have no problem with compressed files, because they can decompress **.Z** files on their provider's machine. But commercial service users have to unpack these files at home, and that takes a utility program like the one we'll find inside **comp430d.zip.**

I won't walk you through the entire process again, but here's the relevant request to send to **ftpmail@decwrl.dec.com:**

```
reply 73537.656@compuserve.com
connect gatekeeper.dec.com
binary
chdir /.2/micro/msdos/simtel20/compress
uuencode
chunksize 49000
get comp430d.zip
quit
/exit
```

You would, of course, alter the request if you were retrieving this file by **ftpmail** through a UNIX provider, or through a commercial on-line service different from CompuServe. Certainly your reply information would then change, as would the chunksize listed here (and you should check with your own commercial service, if you use one, for possible chunksize restrictions).

Macintosh users also need a way to deal with UNIX **.Z** files. The file is called **MacCompress 3.2**. If you're using a Mac, you'll want this file.

• •

What You Need: A Compress/Decompress Program for the Mac

The Program: **MacCompress 3.2**

Where to Get It: Through **ftpmail** from **sumex-aim.stanford.edu.** The directory is */info-mac/util.* The file is **maccompress-32.hqx.** Use the procedures you've learned to acquire this file by sending the proper commands to **ftpmail@decwrl.dec.com.**

• •

Basic ftpmail Commands

Following are the basic commands you can use when requesting a file through **ftpmail.**

connect   Use this command to tell **ftpmail** the site you wish to connect to. As we saw in the above examples, the syntax is simply **connect** *sitename,* as in **connect wuarchive.wustl.edu.** The default host, incidentally, is **gatekeeper.dec.com.**

ascii   Tells **ftpmail** the files you want are regular ASCII text files.

binary   A critical command. Use it when the files to be retrieved are compressed or binary files. If you fail to give this command for such a file, **ftpmail** will be unable to send you the program.

chdir   Allows you to change directories. Note that you are allowed only one **chdir** command per **ftpmail** session.

chunksize   Splits files into chunks according to the size you specify. As mentioned before, CompuServe users must specify **chunksize 49000** to get around the restriction on Internet message size. Other on-line services may have other restrictions, so consult your provider.

compress   Tells **ftpmail** to compress a binary file.

get   Retrieve the file you request. Thus **get geoclock.zip** gets that file according to the commands given previously.

uuencode   Tells **ftpmail** to send you the binary file in **uuencode** format. Don't forget to send this command, or your **uudecode** program won't be able to salvage the file.

FINDING FILES TO RETRIEVE—ARCHIE THROUGH ELECTRONIC MAIL

As you saw in Chapter 5, the **archie** program can be a tremendously useful way to locate files. The good news about using electronic mail as an Internet gateway continues, for **archie** is itself available through e-mail. The idea is to send an e-mail message to an **archie** server, which will conduct the search and send the

Figure 8.13
A list of public access
archie servers.

```
Archie Servers
archie.rutgers.edu: northeastern US
archie.sura.net: southern US
archie.unl.edu: western US
archie.ans.net: ANS network sites
archie.mcgill.ca: Canada
archie.au: Australia and Pacific region
archie.funet.fi: Europe
archie.th-darmstadt.de: Germany
archie.doc.ic.ac.uk: United Kingdom
archie.cs.huji.ac.il: Israel
archie.wide.ad.jp: Japanese
archie.kuis.kyoto-u.ac.jp: Japanese
archie.ncu.edu.tw: Taiwan
archie.nz: New Zealand
```

results back to you. I might, for example, want to contact the SURAnet **archie** server, the same one I consulted in Chapter 5. To do so by mail, I would send mail to **archie@archie.sura.net.** Commands to the server must begin in the first column of the message to be effective.

The **archie** servers mentioned earlier make their services available through electronic mail. To refresh your memory, Figure 8.13 shows the list again.

The message containing your search commands should be sent to **archie@*server*.** Thus, to contact the **archie** server at Rutgers, you'd send mail to **archie@archie.rutgers.edu.**

Tracking Down Sherlock Holmes

An example will make this clearer. As a Sherlock Holmes fan, I might want to look for text files of Arthur Conan Doyle's novels, such as those being compiled by Project Gutenberg and the Online Text Initiative (more about this in Chapter 10). Let's ask **archie** for files containing the name Doyle by sending a message to the above address (leave the subject field blank). Starting at the first column, type **prog doyle** and send the message:

```
: mail archie@archie.sura.net
Subject:
prog doyle
.
```

By return mail, we get a list of sites. I list only the relevant ones in Figure 8.14.

The following are the major commands for using **archie** through electronic mail, along with comments.

compress   This command compresses and **uuencodes** the material sent to you. Upon receiving the material, you must remove everything before the "begin" line and run it through the **uudecode** program. The result, a .Z file, must then be run through uncompress to get the final results.

Figure 8.14
Results of a search for
Arthur Conan Doyle
materials.

```
To: Paul A Gilster -- Computer Focus gilster@rock.concert.net
Subject: archie reply: prog doyle
Status: R


Sorting by hostname


Search request for 'doyle'


    Location: /pub/data/etext
      DIRECTORY rwxrwxr-x        1536   Dec 28 10:31    doyle
    Location: /usr/almanac/lib
      FILE      rw-rw-r--        5255   Apr 24  1992    etext-doyle.tab

Host src.doc.ic.ac.uk   (146.169.2.1)
Last updated 05:03  4 Jan 1993

    Location: /literary/published/usenix/faces/dg-rtp.dg.com
      FILE       r--r--r--      13231  Mar 23  1989    doyle.Z
    Location: /published/usenix/faces/dg-rtp.dg.com
      FILE       r--r--r--      13231  Mar 23  1989    doyle.Z
```

The **compress** command makes sense if you are working with large files, although you won't always know that when you send a request.

help   Can get you out of trouble. If you send a command that **archie** can't understand, you'll receive a help message whether you asked for one or not.

path   Normally, **archie** will return e-mail to the address it extracts from the header of your message. If you find a server unresponsive, adding a path command to the message can help to get things moving. Because a number of different commands can appear in the same message, you can insert this command after your search command. Remember when using more than one command, though, that all commands must begin in column one of the line. Using the **path** command above to specify my address, for example, I'd enter: **path gilster@rock.concert.net**. The e-mail we just sent to **archie.sura.net**, then, would be:

```
% mail archie@archie.sura.net
Subject:
prog doyle
path gilster@rock.concert.net
.
```

prog   This is the search command we encountered in Chapter 5. It looks through the **archie** database to locate any matches to our search term. Note: with an interactive Telnet session, you have the ability to set search terms, as you've just seen. Using mail, the system will default to the UNIX regular expression search type, called **regex.** This makes the search slower, but more likely to find what you need.

quit The **quit** command tells **archie** not to interpret anything past the point where **quit** is inserted. You want to use it if you have an automatically inserted signature file which might contain a term that resembles a command. Notice we also used **quit** when sending commands to **ftpmail,** and for the same reason.

servers This command returns a list of all known **archie** servers.

site This command produces a listing of files at the given site identification. Thus **site uts.mcc.ac.uk** produces a list of all files on the server in question.

whatis Using the **whatis** command allows you to search the software description database for a given substring. The command ignores case.

Using archie by Mail Through CompuServe

Just as we used a commercial on-line service to retrieve files, we can also use one to search for files with **archie.** Just remember to check out your system's local conventions for addressing. We've already seen how to address mail to the Internet from CompuServe. So to search an **archie** server—say, the one at Rutgers—from CompuServe, we would send to this address:

```
>INTERNET:archie@archie.rutgers.edu
```

In a useful file archive called **ftpnet.zip,** located in CompuServe's TapCis Forum libraries, CompuServe whiz Dick Kahane points out an obvious fact: CompuServe users, no matter where they call in from, are connecting to computers in Columbus, OH. So, no matter your location, to minimize net traffic and use the resource closest to you, CompuServe users should tap one of three **archie** servers, as shown in the following CompuServe-style Internet addresses:

```
>INTERNET:archie@archie.unl.edu
>INTERNET:archie@archie.rutgers.edu
>INTERNET:archie@archie.sura.net
```

The first of these is in Lincoln, Nebraska, the second in New Jersey, while SURAnet is based in Maryland. Using geographically nearby sites helps to avoid network congestion.

We've seen how to search for file names that interest us. Let's now search for files indexed under a particular keyword. I'm going to use CompuServe to request an **archie** mail server to locate files indexed under the term **laser.** Figure 8.15 shows how the message will be structured.

As with our **ftpmail** session, I've added a path statement for the return message just as a precaution.[1] The next command is the **whatis** statement, which allows you to search a software description database for a particular word. We follow with the **quit** command and the CompuServe **/exit** command. (This is only to tell CompuServe that we're finishing up the message. It has no Internet function.)

Figure 8.15
A CompuServe **archie**
request.

```
Mail! compose

Enter message. (/EXIT when done)

path 73537.656@compuserve.com
whatis laser
quit
/exit


Send to (Name or User ID):> INTERNET:archie@archie.rutgers.edu
Subject: Recipes

To:   INTERNET:archie@archie.rutgers.edu
From: Paul A. Gilster
Subj: Laser
```

WAIS by Electronic Mail

Another exciting development in resource discovery, WAIS, or Wide Area Information Servers, is also available by electronic mail. This system, discussed at length in Chapter 13, allows you to search for information by using keywords. We'll use Telnet in Chapter 13 to access WAIS and run sample searches. But if you're a mail-only user, you can still use a mail server put together by Jonny Goldman at Thinking Machines Corp. (where the WAIS system was first developed).

The procedure is simple enough. You send a message to **waismail@quake.think.com.** The message should be formatted as follows:

```
search <source-name> keywords
```

source-name stands for the name found in the directory of servers without the **.src** ending that characterizes them. Selected servers are listed in Chapter 15. And the WAIS discussion in Chapter 13 will show how you can search a general database of WAIS servers. A wealth of information is available through them.

You'll receive mail containing the results of the WAIS search. You can then request documents in the form

```
docid
```

where **docid** is a WAIS document identifier.

A sample search will make this clearer. Here's how I ran a WAIS search through e-mail for information. I'm querying the source **nsf-pubs.src** to find anything published by the National Science Foundation on the Internet. Note that I leave the **.src** off the end of the source statement.

```
% mail waismail@quake.think.com
Subject: WAIS Request
search nsf-pubs internet
```

A list of WAIS hits will be returned by electronic mail. Part of the list is shown in Figure 8.16.

Figure 8.16
A mail request for a
WAIS document.

```
Searching: nsf-pubs
Keywords: internet

Result # 1 Score:1000 lines:  0 bytes:  59527 Date:     0 Type: TEXT
Headline: Title  : NSF9119 - STIS User's Guide
DocID: 0 59527 /home/ftp/NSF/genpubs/nsf9119:/home/wais/wais-sources/nsf-
pubs@stis.nsf.gov:210%TEXT

Result # 2 Score: 645 lines:  0 bytes:  29491 Date:     0 Type: TEXT
Headline: Title   : NSF9224--Network Information Services Manager(s) for
DocID: 0 29491 /home/ftp/CISE/program/nsf9224:/home/wais/wais-sources/nsf-
pubs@stis.nsf.gov:210%TEXT

Result # 3 Score: 516 lines:  0 bytes: 103293 Date:     0 Type: TEXT
Headline: Title  : NSF9130 - Undergraduate Level Math Sciences Education
Programs
DocID: 0 103293 /home/ftp/EHR/program/nsf9130:/home/wais/wais-sources/nsf-
pubs@stis.nsf.gov:210%TEXT

Result # 4 Score: 484 lines:  0 bytes:  19403 Date:     0 Type: TEXT
Headline: Title  : NSF Electronic Proposal Submission Project (EPS) Informa-
tion
DocID: 0 19403 /home/ftp/NSF/eps/epsinfo:/home/wais/wais-sources/nsf-
pubs@stis.nsf.gov:210%TEXT

Result # 5 Score: 484 lines:  0 bytes:  17909 Date:     0 Type: TEXT
Headline: Title  : CISE Newsletter, September 1992
DocID: 0 17909 /home/ftp/CISE/letters/lcise921:/home/wais/wais-sources/nsf-
pubs@stis.nsf.gov:210%TEXT

Result # 6 Score: 452 lines:  0 bytes:   4830 Date:     0 Type: TEXT
Headline: Title  : NSF 91-10 STIS Brochure
DocID: 0 4830 /home/ftp/NSF/genpubs/nsf9110:/home/wais/wais-sources/nsf-
pubs@stis.nsf.gov:210%TEXT
```

From this list, we can choose a document we think most useful and retrieve it this way:

```
% mail waismail@quake.think.com
Subject: WAIS Request
DocID: 0 4830 /home/ftp/NSF/genpubs/nsf9110:/home/wais/wais-sources/nsf-
pubs@stis.nsf.gov:210%TEXT
```

I've pasted the document identification directly into my communications program and sent the message on its way. I'll soon receive the needed file in my mailbox.

For now, just note that WAIS searching by mail is workable. You'll learn much more about WAIS, which is one of the most exciting developments on the Internet, in Chapter 13.

SENDING ELECTRONIC MAIL TO OTHER NETWORKS

If you have any doubts that Internet electronic mail opens out to networks across the world, consider the evidence of John J. Chew's *The Inter-Network Mail Guide*, available on the Internet both as a posting in various USENET newsgroups and also by download with anonymous FTP. Chew tracks the ways in which the various commercial providers maintain links to and from the Internet, and his list is growing with each new posting. A glance through it reveals linkages to such varied providers as Geonet Mailbox Systems, BIX, GreenNet, KeyLink, PeaceNet, SprintMail, and AppleLink, to name literally but a few.

Chew's list will come in handy, and I advise you to get a copy.

••

What You Need: A List of Network Interconnections

The Document: **Inter-Network Mail Guide**, by John Chew.

How to Get It: Through anonymous FTP to **ftp.msstate.edu.** The directory is *pub/docs.* The filename is **internetwork-mail-guide.** You can also keep up with changes to this document by monitoring the USENET newsgroups **comp.mail.misc** and **news.newusers.questions.**

••

Now you will learn how to send mail from the Internet to addresses at the major on-line services.

America Online

To send mail from the Internet to America Online, the syntax is **username@aol.com.** The user name should be all lowercase, with spaces removed.

Outgoing messages cannot be any longer than 32K. On the PC version of America Online, incoming mail cannot be any longer than 8K, which effectively prevents your using this service for **ftpmail** file transfers. On the Mac version of America Online, as well as the Apple II version and PC-Link, incoming mail cannot be any longer than 27K. All characters except newline and printable ASCII characters are mapped to spaces. Users are limited to seventy-five pieces of Internet mail in their mailbox at a time.

To send mail from America Online to the Internet, simply enter the Internet address and write your message. Figure 8.17 shows the process in action.

BIX

To send mail from the Internet to BIX, the syntax is *username*@bix.com. To send mail from BIX to the Internet, enter the Internet address preceded by **to** at the **Mail:** prompt. The following is an example of a message being sent from BIX to the Internet:

```
Mail:to gilster@rock.concert.net
Enter subject: Mailing from BIX
Enter text. End with '. <CL>
'
This message is to test BIX's connections to Internet e-mail.
.
send/action:send
Sending..Memo 76679 sent
```

Figure 8.17
Sending a message to
the Internet from
America Online.

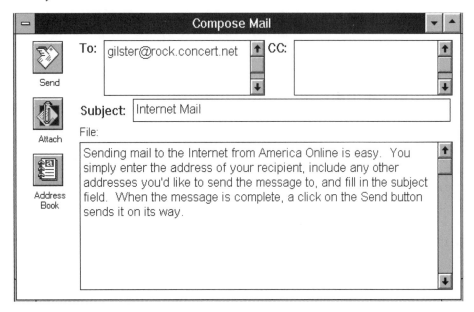

There are no size restrictions on BIX messages to and from the Internet, and no monthly or per-message fee for Internet mail. You can move up to 10 MB per calendar month (in both directions, to and from the Internet), without any additional charges. Beyond that, the charge is one dollar per 100K transferred. Messages can be up to 0.5 MB in length in either direction; longer messages may be truncated.

CompuServe

To send mail from the Internet to CompuServe, the syntax is *usernumber*@**compuserve.com.** CompuServe user numbers contain commas, which must be changed to periods when you send from the Internet. Thus 12345,6789 becomes 12345.6789. To send me a CompuServe message, for example, you'd send to **73537.656@compuserve.com.**

To send mail from CompuServe to the Internet, as just shown, lead off the address with **>INTERNET:** Sending a message to **ftpmail,** then, requires the address:

```
>INTERNET:ftpmail@decwrl.dec.com
```

DELPHI

To send mail from the Internet to DELPHI, the syntax is: *username*@**delphi.com.** To send mail from DELPHI to the Internet, use the word **internet** followed (with no spaces in between) by the recipient's name enclosed in quotes. On DELPHI, to send a message to **ftpmail,** for example, you would address it to **internet"ftpmail@decwrl.dec.com".** The following is a sample message from Delphi to the Internet:

```
MAIL send
To:      internet"gilster@rock.concert.net"
Subj:    Test Message
Enter your message below. Press CTRL/Z when complete, or CTRL/C to quit:
Checking the DELPHI connection to the Internet.
^Z
```

GEnie

To send mail from the Internet to GEnie, the syntax is *username@genie.geis.com.* To send mail from GEnie to the Internet: after entering the Internet address, you are prompted for additional GEnie addresses, copies, and a subject line. You can then enter your text. Figure 8.18 shows a GEnie message to an address on the Internet as it is being composed.

GEnie's Internet mail services cost $3.00 per hour.

MCI Mail

To send mail from the Internet to MCI Mail, the syntax is: *username@mcimail.com.* MCI user names should have spaces removed. Thus **Sam Spade** becomes **Sam_Spade@mcimail.com.** Conversely, it's possible to use an MCI user number. If Sam's number is 123-4567, simply remove the dash. Thus **1234567@mcimail.com.** If there happens to be more than one Sam Spade in the MCI directory, you can reach the desired party by sending to

Sam_Spade/1234567@mcimail.com[2]

Figure 8.18
Sending a message to the Internet from GEnie.

```
Enter Destination GEnie Address or C/R to continue.
?

Would you like to receive a copy of the message? (y/n) ?n

Enter the subject of your Internet message (max 30 characters) or C/R for no sub
ject:
<----------------------------->
?Mailing from GEnie




When you see the prompt, 1>, enter your message.
When you have finished entering your text, use the *S,
to send the Internet message.  Use *X to exit without sending.

Enter Internet text:

Queue#   Item  From        Length   Sent      Subject
    1 6239343  GENIE.MGMT      268 93/05/27 New Pricing Effective July 1st

   1>GEnie prompts the user through the mail process, so sending mail to
   2>the Internet is relatively simple.  You will be prompted for additional
   3>addresses for your message, asked if you'd like a copy of it, and given
   4>space to enter a subject line.
```

Figure 8.19
Sending a message to
the Internet from MCI
Mail.

```
EMS:       INTERNET
      EMS    376-5414 INTERNET                     NRI            Reston

Enter recipient's mailbox information.

MBX:       mike_banks@bix.com

If additional mailbox lines are not needed press RETURN.

MBX:

TO:      Mike Banks
           EMS: INTERNET / MCI ID: 376-5414
           MBX: mike_banks@bix.com

Is this address correct (Yes or No)? y

CC:

Subject: MCI Mail Check

Text: (Enter text or transmit file. Type / on a line by itself to end.)

Mike:

Please let me know if this message gets through OK.  It's routed to
your BIX account via MCI Mail.

Thanks!

Paul
```

To send mail from MCI Mail to the Internet, use the EMS option. Here's how to do it:

- At the TO prompt, type recipient's name and the word EMS in parentheses.
- At the EMS prompt, type **INTERNET.**
- At the MBX prompt, type the recipient's Internet address. Note: if the Internet address exceeds eighty characters in length, you must split the address into multiple MBX lines. The split should occur at one of the following characters: **@ ! %.**
- Only one Internet mailbox may be used with an individual TO or CC recipient.
- Complete the mailing procedure as usual.

Figure 8.19 shows an example of sending a message to an Internet address from MCI Mail.

Prodigy

The Prodigy mail gateway to the Internet is scheduled to be implemented in the second half of 1993.

Mailing Lists and Electronic Journals

A huge variety of mailing lists is available to people with electronic-mail access to the Internet. So much is available here that it would make little sense to try to compress it into a single chapter, much less the tail end of one. The next two chapters, therefore, will explain how you can follow discussions on everything from nuclear physics to medieval archaeology by using your Internet mailbox.

Mailing lists moving across the Internet are available, as are academic discussions routed through gateways with BITNET. A final bonus: a large and growing number of electronic journals can be delivered to your mailbox, often as pointer messages with instructions on how to retrieve the entire issue. These, too, will be explained in the chapters that follow.

A Final Caution

While electronic mail offers rich resources from the Internet, you should be careful about incurring unnecessary expenses. As the next chapter demonstrates, mailing lists can tempt you with a dizzying number of subjects, but their daily message count can be high. If you use a commercial on-line service, you should carefully examine the provisions of your account to see what kind of charges may be involved. Some services carry charges to receive Internet mail, and some may limit the size of files you can store.

CompuServe's mail options are a case in point. The service offers two levels of access. One, a "pay-as-you-go" plan, simply charges you for the on-line time you spend as you retrieve your messages, whether they're from the Internet or somewhere else. The other, the "standard plan," charges a flat rate of $8.95 for a range of basic services. One of these is mail.

Now it gets tricky. While you aren't charged for connect time while using mail under this plan, you are charged by the message for Internet messages. There is a fifteen-cents minimum charge for receiving an Internet message of up to seventy-five hundred characters, with an additional five cents per twenty-five hundred characters. The plan does provide a monthly mail allowance of nine dollars, so the cost of Internet messages could be absorbed up to that amount; you wouldn't, in other words, begin to pay until charges exceed nine dollars.

However, as you learn your way around the Internet, you'll realize that bringing in big text files and binary files for decoding can quickly push you past the limit. Other services may not charge for receiving Internet messages, but may include a storage charge. DELPHI, for example, offers its Internet service for three dollars a month in addition to its regular pricing plans; the Internet option includes a transfer allocation of 10 MB. This refers to the total volume of incoming and outgoing mail messages and FTP files. (Remember that DELPHI has full Internet access and hence provides FTP and Telnet services.) But the service also charges for storage—the first 25,600 characters are free, while each additional 1,024 characters are billed at sixteen cents per month.

The point is, each commercial on-line system has its own billing mechanisms, and considering the volume of traffic the Internet can generate, you should check carefully to be sure you know what your system's requirements are. If you plan to pursue multiple mailing lists, for example, you may well decide you'll save money by opting for a full-service Internet provider offering extensive disk storage and, perhaps, a flat rate for access. You'll also, of course, enjoy the benefits of full Internet access, including Telnet and FTP.

CHAPTER EIGHT NOTES

1. I got this idea from Dick Kahane's **ftpnet.zip** file, which I strongly recommend for Compuserve users. It's in TapCis Forum Library 16, *TAPNEWS/Fact File*. Although written for TapCis users, it's equally applicable to CompuServe members using other communications programs. This file also contains version 4.21 of Richard Marks' freeware MS-DOS implementation of **uudecode.**
2. Thanks to Vinton Cerf for pointing this out to me.

....

BITNET:

The Art of the List

BITNET is a fascinating resource for Internet users, but many long-time network aficionados don't take advantage of its power. This network has proven a smashing success at its primary task, to link universities and create communications links between academic communities. But because it relies on older communications protocols and focuses on academic subjects just as often as more general topics, BITNET isn't glitzy, and it doesn't get the media coverage the Internet is beginning to receive. Let's face it—people don't rush out to get Internet accounts just so they can mine the gateway into BITNET.

What a shame. The information found on BITNET is world-class, and if getting at it is harder than it ought to be, it's up to us to learn how to manage the connection. Besides, BITNET is growing closer to the Internet all the time, with improvements in its basic protocols and new user interfaces sure to emerge in the near future. An excellent resource for those hoping to expand an education or explore an idea, BITNET deserves more attention outside of the academy than it normally gets. The last thing we need is to keep our universities shut off from the give-and-take of the rest of the world. Networks, after all, are designed to make connections, not set up walls. Let's explore.

Why BITNET

My mailbox says it all. An average morning takes me traveling through a wide realm of ideas, one I've tailored expressly to match my interests. A discussion of Anglo-Saxon England—was the burial site at Sutton Hoo a later artifact than is commonly thought? Can contemporary blood types be used to analyze settlement patterns in medieval Iceland? A look at computer networking—what on-line journals are about to be published, and what implications does the field of on-line publishing hold for research in a variety of disciplines? A debate on multicultural ethics—what preconceptions do Americans take with them when they visit Japan? What do the Japanese themselves think of foreign visitors? A question on CD-ROMs: which of the available CD-ROM players is the most reliable?

Messages on all these topics and much more flow to me through BITNET, a computer network set up to foment creativity in the universities and to inspire our leaders in research and education to new and better work. Because of its origins in the academic community, BITNET is intimidating at first blush to users of commercial on-line services like CompuServe and GEnie. Shouldn't a network linking major universities, a tool used for communications between academic specialists, be off-limits for the rest of us? Meeker souls may assume so, and so, too, may some academic users, a few of whom would prefer to keep their discussions entirely to themselves. Human nature is immutable, it seems; once we've found a place we like, it's tempting to close the doors to everyone else.

And then there's the change in vocabulary. Suddenly we're talking about LISTSERVs instead of mailing lists—a vocabulary foreign to many users of the Internet. The way we sign on for discussions, because it's fully automated, is itself intimidating. How do we sign on, and what happens if we make a mistake in what we tell the computer? It's because of questions like these that many Internet users don't take full advantage of the resources available to them on BITNET, or they think of them only as an afterthought. Besides, the thinking goes, isn't BITNET behind the curve when it comes to advanced networking? Does it really have that much to offer?

The answer is, BITNET offers much indeed. And while it's true that its technology isn't state of the art, what counts are the resources behind the machines, and finding a way to reach them. Exploration requires a certain single-mindedness—you don't go into a wilderness thinking you'll only explore those areas that make you most comfortable. As you're about to see when you learn how to tap BITNET's mailing lists and, later, its file archives, this network is a challenge. The advantage you'll gain by using it, though, is immense, because BITNET is a resource like no other.

Connecting roughly 1,500 organizations in fifty-two countries, the network is operated by the Corporation for Research and Educational Networking (CREN), which supports education, research, and development worldwide. BITNET carries electronic mail and mailing list traffic; it also provides for document and program transfer among educational institutions and access to BITNET server machines. For Internet users, there are almost three thousand readily accessible discussion groups on various academic topics, making this unusually fertile ground for the intellectually adventuresome. The notion that such riches would be available to interested parties worldwide would have struck all previous generations of scholars as fanciful nonsense.

BITNET'S BACKGROUND

Created in 1981, BITNET was envisaged as a way of keeping faculty members at our universities in communication with their fellow institutions. For the concept, we thank Ira H. Fuchs, then Vice Chancellor for university systems at the City University of New York (CUNY), and Greydon Freeman, director of the Yale Computing Center at Yale University. Fuchs had IBM's example to look at: he knew that the giant corporation's VNET network connected its programmers, researchers, and managers worldwide, using IBM software and leased telephone lines. As VNET developed, each link added to the chain was responsible for its own connection to the network. VNET became a paradigm for what Fuchs and Freeman foresaw as a communications link for higher education.

CUNY was in some respects the ideal proving ground for such an experiment. Both CUNY and Yale had some experience using network software to connect their own computers; CUNY, in fact, connected nineteen colleges across New York's five boroughs, and the linkage to Yale simply extended its reach. Fuchs and Freeman studied computing facilities at various institutions, concluding that an IBM-based communications protocol would make sense, given the number of users supported by Big Blue's machines. Folding into the concept the notion that computers could be used just as readily for textual data as computer programs, not to mention electronic mail, they began sending letters to schools with major IBM installations, encouraging them to participate in the new network. Despite its reliance on the IBM protocol, the computers on the net range from IBM systems to VAX machines, UNIX workstations, and a number of other computer types, all communicating using the same protocol. Once again, computer networking defeats the parochial limitations of operating systems and hardware.

The philosophy was straightforward: each school was to pay for its own communications link to the network, and each would make it possible for at least one new member to connect to BITNET. And as the network grew, each member agreed to move traffic bound for other members with no charge. BITNET's computers use a "store and forward" method based on an IBM NJE communications protocol—this means that a file goes from one site to another by passing through a series of intermediate nodes.

Moving over 9600-bps leased lines, each file must be sent in its entirety from one node to the next before continuing down the chain. If a connection between two nodes is severed, the file is simply stored until the connection is reestablished. In the absence of alternate routing strategies, a site can therefore be cut off, as can any site relying on mail passing through its computers. Imagine the early network as a tree, with its trunk at CUNY. Traffic to each host had only one path to follow, with the limitations that implies.

The system worked, but problems arose due to the nature of traffic flow in this kind of network pattern, or topology. Slow network connections and a lack of redundancy hampered communications. The solution was to move BITNET traffic using the Internet's protocols, adding the routing redundancy and higher speed connections offered by the TCP/IP network. In 1989, under the name BITNET II, BITNET was reorganized into regions, setting up computers in each as root nodes for that area. These core nodes, in turn, were connected by high-speed data lines, forming in essence a high-speed backbone network for BITNET traffic.

The term "BITNET" stands for "Because It's Time" Network, a moniker that quickly began to prove itself accurate as the net grew. After eighteen months, the fledgling network had reached into twenty universities, one of them—the University of California at Berkeley—providing connections throughout the West Coast. By 1984, a hundred organizations were included, over five hundred by 1989. BITNET's corporate name changed to CREN when it merged with the Computer Science Network, or CSNET (originally funded by the National Science Foundation), in 1989. CSNET was discontinued in 1991, but CREN continues its robust work, organizing BITNET's far-reaching activities in support of education and research in a noncommercial environment.

IBM was more than an inspiration for BITNET; the company also provided initial funding for centralized network services with a 1984 grant. This led to the establishment of BITNIC, BITNET's Network Information Center, and the grant included an IBM mainframe computer which would serve as the central information site for the network. When the grant expired in 1987, BITNET's funding came solely from membership dues. Today, CREN counts some 576 members in the United States and Mexico, including universities, colleges, research laboratories, primary and secondary schools, and government agencies.[1]

But BITNET reaches beyond the United States and Mexico into more than thirteen hundred research sites around the world. Among the most significant BITNET international connections are those to NetNorth in Canada and EARN (the European Academic Research Network) in Europe. Both are loosely considered to be part of BITNET, though in fact each network is maintained individually. NetNorth began as an agreement between eight Canadian universities in 1983, linking IBM mainframe computers. EARN now connects over 750 computers in 24 countries, extending from Europe into Africa and the Middle East. BITNET also links to networks like GulfNet in the Persian Gulf area, RUNCOL in Colombia, ANSP in Brazil and CAREN in Asia.

The list of member institutions included in BITNET, EARN and NetNorth is an impressive one indeed. From the Universidad Nacional de Cordoba in Argentina to the University of Bahrain, from the Pedagogical Institute of Cyprus to the University of Helsinki. There are links to Egypt, Hong Kong, Ireland, Hungary, Iceland, Peru, and India. Never have scholars been provided as useful a communications tool, keeping research up to date and colleagues informed of developments wherever they occur.

BITNET's growth has propelled it into new terrain. Networks are designed to perform precise functions, but they almost always lead to new implementations that couldn't have been thought of by their original designers. So although the communications protocols that drive BITNET are different from those of the Internet, a "gateway" system has allowed users on BITNET to send and receive electronic mail from the Internet. The growth in traffic between the networks encourages the idea that they will one day merge; however, the BITNET protocols do not support direct file transfer between the networks, nor does the nature of their connection allow Internet users to tap BITNET's computers interactively (although it is possible for BITNET users to retrieve files from anonymous FTP sites on the Internet by electronic mail, through a system known as BITFTP).

BITNET AND THE MEDIEVAL UNIVERSITY

Before I explain the concept behind BITNET mailing lists, a few thoughts on what this network signifies. In the early Middle Ages, Europe's schools were structured around a body of common knowledge which the scholar was expected to master. Unlike today's higher education, with its few requirements and curricula targeted toward career goals, early education was based on the premise that students should master knowledge across a broad spectrum.

Their studies were not confined to a specialty like mathematics or grammar, but included rhetoric, the art of speaking well, and communicating. Students were to acquire knowledge of geometry and astronomy, of dialectics and music. These seven liberal arts, known as the Trivium and Quadrivium, encouraged the dissemination of a broad cultural inheritance, and led directly to the scholasticism whose legacy was the great European universities at Paris, Oxford, Bologna, and Salerno. No student, whether studying law, medicine, or philosophy, could proceed without this rich grounding in truths then considered universal.

These notions, alien today, would come to fruition in the Renaissance, perhaps the last era in which people believed it was possible to master all human knowledge. Distant as it seems, the medieval system has much to teach us. Its scope was daring, its aim audacious, and today's intellectual accomplishments, from the equations that took Voyager to Neptune to the communications protocols that drive BITNET and the Internet, descend directly from it.

Today we think in terms of specialties, and indeed, knowledge seems inescapably bounded by the limits of what a single individual can master in a lifetime. But we've become a culture of specialists to our loss, for the cross-linking of knowledge, the fertilization of ideas from a wide range of disciplines, is at the core of human inquiry. There are times as I go through my mail, reading BITNET messages from scholars worldwide on subjects ranging from the *Canterbury Tales* to particle physics research, that I suspect Roger Bacon, Duns Scotus, or Thomas Aquinas would have been right at home with network communications. In this as in other things, they are more modern than we imagine. Our challenge is to equal their curiosity.

WHEN ANALOGIES FAIL

E-mail is remarkably versatile, yet it places few demands upon the imagination. We can relate it to its "real-world" counterpart—the U.S. Postal Service. The analogy is clear and workable. The Postal Service takes a physical letter, examines the address, and delivers it to the person listed at that address. The electronic mail system takes an electronic letter, uses the routing information in its header to track down the recipient, and delivers it to his or her mailbox. True, electronic mail is astonishingly fast, and its improvement over regular postal delivery is obvious. But the basic concept—one-to-one communication through a central delivery mechanism, is one we're all familiar with.

Where e-mail strains the limits of the analogy, though, is when we extend it into new terrain. If one-to-one delivery is what I think of when I speak of electronic mail, then how do we regard the one-to-many communication provided by BITNET's powerful LISTSERV capabilities? Here, we are gathering mail at a central site and then distributing it to a group of interested people, who have specifically requested to receive mail in this way. What the group has in common is a shared interest, and any members of the group may participate in the resulting discussion. This is no longer a one-to-one but a one-to-many form of communication.

The two forms of mail have an evasive boundary, it's true. I can send a message to a colleague across the country and include a list of other recipients by using the **mail** program's carbon copy capabilities; the same could be managed by many other e-mail programs. I can set things up so my recipients know who else is receiving the message, or I can shield that information by using blind carbon copies, as we saw in Chapter 7. But even so, while I have enabled a one-to-many link, I haven't given it the institutional life or structure provided by a mailing list. What I've done informally as a one-time occurrence mailing lists implement as a regular way of disseminating information, with its own set of protocols and responsibilities.

BRINGING ORDER TO THE CHAOS

Back in the 1960s, I discovered the joys of correspondence. In those pre-desktop-computer days, a typewriter was the tool of choice, and I used my Smith-Corona, a beautiful old model passed along in the family since the 1920s, to write letters to fellow science fiction enthusiasts around the world. Each day, the trip to the mailbox was an adventure, because I never knew how many letters might be waiting. I was seldom disappointed, and never happier than when a particularly fat envelope arrived from one of my correspondents, carrying a round robin letter.

These letters weren't one-to-one communications either. You signed on to participate in a group discussion, whose topic could range far and wide. When you joined, it was customary to send a photograph and a brief biography so other people involved in the letter would know who you were. Then the letter would circulate. Each month or so, you received an envelope with letters from seven or eight other people. You read all of them and added your own comments to each. The discussion was public and you received responses from everyone involved in the letter.

Take the round-robin-letter concept I just outlined and extend it into the world of electronic communications. Those same seven or eight people would find it easy to move messages over a network, but the situation could quickly get out of hand. Given that correspondents could reply to everyone and deliver the results the same day, the letter would circulate from person to person as if around the rim of a wheel, with no central source of organization. Instead of one person having the cumulative letter at a time, everyone would have a more or less up-to-date version of it. Anarchy would quickly reign as each correspondent added comments and differing versions shot across cyberspace.

Both BITNET and the Internet have set up structured mailing lists to counter such chaos, and they function remarkably well. A centralized structure is imposed over the circulating material, usually with a single person supervising the entire operation. Instead of bouncing and multiplying across the network, messages flow to the person in charge, who then sees that the discussion is moderated, or at least that each person's contributions become available for all to read. Best of all, this material is then delivered to your electronic mailbox, in the form of a series of messages that keep coming in until you resign from the group in question.

BITNET's MAILING LIST COMMUNITY

Given BITNET's academic background, it's no surprise that the mailing lists you will likely encounter on this network are often research-oriented. BITNET's lists are populated with scientists, teachers, university librarians, and policy analysts. And given the diversity of their studies, the huge range of available topics ensures there will never be a shortage of reading material for the enterprising network participant. These lists proceed without fuss or fanfare. They're a quiet and continuing dialogue between some of the best minds in our culture, one of the academy's best kept secrets.

How do you know what's available? The answer is found in a document maintained by the BITNET Network Information Center, otherwise known as BITNIC, in Washington, DC. This organization maintains a list of BITNET discussion groups which can be had for the asking. The resultant document is large and contains the complete directory of what's current on the mailing list scene. It's a critical document for your network library.

• •

What You Need: A Directory of all BITNET Mailing Lists

The Document: **List of All LISTSERV Lists**

How to Get It: By electronic mail. Send a message to **LISTSERV@BIT-NIC.bitnet.** Leave the subject field blank; in the message itself, enter only **LIST GLOBAL.** The document will be sent to your mailbox. There, you can save it to a file for subsequent reference, printing out, or downloading.

If you need further information, contact

BITNET Network Information Center
1112 Sixteenth St., NW, Suite 600
Washington, DC, 20036
202-872-4200

Incidentally, another useful way to search for LISTSERV lists is to use a WAIS server. WAIS, which we'll examine in Chapter 13, allows you to interactively search the List of Lists. More on using WAIS for this and other search tasks in that chapter.

• •

Figure 9.1 shows a small sample of what you'll see when you receive this list. The section in question, drawn from the O-P portion of the list, covers everything from news in Pakistan to archaeology, from the PageMaker program for desktop publishers to Yale's Organization for Tropical Studies. The name of each list is on the left, followed by the letter L. The network address and description follow on the right.

BITNET lists range widely in subject and structure. Some are general, covering broad topics like philosophy or the outdoors. Others focus with laser-like precision: Early English Drama, Macintosh terminal emulation, Turk-

Figure 9.1
A sampling of the
master list of BITNET
mailing lists maintained
by BITNIC.

```
OS2RZ-L      OS2RZ-L@DOSUNI1      Fragen zu OS2, (lokale Liste, Uni Osnabrueck+
OT_NATL      OT_NATL@ARIZVM1      Theta Tau National Fraternity
OTS-L        OTS-L@YALEVM         Organization for Tropical Studies at Yale Un+
OURASG-L     OURASG-L@RYERSON     Ontario University Registrar's Association D+
OUSSS-L      OUSSS-L@UTORONTO     Ontario University Systems Software Support +
OUTAGES      OUTAGES@ASUACAD      ASU Network Outage Notification
OUTDOR-L     OUTDOR-L@ULKYVM      Outdoor Discussion Group
OVISION      OVISION@VTVM1        ObjectVision, Application Development
OXYGEN-L     OXYGEN-L@MIZZOU1     Oxygen Free Radical Biology and Medicine Dis+
PA_NET       PA_NET@SUVM          Public Administration Network
PACARC-L     PACARC-L@WSUVM1      Pacific Rim Archaeology Interest List
PACE-L       PACE-L@GSUVM1        PACE-L -- PACE degree audit system discussio+
PACIFIC      PACIFIC@BRUFPB       FORUM FOR AND ABOUT PACIFIC OCEAN AND ISLANDS
PACS-L       PACS-L@UHUPVM1       Public-Access Computer Systems Forum
PACS-P       PACS-P@UHUPVM1       Public-Access Computer Systems Publications
PACV-L       PACV-L@DEARN         PACV-L  Discussions list
PAGE-L       PAGE-L@UCF1VM        IBM 3812/3820 Tips and Problems Discussion L+
PAGEIN-L     PAGEIN-L@HEARN       Discussion List for the CEC RARE II PAGEIN p+
PAGEMAKR     PAGEMAKR@INDYCMS     PageMaker for Desktop Publishers
PAINTBOL     PAINTBOL@TCSVM       Paintball discussion list
PAKISTAN     PAKISTAN@ASUACAD     (Peered) The Pakistan News Service
```

ish studies. Some disseminate official information, like severe weather outlooks for various parts of the country. Others are loose discussions where anyone weighs in with an opinion and open debate reigns. Needless to say, the topic has much to do with the level of activity on the mailing list. A controversial subject may generate heated discussions and land fifty messages a day in your mailbox. A quieter list may chug along virtually unnoticed until a flurry of new messages arrive to remind you of its existence.

Incidentally, if you prefer not to scan through the entire global list of BITNET possibilities, there's a shortcut available. Rather than sending the **LIST GLOBAL** command to the BITNIC LISTSERV, try **LIST GLOBAL /TOPIC.** If you were interested, for example, in physics, you might send **LIST GLOBAL /PHYSICS.** Use the same BITNIC address as above. Later, we'll use this searching shortcut to target mailing lists for research purposes. But you really should keep a copy of the global list in your filing cabinet for reference.

THE NICETIES OF BITNET PARTICIPATION

BITNET's mailing lists aren't normal computer bulletin boards, nor should they be treated as such. They provide an opportunity to bridge the seemingly insuperable gap between an academic community too often isolated from society and the community of interested lay people who can benefit from their continuing research. BITNET is a tremendous medium for self-education, for following up on interests you thought you left behind when you left school. It is a medium for exploring ideas and keeping up with breakthroughs in both the humanities and the sciences.

For scholars, the network is a platform for exchanging ideas. Imagine talking to valued colleagues daily, whereas before your conversations were limited to occasional academic conferences. BITNET does exactly what Ira Fuchs and Greydon Freeman intended; it promotes collaboration with distant colleagues and distributes news lightning-fast throughout the research community. The ability to sit in on such a medium is one of the most remarkable features of your access to the Internet and its related outer networks.

So use it well. Remember that serious work is being discussed here; the quality of the ongoing discussion depends directly upon the willingness of participants to bring new ideas to the table and to follow basic rules of propriety. As a BITNET eavesdropper, you should plan on listening and absorbing before you leave any messages. In most of the mailing lists I subscribe to, I'm purely a listener, taking the opportunity to learn from the ongoing discussions. There's no point in jumping in unless you have something genuinely useful to add to the proceedings.

As you examine a new mailing list, then, the idea is to find out what the tenor of the discussion is, follow its byways, and benefit from the expertise you find there. Each mailing list has its own feel, and certain conventions may have emerged to guide its activities. BITNET lists can be surprisingly informal, but the usual caveats about avoiding sarcasm and easily misunderstood comments apply.

Another caveat, and this is a big one: be careful about how you reply to a mailing list. Remember the number of subscribers out there. If you choose to send a message to a particular poster, you should ensure you respond to his or her address only. Mailing lists can become hopelessly clogged with inconsequential messages meant for one pair of eyes only, but accidentally distributed to the entire subscription list by a careless use of the reply function.

This can be more or less of a problem depending upon your relationship to the people subscribing to the mailing list in question. But a sarcastic remark about someone's latest comment which you meant to pass along to a personal friend on the list might have implications for your on-line popularity if it were distributed to everyone. Be cautious, and keep in mind that a mailing list is a public forum, designed for an audience of interested if diverse peers. All will benefit when everyone plays by these simple rules.

In addition, note the following guidelines adopted by CREN as part of its acceptable use policy. Use of CREN networks, says the organization, shall:

- Be consistent with the purposes and goals of the networks.
- Avoid interfering with the work of other users of the networks.
- Avoid disrupting the network host systems (nodes).
- Avoid disrupting network services.

These are, needless to say, broad statements. To place them into context, CREN provides the following examples:

- Messages that are likely to result in the loss of recipients' work or systems are prohibited.
- CREN networks are not to be used for commercial purposes, such as marketing, reselling bandwidth, or business transactions between commercial organizations.
- Advertising is forbidden. Discussion of a product's relative advantages and disadvantages by users of the product is encouraged. Vendors may respond to questions about their products as long as the responses are not in the nature of advertising.
- CREN networks may be used for the provision of services which support the needs and purposes of the CREN networks, and for which a charge

is made, if the network is an optional mechanism for provision of this service for which no additional charge is made, and as long as the use of the service is consistent with the bandwidth of the network and the forwarding hosts. Providers of such information may be non-profit or for-profit organizations.

- "Chain letters," "broadcasting" messages to lists or individuals, and other types of use which would cause congestion of the networks or otherwise interfere with the work of others are not allowed.
- BITNET files will be limited to sizes determined and reviewed periodically. (Note: The current limit is three-hundred-thousand bytes per file transmitted.)

I strongly suggest you get a copy of these guidelines and keep it with your other BITNET materials. Networks rely on our prudent use of their resources.

What You Need: CREN's Guidelines on Network Usage

The Document: **Acceptable Use Policy**

How to Get It: Send mail to **LISTSERV@BITNIC.bitnet.** Leave the subject line blank. In the body of the message, type **CREN NET_USE.**

PUZZLING OUT A BITNET ADDRESS

Armed with your master list of BITNET lists, you're in position to sign on and begin reading. But first let's examine a mailing list address. I'll choose the following entry:

```
TWAIN-L         TWAIN-L@YORKVM1    Mark Twain Forum
```

After all, I'm from Missouri, and Mark Twain is one of my philosophical forebears. To sign up for this list, I'll need to send mail. But to whom? This is not a conventional Internet address; it's a BITNET address we need to disentangle.

The differences? Notice the lack of periods in the address, and the fact that it's all in caps. Notice, too, the lack of a domain name like **.edu** or **.com,** the signifiers used with Internet addresses. Instead, we're looking at a relatively straightforward address statement. To make sense of it, realize that BITNET user names and host names obey certain conventions. They're limited to eight uppercase numbers and letters.

The *node,* or computer in question, has a unique identifier, in this case **YORKVM1.** Each BITNET computer has such a node name, which identifies it to other computers. The user ID, in this case TWAIN-L, is used in conjunction with the node name. Thus we refer to this address as "TWAIN-L at YORKVM1." This information is sufficient to allow another BITNET computer to find the address, but the Internet doesn't yet have enough to work with.

Fortunately, there are basic translation principles to follow. Take the BITNET address and simply add *.bitnet* to the end of it. In the above example, the BITNET node **YORKVM1** thus becomes **YORKVM1.bitnet.** Now the Internet can route traffic as desired. This method will probably work, and you should give it a try, but there are cases where mail addressed using this method will bounce. Some computers understand this short-hand routing, some don't. Here's the alternative. Change the **TWAIN-L@YORKVM1** to **TWAIN-L%YORK-VM1@cunyvm.cuny.edu.** In doing so, you're directing the traffic to a known BITNET gateway into the Internet (the node at CUNY, the Ur of BITNET sites).

There are two addresses to work with in a BITNET list. One is the site to which messages are routed; the other is the LISTSERV address, properly considered the place for administrative messages to go. The Mark Twain list rotates around the address **TWAIN-L@YORKVM1**; that is, this is where messages from participants go, and from which they are dispersed to the entire list. But the address for routine matters of list maintenance is **LISTSERV@YORKVM1.bitnet.**

Memorize that principle: the LISTSERV address is where you send routine administrative requests. Memorize it again. Its use will become clear in what follows.

LISTSERV AND THE PLEASURES OF AUTOMATION

Before sending our sign-up message to the Twain list, a bit of background. A particular protocol must be followed when you subscribe to these lists, not out of some long-standing computer tradition, but because of the necessities of handling automated traffic. For LISTSERVs are indeed automatic. The administrative to and fro involved with signing people up, removing them from lists, and what not, is handled by computerized list functions managed by a server. Remember, a server is simply a program running on a network machine; it has its own user identification and can often accept commands sent by electronic mail.

Most servers you'll deal with run the LISTSERV program written by Eric Thomas, which means the commands are common to all machines running LISTSERV throughout the system. LISTSERV began as a mailing list program created by Ira Fuchs and Daniel J. Oberst, but its quick growth and popularity created problems. The people in charge of the various lists were responsible for signing up new subscribers and deleting those who wanted to leave. For these volunteers, the work load quickly became too heavy to handle.

Revised LISTSERV, which Thomas wrote in 1986, overcame the restrictions of the earlier version by providing new functions. The server could now maintain a list by handling subscription requests automatically, and data files could be maintained as list archives. BITNIC maintains a number of useful files which we'll use to build up our own BITNET library. With both files and electronic mail, our gateway access into BITNET precludes interactive usage of its facilities, so the process requires you to ask the server for specific data through a precise protocol.[2]

The method is simple enough: you send mail to the server in question and the text of your message is interpreted as a command by that machine. Your entry to a BITNET list is handled, then, by sending a properly formatted message to the correct address.

Let's use this method now to retrieve a core document called **BITNET USERHELP.** To get it, contact the BITNET Network Information Center by sending mail to **LISTSERV@BITNIC.bitnet.** Here's how the message will look as sent through the **mail** program:

```
%mail listserv@bitnic.bitnet
Subject:
get bitnet userhelp
.
```

Note that I left the **Subject:** field blank. The command takes up the first line of the message. Sending it, I receive in return a useful document containing material on BITNET's structure, the capabilities of its mailing lists, its links with other networks and more; there's even a suggested reading list.

Here's another document to add to the library.

• •

What You Need: BITNET Background Information

The Documents: **BITNET USERHELP** and **USING BITNET: AN INTRO-DUCTION**

How to Get Them: Through **LISTSERV@BITNIC.bitnet.** Send mail with no subject line, and the one-line message **GET BITNET USERHELP.** For the Introduction, send **GET BITNET INTRO.**

• •

SIGNING ON TO A LIST

To subscribe to the Twain list I need only put the same principles to work. I send a message to **LISTSERV@YORKVM1.bitnet** containing the following request: **SUBSCRIBE TWAIN-L Paul Gilster**

Follow the format exactly, by placing the subscription statement before your name. Note, too, that the name I've entered is my actual name, not my electronic mail address. The LISTSERV is able to pull the information it needs out of the header of the message. Again, you can leave the **Subject:** field of your message blank, as the LISTSERV needs no information there. Send this message—and be sure you're sending to the LISTSERV administrative address rather than the regular mailing list address! You should quickly receive a message back letting you know what happened when you attempted to sign up.

After sending the above mail to **LISTSERV@YORKVM1.bitnet,** I received the message shown in Figure 9.2 (minus extraneous header information).

From this point on, I can expect my mailbox to swell with messages about the sage of Hannibal. Remember, from here on, messages you want to send to the list should be addressed to the list address, not the LISTSERV address. Doing the latter will cause whatever you say to be propagated among the rest of the members of the mailing list, embarrassing for you and aggravating for them, because this is a relatively common occurrence. All mail, then, would go to **TWAIN-L@YORKVM1.bitnet.** (Remember to add *.bitnet* to the address or your mail will be bounced!)

A general principle of computing applies here as well as elsewhere on the network—it's as important to know how to get out of something as it is to get into it. Many newcomers, excited by the wealth of knowledge and subject matter represented in the various kinds of mailing lists, subscribe to so many that their mailboxes contain hundreds of messages a day. Soon the traffic becomes

Figure 9.2
A sample sign-up
message for a BITNET
mailing list.

```
Dear networker,

Your subscription to list TWAIN-L (Mark Twain Forum) has been accepted.

Note: your distribution options have been defaulted as per the "SET TWAIN-L
REPRO" command.

You may leave the list at any time by sending a "SIGNOFF TWAIN-L" command
to LISTSERV@YORKVM1.BITNET (or LISTSERV@VM1.YORKU.CA). Please note that
this command must NOT be sent to the list address (TWAIN-L@YORKVM1) but to
the LISTSERV address (LISTSERV@YORKVM1).

The amount of acknowledgement you wish to receive from this list upon com-
pletion of a mailing operation can be changed by means of a "SET TWAIN-L op-
tion" command, where "option" may be either "ACK" (mail acknowledgement),
"MSGACK" (interactive messages only) or "NOACK".

Contributions sent to this list are automatically archived. You can obtain
a list of the available archive files by sending an "INDEX TWAIN-L" command
to LISTSERV@YORKVM1.BITNET (or LISTSERV@VM1.YORKU.CA). These files can then
be retrieved by means of a "GET TWAIN-L filetype" command, or using the
database search facilities of LISTSERV. Send an "INFO DATABASE" command for
more information on the latter.

Please note that it is presently possible for anybody to determine that you
are signed up to the list through the use of the "REVIEW" command, which re-
turns the network address and name of all the subscribers. If you do not
wish your name to be available to others in this fashion, just issue a "SET
TWAIN-L CONCEAL" command.

More information on LISTSERV commands can be found in the LISTSERV refer-
ence card, which you can retrieve by sending an "INFO REFCARD" command to
LISTSERV@YORKVM1.BITNET (or LISTSERV@VM1.YORKU.CA).

Virtually,

The LISTSERV management
```

overwhelming. To remove yourself from a BITNET list, send mail to the LISTSERV address as before, but include the statement: **SIGNOFF TWAIN-L.** As you see, this information is included in the message from the Twain LISTSERV.

An alternative to resigning, of course, is to become such a whiz at mailbox manipulation that you sift through hundreds of messages a day and find the ones you want to read. I choose the latter course, because try as I may, I can't bring myself to leave many of the good lists. I often skim the message headers of a given list for a month or two without reading anything, but invariably something tweaks my interest and I'm back in.

It's common practice, incidentally, no matter how high your level of interest, to turn off the message flow if you plan to be out of town or otherwise away from your computer connection for any length of time. This prevents you from returning to a mountain of mail. To do so, send a **NOMAIL** command to the relevant LISTSERV. For example, to suspend mail delivery from the TWAIN-L list, I would send:

`SET TWAIN-L NOMAIL`

Figure 9.3
Response to a REVIEW request, giving bacground on the Pacific Rim Archaeology Special Interest list.

```
*    Pacific Rim Archaeology Interest List
*
*+
*
*    Review= Public
*    Subscription= Open
*    Send= Public
*    Notify= Yes
*    Reply-to= List,Respect
*    Files= Yes
*    Confidential= No
*    Validate= Store only
*    X-Tags= Comment
*    Ack= No
*    Stats= Normal,Owner
*    Formcheck= No
*    Notebook= Yes,A,Monthly,Public
*
*    Owner= CROES@WSUVM1,STAFF-L
*    Errors-to= Owner,Postmaster
*
*    PACARC-L Interest Group Distribution List is a
*    discussion group on Pacific Rim Archaeology.
*    The topics include meetings, articles, software,
*    theories, materials, methods, tools, and any topic
*    related to Pacific Archaeology.
*
*    Created April 22, 1988, by Dale Croes
```

To reactivate the list, the command's opposite number is:

`SET TWAIN-L MAIL`

Another tool can be helpful when you're contemplating signing on to a mailing list. By sending a command to the relevant LISTSERV, you can receive information about the intended use of a given mailing list and the subscribers who currently use it (be advised—not all lists support this command). The form to follow is:

`REVIEW` *listname*

Use the LISTSERV address listed for the group you're interested in. To learn more about the Pacific Rim Archaeology Interest List found in Figure 9.1, I'd send the following command to **LISTSERV@WSUVM1.bitnet:**

`REVIEW PACARC-L`

Soon I receive a review message, as found in Figure 9.3. The message will also include a list of subscribers, not shown here.

BITNET ARCHIVES—WHERE THE TREASURE IS

But wait, we're not through with that Twain message. Take another look at it. Contributions to the list, it seems, are archived automatically. An index of the archived files can be obtained by sending this command to the LISTSERV address: **INDEX TWAIN-L.** The files can be retrieved by using yet another command. Now we get an even broader glimpse of the powers of the LISTSERV system. Multiply the hundreds of lists you find in the document you retrieved from BITNIC and then consider the possibilities for archival storage of messages and other information inside those lists. BITNET, far from being a passive message-bouncing system, emerges as a powerful research tool, provided you learn how to use it.

Let's get the index. After sending the **INDEX TWAIN-L** command to **LISTSERV@YORKVM1.bitnet,** I receive the index shown in Figure 9.4.

Figure 9.4
The index to the
TWAIN-L mailing list.

```
*   TWAIN-L FILELIST for LISTSERV@YORKVM1.
*
***************************************************************************
*
*                              rec              last - change
* filename filetype  GET PUT -fm lrecl nrecs   date     time   File description
* -------- --------   --- --- --- ----- -----  -------- -------- ----------------
* :::::::::::::::::::::::::::::::::::::::::::::::::::::::::::::::::::::::::::
*
*   The GET/PUT authorization codes shown with each file entry describe
*   who is authorized to GET or PUT the file:
*
*     ALL = Everybody
*
*:    TWA = 'OWNER(TWAIN-L)'
*
* :::::::::::::::::::::::::::::::::::::::::::::::::::::::::::::::::::::::::::
  TWAIN    RESOURCE  ALL TWA V    75   150 92/07/15 00:35:14 MT Organizations
  TWAIN-L  OLDLOG    ALL TWA V    76   243 92/07/08 11:58:43 Starts 11 Mar 92
  MTP      INFO      ALL TWA V    75   363 92/07/16 20:35:11 MT Project

*
*   NOTEBOOK archives for the list
*   (Monthly notebook)
*                              rec              last - change
* filename filetype  GET PUT -fm lrecl nrecs   date     time   Remarks
* -------- --------   --- --- --- ----- -----  -------- -------- ----------------
---------------
  TWAIN-L  LOG9204   ALL OWN V    74    14 92/04/27 11:06:34 Started on Mon,
27 Apr 1992 08:03:48 -0700
  TWAIN-L  LOG9204D  ALL OWN V    73   146 92/04/24 16:59:28 Started on Fri,
24 Apr 1992 16:56:19 EDT
  TWAIN-L  LOG9205   ALL OWN V    80   262 92/05/31 20:30:51 Started on Wed,
27 May 1992 09:23:36 CDT
  TWAIN-L  LOG9206   ALL OWN V    80  1273 92/06/26 14:42:49 Started on Mon,
1 Jun 1992 08:35:00 LCL
  TWAIN-L  LOG9207   ALL OWN V    80  1424 92/07/30 14:10:15 Started on Wed,
1 Jul 1992 01:13:04 EDT
  TWAIN-L  LOG9208   ALL OWN V    77   189 92/08/27 12:40:28 Started on Thu,
13 Aug 1992 23:14:51 EDT
  TWAIN-L  LOG9209   ALL OWN V    80   402 92/09/30 08:11:10 Started on Wed,
2 Sep 1992 07:54:00 LCL
  TWAIN-L  LOG9210   ALL OWN V    79   260 92/10/27 07:52:34 Started on Wed,
7 Oct 1992 10:25:22 PDT
  TWAIN-L  LOG9211   ALL OWN V    80  1131 92/11/30 20:28:16 Started on Thu,
5 Nov 1992 18:42:54 PST
  TWAIN-L  LOG9212   ALL OWN V    80   820 92/12/11 17:25:06 Started on Tue,
1 Dec 1992 07:51:24 CST
```

Interesting. A set of file archives, retrievable through the LISTSERV itself. Still reading in my original message from the LISTSERV, I note I can retrieve such a file through the **GET TWAIN-L** *filetype* command. To understand what this means, note how the index is structured. The filename and filetype are separated; actually, *filetype* refers to the entries beginning with the word **LOG-.** Evidently the mailing list's activity for each month is catalogued here. Let's get one of these files, **LOG9212,** which should be the list's messages for December 1992. We know we can get it because it's marked **ALL** in the index, and thus available to all comers.

I'll send the command **GET TWAIN-L LOG9212,** sent to the now familiar LISTSERV address, **LISTSERV@YORKVM1.bitnet.** In return, I receive a file containing all the messages that moved across the Twain list during December 1992. Using archival files like these is an excellent way to catch up with a mailing list. If you want to know what the major issues are and how current messages fit in with the previous flow, retrieve a few earlier files and study them. As you can see, BITNET's archival capabilities ensure that no comment made in the list is lost. If I were looking into Mark Twain for research purposes, I could stop here and examine the files maintained in the list.

It is helpful to know that back records of a mailing list are available, but studying each of them could become quite a chore if I were after, say, comments on a particular title. Let's say I want to find what people are saying about *Huckleberry Finn* in these parlous, multi-cultural times. Is there any way to home in on those messages just about Huck? Fortunately, the answer is yes.

LISTSERV's Database Capabilities

Look back at the original sign-up message from the Twain list, where you'll see that not only can we retrieve files, we can search for them using the LISTSERV database function. Remember—we can't use BITNET interactively because of the limitations of the gateway connections between it and the Internet. But the LISTSERV system includes database functions which can be used in so-called "batch" mode, meaning we can construct a complete search, submit it to a LISTSERV, and let the computer at the other end run its procedures, sending us the results. In this way, we can extract what we need from a given list's archives without having to go through the entire index.

To activate the procedure, we must use the LISTSERV Command Job Language Interpreter (CJLI), a set of conventions which the LISTSERV can work with. The following is a sample search I constructed to look for messages containing the word "Huck" in the Twain archives:

```
//
Database Search DD=Rules
//Rules DD    *
Search Huck in TWAIN-L
Index
/*
```

Examine this search routine for a moment. It's not necessary to master all the intricacies of the LISTSERV CJLI to put it to work. The basic template follows:

```
//
Database Search DD=Rules
//Rules DD   *
command 1
command 2
...
/*
```

We'll use this template as our basic search mechanism; LISTSERV understands what it means. I'll focus on the lines marked **command.** As you can see from the preceding sample search, the first command is clear-cut—search for any messages that include the word **Huck.** I've also asked that the results include an index telling us which messages meet the search criteria. We run the search by sending it directly to **LISTSERV@YORKVM1.bitnet.** We get back the list shown in Figure 9.5.

As you can see, we found 68 messages meeting the search criteria, of which I've shown only a few. Of those listed, item number 27 seems germane; it, at least, has the title of the book listed as its subject. Let's also ask for messages 53 and 55, to find out what Huck has been up to in Hollywood and, to wrap it up for now, item 82. To retrieve these messages, we need to send another message to the LISTSERV. Use the same template, only with a different command inserted:

```
//
Database Search DD=Rules
//Rules DD   *
Search Huck in TWAIN-L
Print all of 27 53 55 82
/*
```

As before, we'll receive a message about the status of our request and a file including the information we specified. In this case, we get our four messages, which turn out to be about cinematic treatments of Huck Finn, including one four-hour version shown on Public Television.

There's plenty of material here, but remember, TWAIN-L is but one of the numerous mailing lists available through our Internet gateway into BITNET.

Figure 9.5
Search results from a search of the TWAIN-L database, looking for information on Huckleberry Finn.

```
   Search Huck in TWAIN-L
   -- Database TWAIN-L, 68 hits.

    Index
   Item #   Date    Time   Recs    Subject
   ------   ----    ----   ----    -------
   000011 92/05/31 13:15    26     Re: Hannibal, MO
   000012 92/05/31 19:40    43     Hannibal
   000014 92/06/01 10:07    39     RE: Hannibal
   000027 92/06/05 13:09    37     RE: The Adventures of Mark Twain
   000051 92/06/19 17:39    24     Re: stirring conversation up again -Reply
   000053 92/06/22 08:03    37     Mark Twain in the movies
   000055 92/06/22 09:42    20     Re: Mark Twain in the movies
   000082 92/07/07 13:32    33     Huck Finn
   000084 92/07/08 12:13    24     Old TWAIN-L log file
   000086 92/07/12 13:38    24     MT books in machine-readable form?
```

Browsing through the master list of mailing lists, another possibility emerges for Twain discussions. Because you don't have to be a member of the mailing list to get into its archives, you can explore freely through the wide range of possibilities. Here's the entry for a list specializing in American literature:

```
AMLIT-L          AMLIT-L@MIZZOU1    American Literature Discussion Group
```

Surely there would be more Twain material here. Let's find out. The address is handled just as before. We need to contact not the distribution site, but the LISTSERV; we know, therefore, to mail to **LISTSERV@MIZZOU1.bitnet.** First we'll ask for an index of files in the archive. The command, if previous experience is our guide, should be **INDEX AMLIT-L,** providing AMLIT-L maintains an archive. Bingo. After sending that command to the LISTSERV, I receive back the index shown in Figure 9.6.

Now we know there's an archive here. Let's try something different; we will ask for any messages referring to *A Connecticut Yankee in King Arthur's Court.* Here's the basic search strategy:

```
//
Database Search DD=Rules
//Rules DD    *
Search Connecticut Yankee AND Twain
Index
/*
```

Figure 9.6
A portion of the index
to the AMLIT-L mailing
list.

```
*   AMLIT-L FILELIST for LISTSERV@MIZZOU1.
*
*   Archives for list AMLIT-L (American Literature Discussion Group)
*
*   ::::::::::::::::::::::::::::::::::::::::::::::::::::::::::::::::::::::
*
*   The GET/PUT authorization codes shown with each file entry describe
*   who is authorized to GET or PUT the file:
*
*       ALL = Everybody
*       OWN = List owners
*
*
*   ::::::::::::::::::::::::::::::::::::::::::::::::::::::::::::::::::::::


*
*   NOTEBOOK archives for the list
*   (Monthly notebook)
*                            rec              last - change
   filename filetype  GET PUT -fm lrecl nrecs  date      time    Remarks
   -------- --------  --- --- --- ----- ----- -------- -------- ---------------
   AMLIT-L  LOG9204   ALL OWN V      80  1503 92/04/30 20:16:45 Started on Sun,
   19 Apr 1992 20:18:59 CDT
   AMLIT-L  LOG9205   ALL OWN V      79   790 92/05/31 11:34:09 Started on Fri,
   1 May 1992 01:35:11 CDT
   AMLIT-L  LOG9206   ALL OWN V      79   692 92/06/30 10:29:53 Started on Mon,
   1 Jun 1992 10:38:30 CDT
```

Figure 9.7
A search of TWAIN-L
for *A Connecticut Yankee*
in King Arthur's Court.

```
    Search Connecticut Yankee AND Twain in AMLIT-L
    -- Database AMLIT-L, 1 hit.

    Index
    Item #   Date    Time   Recs   Subject
    ------   ----    ----   ----   -------
    000168 92/08/26 08:14    21    Twain's Conn. Yankee
```

Note that rather than searching under one word only, I asked to see the terms **Connecticut Yankee** (this should save us from people who are merely writing in from Connecticut—their address line might trigger our search), and I added **Twain** into the mix. I capitalize AND because it's, strictly speaking, a *Boolean operator*, otherwise known as a *logical operator*. Named after 19th Century British mathematician George Boole, Boolean operators are used to specify the logical relationship between two concepts. In this case, the relationship is obvious—I want to see files containing both terms.

Figure 9.7 shows what happens when I send this search routine.

Hmmm. Only one hit. Might as well look at it.

```
//
Database Search DD=Rules
//Rules DD   *
Search Connecticut Yankee AND Twain in AMLIT-L
Print all of 168
/*
```

And we retrieve a message discussing Twain's views of science in the novel.

DELVING DEEPER INTO THE DATABASE

Using these LISTSERV database functions isn't exactly elegant. But despite their clunky construction, these search statements can be powerful tools for hunting information, and it behooves people seriously interested in using the networks as research tools to master their command structure. Before proceeding with a more refined search, then, let's consider how to get a complete set of database commands targeted especially to people with little knowledge of database systems. As always, the network helps us build up our on-line library.

• •

What You Need: A Primer on LISTSERV Databases

The Document: **Revised LISTSERV Database Functions**

How to Get It: Through BITNET Network Information Center.

Send command **INFO DATABASE** to **LISTSERV@BITNIC.bitnet.**

• •

You'll receive a lengthy document recounting basic LISTSERV database procedures, including search strategies which allow you to home in on very precise information. BITNET's interface may be ragged, but the quality of the searches you can construct is limited only by your willingness to master its command structure. It would be nice to have interactive access to these databases; we wouldn't have to send multiple jobs to the LISTSERV, searching for information first, then asking for a specific retrieval. But when you consider the range of lists in BITNET and the quality of many of these discussions, getting past the inadequacies of the batch process seems worthwhile.

TAPPING BITNET AS A REFERENCE SOURCE

With the basic search strategy in mind, then, and with knowledge that a huge group of BITNET lists exists, let's consider how we can use BITNET as a ready reference source. We'll choose a subject and send a message to the LISTSERV at the BITNET Information Center, asking it which lists apply most closely to our topic. Then we'll go into the archives and see if we can pull up anything of interest. You never know what might appear; this is like searching a huge library which only yields up its card catalog piece by piece as you move along your research path. Some BITNET searches yield more than you'd expect; others come up disappointingly short. The only way to know is to try.

For purposes of the hunt, assume we're interested in learning more about what's going on with the Hubble Space Telescope. The controversial orbiting observatory has been dogged by problems, yet it seems to be producing some interesting results despite them. What do experts in the field think about Hubble, and what are the chances it will still become the breakthrough telescope of the 1990s, as we had all along assumed it would be?

The first step in the search is to query BITNIC for which lists might apply. To do this, the routine is as follows. We'll send a command to **LISTSERV@BIT-NIC.bitnet:**

```
LIST GLOBAL /TOPIC SPACE
```

The topic is intentionally broad; perhaps there's a list specifically devoted to the Hubble project, but by casting a wide net, we can look through the results and decide which list best meets our criteria. Don't be put off if your initial query yields few or no results. I searched the list first under the term **astronomy** and

Figure 9.8
A search of BITNIC for space-related mailing lists.

```
Excerpt from the LISTSERV lists known to LISTSERV@BITNIC on 18 Dec 1992 10:56
Search string: SPACE


Network-wide ID   Full address      List title
---------------   ------------      ----------
CANSPACE          CANSPACE@UNBVM1   Canadian Space Geodesy Forum
GRAVITY           GRAVITY@UWF       Gravity Topics for Spacetime Course - Spacet+
ISDS              ISDS@UIUCVMD      ISDS Illini Space Development Society List
SEDSNEWS          SEDSNEWS@TAMVM1   News about Space from SEDS
SPACE             SPACE@FINHUTC     (Peered) Space discussions forum
                  SPACE@TCSVM       (Peered) SPACE Digest
                  SPACE@UBVM        (Peered) SPACE Digest
                  SPACE@UGA         (Peered) SPACE Digest
SPACE-IL          SPACE-IL@TAUNIVM  Israeli Space & Remote Sensing List
ST-AUDIT          ST-AUDIT@UWF      Spacetime Topics for Bitnet (Audit List)
```

Figure 9.9
A description of the
SEDSNEWS database.

```
    News about Space from SEDS
  *
  *   SEDSNEWS is an open list for distribution of informational postings
  *   from several space research facilities. VERY ACTIVE. Be sure your mailer
  *   can handle lots of traffic.
  *   This list enhances the SEDS-L list which is an open discussion list.
  *
  *   REVIEW=        PUBLIC          NOTIFY=    YES
  *   Send=          Public          Reply-to=  List,Respect
  *   Subscription=  Open            Stats=     Extended,Public
  *   Formcheck=     Yes             Files=     No
  *   Ack=           No              Mail-via=  Distribute
  *   LOOPCHECK=     NOTOCOUNT       NOTEBOOK=  YES,H,WEEKLY,PUBLIC
  *   Errors-to=     FHD@TAMVM1
  *   Newsgroups=    bit.listserv.sedsnews
  *
  *   Local=TAM*
  *
  *   OWNER= FHD@TAMVM1                          (H. Alan Montgomery)
```

found nothing. But I knew there had to be an active set of discussions on these topics—too many researchers are on-line for there not to be. The choice of **space** as an alternate search term bore fruit, as the results in Figure 9.8 indicate.

The trick now is to decide which of these lists is the most likely to pay off. The News about Space from SEDS looks promising. We'll send a **REVIEW SEDSNEWS** command to **LISTSERV@BITNIC.bitnet.** Figure 9.9 shows the relevant part of the reply. This looks like interesting material. Now we want to retrieve an index of available files. The Twain list has shown us how. We'll send the command **INDEX SEDSNEWS** to **LISTSERV@TAMVM1.bitnet** to see if there's an archive there. And yes, a message returns listing what seem to be extensive logs from 1989 to present. So let's query that database as in the following:

```
//
Database Search DD=Rules
//Rules DD    *
Search Hubble in SEDSNEWS
Index
/*
```

Back comes a remarkable list, some 350 citations on Hubble in this area. Clearly, we've stumbled upon a repository of space information. Figure 9.10 presents just a glimpse of this bounty.

As before, it's easy to pull one of these documents in. Let's get #5427, which talks about Hubble uncovering secrets of galactic evolution. We'll do it this way:

```
//
Database Search DD=Rules
//Rules DD    *
Search Hubble in SEDSNEWS
Print all of 5427
/*
```

Figure 9.10
Results of a search of
SEDSNEWS for
information on the
Hubble space
telescope.

```
005361 92/11/20 06:11  139    NASA Daily News for 11/19/92
005367 92/11/21 00:53  138    NASA Daily News for 11/20/92 (Forwarded)
005392 92/11/25 06:00   64    Hubble, Galileo Briefings Set for Dec. 1
005422 92/11/30 21:19  167    NASA Headline News for 11/30/92 (Forwarded)
005427 92/12/02 02:01  160    HST Uncovers Secrets of Galaxy Evolution
005431 92/12/01 20:28  173    NASA Headline News for 12/01/92 (Forwarded)
005460 92/12/08 19:25  134    NASA Daily News for 12/02/92 (Forwarded)
005479 92/12/08 20:05  100    NASA announces shuttle assignments [N92-?]
005516 92/12/10 13:30  102    WFPC-2 Will Magnify Hubble's Views of the Universe
005361 92/11/20 06:11  139    NASA Daily News for 11/19/92
005367 92/11/21 00:53  138    NASA Daily News for 11/20/92 (Forwarded)
005392 92/11/25 06:00   64    Hubble, Galileo Briefings Set for Dec. 1
005422 92/11/30 21:19  167    NASA Headline News for 11/30/92 (Forwarded)
005427 92/12/02 02:01  160    HST Uncovers Secrets of Galaxy Evolution
005431 92/12/01 20:28  173    NASA Headline News for 12/01/92 (Forwarded)
005460 92/12/08 19:25  134    NASA Daily News for 12/02/92 (Forwarded)
005479 92/12/08 20:05  100    NASA announces shuttle assignments [N92-?]
005516 92/12/10 13:30  102    WFPC-2 Will Magnify Hubble's Views of the Universe
```

Now we receive our first document from SEDS, which turns out to be a lengthy discussion about the early formation of galactic clusters which was originally issued as a NASA press release. We're in business. So far we've just asked this database for information about Hubble, and we got back far too many hits to read through them all. We must find a way to confine our search to a specific set of statements, homing in on what we want.

NARROWING DOWN THE SEARCH

We might, for example, become interested in Hubble's problems with its mirror. What exactly is wrong with it, and what are the prospects for getting it repaired by the space shuttle? To run this search, we need to combine search statements as follows: **Search (hubble AND mirror) AND shuttle in SEDSNEWS.** Here, we've nested our search terms. The computer at the other end will search for every item mentioning both Hubble and the word **mirror**; it will then narrow the field by culling only the hits which also include the word **shuttle**. Let's see what happens.

```
//
Database Search DD=Rules
//Rules DD    *
Search (hubble AND mirror) AND shuttle in SEDSNEWS
Index
/*
```

Figure 9.11 shows the response.

Obviously, the more recent of these postings will be the most useful. Let's get the last two NASA Daily News briefings, and check out 4199, which seems to be a newsletter. It may have useful summary information. We'll change the search strategy to reflect what we need, though again embedding it in the standard search template.

Figure 9.11
A more complex
search for information
on Hubble's mirror,
relating it to a shuttle
repair mission.

```
   Search (Hubble AND Mirror) AND shuttle in SEDSNEWS
-- Database SEDSNEWS, 21 hits.

 Index
Item #  Date      Time   Recs   Subject
------  ----      ----   ----   -------
000541 90/03/28 12:04   149    Nasa News, 3/28/90
000713 90/07/05 18:14    92    NASA Headline News, 7/05/90
000759 90/07/28 19:19    90    NASA Headline News, 7/27/90
000769 90/08/08 15:33    74    THE HUBBLE SPACE TELESCOPE WILL MAKE IMPORTANT
000781 90/08/14 20:34   115    NASA Headline News, 8/14/90
001181 90/12/28 17:47   132    NASA Headline News, 12/27/90
001504 91/04/28 11:12    75    HUBBLE SPACE TELESCOPE COMPLETES FIRST YEAR
002350 91/10/17 17:58   138    NASA Headline News 10/17/91
003119 92/02/10 22:19   509    List of Large Astronomical Projects
003135 92/02/12 03:37   136    space news from Oct 28 AW&ST
003182 92/02/20 05:06    78    space news from Nov 11 AW&ST
003194 92/02/21 07:05   156    space news from Jan 20 AW&ST
003538 92/04/04 01:02   547    Large Astronomical Project Listing (long)
004106 92/06/25 21:58  2479    STS-46 Press Kit (Forwarded)
004199 92/07/06 21:32  1570    SpaceViews - July Boston NSS newsletter
004273 92/07/13 21:17  2680    STS-46 Press Kit [Updated version] (Forwarded)
004976 92/10/06 23:27   129    NASA Daily News for 10/06/92 (Forwarded)
004993 92/10/07 20:24   155    NASA Daily News for 10/07/92 (Forwarded)
005002 92/10/08 21:31   125    NASA Daily News for 10/08/92 (Forwarded)
005367 92/11/21 00:53   138    NASA Daily News for 11/20/92 (Forwarded)
005460 92/12/08 19:25   134    NASA Daily News for 12/02/92 (Forwarded)
```

```
//
Database Search DD=Rules
//Rules DD   *
Search (Hubble AND Mirror) AND shuttle in SEDSNEWS
Print all of 4199 5002 5367 5460
/*
```

By return mail, we receive the desired messages. The oldest of them is *SpaceViews,* the newsletter of the Boston Chapter of the National Space Society. Included is a long discussion of the physics and engineering behind space-based telescopes, helpful indeed if we want to understand what goes on with such a device. We also receive several NASA updates, and a note about a servicing mission to be flown by the shuttle to correct the problems on the Hubble platform. What's happened to Hubble? An "aspherical aberration" in its primary mirror, for one thing. SEDSNEWS is filled with more details, if you're interested.

USING LOGICAL OPERATORS

Notice in the preceding search strategy how we *nested* terms; that is, we've included one set of terms inside another. The command we sent the LISTSERV was **Search (hubble AND mirror) AND shuttle.** The database looked for any documents containing both the terms **hubble** and **mirror.** It then checked for documents meeting that criterion which also contained the term **shuttle.** All of which produced a number of documents that helped us home in on our data.

But if you examine the list of hits from that search, you'll notice some of them are from 1990. Because we want to be as up-to-date as possible, we want to confine our searches to more recent postings. We can do it by including a data range in our search statement. Suppose I've chosen to look for any documents after 1 January 1992. I'd frame the statement:

```
//
Database Search DD=Rules
//Rules DD    *
Search Hubble in SEDSNEWS since 92/1/1
Index
/*
```

In this case we have limited the search to all articles published after a certain date. You might not be as concerned about date limitations in certain fields; searching the TWAIN-L list for messages about Huck Finn, for example, probably wouldn't require you to limit the date so severely. But highly technical subjects which change quickly demand a date strategy.

Maybe you'd like to confine the search within a certain range of dates. Perhaps you read a message you want to recover. You know it appeared some time in January or February 1993, but can't recall the exact day. To set up this kind of search, the following strategy will work:

```
//
Database Search DD=Rules
//Rules DD    *
Search hubble in SEDSNEWS from 93/1/1 to 93/3/1
Index
/*
```

Still not sure if you can find the desired message? We can use an asterisk to create an index of all messages in a given period. The following strategy will create such an index for November 1992, returning all messages from the month.

```
//
Database Search DD=Rules
//Rules DD    *
Search * in SEDSNEWS from 92/11/1 to 92/12/1
Index
/*
```

The **Revised LISTSERV Database Functions** document we retrieved earlier provides a thorough grounding in search strategies. You should print it out now and examine its examples to learn the byways of using logical operators on BITNET, especially if the strategy you need is complicated. Here are two other ways to use Boolean operators to set up a search strategy:

The OR operator: **Search mirror OR shuttle in SEDSNEWS**

Here we've told the LISTSERV to pull any document mentioning the word **mirror** or the word **shuttle**; the two terms don't have to be in the same document for the search to record a hit.

The NOT operator: **Search hubble NOT mirror in SEDSNEWS**

Here we've told the LISTSERV we're interested in a different kind of filtering process. We want messages mentioning Hubble, but are not particularly interested in those discussing its mirror problems. The search strategy above will pull only those Hubble messages without the word **mirror.**

Strategies can be thorny indeed, as a glance through some of the five and six-line examples in **Revised LISTSERV Database Functions** will quickly establish. This is, of course, a major reason why archival resources aren't used more frequently. But the huge list of BITNET mailing lists, if nothing else, should convince you that the material is out there for those willing to make the effort.

ADDING TO THE LIBRARY

Let's take a breather and let our Internet connection to BITNET generate some more reading material for us. Standard documents, like the Twain sign-on message we received, often point in the direction of new files that can help. They're like footprints in the sand; follow them and you'll often uncover unsuspected resources. I keep three-ring binders for printouts of such files, and they get heavy use as I work through the various BITNET commands. Try out your BITNET expertise now by retrieving these files:

....

What You Need: A BITNET Background Document and a Guide to BITNET On-line Etiquette

The Documents: **BITNET Userhelp, Mail Manners**

How to Get Them: Through the BITNET Network Information Center. Send the following one-line messages to **LISTSERV@BITNIC.bitnet:**

GET BITNET USERHELP for the background document.

GET MAIL MANNERS for the etiquette document.

....

The *BITNET Userhelp* document is useful, approaching BITNET basics from the standpoint of the new user. But because we're drawing on BITNET information from an account on the Internet, not all the commands and user tips listed in the document are applicable to us. Remember, our only real link between the Internet and BITNET is our ability to move electronic mail between the two networks; direct file transfer between the two is not possible, nor do BITNET's protocols make interactive access feasible. But read through the document anyway; it's still a goldmine of background information. BITNET is a powerful resource despite its built-in limitations.

The BITNET Network Information Center, it's becoming clear, is a major stop on our quest for information on this network. It makes sense, then, to see what else is available in its archives. Print out the list and keep it with your other BITNET materials. The answers to most BITNET questions can be found in these files.

....

What You Need: An Index of Files at BITNIC

The Document: **LISTSERV Filelist**

How to Get It: Through BITNET Network Information Center.

Send **GET NETINFO INDEX** command to **LISTSERV@BITNIC.bitnet.**
....

To keep up with what's happening around BITNET, a subscription to *NetMonth* magazine is just the ticket. Available by on-line request, it keeps you up to date on the latest BITNET news, and best of all, it's free. *Netmonth* is the kind of tool network users rely on to keep from being overwhelmed by the numerous changes occurring daily throughout the cyberspace continuum.

....

What You Need: A Way to Keep Up With BITNET Happenings

The Document: **Netmonth Magazine**

How to Get It: Send the following command to **LISTSERV@MARIST.bitnet**:

SUBSCRIBE NETMONTH *your full name*
....

And there's a second possibility. BITNEWS is listed in the SRI List of Lists as the official medium of the BITNET Network Information Center; it's used for distributing BITNET news and administrative developments. BITNEWS archives are available on the BITNIC LISTSERV. You may want to consider signing on for this helpful publication.

....

What You Need: A Second BITNET Newsletter

The Document: **BITNEWS**

How to Get It: Send the following command to **LISTSERV@BITNIC.bitnet**:

SUBSCRIBE BITNEWS *your full name*
....

BITNET VIA USENET

Proving once again that the Internet loops around and through itself (a bit like the worm ourobouros, the legendary critter that eats its own tail), it's possible to pull in certain BITNET mailing lists without any direct access to BITNET at all. Certain USENET newsgroups are a redistribution of some of the more popular BITNET lists. The Electronic Music Discussion Group, which the List of All LISTSERV Lists defines as **EMUSIC-L@AUVM**, shows up through USE-NET as **bit.listserv.emusic-l.** The BITNET list on WordPerfect for Windows listed as **WPWIN-L@UBVM** makes a USENET appearance as **bit.list-serv.wpwin-l.** And so on.

The difference? For one thing, only selected BITNET lists are distributed this way. And as opposed to regular BITNET lists, which allow you to receive the periodical postings in your mailbox, USENET access means you must go into the relevant newsgroup and activate a news reader program like **rn** or **trn.** If you read a lot of news groups anyway, this may be the preferred method.

To find out which mailing lists are maintained on USENET, you need an updatable information posting.

• •

What You Need: An Updated List of BITNET Lists on the Internet

The Document: **Bit/Bitlist**

How to Get It: Through the USENET newsgroup **news.answers,** where it's posted periodically.

• •

THE FUTURE OF BITNET

Has BITNET fallen behind the power curve? In many respects, the answer is yes. The nature of the network has hitherto limited it to a maximum transmission speed of 9600 bits per second, whereas other networks are moving toward information exchange in the range of millions of bits per second. As we saw earlier, the failure of a single node can block a BITNET file from going through, while your Internet mail can find an alternate route when one link fails. BITNET doesn't allow Internet users to log on to remote sites in interactive fashion either, a sharp contrast to the powerful capabilities of Telnet and FTP. Such a function is clearly ideal for scholars—witness the growth in interactive use of library catalogs on the Internet.

The BITNET II project, begun in 1989, is an attempt to improve on these limitations by allowing BITNET traffic to move over the high-speed TCP/IP links which drive the Internet. These changes add dynamic routing capabilities and reduce the cost of leased lines. Converting BITNET hosts to TCP/IP also allows an Internet style of addressing, using the domain name system instead of the eight-character names currently used. The difficulties in sending mail from the Internet into BITNET should gradually disappear, firming up its links to the worldwide Internet.

On the level of the individual computer user, these changes will only further emphasize the role of electronic text. I've always had a weakness for magazines, for example. New subscription offers tempt me on a regular basis, and my mailbox is generally stuffed with everything from computer magazines to newsletters on cooking techniques and journals about music and science. But somewhere along the line, as you get involved with network mailing lists, you begin to realize your time isn't infinite. I can read only so much in a given day, and I get so much out of my network participation through BITNET and Internet mailing lists that I'm reluctant to switch any of the lists off.

Is it the end for the printed word at the Gilster household? I doubt it. We've yet to move to a paperless office, despite decades of promises and the bright prospect of high-end scanners and optical-character-recognition software. So I assume there will always be a place for *The Financial Times* and *Bon Appetit*. But the interactive nature of on-line mailing lists, and the certain promise of refined user interfaces in the future, makes them a tough act to top. The growing presence of on-line journals means that more and more of my reading will take place on a computer screen, or through the kind auspices of my laser printer.

These new forms of communications are clearly here to stay, with implications we're only beginning to understand. In the next chapter, we'll look at some different permutations of electronically delivered text. Next stop: the Internet's variant of BITNET's mailing lists, a host of on-line journals, and several projects which make the dissemination of the formerly print-limited word their *raison d'être*.

CHAPTER NINE NOTES

1. These numbers are, of course, changing constantly. They represent the state of things as of March 26, 1993, when updated in a telephone conversation with Ira Fuchs.
2. Mail servers like LISTSERV have been created for UNIX as well. In later chapters and here, I follow what appears to be a growing convention in listing standard LISTSERV in upper case letters; UNIX listserv is referred to in lower case.

Electronic Journals, Mailing Lists, and Project Gutenberg

As we'll see, though the Internet has a bright future in the realms of digitized video and audio, it continues to carry huge amounts of information in purely textual formats. Despite the multimedia hype, conventional ASCII text is far from dead.

BITNET mailing lists, as you saw in the last chapter, provide ready access to the musings of some of the world's more creative thinkers. But mailing lists are hardly limited to BITNET, and those whose interests may not range into the thickets of scholarship nonetheless find plenty to talk about through the adventurous discussion groups available over standard Internet connections. In this chapter, we'll examine these Internet lists, and the vagaries of signing up and maintaining an on-line presence.

Growing directly out of the wide circulation of ideas through text, electronic journals are also coming into vogue, providing unprecedented delivery mechanisms to those interested in a host of specialty topics. As these on-line publications attest, the Internet holds the potential for supplementing traditional publishing techniques and, in many cases, improving on them. From the standpoint of the social welfare—disseminating as much of our cultural inheritance as possible through the most accessible means—nothing beats Project

Gutenberg, an attempt to spread billions of copies of electronic texts worldwide within the next ten years. Add the Online Book Initiative and you have a concerted effort to change the way we view the written word.

Ambitious? Sure, but these and other on-line text projects are thriving. Along with their growth comes a continuing dialogue about the potential for the electronic medium to create a massive repository of cultural information—you can sit in on these deliberations through the contacts this chapter provides. In other words, don't be seduced by sight and sound. The real work of the Internet proceeds through the explosion of ideas, mediated by a delivery system as old as Sumeria—the written alphabet and its digital representation as text.

THE INTERNET'S MAILING LISTS

Not all mailing lists are distributed through BITNET. The mailing lists found on the Internet, including their UUCP-born cousins, constitute one of the most useful information sources available through access to an Internet account. But mailing lists can be hard to find. The new user may not know they exist, much less how to sign on for a particular list. And remember the key dilemma of the network newcomer: the decentralized nature of the Internet ensures that while the information is readily available on-line, the only people who will be able to find it are the people who already know where to look.

Frustrating? You bet. But what you need to know is usually available through your keyboard. In the case of Internet and UUCP mailing lists, there are two places to find information on-line. Stephanie da Silva maintains an on-going list of what's currently available. This is no small feat, since mailing lists are in a state of constant flux, with new ones added as interests coalesce and old ones sometimes dying of attrition. Da Silva is representative of the people who perform yeoman work for the Internet community by bringing some order to the chaos of the networks; the Internet, it's no exaggeration to say, could hardly proceed without them.

To receive da Silva's list, you must subscribe to one of several possible USENET newsgroups—**news.lists, news.announce.newusers, or news. answers**, where the list is posted in parts as it becomes updated. In any case, these lists should be basic subscriptions as you build your Internet library; you'll learn how to sign on to them in Chapter 11. Alternatively, the currently available list of mailing lists is also accessible through a computer site. I also list the massive **List of Interest Groups** compiled and maintained at SRI International Network Information Systems Center in Menlo Park, CA, which is available via FTP.

••

What You Need: A Directory of Internet Mailing Lists

The Documents: **Publicly Accessible Mailing Lists**, by Stephanie da Silva (originally compiled by Chuq Von Rospach); **List of Interest Groups**

How to Get Them: For **Publicly Accessible Mailing Lists,** join the USENET newsgroup **news.lists, news.announce.newusers,** or **news.answers.** Or retrieve it through anonymous FTP to **pit-manager.mit.edu.** The directory is *pub/usenet/news.answers/mail/mailing-lists.* The file names are **part1, part2** and **part3.**

For the **List of Interest Groups,** use FTP to **ftp.nisc.sri.com** (SRI International Network Information Systems Center, Menlo Park, CA). This is a big file, so you may want to get it once for reference, and then rely on the USENET newsgroups to keep you up to date thereafter. The directory is *netinfo.* The filename is **interest-groups.**

....

TOPICS IN PROFUSION

You may be amazed at what is available; as with BITNET, there's an inexhaustible storehouse of topics for discussion. Figure 10.1 describes a mailing list called **alife,** which according to da Silva's list is maintained at a computer at UCLA in California.

Remember the mailing list principle: addresses for routine maintenance and actual list participation are different. The centralized hub of the **alife** list is at UCLA. Electronic mail sent to this specific address will be redistributed to a list of people who have requested to be added. What you see in Figure 10.1 is an address, **alife-request@cognet.ucla.edu,** which is actually one of two mailing list addresses that apply. Note the word **-request** in the midst of the address. This tells you this is the address used to request entry onto the mailing list.

These lists, unlike those on BITNET, are not automated. To join one, you would write to this address and ask permission to be included, and you should include your mailing address in the body of the message, as not all mail headers arrive intact. The **-request** part of the address, then, tells you that this is where administrative details for this mailing list are performed. It plays the same role as the LISTSERV address does in a BITNET list, but you speak, at least in most cases, to a human being instead of a computer.

Figure 10.1
A mailing list description for the Da Silva list.

```
alife
     Contact: alife-request@cognet.ucla.edu

     Purpose: The alife mailing list is for communications regarding
     artificial life, a formative interdisciplinary field involving
     computer science, the natural sciences, mathematics, medicine and
     others.  The recent book _Artificial Life_, Christopher Langton, ed.,
     Addison Wesley, 1989 introduces the scope of artificial life as a field
     of study.  Alife was chartered in February 1990 at the Second Artificial
     Life Workshop, held in Santa Fe & organized by the Center for Nonlinear
     Studies at the Los Alamos National Laboratory and the Santa Fe
     Institute.  The list is intended primarily for low-volume, high-content
     scientific correspondence and as a publically accessible forum for the
     interested members of the public.  Membership as of July 1990 includes
     over 1,200 addresses on four continents.  There is an FTP-accessible
     archives/repository of past traffic, software and papers.  The list
     is maintained by the Artificial Life Research Group, Computer Science
     Department, Lindley Hall 101, Indiana University Bloomington, IN 47405.
     There are conditions on redistribution of the list in order to minimize
     any misunderstanding or exaggeration concerning this new area of study.
```

The other address? Mailing lists use a separate address for the regular message traffic they carry. This is where comments from list members are sent; once there, they are circulated to all other members of the list.

So use the **-request** address for administrative functions only, and be sure to use it when you ask to be added to or deleted from the list. As soon as you begin reading mailing lists you'll realize that a key to keeping them functioning smoothly is this division of basic tasks. People who send requests to join a list to the entire group of subscribers are doing nothing but taking up space in other people's mailboxes. Expect a few sarcastic comments in reply if you make this elementary *faux pas*.

The same is true of deletions. People often sign up for too many lists and then decide they want to be removed. They send a message requesting their removal, often via the regular address rather than through the proper **-request** address. And when the administrator doesn't respond immediately—as is often the case, considering that people have other things to do than maintain mailing lists—a series of increasingly hostile messages follows, each of them going out to the entire list. Not only do the messages serve no purpose (the administrator will certainly honor such a request once he or she encounters it!), they break the continuity of any ongoing discussions and lower the tone of debate for everyone.

Always exercise caution when dealing with a mailing list, whether of the BITNET or the Internet variety. Many postings are limited in nature; you might, for example, want to sent e-mail directly to someone who left a message for the group, informing that person of a particular thought he should have considered, or expressing your unhappiness with one of the other posters on the list. It's easy (too easy, some would say) to use your mail program's reply function to do this, with the result that what you have to say goes not only to your intended recipient, but to the entire list.

There is an axiom among those who fly for a living, saying that there are two kinds of pilots: those who have landed with the gear up, and those who will. Similarly, there are two kinds of mailing list participants: those who have embarrassed themselves with the public promulgation of a private message, and those who will. If you can learn from your mistakes, you'll only do this once.

Figure 10.2 shows some examples, chosen more or less at random, of the kind of mailing lists you'll encounter on the Internet. I've used the descriptions in the da Silva list.

Notice that one of the lists, **Testing-Archive**, collects information which is archived and available for anonymous FTP. So does the **info-high-audio** list, and so did the **alife** list we first looked at. This means the material in the list is being stored on a computer at the site listed; you can download it at your discretion. As we've seen in BITNET's holdings, archives add greatly to the value of on-line communications. Always check to see whether the list you're interested in maintains archives, and if so, how you can access them.

TAPPING AN ARCHIVE

Let's go into the **info-high-audio** archives and generate a list of file possibilities using anonymous FTP. The address is **ftp cs.uiuc.edu.** The da Silva list tells us only that an archive is present somewhere on this computer; to find it, we must ask for directory assistance. Figure 10.3 shows what the session looks like.

Figure 10.2
Examples of mailing lists.

```
argentina
  Contact: argentina-request@ois.db.toronto.edu (Carlos G. Mendioroz)

  Purpose: Mailing list for general discussion and information. By joining
  you can learn about how to make those patties (empanadas) that you miss so
  much, you can discuss on how to 'cebar un buen mate', and of course, on
  how to solve Argentina's most outstanding problems. We don't have a
  regular news service yet, but some members send every now and then a
  briefing. To join send name, e-mail, phone number, address, and topics of
  interest. List contents are primarily in Spanish.

bagpipe
  Contact: pipes-request@sunapee.dartmouth.edu

  Purpose: Any topic related to bagpipes, most generally defined as any
  instrument where air is forced manually from a bellows or bag through
  drones and/or over reeds. All manner of Scottish, Irish, English, and
  other instruments are discussed. Anyone with an interest is welcome.

info-high-audio
  Contact: info-high-audio-request@csd4.csd.uwm.edu (Thomas Krueger)

  Purpose: This list is for the exchange of subjective comments about high
  end audio equipment and modifications performed to high end pieces.
  Techniques used to modify equipment, especially, but not limited to,
  vacuum tube electronics are exchanged. Some comments may be subjective or
  intuitive and may not yet have a measurable basis. Other topics of
  discussion include turntables, arms and cartridges; preamplifiers,
  headamps and cartridge matching; speakers, amplifiers and matching;
  placement of speakers, and room treatments. Any comments that prevent
  an open exchange of ideas and techniques are not encouraged.

  Archives of projects will be maintained on csd4.csd.uwm.edu and available
  via anonymous ftp. Info-High-Audio is bi-directionally gatewayed with the
  USENET newsgroup rec.audio.high-end.

International Trade & Commerce
  Contact: info-request@tradent.wimsey.bc.ca

  Purpose: Discussions of International Trade, Commerce and the global
  economy including postings of company profiles, trade leads and topics
  pertaining to entrepreneurial ventures.

mystery
  Contact: mystery-request@csd4.csd.uwm.edu (Thomas Krueger)

  Purpose: Mystery is a mailing list for mystery and detective fiction.
  Reviews of works and discussions of plot, characterization, and other
  aspects will be discussed. The medium, whether novel, movie, or
  television series, is unimportant.

Testing-Archive
  Contact: testing-archive-request@ernie.cs.uiuc.edu (Brian Marick)

  Purpose: The purpose of Testing-Archive is to collect and archive material
  for software testing practitioners and researchers who are too busy to
  read ongoing discussions. Therefore, typical messages will be abstracts of
  technical reports, announcements of testing tools (both commercial and
  noncommercial), reviews of testing tools, and summaries of discussions
  from other mailing lists or newsgroups. The mailing list will be archived
  and made available for anonymous FTP via
  cs.uiuc.edu:/pub/testing/archiveXX. The list is unmoderated.
```

Figure 10.3
An FTP session to the
info-high-audio
archives.

```
Connected to csd4.csd.uwm.edu.
220 csd4.csd.uwm.edu FTP server (ULTRIX Version 4.1 Tue Mar 19 00:38:17 EST
1991) ready.
Name (csd4.csd.uwm.edu:gilster): anonymous
331 Guest login ok, send ident as password.
Password:
230 Guest login ok, access restrictions apply.
ftp> ls -l
200 PORT command successful.
150 Opening data connection for /bin/ls (128.109.131.2,4779) (0 bytes).
total 6
----------  1 0              0 Oct 24  1991 .rhosts
-rw-r--r--  1 0           1592 Mar 23  1992 Policy
dr-xr-xr-x  2 0            512 Oct 24  1991 bin
dr-xr-xr-x  2 0            512 May 13  1992 etc
d-wxr-xr-x  3 480          512 Dec 22 09:08 incoming
dr-xrwxrwt 25 480         1024 Dec 19 14:48 pub
226 Transfer complete.
remote: -l
321 bytes received in 0.11 seconds (2.7 Kbytes/s)
```

Figure 10.4
A directory listing in
the *pub* directory.

```
ftp> cd pub
250 CWD command successful.
ftp> ls -l
200 PORT command successful.
150 Opening data connection for /bin/ls (128.109.131.2,4780) (0 bytes).
total 3104
drwxr-xr-x  2 4586          512 Nov  8 00:27 bashar
-rw-r--r--  1 501       491551 May  5  1992 bjove.tar.Z
drwxr-xr-x  2 3819         512 Nov  5 21:38 carinhas
drwxr-xr-x  2 1555         512 Oct  1 11:54 ctk
drwxr-xr-x  2 3946         512 Oct 13 16:09 fairlite
-rw-r--r--  1 501        7701 Nov  5  1991 ftphelp
drwxr-xr-x  3 4433         512 Dec 14 16:02 gwc
drwxr-xr-x 20 5304        1536 Dec 28 08:19 high-audio
-rwxr-xr-x  1 5304      362740 Jun 15  1992 icb
-rw-r--r--  1 4494       19724 Dec 28 13:29 inet.services.txt
drwxr-xr-x  2 3975         512 Dec  6 20:00 jspinnow
```

The entries beginning with a **d** are directories; scanning them, we'll choose the one called *pub,* because that's where publications are likely to be. We'll also ask for a directory listing, shown in Figure 10.4, once there to see if we're in the right area.

I've shortened the directory listing purposely; it's a long one. But again, by scanning it, we can determine our likely target. There's another directory here, this one called *high-audio.* Surely it's the one we want. Figure 10.5 gives you a look.

Note that some of these entries are directories; some are files. You know now to tell the difference by looking at the far left of the column; the entries marked with the **d** are directories which contain digest information from previous months, as per their dates. Let's assume that the files on-line in this directory are the most current. We can get one to find out:

Figure 10.5
A directory listing in
the *high-audio* directory.

```
ftp> cd high-audio
250 CWD command successful.
ftp> ls -l
200 PORT command successful.
150 Opening data connection for /bin/ls (128.109.131.2,4806) (0 bytes).
total 1572
drwxr-xr-x  2 5304          512 Oct 25  1991 Digest.1
drwxr-xr-x  2 5304          512 Oct 25  1991 Digest.10
drwxr-xr-x  2 5304          512 Oct 25  1991 Digest.11
drwxr-xr-x  2 5304         1024 Aug 10 12:24 Digest.12
drwxr-xr-x  2 5304          512 May 20  1992 Digest.13
-r--r--r--  1 5304        29456 Nov 27 12:19 dig18.5
-r--r--r--  1 5304        29237 Dec  1 07:59 dig18.6
-r--r--r--  1 5304        51704 Dec  3 07:46 dig18.7
-r--r--r--  1 5304        74855 Dec  7 10:05 dig18.8
-r--r--r--  1 5304        40871 Dec  8 13:28 dig18.9
```

```
ftp> get dig18.9
200 PORT command successful.
150 Opening data connection for dig18.9 (128.109.131.2,4808) (40871 bytes).
226 Transfer complete.
local: dig18.9 remote: dig18.9
41809 bytes received in 2.2 seconds (18 Kbytes/s)
```

And indeed, upon examination, this file turns out to be just what we're after, an archive from the mailing list, providing all the messages handled by the list during the period in question. As you can see from an examination of these truncated directories, there's more than enough material here to keep the high-end audiophile busy for quite some time.

Keeping Up with Mailing Lists

One of the keys to using the Internet successfully is keeping up with new areas of interest as they arise. Therefore, a basic subscription should be to a list called **newlists.** It's designed to tell you about each new list as it appears. Using **newlists,** you'll get in on the ground floor of groups that particularly interest you. You'll find Internet mailing lists on **newlists** as well as new BITNET arrivals, so it's a handy way to keep up with both.

• •

What You Need: Announcements of New Mailing Lists

The Document: **An Internet mailing list called newlists**

How to Get it: Contact Marty Hoag, whose on-line address is **info@vm1.nodak.edu. newlists** functions as a "clearing house" for new mailing lists. Subscribers will get announcements of new lists that are mailed to this list.

• •

Figure 10.6
A new list is announced
on **newlists**.

```
MILHST-L on LISTSERV@UKANVM.BITNET          Military History
         or LISTSERV@UKANVM.CC.UKANS.EDU

    MILHST-L is an unmoderated list provided as a forum for discussion by
    scholars and students of Military History.  It is intended to serve
    Service historians, academic historians, and those for whom military
    history is a non-professional but abiding interest.

    Comments and discussions of the military affairs of any period or
    place are welcome, and social, economic, and political factors are
    considered an integral part of the subject.

    Given the wide scope of the subject, subscribers should take
    particular care to make their subject lines clear and descriptive.

    MILHST-L is an international list and will have no "official"
    language.  Contributors may choose the idion in which they feel most
    comfortable and which they believe will be best suited for
    communicating their thought to the list membership.

    To subscribe, send by e-mail to LISTSERV@UKANVM or
    LISTSERV@UKANVM.CC.UKANS.EDU with the following message in the BODY:

        SUB MILHST-L yourfirstname yourlastname

    Postings should be sent to MILHST-L@UKANVM on BITNET or to
    MILHST-L@UKANVM.CC.UKANS.EDU on the Internet.  and problems should be
    reported to the owners.

    Owners:  Patrick Hughes  JPHUGHES@UKANVM.BITNET
                       or  JPHUGHES@UKANVM.CC.UKANS.EDU
             Lynn Nelson    LHNELSON@UKANVM.BITNET
                       or  LHNELSON@UKANVM.CC.UKANS.EDU
```

Figure 10.6 shows an example of the kind of message (minus the usual header information) you'll receive when the **newlists** mailing list is feeding your mailbox regularly:

Should you decide to subscribe to a list, be advised: there's no guarantee you can get in. Although I've yet to be refused entry to any list (and subscribe to quite a few), there is no automatic right of entry to any of them. For one thing, the moderator and the readers of the list are in charge; how they choose to restrict access is up to them. For another, restricted access may imply not so much a desire to keep people off the list, but a need to conserve system resources. After all, maintaining a mailing list takes time and effort, as well as storage space on the moderator's computers. If such resources are limited, the number of subscribers may need to be capped.

Signing Up for an Internet Mailing List

We will proceed now to sign up for an Internet mailing list. Looking through the various listings, we stumble across one that sounds interesting, shown in Figure 10.7.

Figure 10.7
Description of the
Homebrew mailing list.

```
homebrew%hpfcmr@HPLABS.HP.COM
hplabs!hpfcmr!homebrew  (UUCP)

   The Homebrew Mailing List is primarily for the discussion of the making and
   tasting of beer, ale, and mead.  Related issues, such as breweries, books,
   judging, commercial beers, beer festivals, etc, are also discussed.
   Wine-making talk is also welcome, but non-homemade-wine talk is not.

   Archives are now available from Mthvax.CS.Miami.EDU via the netlib program
   and anonymous ftp; please use anonymous ftp if you can, if not
   send mail to netlib@Mthvax.CS.Miami.EDU with subject index for a
   top level index and help file.

   All requests to be added to or deleted from this list, problems, questions,
   etc., should be sent to homebrew-request%hpfcmr@HPLABS.HP.COM (or UUCP
   hplabs!hpfcmr!homebrew-request).

   Coordinator: Rob Gardner <rdg%hpfcmr@HPLABS.HP.COM>
                          {ihnp4!hpfcla,hplabs!hpfcdc}!rdg  (UUCP)
```

Hmmm, homebrew, and me with a yen for malty, European style ales. This one looks like a natural. Using the principles outlined earlier, we know to look for the word **request** somewhere in this entry, and sure enough, we're advised to direct our inquiries to an entity called homebrew-request%hpfcmr@HP-LABS.HP.COM. The following sample message should get us added to the list:

```
% mail homebrew-request%hpfcmr@hplabs.hp.com
Subject: Subscription
Could you please add me to the mailing list? My
on-line address is gilster@rock.concert.net. Thanks very
much.

Paul Gilster
```

And it shouldn't be long before a return message appears, confirming entry into the mailing list. In the case of the Homebrew Mailing List, I receive two pages of text, including a policy statement on the group which contains guidelines on submissions. Some moderators spend a great deal of time working out new user information and providing general guidelines; others simply fold you into the list of subscribers and let you learn the ropes on your own. In either case, the best procedure is to keep your eyes and ears open as you go. You'll learn a great deal more this way than by immediately jumping into discussions, adding thoughts that may have been expressed months ago.

Another thought: save the guidelines for each list you join and consult them when you need to make changes. Most will remind you about the ground-rules for being removed from the list when and if you decide to leave.

THE ELECTRONIC PUBLISHING EDGE

People have been saying for a long time now that electronic communications would eventually replace paper. In fact, one vision of the early desktop computer days was that computers had rendered paper obsolete. The "paperless office" was a utopian notion; we would all work in offices without filing cabinets, transacting our business on computer terminals, handling all incoming correspondence as electronic mail. Those retrograde souls who persisted in sending us paper mail wouldn't constitute a problem; we'd simply feed their letters into our scanners and work with the digital representations of their work.

The paperless office may yet appear, but not any time soon. Despite advances in scanning technology and optical character recognition, paper is still being generated, aided and abetted by the ease which modern printer technology brings to the process of printing. Nor, despite a drumbeat of theorizing, have electronic news vendors knocked our traditional newspapers out of the running. There's reason for thinking they never will; despite our environmental concerns, it's far more satisfying to have a second cup of coffee over a morning newspaper than while reading a morning computer screen full of news.

But don't count electronic publishing out. The benefits of this medium are so striking that it's certain to grow in importance as the network resources available to it make delivery ever easier. And while we'll leave news gathering and dissemination to a later chapter, our discussion of proliferating text is the ideal place to consider the growth and implications of on-line journals. Those who minimize the importance of BITNET, for example, don't realize how much exciting publishing is going on in its computers, nor do they take advantage of the wealth of research material these ventures are generating every day.

Oxford University Press Takes the Plunge

If you're at all familiar with Oxford University Press, it wouldn't surprise you to learn that the prestigious publishing house has decided to publish a journal called **Postmodern Culture.** After all, the publication sounds like Oxford's cup of tea. It's a peer-reviewed journal of criticism on contemporary literature, aesthetic theory and culture, with an interdisciplinary twist. And while the journal has been published at North Carolina State University since September 1990, it's never had the kind of clout behind it that Oxford will surely provide.

So what's the news? What intrigued the editors of **The News & Observer,** Raleigh's home town paper, enough to give the story prominent placement and a color photo of the journal's editors was this: **Postmodern Culture** is entirely electronic. Its distribution, handled initially by BITNET and thence through Internet connections worldwide, accounts for more than twenty-three hundred subscribers in more than forty countries.

Signing on to **Postmodern Culture** involves sending a message to the relevant LISTSERV; I'll explain how to find such information about this and a host of other on-line journals shortly. For now, however, simply realize that a subscription involves nothing more complicated than receiving the journal in your e-mail inbox when it's published. You're also signed up, in this case, to a list called **PMC-LIST,** which complements the journal itself.

Figure 10.8
A look at
**Postmodern
Culture.**

```
POSTMODERNCULTUREPOSTMODERNCULTURE
P     RNCU   REPO    ODER      E          P O S T M O D E R N
P  TMOD RNCU  U EP S  ODER    ULTU E          C U L T U R E
P     RNCU   UR OS   ODER    ULTURE
P  TMODERNCU  UREPOS  ODER    ULTU E       an electronic journal
P  TMODERNCU  UREPOS  ODER      E          of interdisciplinary
POSTMODERNCULTUREPOSTMODERNCULTURE                  criticism
------------------------------------------------------------
Volume 3, Number 1 (September, 1992)        ISSN: 1053-1920
------------------------------------------------------------


                  SPECIAL FICTION ISSUE


Guest Editor:                    Larry McCaffery

Editors:                         Eyal Amiran, Issue Editor
                                 John Unsworth

Book Review Editor:              Jim English

Managing Editor:                 Nancy Cooke
List Manager:                    Chris Barrett
Editorial Assistants:            John Jenrette
                                 Jonathan Beasley




         ---------------------------------------------------------


                       CONTENTS

AUTHOR & TITLE                                       FN FT


Masthead, Contents, and                      CONTENTS 992
Instructions for retrieving files

Guest Editor's Introduction                  MCCAFFER 992

Kathy Acker, "Obsession"                        ACKER 992

Robert Coover, The Titles Sequence from        COOVER 992
_The Adventures of Lucky Pierre_

Ricardo Cruz, "Five Days of Bleeding"            CRUZ 992

Rikki Ducornet, an excerpt from _Birdland_    DUCORNET 992

Rob Hardin, "Dressed to Kill Yourself"         HARDIN 992

Annemarie Kemeny, "Attempts on Life"           KEMENY 992

Marc Laidlaw, "Great Breakthroughs in         LAIDLAW 992
Darkness (Being, Early Entries From _The
Secret Encyclopaedia of Photography_)"

William T. Vollmann, "Incarnations of the     VOLLMANN 992
Murderer"
```

(continued)

Figure 10.8
(continued)
A look at
**Postmodern
Culture.**

```
POPULAR CULTURE COLUMN:

John Tranter, "Brekdown"                                    POP-CULT 992


FROM: PMC-TALK

Two Threads: Cladistics and Cut-Ups                        PMC-TALK 992
(Excerpted from the Discussion Group
PMC-TALK@NCSUVM, 7/92-8/92)


REVIEWS:

Bill Millard, "Bargaincounterculturalcapitalism:          REVIEW-1 992
Gear and Writhing at the New Music Seminar."
A review of the New Music Seminar and New York
Nights, June 15-21, 1992, New York City.

Russell Potter, "The Black (W)hole of Bataille:           REVIEW-2 992
A Genealogy of Postmodernism?" A review of
_The Accursed Share_ vols. 2 & 3, by Georges
Bataille, and _Heterology and the Postmodern_,
by Julian Pefanis.

Alan Aycock, "Post-Literacy." A review of                 REVIEW-3 992
_Literacy Online: The Promise (and Peril) of
Reading and Writing With Computers_, Myron
Tuman, ed.

Susan Schultz, "Postmodern Promos." A review of           REVIEW-4 992
_A Poetics_, by Charles Bernstein, and _Radical
Artifice: Writing Poetry in the Age of Media_, by
Marjorie Perloff.

Kevin Kiernan, "La Condition McGann." A review            REVIEW-5 992
of _The Textual Condition_, by Jerome McGann.

Rebecca Stephens, "Postmodern Woolf." A review of         REVIEW-6 992
_Virginia Woolf and Postmodernism: Literature in
Quest and Question of Itself_, by Pamela L. Caughie.


Announcements and Advertisements                           NOTICES 992
```

Figure 10.8 shows what an issue of **Postmodern Culture** looks like (I've omitted information about the editorial boards, etc., to focus on the table of contents).

Note the cryptic remarks to the right of each item in the figure. Each article or review possesses a code. Readers may reach into **Postmodern Culture** to retrieve any article; because the material is all in ASCII format, it's easily sent by electronic mail. Provisions are also available to retrieve the entire issue as a package by sending the appropriate command. In other words, the document that appears in your mailbox is actually a pointer, with directions on how to retrieve the rest of the issue.

Postmodern Culture is not Oxford's first venture into the realm of electronic publishing. Indeed, the press set up an electronic publishing research unit in late 1985 and began releasing products into the electronic markets in 1988. According to another on-line publication, **Public-Access Computer Systems News,** Oxford currently produces over fifty electronic packages ranging from general reference materials to science, medicine, the humanities, and social sciences. But **Postmodern Culture** is Oxford's first *networked* electronic publication.

Why would a conservative publishing house like Oxford become so involved in on-line communications? Why, for that matter, would the editors of an academic journal decide networked distribution was the optimum way to reach their readers? If you consider the disadvantages of traditional print media, the answers begin to emerge. A printed and bound journal can take months, even years, to produce, whereas electronic publication is much quicker. Particularly in the fields of science and technology, reducing the lag time before getting material into print can be significant.

On the other hand, the electronic publishing frontier raises questions. If the printed version of a journal presents articles in a single issue for review, should an electronic journal do the same? Or does it make more sense to distribute articles singly, as they arrive? For that matter, should the complete journal, whether composed of single or multiple articles, be sent to subscribers, or should the editors send abstracts only, along with further information about obtaining the bulk of the material, a la **Postmodern Culture**? These questions and more continue to define the debate about the electronic journal.

Our most glittering breakthroughs often have retrograde implications; that is, they call up echoes of a past we thought long abandoned. Think of Charles Dickens, whose novels, giant tomes like *Bleak House* and *David Copperfield*, once appeared in the form of serial publications, a chapter at a time. Electronic publishing lets you release a journal an article at a time, building up a comprehensive collection of material at a central archive site, if that is your chosen method. The technique seems workable, and as we're about to see, has proven itself worthwhile; you get your material while it's "hot off the presses." The real issue for publishers now will be to define their medium.

PACS-L: Electronic Publishing in Action

I discovered an on-line journal I have found most useful by browsing through the network, where I found a BITNET mailing list called **PACS-L**, the Public-Access Computer Systems Forum. The remarks I read implied it was filled with discussions of network issues; in particular, **PACS-L** seemed to be concerned with the electronic dissemination of documents and the significance of the medium. These issues already intrigued me. In fact, I was just then beginning to track Project Gutenberg, a remarkable attempt to create an on-line library of literary works.

The **List of All LISTSERV Lists** we retrieved earlier showed this entry for **PACS-L:**

```
PACS-L          PACS-L@UHUPVM1     Public-Access Computer Systems Forum
```

Using the usual BITNET/Internet conventions: I sent mail to **LIST-SERV@UHUPVM1.bitnet,** with the command **SUBSCRIBE PACS-L Paul Gilster.** In **PACS-L** I learned about **Public-Access Computer Systems News,** an electronic newsletter. Subscribing to the newsletter was equally simple. Send an e-mail message to the same address as before, with the message **SUBSCRIBE PACS-P Paul Gilster. PACS-P** was also listed in the master BITNET list.

```
PACS-P          PACS-P@UHUPVM1     Public-Access Computer Systems Publications
```

A subscription to **PACS-P** brought **Public-Access Computer Systems News** and another publication called **Public-Access Computer Systems Review.** The first of these, according to the information accompanying it, is published irregularly at the University of Houston, and contains news of happenings in the world of electronic publishing. Among the news items in my first issue was the story on Oxford University Press announcing its plans for **Postmodern Culture.**

The concept seemed simple enough: publish a battery of articles on the topic in question and distribute the articles through the network to subscribers rather than by traditional postal methods. The benefits in terms of cost savings and reduced time to destination were clear. After looking through **Public-Access Computer Systems Review,** I began to understand the potential of the medium. Traditional journals include references to articles used in research, but to track them down you have to go to the library. An electronic journal can rely on a text archive, so references are easy to check by calling up the article itself over the network.

Electronic text also speeds retrieval of back issues. Traditional journals stack up in a library or, worse still, in your closet at home. Finding an article in a two-year old issue of a particular journal is a hassle, involving checking dates and page numbers before finding the article. Electronically archived back issues can be made available on-line. A quick scan through the **Public-Access Computer Systems Review** materials made it clear they are doing just that. As with

Figure 10.9
A portion of the index from the PACS server.

```
Amiran, Eyal, and John Unsworth.  "Postmodern Culture: Publishing
in the Electronic Medium."  The Public-Access Computer Systems
Review 2, no. 1 (1991): 67-76.  GET AMIRAN PRV2N1 F=MAIL.

Bailey, Charles W., Jr.  "Electronic Publishing on Networks: A
Selective Bibliography of Recent Works."  The Public-Access
Computer Systems Review 3, no. 2 (1992): 13-20.  GET BAILEY
PRV3N2 F=MAIL.

Bailey, Charles W., Jr., and Dana Rooks, eds.  "Symposium on the
Role of Network-Based Electronic Resources in Scholarly
Communication and Research."  The Public-Access Computer Systems
Review 2, no. 2 (1991): 4-60.  GET BAILEY1 PRV2N2 F=MAIL.
```

the Mark Twain list, the PACS publications contained numerous index files. Back issues were available by sending to the LISTSERV the command:

```
INDEX PACS-L
```

The system works like a charm. For my purposes, finding information on the current state of electronic journals, it would be hard to over-state how useful these electronic archives turned out to be. The **PACS Review** contains numerous articles available on-line. I found Edward M. Jennings' "EJournal: An Account of the First Two Years," Ann Okerson's "The Electronic Journal: What, Whence and When?" and a helpful piece called "Online Journals: Disciplinary Designs for Electronic Scholarship," by Teresa M. Harrison, Timothy Stephen and James Winter.

Figure 10.9 contains a sample of the cumulative index I retrieved from the PACS-L server.

The index went on for several pages, with articles on electronic publishing, information policy at universities, managing a BITNET LISTSERV discussion group, document retrieval systems, and CD-ROM technology. In addition to the feature articles, there were regular columns and reviews of various books, as well as editorials. All in all, it would be hard to locate any better repository of information on this new medium. On-line dissemination leaves traditional modes of publishing in the dust—try going to your local library and tracking down up-to-the-minute data on electronic journals. What a contrast!

To retrieve the files I was interested in using standard BITNET commands, I sent an e-mail message to **LISTSERV@UHUPVM1.UH.EDU,** the address listed on the PACS cumulative index file. (As we've seen, I could also have used **LISTSERV@UHUPVM1.bitnet;** either would have gotten through.) I sent the command **GET BAILEY1 PRV2N2 F=MAIL** to retrieve a very challenging symposium on the uses of the new medium. As you can see from the excerpted index, each file contains a precise accession statement. The **F=MAIL** comment tells the server to send the article through the mail system.

When the article arrived, I saved it as a file using **mail**'s commands (**s** *message-number filename;* i.e., **s 21 bailey** or any file name you choose). I then downloaded the file from the host computer. Alternatively, I could have used the UNIX **more** command to page through it a screen at a time to make sure it was something I could really use before downloading it. And needless to say, this archived material is a powerful repository of information when you add BIT-NET's database search capabilities into the mix.

Finding Other Journals

A subscription to **PACS-L** and its on-line publications is essential for keeping up with the world of electronic publishing. But journal titles aren't always easy to come by, and new ones are being created all the time. You must hustle to accumulate the right information, but as with most Internet information gathering, the project is do-able, if complicated.

One file maintained in the BITNET Network Information Center contains information about electronic journals. Though not as timely as it might be, it's a good place to begin.

Figure 10.10
Descriptions of on-line
journals from the
BITNIC list.

```
Athene

    Athene is a free network "magazine" devoted to amateur fiction written by
    the members of the online community.  Athene does not limit itself to any
    specific genre,  but will publish quality short stories dealing with just
    about any interesting topic, including:

                        science fiction    fantasy
                        religion           mystery
                        computers          humor
                        psychology         sports
                        politics           business

    To  subscribe, mail a request to  Jim McCabe, MCCABE@MTUS5.  Be  sure to
    mention if you want it in ASCII or Postscript.


BioSphere Newsletter

    BioSphere newsletter may be of interest for those of you concerned  about
    the  problems  facing our  environment.  To get a subscription, send this
    command  to LISTSERV@UBVM:  SUB BIOSPH-L your_full_name.


|EJournal
|
|   EJournal  is  an  all-electronic,   Bitnet/Internet distributed,   peer-
|   reviewed,   academic  periodical,   concerning  the  theory and  praxis
|   surrounding  the  creation,   transmission,   storage,   interpretation,
|   alteration  and replication  of  electronic text.   It  also covers  the
|   broader  social,   psychological,  literary,   economic  and  pedagogical
|   implications  of  computer-mediated networks.   Please send  subscription
|   requests to EJOURNAL@ALBNYVMS via mail.


Mednews

    Mednews is  a weekly  electronic  newsletter.      Regular columns consist
    of  medical  news  summary from  USA  Today,    Center For Disease Control
    MMWR, weekly AIDS Statistics from the CDC, plus other interesting medical
       news    items.    To  subscribe,    send  the   following command   to
       LISTSERV@ASUACAD via mail or message:  SUB MEDNEWS Your_Full_Name.


Psychnet

    Psychnet  is  a  weekly  newsletter  keeping   the  psychology  community
    informed  and in contact.  To subscribe, send mail to Robert C. Morecock,
    EPSYNET@UHUPVM1.


|USSR-D
|
|   USSR-D (USSR news and information digest)  is a regular digest of traffic
|   culled from USSR-L  (USSR news & information list),   a public discussion
|   and distribution list dedicated to the dissemination and analysis of non-
|   classified news and  information regarding the Union  of Soviet Socialist
|   Republics and  its past and present  (if not future)   constituent Soviet
|   Socialist  Republics.    To  subscribe  send  the  command   Sub  USSR-D

|   Your_full_name to LISTSERV@INDYCMS.
```

• •

What You Need: A Core List of Electronic Journals

The Document: **BITNET Servers**

How to Get It: Send a **GET BITNET SERVERS** command to **LISTSERV@BITNIC.bitnet.**

This document, incidentally, is a list of network services not limited to electronic journals. It's a useful addition to your file library for BITNET materials.

• •

Figure 10.10 shows descriptions of some electronic journals, as culled from the BITNIC list.

Perhaps the best way to keep up with electronic journals is through the **Directory of Electronic Journals and Newsletters,** compiled by Michael Strangelove at the University of Ottawa. The huge directory includes background information on starting an electronic journal or newsletter, and lists almost one hundred journals in its latest issue. It also includes extensive listings for HyperCard stacks, digest-style newsletters, a bibliography for further reading, and much more. Lengthy descriptions of each publication are particularly valuable, and full instructions are given on how to subscribe.

• •

What You Need: A Resource Guide for Electronic Journals and Related Resources

The Document: **The Directory of Electronic Journals and Newsletters**

How to Get It: Send the following commands to **LISTSERV@ACADVM1.uottawa.ca:**

GET EJOURNL1 DIRECTRY
GET EJOURNL2 DIRECTRY

Note the spelling; it's important.

• •

Looking through this list, I found one item, shown in Figure 10.11, of particular interest to anyone planning to get seriously involved with electronic journals.

A subscription here can be useful indeed, giving you an overview which can tell you when a list is promising, and when you'd just as soon skip it. We could use more review services like this on a wide range of Internet resources.

Another good source for references to electronic journals, mailing lists, USENET newsgroups, and other materials of interest primarily to scholars is the **Directory of Scholarly Electronic Conferences,** edited by Diane Kovacs and a team of directory builders at Kent State University Libraries. This directory is unique in pulling together a wide range of resources.

Figure 10.11
A description of the
List Review Service.

```
> List Review Service <

The LIST REVIEW SERVICE quantitatively and qualitatively explores e-mail
distribution lists (primarily BITNET LISTSERV Lists). The cataract of
information available to those with network access make all but the most
cursory examinations of lists possible.  Akin to book and restaurant reviews,
each issue begins with a narrative description of usually one week's worth of
monitoring, then presents simple statistical data such as the number of
messages and lines, number of queries and non-queries, number of subscribers
and countries represented, list owner, location, and how to subscribe.

The editor sees the publication as a means to cross-fertilize user
perceptions of network resources (i.e., active proselytization for
cyberspace). The service attempts to explore as wide a range of lists as
possible, from the hard sciences to the fuzziest of the humanities.

ISSN: 1060-8192


Posted bi-weekly on LIBREF-L. To subscribe to LIBREF-L, send a single line
message with no subject to Bitnet address LISTSERV@KENTVM or Internet address
LISTSERV@KENTVM.KENT.EDU consisting of: SUBSCRIBE LIBREF-L your_name

Submissions:

No

Related List:

LIBREF-L

Back Issues:

Available by searching the LIBREF-L archives by ISSN (1060-8192), or by
request from the editor of the LIST REVIEW SERVICE.

Contact:

Raleigh C. Muns, Editor, Reference Librarian
SRCMUNS@UMSLVMA.BITNET
Thomas Jefferson Library
University of Missouri-St. Louis
8001 Natural Bridge Rd.
St. Louis, MO 63121
ph: (314) 553-5059
```

What You Need: A Multi-Resource List of Electronic Tools for Scholars

The Document: **Directory of Scholarly Electronic Conferences**

How to Get It: FTP to **ksuvxa.kent.edu.** Files for the directory, including a
Hypercard stack of the entire directory, are available in the *library* subdirectory.

PROJECT GUTENBERG AND THE NEXT PUBLISHING REVOLUTION

Johann Gutenberg, a fifteenth century German printer, is widely credited with being the first European to print with movable type, in the process changing the way books were produced and leading, ultimately, to the enfranchisement of a population of readers—most of whom would not have been able to afford expensive hand-copied books and wouldn't, in many cases, have known how to read them.[1] Ironically, little of Gutenberg himself is known; the man who helped disseminate knowledge like no other left no genuine portrait behind him and details of his life are scant.

Michael Hart was once obscure himself, but now that he's been written up in the *Wall Street Journal* and other prestigious venues, that is changing. His labors on behalf of the on-line dissemination of knowledge are well-known within the Internet community, and if you mention Project Gutenberg even to non-network people, many will acknowledge having heard the name. Hart's work taps Gutenberg for its inspiration in a very pointed way. Like the German printer, Hart is fiddling with technology to improve the way books are produced. If Gutenberg had lived to use the Internet, he'd be more than a little interested in what Hart is doing through Project Gutenberg.

To understand the concept, think about what Gutenberg did. Before his invention, books were rarities, each laboriously copied by hand. To make a second copy of a particular book involved going through the entire process again. Medieval manuscripts are lovely creations, often laid out with an exquisite calligraphy. But their scarcity meant few people owned a book. The invention of movable type allowed books to reach a wider and wider audience, until we reach to the late twentieth century when paperback books are accessible to virtually anyone.

Hart has similar designs on the written word in our day. His goal is to give away a trillion books by 2001 or, to put it more succinctly, to copy the text of some ten-thousand books into digital form and distribute them at no cost to an ever broadening base of readers. His vision is of a society where the great works of literature are available at nominal cost to all.

Hart has been at this for twenty-two years, and he currently presides over an army of several hundred volunteers. They have what some might think the most tedious job in the world, entering whole novels and other works into formats Project Gutenberg can use. (I'm a volunteer, and I'll be working for a while. My book is Boswell's mammoth *Life of Johnson*.)

What happens, meanwhile, to libraries and the people who use them? Hart believes that the libraries of the future will bear the same relation to today's libraries that the best libraries of our culture bear to medieval book collections, where books were chained to the shelves. "It costs me thirty-nine cents to buy a 1.44-MB floppy," he says. "That means if I put *Alice in Wonderland* on there ten times, it costs me four cents per copy. If I compress it, it costs me less than two cents per copy. You're getting close to a penny a book, a virtually free book." This price reduction, Hart noted in an on-line posting, is on the same order of magnitude as the price reductions books experienced after the invention of movable type, with equally dramatic implications for the spread of the electronic word.

Hart explained these notions in a guest editorial in *Database Magazine* in 1990.[2] The library of the future would be searchable by computer, its collections capable of being "transmitted via disks, phone lines or other media at a fraction of the cost in money, time and paper as with present day paper media. These electronic books will not have to be reserved and restricted to use by one patron at a time. All materials will be available to all patrons from all locations at all times." Hart's vision is a far cry from today's libraries, where books are all too often missing from the shelves, information resources bottlenecked at terminals, and media readers ringed by lines of waiting people.

Hart's work flows into the Internet through computers at the University of Illinois campus in Champaign-Urbana, where he has been given computer time despite having no official connection with the school. He's an adjunct professor at Illinois Benedictine College in Lisle, where creating electronic libraries is his sole preoccupation. Although Hart has released a few copyrighted books, copyright restrictions keep him working largely within the public domain, but the copyright issue is continuing to evolve. Will copyright law have to change due to the potential for unauthorized redistribution of electronic documents? Whatever happens, Project Gutenberg must choose its material with care.

To learn more about the rapidly expanding world of on-line libraries and how Project Gutenberg is contributing to their evolution, you can join the project's mailing list.

••

What You Need: A Source of Information on Project Gutenberg

The Document: **The Project Gutenberg Mailing List**

How to Get It: Send the command **SUB GUTNBERG** *your_name* in a message to **LISTSERV@UIUCVMD.bitnet** or **LISTSERV@umd.cso.uiuc.edu.**

••

Once involved, you should note that mail addressed to this list is considered fair game for release in the regular newsletter Hart produces unless you specifically request otherwise. Incidentally, you can also check in through USENET, which makes the mailing list available in the newsgroup **bit.listserv.gutnberg.**

Whether or not you sign up for the mailing list, you can always use FTP to tap the archives, where you can download useful information, such as an index of books currently available (updated regularly through the newsletter) and a file specifically written for new users. Archives of past newsletters, as you would suspect, are also available on-line.

••

What You Need: An Index and New User File for Project Gutenberg

How to Get Them: Through anonymous FTP. FTP to **mrcnext.cso.uiuc.edu** (but not between 10 A.M. and 5 P.M. local time). Information about Project Gutenberg is located in the directory */etext/articles.* For the index, enter **GET INDEX.** For the general user information file, enter **GET NEW.GUT.** This directory contains much additional information about the Project.

••

Project Gutenberg's actual holdings are, of course, available here as well. The directory */etext/etext93* holds books added in that year, just as */etext/etext92* holds the 1992 additions, and so on. Looking through the currently available titles, I found a wide range of familiar authors. Here is Lewis Carroll's *Alice in Wonderland*, Melville's *Moby Dick*, and Hawthorne's *The Scarlet Letter*. Not all entries are prose—Milton's *Paradise Lost* weighs in, about as non-prosaic an entry as you can get. Not all works are literary, either, as *Roget's Thesaurus* and the *CIA World Factbook* attested. There is even a collection of census data and several useful books on the Internet itself, including the first edition of Brendan Kehoe's *Zen and the Art of the Internet,* which made an on-line appearance before becoming a printed book.

Let's look at one of the available texts, H. G. Wells' *The War of the Worlds,* which can be accessed in the */etext/etext92* directory under two file names: **WARW10.TXT** for the straight ASCII version, and **WARW10.ZIP** for the compressed version. (You'll need **PKUNZIP** to extract the file, which is compressed to roughly half its former size by the software.) After several pages of information on Project Gutenberg and a series of legal disclaimers and notes on how to distribute the material, we get to the text itself, as shown in Figure 10.12.

It's quite a story and, as a long-time Wells enthusiast, I heartily recommend another Project Gutenberg holding, *The Time Machine,* which is available in the same directory. I already own copies of both in traditional paper format, of course, so of what use are their digital counterparts? If I were a student, I could use such a text for a wide range of analysis. Even a basic word processor gives me the capability to search for text, so checking on key ideas or concepts by way of performing various kinds of literary analysis should be a snap. More significantly, for those without access to the paper copies, having the text available in this form, readily distributable, is far better than no text at all.

It's a big project, but Project Gutenberg aims high, dominated by a long-term vision. "Somewhere between the present and Star Trek, all that stuff gets into the computer," says Hart. "Nobody ever questions that all the books ever written are in the Enterprise's computer. But nobody ever asks how they got there. We're the ones putting them in."

ASCII Text and the Vernacular

A battle is developing in Internet circles concerning ASCII, the American Standard Code for Information Interchange. An ASCII file is one that contains characters drawn from the ASCII character set, which contained 128 characters in its original form, and twice that in the so-called *extended character set* used in IBM-compatible computing. (The additional characters provide technical, graphics and foreign language capabilities.) The rising controversy involves ASCII as a format for on-line text.

Ponder the issues here. ASCII offers the solution to a problem: how to move textual material between different kinds of computers. After all, from the first days of computing we have lived with incompatible file types, operating systems, and software applications. Think of ASCII as a format for exchanging information. You run a **DOS** machine and your associate down the hall likes a Mac. But

Figure 10.12
The beginning of H.G.
Wells' *The War of the*
Worlds from Project
Gutenberg.

```
The War of the Worlds, by H(erbert) G(eorge) Wells [1898]

    But who shall dwell in these worlds if they be
    inhabited? . . . Are we or they Lords of the
    World? . . . And how are all things made for man?--
        KEPLER (quoted in The Anatomy of Melancholy)




                        BOOK ONE


            THE COMING OF THE MARTIANS



                     CHAPTER ONE


                  THE EVE OF THE WAR


    No one would have believed in the last years of the nineteenth century
that this world was being watched keenly and closely by intelligences
greater than man's and yet as mortal as his own; that as men busied themsel-
ves about their various concerns they were scrutinised and studied, perhaps
almost as narrowly as a man with a microscope might scrutinise the tran-
sient creatures that swarm and multiply in a drop of water.  With infinite
complacency men went to and fro over this globe about their little affairs,
serene in their assurance of their empire over matter.  It is possible that
the infusoria under the microscope do the same.  No one gave a thought to
the older worlds of space as sources of human danger, or thought of them
only to dismiss the idea of life upon them as impossible or improbable.  It
is curious to recall some of the mental habits of those departed days.  At
most terrestrial men fancied there might be other men upon Mars, perhaps in-
ferior to themselves and ready to welcome a missionary enterprise.  Yet
across the gulf of space, minds that are to our minds as ours are to those
of the beasts that perish, intellects vast and cool and unsympathetic,
regarded this earth with envious eyes, and slowly and surely drew their
plans against us.  And early in the twentieth century came the great disil-
lusionment.

    The planet Mars, I scarcely need remind the reader, revolves about the
sun at a mean distance of 140,000,000 miles, and the light and heat it
receives from the sun is barely half of that received by this world.  It
must be, if the nebular hypothesis has any truth, older than our world; and
long before this earth ceased to be molten, life upon its surface must have
begun its course.  The fact that it is scarcely one seventh of the volume
of the earth must have accelerated its cooling to the temperature at which
life could begin.  It has air and water and all that is necessary for the
support of animated existence.

    Yet so vain is man, and so blinded by his vanity, that no writer, up to
the very end of the nineteenth century, expressed any idea that intelligent
life might have developed there far, or indeed at all, beyond its earthly
level.  Nor was it generally understood that since Mars is older than our
earth, with scarcely a quarter of the superficial area and remoter from the
sun, it necessarily follows that it is not only more distant from time's
beginning but nearer its end.
```

an ASCII file is readable on both. And it's readable on the UNIX box at the end of the corridor.

The problem: ASCII, plain and unadorned, can't do some things. I can't underline text in vanilla ASCII, nor can I send italic characters in an e-mail message in ASCII. An electronic text thus misses out on much of the formatting that could make its appearance more elegant and informative. The answer, say some, is to adopt formats like PostScript, a page description language developed by Adobe Systems, Inc. PostScript allows you to print a page including text and graphics, embedding information about each in the document itself. The page is formatted precisely as you'd like it, and you can print out a PostScript document on any printer with a PostScript interpreter. No wonder a segment of the on-line community favors using PostScript or other formatting tools to make electronic text more useful.

But a problem arises immediately. What about people without access to PostScript printers? What happens to the idea of universal text access if you spread around texts so laden with formatting codes that users spend most of their time stripping out irrelevant information rather than using the text? For that matter, what if you compress files in such a way that some users can't figure out how to unpack them?

The problem is not easily managed, and remains the subject of intense on-line debate. As in virtually all aspects of computing, the search for standards defines the limits of the possible.

Dante, Still Divine, and a Host of Other Projects

If Dante Alighieri wasn't a genius, then the word has no meaning. There are those who think the medieval Florentine poet ranks with Homer and Shakespeare in the triad of poetry's greatest luminaries. And certainly, *The Divine Comedy,* a magnificent poem celebrating his love for a woman named Beatrice and illuminating the medieval outlook on life, shows no signs of losing its power despite its age. The tale of the poet's journey through Hell, Purgatory, and Heaven, guided first by the Latin poet Vergil and then by the spirit of his beloved Beatrice, inspired generations of writers with its seemingly effortless *terza rima* verse. And at Dartmouth College, Dante's work has taken on new form.

Dartmouth is home to the Dante Project, an attempt to let scholars and other interested parties examine the poet in new ways. The project has created a searchable database of commentaries on *The Divine Comedy* ranging over six centuries. Scholars who tap the action here can use a variety of search techniques to gather data, saving what could frequently amount to hundreds of hours of manual research. The full text of *The Divine Comedy* is likewise available, and can be queried by a given search term or by line number. Working with Princeton University and the Dante Society of America, Dartmouth is using technology to make the ancient come alive in new and unexpected ways.

The Dante Project is a sterling example of where we're headed. It's esoteric for many of us, but it's an indication of how library resources are being shaped by networked technology to give us insights into textual materials. You can look at the Dartmouth contribution by using Telnet to **library.dartmouth.edu.** At the prompt, enter **connect dante** and you'll be presented with several introductory screens listing the materials available for searching, and then a basic search interface. The system is easy to use but you'd better know your Italian!

Figure 10.13
Recovering a misplaced
sonnet from
Dartmouth's database.

```
Search S5: FIND GENERAL RUIND

 Result S5: 2 sonnets in the
SHAKESPEARE SONNETS
 file.
-1-
Sonnet: 73
  Text: That time of year thou mayst in me behold
When yellow leaves, or none, or few, do hang
Upon those boughs which shake against the cold,
Bare ruin'd choirs, where late the sweet birds sang.
In me thou see'st the twilight of such day
As after sunset fadeth in the west;
Which by and by black night doth take away,
Death's second self, that seals up all in rest.
```

Two other Dartmouth resources should hold your attention if on-line literature is your interest. The college keeps Shakespeare's plays and sonnets available through its Online Library Catalog, with simple search commands for finding that key phrase you're trying to relocate. Telnet to **lib.dartmouth.edu.** At the prompt, enter **select file shakespeare plays** or **select file shakespeare sonnets** depending on your destination. The King James Version of the Bible is also available at the same address. Enter **select file bible** to get there.

I dived into the sonnets database to track down a favorite poem. I couldn't remember the number, but the phrase "bare ruin'd choirs" had potent associations. Figure 10.13 shows what happens when you search this repository. Full instructions for managing the search strategy are provided on-line. They're clunky but usable.

We can add to the equation another active text project with Internet hooks. The Online Book Initiative is run by Software Tool & Die in Brookline, MA (reachable at **obi@world.std.com).** OBI maintains two mailing lists devoted to the issues surrounding its venture, one for discussion of electronic text and other topics, the other for announcements only. Those interested in the growth of this medium may want to explore one or both. You can use anonymous FTP to look at what's available; many of these texts don't duplicate what's on Project Gutenberg.

••

What You Need: Access to the Online Book Initiative archives.

How to Get It: FTP to **world.std.com (192.74.137.5)**. Change to the **obi** directory. You can also find an index of this directory by FTP to **ftp.sura.net (128.167.254.179)**. Change to the **pub/nic directory** and look for **obi.directory.**

••

A look through the directory listings gives you a feel for the breadth of the interests of OBI's contributors. Figure 10.14 shows a brief section of the **obi**

Figure 10.14
Some holdings at the
Online Book Initiative.

```
drwxrwxr-x   2 obi        512 Sep 19  1991 ECPA
drwxrwxr-x   3 obi        512 Jul  6 18:11 EFF
drwxr-xr-x  13 102        512 Aug 22 04:12 Economics
drwxrwxr-x   2 obi        512 Sep 19  1991 Edwin.Abbott
drwxrwxr-x   2 obi        512 Sep 19  1991 Emily.Bronte
drwxrwxr-x   2 obi        512 Sep 19  1991 Ethnologue
drwxrwxr-x   2 obi        512 Sep 19  1991 Ezra.Pound
drwxrwxr-x   2 obi        512 Sep 19  1991 FIPS
drwxrwxr-x   3 obi        512 Sep 19  1991 FSF
drwxrwxr-x   4 obi        512 Oct 14 00:10 Fairy.Tales
drwxrwxr-x   3 obi        512 Dec  6  1991 FoundingFathers
drwxrwxr-x   2 obi        512 Sep 19  1991 GIFNews
drwxr-xr-x   3 102        512 Mar 12  1992 GNU
drwxrwxr-x   2 obi        512 Sep 30 16:27 George.Bush
drwxrwxr-x   2 obi        512 Sep 19  1991 Grimm
drwxrwxr-x   4 obi        512 Oct  4 23:21 HM.recipes
drwxrwxr-x   2 obi        512 Sep 19  1991 Haring
drwxr-xr-x   2 obi        512 Feb 12  1992 Harkin
drwxrwxr-x   2 obi        512 Sep 19  1991 Henry.David.Thoreau
```

directory. Note that each of these entries is itself a directory branching out from the **obi** root.

You'll note from examining the Figure 10.14 that the OBI includes more than classic works of literature. True, it contains works by Emily Bronte and Henry David Thoreau, but George Bush? The OBI's charter is clearly stated in an article project director Barry Shein wrote for the **GNUS Bulletin.**

> There exists huge collections of books, conference proceedings, reference materials, catalogues, etc., which can be freely shared. Some of it is in machine-readable form, much of it isn't. The purpose of the Online Book Initiative is to create a publicly accessible repository for this information, a networker's library.

The OBI has set up two mailing lists, one for general discussion about the issues involved, another for announcements only. To subscribe to either of these lists, send a message to Software Tool & Die as follows.

• •

What You Need: A Mailing List for the Online Book Initiative

How to Get It: Send e-mail to **obi@world.std.com,** asking for entry into either of the lists.

• •

LIVING ON THE TEXTUAL FRONTIER

Electronic text is growing fast, its spread unchecked by any centralized organization. With no single gateway to these materials, users must search widely to find what's being placed on-line. Along with the proliferation of documents are the inevitable hardware concerns that rise with their availability. Even if text is circulating freely, is it as usable as it could be? Display quality is a key factor.

The ergonomics don't always encourage reading a document for hours at a time on a screen where glare and less-than-ideal resolution are problems.

We're still on the frontier of electronic text, with the inevitable squabbles about territorial rights and differing ideologies sometimes encouraging the notion that promoting this medium is more like a range war than a reasoned move into a new form of access. But the technology is changing so fast that circulating texts on the network is becoming easier and easier. High-density storage vehicles, including huge hard disks and optical cartridges, will soon make concerns about the viability of massive text storage seem naive. Enhance these text warehouses with improved search software and you have benefits impossible to have been imagined by readers scant years ago.

Despite the heat debates on these issues often generate, something less than anarchy is going on as we try to determine what standards will govern electronic books. Meanwhile, the journals created on-line seem to be reaching critical mass, with the benefits of archival availability becoming obvious to their readers. These matters are being debated on the Internet's mailing lists and their BITNET-born cousins, making it possible for any of us to take part in the continuing evolution of the printed word.

CHAPTER TEN NOTES

1. The cost of books in the Middle Ages was remarkable by today's standards. According to Michael Hart in a telephone conversation with the author (January 7, 1993), book prices dropped by a factor of 400 as a result of Gutenberg's work. Intriguingly, this is roughly the difference between the cost of today's conventional, paper-bound book and the cost of putting the same book on a 1.44 MB floppy disk.
2. *Database*, December 1, 1991.

11

USENET: Keeping Up with the News

I'm not sure where I'd be without **comp.risks,** a moderated on-line discussion about the hazards associated with computers and high technology. Enthralled with networks, we sometimes forget that computing takes place within a context of social responsibility, and the **comp.risks** newsgroup is a valuable check on unbridled technophilia. On one day, for example, a quick check at postings revealed stories on computer glitches in a recent space shuttle launch attempt, safety-critical software, the security questions surrounding electronic mail, and more. Moderated by Peter G. Neumann, the Forum on Risks to the Public in Computers and Related Systems is sponsored by the ACM Committee on Computers and Public Policy. For those interested, it's also available as a mailing list. Send to **risks-request@csl.sri.com** to join, or keep reading to learn how to keep up with its discussions through USENET.

    comp.risks is but one of a profusion of newsgroups carried on USENET and dedicated to every conceivable subject. In this chapter, we'll look at the variety available to you, and explain how you can sign up for, or more precisely, how you can winnow out, the newsgroups you'd like to read. A number of different programs allow you to manage newsgroup activities, and we'll look at one of them, **trn,** that makes following discussions easier by sorting the messages by subject. Another major topic in this chapter will be the Internet itself, and how keeping up with USENET can help you stay abreast of new developments throughout the networks.

WHAT IS USENET?

USENET is itself a network, but it isn't the Internet. Think of BITNET, an autonomous network with gateway links into the Internet. BITNET traffic flows over the Internet but the two are not synonymous. BITNET uses its own set of protocols, called NJE/NJI; the Internet uses TCP/IP. In the same fashion, USENET traffic moves over the Internet, but it also moves over other networks. USENET began as an implementation of the UNIX-to-UNIX Copy Protocol or UUCP, but today, non-UNIX machines commonly participate in USENET, and UUCP is only one of the mechanisms carrying its traffic. You can get to USENET and take part in its discussions because network interconnections make it possible.

USENET seems to mean "User's Network," although the term is questionable, since USENET's originators created the word from a contraction of "USENIX Network" (USENIX being the largest user group for UNIX). USENET is thought of as "User's Network" today. It was created in my part of the country by two graduate students at Duke University, Jim Ellis and Tom Truscott, in 1979. The first two hosts were, reasonably enough, called **duke** and **unc,** and the initial software to carry the news traffic was written by Steve Bellovin, a graduate student at the University of North Carolina at Chapel Hill. The USENET notion began to spread when its founders distributed the early news software through USENIX.

Today, the network has grown to enormous size with virtually no organizational structure. The key to USENET participation is that anyone, or any organization, can join; the only thing required is another machine with which to communicate. Lacking a central authority, the network likewise lacks any centralized funding. Each host on the network pays for its own transmission costs and allows traffic from other sites to flow. USENET is thus a self-policing network, discouraging commercial use and enforcing certain standards of network etiquette solely by the power of peer pressure. The lack of centralized enforcement can sometimes be exasperating, as heated discussions called "flame wars" spiral out of control and the ratio of noise to signal increases alarmingly on certain newsgroups. For all that, though, USENET provides a vital and compelling destination for network users.

USENET NEWSGROUPS

For the dial-up user, USENET newsgroups will seem in many ways familiar. They're simply discussion areas where ideas can be exchanged. CompuServe users will think in terms of *Forums,* DELPHI users in terms of *Special Interest Groups* or *SIGs,* GEnie users in terms of *RoundTables,* and so on. But the concept is the same. You can post a message on-line and read the responses to it that build up over time. Because numerous people are reading the same material, a collection of such responses begins to accumulate. All the messages written on the same topic are considered to form a *thread;* that is, although they may be posted at different times and interspersed with other messages, they maintain a consistent subject matter.

You can subscribe to a particular newsgroup, page through it using software readers, organize the messages according to threads so you can follow discussions better, add messages commenting on what people have said, and ask questions. Often one thread will branch into another, as subjects begin to diverge and suggest new areas of investigation. A good newsgroup can be a lively place, with well-defined personalities emerging amid an atmosphere of inquiry and excitement. In any case, it's safe to say you won't be bored. The number of newsgroups is increasing constantly (I found almost five thousand the last time I ran a check), and it's likely that even the most abstruse topic will find representation somewhere on USENET.

USENET TOPICS

But there are differences between USENET and commercial on-line services. Perhaps the most obvious is that commercial services keep tighter control over their topics. You might be interested in investing, for example, and become involved in CompuServe's Investor's Forum. If your particular interest was futures trading, you'd find a special message section devoted to the topic; if you chose, you could participate in that section alone. The same forum would have sections for stock traders, the bond market, options, mutual funds, and a host of other investment topics. All of this is inside a single forum, although, to be sure, there are other financial sources on CompuServe.

USENET, on the other hand, boasts a huge variety of newsgroups organized only by a very broad hierarchical structure. They break down into the following categories.

comp Topics for computer professionals and amateur computerists alike. Here you'll find information on hardware systems, software, computer science, and various computer-related subjects. Some examples will illustrate the diversity of the category:

comp.ai   Artificial intelligence discussions.
comp.archives   Descriptions of public access archives.
comp.compression   Data compression algorithms and theory.
comp.dcom.fax   Fax hardware, software, and protocols.
comp.graphics.animation   Technical aspects of computer animation.
comp.lang.c++   The object-oriented C++ language.

sci Research in the sciences is the organizing theme here. These newsgroups are highly specialized and usually followed by professionals in their fields. Some examples:

sci.bio   Biology and related sciences.
sci.engr.biomed   The field of biomedical engineering.
sci.materials   All aspects of materials engineering.
sci.physics.fusion   Fusion, especially "cold" fusion.
sci.virtual-worlds   Modelling the universe.

soc Social issues and world cultures make up the discussions in the **soc** classification. This can be one of the most intriguing areas of USENET, as the international topics draw comment from all over the world. They're especially useful if you try to keep up with the news in a particular country. Alternatively, if you have a sociological bent, you'll

find material about cultural trends. You can see from the following
newsgroups how diverse the **soc** groups can be:

soc.couples   Discussions for couples.
soc.culture.bangladesh   News and comments about Bangladesh.
soc.culture.celtic   Irish, Scottish, Breton, Cornish, Manx, and Welsh
    issues discussed.
soc.roots   Family history research and other genealogical matters.
soc.veterans   Social issues relating to military veterans.

talk   There's no shortage of talk on USENET or, for that matter, on any other
computer network. The ability to put views into widespread
circulation holds a certain compulsive charm to many people, even
those who normally keep their thoughts to themselves when not
on-line. The result is debates, sometimes tendentious, often
interesting, on topics without obvious resolution. Care to sound off
about gun control? Abortion? Health care? You've found the place.
Here are some recent topics:

talk.bizarre   The unusual, bizarre, curious.
talk.philosophy.misc   Philosophical musings on all topics.
talk.politics.mideast   Debate over Middle Eastern events.
talk.religion.misc   Religious and ethical issues.

Remember to bring your sense of humor when you get into these
newsgroups.

news   A critical area, **news** is the section of USENET that focuses on
happenings around the Internet. You'll find announcements of new
newsgroups, changes in software, postings of background files, called
FAQs (**F**requently **A**sked **Q**uestions lists) for particular newsgroups,
and the answers to common questions. Some examples:

news.admin.policy   Policy issues about USENET.
news.announce.important   General announcements of interest to all.
news.future   The future of network news systems.
news.newusers.questions   Questions and answers for users new to
    USENET.

rec   These are the hobbyist groups, such as:

rec.aquaria   Keeping fish and aquaria as a hobby.
rec.arts.drwho   Discussion about the TV character Dr. Who.
rec.arts.movies   Discussions of movies and movie making.
rec.arts.wobegon   Focus on the "Prairie Home Companion" radio show.
rec.aviation.ifr   Flying under Instrument Flight Rules.

misc   This category comprises anything that doesn't fit comfortably within the
other categories. Predictably, its interests are wide and often have
nothing whatsoever to do with computers. Witness the following
examples:

misc.consumers.house   Owning and maintaining a house.
misc.jobs.offered   Announcements of positions available.

misc.rural Issues concerning rural living.
misc.kids Children, their behavior, and activities.

Think of these newsgroup categories as the core of USENET; they're circulated world-wide, although they do not make it into every network with USENET access. Any site can decide not to carry one or more of the groups, so the distribution varies. Remember, USENET lacks a central organization, which means there is no control over who gets a particular news feed or how individual articles are sent out through the net. There are, in fact, a set of alternative hierarchies for newsgroups that have also gained some currency. They're not carried everywhere either, often because they may interest only a limited audience, or because they may be quite lengthy and/or controversial.

alt The **alt** category is broad. Some of these newsgroups are excellent discussion areas; others are trivial. But the idea is to let people say what they want, and you can tune out any newsgroup that doesn't suit your tastes. And be advised: there is some excellent material within the **alt** hierarchy. Some sample groups:

alt.aeffle.und.pferdle German TV cartoon characters.
alt.alien.visitors UFO sightings and more.
alt.books.reviews Book discussions.
alt.gourmand Recipes and cooking.
alt.radio.scanner Radio scanners.
alt.internet.services Questions and news about what's available on the Internet.

Whatever your interest, there's likely to be somebody discussing it in one of the **alt** newsgroups.

bionet High-level, professional discussions among biologists.

bit An interesting and useful grouping, **bit** is the hierarchy where the more popular BITNET mailing lists can be found on USENET. You might want to get involved with these if you'd prefer not to receive BITNET lists in your mailbox.

biz These are groups with a business tilt. As you'd expect, the focus tends to be on computer products and services, but broader items of interest to the business community are also discussed. This is the place to be if you seek news about a new product or an enhancement to an old one. Some examples:

biz.comp.telebit Support of the Telebit modem.
biz.sco.announce SCO and related product announcements.
biz.dec Digital equipment and software.
biz.jobs.offered Position announcements.

clari ClariNet is an electronic publishing service providing a live feed from the UPI wireservice. The news is collected and converted into USENET format before being posted. It's a subscription service so not all servers will offer ClariNet. For those who do, here's an example of the kind of material you'll find in this grouping:

        clari.biz.economy.world   Reports on international economic issues.
        clari.biz.market.dow   Tracks market activity.
        clari.canada.briefs.west   Regional news from Canada.
        clari.feature.mike_royko   The popular Mike Royko column.
        clari.news.europe   European events.

gnu   This group is set up for discussions by and about the Free Software Foundation (FSF). The FSF was established with the charter to remove restrictions on copying, redistributing, and modifying software, meaning anyone could copy and distribute a program without worrying about constraints such as licensing agreements. The Foundation's take on all this is to produce free software replacements for some proprietary software. This project has focused on GNU, an operating system that provides compatibility with UNIX. GNU, another acronym, stands for "**GNU**'s **N**ot **U**NIX."

        gnu.announce   Status and announcements from the Project.
        gnu.emacs.vm.bug   Bug reports on the Emacs VM mail package.
        gnu.misc.discuss   Discussion about GNU and free software.

k12   Discussions of interest to teachers and students from kindergarten through high school. Thus:

        k12.chat.elementary   Informal discussion among elementary students, grades K–5.
        k12.chat.junior   Informal discussion among students in grades 6–8.
        k12.chat.senior   Informal discussion among high school students.

vmsnet   For users of Digital Equipment Corporation's VMS operating system and participants on DECnet, the worldwide network using the DECnet protocols. DECnet is sometimes called the DECnet Internet.

Be advised, too, that local hierarchies exist. **mcnc** and **triangle,** for example, are available at CONCERT-CONNECT here in North Carolina. The first handles traffic of interest to people working at MCNC. The second is of interest to anyone living in the (better known by this term) Research Triangle area—Raleigh, Durham, Chapel Hill. You subscribe to and read these groups the same way you do any newsgroups, but their distribution is limited and postings on them are of local interest.

Useful USENET Lists

Since there are hundreds of newsgroups, how do you know what's out there and, better still, how do you subscribe? The first question is answered by noting there are places on USENET where information about such matters is routinely posted, thanks to the good offices of a battery of volunteers. Somehow these individuals find time in their schedules to produce helpful indices, commentaries, and background information that anyone on the network can use. You will learn how to sign up for USENET newsgroups shortly, but for now, note two sources you'll want to keep in your permanent file. After you have gone through sign-up procedures, you can get them on USENET itself.

What You Need: A Listing of Active USENET Newsgroups

The Documents: **List of Active Newsgroups** (Parts I and II) and **Alternative Newsgroup Hierarchies,** Parts I and II). Gene Spafford developed these lists, at no small cost of time and effort; they're now in the hands of David Lawrence and Mark Moraes.

Where to Get Them: Both lists are regularly posted in a variety of USENET newsgroups: **news.lists, news.groups, news.announce.newusers, news.announce.newgroups, news.answers.** As part of maintaining an active USENET presence, you should plan on subscribing to several. For now, I recommend **news.announce.newusers.** How to subscribe and keep up with such newsgroups forms the subject of the remainder of this chapter.

READING THE NEWS

Dial-up users shouldn't have any problem visualizing what happens when they read USENET newsgroups. The list of newsgroups is located at the service provider's site, and when new users first sign up for an account, you are automatically signed up to all the newsgroups. By using a news reader program located on the host computer at the service provider's site, you can read through these groups in a variety of ways, depending on the capabilities of the news reader you choose. You can resign from newsgroups and sign up for new ones. You can read through older postings, save messages as files for later downloading, include parts of messages in your responses, and tailor your news environment to meet your own needs.

The dial-up process is not terribly different from what happens when you read a DELPHI SIG or a CompuServe Forum. In both, you participate by telling the system to go to the particular area in which you're interested. You read the messages by using system commands, corresponding to the news reader commands you'll use with USENET. You page through the messages, telling the system to present messages by threads, so you read everything on a particular topic before moving on to the next one. If you're a CompuServe user, you may use a program like TAPCIS to automate the process, capturing all your waiting messages, then taking you off-line so you can reply when the meter isn't running, and returning on-line to upload your responses.

With USENET, you have a different set of options to work with. Commercial on-line services have one command structure that allows you to read their forums, unless you use an off-line downloader like TAPCIS. Your USENET access, however, is more flexible. A number of programs can be invoked from the UNIX command prompt to help you read through the newsgroups. Instead of telling the system to take you to a forum or SIG, you tell the service provider's computer to activate one of the news readers, which automatically presents the USENET newsgroups to you. News readers have typically cryptic UNIX-style names; they're called **rn**, or **nn**, or **trn**, or **tin**. All of them give you a basic interface and a way to page through the newsgroups, and all have their virtues.

For the purposes of our discussion, I'll be working with **trn.** The program **trn,** written by Wayne Davison, is commonly available at UNIX sites. Using it is a flexible and intuitive process. As opposed to **rn,** the warhorse of news readers and the most ubiquitous of them all, **trn** provides one crucial advantage: it's a threaded news reader. You can read the newsgroups with **rn,** but you'll be reading them out of subject sequence unless you go to considerable pains to arrange your work session by noting which messages are on what topic and then telling **rn** message by message what you want to read. That process is tedious enough that you won't want to do it more than once. So we'll use **trn** as our newsgroup primer program; later, you may want to evaluate other possibilities.

CONFIGURING TRN

As with **mail** and **elm,** getting **trn** to work is simply a matter of entering its name at the command prompt. But first, there's a problem that needs addressing. If you're a first-time user, you're probably going to find you're subscribed to all the newsgroups at your site. Un-subscribing is easy enough; you just type a **u** at a newsgroup prompt, as we'll see, and you're out of there. But then you realize you're at the top of a very long list, being led through it in prompted fashion one newsgroup at a time. Newsgroup after newsgroup comes up. Do you have to unsubscribe to each one individually?

My first entry into USENET, through The WELL in San Francisco, was an eye-opener. I knew I wanted to read several newsgroups having to do with computer security issues, but I didn't know how to find them. And before I could read anything, I had to page through hundreds upon hundreds of newsgroups, telling each whether I wanted to subscribe to it or not. I did what most novices do in such a situation; I worked through the entire list, the whole time thinking there was probably some easy-to-use mechanism which would allow me to handle the problem in a few minutes, if only I could discover it.

Later, I learned I was right and that I wasn't alone. Every day on newsgroups like **news.newusers.questions,** someone asks how to avoid going through the entire list of newsgroups, unsubscribing to each. The answer is to open up a special file and make some relatively simple changes to it. But this seems like brain surgery to most dial-up users, who are probably more comfortable with a menu structure and a more intuitive command system that lets them sign up for what they want and leave the rest alone. There is also the problem of determining which newsgroups we want to subscribe to in the first place, without having to go through each and read it long enough to make that decision. If it strikes you that USENET and the UNIX tools available aren't designed with user friendliness in mind, you're absolutely right.

Creating .newsrc

Nonetheless, the rewards of USENET are worth the effort, and editing the file in question turns out to be comparatively trivial. Let's plunge ahead by invoking **trn.** Call your service provider and enter **trn** at the command prompt.

```
% trn
```

What you'll see next should look something like Figure 11.1.

Figure 11.1
Invoking **trn** for the
first time.

```
Trying to set up a .newsrc file--running newsetup...

Creating /home/gilster/.newsrc to be used by news programs.
Done.

If you have never used the news system before, you may find the articles
in news.announce.newusers to be helpful. There is also a manual entry for
rn.

To get rid of newsgroups you aren't interested in, use the 'u' command.
Type h for help at any time while running rn.
(Revising soft pointers--be patient.)
Unread news in alt                                           415 articles
Unread news in general                                       340 articles
Unread news in concert.info                                    1 article
Unread news in concert.stats                                   1 article
Unread news in mcnc.cad                                        1 article
etc.

******** 415 unread articles in alt--read now? [+ynq]
```

Now enter a **q** at the prompt, to close **trn.**

```
******** 415 unread articles in alt--read now? [+ynq] q
```

We've just done something significant; the message in Figure 11.1 will help
to understand what it is. At the top line the program tells us it's trying to set up
a file called **.newsrc.** This is going to be a core file for our USENET participation,
because it's responsible for telling the news reader which newsgroups we're
interested in following. When you run **trn** for the first time, the program looks
for this file; if **trn** doesn't find **.newsrc,** it will create it. Contained within the
.newsrc file is the list of newsgroups available through the server at your site.

Generating a Newsgroup List

Let's get that newsgroup list now, because it will help us make decisions about
what we want to subscribe to. Turn on the capture buffer in your communications software. Then, back at the system prompt, enter **cat .newsrc** to cause the
.newsrc file to be scrolled across the screen. The file will be shown without
interruptions. (If you had wanted to pause at the end of every page, you could
have entered a **more .newsrc** command, but in this case we don't want to do
that, because we want a clean copy of the file.)

When the file has finished scrolling and you're back at the command
prompt, turn off your capture buffer and print out the **.newsrc** file. Keep this
list by your side as we proceed to make newsgroup decisions.

Shutting Off the Spigot

Now we'll tackle the problem of too many newsgroup subscriptions. If you look
at the list you've just captured, you'll see how many newsgroups are available
from your service provider. The **.newsrc** file is set up under the assumption that

you are subscribed to each of these. This is why it provided you with the prompt we saw earlier:

```
******** 415 unread articles in alt--read now? [+ynq]
```

In reality, the choices available are greater than the prompt suggests. If you possessed an unusual frame of mind, and really wanted to work through the list of newsgroups one by one, the following would be the choices available to you:

y   Read the articles in question now

n   Don't read these articles now

q   Exit from **trn**

+   Show a listing of available articles

c   Treat all the articles in this group as read

u   Unsubscribe to this newsgroup

Some people like to examine each choice and make a considered decision even if it takes hours or days to work through the entire list. I did this myself, so I understand the impulse. If you choose to set up **trn** this way, call the program back up by entering **trn** at the prompt and proceed to do so. And cancel this afternoon's golf game.

But assuming you'd prefer the simpler solution, let me show you how to edit the **.newsrc** file to remove the problem. I would much rather be signed up to no groups whatsoever, going back to add in the ones I choose to read, than signed up to all of them. We can edit **.newsrc** with the common **vi** text editor to produce exactly this result. As you'll recall from Chapter 7, **vi** is the text editor from hell that causes non-UNIX people to wish they were computing on Macintoshes; it's the flip side of the term user-friendly. So be careful with **vi**. Remember that if you make a mistake, there's an easy way to correct it. We can always erase a bungled **.newsrc** file and then start from scratch. The command would be **rm .newsrc,** at which point we could start the whole process over.

And if this happens to you, a brief word of caution. You may be at the system prompt, deciding to find your **.newsrc** file by running an **ls** command. This is fine, except that when you look at the listing of files in your home directory, you don't see **.newsrc**. Not to worry for **.newsrc** is a hidden file, which will not show up with the standard **ls** filter. To see it, type **ls -a**, the command that lists hidden files along with non-hidden ones.

Getting .newsrc into vi

To call up **.newsrc** in **vi,** type **vi .newsrc.** What you should see will approximate Figure 11.2.

I say "approximate" because these newsgroups are specific to my site at CONCERT-CONNECT, a fact the frequent references to MCNC and CONCERT will make clear. But your **vi** rendition of **.newsrc** will be the same in that it will show the local newsgroups available through your service provider.

To proceed, take a good look at what's on your screen. Each of the newsgroups listed here is followed by a colon.

Figure 11.2
Calling up **.newsrc** in
the **vi** editor.

```
% vi .newsrc
".newsrc" 2271 lines, 44748 characters
alt: 1-62
general: 1-11
concert.info:
concert.services:
concert.stats:
mcnc.ads: 1-1
mcnc.annex:
mcnc.cad:
mcnc.comm:
mcnc.concert.video:
mcnc.convex:
mcnc.corp:
mcnc.dcom:
mcnc.drt:
mcnc.general:
mcnc.ncsulab:
mcnc.pc:
mcnc.programmers:
mcnc.rec:
mcnc.rec.bridge:
mcnc.rec.vollyb:
mcnc.rpm:
mcnc.src:
".newsrc" 2271 lines, 44748 characters
```

```
concert.stats:
mcnc.annex:
mcnc.cad:
mcnc.comm:
```

The colon indicates that these newsgroups are all subscribed to at the moment.
We want to change that by telling **.newsrc** we're not subscribed to any of them.
To do that, we'll turn each of these colons into an exclamation mark. The process
of changing all of one item into another is called a *global replace* and it's not
difficult to do.

Here's how to handle it. You need to get to the colon prompt (:) in **vi**. This
text editor works through two different modes, one a command mode, the other
an insert mode. Command mode allows you to enter commands like the above,
while insert mode is used to add text. Using the **ESC** key will take you out of
insert mode and into command mode.

Begin, then, by pressing the **ESC** key. Now enter a colon (:), followed by the
command shown below. Your command, including the colon, should look like
this on-screen:

`:%s/:/!/`

When you've entered this command, press the **ENTER** key. The substitution will
take place. If you examine the file again, you'll find that the colons have indeed
been replaced by exclamation points.

You can now exit **vi** and save your changes by pressing **ESC** again, followed
by a colon (:) and then **wq**.

`:wq`

This command takes you out of the text editor, leaving you a message like this one:

```
".newsrc" 2382 lines, 47116 characters
%
```

Now you're back at the command prompt.

KNOWING WHAT TO READ

At this point, you are unsubscribed to everything. Now you need to make some additions to **trn;** you have to tell it what *you are* interested in reading. You can begin by calling up the program from the command prompt:

```
% trn
```

You'll see the following message:

```
No unread news in subscribed-to newsgroups. To subscribe to a new
newsgroup use the g<newsgroup> command.

******** End of newsgroups--what next? [qnp]
```

A good thing we have that list of newsgroups, which we can use now to begin our USENET participation. I'll choose **news.announce.newusers** because it's an important stopping-off point for novices. Many of the basic questions you'll have as you wade into USENET will come up again and again here, along with their answers.

To add this newsgroup, tell **trn** to go to that group with the **g** command:

```
******** End of newsgroups--what next? [qnp] g news.announce.newusers
```

You'll get this response:

```
Newsgroup news.announce.newusers is currently unsubscribed to--resubscribe? [yn]
```

The answer is obvious. Choose **y** for yes, and you'll be whisked to the newsgroup. You're not actually *re*subscribing, of course, but **trn** doesn't know that. Choosing **y,** you'll be prompted again:

```
******** 236 unread articles in news.announce.newusers--read now? [+ynq]
```

There may not actually be 236 postings waiting for us to read; many of them may have been taken off-line by the system administrator to save disk space. But my recommendation here would be to reply with a **c.** This command tells **trn** to consider all these messages read; next time you sign on, then, you will start with messages that have accrued since you gave this command.

Our goal right now is to set up **trn** for future use. Your first priority should be to get the relevant groups on your subscription list and then proceed to learn the basics of reading them. Type a **c** at the prompt and you'll see this:

```
Do you really want to mark everything as read? [yn]
```

Choosing the **y** again, and you'll see:

```
Marking news.announce.newusers as all read.

******** End of newsgroups--what next? [qnp]
```

Now you have some reading ahead of you. Take out the printout of the newsgroups we produced earlier and make yourself a cup of coffee. What you want to do is scan through these groups carefully, with an eye toward determining which will be of continuing interest. Your decisions aren't crucial; any group can be subscribed to, unsubscribed from, and resubscribed to at any time. The reason you want to spend some time with this process now is that it's easy to miss an interesting group and then spend months on-line before seeing a reference to it that makes you wish you had joined it long ago. You'll be prompted when new groups are created, so you won't fall behind in your subscriptions to them, but good older groups are easy to miss. So spend some time with your newsgroup list and decide which groups are worth your time.

Then, using the above principles, start signing up. Use the **g** command followed by the name of the newsgroup you want to subscribe to. Some of the groups will be interesting beyond your expectations; you'll be delighted you subscribed to them. Others will be unexpectedly quiet, with only a message or two a week; some won't have any traffic for long periods. Some will be so busy that you'll finally decide you don't have time to spend on them, and you'll unsubscribe. But these are decisions that can only be made with experience, and as you work through your first week or two of USENET activity, you'll begin to see how newsgroups fit into your routine. The beauty of the process is that you can tailor it explicitly to your own interests.

THE CORE NEWSGROUPS

In certain ways, the heading of this section is a misnomer; these newsgroups are not necessarily core groups in the sense that everyone is expected to read them. But some newsgroups can make the life of the new USENET participant a great deal easier. The following lists some I think you'll find rewarding, and I recommend you sign up for them in your first go-around.

news.announce.important   A moderated conference with general announcements of interest to the entire USENET community.

news.announce.newgroups   Announcements of the formation of new newsgroups.

news.announce.newusers   Basic explanations of USENET conventions for new users.

news.answers   Periodic USENET postings appear here, making this a good newsgroup to follow to monitor the network.

news.newusers.questions   Your chance to ask questions. You should avail yourself of this opportunity, as you have USENET experts worldwide standing by to help you.

When you have added the newsgroups that interest you, it's time to exit **trn**. If you followed my advice in signing up for groups (using the **c** command to mark all the messages as read), you will be caught up in all of them; **trn** will show all your newsgroups as read. You should, therefore, be at a prompt like this one:

```
******** End of newsgroups--what next? [qnp]
```

Assuming you are, choose the **q** command now to exit. This should take you back to your system prompt. Because you've marked all your groups as being read, you'll need to let some new messages appear before proceeding. It won't take long; the network remains busy, and the traffic in some newsgroups is remarkably heavy. Come back to USENET later in the day and you should be ready to read the new messages that have accumulated in your absence.

USING TRN TO READ YOUR NEWSGROUPS

One advantage of **trn** is that it's a simple program to use, although it offers options that can make it both more complex and more powerful. As we've seen, you start it by entering **trn** at the system prompt. This time you should be shown a prompt asking you whether you want to read the material in your various newsgroups. It will look like this:

```
Unread news in news.answers                          30 articles
Unread news in news.newusers.questions               12 articles
Unread news in news.software.readers                  5 articles
Unread news in comp.mail.misc                         6 articles
etc.

********   1 unread article in news.answers--read now? [+ynq]
```

As noted before, the suggested commands inside the bracketed box aren't the only possibilities, but they do represent the ones you'll probably use. A **y** will cause the first article to appear. An **n** will skip this newsgroup and take you to the next one. A **q** will quit **trn** altogether.

Choose a **y** now to display the first article. You'll see a screen like the one in Figure 11.3.

This is a USENET message, or part of one; it's also called a posting. We're in the newsgroup **news.answers,** as can be seen from the top of the message header. Notice that this is a moderated newsgroup, meaning messages don't just accumulate here at random, but are sorted and presented through the intervention of a USENET volunteer, who is acting as the publisher of this collected material. Moderated newsgroups, you'll find, often provide more valuable information in less space than their unmoderated cousins, because a good moderator will make sure the material stays on track. In this case, **news.answers** is designed as a repository of periodic postings, usually known as FAQs (for **F**requently **A**sked **Q**uestions); these are lists of the most common queries in each newsgroup, assembled so the group doesn't spend its time answering the same questions over and over.

Newsgroup Header Information

Look more closely at the header and you'll see information not too dissimilar from what appears on a mail message. The message number is followed by a note in brackets telling you how many more unread messages there are in this newsgroup. The header marked **Newsgroups:** tells you that this posting went to other groups besides **news.answers.** It was also sent to **rec.aviation.answers** and **rec.answers.** These groups make sense; we can see the message is a list of frequently asked questions regarding aviation, and thus most likely found in the **rec** category.

The heading **Followup-To: poster** tells you who to contact about this list of questions. In this case, you would write to the person who posted the message. His name is listed after the **Organization:** header; he's Geoffrey G. Peck, a consultant in San Jose, CA. We have his e-mail address, after the **From:** header. The date of the posting is listed, along with the total number of lines. Just below this is a statement of when the file was last modified. This is included because a FAQ is frequently updated, and you want to keep track of which version you should keep and which might be obsolete. Finally, an archive name, **aviation/faq,** tells us you can also find the FAQ at an archive site.

Paging Through a Posting

This **FAQ** is a long posting. Note at the bottom of the screen the statement of where you are in the message:

```
--MORE--(3%)
```

Figure 11.3
A typical USENET
message.

```
news.answers (moderated) #5698 (28 more)                          (1)
Newsgroups: rec.aviation.answers,rec.answers,news.answers          1]
From: geoff@peck.com (Geoff Peck)
[1] Frequently Asked Questions about Aviation (regular posting)
Followup-To: poster
Organization: Geoffrey G. Peck, Consultant, San Jose, CA
Date: Tue Feb 02 03:30:03 EST 1993
Lines: 777


Original-from: geoff@peck.com (Geoff Peck)
Last-modified: 26 Jan 1993 by geoff@peck.com (Geoff Peck)
Archive-name: aviation/faq

This regular posting was last revised January 26, 1993.  Changes since the
last posting are marked by a vertical bar ("|") in the left margin.  ("rn"
and "trn" users may search for new materials using "g^|".)  It answers
frequently asked questions on rec.aviation, and provides a glossary of
frequently-used acronyms, so posters don't need to provide translations of
these terms.  This posting was written by Geoff Peck (geoff@peck.com), with
input from many other netters.  The author takes full responsibility for any
omissions or errors.  (Use of this posting in flight is prohibited.  :-) )
Comments and questions are most welcome.  This article is now being
automatically posted twice per month.  [If you have trouble sending mail to
--MORE--(3%)
```

This tells you there's more to come, and that at present you've read only three percent of the entire message. To proceed, press the **SPACE BAR,** *not* the **RETURN** key. (If you use **RETURN,** you advance one line at a time, which, on a message this size, will quickly cause you to wish you had never heard of USENET!) Each subsequent pressing of the **SPACE BAR** takes you down one more page on the screen.

Now, using the **SPACE BAR** and reading as we go, we could work our way through the entire FAQ. On the other hand, maybe you're not that interested in aviation. To proceed immediately to the next message, you can press the **n** key. Pressing it at any **--MORE--** prompt will take you to the next message. Figure 11.4 shows the next one.

Many of the header fields are identical, although we do note some further information here. Now there's a field for **Keywords:**, which in this case is filled with the term **USENET Amateur Radio**. The **FollowUp-To:** field is different as well; rather than suggesting a reply to the poster of the message, it asks that you send any responses directly to the newsgroup **rec.radio.amateur.misc.** Each newsgroup will have its own conventions about who to reply to and where.

We're also given information about the posting's relationship to previous FAQs. This one has a **Supersedes:** field, meaning the document replaces one called **<1992Dec28.1@ve6mgs.ampr.org>**. This is similar to but more detailed than the **Last-modified:** field of the **rec.aviation** FAQ; it tells us which document is current. We're also told how often to expect a new version, in the **X-Posting-Frequency:** field; a new FAQ appears on the twenty-eighth of every month. Finally, we get the **Last-modified:** date and a version number for this document. This happens to be version 1.00, a fact confirmed in the message,

Figure 11.4
Another USENET message with different fields.

```
news.answers (moderated) #5702 (27 more)              [1]--[2]--[3]--[4]
From: mark@ve6mgs.ampr.org (Mark Gregory Salyzyn)
Newsgroups: rec.radio.amateur.misc,rec.radio.info,rec.answers,news.answers
[1] Amateurs on USENET List  Jan 1993  Part 1 of 4
Summary: List of Amateur Radio Operators that can be reached on USENET
Keywords: USENET Amateur Radio
Date: Thu Jan 28 18:59:59 EST 1993
Followup-To: rec.radio.amateur.misc
Lines: 997
Supersedes: ÂDec28.1@ve6mgs.ampr.org
X-Posting-Frequency: on the 28th of every month

Archive-name: radio/hams-on-usenet/part1
Last-modified: $Date: 1993/01/28 13:00 $
Version: $Revision: 1.00 $

This is the first time this list is posted to news.answers and rec.answers

I would be pleased to take any e-mail updates to this list, preferably at
hams-on-usenet@ve6mgs.ampr.org. I have split this list into four parts. This
First part contains primarily European calls with US call districts 0 and 1.

-- Ciao -- Mark Salyzyn  mark@ve6mgs.ampr.org/adec23.UUCP finally has a
.sig ...
--MORE--(2%)
```

which states this is the first time this FAQ has been posted to **news.answers** and **rec.answers.**

Working Through the Topics

We can see from the bottom of the screen that this is another long document; we've only reached the two-percent mark in our reading of it so far, and again, we can use the **SPACE BAR** to page through the text, or the **n** command to move to the next document. Reading a USENET newsgroup this way is interesting as you begin to learn how the groups are constructed; it shows you what kinds of information are available on them. However, the charm is likely to wear off quickly as you realize how many messages remain in this particular group. And if you look back at the list of groups we encountered when we first started up **trn,** you'll see how much reading is ahead if you continue this way. So let's consider another alternative. I'll press an **n** to abort my reading of this FAQ and move immediately to the next message. Then we'll try something new. With a new message on the screen, enter a plus sign: **+.** The **+** will cause the screen display to change completely. Figure 11.5 shows what you'll see.

Examine the new screen closely. We have a listing of the messages in the **news.answers** newsgroup. Each message is labeled with a single letter at the left margin, along with the name of the poster and, most useful of all, the title of the message. This is helpful indeed. Not only does the listing give us an overview of message traffic on the newsgroup, it also allows us to pick and choose among the messages we'd like to work with. At the bottom of the screen is further information. The **(Mail)** notation is simply a reminder I have mail waiting for me in my mailbox. The **Select threads** statement is another kind of reminder. It tells us that the messages we're looking at here are threaded; that is, they are put together in terms of their content, so we read them in logical

Figure 11.5
A list of messages invoked by the plus (+) key.

```
news.answers          26 articles (moderated)

a Mark Gregory Sal 1 Amateurs on USENET List Jan 1993 Part 3 of 4
  Mark Gregory Sal 1 Amateurs on USENET List Jan 1993 Part 4 of 4
b Philip R. Banks  1 Comp.Sys.Acorn FAQ List Posting (Automatic)
c Ignatios Souvatz 1 comp.protocols.ppp frequently wanted information
d Richard M. Mathe 1 REC.NUDE Nude Beaches Etc. FAQ: California
e Richard M. Mathe 1 REC.NUDE Nude Beaches Etc. FAQ: Not California
f Ilana Stern      1 Sources of Meteorological Data FAQ
g Steve Kotsopoulo 1 X on Intel-based Unix Frequently Asked Questions [FAQ]
i sham             1 R/C Flying: Part 2 of 2/rec.models.rc FAQ
  sham             1 R/C Flying: Part 1 of 2/rec.models.rc FAQ
j John T. Grieggs  1 (01Feb93) comp.graphics Frequently Asked Questions (FAQ
l Tom Schneider    1 Biological Information Theory and Chowder Society FAQ
o Gerben 'P' Vos   1 Acorn ftp and mail-server archives (fortnightly posting
r treese           1 comp.unix.ultrix Frequently Asked Questions
s Chris Hibbert    1 Social Security Number FAQ
t Ralph Johnson Ma 1 rec.models.railroad Fortnightly FAQ (INTRO)
u Mark Kantrowitz  1 FAQ: How to Get Cheap Airtickets 1/2 [Monthly posting]
v Mark Kantrowitz  1 FAQ: How to Get Cheap Airtickets 2/2 [Monthly posting]
w Joel Furr        1 alt.fan.lemurs: Frinkquently Asked Questions

(Mail) -- Select threads -- Top 73% [Z] --
```

order. This saves you from reading part one of a two-part posting, reading several messages in between, and only then getting to part two.

The statement **Top 73%** means you are looking at 73 percent of the message traffic available in this newsgroup. The bracketed Z, or **[>Z]**, means you can read all the messages if you choose. The system is also telling you that this is the default; do nothing more than press the **RETURN** key or the **SPACE BAR** here and you'll be taken to the first message, as though you had marked every message for reading. But before we do that, we will look at the message threads on this page and examine how to read them.

trn is easy to work because message selection is simple. To mark a particular message or thread for reading, simply enter the letter next to it. If I want to read the FAQ **How to Get Cheap Air Tickets,** I note there are two messages and two letters, **u** and **v.** If I enter a **u** and a **v,** the display changes to show these messages have been chosen. A plus sign (**+**) will appear next to them.

```
u+Mark Kantrowitz   1  FAQ: How to Get Cheap Airtickets 1/2 [Monthly posting]
v+Mark Kantrowitz   1  FAQ: How to Get Cheap Airtickets 2/2 [Monthly posting]
```

To read these messages, I press a capital **D.** This marks the unselected articles on the current page as already read. It then displays the articles that were selected. Doing this now, I'll see the first of the selected messages as shown in Figure 11.6. If I choose not to read this message, pressing an **n** will take me to the next message I have selected.

Responding to a Posting by Mail

As you read the newsgroups, you soon become familiar with their conventions and begin to follow ongoing discussions. At some point, you may want to add your own thoughts to what someone else has said. You have two options for

Figure 11.6
A message generated with the **D** command.

```
[1] FAQ: How to Get Cheap Airtickets 1/2 [Monthly posting]
Followup-To: poster
Supersedes: airfare-1.text_725958031@cs.cmu.edu
Nntp-Posting-Host: a.gp.cs.cmu.edu
Organization: School of Computer Science, Carnegie Mellon
Date: Tue Feb 02 02:01:35 EST 1993
Lines: 1298

Archive-name: air-travel/cheap-tickets/part1
Last-Modified: Tue Dec 29 16:40:27 1992 by Mark Kantrowitz
Version: 1.4
Size:  58124 bytes

;;; ************************************************************
;;; Airfare FAQ, Part 1 ***************************************
;;; ************************************************************

This post is a summary of useful information for air travelers. The
focus is on obtaining inexpensive air fares, although other topics are
also covered.
--MORE--(2%)
```

Figure 11.7
Mailing a response to a
USENET message.

```
To: pangloss@swift.com
Subject: Re: C news on ultrix 4.3
Newsgroups: triangle.wizards
In-Reply-To: â@swift.com
Organization: CONCERT-CONNECT -- Public Access UNIX
Cc:
Bcc:


(Above lines saved in file /home/gilster/.rnhead)

(leaving cbreak mode; cwd=/home/gilster)
Invoking command: Rnmail -h /home/gilster/.rnhead


Prepared file to include [none]:
```

doing so. You can respond by sending an electronic mail message to the sender, or you can respond within the newsgroup itself by posting a follow-up message.

Replying by electronic mail is easy. After you finish reading the message you want to respond to, you'll be given a prompt that looks like:

```
(Mail) End of article 41 (of 41)--what next? [npq]
```

Enter an **r** here. This should result in a screen like the one in Figure 11.7.

trn is asking whether I want to include an already prepared file in my answer. The word **none** in brackets means the default is not to include any file; pressing a **RETURN** here will cause the system to assume we don't wish to include one. Now I am prompted about which editor I will use:

```
Editor [/usr/ucb/vi]:
```

The default at CONCERT-CONNECT (and at most system provider sites running UNIX) is **vi.** Again, I can choose this default by pressing the **RETURN** key. At that point, I'll be put into the **vi** editor and can compose my reply.

By pressing the **r** key, I've sent a message to the originator of the posting. If I had chosen to include the original posting for reference, I could have done that by following the same procedure, only using the command **R.**

Responding and Posting in the Newsgroup

If you prefer submitting a follow-up article to the newsgroup rather than responding by electronic mail, that's easily done as well. Use the **f** command at the end of the posting or, if you choose to include the original message, the **F** command. You'll be prompted as follows:

```
(Mail) End of article 41 (of 41)--what next? [npq] f
```

Here's what you'll see:

```
Are you starting an unrelated topic? [yn] n
```

I've entered an **n** at this prompt, to indicate we are staying within the same topic as we write our message; if you choose to start a new topic, you'd choose the **y,** in which case you'd be prompted for the topic. Now we see this:

```
(leaving cbreak mode; cwd=/home/gilster)
Invoking command: Pnews -h /home/gilster/.rnhead

This program posts news to many machines throughout the city.
Are you absolutely sure that you want to do this? [ny]
```

The message asks if we're sure we want to post our message. The newsgroup in question is city-wide, so we're reminded that our posting will go throughout the coverage area—Raleigh, Durham, and Chapel Hill. The message is a reminder that frivolous postings take up bandwidth and should therefore be avoided. Assume we think our posting important enough to merit inclusion in the newsgroup. We choose a **y.**

```
Prepared file to include [none]:
```

As before, we're prompted for a prepared file. We press the **RETURN** key to indicate no file inclusion will be necessary.

```
Editor [/usr/ucb/vi]:
```

And again, we're asked for an editor. Choosing **vi** by simply entering a **RETURN,** we're taken back to the **vi** screen, where we can compose and send our message.

As with responding through electronic mail, we have options for including the original message in our response. To do this, use an **F** instead of an **f** as the follow-up posting command. Figure 11.8 shows what an inserted message looks like.

As you see, the original message is here enclosed with brackets; it's followed by the comment. The reason for doing this is that people sign up for many newsgroups, and it's easy to forget exactly which message a particular posting refers to. Quoting the message ensures that everyone's memory is refreshed.

Figure 11.8
A message inserted inside a reply.

```
news.newusers.questions #9334 (2 + 1 more)                           (1)+-[1]
From: tamerlane@marlowe.renaiss.com (Christopher Marlowe)
\-[1]--[1]
[1] Re: Chatting on Internet ?
Date: Tue Feb 02 15:45:34 EST 1993
Organization: London Guild Hall
Lines: 10


In article K@drg.sotib.ac.uk ghh@egf.sotib.ac.uk (Harald Graham) writes:
I would like a method of online communication with another site on
Internet. I am familiar with telnet and ftp, but I can't see a
possibility of using them for a 'chat' across the net.
Could anybody help?

talk, or ntalk..
---------------------------------------------------------------------------
Disclaimer: It's only my opinion.
(Mail) End of article 9334 (of 9344)--what next? [npq]
```

If you'd like to try out posting without going "live," so to speak, consider a post to the **misc.test** group. It was established for test postings, making it a good place to aim for when you first try out these commands. The recipients are guaranteed to be patient people.

When New Newsgroups Are Created

Newsgroups are being created all the time. Indeed, one of the great pleasures of USENET is the vitality of such entries, as like minds find each other and begin to share common interests. **trn** will notify you when new newsgroups have become available from your server. When this happens, the message differs from the usual one when you first invoke the program. It will look like this:

```
Checking for new newsgroups...

Newsgroup rec.arts.tv.tiny-toon not in .newsrc--subscribe? [ynYN]

Newsgroup k12.news not in .newsrc--subscribe? [ynYN]
```

You now have several options.

Y   Adds all the new newsgroups, putting them at the end of the **.newsrc** file and marking them as groups you want to read.

y   Adds only the newsgroup you've been asked about

N   Adds all new groups to the end of your **.newsrc** file, marking them as unsubscribed.

n   Forgets about the newsgroup entirely.

Once you have answered the question of whether or not you want to subscribe, you'll also have a range of options about where to put each newsgroup. The following prompt will appear:

```
Put newsgroup where? [$^.L]
```

The options are as follows:

^   Puts the newsgroup first among groups you read.

$ Puts the newsgroup last among your groups.

.   Puts the newsgroup before the current newsgroup.

-*newsgroup name*   Puts the newsgroup before the newsgroup you name.

+*newsgroup name*   Puts the newsgroup after the newsgroup you name.

L   Lists newsgroups and their positions.

Growing an Article Tree

Note, incidentally, the small diagram in the top right corner of messages. This is the article "tree" for that message; it shows you how the article fits in with other messages of its thread (you won't see this if the article isn't threaded). All replies branch off from the original messages; in **trn** terminology, "child" articles branch off from "parent" articles. Look at the tree in Figure 11.9.

The numbers in the tree are all the same: ones. This means the subject of the thread hasn't changed during its existence. Read the tree from left to right. The original message is at the left. It has two replies branching off from it. Unread articles are always enclosed in brackets; articles we've read are in parentheses. The article currently being displayed is always highlighted, including its brackets.

Article trees can also be displayed by using the **t** command, as explained later. When a thread grows lengthy, the article tree can become unwieldy, but it gives you a good sense of where the message you're reading stands in relation to what has gone before. For further information on **trn**'s article trees, you can look in the manual for **trn** by giving the command **man trn** at your system provider's command prompt.

Posting a New Message on a Different Topic

Suppose now that we choose to post a new message; our topic will be different than anything now under discussion. We can do this with **trn**'s **f** command as well. As you're reading a newsgroup, use the **$** command to position yourself past the last message in the current group. You should see something like this:

```
End of article 21415 (of 21474)--what next? [npq])
```

Enter a **$** command and you'll receive this prompt:

```
What next? [npq]
```

Figure 11.9
A USENET message with an article tree in the top right corner.

```
news.newusers.questions #13186 (5 + 3 more)                    (1)--[1]--[1]
From: CBARNES@tamvm1.tamu.edu (Chris Barnes)
[1] Re: JPEG viewer
Date: Wed Jul 28 15:13:04 EDT 1993
Organization: Texas A&M University
Lines: 14
X-Newsreader: NNR/VM S_1.3.2

In article <jd$6gk@menudo.uh.edu
cosc18op@menudo.uh.edu (Al Gore) writes:


Which ftp'able JPEG viewer is the fastest for a 386 system?


DVPEG    (archie search on dvpeg4386 for the approprate zip file).


        -------------------------------------------------
Chris Barnes            |    President - Bryan/College Station
cbarnes@tamvm1.tamu.edu |           Retriever Club
(409) 846-3273 (home)   |    "Dedicated to the betterment of
(409) 845-8300 (work)   |             the retrieving breeds"
(Mail) End of article 13186 (of 13208) -- what next? [npq]
```

At this prompt, use the **f** command to begin a message. You'll be prompted for **subject:** and **distribution:**. You will see on-screen:

```
Subject:
```

Enter whatever subject is appropriate. The next prompt will ask how widely this message should be distributed:

```
Distribution:
```

A **RETURN** here enters the default distribution for the newsgroup in question. Remember, the network is worldwide, and the last thing you want is to distribute your posting beyond the boundaries of its applicability. Distribution lists depend on the server you're using, but some common terms follow.

world   The worldwide distribution.

na   Distribution limited to North America.

usa   Distribution limited to the United States.

nc   Distribution limited to North Carolina, etc.

city   Limited to a particular community.

organization   A particular group of local users, etc.

Assume **world** is the default. Should you decide to post to a group with world-wide coverage, but limit your posting to a particular area, you must enter one of these terms in the **Distribution:** field.

Now you'll be asked whether you know what you're doing:

```
This program posts news to thousands of machines throughout the entire
civilized world. Your message will cost the net hundreds if not thousands of
dollars to send everywhere. Please be sure you know what you are doing.
Are you absolutely sure that you want to do this? [ny] y

Prepared file to include [none]:

Editor [/usr/ucb/vi]:
```

After answering a **y** to continue, you're subsequently prompted as to whether you want to include a prepared file. You could do this if you had a file you wanted to fold into the message, but assume you don't. Answer with a **RETURN,** which triggers the default command of **none**. Next you're asked which editor you want to use; the answer again is **RETURN** for the default editor on your system. It's most likely to be **vi**.

Figure 11.10 shows what you see next, a **vi** screen with a series of possible fields to fill out before you begin your message.

As you can see, the **Newsgroups:** and **Subject:** fields have already been filled in by the software. The next fields are:

Summary   Here you can enter a summary of the article you're about to write. Make sure you're precise about this, so people who only read headers will know what they're getting into if they call up your message.

Figure 11.10
The **vi** screen as you
post a new message.

```
Newsgroups: misc.test
Subject: Test - Ignore
Summary:
Expires:
Sender:
Followup-To:
Distribution:
Organization: CONCERT-CONNECT -- Public Access UNIX
Keywords:


~
~
~
~
~
~
~
~
~
~
~
~
"/home/gilster/.article" 11 lines, 168 characters
```

Expires   If you enter a date here, your article will be deleted after this date. Your request may be ignored depending on the site. Can be left blank.

Sender   No need to put anything here unless you're sending the article for someone else. If you are, put your own name in.

Followup-To   This field is where follow-up messages related to your message will be sent. You could put a single newsgroup name here, or else use the word **poster.** That indicates you are collecting comments and will summarize them later. You can leave this blank if you choose.

Distribution   For determining how far the article will travel. You've already answered this, so you can leave it blank.

Keywords   This field might or might not be useful. Some mail readers can use keyword entries entered here. Filling it in is optional.

Having filled out these fields or not as you choose, you can now enter your message using the **vi** editor. When you're through, press the **ESC** key to move into command mode and then enter **:wq** to exit. You'll be prompted like this:

```
Send, abort, edit, or list?
```

Choose an **S** to send your message, an **a** to abort it.

Saving the News

Read USENET for even a few days and you're bound to begin accumulating interesting material you'd like to save. The **s** command will do this for you. At the end of the article you're reading, or the end of one screen of the article, type an **s**. Figure 11.11 shows a message I've decided to save, the FAQ for a newsgroup on audio file formats. I can give the **s** command at the first prompt at the bottom of the screen.

The prompt now changes to the following:

```
End of article 5772 (of 5774)--what next? [npq] s
```

Note that the **s** is intact; **trn** knows I want to save this file, and is asking me for a name for it. After the **s**, I'll include a name:

```
End of article 5772 (of 5774)--what next? [npq] s audio
```

Now the system will note such a file doesn't yet exist. The prompt is:

```
File /home/gilster/News/audio doesn't exist--
     use mailbox format? [ynq]
```

I'm being asked what format to put the file in. If I choose mailbox format by typing a **y**, the file is saved in a way that my mail reader can understand; I could call it up with the **mail -f filename** command to read it. I would see the following prompt:

```
Saved to mailbox /home/gilster/News/audio
```

If I choose no, or **n,** the file is saved just as it looks on the screen, as a file in the corresponding directory:

```
Saved to file /home/gilster/News/audio
```

Figure 11.11
Saving a USENET
message.

```
news.answers (moderated) #5772 (2 more)                              (1)
From: guido@cwi.nl (Guido van Rossum)                               [1]
Newsgroups: alt.binaries.sounds.misc,alt.binaries.sounds.d,comp.dsp,
+        news.answers
[1] FAQ: Audio File Formats (version 2.10)
Date: Wed Feb 03 04:18:01 EST 1993
Followup-To: alt.binaries.sounds.d,comp.dsp
Lines: 1730
Supersedes: audio-fmts_726774133@charon.cwi.nl

Archive-name: audio-fmts/part1
Submitted-by: Guido van Rossum guido@cwi.nl
Version: 2.10
Last-modified: 11-Jan-1993

FAQ: Audio File Formats (version 2.10)
======================================

Table of contents
-----------------

Introduction
Device characteristics
--MORE--(1%) s
```

Using a Saved File

trn has now saved the file for you under the name you specified. You must switch to the directory where it's kept to use it. As you can see from the above, in my system, the directory is */home/gilster/News*, a directory branching off from my home directory. Using the **cd News** command, I switch to that directory and then determine the directory's contents. Use **ls** to do this. You should now see something like the following:

```
comp/    audio    news/
```

The brackets inform us of the presence of subdirectories; here, there are two of them, *comp/* and *news/*. Along with them is the file I saved. I can now download it to my own system for saving on disk, printing, or whatever.

Getting Out of a Newsgroup

Maybe you'd prefer to move out of this newsgroup and on to another before you've finished reading your articles. A **q** will cause **trn** to leave its article selection mode and take you to the next available newsgroup, where you can make a newsgroup selection command. To remind you, this is the newsgroup selection command prompt:

```
********   14 unread articles in news.newusers.questions--read now? [+ynq]
```

No matter what newsgroups you're working with, the prompt is always **[+ynq]**.

If you want to move to a different newsgroup, you can do so with the **g** command at this prompt. **g news.answers** will take me directly there. If I'm not already a subscriber, I'll then be asked if I want to become one.

Exiting trn

A Q entered while you're reading messages will quit the selection process and take you back to the newsgroup selection command for the *current* newsgroup. At the newsgroup selection prompt, you can enter another **q** to quit **trn** altogether.

Four Levels of trn Commands

By now, the command structure of **trn** may be evident. There are several command levels.

1. The first level is the set of commands you can use *at the newsgroup selection prompt*, which is what you see when you enter **trn**, and where you emerge when you finish reading one newsgroup and are on your way to another.

2. The second command set occurs *at the thread level*, where you have a variety of options to manipulate threads.

3. The third set is at the level of *the individual article*, comprising those commands you can use to work with an individual posting, including making a reply to it.

4. The fourth set is the commands available *as you're paging through a multi-page article*. On this level, **trn** is similar to the **more** program, and we need not delve deeply into its command structure. But the other three levels do need our attention.

trn Newsgroup Selection Commands

You've just entered **trn** and encountered a prompt, asking you what you want to do about a particular newsgroup. The prompt looks like this:

```
********   16 unread articles in alt.fan.wodehouse--read now? [+ynq]
```

The following commands will show you what you can do at the *newsgroup selection prompt*. Some of these commands are basic; you'll use them every time you put **trn** to work. Others are obscure, and may never draw your attention, but you may be surprised how useful they can be.

y Read this newsgroup consecutively.

+ Display a thread selector screen.

= List the subjects of the articles in this newsgroup. Unlike the + command, a = will not provide threading. It will simply list the number of each article along with its title. To read a thread, you would have to note the numbers of each article in that thread, then enter each number as you went.

u Unsubscribe from this newsgroup.

c Catch up with all the messages in this newsgroup. This means **trn** will mark all the messages in the group as read.

A Abandon any changes regarding the read or unread status of this newsgroup since you started **trn.** You might use this, for example, if you had decided not to read a set of articles and then changed your mind.

n Go to the next newsgroup containing unread messages.

N Go to the next newsgroup, whether it contains unread messages or not.

p Return to the previous newsgroup with unread news.

P Go to the previous newsgroup, whether it contains unread news or not.

- Go to the previously displayed newsgroup.

1 Go to the first newsgroup.

^ Go to the first newsgroup with unread news.

$ Go to the last newsgroup.

g *name*   Go to the newsgroup matching the name you enter. You can subscribe to new newsgroups by going to them, as we saw earlier.

/*pattern*   Search for a newsgroup matching the pattern you've entered. For example, if I enter **/comp.** at the prompt, I'll see something like this:

```
Searching...
[0 unread in comp.ai.digest--skipping]
[0 unread in comp.archives--skipping]
[0 unread in comp.binaries.hypercard--skipping]
[0 unread in comp.binaries.ibm.pc--skipping]
[0 unread in comp.dcom.telecom.digest--skipping]
[0 unread in comp.mail--skipping]
[0 unread in comp.mail.mhs--skipping]
[0 unread in comp.mail.mhs.arpa--skipping]
********   8 unread articles in comp.mail.misc--read now? [+ynq]
```

trn has skipped those **.comp** groups having no unread messages, flagging the first newsgroup in the **.comp** category where I do have unread messages.

?*pattern*   Search backward for newsgroup matching the pattern you enter. Appending an **r** to either of these searches will cause **trn** to stop at each newsgroup to prompt you whether you want to read it or not, even if it includes no new messages.

l *pattern*   This is a handy command. It searches a list of unsubscribed newsgroups for a particular pattern. Use it, for example, if you're doing research and want to know whether there's a USENET group involved in your topic. Suppose I was preparing a study of Groucho Marx. I might search the USENET groups for **l humor.** Here's what I'd get:

```
Unsubscribed but mentioned in /home/gilster/.newsrc:
alt.humor.oracle
rec.humor
rec.humor.d
rec.humor.flame
rec.humor.funny
rec.humor.oracle
rec.humor.oracle.d
```

m *name*   This command is useful if you want to change the order in which your newsgroups are presented. If you simply type an **m** with no name followed by a **RETURN**, you'll be prompted to move the newsgroup to a new location. Here are the choices:

    ^   Puts the newsgroup first.
    $ Puts the newsgroup last.
    .   Puts it before the current newsgroup.
    -*newsgroup name*   Puts it before that newsgroup.
    +*newsgroup name*   Puts it after that newsgroup.
    L   Lists newsgroups and their positions.

o *pattern*   Displays only those newsgroups matching the pattern you list.

a *pattern*   Displays newsgroups matching your pattern, including unsubscribed newsgroups.

L   Lists contents of current **.newsrc**.

q   Quit **trn**.

x   Quit, restoring **.newsrc** to the way it was before you started **trn**.

trn Thread Selection Commands

This section describes the commands you can use at the *thread level.* They're available to you when you're looking at a screen with the thread titles listed, as follows:

```
a Phil Hill         1   >Mensa - FAQ: What other high-IQ societies are there? [B
b Phil Hill         1   >Mensa - FAQ: Do I qualify for Mensa? How do I Join? [We
c Phil Hill         1   >Mensa - FAQ: What is Mensa? [Weekly]
d Thomas Koenig     1   comp.graphics.gnuplot FAQ (Frequent Answered Questions)
e Brad Templeton    1   Introduction to REC.HUMOR.FUNNY—Monthly Posting
f Nick C. Fotis     1   (2 Feb 93) Computer Graphics Resource Listing : WEEKLY
g Nick C. Fotis     1   (2 Feb 93) Computer Graphics Resource Listing : WEEKLY

(Mail)—Select threads—All [Z>] --
```

At this prompt, you have the following choices:

a-z, 0-9   Select or deselect the thread by its letter or number.

RETURN   Start reading the newsgroup. If no threads are selected, start at the beginning of the group.

Z   Same as **RETURN**. Start reading the newsgroup.

y   This is a toggle switch. If you choose a thread for reading and then change your mind, you can deselect it with a second **y** command.

k   Mark the current thread as killed.

m   Unmark the current thread.

-   Allows you to create a range of numbers, upon which the last marking action takes effect. Thus I could use **m** to unmark a thread, and then enter **a-c** to unmark those numbered postings. This is relatively clumsy to use but it works when you want to unmark a large range of threads.

@   This toggles all thread selections. In other words, if you've marked the first four threads for reading and then enter the **@,** you'll unmark the first four and mark all the rest.

n or **]**   Moves to the next thread.

p or **[**   Moves to the previous thread.

<   Moves to the previous page.

>   Moves to the next page.

^   Moves to the first page.

$ Moves to the last page.

X   Marks any unselected articles as read, and starts reading the articles you have selected.

D   Marks unselected articles as read, and begins reading the articles you have selected. If no articles are marked, a **D** command causes **trn** to proceed to the next page.

J   Marks all articles you have selected as read. Use this command if you change your mind after marking a large number of articles.

/pattern   Search all articles for the pattern you have chosen. Entering **/compuserve**, for example, allows you to search for messages containing the word **compuserve**. If **trn** finds any, it will print the number of the articles, as follows:

```
/compuserve
6952
6953
Done

Selected 2 threads.
```

Pattern searching like this can save you time if you're browsing through a newsgroup for particular information. You can also enter a series of modifiers in the form ***/pattern/modifiers*** to limit your search. For example:

/compuserve/h   Scans headers only for "compuserve."
/compuserve/a   Scans entire articles for "compuserve."
/compuserve/r   Scans previously read articles for "compuserve."

N   Leaves this newsgroup without changing it and proceeds to the next newsgroup.

U   A handy command, **U** switches between read and unread articles. This allows you to toggle back and forth; if you remember seeing an interesting article yesterday that you read but neglected to save, you could use **U** to call up a list of read articles, find your article, and read it again.

L   Changes the **trn** display. Use it as a toggle switch, to move back and forth between a terse mode (no authors shown for the articles), and a verbose mode (authors shown).

q   Quits selection mode.

Q   Quits and returns to newsgroup selection prompt for this newsgroup.

trn Article Selection Commands

This section describes the commands you can use *while a particular article is on-screen*. You have moved past the thread selection commands by choosing an article to read. At the end of the article, you'll see this prompt:

```
(Mail) End of article 2400 (of 2402)--what next? [npq]
```

At this prompt, you have the following choices:

n or **\<spacebar\>**   Move to next unread article. If you're reading a threaded discussion, this moves to the next posting in the discussion on that topic.

N   Moves to next article.

Ctrl-N   Scans for next unread article with same subject.

p   Moves to previously read article.

P   Moves to previous article.

Ctrl-P   Moves to previous unread article with same subject.

>   Reads the next selected thread.

<   Reads the previously selected thread.

t   Displays a diagram of the article in relation to other articles in the thread. This information is normally shown at the top right of a message's first screen.

number   Go to specified article. **9368** takes you to the article with that number in the newsgroup.

/pattern/modifiers   Scans forward for an article matching the pattern you've indicated in the subject line. **?pattern?** scans backwards. With both of these commands, you can use modifiers:

    r   To scan articles you've already read.
    h   To scan headers.
    a   To scan entire articles.
    c   To make case sensitive.

    Examples: **/maps/h** searches forward, examining the headers of messages for the word **maps**. **?maps?r** searches backwards, examining the subject line of articles you've already read for the word **maps**.

f   Submit a follow-up article to the newsgroup. Can also be used to post a new article if you follow the prompts and insert a new topic.

F   Submit a follow-up article which includes the article you're responding to.

r   Reply to the sender of the article by mail.

R   Reply to the sender by mail and include the article.

s   Save to a file. Follow this with a file name. Thus **s library** saves the article to a file called **library**.

w   Save to a file, but without the header.

c   Catch up. Marks all articles in the newsgroup as read.

b   Backs up one page.

^   Go to first unread article.

$ Go to end of newsgroup.

m   Mark article as unread.

M   Mark an article as still unread even after you've exited the newsgroup.

,   Marks the current article as read, along with its replies.

J   Marks the entire thread as read.

=   Lists the subjects of unread articles.

+   Enters thread selection mode.

U   Unread articles. When you give this command, you'll receive a prompt for what you want to mark as unread. The possibilities are:

  + Go back to select thread mode, with all articles marked as unread.
  t Mark this thread's articles as unread.
  s Marks the current article and its descendant articles as unread.
  a Marks all articles in the newsgroup as unread.
  n Use this if you change your mind. It leaves everything as it was.
  u Unsubscribe from the current newsgroup.
  q Quits the current newsgroup.
  Q Quits the current newsgroup but remains at the newsgroup selection prompt for that group.

MOVING PHOTOGRAPHS OVER THE NETWORK

You wouldn't know it to look at them on-line, but some of the postings that move over USENET are actually photographs and graphics. A number of newsgroups handle such traffic, from **alt.binaries.pictures** to **alt.fractals.pictures**. Looking through a file list from **alt.binaries.pictures**, I find such scenes as a sunset, a satellite view of the western United States, a shot of Bruce Lee, and a bit of Chinese art, most of it available in so-called GIF format. GIF stands for **G**raphics **I**nterchange **F**ormat, which has become a standard for storing pictures. Another format you'll see on occasion is JPEG, a storage format with built-in compression to save disk space. Often a graphics file will be zipped; it will sport a **.zip** file suffix, as in **sunset.zip**, and will need to be unpacked before it can be viewed.

How do you move a graphics image over the network? As we saw in Chapter 8, pictures can be shipped as ASCII text. Let's look at an actual graphics file, shown in Figure 11.12, sent as a message over USENET in ASCII format.

This figure shows what you would see if you paged through the message using the space bar. It doesn't look like much, but we can use software on our own computers to put it in shape.

Working with uudecode

To do this, we'll first need to save and download a graphics file. I can use the **s** command as I'm reading the file to save it to the disk on my service provider's computer. Notice that our file contains two parts; many graphics files contain more than this. You must save each part as a separate file. I usually give each saved file an identifiable name. In this case, since we're dealing with a picture of a Sheltie, I'll call the first file **sheltie1.uue** and the second **sheltie2.uue**. Why the **.uue** suffix? If you read the chapter on using the Internet by mail, you'll recall that the suffix is necessary because we're going to use a program, **uudecode**, which requires that suffix on the files it manipulates.

Figure 11.12
The ASCII
representation of a
photograph of a
Shetland Sheep Dog.

```
alt.binaries.pictures #6457 (82 more)
[1]
From: fbruno@ysw526 (F. Bruno)
[1] sheltie.gif [1/2] [a sheltie]
Organization: Lockheed Sanders
X-Newsreader: Tin 1.1 PL4
Date: Thu Jan 28 12:46:48 EST 1993

begin 664 sheltie.gif
M1TE&.#=A\P&# ?        @ !     3 !@  ",4 "   "@ #   #@   #
M #@ $   $@  $ $ $XJ %    %@     %L5 %P@ #@S%V%P[%(G,F@
M &@0 &@8 &@@ &@J '    ' 0 ' 8 ' @ ' H ' V '!# %A(+'15 '9@ '9H
M '@  '@0 '@ '@H '@T 'A"  (1Q (  8 ( @ ( U (!# (!7 (!H !X $H
M ($0 (0H (@= (@U (A  (A( (A5 (A@ (AH &MD,A8K )!5 )!G &A,,42
M&9(U )1  )1( )1P )A5 )A@ )AH )MZ &M!)&] :+'AG*H!Q)XX_'*'A *!P
M ')L-JAH *4P *E[ ()I(++!P +!X +"'  (  &=H66[)](AU5,*Z)&+AXX +B
M +B(  )5X+'!P:(%R1JAAy0'Ez|KF/&*!4 *)@ )A_=ZR(+(&8;!IH ("!
M0@;B9-;;;AP'AQ:/^"^]=_:1   (!x88"(A'MG87]Q7H 8(Ax7(B/bkb0
M-)1M'[")/J^83)b'6:-m%[b2h!x+"02'Mt@ZV$(;b00Xb#+"04+b82*b4
M9)^3  ((9-^)e]4xB @(b(@)"([b04+b84(b(b)"0ak"/8[b77[F@8+bh
M8x5_b\2t"0d)B0b((D(z9G;bh(V:c;BZN)5;BH'# P+"=*J4A*R@
MAZZibKBXP+bP@*"bFkbP=IJ;G[bg@[bPB)N)=jjHI+BPD**FkK"HH)z;b9*'
MC;&QGYB:c:bPJKBXFW3@W+C R+FPG;&YkK"PCK"PL+BXJ*bpn,"Xh,"@L+Bx
MC[c L,"XP,"Xn,"Xj,"Tb+BxL+"Xn+"PN)BIJ"DR,BDP,BDn,"VD+BXn,"X
--MORE-- (2%)
```

Once I've saved both files and exited **trn**, I can download both files with the command **xmodem sbyk sheltie1.uue sheltie2.uue**. Once I have both files on my own hard disk, I'm ready to go to work. I'll first need to get **uudecode**, the software program that can turn this ASCII soup into something a graphics viewer can understand. In Chapter 8, we found it on CompuServe. You can also get it through anonymous FTP from a number of sites. Here's just one:

What You Need: A copy of **uudecode**

Where to Get It: Through anonymous FTP from **wuarchive.wustl.edu**. The directory is *mirrors/msdos/decode*. The file name is **uuexe522.exe**.

Untangling an Image on Your Computer

Once you have a copy of **uudecode**, make sure it and your two graphics files are in the same directory, and that you're at the DOS prompt, to decode them properly. Enter the command **uudecode sheltie1**. (At this point, you don't need to mention the **.uue** extension, for **uudecode** will look for and find it. It will also move immediately on to the second of the two files, decoding it and combining it with the first.) You will then have a workable graphics file that can be called up inside an appropriate graphics viewer.

Tracking Down a File Viewer

Which graphics viewer? Fortunately, numerous viewers are available over the Internet. As we did with **uudecode**, we can use **archie** to find one. Because VPIC is a popular program, we will look for it. At your system's command prompt, then, enter **archie -m 25 vpic** (the **-m 25** statement reduces the number of hits you'll get to 25), assuming you have an **archie** client available through your service provider. If you don't, you can Telnet to the nearest publicly accessible **archie** site. When I ran **archie** recently to find **VPIC**, I tracked down numerous sites for FTP, like this one:

```
Host oliver.sun.ac.za

    Location: /simtel/gif/vpic51.zip
        File -r--r--r-- 00137116 1992 Sep 11 22:00:00 GMT vpic51.zip
```

You'll need to unzip this file as well, and read through its documentation before loading it and putting it to work. But when you do, you'll find that the plain and incomprehensible ASCII program we downloaded from USENET has now turned into a fetching photograph of a Sheltie.

FAQs and How to Find Them

Frequently Asked Questions are those questions that you don't want to tie up bandwidth by asking. They're such common queries that everyone is tired of answering them, and although USENET etiquette implies a forgiving attitude towards novices (indeed, it's part of the credo that experienced users should help newcomers wherever they can), in most cases such help will come in the form of a gentle pointer to the relevant FAQ. After obtaining and reading this document, you may well find your question answered. If, on the other hand, it doesn't appear in the FAQ, then by all means float it past the newsgroup's membership.

Where do you find FAQs? One certain method is to follow the newsgroup in question, where the FAQ will be re-posted sooner or later. Another method is to keep an eye out in **news.answers**, where FAQs are also posted as they arrive.

On the other hand, you may not want to wait for the latest FAQ if you have a question that needs answering now. Fortunately, many newsgroups maintain archives where their FAQs are stored. **comp.ai.news.answers**, for example, offers an archive where you can find its document Frequently Asked Questions About AI. It's archived as **ai-faq/part1**. **news.announce.newusers** offers a FAQ called Answers to Frequently Asked Questions about USENET. It's available in an archive under the name **usenet-faq/part1**.

••

What You Need: An Archive for USENET FAQs

Where to Find It: Via anonymous FTP to **pit-manager.mit.edu**. Change to the directory */pub/usenet/news.answers*.

••

A very useful periodic posting which can keep you up to speed about which newsgroups offer which FAQs is Jonathan I. Kamens' **List of Periodic Informational Postings**. Kamens is one of those USENET volunteers who keep the whole show rolling; we heavy USENET users owe him and his like a considerable debt of gratitude.

••

What You Need: A Way to Keep Up with USENET FAQs

The Document: **List of Periodic Informational Postings**, by Jonathan Kamens

How to Get It: It's available when updated on the newsgroup **news.answers**. Also available through anonymous ftp from **pit-manager.mit.edu** in the *pub/usenet/news.answers/periodic postings* directory. File names are **part1**, **part2**, and so on.

••

USENET RULES OF THE ROAD

Like any other communications medium, from CB radio to smoke signals, USENET has developed its own set of rules and regulations. True, no central organization exists to enforce them, but a broad consensus has emerged regarding the proper way to behave. You'll want to be sensitive to the nuances of the on-line world, not only to avoid potential embarrassment, but to contribute to USENET's growth as a powerful tool for learning, one that only works when everyone concerned makes the necessary effort.

Do You Really Need to Post?

This may seem like an odd question; putting your thoughts on-line for other people to read is what USENET news is all about, but within limits. Think of your local movie theater. You've settled in to enjoy the show, but right behind you is a family who seem to think they're watching the movie in their living room. They comment on every action and carry on a conversation about what happened at work that day. It doesn't take long before your enjoyment of the film is spoiled. It's time to look for a new seat.

A newsgroup can fall prey to the same problems. Some participants jump into conversations without getting a good feel for what's going on, and include messages that may be off the subject not only of the thread, but of the entire newsgroup. In addition to needlessly congesting the network with this traffic, they've broken the continuity of ongoing discussions. So post carefully, and give some thought to what you have to say. The very power of USENET, its international reach to a vast audience, can become a liability if network users don't play by the rules.

Use e-mail Where You Can

Frequently, the best way to send a message is through e-mail. Maybe you'd like to thank someone for her help in answering a question you posted last week.

Why waste network bandwidth on it, when a simple e-mail note would suffice? The most common example of this kind of thing is the "me too" posting. Someone asks whether anyone reading the newsgroup knows a good source for popcorn poppers. Immediately, three other people leave a message saying, in essence, "I want to know the same thing." These messages are superfluous and, if sent at all, should be directed by e-mail to the person posting the original message.

Know Your Destination

Having decided your contribution is worth the bandwidth, think carefully about where you want it to go. The major newsgroups we've examined are posted all over the world, while other groups are regional or local in nature, like the **mcnc** and **triangle** groups I subscribe to. It's one thing to post a favorite recipe on an international cooking newsgroup; it's quite another to post a review of your favorite restaurant on that same group, considering your message will be read by thousands of people who could care less if the Crab Rangoon at Joe's Place in Spokane, WA, is particularly good on Tuesdays.

Use Descriptive Titles for Your Postings

Most of us sign up for more newsgroups than we can possibly read all the way through; that's one advantage of using software that lets us identify articles by title. But the advantage amounts to little when the titles we are presented with are vague or incomprehensible. Then we must call up the article anyway to see what it is or, more likely, simply ignore it altogether. Make your titles count.

Avoid Advertising

USENET grew up in a noncommercial environment with an emphasis upon communications rather than proprietary rights. This noncommercial bias remains today, although there are certain hierarchies, notably the **biz** groups, which challenge the old orthodoxy. You can post a product announcement, for example, as long as you're posting in an appropriate group, like **comp.newprod**. And when making such an announcement, you should stick to the facts rather than hyping the product. A low-key approach designed to inform readers of particular newsgroups about products of interest to them is acceptable. Hawking your company's wares by posting in multiple newsgroups and engaging in blatant advertising is not.

Avoid Flame Wars

Flames are messages stuffed with opinion and argument; flame wars are the verbal equivalent of a cat-fight. There are places, like the **talk** newsgroups, where debate can lead to such wars, and they're fine in their place. But tying up the network with a barrage of personal invective is a sure way to lose the attention of anyone serious about the topic.

Keep Your Signature Short

Signature files are those standard inserts we looked at in the chapter on electronic mail. They usually contain your name, address, and any other pertinent information. Long signatures tie up bandwidth and become exasperating when the same individual uses them over and over in a discussion. In particular, you should avoid wasting everybody's time with crude ASCII drawings or other forms of digital preening.

Exercise Care in Quoting

It's often helpful to quote a message you're responding to, to remind everyone of the context of your posting. But do you really need to quote all three pages of a message, with your comments interspersed between the lines? Choose only the part of the message which is germane to the conversation, adding your comments after it.

News Isn't Always News

What comes across the newswire is hard news. In an era of CNN and satellite communications, we don't need to use USENET to find out what's happening in the way of breaking events. So if the urge strikes you to fire off a message to your favorite newsgroup announcing the latest sports scores or the defeat of an incumbent senator, remind yourself that most of your audience will consider this old news by the time they read it.

Clarity Is All

Because USENET is a nonverbal medium, we lose all the signals normally available to us in conversation. As with electronic mail, remember that a wide audience might not understand messages of exceeding subtlety, and that sarcasm might easily be inferred from a message someone else took as merely humorous. If you're in doubt how something you write might be interpreted, do one of two things:

1. Consider whether your comment should be sent in the first place. (Is there a good reason why you're uneasy?)
2. Consider flagging it with a smiley face like :-) to indicate humor.

If you still like the message but detest smiley faces (good for you!), consider rewriting to avoid unnecessary confusion.

Summarize the Good Stuff

One of the prime directives of USENET computing is to help other people, especially new users. As part of that effort, it's considered good form to create summaries of useful information you've received. If you ask, for example, for help in understanding how a particular issue is being considered by Congress and receive a host of replies, write a summary of the responses and post it on the network for others to see.

Such a summary should be carefully done, however; you don't want to tie up bandwidth by simply pasting all these messages into one slapdash file and shipping it out. Instead, cut out extraneous information, including headers, and compile the responses into a single file. Write a summary that meaningfully pulls together the information, and remember to give credit to the people who helped.

Network etiquette seems like a trivial subject at the beginning, but after you've accumulated some experience with USENET, you'll understand that this cooperative enterprise only works when these basic rules are followed. If you have further questions about how to use the network, you should tap two useful documents which, between them, can solve most on-line questions about manners.

What You Need: A Primer on USENET Etiquette

The Documents: **Rules for Posting to USENET**, by Mark Horton, and **A Primer on How to Work with the USENET Community**, by Chuq Von Rospach.

How to Get Them: Both are posted regularly to **news.announce.newusers** and **news.answers**.

And if you've mastered these rules, another document, written by Brad Templeton, will ensure you never forget them. It's a wickedly funny recitation of the major USENET rules as told through a question and answer session with an on-line etiquette maven. "This is intended to be satirical," says the note at the beginning of the piece. "If you do not recognize it as such, consult a doctor or professional comedian." I doubt, though, that you'll have much difficulty making the distinction.

What You Need: A USENET Etiquette Primer for Laughs

The Document: **Dear Emily Postnews**

How to Get It: It's regularly posted on **news.newusers.questions**.

Resource Discovery: Knowing Where and How to Look

It was an inevitable problem, but its dimensions still stagger. Put information on a hard disk and you can find it using basic retrieval software, some of whose tools are built into the various computer operating systems themselves. Put information on an office network and you can still track it down; there just aren't that many machines to be concerned about. But start widening the network, making it into a company-wide net linking offices in different geographical sites, or spreading it across the ocean to hook up with foreign subsidiaries, and you've made information retrieval a much more dicey proposition.

Then look at information retrieval from the standpoint of the Internet. We learned in Chapter 2 that the Internet isn't really a network at all; it's a metanetwork, a network of networks, subsuming under its spacious mantle a wide variety of hardware and software links through thousands of separate networks, all of which can talk to each other and exchange text and other data. How can you search through this material? There are no central providers, no archives applicable to all these resources. Information can be hiding across town or around the world, and despite your earnest searching, you may not be able to locate it.

That's where search techniques come in, and a new generation of tools designed to work with, not be defeated by, the chaos of widespread network communications. In this and the next two chapters, we'll look at them in their profusion: **archie, gopher,** WAIS, WWW, **veronica,** and more. No single one of them can be said to have solved this dilemma, but together, they offer a measure of control over searching which was unheard of just a few years ago. The fast spread of these tools, gopher in particular, suggests the demand will drive further growth in this arena.

GOPHER TRACKS RESOURCES

What's easier to use, a menu or a blinking prompt? Would you rather work with a list of choices or have to type in a command? There are plenty of people out there, old hands in the computer business, who'd prefer to work with a naked prompt. Give them a **C>** or a **%** to play with and they're happy. But move beyond this core group of UNIX wizards and hard-core MS-DOS types, and you'll find a wider audience with no interest in mastering cryptic computer command structures. Sure, they'll use them when they have to but they'd prefer something more intuitive. This is especially true of the large dial-up community now learning about and beginning to utilize the Internet.

To such people, using the Internet seems like a hit or miss proposition, one based on luck more than skill. There's a grain of truth in this assessment, too. Even old hands will tell you how they "stumbled" upon a great new database, how they "wandered into" a useful FTP site, how they "saw a reference to" a new mailing list. There's no way to quantify this, of course, but looking through my various sources, subscriptions, address books and whatnot, I'd be surprised if I found more than thirty percent of them in any organized fashion. An old professor of mine used to extol the virtues of spending time in the library, whether you need a new book or not. He'd say, "If you just browse the shelves, you'll find things that will jog your thinking, books that will surprise you." He was right, as I long ago confirmed, and what he says applies to the Internet.

gopher Burrows In

Browsing has its drawbacks. It may be fun, but you're probably not getting paid to spend all day prowling around cyberspace. That's where **gopher** comes in. Created at the University of Minnesota, developed by project leader Mark P. McCahill and a team of programmers, **gopher** gives you an interface you can work with, one that can organize and arrange this vast wealth of information into some kind of order. You can look at a **gopher** menu and see at a glance what resources are available to you. You can page through it, going deeper and deeper into its submenus, to explore more specific options. You can then move directly to those resources while staying inside the **gopher** system. Library catalogs, USENET newsgroups, databases on scores of topics—you name it and you can tap into it through **gopher.**

What's fun about all this is that **gopher** shields you from the action. Contrast it to using Telnet to gain access to a particular service. I'll enter the command; say, **telnet archie@sura.net,** and when the connection is made, I'll need to work with the remote computer to extract whatever information I'm after. I've got my work cut out for me, and I'd better understand the commands.

gopher does all this behind the scenes, by letting you make a menu selection. It may seem as if the **gopher** program is doing all the work; what's actually happening is that Telnet is running *behind* **gopher.** In the same way, I could use WAIS to search a remote database, letting **gopher** handle the user interface. The important thing to remember is that **gopher** allows a server to point to another server where a particular document exists. That means **gopher** can include services not just on the local computer, but all over the Internet.

Mark McCahill sees this as one of **gopher's** greatest strengths.

When we designed the user interface, we based it on the fact that the people who work on this project aren't full-time programmers. They spend part of their time programming and part of their time answering questions from users at our campus help facility. So the last thing we wanted to do was to create something that creates more questions for us. When you get 25 percent of all programmers' time spent on answering user questions, you get a good feel for what you can get away with. We did a fair amount of user testing to make sure we weren't confusing people. The strength of **gopher** is that it's simple and painless to use, and that's why it's grown.[1]

A Dynamic Menu Structure

Realize that **gopher** is far from a static thing. Although a menu looks fixed, a declaration of resources from which we must choose, **gopher's** menus are actually dynamic. The first menu you see is based on what the server you've contacted shows you. From that point on, the menu structure depends upon the resources **gopher** is contacting. So while you're looking at a static screen, you're seeing the results of **gopher's** linkages across the Internet. And by making all of these resources available through a single set of commands, **gopher** greatly simplifies the retrieval process.

There must be some use for this kind of tool. Just ask the people who are making **gopher** work. We can track the action through statistics kept at NSFnet, bearing in mind this is only a portion of total Internet traffic. But as of November 1992, **gopher** had become the sixteenth most popular protocol in use on the net, rising from two-hundredth only a year before. The increase in **gopher** traffic volume in that period was forty-four hundred times. By May 1993, it had reached the 12th spot on the list. There is simply no question that tools that can bring a semblance of order to the chaos of cyberspace are in heavy demand.

A First Look at gopher

gopher is relatively easy to use, and there are a number of sites you can reach by way of Telnet to try it out. These include the sites in the accompanying table, listed along with their coverage areas:

Host	Area	Login
consultant.micro.umn.edu	North America	gopher
gopher.uiuc.edu	North America	gopher
panda.uiowa.edu	North America	panda
gopher.sunet.se	Europe	gopher
info.anu.edu.au	Australia	info

gopher.chalmers.se	Sweden	gopher
tolten.puc.cl	South America	gopher
ecnet.ec	Ecuador	gopher
pubinfo.ais.umn.edu	North America	------

If you're accessing the Internet through a provider like DELPHI, you'll need to use Telnet to one of these sites to work with **gopher.** If you're dialing into the Internet through one of the UNIX service providers, you will likely find a **gopher** client already installed on your system. Let's start **gopher,** then, either through Telnet to one of the above sites or by entering **gopher** at the system prompt. What you see next will depend on the server **gopher** is configured to work with. The principles, however, will be the same, despite local differences in content. Figure 12.1 shows the screen I see when I type **gopher** at the CONCERT-CON-NECT prompt.

You can see from the menu what's happening. Because this **gopher** client is located at CONCERT-CONNECT, it calls up information about that network, and provides various useful tips, such as background data on the local **gopher** itself and material designed for new users of the system. The same will happen if you use Telnet to access a **gopher;** calling the **gopher** at **uiuc.edu,** for example, yields a screen with information about the University of Illinois **gopher,** campus events, regional information in and around Champaign-Urbana. Telnet to the University of Iowa address and you'll see menu choices for information about Iowa City, news about the university, and so on.

Along with the local material are menu options to wider sources of information. As you can see from the CONCERT-CONNECT menus, there are entries for Internet Information Servers, Weather Service Forecasts, Requests for Comments (RFCs), and more. Note that all of these end with a slash, which denotes more information to follow. Select Internet Information Servers/, in

Figure 12.1
An Introductory
gopher screen.

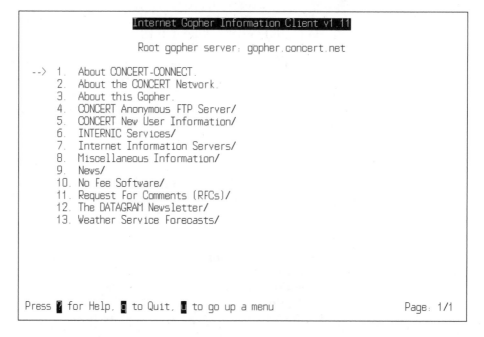

```
              Internet Gopher Information Client v1.11

                  Root gopher server: gopher.concert.net

    --> 1.  About CONCERT-CONNECT.
         2.  About the CONCERT Network.
         3.  About this Gopher.
         4.  CONCERT Anonymous FTP Server/
         5.  CONCERT New User Information/
         6.  INTERNIC Services/
         7.  Internet Information Servers/
         8.  Miscellaneous Information/
         9.  News/
        10.  No Fee Software/
        11.  Request For Comments (RFCs)/
        12.  The DATAGRAM Newsletter/
        13.  Weather Service Forecasts/




    Press ? for Help, q to Quit, u to go up a menu          Page: 1/1
```

Figure 12.2
The submenu for
Internet Information
Servers.

```
┌─────────────────────────────────────────────────────────────────┐
│             Internet Gopher Information Client v1.11              │
│                                                                   │
│                  Internet Information Servers                     │
│                                                                   │
│    --> 1.  Anonymous FTP Site Search - ARCHIE/                    │
│        2.  Campus Information Servers/                            │
│        3.  General Information Servers/                           │
│        4.  On-Line Library Services/                             │
│        5.  Other Gophers/                                         │
│        6.  Phone Books/                                           │
│        7.  WAIS Based Information/                                │
│                                                                   │
│                                                                   │
│                                                                   │
│                                                                   │
│                                                                   │
│                                                                   │
│                                                                   │
│                                                                   │
│                                                                   │
│    Press ? for Help, q to Quit, u to go up a menu    Page: 1/1    │
└─────────────────────────────────────────────────────────────────┘
```

other words, and you'll call up another menu. You can make the selection by using the arrow keys or by entering the line number of the entry you want, followed by a **RETURN**. The small arrow to the left of the menu will move to reflect your current choice. Figure 12.2 shows what we get when we try the submenu for Internet Information Servers.

As you can see, using **gopher** isn't taxing. The relevant actions are laid out for you at the bottom of the screen. At the Internet Information Servers menu, for example, entering a **u** will back you up one screen. A **q** exits the program, and a **?** calls up a help screen showing you the basic **gopher** commands.

All of the menu items in the above screen contain submenus, as we can see by the backslash following each. And if you look over the list, you'll see it's a familiar one. Here's **archie**, for example, ready to help with locating FTP sites and files. WAIS, or Wide Area Information Servers, is a text-searching facility we'll look at more closely in the next chapter. And we have Campus Information Servers, library servers, phone books, even other **gophers** to examine.

Mailing and Saving gopher Files

In the menu we just discussed, we were working with a series of choices, each of which was followed by a slash; we know, therefore, that choosing one of these will lead us to yet another menu. Take a menu item without a slash, on the other hand, and you're asking to see a document. If I were to choose item 3 from the top **gopher** menu in Figure 12.1, I would receive a screen of information about the **gopher** at this site. One way or another, though, making menu choices is moving me closer to the information I'm after. Figure 12.3 shows the information screen I'll get on **gopher** at CONCERT-CONNECT.

Figure 12.3
An information screen
on **gopher**.

```
        CONCERT Network - Network Operations Center, RTP, NC, USA
     ----------------------------------------------------------------------

     This is the main Gopher server at the Concert Network Operations
     Center in the Research Triangle Park, North Carolina.  It is
     maintained by the Internet Operations group.

     This server will be responsible for keeping information for our
     CONCERT-CONNECT users, and for CONCERT Network colleges and universities
     new to the Internet.

     The Address for this gopher is gopher.concert.net at port 70.

     Gopher server and client software for a variety of platforms is available
     in the No Fee Software subdirectory under Gopher Software Distribution.

     If you are the user of a Macintosh or IBM Personal Computer and
     <TEL> directories seem to be empty, it may be that your computer
     will require additional memory for accessing "telnet" services under
     Gopher control.  IBM-type PCs require more than 512K memory.

     For help in using the Internet Gopher, contact Naomi L.T. Courter at
     --More--(96%)[Press space to continue, 'q' to quit.]
```

Home in on the bottom line for a moment. We can press the **SPACE BAR** to finish reading the document. At that point, we'll be given the following series of options:

```
Press <RETURN> to continue, <m> to mail, <s> to save, or <p> to print:
```

Figure 12.4
gopher prompts for a
mail address.

```
     +----------------------------------------------------------------------+
     |                                                                      |
     |  Mail current document to:  gilster@rock.concert.net                 |
     |                                                                      |
     |                             [Cancel ^G] [Accept - Enter]             |
     |                                                                      |
     +----------------------------------------------------------------------+
```

A **RETURN** allows us to continue, which in this case means we will be taken back to the previous menu. Entering **m** is interesting; it will cause **gopher** to mail this document to us, prompting us first for an address, as shown in Figure 12.4.

As you can see, you can send this file to yourself or, for that matter, to someone else. In my case, I'd enter my e-mail address, pressing the **RETURN** key when finished. The file will now make an appearance in my electronic mailbox.

The third option is **s** to save the file. As a dial-up user, this is the option I commonly take, especially for longer files. The **s** option saves the file on CONCERT-CONNECT's computer; I will download it when through with my session for the day. I'll be prompted once again for information on how to save the file, as Figure 12.5 shows.

The client has prompted me for a title for the saved file, suggesting **About_this_Gopher**, because that was the name of the menu selection where I found the file. Alternatively, I can type in any file name I choose. Usually I'll pick something a bit easier to work with than **About_this_Gopher**, shortening it, perhaps, to **gopher.txt** or some such.

What happens if you're using Telnet to connect to **gopher**? Because you don't have an account on the machine you're accessing, you won't be able to save a file there, but mail is still an option. You'd use the **m** command as above, entering your e-mail address, and before long the file would appear.

Finding Files with gopher

Let's look at how **gopher** can help us with an FTP search by choosing menu item 1 from the Internet Information Servers screen (item 8 on the top menu). Now, as shown in Figure 12.6, we're prompted for the type of search we'd like to run.

Figure 12.5
Saving a file using
gopher.

```
+-------------------------------------------------------------------+
|                                                                   |
| Save in file:  About-this-Gopher_                                 |
|                                                                   |
|                             [Cancel ^G] [Accept - Enter]          |
|                                                                   |
+-------------------------------------------------------------------+
```

Saving File...

Figure 12.6
Beginning a search with
gopher.

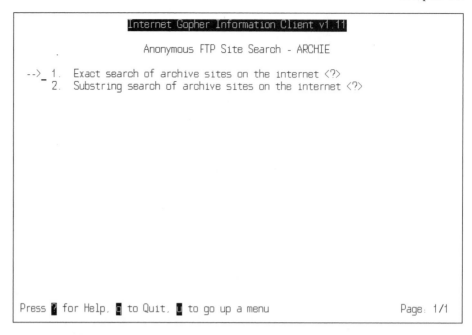

The difference between the two search strategies is that the first looks for
exactly the term we specify. The second will search for that term and find it even
if it's embedded inside another word; it's more exact.

My godson has taken a lively interest in astronomy, and I know there are
some interesting software packages that simulate the solar system and the night
sky. Let's see if we can find one by asking for an exact search, using the term

Figure 12.7
A **gopher** query
screen.

```
         Internet Gopher Information Client v1.11

              Anonymous FTP Site Search - ARCHIE

    --> 1.  Exact search of archive sites on the internet <?>
        2.  Substring search of archive sites on the internet <?>

   +--------------Exact search of archive sites on the internet-------------+
   |                                                                         |
   | Words to search for  astronomy                                         |
   |                                                                         |
   |                              [Cancel ^G] [Accept - Enter]              |
   |                                                                         |
   +-------------------------------------------------------------------------+




   Press ? for Help, q to Quit, u to go up a menu              Page: 1/1
```

Figure 12.8
Results of the
"astronomy" search.

```
┌──────────────────────────────────────────────────────────────────┐
│              ▐Internet Gopher Information Client v1.11▌             │
│                                                                    │
│          Exact search of archive sites on the internet: astronomy  │
│                                                                    │
│   -->_ 1.  Starting Archie Search, patience......                  │
│        2.  ftp.uu.net:/systems/ibmpc/msdos/simtel20/astronomy//    │
│        3.  nctuccca.edu.tw:/Macintosh/UMich-Mac/misc/astronomy//   │
│        4.  nctuccca.edu.tw:/PC-MsDos/Garbo-pc/astronomy//          │
│        5.  sunO.urz.uni-heidelberg.de:/pub/simtel/astronomy//     │
│        6.  nctuccca.edu.tw:/PC-MsDos/UMich-msdos/astronomy//       │
│        7.  swdsrv.edvz.univie.ac.at:/pc/dos/astronomy//            │
│        8.  plaza.aarnet.edu.au:/micros/pc/garbo/pc/astronomy//     │
│        9.  plaza.aarnet.edu.au:/micros/mac/umich/misc/astronomy//  │
│       10.  nctuccca.edu.tw:/PC-MsDos/SIMTEL-msdos/astronomy//      │
│       11.  sunsite.unc.edu:/pub/academic/.cap/astronomy.           │
│       12.  sunsite.unc.edu:/pub/academic/.cap/astronomy.           │
│       13.  sunsite.unc.edu:/pub/academic/astronomy//              │
│       14.  plaza.aarnet.edu.au:/micros/pc/oak/astronomy//          │
│       15.  nic.cic.net:..ub/nircomm/gopher/e-serials/general/science/astronomy// │
│       16.  knot.queensu.ca:/wuarchive/mirrors/msdos/astronomy//    │
│       17.  cs.ubc.ca:/mirror4/msdos/astronomy//                   │
│       18.  athene.uni-paderborn.de:/pcsoft/msdos/astronomy//       │
│                                                                    │
│ Press ▐?▌ for Help, ▐q▌ to Quit, ▐u▌ to go up a menu      Page: 1/2 │
└──────────────────────────────────────────────────────────────────┘
```

astronomy. Choose 1, then, and you'll be prompted to enter a search term, as appears in Figure 12.7.

As you can see, I've entered the search term in the blank. And Figure 12.8 shows what the system calls up.

gopher has located sites containing astronomy programs and data. You can pick one of the selections by moving to it with the arrow keys, and pressing the **RETURN** key to call up the item you choose.

Looking at this list, I'm interested in the second item, because it's in a subdirectory that looks germane: */systems/ibmpc/msdos/simtel20/astronomy//*. This is how a **gopher** search for an FTP site has to proceed; **gopher** isn't perfect, and it can't tell you which of these directories is necessarily the best one for the job. Much of our information gathering, in fact, has to involve trying out likely looking candidates and seeing if they pay off, much as you would browse through books in a bookstore looking for just the title you need. Let's try item 2, then, and see what we can find. The results are shown in Figure 12.9.

Now we're in luck. There are a number of intriguing files here, including one, **skygl352.zip**, which sounds like some kind of planetarium program. To retrieve it, is again a simple matter of putting the arrow to the right of item 18 and pressing another **RETURN**. Now a screen opens and prompts us for information on where to put the file. I've told the system to save the file as **skyglobe.zip**, as shown in Figure 12.10.

gopher now will retrieve the file for me. No need to go out and perform FTP procedures, switching directories, and wandering through the file holdings looking for what I need. **gopher** has managed the entire operation, while keeping the action transparent to me. If I didn't know what was happening, I'd think I had stayed at CONCERT-CONNECT.

You'll notice in the above search that **gopher**, when it had found files meeting my search criteria, also gives me further information. **skygl352.zip** is

Figure 12.9
A set of astronomy
files found by **gopher**.

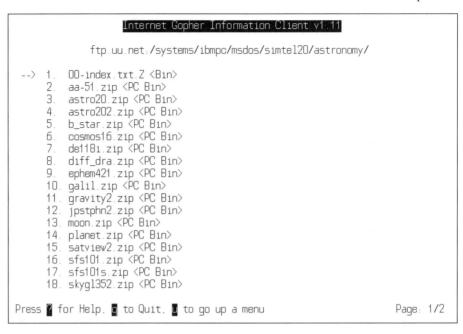

```
           Internet Gopher Information Client v1.11

           ftp.uu.net:/systems/ibmpc/msdos/simtel20/astronomy/

  -->  1.  00-index.txt.Z <Bin>
       2.  aa-51.zip <PC Bin>
       3.  astro20.zip <PC Bin>
       4.  astro202.zip <PC Bin>
       5.  b_star.zip <PC Bin>
       6.  cosmos16.zip <PC Bin>
       7.  de118i.zip <PC Bin>
       8.  diff_dra.zip <PC Bin>
       9.  ephem421.zip <PC Bin>
      10.  galil.zip <PC Bin>
      11.  gravity2.zip <PC Bin>
      12.  jpstphn2.zip <PC Bin>
      13.  moon.zip <PC Bin>
      14.  planet.zip <PC Bin>
      15.  satview2.zip <PC Bin>
      16.  sfs101.zip <PC Bin>
      17.  sfs101s.zip <PC Bin>
      18.  skygl352.zip <PC Bin>

Press ? for Help, q to Quit, u to go up a menu                  Page: 1/2
```

tagged as a binary file in the menu presentation. Here and there in your **gopher** searches, you'll run into the problem of finding a type of file your **gopher** client won't be able to work with. The **gopher+** protocol, now under development at the "Mother Gopher" site at the University of Minnesota, is to be the solution to that problem. The protocol will allow client and server to negotiate the types of data the client can handle.

Figure 12.10
Saving **skyglobe.zip**.

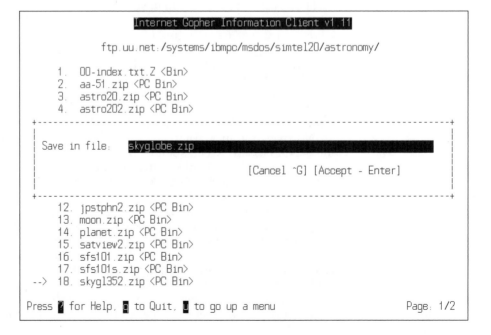

```
           Internet Gopher Information Client v1.11

           ftp.uu.net:/systems/ibmpc/msdos/simtel20/astronomy/

       1.  00-index.txt.Z <Bin>
       2.  aa-51.zip <PC Bin>
       3.  astro20.zip <PC Bin>
       4.  astro202.zip <PC Bin>
  +--------------------------------------------------------------+
  |                                                              |
  |  Save in file:   skyglobe.zip                                |
  |                                                              |
  |                         [Cancel ^G] [Accept - Enter]         |
  |                                                              |
  +--------------------------------------------------------------+
      12.  jpstphn2.zip <PC Bin>
      13.  moon.zip <PC Bin>
      14.  planet.zip <PC Bin>
      15.  satview2.zip <PC Bin>
      16.  sfs101.zip <PC Bin>
      17.  sfs101s.zip <PC Bin>
  -->  18.  skygl352.zip <PC Bin>

Press ? for Help, q to Quit, u to go up a menu                  Page: 1/2
```

If the preceding search sounded faintly familiar, it's because the search for an FTP archive site worked with **archie**. You probably caught on to that when you were prompted for either an exact search match for your search term or a substring search. You'll also run into **gopher** sites where you're simply presented with an alphabetical list of FTP servers. In that case, it's a matter of paging through the list to find a particular source of interest to you. Obviously, a link with **archie** allows **gopher** to be powerfully useful in finding information or programs when you don't know initially where to look.

The gopher Command Structure

In keeping with the theory that good software should be simple to operate, the **gopher** client I've been using boasts relatively few commands; a view of its help message will summon up a scant two screens worth of information. Let's run through the basic functions now, before moving on to see **gopher** in action with other kinds of data search.

To Move the Cursor

Up Arrow   Moves you to the previous line.

Down Arrow   Moves you to the next line.

Return   Displays current item. As we've seen, this "current item" could be a document, or it could be a submenu leading to more choices. Exactly what those choices are will depend on what kind of information source we're accessing.

u   Same as entering a Return.

To Work with Bookmarks

Bookmarks are useful in **gopher**; using them, you can mark where you are in a particular search and return to that location easily. You might not think you need a bookmark, but they're handy for more than jogging your memory. Backing up and down through a sequence of menus is fascinating at first, as you learn what resources are available. After the fifth or tenth time, though, you'd like to find a quicker way to get where you're going. Think of bookmarks as "hot keys;" you can use them to set a marker and then return directly to that page without all the intervening menus. Here are the bookmark commands:

a   Add an item to your bookmark list.

A   Add the current directory/search to the bookmark list.

The difference between the two "add" commands is this: a lowercase **a** command will note a specific item, such as one line from a menu, and will return you immediately to that item upon your request. An uppercase **A** command will return you to an entire screen of information, such as a page from the menu; there, you can make further choices before proceeding.

v   View the current list of bookmarks.

d   Delete a bookmark.

Other gopher commands

s   Saves the current item to a file.

q   Leaves **gopher**, prompting you to be sure that's what you want to do.

Q   Leaves **gopher**, with no prompt.

=   Displays technical information about the item currently being displayed.

O   Allows you to change the options **gopher** is working with.

/   Allows you to search for a particular item in the menu. This command
             will pop up a dialog box asking you to enter the search term. It will
             then search for that term for you, a useful feature on very large menus.

n   Finds the next occurrence of the search term you've specified.

gopher and Telnet

gopher can sift through a wide range of resources in various ways. Choosing,
for example, item 7 from the main screen at CONCERT-CONNECT, *Internet
Information Servers/*, and proceeding from there to choice 3 on the submenu,
General Information Servers/, I can call up a screen listing not only a series of
interesting destinations, but also one that illustrates the various ways **gopher**
goes about getting its information. The screen in question is shown in Figure
12.11.

Figure 12.11
Sources of information
on **gopher**.

```
         Internet Gopher Information Client v1.11

                   General Information Servers

  --> 1.  Automated Data Service - US Naval Observatory <TEL>
      2.  Cleveland Free-Net <TEL>
      3.  Contel DUATS - Pilot info <TEL>
      4.  E-Math - American Mathematical Society <TEL>
      5.  Electronic mail address query program <TEL>
      6.  Federal Information Exchange - Minority On-line Info Service <TEL>
      7.  Food and Drug Administration BBS <TEL>
      8.  Geographic Server - University of Michigan <TEL>
      9.  Guelph's Cosy <TEL>
     10.  HPCwire - High Performance Computing Info <TEL>
     11.  Ham Radio Callbook Server - SUNY at Buffalo <TEL>
     12.  Heartland Free-Net <TEL>
     13.  ISAAC - Advanced Academic Computing Info <TEL>
     14.  Knowbot Information Server <TEL>
     15.  Lunar & Planetary Institute - NASA <TEL>
     16.  NASA SPACELINK <TEL>
     17.  NASA/IPAC Extragalactic Database - NED <TEL>
     18.  NICOL - JvNCnet Network Information Center On-Line <TEL>

Press ? for Help, q to Quit, u to go up a menu            Page: 1/2
```

Noteworthy here are the terms in brackets at the end of each entry. It's useful to know, for example, that we can get into the Cleveland Free-Net with a simple **gopher** choice. How? Through Telnet, coded here as **<TEL>**. Here too are such interesting items as a geographic server from the University of Michigan, NASA's Lunar and Planetary Institute, and a Ham Radio Callbook Server. It's also useful to know when we're trying to locate a hard-to-find astronomical address that item 17 is out there, the NASA/IPAC Extragalactic Database. Let's try it and see how **gopher** handles a Telnet session. We'll move the pointer to item 17 and press the **RETURN** key. And an interesting thing happens, shown in Figure 12.12.

This message gets our attention. It's nothing to worry about. **gopher** is telling us that by setting up a Telnet session, it's losing control over what happens next. There is an escape mechanism available, as shown in the warning message: you can enter a **Ctrl-]** to return to the Telnet prompt. This, followed by a **quit** command, should get you back home to **gopher**, as much as the concept of "home" has meaning in networked cyberspace.

Press **RETURN** to proceed. The following should occur:

```
Trying 134.4.10.118 ...
Connected to denver.ipac.caltech.edu.
Escape character is '^]'.
SunOS UNIX (denver.ipac.caltech.edu)

login:
```

The login for this system is **ned** (see Chapter 15). Entering that, we get to a welcome screen.

**Figure 12.12
gopher's** telnet
reminder.

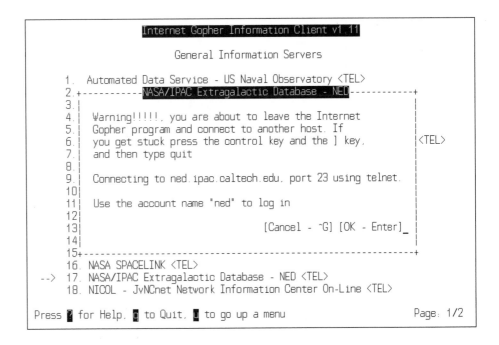

```
           WELCOME TO THE NASA/IPAC EXTRAGALACTIC DATABASE
    At present NED contains extensive CROSS-IDENTIFICATIONS for over 200,000
objects—galaxies, quasars, infrared and radio sources, etc. NED provides
POSITIONS, NAMES, and BASIC DATA (e.g. MAGNITUDES, REDSHIFTS), as well as:
      > BIBLIOGRAPHIC REFERENCES:  (a) provided by SIMBAD for 1983 to 1989
          (b) derived by NED for several journals since January 1990,
      > ABSTRACTS: collected by NED from several journals since 1988,
      > NOTES: from major catalogs such as the RC1, MCG, Hubble Atlas, etc.
```

From here on, we're in NASA's hands. But when we leave the database, we return right back to the **gopher** screen.

gopher and the Public Library

The intriguing thing about using **gopher** is that you're never quite sure what's going to turn up. The resources available are so vast and, in many cases, so surprising, that exploring them can be a full-time occupation. It's useful, for example, to know that **gopher** is one way you can explore the library systems at various universities. More and more libraries are coming on-line all the time, often accessible through Telnet procedures. We've already seen how **gopher** can simplify Telnet; now let's look at some other ways it can help us manage information. I'll choose item 4 from the Internet Information Servers menu, *On-Line Library Services/*. Figure 12.13 shows what we get.

We have an interesting list, offering library catalogs around the world as well as in the United States. But pay particular attention to item 1, listed as American English Dictionary, and followed by a **<?>**. The question mark alerts you to the fact that you're dealing not with a subdirectory but an index. This can be a handy way to search for information indeed. Figure 12.14 shows what we see when we press a RETURN at item 1.

Figure 12.13
A library services menu.

```
               Internet Gopher Information Client v1.11

                         On-Line Library Services

        --> 1.  American English Dictionary <?>
            2.  Asia-Pacific Libraries/
            3.  Electronic Books/
            4.  European Libraries/
            5.  Middle East Libraries/
            6.  North American Libraries/
            7.  North Carolina Libraries/




     Press ? for Help, q to Quit, u to go up a menu          Page: 1/1
```

Figure 12.14
A dictionary search
screen.

```
┌─────────────────────────────────────────────────────────────────────┐
│            Internet Gopher Information Client v1.11                    │
│                                                                       │
│                     On-Line Library Services                          │
│                                                                       │
│   --> 1.  American English Dictionary <?>                             │
│       2.  Asia-Pacific Libraries/                                     │
│       3.  Electronic Books/                                           │
│       4.  European Libraries/                                         │
│  +----------------------American English Dictionary----------------+  │
│  |                                                                  |  │
│  | Words to search for                                             |  │
│  |                                                                  |  │
│  |                               [Cancel ^G] [Accept - Enter]      |  │
│  |                                                                  |  │
│  +------------------------------------------------------------------+  │
│                                                                       │
│                                                                       │
│                                                                       │
│                                                                       │
│                                                                       │
│                                                                       │
│   Press ? for Help, q to Quit, u to go up a menu        Page: 1/1    │
└─────────────────────────────────────────────────────────────────────┘
```

Interesting indeed, for now we can enter a search term to track down a specific word. President Clinton has been described by one columnist as "peripatetic." What does the word mean? We can enter it in the search field and press a **RETURN** to find out. The results are shown in Figure 12.15.

gopher has built another menu, based on the results of the search. In this case, the word we're after and a series of closely related terms (from the phonetic

Figure 12.15
Results of a dictionary
search.

```
┌─────────────────────────────────────────────────────────────────────┐
│            Internet Gopher Information Client v1.11                    │
│                                                                       │
│                American English Dictionary: peripatetic               │
│                                                                       │
│  --> 1.  peripatetic [exact match].                                  │
│      2.  parapet [soundex match].                                    │
│      3.  parfait [soundex match].                                    │
│      4.  perfidious [soundex match].                                 │
│      5.  perfidy [soundex match].                                    │
│      6.  peripatetic [soundex match].                                │
│      7.  perpetrate [soundex match].                                 │
│      8.  perpetration [soundex match].                               │
│      9.  perpetrator [soundex match].                                │
│     10.  perpetual [soundex match].                                  │
│     11.  perpetually [soundex match].                                │
│     12.  perpetuate [soundex match].                                 │
│     13.  perpetuation [soundex match].                               │
│     14.  perpetuity [soundex match].                                 │
│     15.  pervade [soundex match].                                    │
│     16.  powerboat [soundex match].                                  │
│     17.  prefatory [soundex match].                                  │
│     18.  private [soundex match].                                    │
│   Press ? for Help, q to Quit, u to go up a menu        Page: 1/3    │
└─────────────────────────────────────────────────────────────────────┘
```

standpoint, anyway) are provided. Nothing drives home the point more force-fully that **gopher**'s menus are dynamic, changing with new circumstances according to the queries put to it. Choose the first item on the list to get your definition:

```
per.i.pa.tet.ic \.per-*-p*-'tet-ik  \adj : performed or performing
   while moving about : ITINERANT
```

And now we see the justice of the comment, used to describe a president whose jogging is widely observed.

On to the libraries. I'm curious about whether or not P. G. Wodehouse has made much of an impact in the Far East. After all, much of this area was once occupied by British colonial administrators, for whom Wodehouse's Bertie and Jeeves were inspired choices as reading material. Has anything of this fondness for daffy Edwardian behavior remained? An odd question, perhaps, but we can check out the holdings of libraries in the Far East by using **gopher.** I'll find out by returning to the menu of *On-Line Library Services/*, where I can choose item 2, *Asia-Pacific Libraries/*. I'm prompted with a submenu of library choices, as shown in Figure 12.16.

Let's examine item 8, Hong Kong University of Science and Technology, accessible through **gopher**'s Telnet connection. Again, we're prompted that we're about to leave the **gopher** system, and then, after a **RETURN**, delivered to Hong Kong, as shown in Figure 12.17.

The library search is relatively straightforward, and techniques for browsing vary depending on the library you've contacted. For now, I'll just mention that I located such immortal works as *Aunts Aren't Gentlemen*, *Cat-nappers*, *Leave it to Psmith*, and *The Pothunters and Other School Stories*, among others, in Hong Kong, so the works of the master continue to flourish far from his home.

Figure 12.16
Library sources in Asia and the Pacific.

```
┌─────────────────────────────────────────────────────────────────────┐
│              Internet Gopher Information Client v1.11                 │
│                                                                       │
│                      Asia-Pacific Libraries                           │
│                                                                       │
│     -->_ 1.  Australian Bibliographic Network <TEL>                   │
│          2.  Australian Defence Force Academy <TEL>                   │
│          3.  Australian National University <TEL>                     │
│          4.  Curtin University of Technology - Australia <TEL>        │
│          5.  Deakin University - Australia <TEL>                      │
│          6.  Edith Cowan University - Australia <TEL>                 │
│          7.  Griffith University - Australia <TEL>                    │
│          8.  Hong Kong University of Science and Technology <TEL>     │
│          9.  James Cook University - Australia <TEL>                  │
│         10.  La Trobe University - Australia <TEL>                    │
│         11.  Monash University - Australia <TEL>                      │
│         12.  Murdoch University - Australia <TEL>                     │
│         13.  Northern Territory University - Australia <TEL>          │
│         14.  Royal Melbourne Institute of Technology - Australia <TEL>│
│         15.  University of Adelaide - Australia <TEL>                 │
│         16.  University of Canberra - Australia <TEL>                 │
│         17.  University of Melbourne - Australia <TEL>                │
│         18.  University of New England - Australia <TEL>              │
│                                                                       │
│  Press ? for Help, q to Quit, u to go up a menu          Page: 1/2    │
└─────────────────────────────────────────────────────────────────────┘
```

Figure 12.17
Hong Kong University of Science and Technology library catalog opening screen.

```
                    Hong Kong University of Science & Technology    HKUST
                              Library Online Catalog



                         A > AUTHOR
                         T > TITLE
                         S > SUBJECT
                         W > keyWORDS
                         C > CALL NO

                         R > RESERVE Lists
                         I > Library INFORMATION

                         X > Change language to Chinese
                         V > VIEW your circulation record
                         D > DISCONNECT
                      Choose one (A,T,S,W,C,R,I,X,V,D) _


        Students who are graduating this year, and wish to have borrowing privileges
         after graduation can apply for a Library Card at the Circulation Counter.
          ***    The card is free to HKUST graduates, and is renewable annually.   ***
```

Keeping Pace with gopher

Given how handy **gopher** is at these and other search tasks, it would be useful to have a way to keep up with developments in what some developers call "the meta-burrow."

What You Need: A Way to Track **gopher** Developments

The Source: The USENET Newsgroup **comp.infosystems.gopher.**

Look especially for the **gopher** FAQ—Common Questions and Answers about the Internet Gopher. You can retrieve it through anonymous ftp using **pit-manager.mit.edu**. Switch to the directory */pub/usenet/news.answers/*, where the file is **gopher-faq.**

gophers Galore

Another nice thing about **gophers** is that there are so many of them. If I follow the menu structure at CONCERT-CONNECT and go once again to the *Internet Information Servers* screen, I'll notice choice 5, *Other Gophers/*. Working through the menus, I'll be presented with an extensive list. I can look for North Carolina sites, or I can extend my reach to the entire U.S., to South America, to Asia and the Pacific, Europe, and the Middle East.

There's a **gopher**, for example, at National Chung Cheng University, Chia-Yi, Taiwan, R.O.C., and another at TECHNET in Singapore. The University of Western Australia is represented, as is Keio University in Japan. Two Israeli

gophers are readily accessible, while the Universidad de Santiago in Chile and the University de Campinas in Sao Paolo, Brazil are part of the South American contingent. In Europe, the choice is wide, from the DENnet Danish Academic Network to the Department of Physics in Pisa, Italy. Oxford University is here, and so is Stockholm.

The screens I'm given at CONCERT-CONNECT are not indexed; you have to page through them to see what's there. Figure 12.18 shows an example from the North American list.

These are abundant materials for the searching, but wading through screen after screen to find what you're after can be time consuming indeed. Surely there's a better way.

VERONICA SAVES THE DAY

And indeed, there is. Its name is **veronica**. We've already looked at **archie**, the useful tool that helps us find where a given file or computer program can be found among the various FTP sites. **veronica** takes the **archie** concept and applies it to **gophers**. Whereas **archie** lets you do a keyword search to track down a given file, **veronica** provides keyword searches of the titles of gopher items. Given the proliferation of **gophers** and their continuing growth, **veronica** is essential.

An aside: how these tools get named is always interesting. I'm reminded of a conversation with a contact in Washington, DC. She had inquired about my e-mail address, and when I gave it to her, asked the significance of **rock** as the machine name. "Well," I replied, "it's CONCERT-CONNECT, so I guess musical names are appropriate here. There's another machine named **banjo**." She laughed, and said she knew what I was talking about, adding "all our computers are named after tropical fruits." I mention this so you won't be surprised at the

Figure 12.18
A partial list of North American **gophers**.

```
             Internet Gopher Information Client v1.11

                             USA

   -->  1.  All/
        2.  General/
        3.  alabama/
        4.  arizona/
        5.  california/
        6.  colorado/
        7.  connecticut/
        8.  delaware/
        9.  florida/
       10.  georgia/
       11.  hawaii/
       12.  idaho/
       13.  illinois/
       14.  indiana/
       15.  iowa/
       16.  kansas/
       17.  kentucky/
       18.  louisiana/

   Press ? for Help, q to Quit, u to go up a menu        Page: 1/3
```

diversity of machine and program names you're likely to run into on the Internet. As with most matters computational, whimsy plays its role.

Maybe **veronica** is named after Veronica Lake, one of my favorite actresses from Hollywood's golden era. Alas, no. According to its originators, Fred Barrie and Steve Foster at the University of Nevada, **veronica** actually stands for **V**ery **E**asy **R**odent-**O**riented **N**et-wide **I**ndex to **C**omputerized **A**rchives. Of all things, another computer acronym! (And if **veronica** also reminds you of a character from the comic strip Archie, you're not alone).

WHAT VERONICA DOES

If **Veronica** is like **archie** in some ways, it differs significantly in others. **archie** can tell you that the file **earlgrey.zip** is a compressed archive containing tips on how to make good tea; it can tell you exactly where to find it, too. At that point, you have to set up an FTP session to actually retrieve the file. You and **archie** have parted company. **veronica** has no such restraints; she'll go out and get the material directly from the data source. And because you're using a **gopher** client to do all this, the search is simple to manage and as powerful as **gopher** itself.

There are no **veronica** clients; at least, not yet. You get to **veronica** by going through a normal **gopher** client; the two are tightly integrated. You may well find that the **gopher** server accessed by your service provider already has a link to **veronica**, in which case getting a look at the system is easy. But if it doesn't, you can still reach **veronica** in one of two ways:

1. If your system provider offers a **gopher** client, enter **gopher gopher.micro.umn.edu 70** at your service provider's main prompt. This is the gopher at the University of Minnesota. The menu you'll see will present you with a choice labeled *Other Gopher and Information Servers/*. Take it, and from the submenu choose *Search titles in Gopherspace using veronica/*.

2. If you're without a **gopher** client, you can use Telnet to reach one of the anonymous **gopher** clients, as listed earlier in the chapter. Use the site nearest to you to cut down on network lag and reduce system congestion.

What you'll see after taking either of these choices will correspond to what follows.

veronica Goes to Iowa

Let's look at how to put **veronica** to work. Using the gopher at the University of Minnesota, I generate the **veronica** menu in Figure 12.19.

Note the question marks at the end of the last six menu items. These indicate we have a searchable index to work with if we choose that menu item. Items 2 and 3 are documents providing useful information about **veronica** itself. You should read both to keep up with **veronica.**

Notice, too, that items 4 through 6 are listed as searching for **gopher** directories. Actually, a **veronica** search can be restricted to a number of different data types, or combinations of them. You might, for example, search for any mentions of the word **history** which include links to **gopher** directories or Telnet links. For the purposes of this book, I'll show you the simplest **veronica** search

Figure 12.19
The opening **veronica**
menu.

```
┌──────────────────────────────────────────────────────────────────┐
│                  Internet Gopher Information Client v1.11          │
│                                                                    │
│                 Search titles in Gopherspace using veronica        │
│                                                                    │
│     -->  1.                                                        │
│          2.  FAQ:  Frequently-Asked Questions about veronica  (1993/06/24).│
│          3.  How to compose  veronica queries (NEW June 24) READ ME!!.│
│          4.  Search gopherspace for GOPHER DIRECTORIES  (NYSERNet) <?>│
│          5.  Search gopherspace for GOPHER DIRECTORIES  (U. Pisa) <?>│
│          6.  Search gopherspace for GOPHER DIRECTORIES  (UNR) <?>  │
│          7.  Search gopherspace using veronica at NYSERNet <?>     │
│          8.  Search gopherspace using veronica at UNR <?>          │
│          9.  Search gopherspace using veronica at University of Pisa <?>│
│                                                                    │
│                                                                    │
│                                                                    │
│                                                                    │
│                                                                    │
│                                                                    │
│                                                                    │
│  Press █ for Help, █ to Quit, █ to go up a menu         Page: 1/1  │
└──────────────────────────────────────────────────────────────────┘
```

method, which is run by entering a single keyword. But as you progress, you will want to read the **veronica** documents mentioned above, which contain full information about searching under numerous different data types.

Let's give **veronica** a spin now by taking choice 7, which allows us to search through what **veronica** calls "gopherspace"—the cybernetic connections between the **gophers** around the globe. (We could also have opted for choice 8, which searches at the University of Nevada at Reno, where **veronica** was developed.) Choosing menu item 7, then, we see the screen in Figure 12.20.

Before entering a keyword, ponder for a moment what we're dealing with here. **gopher** taps resources throughout the Internet worldwide. Why, then, use **veronica** when **gopher** seems to offer all we need? The answer is as close as the opening screen of whatever **gopher** server you access. At that site, there is usually a mixture of local and more broadly-based information. At CONCERT-CONNECT, as we saw in the beginning, data about CONCERT and its capabilities is provided on the **gopher** menu. We'd like to rummage through gopherspace for this kind of material, locally available but often interesting beyond the audience it was originally intended for.

I went to college in Iowa, for example, so maybe I'd like to check in with what's happening in the land of tall corn. One possibility would be to take the *Other Gophers/* menu item and look through all the **gopher** servers until I found one or more that sported Iowa connections. With **veronica**, all I need to do is ask the question by entering **iowa** as the keyword. Let's try that now, and see the results, as in Figure 12.21.

We see a customized menu generated expressly as the result of our search strategy. The menu format is familiar enough—it's just **gopher**, the interface we've already become familiar with. But look at the menu items—we're a long way from North Carolina, Toto, even though these menu selections are all immediately accessible, just as if they were found on the local **gopher** server.

Figure 12.20
A **veronica** search
screen.

```
        Internet Gopher Information Client v1.11

           Search titles in Gopherspace using veronica

     1.
     2.  FAQ:  Frequently-Asked Questions about veronica  (1993/06/24).
     3.  How to compose  veronica queries (NEW June 24) READ ME!!.
     4.  Search gopherspace for GOPHER DIRECTORIES  (NYSERNet) <?>
   +--------------Search gopherspace using veronica at NYSERNet--------------+
   |                                                                          |
   | Words to search for                                                      |
   |                                                                          |
   |                              [Cancel ^G] [Accept - Enter]                |
   |                                                                          |
   +--------------------------------------------------------------------------+




   Press ? for Help, q to Quit, u to go up a menu              Page: 1/1
```

The breadth of information is noteworthy. We've retrieved selections at the University of Iowa and Iowa State University, an article called "Iowa's Timber-Based Economy," a directory of sawmills, veneer mills, pulp mills, and several items with the slash that tells us we're looking at submenus; they're simply marked *Iowa/*. If you didn't catch it, note particularly the bottom right of the screen, where you'll see that this is, in fact, only page one out of twelve

Figure 12.21
Results of a **veronica**
search under the term
iowa.

```
        Internet Gopher Information Client v1.11

        Search gopherspace using veronica at NYSERNet: iowa

   --> 1.  Iowa/
       2.  Forest statistics for Iowa, 1990.
       3.  Iowa's forest area in 1832: A reevaluation.
       4.  Timber and treaties: The Sauk and Mesquakie decision to sell Iowa.
       5.  Liability on woodlots in Iowa.
       6.  Iowa's timber-based economy: An economic analysis.
       7.  Iowa SCORP: Statewide Comprehensive Outdoor Recreation Plan.
       8.  The timber industry of Iowa - An assessment of timber product out.
       9.  Directory of sawmills, veneer mills, and pulp mills in Iowa.
      10.  Directory of wood-using industries of Iowa.
      11.  Primary forest products industry and timber use, Iowa, 1980.
      12.  Iowa/
      13.  Iowa State University, Dept. of Computer Science/
      14.  iowa/
      15.  Iowa State University, Dept. of Computer Science/
      16.  iowa/
      17.  Iowa State University, Dept. of Computer Science/
      18.  OASIS - University of Iowa Libraries.
   Press ? for Help, q to Quit, u to go up a menu              Page: 1/12
```

possibilities. Clearly, we've struck paydirt in our search for Iowa information. I can almost see the wind rippling through the cornstalks now.

It's interesting to realize one ramification of **veronica**: as we look at the list generated here, we're probably dealing with a variety of **gopher** servers, but we don't have to know which is which. A specific item, such as "The Timber Industry of Iowa," could be coming out of a server in Iowa City, or Ames, or Cedar Rapids, for all we know. And because we're using **gopher** as the client, we can save menu items that seem interesting in our bookmark list, so we can return to them without going through the entire menu tree.

On the other hand, maybe you'd like to know where your information is coming from. We can generate such information with an equal sign command. Entering **=** with the arrow placed to the left of the item in question will tell us what we need. Putting the arrow on item 1, "Iowa," and pressing **=**, this is what I see:

```
Name=Iowa
Type=1
Port=11111
Path=1/Iowa
Host=rodent.cis.umn.edu
```

Now we know the host name for this information: **rodent.cis.umn.edu**. The item "Forest Statistics for Iowa" on the other hand, comes from **minerva.forestry.umn.edu**.

Retrieving text or using any of these menu items works the same as the **gopher** procedures we've already talked about. Figure 12.22, for instance, is the result of placing the arrow on item 19 on page 2 of the menu system (labeled "Buckeyes Run Over Iowa in Rainstorm"), and pressing the **RETURN** key to get information.

Figure 12.22
A sample of Iowa news from **veronica**.

```
Title: Buckeyes run over Iowa in rainstorm

Author: Michael Hughes - Lantern sports writer

Date: 11/02/92

IOWA CITY, Iowa - Adverse weather conditions came over Kinnick
Stadium in Iowa City, Iowa, Saturday, but it wasn't enough to
take the storm out of the Buckeyes in their pursuit of their
third-straight win.

"This is what football is all about," said OSU linebacker Jason
Simmons. "You picture football players and see them all muddy
and in the middle of the rain and out in the weather. It was
fun to play in a game like that."

What made it even more fun for the Buckeyes was the fact that
quarterback Kirk Herbstreit finished the game with a clean jersey.

"I got hit a couple of times, but for the most part the offensive
line protected me and took care of me," Herbstreit said. "After
--More--(25%)[Press space to continue, 'q' to quit.]
```

Note that the search term, **iowa**, is highlighted in the article wherever it occurs. As you can see, pressing the **SPACE BAR** will allow you to continue reading the article. Should you decide to mail or save it, the **m** and **s** keys function as described before.

Finding Something to Read

I find **Veronica** extremely useful in tracking down something I've heard about while eavesdropping on the networks. Spending a lot of time monitoring USENET newsgroups, for example, I often run into references to interesting new offerings. **Fineart Forum** is one of them. All I knew about it was that it was available as an on-line journal, but I didn't know where, or what kind of material it published. **veronica** seemed a natural at trying to locate the journal. I searched under option 6, *"Search gopherspace for GOPHER DIRECTORIES."*. Entering **fineart** as my search term, I retrieved the information shown in Figure 12.23.

This looks promising. I'll choose the entry marked *Fineart Forum/*.

We can see by the backslash that there's another menu behind this level.

Working through these menus, we can actually gain access to the journal as shown in Figure 12.24.

Finding these resources available through a comparatively simple **veronica** source means we can do something about cleaning up our mailbox. Mine, for example, is stuffed every morning with all the journals I subscribe to. When I discovered the **veronica** option, I realized I didn't need all those subscriptions. When I wanted to read something, all I had to do was query the database and track down the relevant journal. Some subscriptions, of course, are necessary; the journals you're most interested in should stay in your mailbox, because you'll be notified every time a new issue comes out. But if your interest is marginal, a **veronica** search is perhaps the best way to go.

Figure 12.23
Results of a search under the term **fineart**.

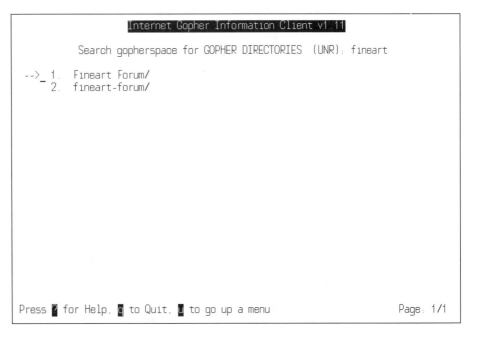

```
           Internet Gopher Information Client v1.11

        Search gopherspace for GOPHER DIRECTORIES  (UNR): fineart

-->_ 1.  Fineart Forum/
      2.  fineart-forum/
```

```
Press ? for Help, q to Quit, u to go up a menu                    Page: 1/1
```

Figure 12.24
A sample of the Fineart
Forum.

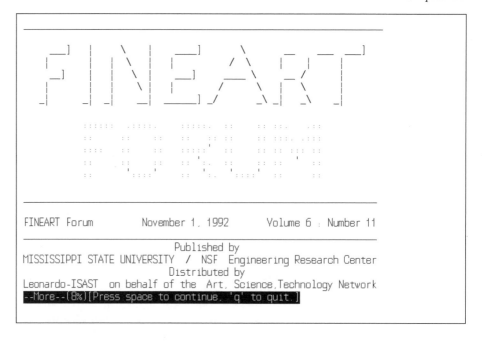

HYTELNET POWER

HYTELNET is a remarkably useful creation, a computer program that's free, available through anonymous FTP, and provides information about using the Internet. If you're using either an IBM-compatible personal computer or a Macintosh to access the Internet, you should look into **HYTELNET**. There are also UNIX and VMS versions available. As a resident program, it can be popped up at a moment's notice to solve the thorniest of navigational problems. We owe Peter Scott, of the University of Saskatchewan Libraries in Saskatoon, a debt of gratitude for this fine tool; Earl Fogel, also at Saskatchewan, created the UNIX and VMS versions. What's available through **HYTELNET**? You can find out where the Free-Nets are, the bulletin board systems, the **gophers**, the WAIS servers, the public libraries; you name it. Figure 12.25 shows you an example of a **HYTELNET** screen after I've asked it for a list of resources.

Notice that the entry labeled "Electronic Books" is highlighted; the number next to it, ELB000, is the active field. I'll press **RETURN** to call up the screen on electronic books, as in Figure 12.26.

Moving through these menus is again done with the cursor keys. I'll put the highlight on Moby Dick and press **RETURN**, retrieving the screen shown in Figure 12.27.

You see how self-referential **HYTELNET** is. It's telling us where to find the book by putting the highlight on yet another reference, **<GOP005>**. Pressing the **RETURN** key with the highlight on that number yields the results shown in Figure 12.28.

Of course, you know now that you don't have to log in through this particular **gopher** if you have access to a **gopher** client yourself; you can even use **veronica**

Figure 12.25
A HYTELNET screen
of resources.

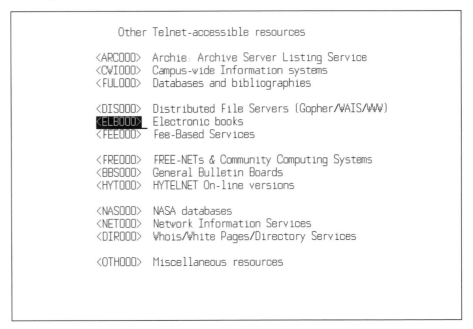

```
                    Other Telnet-accessible resources

             <ARC000>  Archie: Archive Server Listing Service
             <CWI000>  Campus-wide Information systems
             <FUL000>  Databases and bibliographies

             <DIS000>  Distributed File Servers (Gopher/WAIS/WWW)
             <ELB000>  Electronic books
             <FEE000>  Fee-Based Services

             <FRE000>  FREE-NETs & Community Computing Systems
             <BBS000>  General Bulletin Boards
             <HYT000>  HYTELNET On-line versions

             <NAS000>  NASA databases
             <NET000>  Network Information Services
             <DIR000>  Whois/White Pages/Directory Services

             <OTH000>  Miscellaneous resources
```

to track *Moby Dick* down if you choose. The benefit of **HYTELNET** is that you
can run this search quickly through the offices of a resident program, and find
what you need fast.

Figure 12.26
HYTELNET options
for electronic books.

```
                         Electronic Books

    <ELB001> Aesop's Fables
    <ELB002> Alice in Wonderland (Lewis Carroll)
    <ELB023> Antigone (Sophocles)
    <ELB003> Bible (King James Version)
    <ELB004> Book of Mormon
    <ELB005> Concise Oxford Dictionary, 8th Ed.
    <ELB026> Far from the madding crowd (Thomas Hardy)
    <ELB006> Federalist Papers
    <ELB007> Hacker's Dictionary
    <ELB027> Herland (Charlotte Perkins Stetson Gilman)
    <ELB008> Hunting of the Snark (Lewis Carroll)
    <ELB009> Koran
    <ELB010> The Life of Frederick Douglass
    <ELB011> Moby Dick (Herman Melville)
    <ELB012> O Pioneers! (Willa Cather)
    <ELB024> Oedipus at Colonus (Sophocles)
    <ELB025> Oedipus the King (Sophocles)
    <ELB013> Oxford Dictionary of Familiar Quotations (and Modern Q.)
    <ELB014> Oxford Thesaurus
    <ELB015> Paradise Lost (John Milton)
    <ELB016> Peter Pan (J.M.Barrie)
    -- press space for more --
```

Figure 12.27
Tracking down *Moby
Dick* with HYTELNET.

```
                              Moby Dick
                                 by
                           Herman Melville

Available for browsing and searching on the Internet Gopher ▮GOP005▮

This text of Melville's Moby-Dick is based on the Hendricks House
edition. It was prepared by Professor Eugene F. Irey at the University
of Colorado. Any subsequent copies of this data must include this notice
and any publications resulting from analysis of this data must include
reference to Professor Irey's work.
```

Figure 12.28
Site information for
Moby Dick.

```
            Internet Gopher at the University of Minnesota

Telnet CONSULTANT.MICRO.UMN.EDU or 134.84.132.4
login as: gopher

At TERM = (vt100) hit RETURN

Allows remote login to many other Internet sites with LIBTEL.COM. Has
RFCs on-line, campus information, weather service, phone books,
connections to other "gophers", "electronic" books, etc.

The Gopher menu is updated fairly often so it is not shown here. When
using the Gopher hit ? for help.
```

What You Need: A Program Giving you Quick Information about Internet Resources

The Program: **HYTELNET**

Where to Get It: Through anonymous ftp from **access.usask.ca**. Go to the *pub/hytelnet/pc* subdirectory. The file is listed there as **HYTELN65.ZIP**. This number may have changed, indicating a later version has been released.

NOTE: This is a compressed file. To retrieve it, you'll need to enter the word **binary** at the ftp> prompt, as discussed in Chapter 5.

For the Macintosh version: switch to directory *pub/hytelnet/mac*. The file name is **hytelnet.mac.sea.hqx**.

The information necessary for loading **HYTELNET** on your computer comes with the compressed package you'll download. Once installed, the program is called up by pressing a **Ctrl-Backspace** key combination. The **ESC** key then returns the program to background operations, allowing you to proceed with your other work. Alternatively, it's possible to enter **Alt-T** to remove **HYTELNET** from memory. And if you'd prefer to look the system over before you download it, you can access it through Telnet to **access.usask.ca**. Log in as **hytelnet**. The examples I've shown you of Hytelnet at work come from a Telnet session.

Keeping up with Internet resources isn't easy, which means that **HYTELNET** itself must constantly change to reflect new developments. Here's a way to keep up:

 What You Need: A Source of **HYTELNET** News

The Source: The mailing list **HYTEL-L** at the University of Saskatchewan. You can also read new messages in the USENET newsgroup **bit.listserv.hytel-1**.

How to Get It: Send mail to **LISTSERV@KENTVM.bitnet**. The message should read **sub hytel-1** *your name*.

Chapter Twelve Notes

1. Telephone conversation with the author February 1, 1993.

CHAPTER

13

Tracking Down Information

"A cookbook approach just won't work," said Jane Smith, assistant director of the Clearinghouse for Networked Information Discovery and Retrieval. "These tools are changing so fast that as soon as you explain how to use one of them, the information will be obsolete."[1] We were discussing resource finders, tools like WAIS and World Wide Web, which are the subject of this chapter, in the lobby of MCNC's Center for Communications. The Clearinghouse supports and promotes the use of network tools like these. It's even testing a new generation of systems that add features to the WAIS engine, developed by Thinking Machines Corporation, that we'll discuss shortly. And Smith was right.

What to do? Resource discovery is one of the Internet's fastest moving targets. Breakthroughs seem ready to occur in a host of areas, and useful client software is proliferating to take advantage of the deepening information pool. At the same time, battles rage over whose tool is the right one for the job. Maybe you think **gopher** is the information engine for the 1990s; some one else is a fan of the powerful Wide Area Information Servers (WAIS) concept. Others argue that the debate is irrelevant; the tools tie together in a common task, to locate resources and exploit them.

And what models do we use? Should directories of information about the Internet be maintained at some central site? Should they be widely dispersed but connected, allowing for maximum utility and accuracy? Who's in charge of the operation, if anyone, and which standards will come out on top? The answers, as we'll see, don't come easy.

In the meantime, you and I have work to do. Faced with the challenge of the skeet shooter, trying to hit a rapidly moving target with some fast moves and a weapon that sprays shot over a wide area, I'll try to show you a bit of both worlds. On the one hand, there's a publicly accessible WAIS server we can use for practice. Although some of what you see will have changed by the time you access it, the core principles should remain, and my descriptions will give you an idea of what WAIS is all about. We'll also travel by way of Telnet to CERN, the giant European research laboratory, for a look at World Wide Web.

WIDE AREA INFORMATION SERVERS

On-line text, as we saw in earlier chapters, is proliferating. But text, for all its utility, presents formidable retrieval problems. WAIS, the Wide Area Information Servers system, was developed to address such searching. The idea is to let the user search for a combination of keywords by sending search strings to the appropriate WAIS server machines. Each of these servers offers one or more collections of documents available for the search routine. Sources that contain the specified keywords are flagged, and the information is returned in hierarchical order based on the frequency of each keyword and the distance between keywords in the document. The documents your search flags can be requested from the server, and the server will send them to you.

The client/server model is the key. The client is the program you deal with on-screen, entering your queries and refining them; it's what you see as you work with WAIS. The server is where the data you're after is stored. You're using the client to connect with one or more servers each time you run a WAIS search. The benefit of the WAIS protocol, which handles the byplay between client and server, is that it allows the client to work with simple English search terms. The client will convert these into the protocol, which transmits them over the network to the server. On the server end, the results of the search are processed and retransmitted back to the client via the same protocol.

WAIS and the Luck of the Irish

You'll understand WAIS better if you ponder the alternative to using it. There are hundreds of WAIS servers, for example, containing material accessible through other means. A database of recipes can be found through the WAIS database called **usenet-cookbook.src** (the **.src** suffix means you're dealing with WAIS; it stands for "source"). These recipes are largely those that have appeared in the USENET newsgroup **rec.food.cooking**. They're also available at an anonymous FTP site, **gatekeeper.dec.com**.

If all you knew was that a recipe for Irish stew existed somewhere on the Internet, you could go after it in one of two ways. Through anonymous FTP, you'd go to the site. Once on-line there, you could change to the *pub/recipes* directory and look for what you need. Note how directed a process this is. You have to know where the site is, and which directory at that site to examine for what file.

Here's the WAIS alternative: by querying the WAIS source **usenet-cookbook.src**, you could tell your client program to search for the term **irish stew**. The software would handle the protocol conversion and query the server, whereupon a series of articles might be obtained which mention Irish stew. The benefit for you, the end user, is in search time; the WAIS software does the work for you, leaving you with the relatively trivial task of searching through the results to find which of the retrieved titles look close to what you want. Having made that decision, you could then have the full text sent to your mailbox.

Looking for something like Irish stew in a recipe database, you'll likely find that one WAIS search does the trick. Broader search concepts, however, can call for a different technique. Using *relevance feedback*, you can progressively refine your search to track down just the information you need. This allows you to select particular results of the search and mark them as relevant. You can then run the search a second time. The server takes into account the documents you've marked and looks for others which bear similarities to them. This generally means those documents that share a large number of common words.

A New Paradigm for Searching

If you've ever used Dow Jones News/Retrieval, you've experienced something similar in the company's DOWQUEST service, which was the first commercial system to put relevance feedback to work. DOWQUEST brought an entirely new paradigm to the search process. Using standard Boolean search techniques in its older text retrieval services, DJN/R was providing a user interface common to most on-line databases. Users had to specify exact search terms, and used Boolean operators like AND or NOT to show the desired connection between search terms. But DOWQUEST threw away the Boolean connectors. What you asked for was a series of search terms. When a list of hits was returned, you marked particular ones that were close to what you needed and ran the search again, progressively homing in on your target.

Relevance feedback is a powerful search engine; in the hands of skilled searchers, it offers broad retrieval capabilities. But what's even more encouraging is that the technique holds out the promise of effective searching for those without the inclination to master conventional Boolean methods. In that sense, WAIS and relevance feedback point in the direction the Internet at large seems to be taking, toward wider access and a user base which will be served by intuitive, rather than exclusive, tools.

We have researchers at Thinking Machines Corporation, a producer of massively parallel computers and information retrieval engines, to thank for the initial work on the concept; the company's Brewster Kahle conceived WAIS, and it was developed jointly by Thinking Machines, Apple Computer, KPMG Peat Marwick, and Dow Jones and Company. Thinking Machines has made a public-domain version available that will run on many systems; the company also markets a commercial implementation. Kahle, who remains WAIS' guiding light, now runs his own company, WAIS Inc. For him, the definition of his product is a simple one. "WAIS is an infrastructure," Kahle says, "helping people ask novice questions of large collections of information around the world."[2]

A Multitude of Data Sources

The other powerful component of WAIS is its combination of data sources. Putting together a wide variety of databases is useful, but the sheer proliferation of data presents search problems. You might spend your time retrieving what you need from one database, only to realize that two others also contain relevant information. I run into this problem all the time. An online search through CompuServe's Magazine Index Plus database finds an article I need. But I know DIALOG contains databases covering different journal sources; I'll have to try there, too. Only DIALOG and CompuServe use different interfaces, and their billing structures vary widely. Both, in turn, are different from Dow Jones News/Retrieval. Because of this, tracking down articles on a particular concept can take all afternoon, and burn up plenty of money.

Using WAIS, on the other hand, you have the ability to specify multiple databases to be searched sequentially, the results appearing in a list, ranked according to which items most closely meet your criteria. The end user can thus tap a variety of databases through a single user interface and with one search. It's as if I could tell all the information services that I needed to search under a specified set of terms. By running one search, I could query across the board, and would only have one list of results to work with.

WAIS can be powerful indeed, but the very proliferation of data sources creates an inevitable problem. Useful as WAIS servers are, how do you know how to find them? There are currently over four hundred and fifty WAIS databases available on servers throughout the world. Fortunately, there are some ways around the problem. Thinking Machines itself maintains a Directory of Servers. The Directory can be queried like any other WAIS database, returning information on the servers most likely to be useful in finding a given topic.

The WAIS Protocol

Why does WAIS seem to be taking off? A major reason, surely, is the fact that the protocol driving it is open. (The protocol is known as Z39.50 by the National Information Standards Organization; it has been supplemented to meet the needs of full-text information retrieval.) The idea is that WAIS can't work unless there are enough databases out there running the protocol to make this search tool viable. By publishing the specifications for the protocol, Thinking Machines thus spurs development of a wider market. The result: a growing number of information providers who have reason to support the WAIS project and to develop servers that will function under the protocol.

Fortunately, the protocol is hardware independent as well, eliminating the problem of developing a solution under one hardware system and being unable to apply it to others. Since the WAIS software can manage data negotiations with a variety of hardware and software platforms, providers are not constrained by their existing equipment and can develop WAIS servers confidently. Although the original client software was developed, for example, on the Apple Macintosh, programs now exist for a wide variety of operating systems. We should expect this development to continue as WAIS gains in popularity and utility.

The WAIS Support Consortium exists to address questions relating to the spread of WAIS and its future direction. There will be much to consider. Intriguingly, although the basic Z39.50 protocol was developed to manage bibliographical retrieval tasks, it was extended to handle more than text. Internet users will be able to use WAIS to retrieve video and audio materials, provided they have access to the high-end workstations necessary for the job.

A Basic WAIS Search

Let's go right to the source for our first look at WAIS by moving to the WAIS client running at Thinking Machines Corporation. Connecting there will require us to Telnet to **quake.think.com**, entering **wais** as our user name at the **login:**

Figure 13.1
Logging in to WAIS at
quake.think.com.

```
% telnet quake.think.com
Trying 192.31.181.1 ...
Connected to quake.think.com.
Escape character is '^]'.


SunOS UNIX (quake)

login: wais
Last login: Mon Jan 11 05:13:46 from pc05.grida.no
SunOS Release 4.1.1 (QUAKE) #3: Tue Jul 7 11:09:01 PDT 1992

Welcome to swais.
Please type user identifier (optional, i.e user@host): gilster@rock.con-
cert.net
TERM = (vt100)
Starting swais (this may take a little while)...
```

prompt. The variant of WAIS we'll be using here is actually called **swais**, for
"screen WAIS." This is a character-oriented interface, WAIS in its baldest form.
What we'll see at log-in is shown in Figure 13.1.

Browsing WAIS for Sources

What's available through WAIS? After the sign-on at **think.com**, we're presented
with a menu that hints at the possibilities, as shown in Figure 13.2.

You'll note at the top of this list the number of available sources: at the time
of this research, it was 454. The folks at Thinking Machines don't necessarily
know about every WAIS server, but their list is probably the most up-to-date

Figure 13.2
The basic **swais** menu.

```
SWAIS                           Source Selection              Sources: 454
  #            Server                     Source                    Cost
001:  [      archie.au]  aarnet-resource-guide                     Free
002:  [   munin.ub2.lu.se]  academic_email_conf                    Free
003:  [wraith.cs.uow.edu.au]  acronyms                             Free
004:  [   archive.orst.edu]  aeronautics                           Free
005:  [ ftp.cs.colorado.edu]  aftp-cs-colorado-edu                 Free
006:  [nostromo.oes.orst.ed]  agricultural-market-news             Free
007:  [   archive.orst.edu]  alt.drugs                             Free
008:  [   wais.oit.unc.edu]  alt.gopher                            Free
009:  [sun-wais.oit.unc.edu]  alt.sys.sun                          Free
010:  [   wais.oit.unc.edu]  alt.wais                              Free
011:  [alfred.ccs.carleton.]  amiga-slip                           Free
012:  [   munin.ub2.lu.se]  amiga_fish_contents                    Free
013:  [   coombs.anu.edu.au]  ANU-Aboriginal-Studies        $0.00/minute
014:  [   coombs.anu.edu.au]  ANU-Asian-Computing           $0.00/minute
015:  [   coombs.anu.edu.au]  ANU-Asian-Religions           $0.00/minute
016:  [   coombs.anu.edu.au]  ANU-CAUT-Projects             $0.00/minute
017:  [   coombs.anu.edu.au]  ANU-Coombspapers-Index        $0.00/minute
018:  [   coombs.anu.edu.au]  ANU-Local-Waiservers          $0.00/minute

Keywords:

<space> selects, w for keywords, arrows move, <return> searches, q quits, or ?
```

available. If nothing else, it will give you an idea how quickly WAIS is spreading in the Internet community. Also note the range of possibilities here: on this one screen there are databases on acronyms (useful indeed in a rapidly changing telecommunications arena!), aeronautics, agriculture, a WAIS newsgroup, and a network resource guide. And we're still in the A listings.

swais uses a text editor called **ex** which, in keeping with UNIX programs like **mail** and **vi**, offers an inscrutable command structure. It's possible to play around with **swais** without knowing anything about **ex**, but to avoid frustration, you should at least generate a list of basic **swais** commands at the prompt. This is done by typing a question mark (**?**) at the prompt.

What we get in return is a list of the commands in question, as shown in Figure 13.3.

Note that as you scroll through the main **swais** menu, a highlighted bar moves down the screen with every press of the **J** key. This is telling you which of the WAIS databases you're currently on; pressing the **RETURN** key at this point would take you directly into that database and prepare you for a search.

Since our topic is WAIS anyway, let's search the **alt.wais** database. To do so, we'll use the arrow keys to move the highlighted bar to item 10 (these numbers change as new databases are added to the WAIS library). **wais.oit.unc.edu**, a WAIS server at the University of North Carolina, is a database created from the postings in the USENET newsgroup **alt.wais**. Maybe you're beginning to get a feel for how useful WAIS can be at this point. One of the problems with the USENET groups is that to use them as research tools, you have to be able to identify and read older postings. WAIS is showing us how to do just that.

Press the **SPACE BAR**, then, with the highlight on item 10, and you'll see an asterisk pop up by that item. This tells us item 10 is now marked for our use. We can search this database if we can decide on appropriate search terms. Let's try to build up some background information on WAIS. One way to do that is to search for terms like **sources**, which may give us background information on WAIS servers.

Figure 13.3
Retrieving the **swais** help screen.

```
SWAIS                              Source Selection Help
Page:  1

j, down arrow, ^N        Move Down one source
k, up arrow, ^P          Move Up one source
J, ^V, ^D                Move Down one screen
K,  v, ^U                Move Up one screen
###                      Position to source number ##
/sss                     Search for source sss
<space>, <period>        Select current source
=                        Deselect all sources
v, <comma>               View current source info
<ret>                    Perform search
s                        Select new sources (refresh sources list)
w                        Select new keywords
X, -                     Remove current source permanently
o                        Set and show swais options
h, ?                     Show this help display
H                        Display program history
q                        Leave this program
```

Figure 13.4
Beginning the search
with **swais**.

```
SWAIS                              Source Selection              Sources: 454
  #                Server                           Source              Cost
 001:   [          archie.au]   aarnet-resource-guide              Free
 002:   [      munin.ub2.lu.se]  academic_email_conf               Free
 003:   [wraith.cs.uow.edu.au]   acronyms                          Free
 004:   [     archive.orst.edu]  aeronautics                       Free
 005:   [ ftp.cs.colorado.edu]   aftp-cs-colorado-edu              Free
 006:   [nostromo.oes.orst.ed]   agricultural-market-news          Free
 007:   [     archive.orst.edu]  alt.drugs                         Free
 008:   [      wais.oit.unc.edu] alt.gopher                        Free
 009:   [sun-wais.oit.unc.edu]   alt.sys.sun                       Free
 010: * [      wais.oit.unc.edu] alt.wais                          Free
 011:   [alfred.ccs.carleton.]   amiga-slip                        Free
 012:   [      munin.ub2.lu.se]  amiga_fish_contents               Free
 013:   [    coombs.anu.edu.au]  ANU-Aboriginal-Studies     $0.00/minute
 014:   [    coombs.anu.edu.au]  ANU-Asian-Computing        $0.00/minute
 015:   [    coombs.anu.edu.au]  ANU-Asian-Religions        $0.00/minute
 016:   [    coombs.anu.edu.au]  ANU-CAUT-Projects          $0.00/minute
 017:   [    coombs.anu.edu.au]  ANU-Coombspapers-Index     $0.00/minute
 018:   [    coombs.anu.edu.au]  ANU-Local-Waiservers       $0.00/minute


 Keywords: sources

 Enter keywords with spaces between them; <return> to search; ^C to cancel
```

To begin the search, we'll follow the screen directions again, entering a **w** to open up the keywords field. We can enter both **sources** and **wais** as our search term, looking for any entries which contain both words. There's no need to include an **and** in the search; this isn't Boolean searching, and including the word would just set **swais** looking for all documents containing the word **and**. As you can see, WAIS takes some getting used to, particularly if you have any background searching databases by more traditional means.

swais will prompt us for search terms by popping up a keywords field. Here, as shown in Figure 13.4, I've just entered **sources** and am about to enter **wais**.

Pressing the **RETURN** key begins the actual search, which causes the client to translate the search terms through the WAIS protocol and send them to the appropriate server. We wind up with the result shown in Figure 13.5, a list of files WAIS found that contained the desired search terms.

Give this list some scrutiny. There are items here which are clearly germane to the task at hand. The items called **WAIS-discussion digest** look promising; they seem to be archives of one or more of the WAIS mailing lists that circulate in the Internet community. Surely they would contain updated information on new WAIS servers.

We can scroll through this list to examine documents. Retrieving a relevant document is simple enough; we'll simply place the highlight over the document and press the **SPACE BAR**, following the directions at the bottom of the **swais** screen. Soon the message scrolls across the screen.

But before we examine any documents, let's take a closer look at the search results screen and see what it's telling us. You'll note the two columns on the far left. One gives us an ascending list of numbers, the other a score. WAIS is looking for the most likely candidates for our search results. From the information we've given the system, those results with a perfect 1000 score are the closest to what we're looking for (at least as far as our software knows). Indeed, if we start looking at the top of the list, we'll find **WAIS-discussion digest #5** leading all

Figure 13.5
Results of the first
search with **swais**.

```
 SWAIS                              Search Results                  Items: 40
   #     Score    Source                      Title                      Lines
 001:   [1000] (          altwais)  brewster@T Re: WAIS-discussion digest #5    740
 002:   [ 835] (          altwais)  brewster@T Re: WAIS-discussion digest #4    544
 003:   [ 660] (          altwais)  brewster@T Re: WAIS-discussion digest #4    276
 004:   [ 598] (          altwais)  brewster@T Re: WAIS-discussion digest #6    313
 005:   [ 577] (          altwais)  brewster@T Re: WAIS-discussion digest #6    834
 006:   [ 515] (          altwais)  brewster@q Re: Re: document type list an    262
 007:   [ 505] (          altwais)  brewster@q Re: Re: Need help building WA     238
 008:   [ 423] (          altwais)  brewster@q Re: Re: WAIS FAQ part 0 of n:     209
 009:   [ 371] (          altwais)  brewster@T Re: WAIS-discussion digest #4     258
 010:   [ 371] (          altwais)  emv@msen.c Re: WAIS FAQ part 20 of n: FT     101
 011:   [ 361] (          altwais)  brewster@T Re: WAIS-discussion digest #5     312
 012:   [ 319] (          altwais)  brewster@T Re: WAIS-discussion digest #5     153
 013:   [ 309] (          altwais)  trier@slc6 Re: Re: Growth of WAIS Server      67
 014:   [ 299] (          altwais)  brewster@T Re: WAIS-discussion digest #4     417
 015:   [ 299] (          altwais)  brewster@T Re: WAIS-discussion digest #5     412
 016:   [ 257] (          altwais)  brewster@T Re: WAIS-discussion digest #5     195
 017:   [ 247] (          altwais)  bremner@cs Re: Re: Indexing compressed t    1025
 018:   [ 206] (          altwais)  emv@msen.c Re: CFV:   comp.infosystems.wa     61


 <space> selects. arrows move. w for keywords. s for sources. ? for help_
```

comers, and a number of other such digests as well with high priority listings. We can browse through them on-line by pressing the **SPACE BAR** after positioning the highlight bar over the document we want.

WAIS-discussion digest #5 turns out to be an interesting summary of WAIS-related news, including articles on WAIS in commercial settings and a listing of new source materials. But as we look through the assembled materials, perhaps the best document on sources turns out to be another that ranked high on the original **swais** hit list, **WAIS-discussion digest #6**, which includes a useful directory of sources compiled by Chris Christoff. The content of each is examined and they are grouped into categories to make for easy searching.

Christoff's document gives us a broader idea of the range of WAIS servers. Many of them hold materials from various USENET newsgroups. Some contain bibliographies, while others include reports, abstracts, and papers under various subjects, many of them technical in nature. It's natural enough to find a heavy concentration of computer materials here, but there are also resources like ERIC, an archive from the Educational Resources Information Centre, reviews of major works of science fiction, materials on a variety of world religions, useful archives of zipcodes, weather information, documents from such groups as the Electronic Frontier Foundation, Project Gutenberg, and more. You'll find the working documents from the Internet Engineering Task Force here, along with discussions related to the commercialization and privatization of the Internet.

In Chapter 9, I showed you how to search for various BITNET mailing lists. It's satisfying to see such lists becoming available through WAIS. The WAIS procedure is much quicker than going through BITNET search protocols, and provides a higher likelihood that you'll find the information you need. In addition, WAIS remembers search strategies. You can run a search in multiple databases at once, significantly cutting down your search time, and can flag multiple hits to be sent in batch mode to your mailbox.

Taking WAIS South of the Border

Now let's run a more complicated WAIS search, showing off some of the capabilities of **swais**. This time, we'd like to look through more than one database at a time, and we'd like to home in on our target by using relevance feedback techniques. Let's see if we can extract some potentially useful investing information from the WAIS system. In particular, I've heard that Latin America may be an emerging area for economic growth in the early part of the Twenty-first century. If I wanted to learn more about those economies and how to invest in them, how could I use WAIS?

The place to begin is with the Directory of Servers maintained at Thinking Machines; it will give us a chance to scan through the numerous WAIS databases to see which ones are most suited to the task at hand. This directory is also an information center about the WAIS servers themselves; as we'll see, you can learn more about the holdings of each quickly, helping you to make decisions about which may be valuable. Logging in again at the **swais** client at Thinking Machines, then, we look through the menu of servers until we see the entry marked **directory-of-servers**, which is item 150.

The search strategy for the directory is somewhat different from other databases because of the nature of the information it contains. Press the **SPACE BAR** with the highlight on this entry and an asterisk will appear to show that we've selected the **directory-of-servers** as our search target. Pressing the **w** key, as before, pops up the keyword menu, allowing us to enter the search terms we're after. I'll enter several that seem workable, again omitting common words like **and** and **the**. Since Latin America is our focus, let's try that. Our search strategy is **latin america economy stock market**. Figure 13.6 shows the results.

Figure 13.6
Searching for information on Latin American economies; a first run of results.

```
 SWAIS                               Search Results                  Items: 13
    #     Score    Source                    Title                       Lines
 001:    [1000] (directory-of-se)  agricultural-market-news               23
 002:    [ 333] (directory-of-se)  ANU-Asian-Computing                    78
 003:    [ 333] (directory-of-se)  ANU-SSDA-Catalogues                    75
 004:    [ 333] (directory-of-se)  ANU-Thai-Yunnan                        83
 005:    [ 333] (directory-of-se)  ASK-SISY-Software-Information           34
 006:    [ 333] (directory-of-se)  IUBio-flystock-bg                      45
 007:    [ 333] (directory-of-se)  IUBio-flystock-bl                      45
 008:    [ 333] (directory-of-se)  IUBio-flystock-um                      45
 009:    [ 333] (directory-of-se)  US-Budget-1993                         16
 010:    [ 333] (directory-of-se)  White-House-Papers                     22
 011:    [ 333] (directory-of-se)  academic_email_conf                    61
 012:    [ 333] (directory-of-se)  great-lakes-factsheets                 55
 013:    [ 333] (directory-of-se)  uumap                                  26




 <space> selects, arrows move, w for keywords, s for sources, ? for help_
```

But what's this? A number of items clearly don't apply, and some we're just not sure of. Here's one called **agricultural-market-news** which may or may not be useful (does it involve commodities in South America, such as coffee?) Here's another called **IUBio-flystock-bg**. From the acronym and cryptic title, we can't tell much about this one. And surely **great-lakes-factsheets** can't have much to do with our topic? Let's find out.

To learn more about these servers is a simple proposition. Simply press the **SPACE BAR** with the highlight over the server in question, and the directory will produce a background screen on what that server does. Figure 13.7 shows the background screen for **agricultural-market-news**, which does, in fact, take itself out of contention when we inspect it—note that coverage is of the United States only. What's happened here?

A similar inspection of the **IUBio-flystock-bg** entry quickly rules it out as well—it's an "index of the Drosophila fruitfly stocks maintained by the stock center at Bowling Green USA." Has WAIS gone berserk?

Not berserk, perhaps, but running up against its own nature. WAIS is looking for databases that meet our search terms. But we've given it terms that can be interpreted in various ways. When we tell the WAIS directory we want servers dealing with the stock market, we have to bear in mind that WAIS will look just as diligently for the term **stock** as it will for **stock market**. The result is a hit about fruitfly *stocks* which is in no way what we're looking for. But give WAIS credit. If you look at the numerical rankings for these sources to the left of the list, you'll see that all have attained a 333 average save the first, which received 1000. WAIS is telling you that none of these are close matches.

Widening the Search

Maybe we should work on our search terms. We're looking for information about Latin America and its various economies. But we've been too specific thus far

Figure 13.7
Background information about the **agricultural-market-news database**.

```
(:source
 :version  3
 :ip-address "128.193.124.4"
 :ip-name "nostromo.oes.orst.edu"
 :tcp-port 210
 :database-name "agricultural-market-news"
 :cost 0.00
 :cost-unit :free
 :maintainer "wais@nostromo.oes.orst.edu"
 :subjects "business  marketing  commodities agriculture agricultural"
 :description "Server created with WAIS release 8 b3.1 on Oct  5 22:48:47 199
 by wais@nostromo.oes.orst.edu

This server contains the agricultural commodity market reports compiled
by the Agricultural Market News Service of the United States Department
of Agriculture. There are approximately 1200 reports from all over the
United States. Most of these reports are updated daily. Try searching for
'portland grain.'

For more information contact: wais@oes.orst.edu
 "
```

in our search. There may well be large amounts of WAIS information out there in servers whose charter is to cover broader themes. So, rather than searching under **stock market**, let's broaden the search to terms like **economy** and **finance**, leaving **latin america** in the search. We'll go back to our list of sources by pressing the **s** key, as prompted at the bottom of the **swais** screen, and then use the **BACKSPACE** key to back up and erase our previous search terms. Now we'll enter the new ones and once again press the **RETURN** key. The results of that search are shown in Figure 13.8.

This list, however, remains unpromising. What we're running into is that economic and financial information remains relatively untapped by WAIS servers. We've also seen a limitation of WAIS—it pulls up hits with no connection whatsoever with the topic in hand, because of the way it searches for the words we give it to look for. In this case, we're faced with having to look through these sources to see if any of them apply. We can use the **SPACE BAR** to look at each entry and, indeed, the one called **academic_email_conf** may have some interest. It's a database of information about newsgroups and electronic conferences. Although South and Central America do not yet maintain a strong presence on the Internet, let's see if some of these discussion groups have something to show us.

To do this, we'll search the **academic_email_conf** source. We need to move back to our list of sources by pressing the **s** key; then we need to find the relevant source by paging through the **swais** screens, using the page up and page down commands shown in Figure 13.3. Soon we locate the database, use the **SPACE BAR** to place an asterisk by it, and activate the keyword field by pressing the **w** key. One hint: don't forget to use the **SPACE BAR** to deactivate the **directory-of-servers** database when you page up to the **academic_email_conf** list. If you do forget, **swais** will search both directories at once, a result we don't need.

Figure 13.8
Still limited results of a broader search under **economy, finance,** and **latin america**.

```
SWAIS                              Search Results              Items:   9
   #    Score    Source                     Title               Lines
 001:   [1000] (directory-of-se)  Applied-Science-and-Technology    131
 002:   [ 858] (directory-of-se)  ANU-Asian-Computing                78
 003:   [ 858] (directory-of-se)  ANU-Thai-Yunnan                    83
 004:   [ 858] (directory-of-se)  ASK-SISY-Software-Information       34
 005:   [ 858] (directory-of-se)  US-Budget-1993                     16
 006:   [ 858] (directory-of-se)  White-House-Papers                 22
 007:   [ 858] (directory-of-se)  academic_email_conf                61
 008:   [ 858] (directory-of-se)  great-lakes-factsheets             55
 009:   [ 858] (directory-of-se)  uumap                              26




<space> selects, arrows move, w for keywords, s for sources, ? for help
```

Because **swais** has preserved our original search terms, and because we'd like to use them again, all we have to do once we've selected the **academic_email_conf** database is to press the **RETURN** key. Now **swais** returns forty items which meet our criteria, all of them mailing lists or some type of on-line discussion or news feature containing the search terms we're after. We need to look through this list now, shown in Figure 13.9, to see which of these hits seem particularly relevant. For those, we can use relevance searching to sharpen our tools.

Relevance Feedback Techniques

Relevance feedback is easy enough to use. We'll use the **r** command (lowercase only—case is important here) to mark those documents (or, in this case, conferences) we think are close to what we want. Confusingly, you'll see no response on-screen when you do this, but rest assured, **swais** has marked the entries, as we'll see in a moment. **soc.culture.latin.america**, a USENET newsgroup, seems clearly applicable, as does the third entry, which seems to be a mailing list devoted to economic issues. We'll mark both of those with an **r**. Finally, we'll mark the eighteenth entry, a database of economic and financial stories from ClariNet.

Having marked a number of groups, we're not sure which ones we've called relevant and which we've left alone. An **R** command will redraw the screen to show just those entries we thought were significant; another **r** command takes us back to the basic results screen. I like the first entry as well—it's devoted to issues of business and finance, as I can see from pressing the **SPACE BAR** to read its description. So let's mark it with an **r**. Now we have four relevant entries culled from the forty we started with. At this point, we need to rerun the search, letting **swais** go through our results and apply its feedback techniques to the effort.

Figure 13.9
Results of a search of the **academic_email_conf** database.

```
 SWAIS                          Search Results                       Items: 40
    #     Score     Source                    Title                      Lines
 001:   [1000] (academic_email_) ECONOMY@TECMTYVM.MTY.ITESM.MX      ECON    22
 002:   [ 950] (academic_email_) SOC.CULTURE.LATIN-AMERICA;Usenet Newsgro   20
 003:   [ 950] (academic_email_) ECONOMY@TECMTYVM;The economy and economi   20
 004:   [ 750] (academic_email_) CARIBBEAN-ECONOMY@OAKLAND.BITNET           22
 005:   [ 750] (academic_email_) soc.culture.latin-america    Topics about L
 006:   [ 675] (academic_email_) AMERICA;For people interested in how the   17
 007:   [ 675] (academic_email_) IPE@CSF.COLORADO.EDU;International Polit    22
 008:   [ 650] (academic_email_) LASPAU-L@HARVARDA;Latin American Scholar   21
 009:   [ 625] (academic_email_) LASNET@EMX.UTEXAS.EDU;Latin American Stu   26
 010:   [ 625] (academic_email_) clari.biz.finance     Finance, currency, Cor
 011:   [ 475] (academic_email_) rec.music.afro-latin    ?
 012:   [ 425] (academic_email_) CLASSICS@UWAVM;Classics and Latin discus   15
 013:   [ 425] (academic_email_) TML-L@IUBVM;Thesaurus Musicarum Latinaru   15
 014:   [ 425] (academic_email_) MHSNEWS@ICS.UCI                            31
 015:   [ 400] (academic_email_) RURALAM@MSU;Rural America Cluster Evalua   23
 016:   [ 400] (academic_email_) HEGEL@VILLVM;The Hegel Society of Americ   16
 017:   [ 375] (academic_email_) IPE-ISA-L@mach1.wlu.ca         A LISTSER   43
 018:   [ 375] (academic_email_) clari.biz.economy.world      Economy stories
            2


 <space> selects, arrows move, w for keywords, s for sources, ? for help_
```

Figure 13.10
Results of relevance
feedback in generating
a final search list.

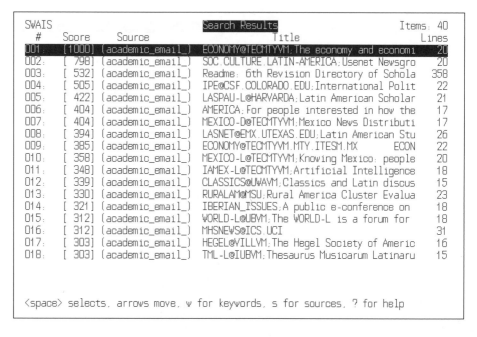

```
 SWAIS                                      Search Results              Items: 40
   #     Score    Source                              Title                 Lines
 001:   [1000]  (academic_email_)  ECONOMY@TECMTYVM: The economy and economi    20
 002:   [ 798]  (academic_email_)  SOC.CULTURE.LATIN-AMERICA: Usenet Newsgro    20
 003:   [ 532]  (academic_email_)  Readme: 6th Revision Directory of Schola    358
 004:   [ 505]  (academic_email_)  IPE@CSF.COLORADO.EDU: International Polit     22
 005:   [ 422]  (academic_email_)  LASPAU-L@HARVARDA: Latin American Scholar     21
 006:   [ 404]  (academic_email_)  AMERICA: For people interested in how the     17
 007:   [ 404]  (academic_email_)  MEXICO-D@TECMTYVM: Mexico News Distributi     17
 008:   [ 394]  (academic_email_)  LASNET@EMX.UTEXAS.EDU: Latin American Stu     26
 009:   [ 385]  (academic_email_)  ECONOMY@TECMTYVM.MTY.ITESM.MX       ECON     22
 010:   [ 358]  (academic_email_)  MEXICO-L@TECMTYVM: Knowing Mexico: people     20
 011:   [ 348]  (academic_email_)  IAMEX-L@TECMTYVM: Artificial Intelligence     18
 012:   [ 339]  (academic_email_)  CLASSICS@UWAVM: Classics and Latin discus     15
 013:   [ 330]  (academic_email_)  RURALAM@MSU: Rural America Cluster Evalua     23
 014:   [ 321]  (academic_email_)  IBERIAN_ISSUES: A public e-conference on      18
 015:   [ 312]  (academic_email_)  WORLD-L@UBVM: The WORLD-L is a forum for      18
 016:   [ 312]  (academic_email_)  MHSNEWS@ICS.UCI                               31
 017:   [ 303]  (academic_email_)  HEGEL@VILLVM: The Hegel Society of Americ     16
 018:   [ 303]  (academic_email_)  TML-L@IUBVM: Thesaurus Musicarum Latinaru     15



 <space> selects, arrows move, w for keywords, s for sources, ? for help
```

To do this, go back to the sources screen (use the **s** command, as prompted at the bottom of the screen). Then run the search again. Although you can't see the relevant items marked as such, **swais** knows they're there and applies them. Again we get forty hits, but this time, as seen in Figure 13.10, the documents are ranked in different order, reflecting the emphases we've told **swais** to put on the search. As before, to get a description of the newsgroups or mailing lists in question, use the **SPACE BAR** to generate the needed information. From this search, we've found a number of conferences we can use to monitor events in Latin and South America. We can sign on to one or more of these using the techniques already discussed in Chapters 9 and 10.

WAIS by gopher

As mentioned earlier, it's possible to access WAIS resources through a **gopher** server. Let's build a hypothetical search. Assume we're in the market for information about music. How do we know what early music sounded like? What about *really* early music, such as what would have been performed in ancient Athens? As in the previous case, I'm constructing the question as I go; my goal is to show you what WAIS is really like, rather than to manufacture searches that have a predesigned outcome. Let's slip into **gopher** and see what we find, measuring the differences between it and **swais** as we travel.

Entering the **gopher** system at MCNC's Concert-Connect service, I notice menu item 7, *Internet Information Servers*. Going to it, I see a menu of possibilities: campus information servers, phone books, and more. I'll choose number 8 on this list, *WAIS Based Information/*. We proceed from there to another menu, which shows various WAIS possibilities, taking item 3, *Everything/*. The list generated by this menu choice will look familiar; it's a list of WAIS servers, not

Figure 13.11
The WAIS menu screen
within **gopher**.

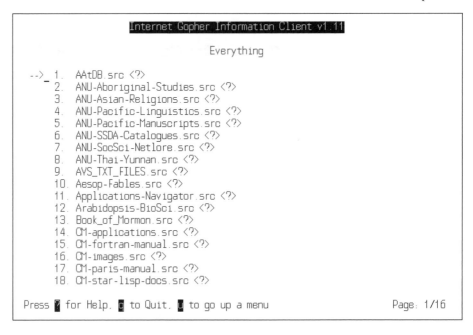

```
┌──────────────────────────────────────────────────────────────────────────┐
│              ▀▀▀▀▀▀▀▀▀▀▀▀▀▀▀▀▀▀▀▀▀▀▀▀▀▀▀▀▀▀▀▀▀▀▀▀▀▀▀▀▀▀▀                     │
│              Internet Gopher Information Client v1.11                       │
│                                                                            │
│                              Everything                                    │
│                                                                            │
│      -->_ 1.   AAtDB.src <?>                                                │
│          2.   ANU-Aboriginal-Studies.src <?>                               │
│          3.   ANU-Asian-Religions.src <?>                                  │
│          4.   ANU-Pacific-Linguistics.src <?>                              │
│          5.   ANU-Pacific-Manuscripts.src <?>                              │
│          6.   ANU-SSDA-Catalogues.src <?>                                  │
│          7.   ANU-SocSci-Netlore.src <?>                                   │
│          8.   ANU-Thai-Yunnan.src <?>                                      │
│          9.   AVS_TXT_FILES.src <?>                                        │
│         10.   Aesop-Fables.src <?>                                         │
│         11.   Applications-Navigator.src <?>                               │
│         12.   Arabidopsis-BioSci.src <?>                                   │
│         13.   Book_of_Mormon.src <?>                                       │
│         14.   CM-applications.src <?>                                      │
│         15.   CM-fortran-manual.src <?>                                    │
│         16.   CM-images.src <?>                                            │
│         17.   CM-paris-manual.src <?>                                      │
│         18.   CM-star-lisp-docs.src <?>                                    │
│                                                                            │
│ Press ▓ for Help, ▓ to Quit, ▓ to go up a menu              Page: 1/16     │
└──────────────────────────────────────────────────────────────────────────┘
```

dissimilar to the one we looked at by way of Telnet through **quake.think.com**.
You can see it in Figure 13.11.

We can query the **directory-of-servers** database using **gopher** just as we did
under the **swais** environment. So let's ask it to find information about music. Which
WAIS servers are likely to help us out? Figure 13.12 shows the search screen as
gopher presents it. We can enter **music** as our search term and we're off.

Figure 13.12
Searching for **music**
using WAIS within
gopher.

```
┌──────────────────────────────────────────────────────────────────────────┐
│              ▀▀▀▀▀▀▀▀▀▀▀▀▀▀▀▀▀▀▀▀▀▀▀▀▀▀▀▀▀▀▀▀▀▀▀▀▀▀▀▀▀▀▀                     │
│              Internet Gopher Information Client v1.11                       │
│                                                                            │
│                              Everything                                    │
│                                                                            │
│       109.  comp.lang.perl.src <?>                                         │
│       110.  comp.lang.tcl.src <?>                                          │
│       111.  comp.multi.src <?>                                             │
│       112.  comp.risks.src <?>                                             │
│ +------------------------directory-of-servers.src------------------------+ │
│ |                                                                        | │
│ | Words to search for  music_                                            | │
│ |                                                                        | │
│ |                           [Cancel ^G] [Accept - Enter]                 | │
│ |                                                                        | │
│ +------------------------------------------------------------------------+ │
│       120.  cosmic-programs.src <?>                                        │
│       121.  cs-techreports.src <?>                                         │
│       122.  cscwbib.src <?>                                                │
│       123.  current.cites.src <?>                                          │
│  -->  124.  directory-of-servers.src <?>                                   │
│       125.  directory-zenon-inria-fr.src <?>                               │
│       126.  disco-mm-zenon-inria-fr.src <?>                                │
│                                                                            │
│ Press ▓ for Help, ▓ to Quit, ▓ to go up a menu              Page: 7/16     │
└──────────────────────────────────────────────────────────────────────────┘
```

Figure 13.13
Results of a search
under the term **music**.

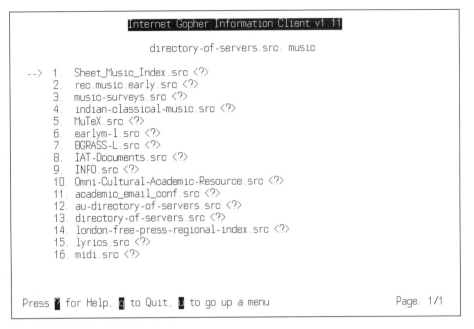

```
            Internet Gopher Information Client v1.11

                directory-of-servers.src: music

    --> 1.  Sheet_Music_Index.src <?>
        2.  rec.music.early.src <?>
        3.  music-surveys.src <?>
        4.  indian-classical-music.src <?>
        5.  MuTeX.src <?>
        6.  earlym-l.src <?>
        7.  BGRASS-L.src <?>
        8.  IAT-Documents.src <?>
        9.  INFO.src <?>
       10.  Omni-Cultural-Academic-Resource.src <?>
       11.  academic_email_conf.src <?>
       12.  au-directory-of-servers.src <?>
       13.  directory-of-servers.src <?>
       14.  london-free-press-regional-index.src <?>
       15.  lyrics.src <?>
       16.  midi.src <?>



    Press ? for Help, ? to Quit, ? to go up a menu            Page: 1/1
```

Another **RETURN** key application produces a list, shown in Figure 13.13, of possible WAIS sites for data on what we're looking for.

Let's take item 2, **rec.music.early.src**, to see if we can learn anything about music in the ancient world. We will launch another search by pressing the **RETURN** key to select that database. At that point, we'll use **greek** as our search

Figure 13.14
Results of refining the
music search with the
term **greek.**

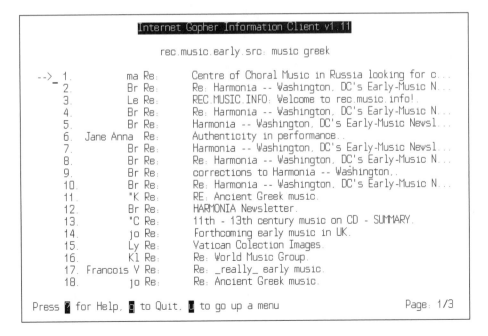

```
            Internet Gopher Information Client v1.11

              rec.music.early.src: music greek

    --> 1.         ma Re:    Centre of Choral Music in Russia looking for c...
        2.         Br Re:    Re: Harmonia -- Washington, DC's Early-Music N...
        3.         Le Re:    REC.MUSIC.INFO: Welcome to rec.music.info!.
        4.         Br Re:    Re: Harmonia -- Washington, DC's Early-Music N...
        5.         Br Re:    Harmonia -- Washington, DC's Early-Music Newsl...
        6.  Jane Anna Re:    Authenticity in performance..
        7.         Br Re:    Harmonia -- Washington, DC's Early-Music Newsl...
        8.         Br Re:    Re: Harmonia -- Washington, DC's Early-Music N...
        9.         Br Re:    corrections to Harmonia -- Washington,.
       10.         Br Re:    Re: Harmonia -- Washington, DC's Early-Music N...
       11.         "K Re:    RE: Ancient Greek music.
       12.         Br Re:    HARMONIA Newsletter.
       13.         "C Re:    11th - 13th century music on CD - SUMMARY.
       14.         jo Re:    Forthcoming early music in UK.
       15.         Ly Re:    Vatican Colection Images.
       16.         Kl Re:    Re: World Music Group.
       17.  Francois V Re:    Re: _really_ early music.
       18.         jo Re:    Re: Ancient Greek music.

    Press ? for Help, ? to Quit, ? to go up a menu            Page: 1/3
```

term and send it to the database. The results, shown in Figure 13.14, are encouraging, listing quite a few hits that might work out.

At this point, you should note the differences on-screen between **gopher** and **swais**. If we generated this same list using a **swais** search, we'd see a numbered list of hits, the possibilities with the highest relevance being labeled 1000. Here we have no such gradation. If we page through this list (we can do so using the **SPACE BAR**, or alternatively, using the **+** and **-** keys), we'll see there are a number of potentially useful entries scattered throughout the list. It's not possible to pull off the top three or four and declare them the best candidates.

What's happening? Well, using WAIS resources, **gopher** has produced a list of useful information, ranking the items according to what it thinks we're after. At this point with **swais**, we would use relevance feedback to home in on items we need. But we have no way to introduce relevance feedback into the equation with **gopher**. The first list we get is the one we're stuck with, which means we'll need to go over that search list from top to bottom.

Another difference: with **swais**, once we generated a list of hits from the **directory-of-servers**, we couldn't just highlight the server or two we wanted and proceed from there. **swais** demanded that we go back to the main server list and highlight the needed servers from it. **gopher** is easier to use. We can query the **directory-of-servers** within it, then use the **RETURN** key to query the databases we need, all without moving back to the main screen. A good thing, too, because some servers available through the **directory-of-servers** are not listed in the rest of the server list. But, unlike **swais**, we cannot use multiple servers at once for our search. That means a WAIS search using **gopher** can be a more time-consuming process, depending on what you need.

Items 11, 17 and 18 catch my eye immediately; they seem to be discussing the question precisely. At this point, I don't have to have memorized the **gopher** commands. Just as with **swais** at **think.com**, I will enter a question mark (**?**) to

Figure 13.15
The basic **gopher** commands for WAIS, listed by entering a **?** command.

```
Bookmarks
---------
a : Add current item to the bookmark list.
A : Add current directory/search to bookmark list.
v : View bookmark list.
d : Delete a bookmark/directory entry.

Other commands
--------------
s : Save current item to a file.
D : Download a file.
q : Quit with prompt.
Q : Quit unconditionally.
= : Display Technical information about current item.
O : change options
/ : Search for an item in the menu.
n : Find next search item.

The Gopher development team hopes that you find this software useful.
If you find what you think is a bug, please report it to us by sending
e-mail to "gopher@boombox.micro.umn.edu".


Press <RETURN> to continue, <m> to mail, <s> to save, or <p> to print:_
```

find out what the command possibilities are. We did this when we were examining **gopher** in Chapter 12. Figure 13.15 shows a partial list of the relevant commands.

The **a** command is promising. It lets us add the current item to a bookmark list. We can use an **a** at each of the first three lines, placing the highlight over each by moving the bar down with the arrow key. Now we've created a separate screen (accessible by a **v** command) of the items we consider the most interesting. An **s** command will then save whichever files we want to keep.

Did the search produce useful results? Definitely. I found a useful message from BITNET's EARLYM-L mailing list on ancient music. Here were summarized the major sources on the subject, giving me enough information to explore as deeply into the material as I might wish.

Another Quick Search with gopher and WAIS

Sometimes WAIS can home in on exactly the information you need. I've owned dogs since I was a kid, and my favorite breed is the Border Collie. I'm lucky enough to have an extremely healthy dog, but I've been around dogs long enough to know that some breeds have health problems which can be passed along to their puppies. So, looking for a new Border Collie, should I be concerned about particular health defects?

I turned to WAIS and **gopher** to find out. Querying the **directory-of-servers**, I asked which databases contained information about **dogs**. Note: I asked first for databases containing data on **border collies**, and was told there were no such databases available. Remember the principle: the **directory-of-servers** is going to give you the general category of information available in each database. I was able to find a database stuffed with dog information, **rec.pets.src**, by keeping my query broadly based.

Figure 13.16
Beginning a search of the **rec.pets.src** database for **border collies**.

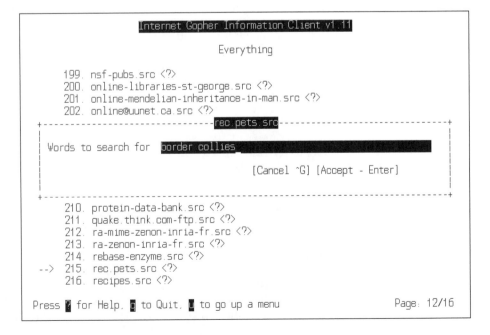

The moral: when you run a search and get no results, ask yourself how to broaden your search terms to the general concept behind the particular datum you hope to find.

rec.pets.src is a compilation drawn from a USENET newsgroup, making it a good source, because theoretically it should contain postings from dog owners and breeders. So I used the **RETURN** key to search this database under the term **border collies**, calling up the search screen as shown in Figure 13.16.

The resultant list was promising indeed. The screen **gopher** showed me indicated a number of messages on Border Collies. Although I paged through the hits, these messages were the only ones that looked germane. I used the **a** command to set up bookmarks, then the **v** command to see my bookmark list. The list is accessed the same way the main list is; you press the **RETURN** key with the highlight on the entry you want to read.

Doing this, I learned that Border Collies can suffer from PRA (progressive retinal atrophy) and juvenile cataracts, inherited diseases that can cause a dog to go blind at an early age. The dogs are also prone to hip problems, and the poster of one message, an obedience trainer, recommended having a Border Collie certified before breeding. A discussion of these issues ensued, all accessible by means of the list of hits I generated from WAIS.

Searches That Puzzle: Use Your Head

The best advice I can give you about WAIS is to keep your expectations under control and use your head. WAIS has all the earmarks of a breakthrough search system, a tool that will begin to gather the vast resources of the Internet into a logically driven, readily searchable whole. But the process is a lengthy one, not likely to be accomplished any time soon. More servers have to come on-line, quite a few more, and the client and server software to manage them will be undergoing a gradual evolution in the direction of ease of use and more intuitive interfaces.

Until the bright future arrives when WAIS searches, no matter which client you use, are as simple as querying your computerized phone directory for the number of a friend, here are some thoughts on how you should use WAIS.

Think in reductionist terms. Since your first queries are likely going to be directed at a master directory of servers, try to remember the basic principles that drive your search. If you're looking for astronomical images of Mars taken by the Viking lander, it may make more sense to query this database of databases under terms like **astronomy** and **space** rather than **mars** and **viking**. The broader context of the search is what you're after, because you're asking the server to provide you with information about which databases specialize in what *category* of knowledge.

Be flexible. I can almost guarantee that the great majority of search strategies anyone runs with WAIS will need to be adjusted before completion. Accordingly, you have to maintain a flexible frame of mind when working with WAIS, as you do with any other form of on-line searching. Prepare to modify your search terms when you retrieve drastically different series of hits than you had expected. Plan to feed WAIS a variety of strategies, examining the results until you think your hit list is close enough for you to begin narrowing it down with relevance feedback techniques. If you're lucky, you may get to this point relatively early in the search process. If you're unlucky, you won't get to it at all, because the information you're after isn't yet available through a server.

Avoid Unrealistic Expectations. Hype tends to be the name of the game, in the computer business more than in most industries. And while the future of WAIS seems unlimited, the present forces us to deal with a gradually growing infrastructure which can't yet meet a wide variety of our research needs. Sometimes you'll be able to home in on what you need with laser-like precision, but many other searches will bring you more ambiguous results, similar to what we found while searching for information on the Latin American economies. We found some good sources which could help us build up background data, but we didn't find any databases specifically targeting our search terms.

All that will change as more and more WAIS servers come on-line, and we'll soon be seeing a growing presence from commercial providers as well. In fact, the real excitement in coming years is going to come from watching the WAIS server list grow larger and larger. For that reason, keep using WAIS. The more skilled you become around its quirks, the more likely you'll be able to draw full power out of it. And as more servers come on-line, the more effective your searching will become.

Learn as you go. Keyword hunting is something of an art; after a while, you get the feel for it, but struggling through those early searches can be a frustrating experience. One way to learn is to look at a document or two containing material you find appropriate to your search. Page through it with an eye toward finding words that appear frequently. These may well be the best keywords to run on your next search. Remember, searching is highly targeted. What you're after may be obvious to you, but not to a computer at the other end of the line. Browsing through a few documents can often supply terms you simply hadn't thought of in your planning.

Stay relevant. Relevance feedback is the most exciting and useful area of WAIS development. As the system now stands, WAIS pulls keywords from your queries and uses them to run its search routines. The problem, as we've seen, can be retrieving small numbers of hits, or at the opposite end, large lists of seemingly irrelevant information. What's needed are refinements in the model used for making the initial query, along with effective means of limiting and specifying categories of information. We'd like, for example, to be able to tell WAIS "show me every document with a date later than July 1, 1993 that contained the words *nuclear* and *reactor* but did not contain the word *weapon*."

WAIS and Its Limitations

If WAIS strikes you as less than perfect, you're right. While you can search under multiple terms, you can't yet limit your search by date, and standard Boolean search procedures aren't available either. But it's clear the trend of WAIS development is in the direction of greater power. WAIS is but a glimpse of the kind of search tools we're moving to on the Internet; its swift acceptance demonstrates how widespread is the need for such tools, and how successfully WAIS has stepped in to meet the need.

Keeping Up with WAIS

This is exciting stuff, on the very edge of development in the Internet community. If you'd like to keep up with what's happening, there are mailing lists which can do the trick.

• •

What You Need: A Way to Keep up with WAIS

How to Do It: Aside from the newsgroup **alt.wais**, already mentioned, you may well find the **wais-discussion** list a lively place to maintain a subscription. Send requests to join to **wais-discussion-request@think.com**. Archives for this group are maintained at the same site through **quake.think.com**, in the directory /pub/wais/wais-discussion/. Another newsgroup of interest is **comp.infosystems.wais**; all discussions on the **wais-discussion** group go to **comp.infosystems.wais** as well.

• •

Brewster Kahle speaks of a future where WAIS has created a new kind of publishing. "WAIS is an infrastructure for helping people not only use remote sources, but helping people make information available," Kahle said. "Everybody has something to say; everybody has a newsletter, a piece of expertise, a favorite recipe. They might be an expert on car types or IBM clones. If we can make a system that helps people share that expertise, we as a societal organism become richer."[3] Kahle's new company, WAIS Inc., should be in the forefront of such developments.

WORLD WIDE WEB: THE PLEASURES OF HYPERTEXT

It wasn't that long ago that hypertext took the computer world by storm, prompted particularly by Apple Computer's introduction of its Hypercard program, a hypertext implementation that brought the new paradigm to the attention of anyone with a Mac, and caused many DOS users to look on with envy. The promise of hypertext seemed bright. Computers can link information in ways that ordinary, sequential reading cannot manage. Why not set up links between key concepts in a text? If you need more information about a certain item, you can click on it to call background material up on the screen.

The notion is closely tied to the name of Ted Nelson, who has for years been the guiding force behind a system called Xanadu, which focuses on creating hypertext by forging such links. Of course, hypertext doesn't have to be limited to text. An encyclopedia might include links to stored audio or video; click on the right place in the entry on Richard Nixon and you might hear his resignation speech, or see him boarding the helicopter for his final presidential ride. Multimedia CD-ROM implementations of this technology provide such audio and video links today, and we're sure to see more as so-called *hypermedia* matures.

World Wide Web, or WWW, is a hypertext project which brings the same sort of information accessibility to the on-line world. As with the evolving WAIS techniques, there are several client programs available to handle WWW connectivity, including a line-oriented version we'll look at here. Developed largely at CERN, the European Laboratory for Particle Physics, WWW is powerful and, like other hypertext media, it's also fun to work with. Not only that—it's audacious. Imagine the metaphor; just as you can link concepts in a hypertext document, you can travel through the Internet's cyberspace using WWW's links. We'll use CERN as our base to experience this concept.

Delving into the Web

CERN's on-line address for World Wide Web Access is **info.cern.ch**, which we'll access by Telnet. Figure 13.17 shows what you'll see when you first sign on.

There's a principle at work here; the easier a resource tool becomes to use, the more powerful it is for the broadest category of users. In the case of World Wide Web, the interface is simplicity itself. You'll note the numbers in brackets following each category. To access information based on those categories, simply enter the number in question, followed by the **RETURN** key. We'd like to know something about the kind of source materials available to us on WWW, for example, so let's try number 2. The next screen gives us a new range of options. Figure 13.18 shows the full listing, which takes up two screens.

That's quite a list, isn't it? It tells us that these categories of resources, ranging from anonymous FTP to WHOIS, from USENET newsgroups to **gopher** and Telnet, are all available and reachable using WWW linkages. And as you can see, each of them contains its own numbers in brackets.

Enter one of these numbers and you're brought through the hypertext tunnel for more information. An important conceptual reminder, one echoed on various CERN screens: there is no "top" to the World Wide Web. If you plan to move

Figure 13.17
The introductory
screen to World Wide
Web.

```
Trying 128.141.201.74 ...
Connected to nxoc01.cern.ch.
Escape character is '^]'.


CERN Information Service
(ttypc on nxoc01)


                                                     Overview of the Web
                            GENERAL OVERVIEW

    There is no "top" to the World-Wide Web. You can look at it from many
    points of view. If you have no other bias, here are some places to start:

    by Subject[1]        A classification by subject of interest. Incomplete
                         but easiest to use.

    by Type[2]           Looking by type of service (access protocol, etc) may
                         allow to find things if you know what you are looking
                         for.

    About WWW[3]         About the World-Wide Web global information sharing
                         project

 Starting somewhere else

    To use a different default page, perhaps one representing your field of
    interest, see  "customizing your home page"[4].

 What happened to CERN?

 1-6, Up, <RETURN> for more, Quit, or Help:
```

Figure 13.18
Looking at World Wide
Web's data sources.

```
DATA SOURCES CLASSIFIED BY TYPE OF SERVICE

  Separate categorizations exist by subject[1] and by organization[2] .

 World-Wide Web[3]     List of W3 servers . See also: about the WWW
                       initiative[4] .

 WAIS[5]               Find WAIS index servers using the directory of
                       servers[6] , or lists by name[7] or domain[8] .

 Network News[9]       Available directly in all www browsers.

 Gopher                Campus-wide information systems, etc. See list of
                       sites[10] , about Gopher[11] .

 Telnet access         See hypertext  Catalogues by Peter Scott[12], list by
                       Scott Yanoff[13] . Also, Art St George's index[14]
                       (yet to be hyperized) etc.

 VAX/VMS HELP[15]      Available using the help gateway[16] to WWW.

 Anonymous FTP         See the ARCHIE[17] -- An index of almost everything
                       available by anonymous FTP. For example of an FTP
                       site, see the uu.net[18] server.

 TechInfo[19]          A CWIS system from MIT. Gateway access thanks to
                       Linda Murphy/Upenn. See also more about techninfo[20]
                       .

 X.500[21]             Directory system originally for eletronic mail
                       addresses. (Slightly uneven view though gateway).

 WHOIS[22]             A simple internet phonebook system.

 Other protocols       Other forms of online data[23] .
 _____

                                                      Tim BL[24]


1-24, Back, Up, Quit, or Help:
```

through it to capture information, you'll find the search is thoroughly interactive. There are as many routes into information as there are search strategies to mine it.

Through the Gateway

Let's move through one of these resource gateways to find out what WWW is doing. Since we've just been discussing WAIS, let's try to pop through at that

Figure 13.19
The introductory WAIS
screen by way of World
Wide Web.

```
Overview -- /WAIS (23/23)
                                W.A.I.S

  The Wide Area Information System project is headed by Brewster Kahle[1] ,
      of Thinking Machines.

   WAIS information is part of the WorldWideWeb by virtue of a gateway[2]

   Databases              Hypertext list sof databases organized by name[3] or
                          by internet domain[4]  or search the master index[5] .

   Technical              Newsgroup[6] .   Archive of talk[7] , archive of
                          discussion[8] digest.

   Documentation          index[9]

   Source                 Release[10] .

   See also: other hypertext related products[11] .

                                                              Tim BL[12]


   1-12, Back, Up, Quit, or Help:
```

juncture. The number in brackets listed in the preceding figure is 5. Figure 13.19 shows what we see when we enter 5.

Again, a menu appears presenting hypertext links into new sources of information. Ask WWW, for example, for more information on the WAIS databases, and you're given the option to present a list of databases by name or Internet domain. Alternatively, it's possible to search the WAIS material to find the proper database to use. What you'll see when you do that is not terribly different from the WAIS screens we've already examined, with this crucial distinction—you're now working with the WWW interface, meaning you can use its commands to find information.

Which commands? WWW really is simple. A list of the relevant commands follows.

Back Moves back to the last document.

BOttom Takes you to the last page of the document.

Help Displays the help page.

HOme Takes you back to the starting document.

List Shows a list of references from the document.

Manual Takes you to the on-line manual for the program.

Next Moves to the next link from the last document.

number Takes you to the referenced document.

Quit Leaves World Wide Web.

Recall Lists the documents you've already looked at.

Recall *number*   Takes you back to a specific document you've previously looked at.

RETURN   Moves one page down.

Top   Returns to the first page of the document.

Up   Moves up one page within the document.

Figure 13.20
World Wide Web
information by subject.

```
INFORMATION BY SUBJECT

  See also arrangements by organization[1] or by  service type[2] . Mail
  www-request@info.cern.ch if you know of online information not in these
  lists....

  Aeronautics            Mailing list archive index[3] .

  Astronomy and Astrophysics
                         Abstract Indexes[4] (down)

  Bio Sciences[5]        separate list .

  Computing[6]           Seperate list.

  Geography              CIA World Fact Book[7] , India: Miscellaneous
                         information[8] , Thai-Yunnan: Davis collection[9] ,

  Law                    US Copyright law[10] .

  Libraries[11]          Lists of online catalogues etc.

  Literature             Project Gutenberg[12] : two classic books a month.
                         See their explanations[13] , the index and
                         newsletter[14] , books published in 1991[15] ,
                         1992[16] , and reserved for the USA[17] .

  Humanities             BMCR classical reviews[18] , Poetry[19] , Scifi
                         reviews[20] . See also electronic journals[21] .

  Mathematics            CIRM library[22] (french)

  Meteorology            US weather[23] , state by state. Also WAIS
                         weather[24] (around MIT :-).

  Music                  MIDI interfacing[25] , Song lyrics[26] (apparently
                         disabled for copyright reasons)

  Physics                High Energy Physics[27],Astrophysics abstracts[28] .

  Politics Economics     US politics[29] . Includes campaign 1992.

  Reference              Roget's Thesaurus[30] . Experimental English

  Religion               The Bible[32] (King James version) , The Book of
                         Mormon[33] , The Holy Qur'an[34]

  Social Sciences        Coombs papers archive[35] .
```

A Sample WWW Search

Let's run through a sample search and see what we can find. You'll recall we had meager results with our earlier search for information about the Latin American economies and the stock market. Let's use the Web's resources to flesh out our knowledge. We can start by asking for a list of WWW sources by subject, which is one of the three offerings on the first menu we're presented, as in Figure 13.20.

Here we find a wide variety of subject matter. *Geography* looks useful; it contains the *CIA World Factbook*, followed by the number 7. Pressing a 7 followed by a **RETURN**, we get a surprise—the Web has taken us to a WAIS server containing this information, as shown in Figure 13.21.

But note: we have a different interface to work with yet again. Just as we had to master **gopher** commands to work with WAIS through that client, we need to use the WWW commands to make this search work.

Fortunately, the Web poses few conceptual difficulties. As can be seen from the bottom of the screen, all that's needed is to enter a search term.

```
FIND ywords>, 1, Back, Up, Quit, or Help: find latin america
```

I've entered **latin america**. In return I'll get a list of hits for Latin America, each of them tagged with a number so I can zip right to them (remember: with **swais**, we would have needed to place the highlight bar over the hit, then pressed the **SPACE BAR** to see it; with **gopher**, we would have used the **RETURN** key to see the hit). I'm particularly interested in Bolivia, which is developing its first stock market. How does its economy stack up today?

By paging through the list of hits for Latin America (use the **RETURN** key for each new page), I can find Bolivia and press the number given (16). At that point, I get multiple screens full of information about the country, and can use

Figure 13.21
A World Wide Web search screen for the *CIA World Factbook*.

```
                                                                    CIA index
                                        CIA

    Specify search words.
    [End]












    FIND <keywords>, Back, Up, Quit, or Help:
```

Figure 13.22
Material about the
Bolivian economy,
generated by World
Wide Web.

```
Economy
Overview: The Bolivian economy steadily deteriorated between
1980 and 1985 as La Paz financed growing budget deficits by expanding
the money supply and inflation spiraled--peaking at 11,700%. An austere
orthodox economic program adopted by newly elected President Paz
Estenssoro in 1985, however, succeeded in reducing inflation to between
10% and 20% annually since 1987, eventually restarting economic growth.
President Paz Zamora has retained the economic policies of the previous
government, keeping inflation down and continuing the moderate growth
begun under his predecessor. Nevertheless, Bolivia continues to be one of
the poorest countries in Latin America, and it remains vulnerable to
price fluctuations for its limited exports--agricultural products,
minerals, and natural gas. Moreover, for many farmers, who constitute
half of the country's work force, the main cash crop is coca, which is
sold for cocaine processing.


Back, Up, <RETURN> for more, Quit, or Help:
```

the **RETURN** key to page through this information. Figure 13.22 shows a sample screen about the Bolivian economy.

Inflation was certainly a problem in the mid-1980s, reaching 11,700 percent in 1985! However, a government austerity program seems to have whipped these price increases, and economic growth accelerated under President Paz Zamora. Numerous further screens tell the story in detail.

The *CIA World Factbook*, of course, is only one of the sources we can use. Let's move back up to the sources screen and consider another topic and another source. We can use the **recall** command to do this; it will generate a list of the documents we have looked at so far.

```
R  1)    in Overview of the Web
R  2)    in Subject listing
R  3)    CIA index
R  4)    in latin america (in CIA)
R  5)    Document
```

With this list on-screen, we can give a **recall *n*** command, where *n* is the number of the screen we wish to return to. Thus **recall 2** takes us back to the subject listing.

The Web and the Boat

The Web is a fascinating place to prowl; you never know what you're going to find. And depending on the server it accesses, the information you locate can be quite relevant to day-to-day concerns. Take politics. A mini-firestorm blew up when (then) President-elect Clinton announced he had changed his mind about the Haitian boat people. Should they be given asylum in the United States or not? Had he truly contradicted a campaign pledge when he said he was against letting Haitian refugees into this country, for fear that thousands would come?

Looking around the subject menu, we find the Web's area called *Politics Economics*. The information there is wide-reaching, and includes, as shown in Figure 13.23, indices of speeches made by the two major candidates in the 1992

Figure 13.23
World Wide Web
materials on politics
and economics.

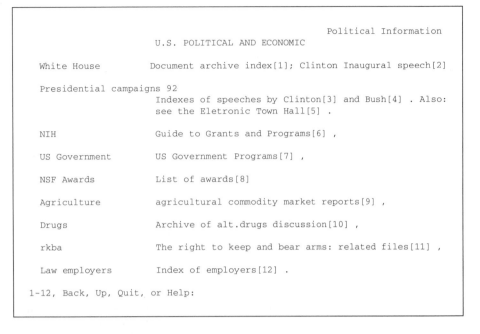

```
                                                  Political Information
                        U.S. POLITICAL AND ECONOMIC

    White House          Document archive index[1]; Clinton Inaugural speech[2]

    Presidential campaigns 92
                         Indexes of speeches by Clinton[3] and Bush[4] . Also:
                         see the Eletronic Town Hall[5] .

    NIH                  Guide to Grants and Programs[6] ,

    US Government        US Government Programs[7] ,

    NSF Awards           List of awards[8]

    Agriculture          agricultural commodity market reports[9] ,

    Drugs                Archive of alt.drugs discussion[10] ,

    rkba                 The right to keep and bear arms: related files[11] ,

    Law employers        Index of employers[12] .

    1-12, Back, Up, Quit, or Help:
```

elections. Let's tap into the database to find out what Clinton had to say about Haiti during the campaign itself.

Entering a **3** to move to the Clinton index, we're once again sent to a WAIS server. We can search it using standard WWW methods. Let's search under **haiti**. Doing this generates the screen shown in Figure 13.24.

And by following through and choosing the most relevant document, the one labeled 1000, we find the statement shown in Figure 13.25.

Figure 13.24
Materials listed under
the search term **haiti**
by World Wide Web.

```
                              HAITI

    Index clinton-speechess contains the following 9 items relevant to 'haiti'.
    The first figure for each entry is its relative score, the second the number
    of lines in the item.

    1000     32          HAITI: Statement - 5/27/92[1]
     333    217          IMMIGRATION: Position Paper[2]
     278    507          NATIONAL SECURITY: Position Paper[3]
     278    601          VARIOUS TOPICS: Speech - Atlanta, GA - 9/9/92[4]
     278    307          VARIOUS TOPICS: Speech - Boston, MA - 9/25/92[5]
     278    148          POVERTY: Position Paper - 10/8/92[6]
     278    518          ACCEPTANCE SPEECH: William Clinton[7]
     278    566          RACE RELATIONS: Speech - Washington D C - 6/13/92[8]
     278    466          FOREIGN AFFAIRS: Speech - Los Angeles, CA - 8/13/92[9]

        [End]



    FIND <keywords>, 1-9, Back, Up, Quit, or Help:
```

Figure 13.25
A retrieved campaign statement by candidate Clinton, found through World Wide Web.

```
Statement by Governor Bill Clinton on Haitian Refugees

I am appalled by the decision of the Bush administration to pick up fleeing
Haitians on the high  seas and forcibly return them to Haiti before consid-
ering their claim to political asylum.  It was bad enough when there were
failures to offer them due process in making such a claim.  Now  they are
offered no process at all before being returned.

This policy must not stand.  It is a blow to the principle of first asylum
and to America's moral  authority in defending the rights of refugees
around the world.  This most recent policy shift is  another sad example of
the Administration's callous response to a terrible human tragedy.
```

An interesting thought: will WWW and tools of its ilk make politicians more careful about what they promise?

The Web Reconsidered

WWW sports a slick interface, but there's a problem. The Web's resources are all conventional data gathering engines (as much as anything in this fast-moving field can be called "conventional"). What if we could take the statement above and pop up hypertext links inside it? What if most of the documents we were able to retrieve were *themselves* hypertextual in nature? Hypertext editors are in their infancy, as is the Web itself, so we can't expect their full power to be on display just yet. But there's no question this technology has quite a role to play in future developments.

The Web Drawn Back upon Itself

By now, experience has taught us that the Internet is a tremendous self-referential engine; nothing makes that more obvious than putting World Wide Web to work using its hypertext linkages to elicit still further data. So let's find out which documents would be useful for our file libraries by searching the Web for references to itself. Again, we'll go into the Web and have a look around. The first thing you'll notice is that the opening screen offers an option for immediate assistance. Item number 3:

```
About WWW[3]              About the World-Wide Web global information sharing
                             project
```

Prowl around in this wormhole for a few minutes and you'll find plenty of useful information, most particularly a bibliography on the Web as found in both technical and popular literature. Let's retrieve it now.

....

 What You Need: A Bibliography of WWW Related Materials

The Document: **World-Wide Web Bibliography**

How to Get It: Via WWW at Telnet **info.cern.ch**. Choose option 3 and look for

```
Bibliography[21]        Paper documentation on  W3 and references.
```

Choose 21 to view this document, which you can capture on-screen with your software.

. . . .

Of interest here is the scarcity of entries in this bibliography; clearly, the Web has plenty of room to grow. There's also a useful on-line history of Web activity for you to follow. A number of the documents found in the bibliography can be retrieved through anonymous FTP to **info.cern.ch**. Most are in PostScript format, however.

Internet Services and Their Limitations, Through the Web

Examine the services available through the Web and you'll find a very familiar list. The screen shown in Figure 13.26, for example, is what you see if you opt for FTP.

You've also got access to WHOIS, the directory services offered by X.500, USENET news, Campus Wide Information Servers, and more. Not all of these options are reachable through a dial-up connection. Try to use **archie**, for example, and you'll get a statement like the following:

```
Sorry, but the service you have selected is one
to which you have to log in. If you were running www
on your own computer, you would be automatically connected.
For security reasons, this is not allowed when
you log in to this information service remotely.
```

You will, however, learn the address of the site so you can Telnet there yourself, once you've left WWW.

Directories at anonymous FTP sites can likewise be searched, but their files can only be read on-line; they can't be retrieved. This is where a full network connection would come in handy. You could set up a client WWW program on your computer, at which time the software would proceed to make the FTP or Telnet connection of your choice. With a public browser like the one at CERN, this can't be done.

Nonetheless, reading files on-line can be helpful. What you'll see if you access FTP information is the following kind of screen, which I chose from a menu of FTP sites:

```
                                               FTP Directory of //think.com/
                                /

HPFF[1]          README[2]       Sse[3]        bin[4]          cm[5]
dev[6]           etc[7]          gnus[8]       incoming[9]     jpeg[10]
lost+found[11]   mail[12]        pub[13]       public[14]      random[15]
space-comp-std[16]               think[17]     tmp[18]         users[19]
usr[20]          uucp[21]        var[22]       wais[23]

       [End]
```

Each directory can be called up. I can select the */pub* directory by entering **13**. The following is what I get:

Figure 13.26
The introductory
screen into FTP
resources offered by
World Wide Web.

```
A TO E: EXHAUSTIVE LIST OF FTP SITES


a.cs.uiuc.edu[1]                            128.174.252.1    US -5
90/08/22
Admin: Univ. of Illinois - Urbana-Champaign
Files: TeX; dvi2ps; gif; texx2.7; amiga; GNUmake; GNU


a.psc.edu[2]                                128.182.66.105   US -5
90/12/31
Admin: Pittsburgh Supercomputing Center
Files: GPLOT; GTEX


aarnet.edu.au[3]                            139.130.204.4    AU +10
92/12/20
Admin: Australian Academic & Research Network
Files: Australian AARNET network stats


acacia.maths.uwa.oz.au[4]                   130.95.16.2      AU +8
92/12/20
Admin: Univ. of Western Australia


acfcluster.nyu.edu[5]                       128.122.128.11   US -5
91/01/02
Admin: New York Univ.
Server: 128.122.128.17, 128.122.128.16
Files: VMS UUCP; news; DECUS library catalog; vsmnet.sources; info-vax code
1-228, Back, Up, <RETURN> for more, Quit, or Help: Back
```

```
                                           FTP Directory of //think.com/pub
                              /PUB

Parent Directory[1]            1000Mile.hqx[2] HPFF[3]
MicroEmacs.sit.hqx[4]          animal-rights[5]               aviation[6]
caia-93[7]      cellular-automata[8]           cmost[9]       cvs[10]
deboer-adoption-story[11]      disinfectant[12]               gurps[13]
j[14]           kurt[15]       libernet[16]    moose[17]      muzic.nsf[18]
pc532[19]       pmdc.tar.Z[20] pps.shar[21]    radio[22]      sgi[23]
terryd[24]      top-2.5.tar.Z[25]              wais[26]       weather[27]
xjug.tar.Z[28]  xpbiff[29]

    [End]
```

As you can see, each directory and file has its own number. I can move, for
example, into the */wais* subdirectory by choosing 26. There, I can call up the file
I need:

```
                                           FTP Directory of //think.com/wais
                              /WAIS

Parent Directory[1]            README[2]       WAIS-Corporate-Paper.sit.hqx[3]
WAIStation-Canned-Demo.sit.hqx[4]              WAIStation-NeXT-1.9.1.README[5]
WAIStation-NeXT-1.9.1.tar.Z[6] WAIStation-NeXT-1.9.6.README[7]
WAIStation-NeXT-1.9.6.tar.Z[8] WAIStation-README[9]
WAIStation-User-Guide.sit.hqx[10]             Z3950[11]
bibliography.txt[12]           doc[13]         ir-book-sources[14]
motif-a1.tar.Z[15]             old[16]         wais-8-b5.1-swais-patches[17]
```

```
wais-8-b5.1.tar.Z[18]          wais-corporate-paper.text[19]
wais-for-mac-1.1.sea.hqx[20]   wais-sources.sea.hqx[21]
wais-sources.tar.Z[22]
```

```
[End]
```

By choosing item 12, for example, I can read the file **bibliography.txt** on-screen. It's an ASCII file, so the process is painless. However, if I asked to see a compressed file, I'll see nothing but strange-looking characters. Be sure to check those file extensions!

CHAPTER THIRTEEN NOTES

1. From an interview at the Clearinghouse for Networked Information Discovery and Retrieval at MCNC, Research Triangle Park, NC, January 19, 1993.
2. Telephone interview with Brewster Kahle January 24, 1993.
3. *Ibid.*

CHAPTER
14

An Internet Toolbox

To call the Internet a maze of contradictions is to state the obvious. Even as excitement builds and new participants sign on to the networks, there comes a realization that Internet tools are still in their infancy. Because of its history as a gradually interconnecting network of networks, the Internet can't boast any unified command structure. Improvements come from below, through the efforts of creative talents like Brewster Kahle, Mark McCahill, and the team that developed World Wide Web. They and their numerous counterparts are helping us to find new ways to pull information out of cyberspace.

In this chapter, we'll examine a number of other tools that make it easier to get around this uncharted domain. While they're each capable of being used on their own, tools like **netfind** or WHOIS point in a common direction. Think of the phone book analogy, as do most people who work with these applications; the common nickname for this category, in fact, is *white pages*. They're under development to help us track down people on the network.

Currently, much discussion rages over how such finder mechanisms should function, and what the best format and strategy for a network-wide directory system should be. It's likely that trial and error will resolve these issues at some point in the not-so-distant future. But for now, we must work with what we have, and many of these tools are powerful indeed. You'll want to get to know each.

You'll also discover that network tools can perform multiple functions. **finger**, for example, is a handy way to track down people whose name you already know at a given site; you can even check to see if they're on-line at the moment. But **finger** can also be used to tap servers for specialized information. Let's begin, then, with a look at **finger** and how it can point to the information you need.

339

FINGER FINDS PEOPLE AND INFORMATION

You can find out who else is logged in to the system you're using by entering **finger** at the system prompt. You'll get a list of active users, like the following (although I've changed the names):

```
Login      Name                        TTY    Idle    When        Where
dwight     Dwight Eisenhower --        p0             Mon 08:20   nb1.concert.net
nocs       Network Operations C        p1     58      Mon 08:27   elvis.concert.ne
gkc        G K Chesterton -- Pe        *p2            Mon 08:53   nb1.concert.net
bogart     Humphrey Bogart -- Y        p3     4       Mon 08:28   nb-clt.concert.n
pablo      Paul A Gilster -- Co        p6             Mon 09:25   nb1.concert.net
walt       Walter Johnson -- Wa        p7     1       Mon 09:19   nb2.concert.net
manny      Emmanuel Kant -- Cr         p8     9       Mon 08:38   boogie.concert.n
jackson    Jack Benny -- cbs ra        p9     4d      Wed 14:07   mayur.mc.duke.ed
```

finger can also reach out into the network if you use it in conjunction with a user name. Here's what I get when I **finger** my address at The World:

```
% finger pag@world.std.com
[world.std.com]
world -- The World -- Public Access UNIX -- Solbourne 5E/900 OS/MP 4.1A.3
 10:22am  up  8:43,  38 users,  load average: 2.16, 2.59, 2.88

pag     . Paul A Gilster         Login Fri 16-Apr-93 8:45AM from rock.concertt
 [4597,4597]  /users/pag;  Group: pag
 Groups: pag

 pag has new mail as of Fri 16-Apr-93 9:47AM
```

What you get from a **finger** search varies depending on how much information is available at the site. **finger** may list the login name, full name, office location and phone number, login time, idle time, time mail was last read, and the contents of the *.plan* and *.project* files from the home directory of current users. But what one site does may not parallel what another puts on-line. In many cases, **finger** has been disabled for security reasons; in others, an on-line directory is yours for the asking. The best way to find out is to try **finger** to see what you get.

In addition to using it to track down information about a specific user, you can also ask for information about all the users at a particular remote site, using the command **finger @***sitename*. **finger @med.unc.edu**, then, produces a list similar to the one from CONCERT-CONNECT, showing who's currently logged in at UNC's Medical School.

What happens if you don't know the login name for the user in question? No problem. You can type in part of the person's name and **finger** will produce a list of possible hits. Entering **finger g** at CONCERT-CONNECT, for example, produces a list of everyone with a **G** as their middle initial. Entering **finger wilson** gives me a list of everyone with the name Wilson who's currently logged on, even if their login names are "trw" and "gwilson." Again, it's necessary to point out that **finger** searches like this may or may not work depending on the site. This makes **finger** an imperfect tool, if a useful one.

But **finger** has other tricks to work with. It can be used to tap into a wide range of information. Try the following command: **finger quake@geophys.washington.edu**. Instead of being sent information about a particular user at the site, you'll get an update on recent earthquake activity, as shown in Figure 14.1.

Figure 14.1
Results of a **finger**
command to
quake@geophys.wash
ington.edu.

```
[geophys.washington.edu]
Login name: quake      In real life: Earthquake Information

Directory: /u0/quake              Shell: /u0/quake/run_quake

Last login Sat Feb  6 08:40 on ttyi2

New mail received Fri Feb  5 18:48:22 1993;

   unread since Sun Sep  6 14:58:12 1992

Plan:

Information about Recent earthquakes are reported here for public use.

Catalogs are available by anonymous ftp in geophys.washington.edu:pub/seis-

DATE-TIME is in Universal Stardard Time which is PST + 8 hours, LAT and

LON are in decimal degrees, DEP is depth in kilometers, N-STA is number

of stations recording event, QUAL is location quality A-good, D-poor, Z-from

automatic system and may be in error.


Recent events reported by the USGS National Earthquake Information Center

  DATE-TIME (UT)   LAT    LON    DEP   MAG        LOCATION AREA

  93/01/26 20:32  23.0N  101.2E   33   5.7    MYANMAR-CHINA BORDER REGION

  93/02/02 16:05  42.5N   86.1E   33   5.7    NORTHERN XINJIANG, CHINA

  93/02/05 07:32  11.3S  166.1E   50   5.7    SANTA CRUZ ISLANDS

  93/02/05 07:15  12.6N  141.8E   33   5.7    SOUTH OF MARIANA ISLANDS

  93/02/07 13:27  37.6N  137.3E   33   6.3    NEAR WEST COAST OF HONSHU, JAPAN


Recent earthquakes in the Northwest located by Univ. of Wash. (Mag  2.0)

DATE-TIME (UT)  LAT(N) LON(W)   DEP  MAG N-STA QUAL

93/01/07 22:06  47.58  121.50  14.4  3.4  48    B FELT 6.9 km  SW of Skykom

93/01/10 23:16  46.46  122.26  16.1  2.0  37    A  9.1 km    S of Morton

93/01/26 17:05  47.36  122.68  23.1  3.0  49    B FELT 2.6 km  S of Bremerton

93/01/29 14:29  45.41  118.93   3.1  2.0  10    C  9.7 km SSW of Pendleton,OR

93/02/03 00:48  48.61  123.00  10.4  2.0  16    B  2.7 km   NE of Victoria,BC
```

There aren't too many **finger** sites available yet that provide this kind of information, but those currently accessible are interesting. You'll find the Top 40 on the pop charts (**finger buckmr@aix.rpi.edu**), NASA's Headline News (**finger nasanews@space.mit.edu**), and tropical storm forecasts (**finger fore-cast@typhoon.atmos.colostate.edu**). These and other **finger** sites are listed in Chapter 15.

NSLOOKUP

Although it's not available at all sites, **nslookup** can provide information on Internet domain name servers. Ever wondered, for example, what the government calls its computers? Let's find out by using **nslookup**. After calling up the program by entering **nslookup** at the UNIX prompt, I'm given the program's own prompt, a simple >. I'll tell **nslookup** I want to examine the domain **house.gov** by using the server there.

```
> server house.gov
Default Server:  house.gov
Address:  137.18.128.6
```

I can use the **ls** command to get further information. By entering **ls house.gov**, I get a list of the host computers used there. It's a huge list; here's just a bit of it:

```
quorum_router                137.18.24.31
carbon                       137.18.128.7
CS/1IPSN                     137.18.24.16
GejdensonFP                  137.18.90.1
GejdensonFP                  137.18.240.48
mac_pacic                    137.18.240.74
RoseSvr                      137.18.240.89
ts2652-1                     137.18.24.19
ts2652-2                     137.18.24.22
ts2652-3                     137.18.24.23
ts2652-4                     137.18.24.24
WIND                         137.18.240.218
```

nslookup is no problem to use. The following describes the basic commands.

root   Sets the default server to the root. The root server has the top-level domain information.

server *name*   Sets the default server.

ls *name*   Lists the names of host computers that are servers for that domain. You can set this up as a file by using the **command ls** *name* > *filename*. In the previous example, using this command would have prevented most of the output from running off the screen. Instead, we would have a file which could then be read with the next command.

view *file*   Sorts the output from the **ls** command and lets us view it with the **more** program.

finger *name*   Fingers the host you specify.

The latter command, of course, is how **nslookup** ties into our search for users. Having identified the hosts at a particular domain, you can then find out who is using a host, or ask whether a specific user is doing so, using the **finger** commands.

NETFIND

Another useful network tool is **netfind**, which offers searching for individuals by name and domain. To try **netfind,** Telnet to **bruno.cs.colorado.edu**. Log on as **netfind** with no password. There are also a number of alternative servers available; using the one closest to you makes sense and conserves network resources. The list of alternative servers follows.

archie.au   (AARNet, Melbourne, Australia)

bruno.cs.colorado.edu   (University of Colorado, Boulder)

dino.conicit.ve   (NCT & Scien. Research, Venezuela)

lincoln.technet.sg   (Technet Unit, Singapore)

malloco.ing.puc.cl   (Catholic University of Chile, Santiago)

monolith.cc.ic.ac.uk   (Imperial College, London, England)

mudhoney.micro.umn.edu   (University of Minnesota, Minneapolis)

netfind.oc.com   (OpenConnect Systems, Dallas, Texas)

redmont.cis.uab.edu   (University of Alabama at Birmingham)

nic.uakom.sk   (Slovak Academy of Sciences, Republic of Slovakia)

Figure 14.2 shows what I see when I log on at **redmont.cis.uab.edu**, at the University of Alabama at Birmingham.

Figure 14.2
Logging in to a **netfind** server.

```
========================================================
Welcome to the UAB Netfind server.
========================================================

Alternate Netfind servers:
      archie.au (AARNet, Melbourne, Australia)
      bruno.cs.colorado.edu (University of Colorado, Boulder)
      malloco.ing.puc.cl (Catholic University of Chile, Santiago)
      mudhoney.micro.umn.edu (University of Minnesota, Minneapolis)
      netfind.oc.com (OpenConnect System, Dallas, Texas)
      sun.uakom.cs (Slovak Academy of Sciences, Czech and Slovak Fed. Repub.)


I think that your terminal can display 24 lines.  If this is wrong,
please enter the "Options" menu and set the correct number of lines.

Top level choices:
      1. Help
      2. Search
      3. Seed database lookup
      4. Options
      5. Quit (exit server)
```

Using **netfind** is simple; you enter keywords about the person in question. I'm looking, for example, for a friend of mine who teaches at a university in New Jersey. I could search under terms like these: **benfield** (his last name) **montclair new jersey**. Running this search, I see what is shown in Figure 14.3.

The process goes on for several screens. **netfind** is checking domains, and then hosts. In the domain part of the search, **netfind** is looking for mail forwarding information, while in the host part, it's performing **finger** searches into the hosts. The information produced by the search includes any problems **netfind** ran into running its search, information about the most promising e-mail address for the person in question and a statement of when and where the person most recently logged on. Ultimately, we find what we're looking for:

```
SUMMARY:
- The most promising email address for "benfield"
  based on the above search is
  benfield@nemo.montclair.edu.
```

Let's go back to the search strategy for a moment, now that we've found our man. **netfind** is structured so that the first thing you enter should be a name. It can be a first or last name; it can be a login name, for that matter, but you can only specify one name at a time. The name is then followed by a set of keywords describing where the person works. Here you have some latitude. You can enter the name of the institution, as we did above when we searched for **montclair**. You can enter a city name, a state, a country. What you can't do, however, is enter the host part of a domain name. If you were searching for me and knew I worked on a machine named **rock**, that information wouldn't help you find me, but the rest of the information would.

Note, too, that **netfind** is keyword-driven. We could find Mr. Benfield if we searched under **benfield montclair edu**, but we can't search domains per se; the search can't read, in other words, **benfield montclair.edu**. Notice another

Figure 14.3
Running a **netfind** search.

```
Enter person and keys (blank to exit) -- benfield montclair new jersey
( 0) check_name: checking domain ami.com.  Level = 0
( 1) check_name: checking domain edg.com.  Level = 0
( 2) check_name: checking domain montclair.edu.  Level = 0
( 2) get_domain_addr: Got nameserver adam.montclair.edu
( 3) check_name: checking nameserver adam.montclair.edu.  Level = 2
The domain 'ami.com' does not run its own name servers,
        and there is no aliased domain IP address for this domain.
        - Skipping domain search phase for this domain.
The domain 'edg.com' does not run its own name servers,
        and there is no aliased domain IP address for this domain.
        - Skipping domain search phase for this domain.
( 3) do_connect: Finger service not available on host adam.montclair.edu
        - Cannot do user lookup.
------
Search of domains completed.  Proceeding to search of hosts.
------
( 3) check_name: checking host mozart.montclair.edu.  Level = 0
( 4) check_name: checking host apollo.montclair.edu.  Level = 0
( 6) check_name: checking host icarus.montclair.edu.  Level = 0
```

significant aspect of **netfind**. If you don't already have a pretty good idea where to find a person, you won't find him or her with **netfind**. Think of it as a tool that helps you zero in on a target you've already got in your sights, rather than one that lets you shoot wildly, hoping to hit something along the way. The other **netfind** limitation: the fact that some sites disable **finger**, so **netfind** can't track down anything to work with.

Nonetheless, the system does have impressive coverage. As of late 1992, **netfind** could locate users in over nine-thousand domains, including people in such exotic locales as Iceland, Estonia, Tunisia, and Antarctica. That translates, according to **netfind**'s originator, Michael F. Schwartz, to about 5.5 million people. Schwartz's logs show that users in 3813 sites in 41 countries have either tried the University of Colorado **netfind** server or have retrieved the software. Schwartz adds, "I see an average of 1380 logins per day to use the University of Colorado **netfind** server (each login could do several searches), and there are 8 alternate **netfind** servers in 6 countries (see the login banner at the University of Colorado server for a list of them), plus whoever sets up their own local clients."[1]

USING WHOIS

Originally set up as a database of registered information running at a single ARPANET Network Information Center, WHOIS is now spread over the Internet; there are many sites making this information available through servers. Each record contains a unique identifier, a name, and other fields depending on the type of information it contains. What's in a WHOIS database? Anything from domains, hosts, and networks, to the people on them.

The original WHOIS database was maintained at the Defense Data Network Network Information Center by Government Systems, Inc., of Chantilly, VA. With the arrival of the new INTERNIC services in 1993, however, this site had become out of date for civilian registrations.

The new host for WHOIS searches is **rs.internic.net**. We can access the site through Telnet, as in Figure 14.4.

As you can see, we have a range of options. Choosing **WHOIS**, we get the following screen:

```
NIC, SunOS Release 4.1.1 (NIC) #1:
Cmdinter Ver 1.2 Mon Feb  8 14:50:43 1993 EST
@ whois
= Connecting to id Database . . . . . .
Connected to id Database
NIC WHOIS Version: 2.10 Mon, 8 Feb 93 14:50:51

  Enter a handle, name, mailbox, or other field, optionally preceded
  by a keyword, like "host diis". Type "?" for short, 2-page
  details, "HELP" for full documentation, or hit RETURN to exit.
---> Do ^E to show search progress, ^G to abort a search or output <---
Whois: cerf, vinton
```

Now we can ask for a particular person. I've queried this database about Vinton Cerf, the president of the Internet Society. Quickly I have a response:

Figure 14.4
Logging on for a
WHOIS search at the
INTERNIC.

```
%: telnet rs.internic.net
Trying 198.41.0.5 ...
Connected to rs.internic.net.
Escape character is '^]'.


SunOS UNIX (rs) (ttyq5)

Termial type = [vt100]
Current sysload is 1.98
*******************************************************************************
* -- InterNIC Registration Services Center  --
*
* For gopher, type:                   GOPHER
_
* For wais, type:                     WAIS search string
_
* For the *original* whois type:      WHOIS [search string]
_
* For the X.500 whois DUA, type:      X500WHOIS
_
* For registration status:           STATUS   number
_
*
* For user assistance call (800) 444-4345 | (619-455-4600 or (703) 742-4777
* Please report system problems to ACTION@rs.internic.net
*******************************************************************************
Please be advised that the InterNIC Registration host contains INTERNET
Domains, IP Network Numbers, ASNs, and Points of Contacts ONLY. Please
refer to rfc1400.txt for details (available via anonymous ftp at
either.nic.ddn.mil [/rfc/rfc1400.txt]  or ftp.rs.internic.net
[/policy/rfc1400.txt]).
Cmdinter Ver 1.3 Fri Apr 16 11:04:42 1993 EST
[vt100] InterNIC
```

```
Cerf, Vinton G. (VGC)            CERF@NRI.RESTON.VA.US
   Corporation for National Research Initiatives
   1895 Preston White Drive, Suite 100
   Reston, VA 22091
   (703) 620-8990 (FAX) :

   Record last updated on 05-Mar-93.
```

If you're not sure of a person's full name, you can enter a last name, and WHOIS will produce a list of possibilities, from which you can choose the person you're after.

It's very possible that your service provider offers a WHOIS client program. If so, the usage is **whois [-h *host*] *name.*** A search for Dr. Cerf through the INTERNIC would thus appear **whois -h rs.internic.net cerf**. With a client program, you have the advantage of being able to easily contact a wide variety of **WHOIS** databases. The **-h** command is what makes this possible.

One caution: using the **whois** command by itself will likely search the database at **nic.ddn.mil**. Due to the recent changes involved in the creation of the new INTERNIC, this database will be up to date for MILNET addresses only. Use **rs.internic.net** as the site name to query the INTERNIC.

It would be useful to acquire a list of **WHOIS** servers.

What You Need: A List of WHOIS Servers

The Document: **The List of Internet WHOIS Servers**

How to Get It: Through anonymous FTP from **sipb.mit.edu**. The directory is *pub/whois*, and the file name is **whois-servers.list**.

Here's a small portion of the list:

```
uc.edu                      University of Cincinnati C=US
thor.ece.uc.edu             University of Cincinnati C=US
directory.ucdavis.edu       University of California at Davis C=US
uchicago.edu                University of Chicago C=US
oac.ucla.edu                University of California at Los Angeles C=US
whois.ucsb.edu              University of California at Santa Barbara C=US
ucsd.edu                    University of California at San Diego C=US
```

The entire list has reached well over one-hundred entries. If you are looking for someone at a particular institution, then, you can check this list to determine whether that school or organization makes a directory available. You can then specify that directory as the one you'll search with the **WHOIS** client. If I wanted to search the University of California at Santa Barbara WHOIS server for someone named Smith, for example, I'd use the command **whois -h who-is.ucsb.edu smith**. There are, as it turns out, quite a few of them.

USING THE NETMAIL DATABASE

The Merit Network NetMail database provides information for a university or other organization's mail site names, covering BITNET, UUCP, and the Internet. Ask it, for example, for a list of mail sites at **unc.edu**, the University of North Carolina at Chapel Hill academic computing center, and it produces this:

```
There are 5 sites found for UNC.EDU


Internet Sites:
  CS.UNC.EDU
  DOPEY.CS.UNC.EDU
  SAMBA.ACS.UNC.EDU
  THORIN.CS.UNC.EDU
  UNCLEV.UNCH.UNC.EDU
```

To use the Merit database, **telnet hermes.merit.edu**. At the **Which Host?** prompt, type **netmailsites**. You'll be given the opportunity to search three times on any single connection.

You can use this database in several ways. If you already know the e-mail address, you can enter the address (using the part after the **@**) to see if it is a known site name. Alternatively, you can enter a location. The database searches for exact words, but you can add a **?** to the end of an entry to make it look for any words matching a wider description. An entry like **richmond**, for example, is very specific. The entry **rich?** will search for any word beginning with **rich** but having any other possible endings. Thus you might find Richmond, Richland, Richebourg, and so on.

Entering **north carolina** as my search term, I receive a list of 39 sites, from the North Carolina State University Department of Nuclear Engineering to a UUCP connection at the Sun Microsystems North Carolina sales office. Entering **univ? missouri** as my search terms, I receive a list of 24 sites in the University of Missouri system, as below:

```
UMRVMB                     University of Missouri Rolla Campus
UMRVMC                     University of Missouri Rolla Campus
UMRVMD                     University of Missouri Rolla Campus
UMSLVAXA                   University of Missouri St Louis Campus
UMSLVMA                    University of Missouri St Louis Campus
UMSLVMB                    University of Missouri St Louis Campus
UMVMA                      University of Missouri Central Facility
```

This information is shown in the default terse mode, giving the site name and name of the institution. A **set verbose** command provides full information on each site. Having set that, for example, I see a fuller listing for one of the computers at the University of Missouri's St. Louis campus:

```
UMSLVMB
     Alternate Name(s):
     CPU: IBM 4381
     OS: VM/SP
     University of Missouri St Louis Campus
        Office of Computing and Telecommunications;St. Louis, MO
        63121-4499 US
```

Figure 14.5
Tracking down phone books with **gopher**.

FINDING PEOPLE WITH CSOs

gopher can help us with another form of directory service. Looking around the **gopher** menus, you've probably run into items labeled **<CSO>**. These are name servers; i.e., they can be used to find people by querying a database. **gopher's** ability to search these data repositories can help us locate people quickly, and we can uncover quite a few directories if we prowl around.

Using the **gopher** at CONCERT-CONNECT, I can move to the *Internet Information Servers/* screen, where I'll choose item 6, *Phone Books/*. In the submenu, item 3 catches my eye. It's labeled *Phone books at other institutions/*. Choosing it, I'll see the screen shown in Figure 14.5.

Let's choose item 8, *North America/* and see what we get. Figure 14.6 shows a partial list (the entire list is twelve screens long).

Some of these entries are revealed as indices by the **<?>** following their names. We'll focus on the **<CSO>** entries. The son of a friend of mine attends Cornell University in Ithaca, New York. Let's see if we can find him. We'll choose item 28 and press **RETURN**. The interesting screen shown in Figure 14.7 appears.

This is a form we can fill in to find the person we need. I'll enter my friend's son's name thus: **christopher allen**, followed by a **RETURN**. I enter the name this way because I know he goes by "Chris," but I'm not sure whether that or his full name would be listed in the index. If he's entered as "Christopher," I'll be OK, and indeed, his name appears.

```
        name: Christopher John Allen
 send_email_to: cja1@cornell.edu
     nickname: callen
```

Figure 14.6
A partial listing of North American phone book entries.

```
    Internet Gopher Information Client v1.11

                  North America

--> 1.  American Mathematical Society Combined Membership List <?>
    2.  Arizona State University <?>
    3.  Auburn University <?>
    4.  Bates College <CSO>
    5.  Baylor College of Medicine <?>
    6.  Board of Governors Universities (Illinois) <CSO>
    7.  Boston University <CSO>
    8.  Bradley University <?>
    9.  Brigham Young University <CSO>
   10.  Brown University <CSO>
   11.  Bucknell University <CSO>
   12.  Bull HN Information Systems <?>
   13.  California Institute of Technology <?>
   14.  California State University - Fresno <?>
   15.  California State University - Hayward <?>
   16.  California State University - Sacramento <?>
   17.  Calvin College <CSO>
   18.  Cambridge Computer Associates <?>

Press ? for Help, q to Quit, u to go up a menu        Page: 1/12
```

Figure 14.7
The data entry screen
for the directory at
Cornell University.

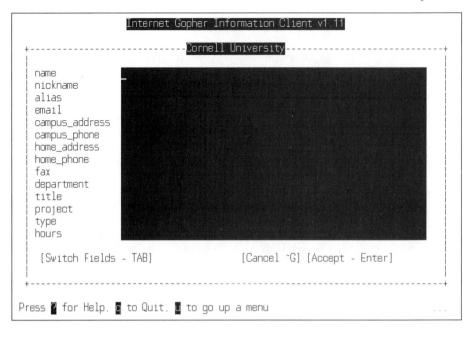

```
         Internet Gopher Information Client v1.11

+-----------------------------Cornell University---------------------------+
|                                                                          |
|  |  name                                                                 |
|  |  nickname     _                                                       |
|  |  alias                                                                |
|  |  email                                                                |
|  |  campus_address                                                       |
|  |  campus_phone                                                         |
|  |  home_address                                                         |
|  |  home_phone                                                           |
|  |  fax                                                                  |
|  |  department                                                           |
|  |  title                                                                |
|  |  project                                                              |
|  |  type                                                                 |
|  |  hours                                                                |
|  |                                                                       |
|  |  [Switch Fields - TAB]              [Cancel ^G] [Accept - Enter]      |
|  |                                                                       |
+--------------------------------------------------------------------------+

Press ? for Help, q to Quit, u to go up a menu              . . .
```

```
campus_address: 521 Sheldon Ct.
              : Ithaca, NY 14850
 campus_phone: 3-7901
      project: try and make it to the summer
```

These CSO searches can also use wild-cards. If I had chosen to, I could have tried **ch* allen** to see what the system would come up with. I could have used **chris* allen**, for that matter, since the first five letters of Christopher and Chris are identical. A wild card asterisk simply indicates the system should try to find anything that matches the letters I've typed, along with any other letters that might follow them. I might thus have encountered a Charles Allen using my **c* allen** search strategy. The **?** wildcard, incidentally, does not work with CSO name servers.

Note in the example that you aren't restricted to searching by name. If I had remembered that my friend's son had an electronic mail address of **cjal@cornell.edu**, I could have entered that in the relevant field and pulled up the same information. The fields available for searching are name, phone number, and e-mail address; not all items in the above entry are indexed. But being able to search in these fields should retrieve the information you need in most cases. Because they're popular at universities, CSO servers can be a fast and easy way to track people down, especially when used through the kind offices of **gopher**.

KNOWBOTS AND THE INTELLIGENT DIRECTORY

Using **gopher** was easy; its menu structure helped us through the complexities of a CSO search. Also offering a consistent user interface is the Knowbot Information Service, which provides a single format to help you access different kinds of user directory services. While **gopher** sets up a series of menus, from which you choose the information source you'll work with, Knowbot Information Service's **netaddress** program can itself go out and request information from a variety of sources. The two hit many of the same sources, too; **gopher** can query CSO servers, WHOIS, netfind, WAIS, and X.500 (more about X.500 later in this chapter). **netaddress** can pull data from WHOIS servers, a variety of campus directory systems, the X.500 project run by NYSERNet, **finger**, and a directory service offered by MCI Mail.

"Knowbots" are programs that can hunt down information no matter what its format; the ultimate goal is a Knowbot that can cruise the Internet looking virtually anywhere for whatever data you specify. We're not at that point yet, but developments in this field are exciting. The WAIS concept is similar in one sense; WAIS provides a consistent interface to a variety of different databases. The beauty of a true Knowbot is that it would be easier to use than WAIS. It would know what you wanted and be able to find it without any subsequent user intervention. In addition to Knowbot Information Service in Reston, VA, the Knowbot concept is being explored by SandPoint Corporation of Cambridge, MA, and Advanced Research Technology of Rosemont, PA.

You can try out Knowbot Information Services' **netaddress** program by Telnet either to **nri.reston.va.us 185** or **sol.bucknell.edu 185**. At either address, you can use a single query to set off a search through a variety of information services, with the results presented in a uniform format. The search syntax is simple. At the **>** prompt, you enter a name. Given this command, the service will search for the name in question. Entering the name **stroud** at the prompt, I received a list of 21 people with that last name, alphabetized, and including organization name, city, state, e-mail address, and other information.

You can also use a Knowbot to narrow in on a person when you know something more than the person's name. If, for example, the target of your search was a user of MCI Mail, you could tell Knowbot to search that database using the **service** *directory* command—**service mcimail** does the trick. You can then run the address search knowing the results will be constrained to include only those people in the MCI Mail database.

The following describes the basic Knowbot commands.

service   Adds a given directory service to the list of services searched by **netaddress**. If you don't specify a particular service, **netaddress** will use a default list of services.

services   Lists the services available through **netaddress**.

org   You can search using organization as a qualifier; **org digital equipment**, for example, calls up only those people who list that company as their organization.

country   Constraining your search by country lets you pull up everyone on a specific directory from a given country.

ident   Allows you to search for a service-specific identifier instead of a user name. I might want to search for a user named Charles Johnson under his username **cjohn**, for example.

query   Entering **query** *username* is the same as simply entering the username at the **>** prompt. It simply tells **netaddress** this is the name to search for.

quit   Quits **netaddress**.

The results of a **netaddress** search are also available by e-mail. You can send a message to either **netaddress@nri.reston.va.us** or **netaddress@sol.buck-nell.edu.** The body of the message is processed as a command input to **netaddress,** and the results are then mailed back to you.

Digging Out a Name from USENET

Perhaps you've been reading USENET newsgroups for a while now and would like to contact someone whose name you ran across in one of them. But you don't know the person's e-mail address. Fortunately, all is not lost. An address database tapping USENET newsgroups can be found at **pit-manager.mit.edu**. This database is easy to use and can be queried by e-mail, making it ideal for those without full Internet access.

Send a message to **mail-server@pit-manager.mit.edu**. In the body of the message, enter **send usenet-addresses/***name*, where *name* is either a first or last name of the person you're looking for. I might send, for example, a message like **send usenet-addresses/gilmore** to track down a USENET poster with that last name. One caveat: characters like apostrophes have to be replaced with a period for the search to work. "O'Toole" becomes **o.toole** in the search command.

Need more than one person's address? You can send multiple requests by putting them on separate lines in the same message, but each will be answered in a separate reply. You can also tap into this database with a WAIS search. Telnet to **quake.think.com** and run **swais**, as discussed in Chapter 13. By searching the Directory of Servers, you'll be able to find the server at **pit-manager.mit.edu** which contains the information (it's called **usenet-addresses**). You can search it using standard WAIS methodology. This method is preferred over e-mail, but not everyone has full Internet access.

BITNET Names

Tracking down someone on BITNET can get interesting. Fortunately, many BITNET sites have name servers which you can query. You'll want to get a list of these sites.

••

What You Need: A List of BITNET Name Servers

The Document: **BITNET Servers**

How to Get It: Send e-mail to **LISTSERV@BITNIC.bitnet**. Include the command **send bitnet servers** in the body of the message.
••

To find someone on BITNET, you can send e-mail to the relevant server. Leave the subject field blank and make your request the first line of the message. Trying to find John Smith at American University, for example, I would send a message to **LISTSERV@AUVM.bitnet**, an address I've taken from the BITNET Servers file.

```
% mail listserv@auvm.bitnet
Subject:
whois smith, john
```

CAMPUS WIDE INFORMATION SYSTEMS

Another alternative if you're looking for someone at a college or university is to find out whether that institution maintains an on-line information service. Campus Wide Information Systems (CWIS) are becoming more prevalent all the time, and many of them are excellent. I frequently use the **gopher** at MCNC to look through these systems. Many **gophers** contain CWIS information (you can search using **veronica** to track these down). In addition, there is a WAIS server, **cwis-list.src**, containing a searchable list of CWIS servers prepared by Judy Hallman at the University of North Carolina at Chapel Hill. You can search it through Telnet to **quake.think.com** (log in as **wais**, as explained in Chapter 13). If the campus you're interested in has a CWIS, you'll find it on the list. Another good source is Peter Scott's **HYTELNET** program, which lets you choose the CWIS you want to go to and can perform the connection without further user intervention when you log on to it using **telnet access.usask.ca**. Log on as **hytelnet**.

Judy Hallman's list of CWIS servers is also available through anonymous FTP, and it's a handy thing to have if you think you'll be trying to track down campus addresses.

•••

What You Need: A List of CWIS Servers

The Document: **CWIS-L**

How to Get It: Through anonymous FTP to **ftp.oit.unc.edu**. Look in the directory *pub/docs/about-the-net/cwis*. The file is **cwis-l**.
•••

Just what is a CWIS? It's a repository of campus information which can be reached by any workstation at the university that has communications capability. These services vary from school to school, not only in terms of content but also in terms of the software that drives them. But you can expect to find menu-driven systems allowing you to choose information on campus events and services, lists of job openings and housing possibilities, class schedules, directories of faculty and students, grant opportunities, and more. Frequently, the system will be set up to enable electronic mail or discussion groups, though such services are generally only available to registered users. You may also find library search capabilities open to the public.

It would be unthinkable to discuss CWIS without making mention of Cornell University, whose CUINFO has been on-line for over a decade thanks to the dedicated work of Steven L. Worona. While earlier systems had become available, including services at the University of Illinois at Champaign-Urbana and Stanford University, Cornell's may have been the first real bridge to the non-mainframe community, and today it stands as an exemplar of what a well-designed campus system can achieve. You can reach CUINFO using **tn3270 cuinfo.cornell.edu 300**. Figure 14.8 shows the opening screen.

Figure 14.8
The opening screen
from the CWIS at
Cornell University.

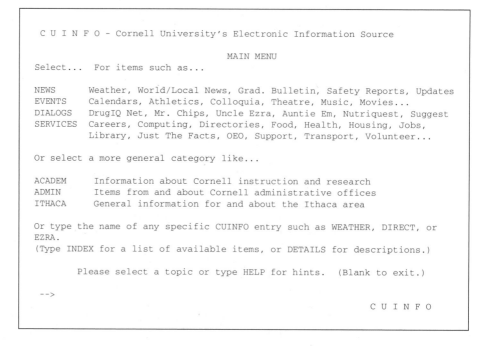

```
    C U I N F O - Cornell University's Electronic Information Source

                              MAIN MENU
    Select...  For items such as...

    NEWS      Weather, World/Local News, Grad. Bulletin, Safety Reports, Updates
    EVENTS    Calendars, Athletics, Colloquia, Theatre, Music, Movies...
    DIALOGS   DrugIQ Net, Mr. Chips, Uncle Ezra, Auntie Em, Nutriquest, Suggest
    SERVICES  Careers, Computing, Directories, Food, Health, Housing, Jobs,
              Library, Just The Facts, OEO, Support, Transport, Volunteer...


    Or select a more general category like...

    ACADEM     Information about Cornell instruction and research
    ADMIN      Items from and about Cornell administrative offices
    ITHACA     General information for and about the Ithaca area


    Or type the name of any specific CUINFO entry such as WEATHER, DIRECT, or
    EZRA.
    (Type INDEX for a list of available items, or DETAILS for descriptions.)


        Please select a topic or type HELP for hints.  (Blank to exit.)

    -->
                                                        C U I N F O
```

This screen should give you a feel for the wide variety of information
available here. Each of these menu items contains submenus. Figure 14.9 shows
the menu for SERVICES, with all its associated submenus.

Figure 14.9
The services menu at
Cornell.

```
                          CUINFO -- Services

    Title           Contents              Title            Contents
    ---------  -----------------------    ---------  -----------------------
    CAREER     Cornell Career Center      MEDIA      Media Services Information
    CDO        ABEN Alumni Network        OEO        Office of Equal Opportunity
    COMPUTING  Computing at Cornell       ORGS       Stud. Organization Directory
    C-STORE    Campus Store Information   PERSONNEL  Univ. Human Resource Service
    DIRECTORY  Cornell Directories        PHONE-MENU Local Food Delivery Menus
    ENGINEER   Internat. Programs in Eng. RADIO-TV   Local Area Radio/TV Listings
    EXT-PUB    Coop. Ext. Pub. List       SAFETY     Public Safety Items
    FAMILY     Work and Family Issues     SCOLA      Satellite Comm. for Learning
    FAO        Financial Aid Office       SEO        Student Employment Office
    FOOD       On- and Off-Campus Eating  SUPPORT    Student Services, Uncle Ezra
    HEALTH     Gannett Health Center      TAKENOTE   TakeNote Course Listing
    HOUSING    On- and Off-Campus Housing TEXTBOOKS  Textbook Information
    IMS        Instructional Materials    TRANSPORT  Air/Bus/Train Schedules
    JUST       Access "Just The Facts"    TRAV-AGENT Airline Reservation Requests
    LIBRARY    Library Information        VOLUNTEER  Openings for Volunteers

               Please select a title.  (Blank for previous menu.)

    -->
                                                        C U I N F O
```

Figure 14.10
Directory services
menu at Cornell.

```
Cornell Directories

  Students: STUDENT listed by last name      F-STUDENT listed by first-name
  Fac/Staff: STAFF   listed by last name      F-STAFF listed by first name
            E-STAFF listed by e-mail address  D-STAFF listed by department

Other Directories:  CISER for social scientists
                    FRAT-SOR for fraternities, sororities, small living units
                    MEDICAL for Cornell University Medical College
                    LIFE for Student Life Union Telephone List

Information for CUINFO's Student Directory listings comes from the Office
of the Registrar (222 Day Hall, 255-4232).  Staff Directory listings are
provided by the Office of Telecommunications (200 CCC, 255-3305).  The
CISER directory comes from the CISER office (201 Caldwell 255-4801).
Medical Directory listings are provided by the Office of Academic Computing,
Cornell University Medical College, NYC (212-746-4622).
Student and Staff directory data is updated weekly.

            Please select a title.  (Blank for previous menu.)


  -->
                                                      C U I N F O
```

Of particular note is the **SUPPORT** category, which contains a listing for
something called Uncle Ezra. This innovative counseling service has proven so
successful that it has spread to other universities. As you can see from the menus
at CUINFO, there is very little that isn't available to campus users. For those of
us logging on from the outside to find an address, the **DIRECTORY** submenu
pops up a quick way to locate our people, as shown in Figure 14.10.

It's necessary to point out that there is no standard for Campus Wide
Information Systems as yet; the variety of user interfaces is wide. Figure 14.11,
for example, is the opening screen from the CWIS at Appalachian State University in Boone, North Carolina.

Here again, we have an easy to use menu system with choices leading to
submenus and eventually to text. No matter which software implementation you
run into, CWIS systems are a great way to find people, and their growth into
broader forms of information implies an interesting convergence with the
Free-Net systems we discussed in Chapter 3.

Because CWIS systems are an exciting area of Internet development, it
would be useful to find a way to keep up with the field. Fortunately, that's easy.

What You Need: A Mailing List for CWIS Systems

The List: CWIS-L

How to Get It: Send e-mail to **LISTSERV@WUVMD.bitnet**. Include in your
message **subscribe cwis-l your name**. Leave the Subject: field blank.

Figure 14.11
Introductory screen
from the CWIS at
Appalachian State
University.

```
        Welcome to the Appalachian State University VideoText System

     This is an electronic bulletin board for the use of Students, Faculty,
       Staff, and Visitors. ONLY HIGHLIGHTED OPTIONS ARE AVAILABLE.

  SELECT 95 TO FIND INFORMATION QUICKLY
        1) Directories              10) Ask Uncle Sigmund
        2) Employment               11) Scholarly Resources
        3) Calendars and Events     12) Academic Programs/Courses/Seminars
        4) News                     13) Buy/Sell/Trade etc
        5) Facts About Appalachian  14) Career Development Services
        6) Libraries at Appalachian 15) Other Information Systems
        7) Univ Policies/Procedures 16) List Todays' Activities
        8) Computer Information      17) APPALCART ROUTES
        9) Student Activities & Programs 95) INDEX

         Please enter the number of your choice and press the Return key!

                        NEW ITEMS?   PRESS <RETURN>
     QUESTIONS? SUGGESTIONS? Call E. Jones 704 262-6276 or email JONESEL.

  Commands:  H=Help M=Main E=Exit F=Find Left-Arrow=Previous Return=Next

  ASU Commands>_                         Backup=PF3  Help=HELP  Exit=PF1-KDOT
```

X.500 AND THE CONQUEST OF PARADISE

Developed by the CCITT (Consultative Committee for International Telegraph
and Telephone) and the ISO (International Standards Organization), X.500 is a
distributed directory standard. X.500 makes it possible to refer to people by a
"distinguished name," which can be retrieved from an X.500 directory and
mapped onto the appropriate mailbox address. Currently, X.500 is being de-
ployed, but not as widely as its proponents initially hoped due to early problems
in implementation. The critical need will be for enough sites to begin using X.500
so that the amount of data available becomes genuinely useful.

PARADISE is an experimental X.500 service which can be accessed through
Telnet to **paradise.ulcc.ac.uk**. Log on as **de**. Once on-line, you can search for
information about people and organizations, retrieving electronic mail addresses, telephone and fax numbers, and more. Your job is to provide name
information and the location of the person. The directory service will run a
search to find information that matches your search commands. As of mid 1991,
there were over four-hundred participating organizations and some 350,000
entries in the directory. Naturally, the directory service won't do you any good
if the people you're looking for don't work for organizations that are taking part
in the project.

Figure 14.12 shows what you'll see when you Telnet to the **PARADISE** server.

Two types of search are available. A simple search is used when you're
looking for a specific person, department, or organization, and the prompts
mentioned above help you home in. A more powerful search method for multiple
organizations lets you search when you know the name of the person and their
country, but don't know the name of their organization. In this case, the program
searches widely through organizations to match the string you've entered; if you

Figure 14.12
The entry screen at
the PARADISE server.

```
Trying 128.86.8.56 ...
Connected to paradise.ulcc.ac.uk.
Escape character is '^]'.


SunOS UNIX (found.paradise.ulcc.ac.uk)

login: de
SunOS Release 4.1.1 (DUA) #5: Tue Jun 9 08:28:49 BST 1992

               Welcome to PARADISE - the COSINE Directory Service

Connecting to the Directory - wait just a moment please ...
You can use this directory service to look up telephone numbers and elec-
tronic
mail addresses of people and organisations participating in the Pilot
Directory Service.

Select the mode you would like:

S  Simple queries - if you know the name of the organisation you want to
search
                    (this is how the interface always used to behave)

P  Power Search - to search many organisations simultaneously

I  Brief instructions explaining the program modes and how to use the pro-
gram

?  The help facility - usage and topics

Q  To quit the program

Enter option:
```

omit the organization name entirely, it will search through the entire list of
organizations in that country.

Begin by typing in the name of the person you're looking for, either as a full
name or just a last name. You move through several fields in such a search, being
prompted for department, organization, and country. Here's what a simple
search screen looks like, as shown in Figure 14.13.

You answer at the prompt with a name; you're then prompted for the
remaining fields.

THE MOTHER OF ALL DIRECTORIES

In January 1993, AT&T announced it had signed a cooperative agreement with
the National Science Foundation to develop the next generation of directory for
NSFNET. Just as the Internet is a network of networks, the new directory is seen
as a directory of directories, pointing to the wealth of information sources on
the network. Included are key data like FTP sites, lists of servers, lists of
directories of various kinds, library catalogs, and other material. The notion is
to make all of this easy to get to by creating simple user interfaces. In addition,
AT&T plans to use the X.500 specification to create directory services listing
users of the Internet and resources available on-line.

Figure 14.13
A sample search in
PARADISE.

```
You will be prompted to type in:

:- the NAME of the person for whom you are seeking information
:- their DEPARTMENT (optional),
:- the ORGANISATION they work for (optional if power searching), and
:- the COUNTRY in which the person or organisation is based.

On-line HELP is available to explain in more detail how to use the
Directory Service.  Please type ?INTRO (or ?intro) if you are not familiar
with the Directory Service.

?          for HELP with the current question you are being asked
??         for HELP on HELP
q          to quit the Directory Service (confirmation asked unless at the
           request for a person's name)
Control-C  abandon current query or entry of current query

Simple query mode selected
Person's name, q to quit, * to browse, ? for help
:-
```

Two other organizations, General Atomics and Network Solutions Inc., are involved; they'll all work together under the rubric INTERNIC. The current agreement is for a five-year period, during which time the already unsettled question of resource and people discovery is likely to get even more controversial. Is AT&T's approach the right one, and is a centralized directory structure the optimum way of organizing Internet information for the benefit of all?

Many network tools, after all, like **gopher**, **netfind**, or WAIS, work under the distributed model. **gopher** doesn't function because it taps into a primary database; rather, it has been designed to work with information in a variety of formats clustered in sites around the world. Working from the top down may be a model that appeals to one set of planners, but going into uncharted waters and bringing the information back home is another way of approaching the task. The kinds of decisions that will be made over these issues will shape the Internet as it evolves toward linkage with the national communications network called the NREN—the National Research and Education Network.

You can use the new INTERNIC Directory and Database Services to consult an X.500 directory. Telnet to **ds.internic.net**. Use a user id of **x500** with no password. You can also use a public access **netfind** program here. Telnet to the same site, and use a user id of **netfind** with no password.

REAL-TIME CONVERSATION

You're not limited to electronic mail when you want to contact someone on the Internet. A handy program called **talk** actually lets you go "live." You type on your keyboard; your friend types on his, both of you sitting at your terminals at the same time. In this way, it's possible to maintain an active conversation, very similar to what happens on the commercial networks when people use the "chat" or "conferencing" capabilities. These services have become very popular on CompuServe, BIX, and DELPHI.

To run **talk**, simply give the address of the person you want to talk to. **talk summers@alphabettica.com**, for example, displays a message on your friend's screen that you're available for a chat. By responding in like fashion, she can initiate a two-way discussion. Because incoming text can confuse whatever you're trying to enter, the **talk** program gets around the problem by giving you a split screen to work with. You see what you enter at the top of the screen, while your friend's response appears on the bottom.

talk is enjoyable, if trivial, once you've worked out the kinks. It's difficult, for example, to handle pauses in a conversation. Without verbal cues or physical gestures, you don't really know whether you're supposed to say something or whether your correspondent is simply gathering her thoughts before continuing. Then, too, there's the question of productivity. You find after a while that simultaneous typing doesn't produce a very high information flow; you can ratchet up the content by ten or so if you simply pick up the phone and call this person. Nonetheless, as a diversion from a long day at the office, **talk** has its charms.

One-to-one conferencing is the easiest way to start this kind of interactive discussion, but you can also get involved with multiple parties. If you have any CompuServe or DELPHI experience, you'll recall that numerous users often gather in the various forums or Special Interest Groups to hold regular conferences. Here the strains of the on-line medium as applied to conversation really show. Because so many people have access to their keyboards at the same time, conventions are used to regulate the traffic. A formal conference, for example, might require each user to enter **ga** for "go ahead" after concluding his or her thoughts. Questions could be signaled by a **?**, which would indicate to the moderator that a particular person wanted to speak. The moderator's job is to monitor the flow of the conversation.

On the other hand, many such conferences are entirely free-form, with people chipping in where and when they please. This can lead to virtual anarchy on-screen, but there are those who thrive on it, forming on-line friendships and exploring ideas. The Internet, too, makes multiple party conferencing a reality; its implementation is known as **Internet Relay Chat**, or IRC. To try out IRC, you can reach a public client program through Telnet to **irc.demon.co.uk** or **sci.dixie.edu 6668**. There, you can learn more about how IRC works.

A number of IRC servers are available, including the following:

```
csa.bu.edu
ucsu.colorado.edu
irc.caltech.edu
ug.cs.dal.ca
nic.funet.fi
vesuv.unisg.ch
munagin.ee.mu.oz.au
sunsystem2.informatik.tu-muenchen.de
```

Many UNIX-based systems will also offer you the option of calling IRC up from the command prompt. You can invoke it by entering **irc**. If you wish to use a nickname dissimilar from your login name, enter the command **irc** *nickname* instead. Figure 14.14 shows what you'll see in a typical IRC chat session, which I began by entering **irc** at the command prompt on my account at The World.

Look at the screen in Figure 14.14, which contains some interesting information. You'll see there were some 1455 users and 517 "invisible" users on 162 servers worldwide at the moment I initiated **IRC**. Invisible users, it turns out, are users who are on secret or hidden channels; their name does not turn up in

Figure 14.14
Beginning of an IRC
session.

```
*** Connecting to port 6667 of server world.std.com
*** Welcome to the Internet Relay Network, pag
*** Your host is world.std.com[world], running version 2.7.2g
*** If you have not already done so, please read the new user information
+/HELP NEWUSER
*** This server was created Wed Mar 3 1993 at 12:38:04 EST
*** There are 1455 users and 517 invisible on 162 servers
*** 69 users have connection to the twilight zone
*** There are 497 channels.
*** I have 2 clients and 1 servers
MOTD - world.std.com Message of the Day -
MOTD -
MOTD -                     Welcome to World's IRC server
MOTD -
MOTD -       For additional details on IRC, check 'help irc' on World.
MOTD -         Topics include a guide to basic commands and a schedule
MOTD -             of special IRC discussions for World customers.
MOTD -
MOTD -
* End of /MOTD command.
*** Mode change "+i" for user pag by pag
```

a list of active users. The 69 users who have a "twilight zone" connection are
IRC operators. With 1455 users talking, conceivably, at once, the message traffic
is overwhelming. To provide some order for this chaos, the IRC space is divided
into channels, the number of which is unlimited. Each is designed to accommodate 10 users, except for channels 1–9, which have no such restrictions.

We can generate a list of available channels by using the **/list** command.
Doing this for the entire list creates many screens full of channels, of which I'll
show you only a small percentage, in Figure 14.15.

Figure 14.15
Partial list of available
IRC channels.

```
*** #TUEBINGEN 8       Haengen wir den Chauvi raus ...
*** #Konstanz  4
*** #report    1
*** #ccc       1       Chaos Computer Club - Ulm
*** #amigager  4
*** #OS/2      4
*** Prv        5
*** #linux     13      Free 386 Un*x/X11/tcp ++ (/msg linuxbot help)
*** #meditatio 4
*** #nippon    10      TGIF!!!  Let's party!
*** #malaysia  36      WOI..BALIK STUDY SEMUA!!!!
*** #Services  7
*** #Amiga     29      Cryo has an A1200 to add to his orphan collection
*** #eu-opers  15      European IRC operators' hangout
*** #AmigaSwe  2
*** #BTHS      1
*** #Kristanzo 2
*** #espanol   31      ALEJANDRO SANZ
*** #bondage   17      Hat to da Back
*** #Turks     6
*** #Twilight_ 28      tzoper is a boojum snark!
[1] 14:58 pag (+i)* type /help for help
```

Figure 14.16
An example of an IRC
session in progress.

```
<Kemal> bull: hirvonen@ucsvax.ucs.umass.edu   I am in Australia actually, we
+just talk a lot

<RingMan> kemal:do oyu like reading, sports?
<Aedes> hi euph
<Kemal> ringman: I read an awful lot
*** Fuzzie (EROBERTS@192.203.164.120) has joined channel #canada
<Fuzzie> hi all :)
<Euphrasie> hello!!
<Renard> hiya fuzz
<Euphrasie> hi fuzzie!!
<RingMan> Kemal:can I suggest a good book?
<Cheaka> kemal-all i can say is,don't worry about it things will  work
+themselves out for you. sure life can be hard at times but they always work
+themselves out in the end
```

You can join a channel with the **/join** command. This is where things get hard to follow. You have to develop a certain tolerance for nonsequential text. Figure 14.16 shows, for example, what I saw on-screen recently when I joined a channel called *canada*.

This probably gives you a bit of the flavor of IRC. The screen is split so that you can enter your own comments at the bottom, which will then be seen by everyone. There are also commands for a wide range of options including private conversations, generating help screens (use the **/help** command), finding out who is on-line, and more.

••

What You Need: An IRC Tutorial

Where to Get It: Through anonymous FTP from **cs.bu.edu**. The directory is *irc/support*. The files are all labeled **tutorial**. Do an **ls tutorial*** command to see them.
••

There's also a useful Frequently Asked Questions list for the USENET newsgroup **alt.irc**.

••

What You Need: Further Information on Internet Relay Chat

The Document: Frequently Asked Questions list for the **alt.irc** newsgroup.

How to Get It: Through anonymous FTP to **pit-manager.mit.edu**. The directory is *pub/usenet/news.answers*. The file is **irc-faq**.
••

The following describes some of the basic IRC commands. Preceding a command with a backslash ensures that it's treated as a command, and not as a message which will be sent to other participants.

/bye   Synonymous with **/quit**, this command allows you to leave any channel at any time.

/invite *nickname*   Sends a message to someone on a different IRC channel that you'd like them to meet you on your channel.

/join #*channel-name*   Lets you join the channel of your choice. All channel names include a # sign in front. Note: you can also create your own channel by the command **/join #channel-name** where you're entering the name of the channel you want to create.

/list   Lists all available channels for IRC.

/msg *nickname*   Allows you to send a private message to a person.

/summon *username*   Invites someone who is not using IRC to join you in chatting. Note: this requires the user name at the person's site, rather than an IRC nickname. Thus **/summon flr@samson.utn.edu** summons that person to a chat.

/who #*channel*   This command tells you which users are participating in a given channel. The listing includes the person's nickname, along with an electronic mail address.

/whois *username*   Gives you the identity of anyone on the channel.

Well-Populated Dungeons

The Internet provides ample opportunities for recreation, including on-line versions of backgammon and chess, addresses for both of which can be found in Chapter 15. But one category of recreation deserves special mention here, since it ties in so closely with Internet Relay Chat (think of it as IRC with superimposed organization). The cryptic acronym MUD stands for Multi-User Dungeon, which in turn stands for role-playing games based on text. You might do most anything in such a game, from going off to an idyllic landscape to meditate, to slaying dragons and rescuing maidens. As you proceed by way of Telnet, you receive a series of choices about your next action and you enter your reply. The system considers your reply and acts upon your command.

A wild variety of MUDs exist, springing from the original MUD created by Richard Bartle and Roy Trubshaw at the University of Essex in England. With new versions appearing frequently, it's helpful to keep up with the MUD community by tapping a USENET newsgroup devoted to such things.

• •

What You Need: A Way to Keep up with MUDs

The Newsgroup: **rec.games.mud.announce**. You can also try **alt.mud**. You'll also find a FAQ, **games/mud-faq/part1**, **games/mud-faq/part2**, and **games/mud-faq/part3** in the FAQ archive at **pit-manager.mit.edu**.

• •

CHAPTER FOURTEEN NOTES

1. Electronic mail message to the author February 8, 1993.

15

A Directory
of Internet Resources

It's interesting to speculate how big a volume it would take to create a truly complete Internet directory, listing every conceivable resource from **FTP** sites, **WAIS** servers, mail servers, Telnet destinations, and more. Whatever the answer, a single chapter like this one can only hope to suggest useful and interesting material for your browsing and reference. Inevitably, many of the sites here, especially the Telnet sites, reflect my own parochial interests, though I've attempted to broaden their scope by working in what seem to be popular destinations as reflected in some of the directory materials listed below.

ARCHIE SITES

These are public access **archie** sites. Choose the one nearest you to prevent network congestion.

> **archie.rutgers.edu**: northeastern U.S.
> **archie.sura.net**: southern U.S.
> **archie.unl.edu**: western U.S.
> **archie.ans.net**: ANS network sites
> **archie.mcgill.ca**: Canada
> **archie.au**: Australia and Pacific region
> **archie.funet.fi**: Europe
> **archie.th-darmstadt.de**: Germany
> **archie.doc.ic.ac.uk:** United Kingdom

archie.cs.huji.ac.il: Israel
archie.wide.ad.jp: Japan
archie.kuis.kyoto-u.ac.jp: Japan
archie.ncu.edu.tw: Taiwan
archie.nz: New Zealand

BITNET Mailing Lists

BITNET's resources are rich indeed. Consult the following directory files to help you find material matching your own interests.

Directory of Scholarly Electronic Conferences

A comprehensive listing of academic conferences divided into four general categories, with the liberal arts section presented in subsections. Compiled by Diane K. Kovacs.
Access: **ftp ksuvxa.kent.edu**. Directory: *library*. Because the directory is maintained in parts, it's advisable to download and read the file **ACADLIST README** for further information about which parts you need and how to download them.

Listserv Lists

Collects all mailing lists available by way of BITNET.
Access: Send electronic mail to **LISTSERV@BITNIC.bitnet**. Leave subject field blank. The body of the message should read **list global**.

Campus Wide Information Systems

Campus-wide information systems are proliferating, with news of interest to the local university and college communities, and often, gateways into library systems and information attractive to a wider audience. The basic document on these systems is Judy Hallman's "Campus Wide Information Systems." You can retrieve this list of campus systems and Free-Net bulletin boards worldwide, along with login instructions, through anonymous FTP as follows.
Access: **ftp ftp.oit.unc.edu**
Directory: *pub/docs/about-the-net/cwis*
File: **cwis-l**

Meanwhile, here are some sample CWIS systems to get you started:

Arizona State University PEGASUS and ASEDD

Contains a directory to university staff and the Arizona State Economic Development Database.
Access: **tn3270 asuvm.inre.asu.edu**
Login: **helloasu**

CUINFO: Cornell University's Campus/Regional Information System

Provides information on campus and regional events. Tracks weather, calendars, services and administrative news.
Access: **tn3270 cuinfo.cornell.edu 300**

HOLY CROSS

Contains campus catalog for Holy Cross, along with its student handbook, campus libraries, a course guide, news and entertainment, athletics, and various directories.
Access: **telnet hcacad.holycross.edu**
Login: **view**
Password: **view**

NORTH CAROLINA STATE UNIVERSITY HAPPENINGS!

Contains the University Infobook, with information broken down by schools and departments. Also faculty and student directories, computing center news, and NCSU library information, as well as a variety of newsletters.
Access: **telnet ccvax1.cc.ncsu.edu**
Login: **info**

PENNSYLVANIA STATE UNIVERSITY

Local information and schedules. Weather forecasts, news of cultural events, campus directories, and student services.
Access: **tn3270 psuvm.psu.edu**
Login: Enter **EBB** on the COMMAND line

RUTGERS UNIVERSITY

Course catalogs, university activities, computer services, on-line library catalog, weather, and news.
Access: **telnet info.rutgers.edu**

SUINFO: SYRACUSE UNIVERSITY CAMPUS INFORMATION SYSTEM

A campus system providing catalogs and local news. Other offerings include Educational Resources Information Clearinghouse (ERIC database), as well as archived information from a number of BITNET discussion groups.
Access: **telnet acsnet.syr.edu**
Login: Tab to the command line (you'll tab right past the **logon** and **password** lines) and enter **suinfo**.

TILBURG UNIVERSITY, NETHERLANDS, KUBGIDS

On-line public access library catalog, along with a series of databases holding information on computer science, economics, and business.
Access: **telnet kublib.kub.nl**
Login: **kubgids**

UNIVERSITY OF MINNESOTA TWIN CITIES

A CWIS run through a **gopher** at the University of Minnesota, with the usual **gopher** benefits of access to services like FTP, **archie** and WAIS. This is where **gopher** started. The campus information is available in this format, along with a wide variety of computer-related information.
Access: **telnet consultant.micro.umn.edu**
Login: **gopher**

UNIVERSITY OF NORTH CAROLINA AT CHAPEL HILL, OFFICE OF INFORMATION TECHNOLOGY INFORMATION CENTER

Included in the campus news here are university newsletters, a campus directory, and material from UNC's Office of Public Information.
Access: **telnet info.acs.unc.edu**

UNIVERSITY OF PENNSYLVANIA—PENNINFO

Along with directories and campus calendars, this system contains an abundance of information on computing topics including Internet-related material. Access to library catalogs and articles from campus publications can be found here.
Access: **telnet penninfo.upenn.edu**

DIRECTORIES

AARNET RESOURCE GUIDE

An Australian version of the Internet Resource Guide. Available through anonymous FTP from **aarnet.edu.au**.
Directory: *pub/resource-guide*
File: **resource_guide_archives.txt**

A CRUISE OF THE INTERNET

This is a software program written as a basic tutorial to Internet services.
Access: **ftp nic.merit.edu**
Directory: *resources*
File: **merit.cruise.readme.txt** has information about how to download the complete package.

ELECTRIC MYSTIC'S GUIDE

An intriguing and exhaustive compendium of Internet sites with a religious theme.
Access: **ftp panda1.uottawa.ca**
Directory: *pub/religion*
File: **electric-mystics-guide***

A GUIDE TO INTERNET/BITNET

This is a three-part guide, compiled by Dana Noonan, containing listings of on-line library catalogs in the United States as well as abroad, with news about special collections and a tutorial on use.
Access: **ftp vm1.nodak.edu**
Directory *nnews*
Files: **GUIDE1.NNEWS, GUIDE2.NNEWS, GUIDE3.NNEWS**

HYTELNET

Peter Scott's hypertext program for locating Internet resources. Can run as a memory-resident program under MS-DOS; a Macintosh and an Amiga version are also available.
Access: **ftp access.usask.ca**
For the Macintosh version:
Directory: *pub/hytelnet/mac*
File: **hytelnet.mac.sea.hqx**

For MS-DOS:
Directory: *pub/hytelnet/pc*
File: *hyteln65.zip*
For the Amiga version:
Directory: *pub/hytelnet/amiga*
File: **Ami-HyTelnet.lha**
Note: file numbers change as new versions are released.

INDEX OF RFCS
A listing of all RFCs created since the beginning of ARPANET.
Access: **ftp ftp.nisc.sri.com**
Directory: *rfc*
File: **rfc-index.txt**

INFORMATION AVAILABLE ON THE INTERNET: A GUIDE TO SELECTED SOURCES
Compiled by the SURAnet Network Information Center. Lists information sources on the Internet.
Access: **ftp ftp.sura.net**
Directory: *pub/nic*
File: **infoguide.6-93.txt**
Note: these numbers change as subsequent editions are released.

INFORMATION SOURCES: THE INTERNET AND COMPUTER-MEDIATED COMMUNICATION
John December has compiled this list of pointers to Internet information. It's a basic list for your file library.
Access: **ftp ftp.rpi.edu**
Directory: *pub/communications*
File: **internet-cmc**

INTERNET RESOURCE GUIDE
A large and extremely quirky index to resources on the Internet, containing listings of a variety of computational resources, library catalogs, archive sites, on-line address books, and networks connecting to the Internet. Dial-up users will find it easiest to retrieve on-line as a single text file totaling almost 600K.
Access: **ftp ds.internic.net**
Directory: *resource-guide*
File: **wholeguide.txt**
Be advised: this file contains control characters that making viewing parts of it with a text editor problematical.

THE MAASINFO DIRECTORIES
Compiled by Robert E. Maas, **MaasInfo.TopIndex** is an index to major Internet services (nicknamed the "Index of Indexes"), while **MaasInfo.DocIndex** is an index of Internet documents and tutorials. These are among the most helpful directory documents available on the Internet, although the formatting makes them hard to read.
Access: **ftp ftp.unt.edu**
Directory: *articles/maas*
Files: **maasinfo.docindex** and **maasinfo.topindex**

NixPub Long Listing—Public/Open Access Unix Sites

An annotated list with description and contact information. Posted to USENET groups **comp.misc**, **alt.bbs. alt.bbs.lists**.
Access: **ftp pit-manager.mit.edu**
Directory: *pub/usenet/comp.misc*.
File: **Nixpub_Posting_(Long)**
There is also a shorter version in the same directory, with the file name **Nixpub_Posting_(Short)**.

Public Dialup Internet Access List

A useful list of public access service providers maintained by Peter Kaminski. Note: this list contains only sites offering FTP or Telnet services; sites offering news and mail only need to be found using the NixPub list posted above.
Access: **ftp ftp.netcom.com**
Directory: */pub/info-deli/public-access*
File: **pdial**

Special Internet Connections

A frequently updated list of services available over the Internet. Compiled by Scott A. Yanoff and posted to the USENET newsgroups **alt.internet.services, comp.misc, biz.comp.services, alt.bbs.internet, news.answers.** Indispensable.
Access: **ftp csd4.csd.uwm.edu**
Directory: *pub*
File: **inet.services.txt**

Surfing the Internet: An Introduction

A useful and light-hearted tour of Internet resources. Highly recommended.
Access: **ftp nysernet.org**
Directory: *pub/resources/guides*
File: **surfing.2.0.2.txt**

Using Networked Information Sources: A Bibliography

Deirdre Stanton's bibliographical guide.
Access: **ftp infolib.murdoch.edu.au**
Directory: *pub/bib*
File: **stanton.bib**

Zamfield's Wonderfully Incomplete, Complete Internet BBS List

A list of bulletin board systems available on the Internet. Posted twice monthly on **alt.bbs.internet**.
Access: **ftp wuarchive.wustl.edu**
Directory: *pub*
Also available by electronic mail from **zamfield@dune.ee.msstate.edu**.

FINGER SITES

DATABASES QUERIES
This finger server allows you to search databases. For more information, retrieve the help file as follows.
Access: **finger help@dir.su.oz.au**

EARTHQUAKE INFORMATION
Information about recent earthquake activity.
Access: **finger quake@geophys.washington.edu**

NASA HEADLINE NEWS
A summary of daily press releases from NASA.
Access: **finger nasanews@space.mit.edu**

STD HOURLY AURORAL ACTIVITY STATUS REPORT
This is a regular report on auroral activity; reports are made hourly and watches and warnings are listed.
Access: **finger aurora@xi.uleth.ca**

SEASONAL HURRICANE FORECASTS
Hurricane data.
Access: **finger forecast@typhoon.atmos.colostate.edu**

FTP SITES

Here are a handful of interesting sites. Your own list of favorite destinations will grow as you try these and others.

ECIX—ENERGY AND CLIMATE INFORMATION EXCHANGE
This is the FTP site for the Institute for Global Communications, which hosts EcoNet, PeaceNet, and ConflictNet. You can download files on efficient energy use and environmental issues, with policy statements, newsletters, and other materials on the environment.
Access: **ftp igc.apc.org**

GENERAL ACCOUNTING OFFICE REPORTS ARCHIVE
Includes reports (full-text) from the U.S. General Accounting Office. This is a pilot project to determine whether there is sufficient interest to warrant making all GAO reports available over the Internet.
Access: **ftp cu.nih.gov**

MUSIC ON THE NET: LYRIC AND DISCOGRAPHY ARCHIVE
A compendium of song lyrics and discographies collected at the University of Wisconsin–Parkside. Over 225 discographies and 1,000 songs.
Access: **ftp vacs.uwp.edu**

NASA ARCHIVES

NASA press releases are available here, along with data files and images, plus indices to NASA information. This is a fine source of material about the space program; the collection of GIF images is remarkable, with images from missions from Voyager to the shuttle. Shuttle mission status reports plus material on Magellan, Galileo, and other projects.
Access: **ftp ames.arc.nasa.gov**

THE OAK REPOSITORY

A service of Oakland University, Rochester, MI, this is an Internet site with extensive holdings in PC and UNIX software.
Access: **ftp oak.oakland.edu**

PROJECT HERMES: U.S. SUPREME COURT OPINIONS

Contains full text of U.S. Supreme Court opinions. Text is available in both ASCII format as well as ATEX, a document processing and typesetting format.
Access: **ftp ftp.cwru.edu**
Directory: *hermes*

SIMTEL20

Owned and operated by the U.S. Army at White Sands Missile Range, NM, this site contains a massive collection of public domain and shareware software for a wide range of computers and operating systems.
Access: **ftp wsmr-simtel20.army.mil**

SURANET FTP SERVER

A useful compendium of basic Internet materials, with tutorial information on common procedures and more.
Access: **ftp ftp.sura.net**

UNIVERSITY OF MICHIGAN SOFTWARE ARCHIVES

Collections of public domain, freeware, and shareware. Operating systems include Macintosh, IBM PC, Apple 2, Atari, and NeXT.
Access: **ftp archive.umich.edu**

WASHINGTON UNIVERSITY PUBLIC DOMAIN ARCHIVES

Huge collection of public domain and shareware software for PCs, Macintoshes, and a wide variety of other hardware. Contains "mirrored" archive of the SIMTEL20 holdings. A valuable source for software.
Access: **ftp wuarchive.wustl.edu**

GOPHER SITES AVAILABLE THROUGH TELNET

To log on at these **gopher** sites, use **gopher** as your login name unless advised otherwise. The number of **gopher** sites available through Telnet is growing. This list includes only some of them.

```
telnet consultant.micro.umn.edu
telnet panda.uiowa.edu. Login: panda
telnet grits.valdosta.peachnet.edu
```

```
telnet gopher.uiuc.edu
telnet fatty.law.cornell.edu
telnet cat.ohiolink.edu
telnet gopher.ora.com
telnet info.anu.edu.au. Login: info
telnet tolten.puc.cl
telnet gopher.denet.dk
telnet gopher.th-darmstadt.de
telnet ecnet.ec
telnet ecosys.drdr.virginia.edu
telnet gopher.isnet.is
telnet siam.mi.cnr.it
telnet sunic.sunet.se
telnet gopher.chalmers.se
```

INTERNET MAILING LISTS

The extensive listing of mailing lists maintained at SRI International is quite a read, but going through it carefully can alert you to many interesting news-groups you might not otherwise hear about. So make acquiring the "List of Lists" an early goal.

LIST OF INTEREST GROUPS
Mammoth listing of mailing lists on the Internet and BITNET. Maintained at SRI International NISC.
Access: **ftp ftp.nisc.sri.com**
Directory: *netinfo*
File: **interest-groups**

PUBLICLY AVAILABLE MAILING LISTS
Compiled by Stephanie da Silva, this useful publication catalogs mailing lists in three parts. Posted on USENET **newsgroups news.lists**, **news.announce.new-users.**
Access: **ftp pit-manager.mit.edu**
Directory: *pub/usenet/news.announce.newusers*
Files: **Publicly_Accessible_Mailing_Lists,_Part_I**
      Publicly_Accessible_Mailing_Lists,_Part_II
      Publicly_Accessible_Mailing_Lists,_Part_III

INTERNET RELAY CHAT AND OTHER INTERACTIVE SITES

BACKGAMMON PLAYING
The first Internet backgammon server is surely the harbinger of more interactive sports to come.
Access: **telnet 134.130.130.46 4321**
Login: **guest**

CHAT: CONVERSATIONAL HYPERTEXT ACCESS TECHNOLOGY
This is a natural language information system using technology developed by Communications Canada. Information is available on AIDS, epilepsy, and the Canadian Department of Communications. There are also two intriguing natural

language programs, one called Alice, the other Maur. In the first, you hold a simulated conversation with a student at a university; in the second, you converse with a dragon.
Access: **telnet debra.dgbt.doc.ca**
Login: **chat**

INTERNET CHESS SERVER

This system lets you play chess through the Internet against real-time human opponents. You can maintain a clock, compute player ratings, watch games in progress, choose from a variety of display styles, and talk to other users of the system while you're on-line. A series of help files (enter **help**) walk you through the basic features.
Access: **telnet valkyries.andrew.cmu.edu 5000**

INTERNET RELAY CHAT

This is a public client allowing you to try out Internet Relay Chat. It's often busy and hard to get into.
Access: **telnet bradenville.andrew.cmu.edu**
Other sites: **ircclient.itc.univie.ac 6668**
                 irc.ibmpcug.co.uk 9999

INTERNET GO SERVER

An interactive game of GO.
Access: **telnet icsib18.icsi.berkeley.edu 6969**
Login: choose on-line

MONOCHROME

A multi-user messaging system. You can log on as a guest, or send an e-mail message to gain full access to the system.
Access: **telnet mono.city.ac.uk**
Login: **mono**
Password: **mono**

LIBRARY CATALOGS

If you're tracking Internet connectivity to libraries, you'll want to retrieve Charles Bailey's directory, which also contains much of interest to on-line publishers.

LIBRARY-ORIENTED COMPUTER CONFERENCES AND ELECTRONIC SERIALS

Compiled by Charles W. Bailey, Jr. Contains material of interest to those involved in electronic publishing and Internet connections to libraries.
Access: **ftp noc.sura.net**
Directory: *nic*
File: **info-servers**

Computerized library catalogs are becoming more common every day, in the form of On-Line Public Access Catalogs, or OPACs. These systems provide you with the chance to search a given library's holdings free of charge. They do **not** give access to the books or journals in the catalogs.

Here are some directory materials to help you get a handle on on-line library catalogs:

CATALIST

Richard Duggan's hypertext program which creates browsable links using the **University of North Texas' Accessing On-line Bibliography Databases** material. Runs under Microsoft Windows.
Access: **ftp zebra.acs.udel.edu**
Directory: *pub/library*
File: The file **readme.txt** contains complete information.

INTERNET ACCESSIBLE LIBRARY CATALOGS AND DATABASES

This list was compiled by Art St. George and Ron Larsen, and lists over one hundred library catalogs available on the Internet. Also contains information on Campus Wide Information Systems and Free-Nets.
Access: **ftp ariel.unm.edu**
Directory: *library*
File: **internet.library**

UNIVERSITY OF NORTH TEXAS' ACCESSING ON-LINE BIBLIOGRAPHY DATABASES

This is Billy Barron's list of worldwide libraries with on-line access to their catalogs, including login instructions and a useful appendix on common library systems.
Access: **ftp ftp.unt.edu**.
Directory: *library*
File: **libraries.txt**
A sampling of Internet-accessible library catalogs:

BISON: SUNY BUFFALO ONLINE CATALOG

BISON stands for Buffalo Information System Online. The system contains information about holdings of the University Libraries of the University of Buffalo. Provides descriptions, call numbers, and availability.
Access: **telnet bison.cc.buffalo.edu**

CARL: COLORADO ALLIANCE OF RESEARCH LIBRARIES

Access to a wide variety of databases. You can search through academic and public library on-line catalogs, current article indices like UnCover and Magazine Index, the Academic American Encyclopedia, the Internet Resource Guide, and more. Gateways to other library systems as well. Access is limited for some items.
Access: **telnet pac.carl.org**

CUNYPLUS: CITY UNIVERSITY OF NEW YORK ONLINE CATALOG

An on-line catalog providing holdings of many City University of New York campus libraries. Like BISON, this is a NOTIS catalog, with a standard command set.
Access: **tn3270 128.228.1.2**
At the command line, enter **dial vtam**. From the VTAM menu, move to CUNYPLUS and press **RETURN**. Enter **lucu** to start CUNYPLUS.

ELIXIR: SUNY BINGHAMTON ONLINE CATALOG

Provides access to holdings of SUNY Binghamton. A NOTIS-based catalog with standard command structure. Access to some features is restricted to users with a valid SUNY Binghamton ID.
Access: **tn3270 bingvmb.cc.binghamton.edu**
Enter **dial vtam** at command line, and **elixir** at the vtam menu.

LIBRARY OF CONGRESS CATALOGING BY DRA

This unique service allows searching through almost four million titles in the Library of Congress database maintained by Data Research Associates, Inc. Here you'll find records from materials distributed by the Cataloging Distribution Service of the Library of Congress, including books, maps, music, serials, and visual materials. You can search by author, title, ISBN, and other fields.
Access: **telnet dra.com**

LIBS: SONOMA STATE UNIVERSITY

A wealth of on-line services are available at this address. United States library catalogs provide listings by state and information on how to use the systems. You can also access Campus Wide Information Systems across the country. Databases available through the service allow you to search for information on everything from agriculture to business and market conditions, as well as scientific topics.
Access: **telnet nessie.cc.wwu.edu**
Login: **LIBS**

MELVYL: CATALOG DIVISION OF LIBRARY AUTOMATION

This is a catalog of monographs and serials held by the nine University of California campuses and affiliated libraries. Represents nearly eleven million holdings in the university system, the California State Library, and the Center for Research Libraries. Also provides access to MEDLINE and Current Contents, and gateways to many other systems. Access to some databases is restricted.
Access: **telnet melvyl.ucop.edu**

NYPLNET: NEW YORK PUBLIC LIBRARY ONLINE CATALOG

Offers databases covering New York Public Library branch libraries catalog and metropolitan Inter-Library Cooperative System Regional Catalog, along with the library's Dance Collection Catalog.
Access: **telnet nyplgate.nypl.org**
Login: **nypl**
Password: **nypl**

OASIS: THE UNIVERSITY OF IOWA LIBRARIES

Contains over one million bibliographic records. Includes all catalogued materials in the main library and eleven departmental libraries published since 1980. Includes Law Library and government materials.
Access: **telnet oasis.uiowa.edu**.
Enter 1 at the menu for OASIS access.

OCLC: WORLD'S LARGEST BIBLIOGRAPHIC DATABASE

Provides access to over twenty-two million books and library materials on the OCLC union catalog, along with other databases, both commercial and noncommercial. Authorization and password are required to use this service.
Access: **telnet epic.prod.oclc.org**

PRINCETON UNIVERSITY ONLINE MANUSCRIPTS CATALOG

Over fifty-six thousand records, ranging from individual letters of George Washington to collections of material like the papers of publisher Charles Scribner's Sons.
Access: **telnet pucc.princeton.edu**
Login: Press **RETURN**, then enter **folio**.

PURDUE UNIVERSITY THOR

On-line database of material in the Purdue University Libraries. Contains all serials and books added to the libraries after June 1976.
Access: **tn3270 lib.cc.purdue.edu**

UNIVERSITY OF SASKATCHEWAN LIBRARIES

Offers a wide range of offerings; among others, you'll find U.S. government publications, special collections, university archives, early Canadiana, the history of photography, landmarks of science, the Canadian Education Index, and an index to the Saskatoon newspaper.
Access: **telnet sklib.usask.ca**
Username: **SONIA**

VICTORIA UNIVERSITY OF WELLINGTON LIBRARY

Offers the catalog of the university library.
Access: **telnet library.vuw.ac.nz**
At the **LOGON PLEASE:** prompt, enter **OPAC**, followed by a **RETURN**.

MAIL RESOURCES

If you're planning to use electronic mail to retrieve files, you should download the following file first:

FTP MAIL SERVERS

Among other things, this file contains a handy list of mail servers, from which you can retrieve files by mail if you lack access to FTP. Compiled by Jonathan Kamens.
Access: **ftp pit-manager.mit.edu**
Directory: *pub/usenet/news.answers*
File: **finding-sources**

The following is a potpourri of Internet services available through electronic mail.

ALMANAC

This information server answers electronic mail requests. Includes USDA market news, reports, newsletters, journals, and articles on agricultural science.

Access: Send e-mail to one of the following addresses, including the message **send guide** in the body of the letter.

```
almanac@esusda.gov
almanac@oes.orst.edu
almanac@ecn.purdue.edu
almanac@silo.ucdavis.edu
almanac@ces.ncsu.edu
```

AMATEUR RADIO RELAY LEAGUE

You will be sent information on how to retrieve information on amateur radio operations, including how to get an amateur license, examinations and requirements, the nature of RF radiation, and data on other ham radio FTP sites.
Access: e-mail to **info@arrl.org**.
Leave the Subject: field blank and enter **help** in the message field.

BIBLIOGRAPHIC MAILSERVER FOR ARTIFICIAL INTELLIGENCE LITERATURE

A service of the University of Saarbruecken, Germany, this mailserver allows users to retrieve bibliographical information about artificial intelligence publications. You can retrieve further information by sending e-mail to the following address:
Access: **mail lido@cs.uni-sb.de**
Subject: **lidosearch info english**. Leave the body of the message blank.

CANCERNET: THE NATIONAL CANCER INSTITUTE

This is a useful way to keep up with news about cancer using electronic mail. It uses the NCI's Physician Data Query system to make available updates in both English and Spanish. You can also obtain a list of patient publications available from the Office of Cancer Communications.
Access: electronic mail to **cancernet@icicb.nci.nih.gov**. Leave the subject field blank. In the body of the message, enter **help** to receive current information. This will get you a CancerNet contents list, which you can use to request specific items of information. These include PDQ State-of-the-Art Treatment Statements (For Physicians), PDQ Patient Information Statements, PDQ Supportive Care Statements, and PDQ Cancer Screening Guidelines.

COMSERVE: THE HUMAN COMMUNICATIONS FORUM

An electronic information service focusing on communications studies. Announcements are periodically distributed in issues of its electronic news bulletin. Maintains indices of articles on communications studies, along with a directory service for users.
Access: **mail comserve@vm.ecs.rpi.edu**
To obtain a description of Comserve commands, send mail with the following command in the message field: **send comserve helpfile**.

DIPLOMACY

A wide variety of Diplomacy games, including variants like Chaos (34 players), Britain (Britain starts with six armies), and Fleet_Rome (Rome begins with a fleet instead of an army), are available for playing through electronic mail. You

can learn more about the process by sending e-mail with the single statement **help** in the body of the message to one of the Diplomacy sites.
Access: **mail judge@morrolan.eff.org**
Other possibilities: **judge@gu.uwa.edu.au; judge@shrike.und.ac.za; judge@u.washington.edu.**

FAXGATE

A subscription service allowing you to send faxes by computer. You can retrieve further information by electronic mail.
Access: **mail faxgate@elvis.sovusa.com**
In body of message, enter **help**.

FTP BY MAIL

To retrieve files when you don't have FTP capability, use e-mail.
Access: **mail ftpmail@decwrl.dec.com**
Leave the subject field blank. In the body of the letter, enter **help** on the first line, **quit** on the second. This will generate a file with instructions on using the system.

GENBANK

Information on genetics available through a comprehensive database. This service is available through three addresses:
Access: **mail gene-server@bchs.uh.edu**
Other sites: **retrieve@ncbi.nlm.nih.gov** and **blast@ncbi.nlm.nih.gov**
Enter **help** in the Subject: field.

NETLIB

Mathematical and other scientific software is available through a gateway machine at Oak Ridge National Laboratory in Oak Ridge, TN.
Access: **mail netlib@ornl.gov**
Leave the subject field blank. In the body of the letter, write **send index**.

REDUCE

The symbolic algebra system REDUCE is supported by an on-line software library.
Access: **mail reduce-netlib@rand.org**
Leave subject field blank. In message, write **send index**.

SID'S MUSIC SERVER

This is a server specializing in live recordings and hard-to-find music. Send mail for more information.
Access: **mail mwilkenf@silver.ucs.indiana.edu**
In the subject field, enter **boothelp**.

STATLIB

This is a system for the distribution of statistical software by electronic mail. A wide variety of datasets and programs is available.
Access: **mail statlib@lib.stat.cmu.edu**
Leave the subject field blank. In the message, write **send index**.

TUGLIB

Software from the TeX User Group. TeX is a powerful text formatter widely used in the computer science community.
Access: **mail tuglib@science.utah.edu**
Leave subject field blank. In the message, write **send index**.

USENET ORACLE

The answer to all your questions is to be found here. By sending mail to the USENET oracle, you can quickly find out what this inscrutable being, distantly related to the oracle at Delphi, thinks about your problems.
Access: **mail oracle@cs.indiana.edu**
Enter **oracle most wise, please tell me** in the subject field. The body of the message should contain only your question. You may be asked to answer a question yourself as a way of thanking the oracle for its help.

ON-LINE JOURNALS AND NEWSLETTERS

On-line journalism is a rapidly growing field. The first stop in exploring it is to acquire the following directory:

DIRECTORY OF ELECTRONIC JOURNALS AND NEWSLETTERS

Directory containing scholarly lists and electronic newsletter titles. Compiled by Michael Strangelove.
Access: electronic mail to **LISTSERV@ACADVM1.uottawa.ca**
Leave subject field blank. In body of message, write

```
GET EJOURNL1 DIRECTRY
GET EJOURNL2 DIRECTRY
```

spelled exactly as shown.

Here are some interesting journals to begin your reading:

ALAWON

This is an on-line journal produced irregularly by the American Library Association. It is available without charge and only accessible in electronic form.
Access: **mail LISTSERV@UICVM.uic.edu**
In the message, enter **subscribe ala-wo** *yourname.*

ARACHNET ELECTRONIC JOURNAL OF VIRTUAL CULTURE

A multidisciplinary approach to virtual culture, which the journal defines as "computer-mediated human experience, behavior, thought, meaning, action or interaction..."
Access: **mail LISTSERV@KENTVM.bitnet**
In the body of the message, enter **sub arachnet** *yourname.*

CU-DIGEST

This weekly newsletter covers a broad range of computing issues, with special attention to social and ethical implications.
Access: **ftp.eff.org**
Directory: *pub/cud/cud*

CURRENT CITES

Useful citations from various journals concerned with networks and information technology.
Access: **ftp a.cni.org**
Directory: *current.cites*

DISTED: ONLINE JOURNAL OF DISTANCE EDUCATION

Distance education involves using radio, television, computers, and other techniques to reach wider geographical areas. Can involve anything from grade school classes to post-secondary education and adult education.
Access: electronic mail to **listserv@uwavm.bitnet**
Your message should contain the command **sub disted your_full_name**.

FINEART FORUM

A lively electronic journal tracking the arts.
Access: **mail fast@garnet.berkeley.edu**

INTERNET/NREN BUSINESS JOURNAL

Focusing on commercial uses and development of the network.
Access: **mail listserv@poniecki.berkeley.edu**
In the message, enter **sub ibj-1** *your name*

INTERNET WORLD

Available by subscription from Meckler Associates and edited by Daniel Dern, **Internet World** tracks network developments. It is distributed nine times per year.
Access: Obtain information by way of **meckler@tigger.jvnc.net**.

INTERPERSONAL COMPUTING AND TECHNOLOGY

Studying the nature of the electronic journal.
Access: **mail LISTSERV@GUVM.bitnet**
In the message, enter **subscribe ipct-l** *yourname*.

MATRIX NEWS

Contact **mids@tic.com** for further information about subscribing to this on-line journal, which is particularly strong at tracking network growth, and provides interesting reviews and commentary.

POSTMODERN CULTURE

Literary and cultural studies, with an emphasis on an interdisciplinary approach to contemporary literature, theory, and culture.
Access: **mail listserv@listserv.ncsu.edu**. In the message, type **sub pmc** *your name*.
Or you can use FTP for back issues. **ftp ftp.ncsu.edu**.
Directory: *pub/pmc-list*

PSYCHE

A journal discussing the nature of human consciousness, with perspectives from cognitive science, philosophy, psychology, neuroscience, artificial intelligence, and anthropology.
Access: **mail LISTSERV@nki.bitnet**
In the message, enter **subscribe psyche-l** *yourname*.

REACH: RESEARCH AND EDUCATION APPLICATIONS OF COMPUTERS IN THE HUMANITIES NEWSLETTERS

A useful information source on network tools, with news of information groups worldwide, and articles on computers and networks.

Access: **ftp ucsbuxa.ucsb.edu**

Both current issues and back numbers are available here. Change to directory *hcf*.

TELNET RESOURCES

Agriculture

ATI-NET

This is the Advanced Technology Information Network, designed to provide information about markets in California. Data on agricultural markets, international exporting and the educational community is available here. Includes biotechnology information. Individual systems provide information for the agricultural market, international exporting, and the educational community.

Access: **telnet caticsuf.csufresno.edu**

Login: **super**

CLEMSON UNIVERSITY FORESTRY AND AGRICULTURAL NETWORK

A battery of information on everything from weather to economics, from plants and engineering to home, health, and family. Also includes a section on K–12 education.

Access: **telnet eureka.clemson.edu**

Login: **PUBLIC**

PENPAGES

A database of economic materials related to agriculture, including market news and newsletters. Provided by the College of Agricultural Sciences at Pennsylvania State University. Coverage of livestock auctions, Chicago Mercantile exchange futures, and reports on a wide variety of agricultural products. You can even track news on fruit, vegetables, and flowers. Includes a database on food and nutrition. Textual materials can be searched using Boolean keyword methods.

Access: **telnet psupen.psu.edu**

Login: **PNOPTA**

Aviation

GTE CONTEL DUAT SYSTEM

Two systems, one for certified pilots, the other for nonpilots. This service gives you access to weather briefings, both locally and along the route of flight. It also includes a comprehensive flight planning system which computes a flight log. The planner can produce a route automatically, or it can be given an origin, intermediate points and destination, producing a shortest-path route. Uses the FAA database of airways, airports, and navigation aids for the continental United States.

Access: **telnet duat.gtefsd.com** (pilots only)

       telnet duats.gtefsd.com (nonpilots or pilots)

Business

IOWA ELECTRONIC MARKET

Looking to learn more about the financial markets? The Iowa Electronic Market allows you to speculate safely. You can set up a trading account and trade a variety of contracts. The Iowa Earnings Market includes portfolios based on the quarterly earnings per share of specific companies. The Iowa Economic Indicators Market works with fluctuations between the Mexican peso and the U.S. dollar. Short sales and margin purchases are not allowed.

Access: **telnet ipsm.biz.uiowa.edu**

STOCK MARKET REPORT

a2i Communications offers a free market report in its guest menu; this is a public-access UNIX provider which also gives you full sign-up information and other particulars here. The stock market news is largely set up to track the communications and computer industries.

Access: **telnet a2i.rahul.net**
Login: **guest**

Communications

IGC: INSTITUTE FOR GLOBAL COMMUNICATIONS

The on-line home for the environmental and peace movements, providing communications services and access to a variety of networked information. IGC is the Institute for Global Communications. It includes PeaceNet, EcoNet, ConflictNet, and HomeoNet. A subscription to PeaceNet provides access to EcoNet and ConflictNet. This service charges a monthly subscription fee.

Access: **telnet igc.org**
Login: **new**. At the **password** prompt, press **RETURN** to begin the registration process.

NICOL: JvNCNET NETWORK INFORMATION CENTER ON-LINE

NICOL is a user-friendly menu-driven application which makes finding Internet resources a simple matter. On this service, you can move around the menus to examine information about the Internet Society, Internet library resources, Requests for Comments, and much more.

Access: **telnet nisc.jvnc.net**
Login: **nicol**

WASHINGTON UNIVERSITY SERVICES

This broad-based site offers you a huge range of network services, from library catalogs, both foreign and domestic, to government libraries, publicly accessible databases, Campus Wide Information Systems, and more. It's a good place to become familiar with as you learn your way around the Internet, suggesting sites for future direct Telnet activity.

Access: **telnet wugate.wustl.edu**
Login: **services**

Computer Information

HEWLETT-PACKARD CALCULATOR BBS

HP uses this system to support its calculator customers. A variety of conferences are available for customers, as is a download area.
Access: **telnet hpcvbbs.cv.hp.com**
Login: **new**

HPCWIRE

This is the High Performance Computing daily news and information service, which tracks developments in the field of workstations through super-computers. This database includes daily news summaries, information on Internet developments related to supercomputing, newsletters on high performance computing topics, and forums for developers. Trade show and news of hardware developments is also available. You can also use HPCwire's Executive Wrap-Up to have stories on this topic sent to your electronic mailbox every week.
Access: **telnet hpcwire.ans.net**
Login: **hpcwire**

UNIVERSITY OF NORTH CAROLINA AT CHAPEL HILL BULLETIN BOARD SYSTEM

Electronic mail, software, access to USENET newsgroups, and library catalog searching. Of particular interest is LIBTEL, an information resource access system which allows you to search library catalogs worldwide using an intuitive user interface. The system also taps the Library of Congress catalogs maintained by Data Research Associates. Users likewise can Telnet into a variety of bulletin board systems, and use **gopher**, World Wide Web, and **HYTELNET**.
Access: **telnet bbs.oit.unc.edu**
login: **bbs**

Education

AEDNET: THE ADULT EDUCATION NETWORK

An international electronic network focusing on adult education, intended for academics as well as a lay audience. Activities include discussion groups and special events. AEDNET also produces *New Horizons in Adult Education*, an electronic journal.
Access: **mail aednet@suvm.bitnet**
Include your full name and user identification. You will receive further information about AEDNET.

AMERICAN PHILOSOPHICAL ASSOCIATION: THE ELECTRONIC AGORA

This system serves philosophers involved in the APA. Contains calendars of events, information about grants and fellowships, a directory of members, and other resources.
Access: **telnet atl.calstate.edu**
Login: **apa**

Dartmouth Dante Project

As described in Chapter 10, the Dartmouth Dante Project is particularly exciting for Renaissance scholars. It's a full-text database containing not only Dante's *Divine Comedy* but also centuries worth of commentary. This database is a showcase for what can be done in a variety of disciplines with fast search software and wide access to core materials.
Access: **telnet library.dartmouth.edu**
This will take you into the Dartmouth College Library Online System. At the prompt, enter **connect dante**.

ISAAC: Information System for Advanced Academic Computing

This system has been established to provide information for IBM computer users about software and hardware useful for research and instruction in higher education. ISAAC is free for faculty, staff, and students in higher education. You can register for use on-line.
Access: **telnet isaac.engr.washington.edu**
Login: **register**

National Education Bulletin Board System

This system is operated by the National Education Supercomputer Program. It's a collection of conferences you can access including forums on education and colleges, as well as telecommunications and other computing topics.
Access: **telnet nebbs.nersc.gov**
Login: **new**
You'll be prompted for additional information to set up a user identification and password.

Newton: Argonne National Laboratory's Division of Educational Programs

An educational BBS for use by teachers and students across the nation. Especially applicable for those working in the sciences and mathematics.
Access: **telnet newton.dep.anl.gov**
Login: **cocotext**

University of Maryland Information Service

Offers access to **gopher** and a number of Internet resources including an on-line library catalog and a campus directory.
Access: **telnet info.umd.edu**
Login: **info** to get the campus directory; **gopher** to access Internet resources.

Geography

Geographic Server

Geographic information offered by city or area code. Data comes from U.S. Geological Survey and the U.S. Postal Service. The database includes all U.S. cities, counties, and states, as well as some U.S. mountains, rivers, lakes, and

national parks. Queries should generally look like the last line of a postal address, as in "Dunn, NC 28334". This produces information including population, latitude/longitude, elevation and more.
Access: **telnet martini.eecs.umich.edu 3000**

GLOBAL LAND INFORMATION SYSTEM (GLIS)

An interactive source of information useful for earth science and global change studies. Includes geographic coverage maps and other images.
Access: **telnet glis.cr.usgs.gov**
Login: **guest**

INFO-SOUTH LATIN AMERICAN INFORMATION SYSTEM

Useful material on the social, political, and economic conditions in South America. The range of topics is wide, covering everything from banking to defense, from foreign trade to science and technology. Sources include newspapers and journals published worldwide.
Access: **telnet sabio.ir.miami.edu**

Government Information

FDA: THE FDA ELECTRONIC BULLETIN BOARD

This BBS, provided by the Food and Drug Administration, contains a large repository of information related to the agency's mission. It includes news releases, a drug and device product approvals list, current information on AIDS, an FDA consumer Magazine index and selected articles, and an index of FDA news releases. Speeches given by the FDA commissioner and deputy are also available here, as is Congressional testimony by FDA officials. An on-line manual for using the system is available.
Access: **telnet fdabbs.fda.gov**
Login: **bbs**

FEDERAL INFORMATION EXCHANGE

Contains FEDIX, an information system linking federal government agency information with colleges and universities, and MOLIS, the Minority On-line Information Service, with current information about historically black colleges and universities. A wealth of information on federal education and research programs, scholarships, fellowships and grants, as well as news.
Access: **telnet fedix.fie.com**
Login: **fedix**

Legal Information

LAWNET: COLUMBIA LAW SCHOOL PUBLIC INFORMATION SERVICE

Provides legal information and access to catalogs. You can search the law school library system called PEGASUS. Other options include the main library catalog at Columbia, as well as textual data on law firms, US courts, and other material.
Access: **telnet sparc-1.law.columbia.edu**
Login: **lawnet**

LIBERTY: WASHINGTON AND LEE UNIVERSITY UNIVERSITY COMPUTING

The LIBERTY system is a wide-ranging storehouse of data. The opening menu takes you to WAIS databases (both through a **swais** interface and a local menu), the World Wide Web, **netfind**, USENET, and more. The Directory of Scholarly Electronic Conferences maintained by Diane Kovacs is available for searching. Also, a wide variety of legal information includes a legal resource index and the Wilsonline Index to Legal Periodicals. Also available: the Business Start-Up Information Database.

Access: **telnet liberty.uc.wlu.edu**
Login: **lawlib**

Mathematics

E-MATH: THE AMERICAN MATHEMATICAL SOCIETY'S E-MATH SYSTEM FOR ELECTRONIC COMMUNICATION AND INFORMATION DELIVERY

This system provides a variety of features for the mathematical community, including directory information, professional opportunities, a database of mathematical documents, and software. e-MATH also provides **gopher** and WAIS access to Internet resources.

Access: **telnet e-math.ams.com**
Login: **e-math**
Password: **e-math**

Medicine

E.T.NET: THE NATIONAL LIBRARY OF MEDICINE

Includes discussions on technology in health sciences education, as well as conferences on digital imaging, computer assisted instruction, nursing care research, and interactive technology. Also a collection of health sciences shareware.

Access: **telnet etnet.nlm.nih.gov**
Login: **etnet**

Meteorology

NOAA EARTH SYSTEM DATA DIRECTORY

This is an information resource for identification, location, and overview descriptions of Earth Science Data Sets. Managed by the National Oceanic and Atmospheric Administration.

Access: **telnet nodc.nodc.noaa.gov**
Login: **NOAADIR**

UNIVERSITY OF MICHIGAN WEATHER UNDERGROUND

From the College of Engineering, University of Michigan, a wealth of data. U.S. forecasts and climate data, current weather observations and long range forecasts, Canadian weather, earthquake reports, and severe weather outlooks, among much else. The system is easy to use and powerful.

Access: **telnet downwind.sprl.umich.edu 3000**

Recreation

HAM RADIO CALLBOOKS

A database of ham radio call-signs established at the University of Buffalo by Devon Bowen, KA2NRC. Enter **help** for information. You can filter searches by call-sign, city, first name, last name, street address, etc.
Access: **telnet callsign.cs.buffalo.edu 2000**

MICROMUSE

Research into virtual realities. Players can connect to the computer, adopt a personality and character of their own, and enter into a cyberspace world. Everything has a few lines of textual description which is displayed when a player looks in that direction. Adventures based on Narnia books; recreation of Wizard of Oz, a Logic Quest game, and more.
Access: **telnet michael.ai.mit.edu**
login: **guest**

PROFESSIONAL SPORTS SCHEDULES

You can track the schedules of professional teams here, either for a single day or a season. Available sports and their addresses are shown below:
NBA schedules: **telnet culine.colorado.edu 859**
NHL schedules: **telnet culine.colorado.edu 860**
Baseball schedules: **telnet culine.colorado.edu 862**
NFL schedules: **telnet culine.colorado.edu 863**

TRADE WARS WORLD

A multi-player on-line game is available on this bulletin board system. You can play a "scratch" game to learn the ropes, notifying the system operator when you think you're ready to take on more experienced players.
Access: **telnet nelsons.cern.ch 2002**

Science

LUNAR AND PLANETARY INSTITUTE

The LPI is located near NASA's Johnson Space Center, and houses extensive collections of lunar and planetary data, along with an image processing facility and library. This system gives you access to a Lunar and Planetary Bibliography as well as a Mars Exploration Bulletin Board.
Access: **telnet lpi.jsc.nasa.gov**
Login: **LPI**

NASA SPACELINK: SPACE-RELATED INFORMATIONAL DATABASE

This is a database of space information provided by the Marshall Space Flight Center, Huntsville, AL. Includes NASA news, aeronautics, space exploration, NASA educational services, classroom materials, information on technology transfer and more. Provides easy access to current and historical NASA materials. Teachers and other callers can leave questions and comments for NASA.
Access: **telnet spacelink.msfc.nasa.gov** or **xsl.msfc.nasa.gov**

NNDC ONLINE DATA SERVICE

Managed by the National Nuclear Data Center at Brookhaven National Laboratory, the NNDC database contains information of interest to scientists involved in physics and related fields.
Access: **telnet bnlnd2.dne.bnl.gov**
Login: **nndc**

NSSDC'S ONLINE DATA AND INFORMATION SERVICE

A database provided by the National Space Science Data Center. Includes planetary science and Magellan Project information, along with newsletters and other on-line data sources.
Access: **telnet nssdc.gsfc.nasa.gov**
Login: **nodis**

OCEANIC: THE OCEAN INFORMATION CENTER

A database of oceanographic and marine study materials. Provides access to oceanic research materials, a directory of researchers in the field, and a schedule of research cruises.
Access: **telnet delocn.udel.edu**

SDDAS: THE DATA DISPLAY AND ANALYSIS SYSTEM OF THE DIVISION OF INSTRUMENTATION & SPACE SCIENCES AT SOUTHWEST RESEARCH INSTITUTE

A variety of space sciences and other data.
Access: **telnet espsun.space.swri.edu 540**

STIS: SCIENCE AND TECHNOLOGY INFORMATION SYSTEM

Provides a way to search through publications of the National Science Foundation and materials related to its activities. Access to NSF's press releases is one good way to keep up with events of importance to the Internet at large. You'll also find reports from the National Science Board here, along with descriptions of research projects NSF is funding. Documents can be searched on-line, and materials can be retrieved either through anonymous FTP or delivered by electronic mail.
Access: **telnet stis.nsf.gov**
Login: **public**

Sociology

LOUIS HARRIS DATA CENTER: THE INSTITUTE FOR RESEARCH IN SOCIAL SCIENCE

A database containing data from the Harris Organization, along with other polling information. Over 750 Harris polls are located here, providing insights into American society. Users can search the text of all Harris Survey questions back to roughly 1960 looking for particular topics.
Access: **tn3270 uncvm1.oit.unc.edu**
Log in: **irss1** or **irss2**
Password: **irss**

SSDA: Aleph/Hebrew University Social Science Data Archive Catalog

A useful compendium of information from Israel, available for searching. Find information on financial conditions, government and political issues, and a wide variety of sociological data, from housing to household behavior, and immigration and absorption patterns.
Access: **telnet har1.huji.ac.il**

Software

ZIB Electronic Library

A library of software organized into libraries, with access to other software caches.
Access: **telnet elib.zib-berlin.de**
Login: **elib**

USENET

Alternative Newsgroup Hierarchies

Descriptions of alternative newsgroup hierarchies, from *alt* and *bionet* to *clarinet* and *gnu*. Posted on USENET newsgroups **news.lists**, **news.groups**, **news.announce.newusers**. Also available as follows:
Access: **ftp pit-manager.mit.edu**
Directory: *pub/usenet/news.announce.newusers*
File: **Alternative_Newsgroup_Hierarchies**

List of Active Newsgroups

A key directory of newsgroups maintained by David Lawrence and Mark Moraes; includes short descriptions of each group. Posted to USENET newsgroups **news.lists**, **news.groups**, **news.announce.newusers**.
Access: **ftp pit-manager.mit.edu**
Directory: *pub/usenet/news.announce.newusers*
File: **List_of_Active_Newsgroups**

List of Periodic Informational Postings

This is a compilation of Frequently Asked Questions for the USENET newsgroups; it's maintained by Jonathan I. Kamens. The list reflects postings available at the ftp site.
Access: **ftp pit-manager.mit.edu**
Directory: *pub/usenet/news.answers/periodic-postings*
Files: **part1**, **part2**, **part3**, **part4**, **part5**

Regional Newsgroup Hierarchies

Newsgroups that are restricted to local geographical areas. Posted to USENET newsgroups **news.lists**, **news.groups**, **news.announce.newusers**.
Access: **ftp pit-manager.mit.edu**
Directory: *pub/usenet/news.announce.newusers*
File: **Regional_Newsgroup_Hierarchies**

WAIS Databases

The list of WAIS databases here is merely suggestive of the growing WAIS presence on the Internet. I've attempted to give you an idea of the range of material available.

Astronomy

astro-images-gif.src
Sources of astronomical images in GIF format.

Biology

biology-journal-contents.src
Periodical references to journals on molecular biology.
bionic-databases-limb.src
A list of databases available to molecular biologists.

Business

agricultural-market-news.src
Agricultural commodity market reports from the U.S. Department of Agriculture.
usda-rrdb.src
U.S. Dept. of Agriculture economic research.

Computer Hardware

alt.sys.sun.src
Archived news articles from **alt.sys.sun** newsgroup.
archie.au-mac-readmes.src
Index of files for the Macintosh archive on **archie.au.**
archie.au-pc-readmes.src
Index of files for the Amiga archives on **archie.au.**
ibm.pc.FAQ.src
Information about IBM PC systems.
info-mac.src
An archive of the **info.mac** discussion forum.
NeXT.FAQ.src
Information about NeXT computer systems.

Computer Science

cacm.src
Communications of the ACM.
comp.archives.src
An index of articles on software posted to **comp.archives.**
nren-bill.src
The High Performance Computing Act of 1991.
risks-digest.src
Collection of the RISKS digest which discusses the risks involved with using computers.

Education

bit.listserv.cwis-l.src
An archive of Campus Wide Information Systems.
ERIC-archive.src
Material from the Educational Resources Information Centre.
kidsnet.src
An archive on computer networking for children and their teachers.

gopher

alt.gopher.src
Archive of the **alt.gopher** newsgroup.

Humanities

bryn-mawr-classical-review.src
Reviews of books on Latin and Greek classical literature.
humanist.src
Archive of the humanist discussion list maintained at Brown University.
journalism.periodicals.src
The Journalism Periodicals Index.
poetry.src
Complete poems of Shakespeare and Yeats.
proj-gutenberg.src
Documents produced by Project Gutenberg.
roget-thesaurus.src
Roget's Thesaurus, provided by Project Gutenberg.
sf-reviews.src
Science fiction reviews.

Law

eff-documents.src
Documents from the Electronic Frontier Foundation.
supreme-court.src
U.S. Supreme Court decisions.

Libraries

current.cites.src
Index of journals on electronic publishing, optical disk technologies, computer networking, and information transfer.
hytelnet.src
Information sources accessible by TELNET.
online-libraries-st-george.src
The St. George's directory of libraries and CWIS's.

Meteorology

weather.src
Weather information, including surface analysis weather system maps.

Music

lyrics.src
The lyrics for a selection of contemporary music.

Networks

aarnet-resource-guide.src
A copy of the AARNet Resource Guide.
comp.dcom.fax.src
Archive of **comp.dcom.fax** newsgroup.
com-priv.src
Discussions about issues related to the commercialization and privatization of the Internet.
file-archive-uunet.src
Directory listing of the archive on **uunet.uu.net**.
internet_info.src
Texts, guides, and information on Internet use and etiquette.
internet-resource guide.src
Guide to using the Internet.
internet-rfcs.src
Internet Request for Comments documents.
lists.src
Several master lists of newsgroups, mailing lists, electronic serials and journals.
matrix_news.src
Material from **Matrix News**, a network newsletter.
netinfo-docs.src
Files on accessing the Internet and its resources.
rfc-index.src
An index of the list of Internet RFCs.
uunet.src
UUNET directory listing of FAQs from all newsgroups.

Politics

world-factbook.src
The 1990 World Factbook produced by the CIA, with information on countries and cities.

Religion

bible.src
King James version of the Bible.
Quran.src
The Koran.

Software

comp.binaries.src
An archive for the **comp.binaries** newsgroup.
jargon.src
Collection of computer terms.
unix.FAQ.src
Information about UNIX.
unix-manual.src
Manual pages for UNIX.
wuarchive.src
The directory listing of the software archive at
wuarchive.wustl.edu.

WAIS

alt.wais.src
Articles from the **alt.wais** newsgroup.
directory-of-servers.src
Directory of servers at **quake.think.com.**
unc-directory-of-servers.src
University of North Carolina directory of WAIS servers.
wais-discussion-archives.src
An electronic discussion forum about WAIS.
wais-talk-archives.src
Informal discussions about WAIS.

WHITE PAGES DIRECTORIES

White Pages are directories of users. They usually contain information on e-mail address and telephone numbers, as well as postal addresses, and can be searched.

WHOIS SERVERS

Listing WHOIS servers on the Internet; compiled by Matt Power. Appears on USENET newsgroup **info.nets**.
Access: **ftp sipb.mit.edu**
Directory: *pub/whois*
File: **whois-servers.list**

The following are the basic White Pages options.

INTERNIC DIRECTORY AND DATABASE SERVICES

Directory services using X.500 technology provided through a variety of interfaces by AT&T.
Access: **mail mailserv@ds.internic.net**
In body of message, enter command **help**. This will generate a list of mail server commands. Or, **telnet ds.internic.net**. This will take you to the INTERNIC Directory and Database Services Telnet Interface Main Menu. You will be prompted from there to conduct a search for persons or institutions.

KNOWBOT INFORMATION SERVICE

A single query here can search through a variety of sources including the INTERNIC database and MCI Mail.
Access: **whois -h nri.reston.va.us**
Or Telnet to **nri.reston.va.us 185**

NASA AMES RESEARCH CENTER ELECTRONIC PHONE BOOK

This is an electronic directory of NASA employees, searchable by using **WHOIS**.
Access: **whois -h x500.arc.nasa.gov** *name*

NETFIND

Allows you to search for people by name and domain.
Access: **telnet** to **bruno.cs.colorado.edu** (log on as **netfind**)
Or go to one of the following sites:
archie.au (AARNet, Melbourne, Australia)
bruno.cs.colorado.edu (University of Colorado, Boulder)
dino.conicit.ve (NCT & Scien. Research, Venezuela)
lincoln.technet.sg (Technet Unit, Singapore)
malloco.ing.puc.cl (Catholic University of Chile, Santiago)
monolith.cc.ic.ac.uk (Imperial College, London, England)
mudhoney.micro.umn.edu (University of Minnesota, Minneapolis)
netfind.oc.com (OpenConnect Systems, Dallas, Texas)
nic.uakom.sk (Slovak Academy of Sciences, Republic of Slovakia)
redmont.cis.uab.edu (University of Alabama at Birmingham)

NYSERNET/PSI ONLINE X.500 DIRECTORY

A useful on-line directory of personnel covering some 88 organizations in the United States. Includes name, electronic mail address, postal address, telephone number, and job title. Supports the OSI X.500 directory standard.
Access: **telnet wp.psi.com**
Login: **fred**

PARADISE—THE COSINE DIRECTORY SERVICE

An experimental X.500 service in the United Kingdom providing information about people and organizations.
Access: **telnet paradise.ulcc.ac.uk**
Login: **de**

WHOIS

A large number of sites now run WHOIS servers, providing database services about people and associated information.
Access: **whois -h** *site person,* where **site** is the server site, and **person** is the name of the person you're searching for. You can use **WHOIS** to access the INTERNIC with the **whois -h rs.internic.net** command. To search for a MILNET address, use **whois -h nic.ddn.mil**.

The Future of the Internet

Anyone who has lived through the incredibly short evolution of the personal computer knows how hazardous it is to predict the future. Nonetheless, certain trends seem certain to gather momentum as the Internet continues to grow. Experiments in audio and the transmission of video images, including live broadcasts from Internet Engineering Task Force meetings received worldwide over the so-called multicast backbone (MBONE), point to a bright future for multimedia messaging and the delivery of a new category of product over a medium once isolated to text. The appearance of Internet Talk Radio in March 1993 only confirms this movement, as listeners worldwide gained access to a half-hour show on the Internet delivered via binary data.

We're also moving toward something called the National Research and Education Network, an overlay on the existing Internet that has the promise of vastly increasing bandwidth and promoting a host of services into the home. Precisely what shape the NREN will take isn't clear, and is the subject of continuing controversy. But in some fashion, wider access to computer networks, along with the benefits of digital audio and video, will change the way business and home users gain information, with inescapable consequences for our libraries, our schools, and our government.

Access is the issue—who gets to take advantage of these wondrous new capabilities? Part of that question is already being answered, in the form of the surge in dial-up users of the Internet. A few years ago, getting Internet access meant working for an organization whose network was already connected. That usually meant a school, or a research laboratory, or a government organization, and it always meant one network tying into a larger network, which is, after all, where the name "Internet" comes from.

Today, we're moving into the era of the individual user. As we've seen, getting an individual account on the Internet is easier than it's ever been, because a new class of service provider has moved onto the market. This is a trend that's sure to accelerate, and as it does, the Internet will begin to open up. Network visionaries sometimes speak of Internet connections becoming as common as telephone jacks; buy a new home and your Internet hookup is already wired in. This seems fanciful at present, but the enfranchisement of the individual user is a step in that direction, and powerful demand may well validate the concept over the course of the coming decade.

COMMERCE TAKES TO THE DATA PACKETS

All of which represents quite a change for the Internet. It wasn't that long ago that Internet access belonged to faculty members at universities, research scientists, and similarly restricted population groups. That image, of a sober, almost staid network buzzing with arcane discussions limited to a highly select audience, is gradually changing. How else to explain the cartoon character Dilbert, who appeared being "sucked into cyberspace" in one of the newspaper strip's more colorful episodes. At the end of the cartoon, readers found a message from the artist: "Internet ID: scottadams@aol.com." The message elicited an appreciative ripple on the network, as denizens of several different mailing lists commented on the widening popularity of their favorite medium.

Nor is the new attention on the Internet limited to artists. One day in February 1993, the *Palo Alto Weekly* carried a full-page advertisement for the Alain Pinel Realty Company of Saratoga, CA. The ad featured photographs of each of the 35 realtors who work for the agency. Under each picture was an Internet address. The notion that you might be able to bring the Internet into your discussions with the local realtor startled some, but ponder this: the great bulk of the Internet consists of local area networks, or LANs, inside larger companies. And while some parts of the Internet do exclude commercial activities, others do not. Anyone hoping to move commercial traffic over the Internet has the option of using a provider that places no restrictions on the type of content carried.

Thus the explosion in commercial use. In fact, while fifty percent of connected hosts are governmental or academic in nature, fully nine out of ten new connections go to commercial sites.[1] Want to order a book on-line? You can do so on the Internet, through the Online Book Store at Software Tool & Die. Want to cut publishing costs and make life easier on editors? Addison-Wesley already uses the Internet to receive book proposals and perform basic copy editing chores. So does Oxford University Press, just down the road from me in Cary, NC. A number of large corporations, including General Motors and General Electric Co., are using the Internet to aid in corporate research, not to mention benefiting from electronic mail communications. Apple Computer has even made its System 7 operating system available by anonymous FTP from **apple.com**.[2]

"By June of 1991," says Internet Society president Vinton Cerf, a key figure in the development of the original TCP/IP protocols, "50 percent of all registered hosts on the system were commercial. That's an important metric; commercial use is the Internet's fastest growing component."[3] *Infoworld* estimates that some five-hundred thousand new commercial users now prowl the network.[4]

THE INTERNET AND THE FUTURE OF THE NEWSPAPER

The number of personal computers in the homes and offices of America continues to swell, even as the number of newspaper subscribers dwindles. Somewhere in there, given the continuing need for in-depth news, is an opportunity, and ClariNet Communications Corp. of Cupertino, CA, has seized it. Its ClariNet is a commercial news service which draws on United Press International and a host of other sources including Newsbytes, a computer press service, to present the news in electronic form on the Internet.

A network that wants to distribute ClariNet News signs a contract with the company, which allows it to carry a series of newsgroups on USENET with the prefix *clari*. By subscribing to particular groups of interest, the network user can create a customized news service, targeting precisely what the user is interested in and ignoring the rest. The news stories then appear as individual items in the groups subscribed to. More information on ClariNet can be obtained by sending e-mail to **info@clarinet.com**.

Included in the newsgroups are headlines, business, and financial coverage, and syndicated columns from the likes of Mike Royko and Dave Barry. Clari-News is the basic electronic newspaper from United Press International, distributed in one hundred newsgroups based on subject matter. There are also special groups like TechWire, with stories on science and technology; ClariNews-Biz, with stock market reports, economic indicators and corporate news; the aforementioned Newsbytes, and a variety of local options.

Another provider, the Msen Reuters News Service in Ann Arbor, MI, has begun offering its clients access to the Reuters News Wire and Business News Wire, likewise delivered directly to computers and workstations. Reuters news, broken into areas such as financial, international, and other categories including the Reuters Business Diary, is moved in the form of USENET newsgroups, much like ClariNet.

HPCwire, a service of Select News in San Diego, CA, is another interesting entry in this field, offering news stories of interest to the high performance computing community. The mechanism here is delivery through electronic mail. Subscribers contact the service (**sub@hpcwire.ans.net**) to receive regular mailings which list the articles available in that issue. They can then choose what they want to read and respond with an electronic mail message requesting those specific articles.

Services like ClariNet and Msen Reuters News Service are provided on a subscription basis; your service provider may or may not have them. But the potential of the Internet as an information delivery tool for news services is clear; delivery services bring a more structured format to the chaos of USENET, and offer a unique way of filtering the news for people whose time is short (and whose isn't?). We're probably going to see an explosion in the delivery of such materials, spreading outward from the highly focused academic newsletters and journals now commonly available to services with an emphasis on high readership potential.

MAKING MAIL COME ALIVE

Electronic mail on the Internet must follow certain format requirements, as outlined in RFC 822. The basic prerequisite is for the message header and body to consist only of 7-bit ASCII characters, which is why, when we want to send a program or a graphics file by e-mail, we have to encode and decode it, moving to and from basic ASCII. As we saw in Chapter 8, a program thus encoded can be examined in this ASCII format, though it will seem to be no more than a string of meaningless characters. The **uudecode** program is then applied to pop this ASCII alphabet soup back into the format we were expecting—a working program.

In keeping with the idea that sound and video are going to become increasingly important on the Internet, it's no surprise to find a new standard developing for attaching such enclosures within e-mail messages. The standard is called MIME—it stands for **M**ulti-purpose **I**nternet **M**ail **E**xtensions, and it allows for the creation of multimedia mail incorporating sound and video. RFC 1341, "MIME: Mechanisms for Specifying and Describing the Format of Internet Message Bodies," by N. Borenstein and N. Freed, presents the specifications which make this possible.[5]

The idea behind MIME is that the sound and/or video materials attached to a given message are not actually sent until the recipient asks for them. The message, then, is a file that locates the appropriate binary materials for transmission as it needs them.

Dial-up users, unfortunately, can't enjoy the fruits of this emerging technology. Not yet, anyway. However, the MIME specification is flexible enough to present the message contents as a plain message (with notation of materials which could not be displayed), so you would at least know you were in the presence of MIME. A SLIP or other full network connection would allow you to proceed with the nontextual materials in such a message if you were using a MIME-compliant mail reader. You would be prompted on whether you wished to continue with FTP file retrieval of the audio or video materials.

INTERNET TALK RADIO

If a "message" can contain nested audio and video submaterials, we are beginning to redefine what we mean by the term. A similar refocusing is changing our understanding of the term "publication." Traditionally, of course, publishing meant using a printing press to produce what we computer types call hard copy. Electronic publishing changed the rules by making journals and other textual information available on demand through computer networking.

Now MIME and an exciting technology known as *multicasting* are bringing the potential for sight and sound to the average workstation. It was inevitable, then, that a consumer-oriented medium would develop, utilizing audio over the network; it stretches our definition of the term "radio." Internet Talk Radio is that service, an information provider in radio magazine format, sort of an "All Things Considered" for Internet consumption.

The brain child of author and Internet world traveler Carl Malamud,[6] Internet Talk Radio is distributed on the network itself as a massive audio file—roughly 15 MB total—professionally produced and transported worldwide on the network. The talk is technical, though Malamud aims to work on topics you won't find in the standard trade press. This is an insider's view of the Internet, including such features as "Geek of the Week," in which prominent network figures are interviewed. Although saved in a Sun Microsystems audio format, the show can be translated by utility programs for playback on a Macintosh or a PC.

What else might you find on Internet Talk Radio? Malamud speaks of travel information and restaurant reviews as one possibility, with additional features on mailing lists and books, as well as coverage of key industry functions. Internet Talk Radio could develop into a useful and diverting information forum if its current plans to summarize technical topics go through. Beyond that, ITR offers the promise of a new medium, one that borrows the best of its chosen metaphor—radio—and brings to it the flexibility of computer processing and distribution. As the first attempt to bring regular organized news and information by means of audio into the computer information flow, Malamud's new effort will be something to track carefully.

More information on audio formats is available through anonymous FTP. The following file can help:

What You Need: Background Information on Audio File Formats

The Document: **FAQ: Audio File Formats**.

Where to Get It: Through anonymous ftp at **ftp.cwi.nl**. The directory is */pub*. The file is **AudioFormats2.10**.

Unfortunately, the size of the Internet Talk Radio files makes them impractical for dial-up users; one show would exceed most people's storage allotment. But the operative principle, that the Internet can carry sound as readily as text, is demonstrated by the project. The key issue is size, which raises a question unlikely to be resolved any time soon—is the movement of massive audio files over the network a brainstorm or simply a colossal waste of bandwidth, considering that a text file of the half-hour show's proceedings could convey the same information in a package that seems, by comparison, minute? If you're intrigued by such issues, you may want to listen in to the discussion on **alt.internet.talk-radio**, a USENET newsgroup which has sprung up around the new offering.

IP MULTICASTING—THE INTERNET BY SIGHT AND SOUND

Attendees at the Internet Engineering Task Force's meeting in Boston in July 1992 weren't the only ones who could follow the proceedings. Ninety-five workstations in ten countries, from Australia to Canada to Japan, the United Kingdom, and the United States, received live audio from the site, using built-in audio hardware and special software; an additional seventy-five workstations received slow-frame-rate video, which was displayed after decompression at each machine. IETF's November 1992 meeting in Washington, DC, saw a similar demonstration of the Internet's ability to move real-time audio and video to a geographically dispersed audience.[7]

While it may raise eyebrows at first, the idea of transporting such signals over a network makes sense. If you can digitize a message or a still image, you can also digitize a voice or a video clip of someone delivering a speech. And while the participants in these IETF experiments share a common enthusiasm, they also agree a significant number of resource management issues must be addressed before real-time Internet audio and video will become commonplace.

Not all routers carrying Internet traffic, for example, can support audio and video multicasting, making it necessary for Steve Casner and Steve Deering—the Internet's audio/video team—to construct what Casner called "a virtual multicast network of tunnels layered on top of the physical backbone and regional networks."[8] Multicasting, then, has given rise to a new backbone—the MBONE, for **M**ulticast **B**ackb**one**—which will serve as a testbed for continued audio and video experimentation.

Because of the high bandwidth demands of these projects, the MBONE functions almost like an old-fashioned telephone tree.[9] Multicast technology configures network routers so they know about the special communications channels for this traffic. When someone on that communications channel sends a packet to a multicast address, the routers that are part of the multicast "tree" copy the packets to the appropriate routers further down the tree, or to the ultimate hosts as the case may be. Traffic is delivered only as necessary.

Why the term "multicast?" A *broadcast* is sent out to everyone; a *unicast* goes from one point to another. A multicast, by logical extension, is the movement of information from point to multipoint, traveling only to specified destinations on the Internet. Video thus far is slow, some two to six frames per second. "It's a bit like watching a movie from 1910," comments Vinton Cerf. "But that's partly a function of available bandwidth. There's a lot of compression going to get this to work."[10]

What's ahead for the Internet as the multicast idea begins to solidify? One obvious development, according to Cerf, is the likelihood of services charging depending on the type and quantity of their traffic. It's one thing to route text data in ASCII files across the Internet. But what happens when particular sites need to consume vastly higher amounts of bandwidth as part of their activities? Distinctions between the kind of data moved and the cost of moving it are bound to become sharper in coming years.

Right now you need a sophisticated workstation to receive these transmissions—Casner and company have been working with Sun SPARCstations and Silicon Graphics Indigo machines, and it's clear that these cutting edge technologies will remain experimental for some time to come. But if you're intrigued by the possibility of audio and video over a networked computer, you may want to read the technical details in a document Steve Casner has developed. It's available by anonymous FTP.

....

What You Need: The Technical Details on Multicasting

The Document: **Frequently Asked Questions on the Multicast Backbone (MBONE)**

How to Get It: via anonymous FTP from **gum.isi.edu.** The directory is *share/mbone*. The file is **faq.txt**.

....

THE EVOLUTION OF THE NREN

As new technologies enter adolescence and commercial activity increases, the Internet faces a bevy of issues. The complicated relationship between NSFNET and ANS is pivotal to understanding what will happen. One strong possibility, according to Bill Washburn, executive director of the Commercial Internet Exchange Association, is that subsidies to ANS will eventually be eliminated as NSF moves out of the position of funding the backbone.[11] Will NSF provide money to different regional networks so that they can choose their own best route onto the Internet?

No matter what the answer, changes in subsidies for university networks would place the burden upon the regional networks and the universities linked to them to find ways to pay for their own operations, distributing the costs as broadly as possible. NSF, meanwhile, would likely put its money into a substantially reduced backbone network that would be used to connect supercomputer sites nationwide.

What of ANS itself, with its corporate involvement from IBM and MCI? Is the future of the Internet inevitably tied to corporation-funded research, producing high-speed testbeds for new technology and, in the process, improving the corporations' competitive position? If so, how is a balance to be struck between business interests and the public welfare? These issues continue to be debated as the National Information Infrastructure, of which the NREN is to be only a part, takes shape in the minds of its proponents.

Raising the Speed Limit on the Data Highway

The vision the NREN encompasses is one of power and utility. Actively supported by Vice-President Al Gore, this network is to be a high-speed data communications medium linking not just universities, research centers, and government agencies, but secondary and even elementary schools to information resources. Gore, then a senator, was instrumental in lobbying for the fiber-optic links that would become the NSFNET backbone in the 1980s. It was in November 1987 that the Federal Coordinating Committee for Science Engineering and Technology proposed the NREN in a report to Congress. The idea seemed simple: we already had a collection of computer networks, mostly academic and research-oriented, that moved data across a backbone of connections at some fifty-six thousand bits per second. The NREN proposal was to increase that speed up to as much as a billion bits per second by the mid 1990s. Once built, the network would be commercialized, allowing the federal government to turn over operations to private companies.

This would be a fast network indeed. One billion bits per second, or one gigabit, is a speed which would allow you to send three-hundred copies of *Moby Dick* over the network every second. No wonder the NREN's most fervent backers, including the Vice-President, see the visionary network as a national data highway, and liken it to the interstate highway system in terms of its effect upon economic growth for all regions of the country. It was Senator Gore who was responsible for getting the idea through Congress in the form of the High-Performance Computing and Communications Act of 1991, which provided 2.9 billion dollars over five years toward the NREN. The High Performance Computing and High Speed Networking Applications Act of 1993, sponsored by Rep. Richard Boucher (D. W.Va), expands the Gore bill to include access to health-care facilities and schools at all levels.

Why an NREN? Gore sees it as vital to maintaining our technological superiority in a world where competition in high-tech can only grow stronger.

And while a large number of academic and research organizations around the country are presently connected to the Internet, there are still gaps. Although major universities invariably have access, an Internet account is a luxury for students and faculty at many smaller colleges, and generally out of the question for high-school and grade-school teachers and students. An information super-highway is all about access, about bringing these resources to the researchers and educators who need them. The NREN would attempt to connect all academic and research organizations as well as all government agencies. In that sense, the NREN is seen as the logical development of the present-day NSFNET and indeed, NSFNET is now officially known as the Interim NREN, the base upon which tomorrow's network will be built.

A Vision of a New Network

The NREN concept revolves around a series of computer capabilities, augmented by connections to powerful hardware resources like supercomputers. These features, all of them available in some form today, could be enhanced and distributed throughout society, reaching from laboratories and universities to two- and four- year colleges. They include electronic mail, high resolution graphics, full-motion video, and sound. They include computer libraries which could be tapped to provide information on almost any subject. "By the end of the decade," writes Gordon Cook, "the NREN may become, on a national level, the most powerful tool ever created for finding, manipulating and disseminating information."[12] Cook edits the **COOK Report on Internet —> NREN**, a regular newsletter on network development, and he is deeply concerned about how decisions made today will affect the future course of the project.

What could you do with such a network? As opposed to the exchange of electronic mail, the NREN offers the possibility of *interactive* audio and video. Imagine researchers separated by geography using their computer screens to work on intricate specifications in real-time, making dynamic changes to plans and working out new strategies based on visual data at each workstation. Such a network would also handle video telephone connections, so that each researcher could talk to his opposite number on-screen, and see that person responding (whether this is a genuine advantage or not is a matter for speculation).

Not just drawings could be examined in this way, of course, but also medical imagery including patient records and X-rays, which could be analyzed by specialists no matter what their physical location. Now extend the idea into the realms of art, of literature, of entertainment. If video and voice can flow over the network, so can music, or plays, or poetry readings. Pipe such traffic into the home through fiber-optic links and you complete a transition, taking the Internet from a specialist's tool to the primary communications medium for a computerized society.

Powerful support has arisen in the networking community for applications like these. Putting NREN capabilities into primary and secondary schools could bring a wealth of library tools to students; corporations could readily tap available databases. The grandest vision incorporates a truly national network which would include community access at all levels of society. Indeed, the enthusiastic response to the NREN concept in the library and K–12 education communities bodes well for the development of multimedia and remote learning, using network tools that will take advantage of the NREN's broad bandwidth. Such tools might include knowledge robots—knowbots, which would be sent through the network to obtain specific information for their users, as well as electronic directories with the addresses of users and services, along with user interfaces that don't restrict access to the technologically sophisticated.

It's a staggering vision—students routinely logging on to the Library of Congress, laboratory researchers exchanging high-resolution imagery in pursuit of medical breakthroughs—but there remain serious questions about how such a network is to be organized. We've seen that the present-day Internet, despite its explosive growth in recent months, remains difficult to use and, for a broad spectrum of non-networked individual users, challenging to access. Tapping it requires relatively arcane knowledge of commands and procedures which most network operations centers are unable to explain to the novice. Documentation is both sparse and technically intimidating, which is why books like these are necessary. The ever-changing dynamics of network tools ensures there will be no early end to such needs.

A Question of Access

The inevitable question, then, is who will use the NREN? Raising the Internet's speed limit into the gigabit range is unquestionably important, but prudent policy also dictates we address some of the network's shortcomings, or the NREN will emerge as the tool of a technological elite, effectively off-limits save for those savvy enough to capitalize on it. What we need, say some observers, more than network speed, is attention to user interface issues. Why build a network if the majority of potential users can't figure out how to use it? Why build it, for that matter, if access is in the hands of an entrenched elite whose self-interest dictates restricting it to like-minded specialists?

Tom Grundner, director of the National Public Telecomputing Network in Cleveland, recalls reading a string of messages about the NREN from academics worried about the general public gaining access, one of which concluded, "Why should we let them use it at all?" It's not an attitude Grundner finds amusing. "Academic computing centers are designed to provide services to the people who work there and 35 of their buddies," Grundner said. "They don't care if anybody else on campus ever has access to this stuff, much less whether the public at large does. The worst nightmare of the academic computing people would be to have the Internet opened up to anyone who wanted to have access to it."[13] All of which raises the ire of this electronic populist—Grundner notes that it's usually public tax dollars that make academic computing centers possible.

As for the NREN in its current state of development, Grundner opposes it, saying it lacks a coherent vision for the development of community computer systems. Instead, his energies are applied to the development of Free-Nets, those computer networks, examined in Chapter 3, which link the public to Internet resources while offering abundant community information and a user-friendly interface. Grundner is trying to put networking within reach of anyone with a modem. It will do us little good, he thinks, to train students to use a network if, as soon as they graduate, their access to its resources is cut off.

For his part, Gordon Cook continues to be a provocative gadfly, holding NREN planners' feet to the fire to explain their actions. In an incisive study called "The National Research and Education Network: Whom Shall It Serve?", Cook argues that the NREN project has suffered from a lack of direction and focus. While the High Performance Computing and Communications legislation called for the network to be privatized after five years, the National Science Foundation's ongoing improvements to the network backbone have already brought private corporations into play, well ahead of the intent expressed in the legislation.

Who's Going to Build It?

An equally critical consideration is, who is going to build the data superhighway? Is the NREN to be, like the interstate highway system, a structure built by the government but otherwise unregulated? Or is it to follow the model of the national power grid, and be a privately constructed network submitting to federal and state regulation so that affordable access is guaranteed? Already the two camps are taking the field, with Vice-President Gore arguing that the private sector may not be willing to take on such a risky investment, and that if it did, the danger of the NREN's becoming restricted in its access is too great. Gore argues for a government-constructed public network regulated and managed for all Americans to use.

Building the NREN is no small undertaking. Moving data networks like this one into the home requires replacing the copper telephone wires which currently feed most homes with high-capacity fiber-optic cables. While most long-distance lines have already undergone such conversion, the so-called "local loop" between the home and the local telephone switch remains largely copper-based, and thus of insufficient bandwidth to carry the huge dataflow proposed by the NREN. Telephone equipment at both the long-distance and local levels would need upgrading as well to handle the required bandwidth and stand up to the anticipated traffic flow. Critical to the discussion is the meeting ground between private investment and universal access, a murky terrain whose cartography is under active investigation.

While some computer companies look forward to the possibility of increased equipment sales because of the NREN, other firms are concerned about the federal government's role in developing the network. AT&T is but one company uneasy about the potential of the government's creating a network which would operate in competition with the established telecommunications carriers. And at the Electronic Frontier Foundation, Lotus Development Corporation founder Mitchell D. Kapor thinks the whole enterprise offers too grandiose a vision. Kapor insists that Integrated Services Digital Network (ISDN) technology, capable of being carried over standard copper wires, offers the best hope of making many of these services available to the widest possible audience. The ISDN choice would also offer significant cost savings over the full NREN proposal.

Whatever the merits of ISDN, the Electronic Frontier Foundation (EFF) is an organization worth your attention. Founded in 1990, EFF advocates freedom of expression in digital media and the application of constitutional principles to computer communications. While the EFF is perhaps best known for its role in the successful lawsuit of software game publisher Steve Jackson against the U.S. Secret Service, the organization is also active in shaping debate over such issues as the emerging National Research and Education Network, privacy in computer communications, and the emergence of on-line "virtual" communities.

To learn more about the EFF, contact:

Electronic Frontier Foundation
1001 G Street NW, Suite 950 East
Washington, DC 20001
Voice: 202-347-5400
Fax: 202-393-5509
E-mail: **eff@eff.org**

A Truly Global Network

We think of the Internet as a global network, and indeed it is; we can send and retrieve messages and files from just about anywhere with a network connection. But that's just the point. Is the Internet destined to be a tool of the economically advantaged, or will nations in the developing world gradually take their place among the network's citizenry?

No one can drive a network into an environment where computers are nonexistent, but it's clear from recent Internet meetings that drawing attention to the network's advantages can have a quickening effect on the state of the art wherever such meetings are held. Vinton Cerf points out that holding a meeting of the Internet Society in San Francisco offers few technological challenges, but that hosting one in Prague, where the 1994 meeting is scheduled, will make demands upon the infrastructure of a recovering nation. "Our hope," says Cerf, "is that as we hold meetings like this, there will be some leave-behind effect, that investment will persist beyond the period of the meeting."

The Internet Society also sponsors a committee on technology in developing countries, part of whose objective is to supply educational materials to researchers and engineers in key locations worldwide. An annual workshop provides training in the installation and use of the network to participants from countries with scant Internet deployment. Clearly, the development of the Internet Society itself is a symptom of the network's coming of age, as it moves from the necessary management of engineering issues to the broader implications of technological change.

The goal of an emerging global network must be access to those places where information is least available. Just as no NREN vision without comprehensive access is compelling, no global communications strategy without an aggressive campaign of technological enfranchisement makes sense. We've seen how much we can do with a desktop personal computer and a dial-up connection to the Internet. Imagine these benefits translated to countries where libraries are scarce, books rare, researchers and scientists disconnected from the work of their peers. The Internet's future is bright, but no one committed to the social benefits of computer networking will deny there's plenty of work to be done.

Chapter Sixteen Notes

1. Ubois, Jeff. "What is Acceptable Internet Use?" *MacWEEK*, Vol. 6, No. 34, September 28, 1992, 30.
2. A fine, current discussion of commercial uses of the Internet is provided in John Quarterman's "What Can Businesses Get Out of the Internet?" *ComputerWorld*. February 22, 1993, 81–83.
3. Telephone conversation with Vinton Cerf April 23, 1993.

   4. Gerber, Cheryl. "Booming Commercial Use Changes Face of Internet." *Infoworld,* April 12, 1993, 1.
   5. The best discussion of MIME that I've run across is in Rose, Marshall T., *The Internet Message: Closing the Book with Electronic Mail.* Englewood Cliffs, NJ: PTR Prentice Hall, 1993, 207–227.
   6. Malamud's *Exploring the Internet* is one of the most curious, and hugely enjoyable, books ever written about the Internet. Malamud physically travels to Internet sites worldwide, along the way talking to major network figures and sampling restaurants from every cuisine imaginable.
   7. Ron Frederick's "IETF Audio & Videocast." *Internet Society News* Vol. 1, No. 4, 19 tells this story.
   8. Casner, Steve. "Second IETF Internet Audiocast." *Internet Society News* Vol. 1, No. 3, 23.
   9. This comparison, and much of the material in this paragraph, derive from a telephone interview with Internet Society president Vinton Cerf, April 22 and 23, 1993.
  10. Telephone interview April 22, 1993.
  11. Interview with Bill Washburn 8 March 1993.
  12. From Gordon Cook's *The National Research and Education Network: Whom Shall It Serve?* Ewing, NJ: COOK Network Consultants, 1992. Cook's **COOK Report on Internet —> NREN** tracks developments in this area regularly, and is indispensable reading for anyone seriously interested in policy decisions regarding computer networking. It is available from Cook; send e-mail to **cook@path.net**.
  13. Telephone interview with Tom Grundner January 21, 1993.

Bibliography

Abernathy, Joe. "What Is To Be Done?" The Village Voice, December 22, 1992, 56.

Anthes, Gary H., and Joanie M. Wexler. "Industry Looks to Clinton Regime to Accelerate Technology Highway." *ComputerWorld*, January 25, 1993, 1.

Arms, Caroline R. "A New Information Infrastructure." *Online*, September 1990, 15.

_____. "Using the National Networks: BITNET and the Internet." *Online*, September 1990, 24.

Aupperle, Eric M. "Changing Eras: Evolution of the NSFNET." *Internet Society News*, Winter 1993, 3.

_____. "Internet and NSFNET's Evolution." *Internet Society News*, Summer 1992, 2–3.

Banks, Michael A. *The Modem Reference*. 3rd ed. New York: Brady Publishing, 1992.

Barlow, John Perry. "Crime and Puzzlement: Desperadoes of the DataSphere." *Whole Earth Review*, Fall 1990, 45–57.

Beaver, David. "Pushing Beyond Paper." *MacUser*, January 1993, 215–221.

Benedikt, Michael, ed. Cyberspace: First Steps. Cambridge, MA: MIT Press, 1991.

Berners-Lee, Tim. "A Summary of the WorldWideWeb System." *ConneXions: The Interoperability Report*, July 1992, 26–27.

Bernt, Phyllis, and Martin Weiss. *International Telecommunications*. Carmel, IN: SAMS Publishing, 1993.

Bishop, Ann P. "The National Research and Education Network (NREN): Update 1991." *ERIC Digest*, December 1991.

Brandt, D. Scott. "Accessing Electronic Journals." *Academic and Library Computing* Vol. 9, No. 10, November/December 1992, 17–20.

Calem, Robert E. "The Network of All Networks." *New York Times*, 6 December 1992, 12F.

Cerf, Vinton G. "Networks." *Scientific American*, September 1991, 72–81.

Clements, Charles, M.D. "HealthNet Connects Africa to Vital Medical Data." *Satellite Communications*, January 1992, 18–21.

Comer, Douglas E. *Internetworking with TCP/IP Vol. I: Principles, Protocols, and Architecture*. Englewood Cliffs, NJ: Prentice Hall, 1991.

Denning, Peter J. *Computers Under Attack: Intruders, Worms and Viruses*. Reading, MA: Addison-Wesley, 1990.

Derfler, Frank J., Jr. *PC Magazine Guide to Connectivity*. 2nd ed. Emeryville, CA: Ziff-Davis Press, 1992.

Dern, Daniel P. *The New User's Guide to the Internet*. New York: McGraw-Hill, 1993.

_____. "Applying the Internet." *BYTE Magazine*, February 1992, 111–118.

Deutsch, Peter. "Resource Discovery in an Internet Environment—the archie Approach." *Electronic Networking: Research, Applications, and Policy"* Vol. 2, No. 1, Spring 1992, –51.

Duncan, Ray. "Roaming the Internet." *Dr. Dobb's Journal*, February 1993, 31–32.

_____. "Roaming the Internet, Part 2." *Dr. Dobb's Journal*, April 1993, 127.

Ebersman, Paul. "Making the Internet Connection." *UnixWorld*, June 1992.

Fisher, Sharon. "Whither NREN?" *BYTE Magazine*, July 1991, 181–189.

Frey, Donnalyn, and Rick Adams. *!%@:: A Directory of Electronic Mail Addressing and Networks*. Sebastopol, CA: O'Reilly & Associates, Inc., 1990.

Franks, John. "What Is an Electronic Journal?" Posted on PACS-L mailing list January 1993.

Gerber, Cheryl. "Booming Commercial Use Changes Face of Internet." *Infoworld*, 12 April 1993, 1.

Gibson, William. *Neuromancer*. New York: Ace Books, 1984.

Goos, Anke and Daniel Karrenberg. *The European R&D E-Mail Directory*. Buntingford, United Kingdom:EurOpen, 1990.

Gore, Albert. "Infrastructure for the Global Village." *Scientific American*, September 1991, 150–153.

Grundner, Tom. "Whose Internet Is It Anyway?—A Challenge." *Online*, July 1992, 6–10.

Habegger, Jay. "Understanding the Technical and Administrative Organization of the Internet." *Telecommunications*. Vol. 26, No. 4, April 1992, S12.

Hafner, Katie and John Markoff. *Cyberpunk*. New York: Simon & Schuster, 1991.

Hardie, Edward T.L. and Vivian Neou, eds. *Internet: Mailing Lists*. Englewood Cliffs, NJ: PTR Prentice Hall. 1993.

Harrison, Teresa M., Timothy Stephen and James Winter. "Online Journals: Disciplinary Designs for Electronic Scholarship." *Public-Access Computer Systems Review*, Vol 2, No. 1, 25–38.

Horvitz, Robert. "The USENET Underground." *Whole Earth Review*, Winter 1989, 112–115.

Jackson, Mary E. "Document Delivery Over the Internet." *Online*, March 1993, 14–21.

Jacobsen, Ole J. "ConneXions—The Interoperability Report." *Internet Society News*, Winter 1993.

Jennings, Edward M. "EJournal: An Account of the First Two Years." *Public-Access Computer Systems Review,* Vol 2, No. 1, 91–110.

Johnson, Johna Till. "The Internet Opens Up to Commercial Use." *Data Communications,* March 1993, 55–60.

Kahin, Brian, ed. *Building Information Infrastructure: Issues in the Development of the National Research and Education Network.* New York: McGraw-Hill Primis, 1992.

Kahle, Brewster. "WAIS: Wide Area Information Servers." *NSF Network News,* No. 11, March, 1992, 1–2.

Kapor, Mitch. "Civil Liberties in Cyberspace." *Scientific American,* September 1991, 158–164.

Karraker, Roger. "Highways of the Mind." *Whole Earth Review,* Spring 1991, 4–11.

Kehoe, Brendan P. *Zen and the Art of the Internet: A Beginner's Guide to the Internet.* Chester, PA: Widener University, 1992.

Kochmer, Jonathan. *Internet Passport.* Bellevue, WA: NorthWestNet Academic Computing Consortium, Inc. 1993.

Krol, ed. *The Whole Internet User's Guide & Catalog.* Sebastopol, CA: O'Reilly & Associates, Inc., 1992.

Landweber, Larry. "International Connectivity." *Internet Society News,* Vol. 1, No. 2, Spring 1992, 49–52.

Lane, Elizabeth S., and Craig A. Summerhill. *An Internet Primer for Information Professionals: A Basic Guide to Networking Technology.* Westport, CT: Meckler Corp., 1993.

LaQuey, Tracy L., with Jeanne C. Ryer. *The Internet Companion.* Reading, MA: Addison-Wesley Publishing Co., 1992.

_____. *The User's Directory of Computer Networks.* Burlington, MA: Digital Press, 1990.

Levy, Steven. *Hackers: Heroes of the Computer Revolution.* Garden City, NY: Anchor Press/Doubleday, 1984.

Lynch, Daniel C. and Marshall T. Rose. *Internet System Handbook.* Reading, MA: Addison-Wesley Publishing Co, 1993.

Malamud, Carl. *Exploring the Internet: A Technical Travelogue.* Englewood Cliffs, NJ: PTR Prentice Hall, 1992.

Malamud, Carl. *Stacks: Interoperability in Today's Computer Networks.* Englewood Cliffs, NJ: Prentice-Hall, 1992.

Malkin, Gary, and April Marine. "FYI on Questions and Answers: Answers to Commonly Asked New Internet User Questions." RFC 1325 (FYI 4), May 1992.

McCahill, Mark. "The Internet Gopher: A Distributed Server Information System." *ConneXions: The Interoperability Report,* Vol. 6, No. 7, July 1992, 10–14.

McClure, Charles R., Ann P. Bishop, Philip Doty, and Howard Rosenbaum. *The National Research and Education Network (NREN): Research and Policy Perspectives.* Norwood, NJ: Ablex Publishing Corp., 1991.

Marine, April. *Internet: Getting Started.* Englewood Cliffs, NJ: PTR Prentice Hall. 1993.

_____. "Demystifying the Internet." *Open Systems Today,* September 21, 1992, 86.

Markoff, John. "Turning the Desktop PC Into a Talk Radio Medium." *New York Times,* March 4, 1993, A1.

_____. "Building the Electronic Superhighway." *New York Times,* January 24, 1993, Sec. 3, 1.

_____. "The Staggering Scope of the Internet." *Digital Media: A Seybold Report,* April 20, 1992, 19.

Mockapetris, Paul. "Domain Names—Concepts and Facilities." RFC 822. August 13, 1982.

Moore, Michael A., and Ronald M. Sawey. *BITNET for VMS Users.* Burlington, MA: Digital Press, 1992.

Nickerson, Gord. "Computer Mediated Communication on BITNET." *Computers in Libraries,* February 1992, 33–36.

NYSERNet Inc. *NYSERNet New User's Guide to Useful and Unique Resources on the Internet.* Syracuse, NY: NYSERNet, 1992.

Okerson, Ann. "The Electronic Journal: What, Whence and When?" *Public-Access Computer Systems Review* Vol. 2, No. 1, 5–24.

Parkhurst, Carol A., ed. *Library Perspectives on NREN: The National Research and Education Network.* Chicago: LITA, 1990.

Peek, Jerry, Tim O'Reilly and Mike Loukides. *UNIX Power Tools.* Sebastopol, CA: O'Reilly & Associates/Bantam Books. 1993.

Quarterman, John S. *The Matrix—Computer Networks and Conferencing Systems Worldwide.* Burlington, MA: Digital Press, 1990.

_____. "What Can Businesses Get Out of the Internet?" *ComputerWorld,* February 22, 1993, 81–83.

Raymond, Eric, and Guy L. Steele, Jr. *The New Hacker's Dictionary.* Cambridge, MA: MIT Press, 1991.

Rose, Marshall T. *The Internet Message: Closing the Book with Electronic Mail.* Englewood Cliffs, NJ: PTR Prentice Hall, 1993.

Schrage, Michael. "Betting Billions on a Long Shot to Boost U.S. Competitiveness." *Washington Post,* February 26, 1993.

Schulman, Mark. *Introduction to UNIX.* Carmel, IN: Que Corp., 1992.

Schwartz, Michael F. "Which White Pages Service is Appropriate for My Site?" *Internet Society News,* Vol. 1, No. 4, Winter 1993, 19–21.

Stanton, Deirdre E. "Using Networked Information Sources: A Bibliography." Anonymous FTP from **infolib.murdoch.edu.au**.

Sterling, Bruce. *The Hacker Crackdown: Law and Disorder on the Electronic Frontier.* New York: Bantam, 1992.

Stoll, Clifford. *The Cuckoo's Egg: Tracking a Spy Through the Maze of Computer Espionage.* New York: Doubleday, 1989.

SURAnet Network Information Center. "SURAnet Guide to Selected Internet Resources." College Park, MD: SURAnet, 1993.

Taubes, Gary. "Publications by Electronic Mail Take Physics by Storm." *Science* 259, February 26, 1993: 1246–1248.

Tennant, Roy, John Ober and Anne G. Lipow. *Crossing the Internet Threshold: An Instructional Handbook.* Berkeley, CA: Library Solutions Press, 1993.

_____. Tennant, Roy. "Internet Basics." *ERIC Digest,* September 1992.

Ubois, Jeff. "What is Acceptable Internet Use?" *MacWEEK,* September 28, 1992, 30.

U.S. Congress. High-Performance Computing Act of 1991. Public Law 102–194. Washington, DC: U.S. Government Printing Office, S.272

Vinge, Vernor. *A Fire Upon the Deep*. New York: TOR Books, 1992.

Weiser, Mark. "The Computer for the 21st Century." *Scientific American,* September 1991, 94–104.

Wylie, Margie. "Internet of the Future May Be a One-Stop Information Shop." *MacWEEK,* January 25, 1993.

Dial-Up Internet
Service Providers

This appendix is basically two lists, one of Internet service providers, the other of public access UNIX sites. It draws on several sources.

Chief among them are Peter Kaminski's Public Dialup Internet Access List (PDIAL) and Phil Eschallier's NixPub Long Listing of Public/Open Access UNIX Sites. I have supplemented both with additional information, particularly in the realm of overseas providers. My intent was to create a list of maximum utility to modem users interested in accessing the Internet.

A WORD ON SOURCES

Peter Kaminski's PDIAL is widely distributed on the Internet, and is Copyright 1992-1993 by Peter Kaminski. Material drawn from it is used here with his permission.

PDIAL focuses on dial-up service providers which offer full Internet access, including ftp and Telnet capabilities as well as electronic mail. The NixPub list takes a different tack; as a listing of public access UNIX sites, it includes full access Internet providers as well as UNIX systems offering electronic mail and USENET newsgroups only. It also lists UNIX systems with no Internet connectivity whatsoever.

Why list sites without any Internet connectivity here? Because UNIX systems are those most likely to provide local access to electronic mail to the

Internet, and perhaps other services, in the future. Any of the NixPub sites are therefore worth watching as possible future providers of some form of Internet connectivity.

In the material that follows, I have removed duplicate references from the two lists and have broken their lists of providers down by country, with the United States listed first. It was possible to gather more information from some systems than others; in each case, I list as much as I know. Both PDIAL and NixPub have been supplemented by contacts with service providers overseas, many of whom were kind enough to forward information about their services. The growth in overseas dial-up access, particularly in Europe through EUnet, is heartening news.

OBTAINING UPDATED LISTS

There are various ways to obtain the frequently updated PDIAL. The list is posted to the USENET newsgroups **alt.internet.access.wanted**, **alt.bbs.lists**, **alt.online-service**, **ba.internet** and **news.answers**.

Alternatively, you can retrieve it by sending e-mail to **info-deli-server@netcom.com**. Enter **send pdial** as the subject of your message. To receive future editions as they are published, send e-mail with the subject **subscribe pdial** to **info-deli-server@netcom.com**.

NixPub Long Listing, Phil Eschallier's list of Public/Open Access UNIX Sites, is likewise available on-line. It is regularly posted to the USENET newsgroups **comp.misc**, **comp.bbs.misc** and **alt.bbs**. To subscribe to the NIXPUB-LIST mailing list, send e-mail to **mail-server@bts.com**. Enter as your message **subscribe nixpub-list** *your name*.

The same address may be used to retrieve the current list. Send e-mail to **mail-server@bts.com** with the message **get pub nixpub.long** or **get pub nixpub.short**, depending on which version you want. Finally, the NixPub list is available by anonymous ftp from **vfl.paramax.com**. The directory is *pub/pubnet*. The file name is **nixpub.long** or **nixpub.short**.

The following notice appears on the NixPub list, and is repeated here at the request of Phil Eschallier: "The "nixpub" listings are (C) Copyright 1993, Bux Technical Services. This publication is released for unlimited redistribution over any electronic media providing it remains in its original form. Publishing, removing this copyright notice, or in any way revising this document's contents is forbidden without written consent from the owner."

The material drawn from the NixPub list is used here, with some deletions where redundancies occured, with the permission of Phil Eschallier. I have chosen to maintain the formatting he uses in NixPub for these entries to differentiate between public access UNIX sites and full access service providers.

DIAL-UP SERVICE PROVIDERS

United States

The following is a list of full access Internet providers, offering electronic mail, ftp and Telnet, drawn primarily from the PDIAL list with a few supplements. Immediately following it is a list of public access UNIX sites, as found in the NixPub list.

A2I COMMUNICATIONS

1211 Park Avenue, Suite 202
San Jose, CA 95126
Voice: n/a
Dial-Up: 408-293-9010 (v.32, v.32 bis) or 408-293-9020 (PEP). Use *guest* to log in.
Area codes: 408
Local access: California: Campbell, Los Altos, Los Gatos, Mountain View, San Jose, Santa Clara, Saratoga, Sunnyvale
Fees: $20/month or $45/3 months or $72/6 months.
E-mail: **info@rahul.net**

ANOMALY—RHODE ISLAND'S GATEWAY TO THE INTERNET

Small Business Systems, Inc.
Box 17220, Route 104
Smithfield, RI 02917
Voice: 401-273-4669
Dial-Up: 401-331-3706 (v.32) or 401-455-0347 (PEP)
Area codes: 401
Local Access: Rhode Island: Providence/Seekonk
Fees: $125/6 months or $200/year; Education rates are $75 for 6 months or $125/yr.
E-mail: **info@anomaly.sbs.risc.net**

BIX

General Videotex Corp.
1030 Massachusetts Ave.
Cambridge, MA 02138
Voice: 800-695-4775
Dial-Up: 800-695-4882. Log in as *bix*. Enter *bix.news* at the Name? prompt. Complete the registration.
Area Codes: 617, PDN.
Local Access: nationwide
Fees: $20/mo for 20 hours off-peak ($9 per hour prime time); $1.80/hr thereafter; $13/mo membership fee. Or $9 per hour prime time, $3/hr off-peak ($2/hr direct dial or $1/hr via Telnet) plus $13/mo fee.
E-mail: **bix@genvid.com**

CAPCON LIBRARY NETWORK

1320 19th St. NW, Suite 400
Washington, DC 20036
Voice: 202-331-5771
Dial-Up: contact for number
Area Codes: 202, 301, 410, 703
Local Access: District of Columbia, suburban Maryland & northern Virginia. About to go nationwide.
Fees: $35 start-up plus $150/yr plus $24/mo for first account from an institution (if paid annually in advance; otherwise, $30/mo); $35 start-up plus $90/yr plus $15/mo for additional users (if paid annually; otherwise $18/mo). 20 hours/mo included, additional hours $2/hr. CAPCON member rates lower
E-mail: **capcon@capcon.net**

CLASS
Cooperative Library Agency for Systems and Services
1415 Koll Circle, Suite 101
San Jose, CA 95112-4698
Voice: 800-488-4559
Dial-Up: Contact for number. CLASS serves libraries and information distributors only.
Area codes: 800
Fees: $10.50/hour and $150/year for first account; $50/year each additional account and $135/year CLASS membership.
E-mail: **class@class.org**

COLORADO SUPERNET
Colorado School of Mines
1500 Illinois
Golden, CO 80401
Voice: 303-273-3471
Dial-Up: Contact for number
Area codes: 303, 719
Local Access: Colorado: Ft. Collins, Boulder/Denver, Colorado Springs
Fees: $1/hour off-peak, $2/hour peak ($250 max/month) plus $20 sign-up fee
E-mail: **info@csn.org**

COMMUNITY NEWS SERVICE
1715 Monterey Rd.
Colorado Springs, CO 80910
Voice: 719-579-9120
Dial-Up: 719-520-1700
Area codes: 303, 719, 800
Local Access: Colorado: Colorado Springs, Denver and continental via 800 service
Fees: $1/hour; $10/month minimum plus $35 signup
E-mail: **klaus@cscns.com**

CONCERT-CONNECT
3021 Cornwallis Rd.
Research Triangle Park, NC 27709
Voice: 919-248-1999
Dial-Up: Contact for number
Area codes: 704, 919
Local Access: North Carolina: Asheville, Chapel Hill, Charlotte, Durham, Greensboro, Greenville, Raleigh, Winston-Salem, Research Triangle Park
Fees: $30/month plus $50 sign-up fee.
E-mail: **info@concert.net**

CR LABORATORIES DIALUP INTERNET ACCESS
P. O. Box 326
Larkspur, CA 94977
Voice: 415-381-2800
Dial-Up: 415-389-8649

Area Codes: 415, 510, 602, 707, 800
Local Access: CA: San Francisco Bay area, San Rafael, Santa Rosa. AZ: Phoenix,
Scottsdale, Tempe, Glendale. 800 numbers in Continental US
Fees: $17.50/month plus $19.50 signup
E-mail: **info@crl.com**

CTS NETWORK SERVICES (CTSNET)

1274 Vista Del Monte Dr.
El Cajon, CA 92020-6830
Voice: 619-593-9597
Dial-Up: 619-593-6400 (HST); 619-593-7300 (V.32bis); 619-593-9500 (PEP).
619-220-0836. 619-220-0853. 619-220-0857. Log in as *help*.
Area Codes: 619
Local Access: CA: San Diego, Pt. Loma, La Jolla, La Mesa, El Cajon, Poway,
Ramona, Chula Vista, National City, Mira Mesa, Alpine, East County
Fees: personal: $10-23/mo, $15 start-up; commercial: $20-45/mo, $15 start-up
E-mail: **info@crash.cts.com**, **support@crash.cts.com**

THE CYBERSPACE STATION

204 N. El Camino Real, Suite E626
Encinitas, CA 92024
Voice: n/a
Dial-Up: 619-634-1376; login as **guest**
Area codes: 619
Local Access: California: San Diego
Fees: $15/month plus $10 startup or $60 for six months
E-mail: **help@cyber.net**

DELPHI

1030 Massachusetts Ave.
Cambridge, MA 02138
Voice: 800-544-4005
Dial-Up: 800-365-4636. Enter *JOINDELPHI*. Password: *INTERNETSIG*.
Area Codes: 617, PDN
Local Access: MA: Boston. KS: Kansas City.
Fees: $10/mo for 4 hours or $20/mo for 20 hours plus $3/mo for Internet Services.
E-mail: **walthowe@delphi.com**

DIAL N' CERF, DIAL N' CERF AYC

P. O. Box 85608
San Diego, CA 92186-9784
Voice: 800-876-2373; 619-455-3900
Dial-Up: Contact for number
Area codes: 213, 310, 415, 510, 619, 714, 818
Local Access: California: Los Angeles, Oakland, San Diego, Irvine, Pasadena,
Palo Alto
Fees: $5/hour ($3/hour on weekend) plus $20/month plus $50 startup or
$250/month flat-rate for AYC
E-mail: **help@cerf.net**

DIAL N' CERF USA

P. O. Box 85608
San Diego, CA 92186-9784
Voice: 800-876-2373; 619-455-3900
Dial-Up: Contact for number
Area codes: 800
Local Access: Wherever 800 service is available
Fees: $10/hour ($8/hour on weekend) plus $20/month.
E-mail: **help@cerf.net**

ESKIMO NORTH

P. O. Box 75284
Seattle, WA 98125-0284
Voice: 206-367-7457
Dial-Up: 206-367-3837 at 300-2400 bps; 206-362-6731 at 9600/14.4; 206-742-1150 for World Blazer modems
Area Codes: 206
Local Access: WA: Seattle, Everett
Fees: $10/month or $96/year
E-mail: **nanook@eskimo.com**

EXPRESS ACCESS—ONLINE COMMUNICATIONS SERVICE

6006 Greenbelt Rd. #228
Greenbelt, MD 20770
Voice: 301-220-2020
Dial-Up: 301-220-0462; 410-766-1855. Log in as **new**.
Area codes: 202, 301, 410, 703
Local Access: Northern Virginia, Baltimore, Washington DC
Fees: $25/month or $250/year
E-mail: **info@digex.com**

GREBYN CORPORATION

P. O. Box 497
Vienna, VA 22183-0497
Voice: 703-281-2194
Dial-Up: 703-281-7997; log in as **apply**.
Area Codes: 202, 301, 703
Local Access: Northern VA, Southern MD, Washington DC
Fees: $30/month
E-mail: **info@grebyn.com**

HALCYON

P. O. Box 555
Grapeview, WA 98546
Voice: 206-955-1050
Dial-Up: 206-382-6245. Log in as **new**.
Area Codes: 206
Local Access: Seattle, WA
Fees: $200/yr or $60/quarter plus $10 startup fee
E-mail: **info@halcyon.com**

HOLONET

Information Access Technologies, Inc.
46 Shattuck Square, Suite 11
Berkeley, CA 94704-1152
Voice: 510-704-0160
Dial-Up: 510-704-1058
Area Codes: 510, PDN
Local Access: California: Berkeley
Fees: $2/hour off-peak, $4/hour peak; $6/month or $60/year minimum.
E-mail: **info@holonet.net**

IDS WORLD NETWORK

11 Franklin Rd.
East Greenwich, RI 02818
Voice: 401-884-7856
Dial-Up: 401-884-9002; 401-785-1067
Area Codes: 401
Local Access: Rhode Island: East Greenwich; northern RI
Fees: $10/month or $50/half year or $100/year
E-mail: **sysadmin@ids.net**

INSTITUTE FOR GLOBAL COMMUNICATIONS/IGC NETWORKS (PEACENET, ECONET, CONFLICTNET, LABORNET, HOMEONET)

18 De Boom St.
San Francisco, CA 94107
Voice: 415-442-0220
Dial-Up: 415-322-0284. Log in as *new*.
Area Codes: 415, 800, PDN
Local Access: CA: Palo Alto, San Francisco
Fees: $10/mo plus $3/hr after first hour
E-mail: **support@igc.apc.org**

INTERCON SYSTEMS CORP.

950 Herndon Parkway, Suite 420
Herndon, VA 22070
Voice: 703-709-5500 Ext. 551; 800-638-2968
Dial-Up: Contact
Area Codes: PDN
Fees: $29/month plus $29.95 one-time charge for software for WorldLink Basic Service; $39/mo. for 9600 bps access.
E-mail: **comment@intercon.com**

THE JOHN VON NEUMANN COMPUTER NETWORK—DIALIN' TIGER

JvNCnet-Princeton University
B6 von Neumann Hall
Princeton, NJ 08544
Voice: 800-358-4437; 609-258-2400
Dial-Up: Contact for number
Area Codes: 201, 203, 215, 401, 516, 609, 908
Local Access: New Jersey: Princeton and Newark; Pennsylvania: Philadelphia;

New York: Garden City, NY; Connecticut: Bridgeport, New Haven & Storrs;
Rhode Island: Providence
Fees: $99/month plus $99 startup (PC or Mac SLIP software included; shell is
additional $21/month)
E-mail: **info@jvnc.net**

THE JOHN VON NEUMANN COMPUTER NETWORK—TIGER MAIL & DIALIN' TERMINAL

JvNCnet-Princeton University
B6 von Neumann Hall
Princeton, NJ 08544
Voice: 800-358-4437; 609-258-2400
Dial-Up: Contact for number
Area Codes: 800
Local Access: Wherever 800 service is available
Fees: $19/month plus $10/hour plus $36 startup (PC or Mac SLIP software
included)
E-mail: **info@jvnc.net**

MAESTRO

29 John St., Suite 1601
New York, NY 10038
Voice: 212-240-9600
Dial-Up: 212-240-9700. Log in as *newuser*.
Area Codes: 212, 718
Local Access: NY: New York City
Fees: $15/mo or $150/yr
E-mail: **info@maestro.com**; **staff@maestro.com**; **rkelly@maestro.com**,
ksingh@maestro.com

MCSNET

3217 N. Sheffield
Chicago, IL 60657
Voice: 312-248-8649
Dial-Up: 312-248-0900 (v.32bis); 312-248-0970 (v.32bis); 312-248-6295 (PEP)
Area Codes: 312, 708, 815
Local Access: IL: Chicago
Fees: $25/mo or $65/3 months; $30/3 months for 15 hours/mo.
E-mail: **info@genesis.mcs.com**

MERIT NETWORK, INC.—MICHNET PROJECT

University of Michigan, Institute of Science and Technology
2200 Bonisteel Ave.
Ann Arbor, MI 48109
Voice: 313-764-9430
Dial-Up: Contact for number
Area Codes: 313, 517, 616, 906, PDN
Local Access: Michigan; Massachusetts: Boston; Washington, DC
Fees: $35/month plus $40 signup
E-mail: **info@merit.edu**

MINDVOX

Phantom Access Technologies, Inc.
1562 First Avenue, Suite 351
New York, NY 10028
Voice: 212-989-2418
Dial-Up: 212-989-4141 (2400 bps); 212-989-1550 (9600 bps); log in as **mindvox** or **guest**.
Area Codes: 212, 718
Local Access: New York: New York City
Fees: Between $15-20/month. No startup fee.
E-mail: **info@phantom.com**

MSEN, INC.

628 Brooks St.
Ann Arbor, MI 48103
Voice: 313-998-4562
Dial-Up: Contact for number
Area Codes: 313
Local Access: SE Michigan
Fees: $5/month plus $2/hour or $20/month for 20 hours
E-mail: **info@msen.com**

MV COMMUNICATIONS, INC.

P. O. Box 4963
Manchester, NH 03108-4963
Voice: 603-429-2223
Dial-Up: contact for numbers
Area codes: 603
Local Access: many New Hampshire communities
Fees: $5.00/mo minimum plus variable hourly rates.
E-mail: **info@mv.com**

NEARNET

10 Moulton St.
Cambridge, MA 02138
Voice: 617-873-8730
Dial-Up: Contact for number
Area Codes: 508, 603, 617
Local Access: Massachusetts: Boston; New Hampshire: Nashua
Fees: $250/month
E-mail: **nearnet-join@nic.near.net**

NEOSOFT'S SUGAR LAND UNIX

3408 Mangum
Houston, TX 77092
Voice: 713-684 5969
Dial-Up: 713-684-5900
Area Codes: 713
Local Access: Texas: Houston. About to expand to St. Louis and New Orleans.
Fees: $29.95/mo.
E-mail: **info@neosoft.com**

NETCOM ONLINE COMMUNICATION SERVICES, INC.

4000 Moorpark Ave., No. 209
San Jose, CA 95117
Voice: 408-554-8649
Dial-Up: 206-527-5992; 214-753-0045; 310-842-8835; 408-241-9760; 408-459-9851; 415-328-9940; 415-985-5650; 503-626-6833; 510-426-6610; 510-865-9004; 619-234-0524; 714-708-3800; 916-965-1371.
Area Codes: 206, 213, 310, 408, 415, 503, 510, 619, 818, 916
Local Access: California: San Francisco Bay area, Santa Cruz, Los Angeles, Irvine, San Diego, Sacramento. OR: Portland. TX: Dallas/Fort Worth. WA: Seattle.
Fees: $19.50/month plus $20 signup
E-mail: **info@netcom.com**

NORTH SHORE ACCESS

145 Munroe St., Suite 405
Lynn, MA 01901
Voice: 617-593-3110
Dial-Up: 617-593-5774 (V.32, PEP). Log in as *new*.
Area Codes: 617, 508
Local Access: MA: Wakefield, Lynnfield, Lynn, Saugus, Revere, Peabody, Salem, Marblehead, Swampscott
Fees: $10/mo includes 10 hours connect time, $1/hr thereafter
E-mail: **postmaster@northshore.ecosoft.com**

NORTHWEST NEXUS INC.

P. O. Box 40597
Bellevue, WA 98015-4597
Voice: 206-455-3505
Dial-Up: contact for numbers
Area Codes: 206
Local Access: WA: Seattle
Fees: $10/mo for first 10 hours plus $3/hr; $20 start-up
E-mail: **info@nwnexus.wa.com**

OARNET

1224 Kinnear Rd.
Columbus, OH 43212
Voice: 614-292-0700
Dial-Up: Contact for number
Area Codes: 614, 513, 419, 216, 800
Local Access: Ohio: Columbus, Cincinatti, Cleveland, Dayton; also 800 service
Fees: $4/hour to $330/month
E-mail: **nic@oar.net**

OLD COLORADO CITY COMMUNICATIONS

2502 West Colorado Ave.
Suite 203
Colorado Springs, CO 80904
Voice: 719-632-4848, 719-593-7575, 719-636-2040

Dial-Up: 719-632-4111
Area Codes: 719
Local Access: CO: Colorado Springs
Fees: $25/month
E-mail: **dave@oldcolo.com**; **thefox@oldcolo.com**

PANIX PUBLIC ACCESS UNIX

110 Riverside Dr.
New York, NY 10024
Voice: 212-877-4854
Dial-Up: 212-787-3100. Log in as **newuser**.
Area Codes: 212, 718
Local Access: New York: New York City
Fees: $19/month or $208/year plus $40 signup
E-mail: **alexis@panix.com, jsb@panix.com**

PATHWAYS

Pandora Systems
1903 Broderick #4
San Francisco, CA 94115
Voice: 415-346-4188
Area Codes: 415, PDN
Local Access:
Fees: $25 sign-up; $8/mo plus $8/hr peak, $5/hr off-peak, $3/hr via Internet, or
$3/hr by direct dial modem access
E-mail: **info@path.net**

PERFORMANCE SYSTEMS INTERNATIONAL, INC. (PSI)

PSI's World-Dial Service
Voice: 703-620-6651
Dial-Up: send e-mail to **numbers-info@psi.com**
Area Codes: PDN
Local Access:
Fees: $9/month minimum plus $19 startup
E-mail: **all-info@psi.com, world-dial-info@psi.com**

PERFORMANCE SYSTEMS INTERNATIONAL, INC. (PSI)

PSILink—Personal Internet Access
Voice: 703-620-6651
Dial-Up: Contact for number
Area Codes: PDN
Local Access:
Fees: $29/month plus $19 startup (PSILink software included)
E-mail: **all-info@psi.com, psilink-info@psi.com**

THE PORTAL SYSTEM

20863 Stevens Creek Boulevard, Suite 200
Cupertino, CA 95014
Voice: 408-973-9111
Dial-Up: 408-973-8091 high speed; 408-725-0561 at 2400 bps; log in as **info**.

Area Codes: 408, 415, PDN
Local Access: CA: Cupertino, Mountain View, San Jose
Fees: $19.95/month plus $19.95 signup fee
E-mail: **cs@cup.portal.com, info@portal.com**

PREPNET

305 S. Craig St., 2nd Floor
Pittsburgh, PA 15213
Voice: 412-268-7870
Dial-Up: Contact for number
Area Codes: 215, 412, 717, 814
Local Access: PA: Philadelphia, Pittsburgh, Harrisburg
Fees: $1,000/year membership. Equipment: $325 one-time fee plus $40/month
E-mail: **prepnet+@andrew.cmu.edu**

RAINDROP LABORATORIES

Voice: n/a
Dial-Up: 503-293-1772 (2400); 503-293-2059 (v.32, v.32 bis). Log in as *apply*.
Area Codes: 503
Local Access: OR: Portland, Beaverton, Hillsboro, Forest Grove, Gresham, Tigard, Lake Oswego, Oregon City, Tualatin, Wilsonville
Fees: $6/month (i hr/day limit)
E-mail: **info@agora.rain.com**

TELERAMA BBS

P. O. Box 19026
Pittsburgh, PA 15213
Voice: 412-481-3505
Dial-Up: 412-481-5302; log in as **new**.
Area codes: 412
Local Access: PA: Pittsburgh
Fees: $6/mo for 10 hours, 60 cents/hr thereafter.
E-mail: **info@telerama.pgh.pa.us**

TEXAS METRONET

860 Kinwest Pkwy., Suite 179
Irving, TX 75063-3440
Voice: 214-401-2800
Dial-Up: 214-705-2902 at 9600 bps; 214-705-2917 at 2400 bps; login with **info/info** or **signup/signup**
Area Codes: 214
Local Access: TX: Dallas
Fees: $10-50/month plus $20-30 startup fee
E-mail: **srl@metronet.com**

THE META NETWORK

2000 N. 15th St., Suite 103
Arlington, VA 22201
Voice: 703-243-6622
Dial-Up: contact for numbers

Area Codes: 703, 202, 301, PDN
Local Access: Washington, DC metro area
Fees: $20/month plus $15 sign-up first month
E-mail: **info@tmn.com**

UUNORTH

3555 Don Mills Rd.
6-304 Willowdale, ON M2H 3N3
Voice: 416-225-8649
Dial-Up: contact for numbers
Area Codes: 416, 519, 613
Local Access: ON: Toronto
Fees: (In Canadian dollars) $20 start-up plus $25 for 20 hours off-peak plus
$1.25/hr OR $40 up to 5 hr/day plus $2/hr OR $3/hr
E-mail: **uunorth@uunorth.north.net**

WARIAT

APK—Public Access UNI* Site
19709 Mohican Ave.
Cleveland, OH 44110
Voice: 216-481-9428
Dial-Up: 216-481-9436 at 2400 bps; 216-481-9425 (v.32bis, SuperPEP)
Area codes: 216
Local Access: OH: Cleveland
Fees: $35/month, $200/6 months, $20 signup
E-mail: **zbig@wariat.org**

THE WHOLE EARTH 'LECTRONIC LINK (THE WELL)

27 Gate Five Road
Sausalito, CA 94965
Voice: 415-332-4335
Dial-Up: 415-332-6106
Area Codes: 415, PDN
Local Access: CA: Sausalito
Fees: $15/month plus $2/hour
E-mail: **info@well.sf.ca.us**

THE WORLD

Software Tool and Die
1330 Beacon St.
Brookline, MA 02146
Voice: 617-739-0202
Dial-Up: 617-739-9753; log in as **new**.
Area Codes: 617, PDN
Local Access: Massachusetts: Boston
Fees: $5/mo plus $2/hour or $20/mo for 20 hours
E-mail: **office@world.std.com**

WYVERN TECHNOLOGIES, INC.
211 East City Hall Ave.
Suite 236
Norfolk, VA 23510
Voice: 804-622-4289
Dial-Up: 804-627-1828 (Norfolk); 804-886-0662 (Penninsula)
Area Codes: 804
Local Access: VA: Norfolk, Virginia Beach, Portsmouth, Chesapeake, Newport
News, Hampton, Williamsburg
Fees: $15/mo or $144/yr, $10 start-up
E-mail: **system@wyvern.com**

Area Code Summary

201	jvnc-tiger
202	CAPCON
202	express
202	grebyn
202	tmn
203	jvnc-tiger
206	eskimo
206	halcyon
206	netcom
206	nwnexus
212	maestro
212	mindvox
212	panix
213	dial-n-cerf
213	netcom
214	metronet
215	jvnc-tiger
215	PREPnet
216	OARnet
216	wariat
301	CAPCON
301	express
301	grebyn
301	tmn
303	cns
303	csn
310	dial-n-cerf
310	netcom
312	genesis
313	michnet
313	MSen
401	anomaly
401	ids
401	jvnc-tiger
408	a2i
408	netcom

408 portal
410 CAPCON
410 express
412 PREPnet
412 telerama
415 crl
415 dial-n-cerf
415 IGC
415 netcom
415 portal
415 well
416 uunorth
419 OARnet
503 agora.rain.com
503 netcom
508 anomaly
508 nearnet
508 northshore
510 crl
510 dial-n-cerf
510 holonet
510 netcom
513 OARnet
516 jvnc-tiger
517 michnet
519 uunorth
602 crl
603 MV
603 nearnet
609 jvnc-tiger
613 uunorth
614 OARnet
616 michnet
617 delphi
617 nearnet
617 northshore
617 world
619 crash.cts.com
619 cyber
619 dial-n-cerf
619 netcom
703 CAPCON
703 express
703 grebyn
703 tmn
704 rock-concert
707 crl
708 genesis
713 sugar
714 dial-n-cerf

717 PREPnet
718 maestro
718 mindvox
718 panix
719 cns
719 csn
719 oldcolo
800 class
800 cns
800 crl
800 csn
800 dial-n-cerf-usa
800 IGC
800 jvnc
800 OARnet
804 wyvern
814 PREPnet
815 genesis
818 dial-n-cerf
818 netcom
906 michnet
908 express
908 jvnc-tiger
916 netcom
919 rock-concert
PDN bix
PDN delphi
PDN holonet
PDN IGC
PDN michnet
PDN pathways
PDN portal
PDN psi-world-dial
PDN psilink
PDN tmn
PDN well
PDN world

U.S. PUBLIC ACCESS UNIX SITES BY STATE

Here, as elsewhere in the appendix, public access UNIX sites are drawn from the NixPub list and presented in the following format:

Updated Last	Telephone #	System Name	Location		Speed Range	Hours
03/93	602-293-3726	**coyote**	Tucson	AZ	300-FAST	24

FTK-386, ISC 386/ix 2.0.2; Waffle BBS, devoted to embedded systems programming and u-controller development software; E-Mail/USENET; UUCP and limited USENET feeds available;

Contact: E.J. McKernan (**ejm@datalog.com**).
bbs: ogin: bbs (NO PWD)
uucp: ogin: nuucp (NO PWD)

03/93   602-649-9099^   **telesys**   Mesa   AZ   1200-FAST   24
SCO UNIX V/386 3.2.4; Telebit WorldBlazers; TeleSys-II Unix based BBS (no
fee) login: bbs; Unix archives available via BBS or ANON UUCP; Shell Accounts
available for full access USENET, email (fees); Phoenix Matchmaker with more
than 9000 members (fees) login: bbs Regional supplier of USENET Newsfeeds;
uucp-anon: nuucp NOPWD;
Contact: **kreed@tnet.com** or **...!ncar!noao!enuucp!telesys!kreed**

03/93   602-991-5952   **aa7bq**   Scottsdale AZ   300-2400   24
Sun 4, SunOS 4.1.2; NB bbs system; 900 meg online; Primarily Ham Radio
related articles from usenet (Rec.radio.amateur.misc), complete Callsign
Database, Radio and scanner modifications, frequency listings, shell access by
permission, No fees, Free classifie ads, Local e-mail only.
Login: bbs (8N1) or
Login: callsign for callsign database only. Don't use MNP!
For additional info contact **Fred.Lloyd@West.Sun.COM**

03/93   408-245-7726^   **uuwest**   Sunnyvale   CA   300-FAST   24
SCO-XENIX, Waffle. No fee, USENET news (news.*, music, comics, telecom,
etc) The Dark Side of the Moon BBS. This system has been in operation since
1985.
Login: new Contact: (UUCP) **ames!uuwest!request** (Domain) **request@darks-
ide.com**

03/93   408-249-9630^   **quack**   Santa Clara CA   300-FAST   24
Sun 4/75, SunOS 4.1.3; 3 lines: First two are Zyxel U-1496E (300-2400,
v.32bis/v.42bis), third is a Worldblazer (same and add PEP); Internet connectivity; Shell—$10/mo; New users should login as 'guest';
Contact: **postmaster@quack.kfu.com**

04/93   408-423-4810   **deeptht**   Santa Cruz CA   300-FAST   24
4 dialin lines (2 2400 at 423-4810, 2 v32 at 423-1767), 486/40+32M, 2 GB disk
space including a large part of the uunet source archives, SCO UNIX 3.2v4.1,
C/Pascal/Fortran/BASIC compilers, TinyMud, rn/trn.
Domain name: **deeptht.armory.com** (and alias armory.com).

03/93   408-423-9995   **cruzio**   Santa Cruz CA   1200-2400   24
Tandy 4000, Xenix 2.3.*, Caucus 3.*; focus on Santa Cruz activity (ie directory
of community and goverment organizations, events, ...); USENET Support;
Multiple lines; no shell; fee: $15/quarter.
Contact: **...!uunet!cruzio!chris**

03/93   408-458-2289   **gorn**   Santa Cruz CA   300-FAST   24
Everex 386, SCO xenix 2.3.2; 2 lines, -2837 telebit for PEP connects; Standard
shell access, games, email injection into the internet, up to date archive of
scruz-sysops information, upload/download, usenet news including scruz.*

heircarchy for santa cruz area information; UUCP set up on as-requested; No charge, donations accepted; newuser: log in as "gorn" and fill out online form. Contact: **falcon@gorn.echo.com**

03/93   408-739-1520^   **szebra**   Sunnyvale   CA   300-FAST   24
386PC, AT&T SVR4v3; Trailblazer+; Full Usenet News, email (Internet & UUCP), first time users login: bbs, shell access/files storage/email available (registration required); GNU, X11R4 and R5 source archives. viet-net/SCV and VNese files/sftware archives.
contact: **tin@szebra.Saigon.COM** or **{claris,zorch,sonyusa}!szebra!tin**

03/93   415-826-0397^   **wet**   San Francisco CA   1200-FAST   24
386 SYS V.3. Wetware Diversions. $15 registration, $0.01/minute. Public Access UNIX System: uucp, PicoSpan bbs, full Usenet News, Multiple lines (6), shell access. Newusers get initial credit!
contact:**{ucsfcca|hoptoad|well}!wet!editor** (Eric Swanson)

03/93   415-949-3133^   **starnet**   Los Altos   CA   300-FAST   24
SunOS 4.1. 8-lines. MNP1-5 and v42/bis, or PEP on all lines. Shell access for all users. USENET—900+ groups. E-mail (feeds available). smart mail. Publically available software (pd/shareware). $12/mo. Contact: **admin@starnet.uucp** or **...!uunet!apple!starnet!admin**

03/93   415-967-9443^   **btr**   Mountain View CA   300-FAST   24
Sun (SunOS UNIX), shell access, e-mail, netnews, uucp, can access by Telenet PC Pursuit, multiple lines, Telebit, flat rate: $12.50/month. For sign-up information please send e-mail to Customer Service at **cs@btr.com** or **..!{decwrl,fern-wood,mips}!btr!cs** or call 415-966-1429 Voice.

03/93   510-294-8591   **woodowl**   Livermore   CA   1200-FAST   24
Xenix/386 3.2.1. Waffle BBS, Usenet Access; Reasonable users welcome. No fee; For more information contact: **william@woodowl.UUCP**, **lll-winken!chumley!woodowl!william**, or call and just sign up on system.

03/93   510-530-9682   **bdt**   Oakland   CA   1200-FAST   24
Sun 4, SunOS 4.1; BBS access to Usenet news, E-mail (Internet and UUCP). PEP/V.32 on 510-530-6915. First time users login: bbs. Unix, Atari ST, and IBM-PC sources and PD/shareware. $35 annual fee. 30-day free trial. Newsfeeds and UUCP access by special arrangement. Contact: David Beckemeyer **david@bdt.com**

03/93   510-623-8652^   **jack**   Fremont   CA   300-FAST   24
Sun 4/470 running Sun O/S 4.1.1 offers downloading of netnews archives and all uploaded software. Each user can log in as bbs or as the account which they create for themselves. This is a free Public Access Unix System that is part of a network of 4 machines. The primary phone line is on a rotary to three other lines.

03/93   619-278-8267   **cg57**   San Diego   CA   1200-FAST   24
i386 Unix (SysV3.2), GDXBBS Software (login as bbs); Worldblazer on dial-in, -3905 Telebit Trailblazer Plus, -9837 Courier HST (450 Backchannel); BBS is

free; Over 600 meg of downloadable software (UNIX/386BSD/Linux and DOS systems + Soundblaster files); Shell accounts available for $30 for 6 months; Full (USENET) news feed, smart mailer and uucp accounts available after July 1993.
Contact: **steve@cg57.uucp**

03/93   619-453-1115^   **netlink**   San Diego   CA   1200-2400   24
i386 Unix system, provides access to email and over 800 Usenet newsgroups through Waffle BBS interface (no shell). Multiple lines, NO FEE for basic access. Higher access available for a donation. Mail feeds available.
Login: bbs Contact: **system@netlink.cts.com**

03/93   714-635-2863^   **dhw68k**   Anaheim   CA   1200-FAST   24
Unistride 2.1; Trailblazer access; 2nd line -1915; No fee; USENET News; /bin/sh or /bin/csh available

03/93   714-821-9671^   **alphacm**   Cypress   CA   1200-FAST   24
386—SCO-XENIX, no fee, Home of XBBS, 90 minute per login, 4 lines, Trailblazer pluses in use.
uucp-anon: login: nuucp NO PASSWD

03/93   714-842-5851^   **conexch**   Santa Ana   CA   300-2400   24
386—SCO Xenix—Free Unix guest login and PC-DOS bbs login, one hour inital time limit, USENET news, shell access granted on request & $25/quarter donation. Anon uucp: ogin: nuucp NO PASSWD. List of available Unix files resides in /usr3/public/FILES.

03/93   714-894-2246^   **stanton**   Irvine   CA   300-2400   24
80386-25, SCO Xenix-386, 320mb disk, 2400/1200/300 MNP supported; E-Mail & USENET; Fixed fee $20/yr; X11R4 archive and many packages ported to Xenix 386; C development system (XENIX/MSDOS), PROCALC 1-2-3 clone, FOXBASE+; anon uucp: ogin: nuucp, no word

03/93   818-287-5115^   **abode**   El Monte   CA   2400-FAST   24
XENIX 2.3.3; 2400-9600 Baud (Telebit T1000 PEP); Fee of $40 per year; Users get access to shell account, C compiler, email, usenet news, games, etc. Send email to contact name below for more information.
Contact: **eric@abode.ttank.com (cerritos.edu!ttank!abode!eric)**

03/93   818-367-2142^   **quake**   Sylmar   CA   300-FAST   24
ESIX/386 3.2D running Waffle; Telebit WorldBlazer on dial-in line, 818-362-6092 has Telebit T2500; Usenet (1000+ groups), Email (registered as quake.sylmar.ca.us), UUCP/UUPC connections; Rare Bird Advisories, Technomads, more; $5 a month if paid a year at a time. New users login as "bbs", then "new". One week free to new users.

03/93   818-793-9108^   **atrium**   Pasadena   CA   300-2400   24
Xenix/386 2.3.3; International pen-pal service; login: mm
Contact: **sysop@atrium.ucm.org**; multi-lines

03/93   916-649-0161^   **sactoh0**   Sacramento CA   1200-FAST   24
3B2/310 SYVR3.2; SAC_UNIX, sactoh0.SAC.CA.US; $2/month; 3 lines, v.32 on
722-6519, TB+ on 649-0161, 2400/1200 baud on 722-5068; USENET, E-Mail,
some games; login: new
Contact: **root@sactoh0.SAC.CA.US** or ..**ames!pacbell!sactoh0!root**

03/93   916-923-5013   **rgm**   Sacramento CA   1200-FAST   24
486SX-25. 200mb. Coherent 386 v4.0.1; Dedicated incoming HST line. Full
Bourne/Korn shell accessfor all users. Internet mail, limited Usenet (requests
encouraged). Mail & news feeds available. $2/mo. for light mail/news users.
login: new; Contact **root@rgm.com**

03/93   303-871-3324^   **nyx**   Denver   CO   300-FAST   24
A sort of "social experiment" aimed at providing Internet access to the public
with minimal operational costs with a "friendly" front end (a home-made menu
system). Completely donation and volunteer operated, no user fees at all. Log
in as 'new' to create an account. Equipment: Sun SparcServer II + Pyramid 90x,
~6Gb disk space, 16 phone lines (+ network logins; usually ~50 users logged in).
Public domain file area, private file area, games, full USENET news, internet
e-mail. Provides shell and more network access with proof of identity.
Contact: Andrew Burt, **aburt@nyx.cs.du.edu**

03/93   203-661-1279   **admiral**   Greenwich CT   300-FAST   24
SCO Unix 3.2.2. (HST/V32) 203-661-2873, (PEP/V32) 203-661-1279, (V32) 203-
661-0450, (MNP6) 203-661-2967. Magpie BBS for local conversation and Waffle
for Internet mail/Usenet news. Interactive chat and games. BBS name is "The
Grid." Willing to give newsfeeds and mail access. Shell (tcsh, ksh avail) accounts
available at no charge. Direct connect to Internet site (Yale) via UUCP. 230 megs
disk space. For more information contact **uunet!admiral!doug** (Doug Fields)
or **fields-doug@cs.yale.edu**.

03/93   407-299-3661^   **vicstoy**   Orlando   FL   1200-2400   24
ISC 386/ix 2.0.2. Partial USENET, e-mail (feeds available); Login as bbs, no passwd
(8N1); Free shell access; Orlando BBS list, games; cu to Minix 1.5.10 system
(weather permitting); USENET includes Unix/Minix source groups. Contact:
uunet!tarpit!bilver!vicstoy!vickde or **vickde@vicstoy.UUCP** (Vick De Giorgio).

03/93   407-438-7138^   **jwt**   Orlando   FL   1200-FAST   24
80386/33, System V.3.2, Waffle BBS, no shell access, two lines, V.32, V.32bis,
PEP, Usenet news, no fee, login as "bbs".
Contact: **john@jwt.UUCP** (John W. Temples)

03/93   904-456-2003   **amaranth** Pensacola   FL   1200-FAST   24
ISC Unix V/386 2.2.1 TB+ on dialin. XBBS no fee. limited NEWS, E-mail
For more info: Jon Spelbring **jsspelb@amaranth.UUCP**

03/93   217-789-7888   **pallas**   Springfield IL   300-FAST   24
AT&T 6386, 600 meg disk space; 4 lines w/ USRobotics Dual Standard modems;
BBS available at no fee (UBBS), shell access for $50/year; E-Mail, Usenet; "guest"
login available.

03/93   309-676-0409   **hcs**   Peoria   IL   300-FAST   24
VAX/BSD SGI/SV Network—Public Access UNIX Systems—Mult.Lines / 1.8GB
386 bbs (Free). Network Fee structure based on usage with $0.02 minute
connection. Shells (sh,ksh,csh,tcsh,bash) Compilers (C,Pascal, Fortran,Lisp,Ratfor oths), games, File and Pic. Libs., UUCP and USENET access
with NetNews (nn reader), U.S. Patent and other databases, general timesharing
and programmed on-line applications. Self register.
Contact: Victoria Kee {**uunet!hcsvax!sysop   sysop%hcsvax@uunet.uu.net**}

03/93   312-248-0900   **ddsw1**   Chicago   IL   300-FAST   24
80386 systems, ISC 2.2; guest users 1 hr daily in AKCS BBS; fee for shell, Full
Usenet access, unlimited use, and offsite mail; Authors of AKCS bbs; 1.5GB
storage, fee $75/year or $20/bi-monthly, 19200 V.32/PEP available on (312)
248-6295 anonymous uucp (nuucp) from 12 midnight to 6 AM, ~/DIREC-
TORY/README for info on anon uucp. Newsfeeds and mail connections available; Internet access in the works (PLEASE contact us if interested).
Contact: Karl Denninger (**karl@ddsw1.MCS.COM**)

03/93   312-282-8606^   **gagme**   Chicago   IL   300-FAST   24
3B2/400—System V 3.2. E-mail, netnews, sources, access to anonymous ftp,
GIFs, UUCP, local message base, games, etc. PEP and V.32 available for logins
and UUCP. Send mail to **info@gagme.chi.il.us** for more information.

03/93   312-283-0559^   **chinet**   Chicago   IL   300-FAST   24
'386, SysVr3.2.1; Multiple lines including Telebit and HST; Picospan BBS (free),
USENET at $50/year (available to guests on weekends).

03/93   708-425-8739   **oaknet**   Oak Lawn   IL   300-FAST   24
386 Clone running AT&T System V release 3.2.1, no access charges. Free shell
accounts, USENET news, and internet email...
Contact: **jason@oaknet.chi.il.us**, Jason Vanick (708)499-0905 (human).

03/93   708-833-8126^   **vpnet**   Villa Park   IL   1200-FAST   24
386 Clone—Interactive Unix R2.2 (3.2), Akcs linked bbs FREE, inclu- ding many
selected Usenet groups. Shells are available for a minimum $60/year contribu-
tion; under 22, $30. Includes access to our FULL Usenet feed. Well connected.
Five lines including three Trailblazers. Two hunt groups—V.32 modems call
708-833-8127 (contributors only).
Contact: **lisbon@vpnet.chi.il.us**, Gerry Swetsky (708)833-8122 (human).

03/93   708-879-8633   **unixuser**   Batavia   IL   300-FAST   24
386, w/ Linux/Waffle; v.32[bis] support; Linux downloads; Limited free use; Paid
subscribers get Internet mail access, some USENET groups; Subscription is
$25/year; CDROM disk available—changes monthly; Shell accounts are avail-
able.

03/93   708-983-5147   **wa9aek**   Lisle   IL   1200-FAST   24
80386, UNIX V.3.2.3; XBBS for HAM radio enthusiasts; 1.5 Gigabytes online;
Multiple lines, dial in—USR HST DS V.32bis/42bis, 8138—Tb T2500; Login as
bbs (8-N-1).

03/93   812-333-0450   **sir-alan**   Bloomington IN   1200-FAST   24
SCO UNIX 3.2; no fee; TB+ on 333-0450 (300-19.2K); archive site for
comp.sources.[games,misc,sun,unix,x], some alt.sources, XENIX(68K/286/386)
uucp-anon: ogin: nuucp password: anon-uucp uucp-anon directory: /u/pdsrc,
/u/pubdir, /u/uunet, help in /u/pubdir/HELP
Contact: **miikes@iuvax.cs.indiana.edu** (812-855-3974 days 812-333-6564 eves)

03/93   812-421-8523   **aquila**   Evansville   IN   300-2400   24
80386, SCO Unix; Second line is -1963; Games, mail, and Unix classes-by-mail;
System has a "BBS Mall" of varied topics—several BBSs under a single system.
Anonymous uucp/mail: nuucp password. Contact: **info@aquila.uucp**

03/93   502-231-5908   **compunet** Louisville   KY   300-FAST   24
386 clone, Interactive System V 3.2, 2 gig. Also 502-231-5910, both lines support
V.32 and HST. Carrying most USENET groups, Shell access, multi-user games(
including The Realm(c)) multi-user chat, downloads including the AB20 and
SIMTEL20 CD-ROMS, and more. Rate info available via a guest information
account.

03/93   606-233-2051   **lunatix**   Lexington   KY   300-2400   24
SCO Unix 3.2.2. 2 2400 baud lines. V32bis later in the fall. Home grown Pseudo
BBS software. Multiuser games, Full USENET Feed on tap, USENET Feeds
available. Shells available, No Fees.

03/93   301-924-5998   **highlite**   Laurel   MD 1200-FAST   24
Equip ???; Gotham Communications Research. Washington, DC METRO calling area; Northern VA and Southern MD included; Login as guest (password
guest); 8N1; $10/month or $100/yr, 20 free hrs/month (then $1/hour); Usenet
news; Internet E-mail; Shell access; All modems V.32 or faster.
Contact: Dave at **uunet!highlite!dlreed** or **dlreed@gotham.com**

03/93   410-661-2598   **wb3ffv**   Baltimore   MD 1200-FAST   24
80486, UNIX V.3.2.x; XBBS for HAM radio enthusiasts; 1.6 Gigabytes online;
Multiple lines, dial in—TB WorldBlazer, 2475—USR HST DS V.32bis/42bis,
2648—Tb+ PEP; Some USENET; Anon-UUCP available; Login as bbs (8-N-1).

07/93   410-893-4786   **magnus1** Belair   MD 300-FAST   24
Equip ???, UNIX 3.3.2; ksh, csh, sh; Multiple lines; $45.00/yr; E-Mail/USENET; 'C',
Pascal, Fortran, Cobol, Basic development systems; Interactive chat and games;
Files for download; USA Today, Online Magazines, Daily Business News; PC
Catalog; Local Online Forums as well; as Technical Help; Clarinet News; No limits.
Contact **magnus1!cyndiw@uunet.UU.NET**

06/93   508-664-0149   **genesis** North Reading MA 300-FAST   24
SVR3 UNIX; Internet mail; Usenet News; No Fees; Shell access and menu
system; Three lines; One hop from the Internet; HST and V.32bis; UUCP feeds
available. Contact: **steve1@genesis.nred.ma.us** (steve belczyk).
Automated reply: **info@genesis.nred.ma.us**

03/93   508-752-9121   **schunix**   Worcester   MA   2400-FAST   24
5 lines ,SUN 4/75(Sparc 2), SunOS 4.1.1(BSD),1.9GB; 2400 buad on dial-in, 14.4k (T3000) on -8305; Shell, Usenet, E-mail, $15/month or $150/yr for up to 1 hr/day, 1 time Reg fee of $10; 5 megabyte quota; 4 week free trial; login as "guest" Contact: ...**!uunet!lectroid!jjmhome!schu@schunix.uucp** (Robert Schultz) SCHUNIX c/o Ostrow Electric, 9 Mason Street, Worcester, MA 01609 Voice: 508-752-4522

03/93   313-623-6309   **nucleus**   Clarkston   MI   1200-2400   24
AMI 80386—ESIX 5.3.2, large online sources archive accessable by anonymous UUCP, login: nuucp, nucleus!/user/src/LISTING lists available public domain/shareware source code.
Contact: **jeff@nucleus.mi.org**

03/93   313-761-3000   **grex**   Ann Arbor   MI   300-FAST   24
Sun 2/170 with SunOS 3.2. Full Usenet feed, Internet e-mail, shell accounts, on-line games, PicoSpan, UUCP accounts. Voluntary donation ($6/month or $60/year) for coop membership and Usenet posting access. 6 lines, 300MB. Cooperatively owned & operated by Cyberspace Communications.
Contact: **info@cyberspace.org**

06/93   313-996-4644^   **m-net**   Ann Arbor   MI   300-2400   24
486—BSDI, open access; run by Arbornet, tax-exempt nonprofit; donations tax deductible; dues for extended access; user supported; 15 lines; Picospan conferencing; 500 MB disk; Internet e-mail; UUCP available; free shell access, C compiler, multiuser party, games (including nethack, empire, rotisserie baseball); M-Net 10 year anniversary in June, 1993! Access from the Internet: telnet **m-net.ann-arbor.mi.us**
contact: **help@m-net.ann-arbor.mi.us**

03/93   517-487-3356   **lunapark**   E. Lansing   MI   1200-2400   24
Compaq 386/20 SCO-UNIX 3.2, lunabbs bulletin board & conferencing system, no fee, login: bbs password: lunabbs. Primarily UNIX software with focus on TeX and Postscript, also some ATARI-ST and IBM-PC stuff 2400/1200—8 N 1
Contact: ...**!{mailrus,uunet}!frith!lunapark!larry**

03/93   517-789-5175   **anubis**   Jackson   MI   300-1200   24
Equip ???, OS ???; 1200 baud dial-in (planning on 19.2kbps); UUCP connections to the world, PicoSpan BBS software, Teleconferencing, C programming compiler, 3 public dial-in lines, Online games;
Contact: Matthew Rupert (**root@anubis.mi.org**).

03/93   616-457-1964   **wybbs**   Jenison   MI   300-FAST   24
386—SCO-XENIX 2.3.2, two lines, XBBS for new users, mail in for shell access, usenet news, 150 meg storage, Telebit. Interests: ham radio, xenix AKA: Consultants Connection Contact: **danielw@wyn386.mi.org** Alternate phone #: 616-457-9909 (max 2400 baud). Anonymous UUCP available.

03/93   906-228-4399   **lopez**   Marquette   MI   1200-2400   24
80386, SCO Xenix 2.3.4; Running STARBASE II Software. Great White North
UPLink, Inc. (Non Profit) 100+ local rooms, PLUS USENET, Multi Channel
Chat, 5 ports, $30 yr, flat rate for full access to net news, mail. Upper Michigan's
ORIGINAL BBS (since 1983)
Contact: Gary Bourgois ...**rutgers!sharkey!lopez!flash (flash@lopez.UUCP)**

03/93   612-473-2295^   **pnet51**   Minneapolis MN   300-2400   24
Equip ?, Xenix, multi-line, no fee, some Usenet news, email, multi-threaded
conferencing, login: pnet id: new, PC Pursuitable
UUCP: {**rosevax**, **crash**}**!orbit!pnet51!admin**

03/93   603-448-5722   **tutor**   Lebanon   NH 300-FAST   24
Altos 386 w/ System V 3.1; Limited newsfeed; E-Mmail and USENET available
via UUCP.
Contact: **peter.schmitt@dartmouth.edu**

03/93   201-759-8450^   **tronsbox**   Belleville   NJ   300-FAST   24
Generic 386, UNIX 3.2; Provides shell for some users, USENET, E-Mail (feeds
available) at $15 a month flat; Multiple line (-8568 300—2400 baud).

06/93   908-937-9481   **digex**   New Brunswick NJ   300-FAST   24
Express Access Online Communications. SunOS shell, full Usenet, and e-mail
$15/month or $150/year; Internet services include telnet, FTP, and IRC w/
news/mail $25/month or $250/year; includes unlimited usage 3am—3pm and 1
hour between 3pm and 3am. Login as new (no password) for info and account
application, major credit cards accepted. Telnet to **cnj.digex.com** or mail to
info@cnj.digex.com for more info; voice phone 1-800-546-2010.

03/93   212-420-0527^   **magpie**   NYC   NY 300-FAST   24
?—UNIX SYSV—2, Magpie BBS, no fee, Authors: Magpie/UNIX,/MSDOS No
Shell; Muli-line (using Telebit Worldblazers) plus anonymous uucp;
Contact: Steve Manes, **manes%magpie@nycenet.nycenet.edu**

03/93   212-675-7059^   **marob**   NYC   NY 300-FAST   24
386 SCO-XENIX 2.2, XBBS, no fee, limit 60 min; Telebit Trailblazer (9600 PEP)
only 212-675-8438;
Contact: {**philabs|rutgers|cmcl2**}**!phri!marob!clifford**

06/93   516-586-4743   **kilowatt**   Deer Park   NY 2400-FAST   24
Consensys SVR4 running on a clone 80486-33. 516-586-4743 for Telebit World-
Blazer, 516-667-6142 for a Boca V.32bis. Providing FREE USENET email/news
to the general public. FREE feeds available with a selection of all of alt, biz,
comp, rec, talk, sci, soc, and vmsnet newsgroups ... using UUCP or QWK-pack-
ets. Contact: Arthur Krewat 516-253-2805 **krewat@kilowatt.UUCP** or
krewat@kilowatt.linet.org Telnet/Ftp not available here, so don't even ask!

03/93   518-237-2163   **tnl**   Troy   NY 300-FAST   24
80386 w/ SCO XENIX. No Fee. Full shell, USENET, BBS, games, optional menus, 2 hr limit. Login as 'new' for an account, no valid. "The Northern Lights." Contact: **norstar@tnl.com** (Daniel Ray)

03/93   518-346-8033   **sixhub**   upstate   NY 300-2400   24
PC Designs GV386. hub machine of the upstate NY UNIX users group (*IX) two line reserved for incoming, bbs no fee, news & email fee $15/year Smorgasboard of BBS systems, UNaXcess and XBBS online, Citadel BBS now in production. Contact: **davidsen@sixhub.uucp**.

03/93   716-634-6552   **exuco1**   Buffalo   NY 300-FAST   -24
SGI Iris Indigo; 2 Lines, both Telebit WorldBlazers (on a hunt) [PEP Answer sequence last]; "The Buffalo Computer Society", Western New York's first Public Access UNIX; Mon-Fri 6:00pm-7:00am EST, 24 Hours on Weekends; No Fee; E-Mail/USENET Come March '93—will be running on several DEC Vaxen running BSD 4.3, and MANY MANY MANY more lines.

04/93   718-729-5018   **dorsai**   NYC   NY 300-FAST   24
80386, ISC 386/ix, Waffle bbs; Live Internet connection; 3 phone lines (V.32bis for contributors); no shell (yet); BBS with over 250 non-Usenet newsgroups, 1.2 gb of mac, ibm, amiga, cp-m, appleII, cbm files; BBS is free, $25/yr for UseNet access, (180 min/day), $50/yr for extended gold access (300 min/day); $?? for platinum access (i.e. ftp/telnet/irc/etc); Full news and mail feed from uupsi; login through bbs.
Contact: **postmaster@dorsai.com**

03/93   216-582-2460^   **ncoast**   Cleveland   OH 1200-FAST   24
80386 Mylex, SCO Xenix; 600 meg. storage; XBBS and Shell; USENET (news-feeds available), E-Mail; donations requested; login as "bbs" for BBS and "makeuser" for new users. Telebit used on 216-237-5486.

03/93   513-779-8209   **cinnet**   Cincinnati   OH 1200-FAST   24
80386, ISC 386/ix 2.02, Telebit access, 1 line; $7.50/Month; shell access, Usenet access; news feeds available; login: newacct password: new user to register for shell access

03/93   614-868-9980^ **bluemoon**   Reynoldsburg OH 300-FAST   24
Sun 4/75, SunOS; 2.2gb; Leased line to the Internet; Multiple lines, HST Dual on -9980 & -9982, Telebit T2500 on -9984; 2gb disk space; Bluemoon BBS—supporting UNIX, graphics, and general interest; Full USENET, gated Fidonet conferences, E-Mail;
Contact: **grant@bluemoon.uucp** (Grant DeLorean).

06/93   503-220-0636^   **techbook** Portland   OR 300-FAST   24
SPARCstation, SunOS 4.1.3, 1.5GB disk; 10 lines and support PEP/V.32 and V.32bis; E-Mail/USENET; Shell access for $60 / year includes Korn, C, or tcsh; $90 / year includes full internet (ftp, telnet, irc, mud) access; apply with "new" or email **info@techbook.com**

03/93   503-297-3211^   **m2xenix**   Portland   OR   300-FAST   24
'386/20, Xenix 2.3. 2 Lines (-0935); Shell accounts available, NO BBS; No fee;
E-mail, USENET News, program development.
Contact: ...**!uunet!m2xenix!news** or on Fido at 297-9145

03/93   503-632-7891^   **bucket**   Portland   OR   300-FAST   24
Tektronix 6130, UTek 3.0(4.2bsd-derived). Bit Bucket BBS no longer online.
Modem is Telebit Trailblazer+ (PEP). Users intereseted in access to Unix should
send EMail to rickb@pail.rain.com. $30/year access fee includes USENET News,
EMail (fast due to local Internet access), and access to all tools/utilities/games.
Internet 'ftp' available upon request. UUCP connections (1200, 2400, 9600V.32,
9600PEP, 19200PEP) available (through another local system which is not
publically available) to sites which will poll with reasonable regularity and
reliability.

07/93   215-348-9727   **jabber**   Doylestown PA   300-FAST   24
80386, ISC 386/ix 3.0; Trailblazer+ (PEP) on dial in line, Worldblazer (V.32[bis]
and TurboPEP) on -8129, T-3000 (V.32[bis]) on -1932; No fee services: "*NIX
Depot" BBS, BBS for UNIX/Xenix users; Fee services: UUCP feeds, providing
access to Internet E-mail and full USENET News (2650+ groups); Anonymous
UUCP available for access to the latest nixpub lists, please see the footer of this
list for more details.
Contact: Phil Eschallier (**phil@bts.com**).
anon-uucp: ogin: nuucp (No passwd)

07/93   215-539-3043^   **cellar**   Trooper/OaksPA   300-FAST   24
DTK 486/33, SCO Unix 3.2, Waffle BBS—The Cellar BBS, no shell; USR Dual-
Standard modems, five lines and growing. BBS is free; net news (full feed) and
net mail by subscription. $10/mo, $55/6-mo, or $90/yr. Fancies itself to be more
of a colorful "electonic community" than the best plug into the net, and as such,
it features a lively local message base. But it also generally carries the latest
Linux distribution, just to prove it hasn't forgotten its hacker roots.
Contact: Tony Shepps (**toad@cellar.org**).

03/93   814-353-0566   **cpumagic** Bellefonte   PA   1200-FAST   24
80386, ESIX 4.0.3a (SVR4); Dual Standard (v.32/v.32bis/HST); The Centre
Programmers Unit BBS, custom BBS software (Micro Magic); Files available:
UNIX, GNU, X, ESIX, MSDOS tools and libraries; No fee but up/download ratios
enforced.
Contact: Mike Loewen at **mloewen@cpumagic.scol.pa.us**
or ... **psuvax1!cpumagic!mloewen**

03/93   605-348-2738   **loft386**   Rapid City   SD   300-FAST   24
80386 SYS V/386 Rel 3.2, Usenet mail/news via UUNET, UUNET archive access.
NO BBS! News feeds avaliable. 400 meg hd. Fees: $10/month or $25/quarter.
Call (605) 343-8760 and talk to Doug Ingraham to arrange an account or email
uunet!loft386!dpi

03/93   615-288-3957   **medsys**   Kingsport   TN 1200-FAST   24
386 SCO-UNIX 3.2, XBBS; No fee, limit 90 min; Telebit PEP, USENET, 600mb;
login: bbs password: bbs anon uucp—medsys Any ACU (speed) 16152883957
ogin: nuucp Request /u/xbbs/unix/BBSLIST.Z for files listing
Contact: **laverne@medsys** (LaVerne E. Olney)

03/93   615-895-4675   **raider**   Murfreesboro TN 1200-FAST   24
Featuring UniBoard 1.10. BBS accounts are free and available to the general
public with most of the capabilities on first call. We also provide mail, shell, and
USENET links. One hop from Internet. Complete source and binary archives
available. No annual member fees for shell or uucp accounts. 615-895-4675 is
Intel 14400-EX modem using V.32/V.32bis/V.42/V.42bis. For more info contact
root@raider.raider.net, or log into bbs and leave mail for 'root'. UniBoard BBS
system is *FULLY* integrated with USENET News and Internet-gatewayed
email system! Other features include color, ANSI control sequences, and full-
screen message editor.

03/93   214-436-3281^   **sdf**   Dallas   TX   300-FAST   24
i386-25, ISC 2.0.1; sdf public access Unix. 4-line rotary, 2400 bps, 14.4k (436-
4259), PEP (436-5935). No fees but supported entirely by donations. Shell
accounts, UUCP mail and news feeds available. Providing access to Internet
mail, 1600+ newsgroup full-feed UseNet, online games, RoundTable online chat,
programming utilities, and more. Login as "new" for sample access and/or
immediate account registration.
Contact: **admins@sdf.lonestar.org**

03/93   512-346-2339^   **bigtex**   Austin   TX   FAST   24
SysVr3.2 i386, anonymous shell, no fee, anonymous uucp ONLY, Telebit
9600/PEP; Mail links available. Carries GNU software. anon uucp login: nuucp
NO PASSWD, file list /usr3/index anon shell login: guest NO PASSWD, chroot'd
to /usr3
Contact: **james@bigtex.cactus.org**

03/93   713-480-2686^   **blkbox**   Houston   TX   300-FAST   24
486/33, SCO Open Desktop; 5 lines, all V32[bis]/V42[bis]; E-Mail/USENET
(4500+ groups); 25 online adventure games, IRC, SLIP/PP; $21.65 / month for
full shell access.
Contact: Marc Newman (**mknewman@blkbox.com**)

03/93   713-668-7176^   **nuchat**   Houston   TX   300-FAST   24
i386; USENET, Mail, Shell Access; 300M On-line; Trailbazer Used; No fee.

03/93   801-566-6283^   **bitsko**   Salt Lake City UT 300-FAST   24
80486, UHC UNIX SVR4; Bitsko's Bar & Grill BBS; Telebit; No fee; Unidel;
Usenet news; Internet mail; Citadel-net gateway and local feeds available;
Source system for Unidel, a Citadel-like newsreader and UNIX BBS, and uccico,
a UNIX-side Citadel-net gateway.
Contact: **ken@bitsko.slc.ut.us** (Ken MacLeod)

04/93   703-528-4380   **sytex**   Arlington   VA   300-FAST   24
ISC Unix, UUCP, Waffle BBS, 5 lines. Login as "bbs". Mail, usenet news, ftp
available via ftp-requests though UUnet. Serving Washington DC, Northern
Virginia, Southern Maryland. First year startup Charter member accounts
available for $120. Gives fullest access as the system develops.

06/93   703-551-0095   **ukelele**   Woodbridge VA   300-FAST   24
Genuine Computing Resources. SVR4/386. Calling area includes District of
Columbia, Fairfax Cty, Prince William Cty, Manassas, and ries, VA. Shell, Full
Usenet, Internet E-Mail. $15/month for access to (703)551 exchange, $10/month
for (703)878 access. All lines V.32bis or higher. You get 1 hour/day connect time
and 1.5MB disk storage. Direct Internet connectivity expected soon without rate
increase for existing users. Login as 'guest' or send mail to **info@gcr.com** for
further details. For human interaction send mail to **cjl@gcr.com**. News and mail
feeds also considered.

03/93   703-803-0391^   **tnc**   Fairfax Station   VA   300-FAST   24
Zenith Z-386, SCO Xenix; 120 MB HDD; 12 lines, tb+ for UUCP only; "The Next
Challenge"; Usenet, mail, Unique (sysop written) multi-user space game; No
Shell; Free and user supported—No fee for light mail and usenet; Subscription
required for game and unlimited mail and usenet at $25 / year;
Contact: Tom Buchsbaum (**tom@tnc.UUCP** or **uunet!tnc!tom**).

06/93   900-468-7727   **uunet**   Falls Church VA   300-FAST   24
Sequent S81, Dynix 3.0.17(9); UUNET Communication Services; No Shell;
Anonymous UUCP, fee $0.40/min—billed by the telephone company, login: uucp
(no passwd); Multiple lines, PEP and V.32 available; grab "uunet!~/help for more
info" ... Full internet mail and USENET access via subscriber UUCP accounts.
Contact: **info@uunet.uu.net** or call [voice] 703-204-8000.

03/93   206-747-6397^   **seanews**   Redmond   WA   1200-FAST   24
Xenix 386 2.3.2. SEANEWS is a free public service, providing access to Usenet
and Internet mail. There are no games, very limited files, etc. However
SEANEWS does have up-to-date Usenet news and excellent mail-handling
capability.

03/93   414-241-5469^   **mixcom**   Milwaukee   WI   1200-FAST   24
80386, SCO UNIX 3.2; MIX (Milwaukee Internet eXchange); $9/mo access to
Internet services including email, Usenet BBS and file archives; MIX has
comprehensive and easy to use menus, along with shell access; Multiple lines;
login as 'newuser' password 'newuser'.
Contact: Dean Roth (**sysop@mixcom.com**) [414-962-8172 voice]

03/93   414-321-9287   **solaria**   Milwaukee   WI   300-2400   24
Sun 3/60LE, SunOS 4.1. Internet E-mail, limited USENET news, shell access,
Telebit WorldBlazer soon. Feeds available. Donations requested, registration
required. One hop off of the Internet.
Contact: **jgreco@solaria.mil.wi.us** (Joe Greco) or log in as "help"

06/93   414-342-4847   **solaria**   Milwaukee   WI   300-FAST   24
Sun 3/60LE, SunOS 4.1. Internet E-mail, limited USENET news, shell access, feeds available, donations requested, registration required. One hop off of the Internet.
Contact: **jgreco@solaria.mil.wi.us** (Joe Greco) or log in as "help"

06/93   414-734-2499   **edsi**   Appleton   WI   300-FAST   24
IBM PS/2 Model 55SX, SCO Xenix 2.3.2; Running STARBASE II Software. Enterprise Data Systems Incorporated (Non-profit). 100+ local rooms, PLUS USENET, Multi Channel Chat, 9 ports, $15 yr, flat rate for full access to net news (no alternet yet), mail. The Fox Valley's only public access Unix based BBS.
Contact: Chuck Tomasi (**chuck@edsi.plexus.COM**)

03/93   608-246-2701   **fullfeed**   Madison   WI   FAST   24
Sun SPARC station SLC, 16Mb RAM, 1Gb disk, SunOS 4.1.1, Telebit WorldBlazers; operated by FullFeed Communications; USENET/E-Mail, UUCP plus other digital communication services; login: fullfeed; UUCP starts at $24/month, shells cost $16/month; No-cost, limited-term, evaluation accounts are setup over the telephone; FullFeed plans to offer Internet connections (SLIP, PPP, 56Kbps) within 6 months.
Contact "**SYSop@FullFeed.Com**" or call +1-608-CHOICE-9 (voice).

03/93   608-273-2657   **madnix**   Madison   WI   300-2400   24
486, MST UNIX SysV/386, shell, no fee required, USENET news, mail, login: bbs
Contact: **ray@madnix.uucp**

INTERNET ACCESS WORLDWIDE

Australia

Connect.Com.AU Pty Ltd.
Voice: +61 3 5282239
Dial-Up: Contact for number
Area Codes: +61 3, +61 2
Local Access: Australia: Melbourne, Sydney
Fees: AUS$2000/yr (1 hr/1 day), 10 percent discount for AUUG members; other billing negotiable
E-mail: **connect@connect.com.au**

04/93   +61-2-837-1183   **kralizec**   Sydney   AU   1200-FAST   24
Sun 3/50, SunOS 4.0; 470mb disk; V.32/MNP-5 modem; Dialup access to Internet E-mail & USENET; mail-based FTP. 80-100 Mb software online for download. Full C-shell access to all members. No joining fee. Usage fee $50 for 50 hours connect time. Voice number +61-2-837-1397. Home of IXgate—Internet to Fidonet gateway—also Fido 713/602.
Contact: **nick@kralizec.zeta.org.au**

Austria

EUnet Austria Ltd
Michael Haberler
A-1010 Vienna, Austria, Schottenring 33
Voice: +43 (1) 3174969
Fax: +43 (1) 3104462
E-mail: **mah@eunet.co.at**

Belgium

EUnet Belgium
Pierre Verbaeten, Jean Huens, Hans Baele
p/a K.U.leuven
Dept. Computerwetenschappen
Celestijnenlaan 200A
B-3001 Leuven, Belgium
Voice: +32 16 20 10 15
Fax: +32 16 20 53 08
E-mail: **pr@Belgium.EU.net**

Bulgaria

EUnet Bulgaria
Network Support
Daniel Kalchev
Digital Systems / EUnet Bulgaria
Neofit Bozveli 6
BG-9000 Varna, Bulgaria
Phone: +359 52 259135
Fax: +359 52 234540
E-mail: **pr@Bulgaria.EU.net**

Canada

Communications Accessibles Montreal
Voice: 514-923-2102
Dial-Up: 514-281-5601 (v.32 bis, HST); 514-738-3664 (PEP); 514-466-0592 (v.32)
Area codes: 514
Local Access: Quebec: Montreal, Laval, South-Shore, West-Island
Fees: $25/mo Canadian
E-mail: **info@cam.org**

PUCnet Computer Connections
10215 178th St.
Edmonton, AB T5S 1M3
Voice: 403-448-1901
Dial-Up: 403-484-5640 (v.32 bis). Log in as *guest*.

Area Codes: 403
Local Access: AB: Edmonton and surrounding communities in the Extended Flat Rate Calling Area
Fees: $Cdn 20/mo for 20 hours of connect time plus $5/hr (for direct internet services such as ftp and telnet) plus $10 sign-up
E-mail: **info@pucnet.com** or **pwilson@pucnet.com**

03/93   403-569-2882   **debug**   Calgary   AB   300-FAST   24
386, SCO-Xenix; Login: gdx; Telebit, HST, V.32bis, MNP-5 supported; 6 phone lines: (403) 569-2882, 569-2883, 569-2884, 569-2885, 569-2886; System runs modified GDX BBS software; Services: Usenet, Internet email, IRC, local-chat, 50+ games, legal-forms, programming, ftp-via-email, and much more; Fee: $10/month-3hrs/day to $25/month-24hrs/day; Visa & Amex accepted. Demo accounts with limmited access are free.
Contact: Rob Franke **root@debug.cuc.ab.ca**

03/93   416-249-5366   **r-node**   Etobicoke   ON   300-FAST   24
80386, ISC SV386; SupraModem2400 on Dial-in line, Worldblazer and Cardinal2400 on other two lines; No fee services: Uniboard BBS for BBS users; shell access for those who ask; Fee services: access to subsequent lines, unlimited dl/ul access; full USENET News and International E-mail access through Usenet/Internet mail; Free UUCP connections;
Contact: Marc Fournier (**marc@r-node.gts.org**)

03/93   416-461-2608   **tmsoft**   Toronto   ON   300-FAST   24
NS32016, Sys5r2, shell; news+mail $30/mo, general-timesharing $60/mo All newsgroups. Willing to setup mail/news connections. Archives:comp.sources.{unix,games,x,misc}
Contact: Dave Mason <**mason@tmsoft**> / Login: newuser

03/93   514-435-8896   **ichlibix**   Blainville Queb CA   300-FAST   24
80386, ISC 2.2.1; 2400 bps modem on dial in, HST DS on -2650; BBS program is Ubbs (RemoteAccess Clone)—named Soft Stuff, no shell; No fees required but are recommended for more access ($25-$75/yr); Files for both dos and UNIX + a lot of binaries for ISC; Possibility to send/receive UUCP mail from the BBS

03/93   604-576-1214   **mindlink**   Vancouver   BC   300-FAST   24
80386 w/ SCO Xenix; 14 lines, 660 Meg disk space, TB+ & 9600 HST available; No shell; Fee of $45/year for BBS access; E-Mail, USENET, hundreds of megs of file downloads; Operating since 1986.

04/93   613-724-9817   **latour**   Ottawa   ON   300-FAST   24
Sun 3/60, SunOS 4.1, 8meg Ram, 660 meg of disk; 2nd line v.32[bis]; No BBS; Unix access rather than usenet; Login as guest for a shell (send mail to postmaster asking for an account); Anon uucp is login as 'anonuucp' (/bin/rmail is allowed)—Grab ~uucp/README[.Z] for an ls-lR.

03/93   613-837-3029   **micor**   Orleans   ON   300-FAST   24
386/25, 600 Meg, Xenix 2.3.2, USENET, email, 2 phone lines fee required to get more than 15 mins/day of login and to access additional phone lines. Available:

bbs accounts (waffle) or shell accounts.
Contact: **michel@micor.ocunix.on.ca** or **michel@micor.uucp**, Michel Corm-
ier.

CIS

EUnet Relcom—Former Soviet Union
Voice: +7 095 1983796
Fax: +7 095 1964984
E-mail: **postmaster@ussr.eu.net** or **ip-op@ussr.eu.net**

Czech Republic

EUnet Czech Republic
Dr. Pavel Rosendorf
COnet spol. s r.o.
Technicka 3
166 28 Prague
Czech Republic
Voice: +42 2 332 3242
Fax. +42 2 311 6278
E-mail: **prf@vscht.cz**

Denmark

EUnet Denmark/DKnet
Symbion
Fruebjergvej 3
2100 Copenhagen O
Denmark
Voice: (+45) 39 17 99 00
Fax : (+45) 39 17 98 97
E-mail: **netpasser@denmark.eu.net**

Finland

EUnet Finland Ltd
Punavuorenkatu 1
FI-00120 Helsinki
Finland
Voice: +358 0 400 2060
Fax. +358 0 622 2626
E-mail: **helpdesk@EUnet.fi**

04/93   +358-0-455-8331 clinet   **Espoo**   FI   300-FAST   24
Sun 3/60 16M/1G + Motorola M8[48]00-hybrid 32M/300M (terminal server,
mostly), SunOS (4.1.1); Multi-line -8331 (V32bisMNP), -8332 (V32MNP) &
-8778 (V32), 4 lines starting at -8688 (V22bis); custom software (locally written),

conferences, menu system, other stuff; TCP/IP connected with IRC, USENET (all groups), E-Mail, shell access, common UNIX software, programming; $10/mo including at least 1hr of daily time ($0.25/hr if all lines busy). login as 'new'. Since 1987.
Contact: **clinet@clinet.fi**.

France

EUnet France
M. Laurent Bloch
Fnet, EUnet-France
11 Rue Carnot
94270 Le Kremlin Bicetre, France
Voice: +33 1 45 21 02 04
Fax: +33 1 46 58 94 20
E-mail: **contact@France.EU.net**

Germany

EUnet Deutschland Gmb
Emil-Figge-Strasse 80
D-44227 Dortmund
Tel: +49 231 972 00
Fax: +49 231 972 1111
E-mail: **info@germany.eu.net**

04/93   +49-30-694-61-82 **scuzzy**   Berlin   DE   300-FAST   24
80486/33, ISC 3.0; HST 14400/v.42bis on the first, HST 14400/V.32bis/V.42bis Modems on other dial-in lines; Large library of source code including 386BSD, GNU, TeX, and X11—will distribute on tapes (grab /src/TAPES for the order form, /src/SERVICE for info about support for Free Software). Bulletin Board System with possible full Internet access, i.e. email, USENET, IRC, FTP, telnet (grab /src/BBS for info, or login as 'guest'); Login as 'archive' for x/y/z-modem and kermit transfers; Anonymous UUCP available, grab /src/README for initial info;
Contact: **src@contrib.de** (Heiko Blume)
anon uucp: ogin: nuucp word: nuucp

04/93   +49-40-494867   **isys-hh**   Hamburg   DE   300-FAST   24
Intel 80486/33/1050—SCO Unix 3.2V2.0 (ODT 1.1.0n);
Shells: msh, sh, csh, ksh; nn for newsreaders, ELM for mail
Contact: **mike@isys-hh.hanse.de** (Michael Loth)

04/93   +49-69-308265   **odbffm**   Frankfurt/Main DE   300-FAST   24
Altos 386/2000, Telebit Modem, Public Access Unix; only shell accounts, no bbs software. Mail and news access (currently via UUCP, Internet planned).
Contact: **oli@odb.rhein-main.de**, voice +49 69 331461, fax +49 69 307682

Greece

EUnet Greece
Foundation of Research and Technology—Hellas
Institute of Computer Science (FORTH-ICS)
P.O.Box 1385, Heraklio, Crete Greece 711 10
Voice: +30 81 221171, 229302
Local Access: Athens, Thessaloniki, Heraklio and Patras
E-mail: **stelios@ics.forth.gr**

Hungary

Hungarian EUnet Backbone
Computer and Automation Institute of the Hungarian Academy of Sciences
H-1132 Budapest, Victor Hugo str. 18-22
Hungary
Voice: +36 1 1497986
Fax: +36 1 1297866
E-mail: **postmaster@Hungary.EU.net**

Iceland

EUnet Iceland
Marius Olafsson
SURIS/ISnet
Taeknigardi, Dunhaga 5
107 Reykjavik
Iceland
Voice: 354 1 694747
Fax: 354 1 28801
E-mail: **isnet-info@isgate.is**

Ireland

IEunet Ltd,
Innovation Center,
O'Reilly Institute,
Trinity College,
Dublin 2,
Ireland.
Voice: +353-1-6719361
Fax: +353-1-6798039
E-mail: **info@ieunet.ie**

Italy

EUnet Italy
Alessandro Berni
IUnet c/o DIST
Via Opera Pia, 11a
16145 Genova, Italy
Voice: +39 10 3532747
Fax: +39 10 3532948
E-mail: **pr@Italy.EU.net**

04/93   +39-541-27135 **nervous**   Rimini (Fo)   IT   300-FAST   24
386/33, 1GB, ISC 386ix; Menu driven BBS, no shell; Directly connected with
uunet.uu.net, UnixBBS Development Site, full USENET access thru menu-
driven BBS (no shell logins), lots of unix sources and erotic images, no fees
required for file download
Contact: **pizzi@nervous.com**

Japan

InetClub
2-1-15 Ohara Kamifukuoka-shi
Saitama 356
Japan
Voice: +81 492 66 7313
Fax: +81 492 66 7510
E-mail: **kddlab.kddlabs.co.jp**. Subject: **help**

Internet Initiative Japan
Hoshigaoka Bldg.
2-11-2 Nagata-cho
Chiyoda-ku
Tokyo 100
Japan
Voice: +81-03-3580-3781
Fax: +81-03-3580-3782
E-mail: **info@iij.ad.jp**

Aegis
Kyoto
Japan
E-mail: **davidg@aegis.org**

Luxemburg

EUnet Luxemburg
Jacques Kirsch
Voice: +352 470261 361
Fax: +352 470264
E-mail: **postmaster@luxemburg.eu.net**

Netherlands

EUnet Netherlands
Martijn Roos Lindgreen
Stichting NLnet
Kruislaan 413
1098 SJ Amsterdam
Voice: +31 20 592 4245
Fax: +31 20 592 4199
E-mail: **pr@Netherlands.EU.net**

New Zealand

04/93   +64-4-389-5478 **actrix**   Wellington NZ 300-FAST   24
Zenith 386/33MHz w/ ISC 386/ix 2.02; Actrix Information Exchange—New
Zealand's first Public Access UNIX. 750 Mb disk; 3 lines, USR Courier HST
(T2500 due December 1990, X25 in '91). Fee: NZ$54 p.a. - offers heavily modified
XBBS with USEnet and Fidonet, e-mail (elm), hundreds of file areas divided
into sections for UNIX, MS-DOS, Amiga, Atari, Apple //, Macintosh, CP/M etc.
Shell w/ many extras available via 'Enhanced subscription'. Planned to join APC
(PeaceNet/EcoNet);
Contact: **paul@actrix.gen.nz** (Paul Gillingwater) PO Box 11-410, Wgtn, NZ

04/93   +64-4-564-2314 **cavebbs**   Wellington NZ 1200-FAST   24
AT&T 3B2/400 w/SysV 3.2; The Cave MegaBBS System. 144MB disk; 1 line. v32
MNP5/v42bis. Free access for paid users of the main Cave DOS-based system,
4 lines on +64-4-564-3000. Shell accounts with elm mailer and rn/trn newsread-
ers. News and email hub for local sites in the welly domain. The Cave runs using
KiwiBoard s/w on a 386/33 to provide local messaging and 825MB of PC files;
Contact: **clear@cavebbs.welly.gen.nz** (Charlie Lear), Box 2009 Wellington, NZ,
phone/fax +64-4-564-5307

Norway

EUnet Norway
Arne Asplem
Forskningsparken
Gaustadallen 21
N-0371 Oslo, Norway
Voice: +47 22 958327
Fax: +47 22 604427
E-mail: **pr@Norway.EU.net**

Portugal

EUnet Portugal
Dr. Jose' Legatheaux Martins
c/o PUUG—Portuguese Unix Users Group
Av. 24 de Julho 134—7o

1300 LISBOA
PORTUGAL
Voice: +351 1 395 06 42
Fax: +351 1 397 18 76
E-mail: **pr@Portugal.EU.net**

Romania

EUnet Romania
Liviu Ionescu
Adcon Telemetry
Voice: +40 1 3126886
Fax: +40 1 3126668
E-mail: **ilg@adcon.ro**

Slovakia

EUnet Slovakia
Gejza Buechler
c/o Comenius University Bratislava
Faculty of Mathematics and Physics
Computing centre
Mlynska dolina
Bratislava
842 15
Slovakia
Voice: +42 7 377 434 or +42 7 725 306
Fax: +42 7 377 433 or +42 7 725 882
E-mail: **gejza@Slovakia.EU.net**
nic-hdl: GB224

Ivan Lescak
c/o Comenius University Bratislava
Faculty of Mathema
Computing centre
Mlynska dolina
Bratislava
842 15
Slovakia
Voicw: +42 7 725 306
Fax: +42 7 725 882
E-mail: **ivan@Slovakia.EU.net**
nic-hdl: IL2

Slovenia

NIL Systems Integration and Consulting Ltd.
Jozek Gruskovnjak
Leskoskova 4
61000 Ljubljana

Slovenia
Voice: +38 61 105 183
Fax: +38 61 105 381
E-mail: **pr@Slovenia.EU.net**

Spain

EUnet Spain
Jose A. Manas
Goya Servicios Telematicos S.A.
Clara del Rey 8, 1o 7
E-28002 Madrid, Spain
Voice: +34 1 413 48 56
Fax: +34 1 413 49 01
E-mail: **postmaster@spain.eu.net**

Sweden

Swipnet AB
Olle Wallner
Box 62, S-164 94
Kista, Sweden
Voice: +46 8 632 40 40
wallner@swip.net

Switzerland

EUnet Switzerland
CHUUG/EUnet Switzerland
Zweierstrasse 35
CH-8004 Zuerich
Switzerland
Voice: +41 1 291 45 80
Fax: +41 1 291 46 42
E-mail: **pr@switzerland.eu.net**

04/93   +41-61-8115492 **ixgch**   Kaiseraugst CH 300-FAST   24
80386, SCO XENIX SV2.3.3, USR-DS (-V.32); Host: ixgch.xgp.spn.com (Ixgate
Switzerland); Organization: XGP Switzerland & SPN Swiss Public Network;
Public UI: PubSh (Public Shell), free!; Services among others: UUCP feeds for
Internet Mail and Usenet News, Swiss BBS-List Service, Ixgate-Archive
(RFCs,NIC-docs,non-comp-areas etc.), anonymous UUCP, CHAT conference,
TALK software and more. BTW: V.32bis connections soon! General info: mail to
service@spn.com (Subject: help).
Contact: **sysadm@xgp.spn.com** (...**!gator!ixgch!sysadm**)

Tunisia

EUnet Tunisia
Mondher Makni
IRSIT, BP 212
2 Rue Ibn Nadime
1082 Cite Mahrajane
Tunis, Tunisia
Voice: +216 1 787 757 / 288 805
Fax: +216 1 787 827
Telex: 14570 IRSIT-TN
E-mail: **mondher@tunsia.eu.net**

United Kingdom

Demon Internet Systems (DIS)
42 Hendon Lane
Finchley
London N3 1TT
Voice: +44 (0)81 349 0063
Dial-Up: +44 (0)81 343 4848
Area Codes: +44 (0)81
Local Access: London
Fees: GB Pounds 10.00/month; 132.50/yr (including 12.50 start-up charge). No
on-line charges.
E-mail: **internet@demon.co.uk**

The Direct Connection
Voice: +44 (0)81 317 0100
Dial-Up: +44 (0)81 317 2222
Area Codes: +44 (0)81
Local Access: London
Fees: GB Pounds 10/mo and up. No on-line charges. GB Pounds 7.50 sign-up
fee.
E-mail: **helpdesk@dircon.co.uk**

EUnet GB
Rooms G01/G02, KRDBC
University of Kent Campus
Canterbury, Kent CT2 7PB
United Kingdom
Voice: +44 227 475497
Fax: +44 227 475478
E-mail: **postmaster@britain.eu.net**

PIPEX
Voice: 0223 250120
Fax: 0223 250121
E-mail: **pipex@pipex.net**

UK PC User Group

Voice: +44 (0)81 863 6646
Dial-Up: +44 (0)81 863 6646
Area Codes: +44 (0)81
Local Access: London
Fees: GB Pounds 15.50/mo or 160/yr plus 10 start-up (no time charges)
E-mail: **info@ibmpcug.co.uk**

04/93   +44-734-34-00-55**infocom**   Berkshire   UK   300-FAST   24
80486, SCO UNIX 3.2.2; BBS, Teletext pages; 2nd line 32-00-55; Internet
Mail/USENET at HOME using FSUUCP (DOS)/UUCP; Max 60.00 + V.A.T. per
annum, this will also be the charge when internet access (i.e. ftp & telnet arrive
shortly), this level includes UUCP Login & a BBS Login account, if you choose
UUCP transfers this can save a lot of connection charges from those nasty
telephone companies. File Upload & Download, no quotas; Some services are
free and some are pay; login as 'new' (8-N-1) ... on-line registration, password
sent by mail;
Contact: **sysop@infocom.co.uk** or mail <**information@infocom.co.uk**> with
"general" in the subject line or Fax +44 734 32 09 88

04/93   +44 81 893 4088 **HelpEx**   London   UK   300-2400   24
SunOS 4.1, V32/V42b soon. Mail, news and UNIX shell (/usr/ucb/mail, ream; rn;
sh, csh, tcsh, bash) UK#5 per month. 500 USENET groups currently and
expanding. All reasonable mail and USENET use free. Beginner's pack available.
Mail for contract and charges documents. One month free trial period possible.
Mail and news feeds. ***SUITABLE FOR BUSINESS USE TOO.***
Contact: **HelpEx@exnet.co.uk**, or voice/FAX +44 81 755 0077 GMT 1300-2300.

Index

455

Internet Society

APPLICATION FOR MEMBERSHIP

To: Internet Society

Please enroll me as a member of the Internet Society. I understand that membership entitles me to receive the quarterly Internet Society News, reduced fees for attendance at Internet Society conferences and other benefits. Membership privileges will be for twelve months from the receipt of payment. I am applying for

___ regular membership at $70.00

___ student membership at $25.00 (please send proof of status)

NAME: _____

POSTAL ADDRESS: _____

_____

_____

_____

INTERNET ADDRESS: _____

___ Please bill me.

___ Payment is included with this application as below.

PAYMENT INFORMATION: Payment of Internet Society annual dues may be made via check, money order, credit card or wire transfer.

For **credit card** payments:

___ AMEX ___ VISA ___ MC ___ DINERS ___ CARTE BLANCHE

Card Number: _____

Expiration Date: _____

Signature: _____

Send **wire transfers** to:

Bank: Riggs Bank of Virginia
Merrifield Office
8315 Lee Highway
Fairfax, VA   22031   USA

Bank ABA Number: 056001260

Account Number: Internet Society
14838710

Send via **e-mail** to: isoc@isoc.org
File headers will be accepted as signatures.

or **fax** to: (703) 620-0913

or **mail** to: Internet Society
Suite 100
1895 Preston White Drive
Reston, VA   22091   USA

Internet Society

APR 2 8 1996	DATE DUE	
APR 2 4 1997		
NOV 2 5 1997		

TK 5105.875 .I57 G55 1993
Gilster, Paul, 1949-
The Internet navigator
                      94-2196

PJC LEARNING RESOURCES CENTER DH